Tapping the Green Market

PEOPLE AND PLANTS CONSERVATION SERIES

Series Editor
Martin Walters

Series Originator
Alan Hamilton

People and Plants is a joint initiative of WWF,
the United Nations Educational, Scientific and Cultural Organization (UNESCO)
and the Royal Botanic Gardens, Kew
www.rbgkew.org.uk/peopleplants

Titles in the series

Applied Ethnobotany: People, Wild Plant Use and Conservation
Anthony B Cunningham

Biodiversity and Traditional Knowledge: Equitable Partnerships in Practice
Sarah A Laird (ed)

People, Plants and Protected Areas: A Guide to In Situ *Management* (reissue)
John Tuxill and Gary Paul Nabhan

Plant Invaders: The Threat to Natural Ecosystems (reissue)
Quentin C B Cronk and Janice L Fuller

Tapping the Green Market:
Certification and Management of Non-Timber Forest Products
Patricia Shanley, Alan R Pierce, Sarah A Laird and Abraham Guillén (eds)

Uncovering the Hidden Harvest: Valuation Methods for Woodland and Forest
Resources
Bruce M Campbell and Martin K Luckert (eds)

Forthcoming titles in the series

Ethnobotany: A Methods Manual (2nd edition)
Gary J Martin

Tapping the Green Market

Certification and Management of Non-Timber Forest Products

*Edited by Patricia Shanley, Alan R Pierce,
Sarah A Laird and Abraham Guillén*

Earthscan Publications Ltd,
London • Sterling, VA

First published in the UK and USA in 2002 by
Earthscan Publications Ltd

ISBN: 1 85383 810 1 paperback
      1 85383 871 3 hardback

Typesetting by MapSet Ltd, Gateshead, UK
Printed and bound in the UK by The Bath Press
Cover design by Yvonne Booth
Cover photo by Esther Katz/CIFOR
Panda symbol © 1986 WWF
® WWF registered trademark owner

For a full list of publications please contact:
Earthscan Publications Ltd
120 Pentonville Road
London N1 9JN, UK
Tel: +44 (0)20 7278 0433
Fax: +44 (0)20 7278 1142
Email: earthinfo@earthscan.co.uk
Web: **www.earthscan.co.uk**

22883 Quicksilver Drive, Sterling, VA 20166–2012, USA

Earthscan is an editorially independent subsidiary of Kogan Page Ltd and publishes in association
with WWF-UK and the International Institute for Environment and Development

A catalogue record for this book is available from the British Library

Library of Congress Cataloging-in-Publication Data

Tapping the green market : certification and management of non-timber forest products / edited
by Patricia Shanley ... [et al.].
      p. cm. — (People and plants conservation series)
  Includes bibliographical references (p.   ).
  ISBN 1-85383-871-3 (hardback) — ISBN 1-85383-810-1 (pbk.)
   1. Non-timber forest products—Certification. I. Shanley, Patricia, 1955- II. People and
plants conservation series (Earthscan Publications Ltd.)

SD543 .T26 2002
338.1'74987—dc21

                                        2001006716

Contents

List of figures, tables and boxes   *viii*
About the contributors   *x*
The NTFP certification project team   *xiii*
The People and Plants initiative *by Alan Hamilton*   *xv*
People and Plants partners   *xvi*
Acknowledgements   *xvii*

Section I: Overview

Introduction *by Patricia Shanley, Sarah A Laird, Alan R Pierce and
 Abraham Guillén*   3

1   The rise of certification, the current state of the playing field for NTFP
    certification programmes and future prospects *by Jamison B Ervin and
    Patrick Mallet*   7
2   The process of drafting and revising guidelines for NTFP certification
    by Patricia Shanley and Sarah A Laird   20
3   Summaries of the field-testing results in Mexico, Bolivia and Brazil
    by Abraham Guillén   28

Section II: NTFP species profiles from around the world

Introduction *by Patricia Shanley, Alan R Pierce, Sarah A Laird and
 Abraham Guillén*   47

Latin America

4   Chicle (*Manilkara zapota*) *by Peter W Alcorn*   49
5   Brazil nut (*Bertholletia excelsa*) *by Enrique G Ortiz*   61
6   Palm heart (*Euterpe* spp.) *by Dennis Johnson*   75
7   Pau d'arco (*Tabebuia* spp.) *by M Constanza von der Pahlen*   85
8   Cat's claw (*Uncaria guianensis* and *U. tomentosa*) *by Miguel N Alexiades* 93
9   Breu resin (*Protium* spp.) *by Campbell Plowden*   110
10 Titica vine (*Heteropsis* spp.) *by Campbell Plowden*   116
11 Amapá (*Parahancornia* spp. and *Brosimum* spp.) *by Campbell Plowden* 123
12 Copaíba (*Copaifera* spp.) *by Campbell Plowden*   126
13 Sangre de drago (*Croton lechleri*) *by Miguel N Alexiades*   136

Eastern North America

14 Fiddlehead ferns (*Matteucia struthiopteris*) by *Alan R Pierce*   156
15 Maple syrup (*Acer saccharum*) by *Alan R Pierce*   162
16 American ginseng (*Panax quinquefolius*) by *Alan R Pierce*   172

The Mediterranean region

17 Mastic gum (*Pistacia lentiscus*), cork oak (*Quercus suber*), argan (*Argania spinosa*), pine nut (*Pinus pinea*), pine resin (various spp.) and chestnut (*Castanea sativa*) by *Yorgos Moussouris and Pedro Regato*   183

Sub-Saharan Africa

18 Griffonia (*Griffonia simplicifolia*) by *Kodzo Gbewonyo*   200
19 Baobab bark (*Adansonia digitata*) by *Claudia Romero, Isla Grundy, Bruce Campbell and Anthony B Cunningham*   208
20 Yohimbe (*Pausinystalia johimbe*) by *Terry C H Sunderland, Marie-Laure Ngo-Mpeck, Zacharie Tchoundjeu and Sarah A Laird*   215

Africa and Asia

21 Rattan (various spp.) by *Terry C H Sunderland and John Dransfield*   225
22 Amla (*Phyllanthus emblica*) by *Ganesan Balachander*   240
23 Sumatra benzoin (*Styrax* spp.) by *Esther Katz, Carmen García and Marina Goloubinoff*   246

Other initiatives

24 Sustainable harvesting of epiphytic bromeliads in the highlands of Chiapas, Mexico: a pilot study by *Jan H D Wolf and Cornelis J F Konings*   257
25 Reducing the ecological footprint of the 'wooden rhino': the case for certification of Kenyan woodcarvings by *Susanne F Schmitt and Anthony B Cunningham*   259

Section III: The core elements of NTFP certification

26 Ecological issues by *Alan R Pierce and Patricia Shanley*   267
27 Social issues by *Alan R Pierce*   283
28 Subsistence issues by *Alan R Pierce*   299
    Space outside the market: implications of NTFP certification for subsistence use – a northern case study from the Upper Peninsula Region, US by *Marla R Emery*   302
    The interface of timber and non-timber resources: declining resources for subsistence livelihoods – a southern case study from Brazilian Amazonia by *Patricia Shanley, Leda Luz and Margaret Cymerys*   313
29 Marketing issues by *Sarah A Laird and Abraham Guillén*   322
30 Technical issues by *Abraham Guillén, Alan R Pierce and Richard Z Donovan*   337

Contents

Section IV: Conclusions and recommendations

31 Conclusions and recommendations *by Patricia Shanley, Sarah A Laird,*
   Alan R Pierce and Abraham Guillén   353

Appendices

I   Generic guidelines for assessing the management of NTFPs
     by the NTFP certification project team   366
II   Species-specific NTFP certification guidelines for the production of maple
     syrup *by Alan R Pierce*   386
III Resource directory   399

Acronyms and abbreviations   403
References   407
Index   440

List of figures, tables and boxes

Figures

22.1	A value chain of amla fruits: from forest fruits to pickles	245
23.1	National and export markets for benzoin	254
28.1	NTFP exchange-value continuum	303
28.2	Product types and livelihood uses of Michigan NTFPs	307
28.3	1986–1995 average annual unemployment: Upper Peninsula (UP), Michigan (MI) and US rates	308
28.4	1995 unemployment fluctuations: Upper Peninsula (UP), Michigan (MI) and US rates	309
28.5	Number of species extracted by the timber industry in eastern Amazonia, Pará, Brazil	318
28.6	Fruit consumption in three Capin River communities, Pará, Brazil	318

Tables

1.1	Comparison of NTFP certification programmes	15
6.1	Commercialized *Euterpe* species	82
6.2	Non-commercialized *Euterpe* species	83
8.1	Differences between *U. tomentosa* and *U. guianensis*	96
15.1	Canadian and US production of maple syrup, 1997 and 1998	169
17.1	Annual resin production in Southern Europe, 1982 and 1997	194
20.1	Diagnostic bark characters of *P. johimbe* and *P. macroceras*	220
21.1	The rattan genera: number of species and their distribution	227
21.2	Available rattan floras by region to date	228
21.3	Some traditional uses of rattans, excluding cane	229
21.4	The major commercial species of rattan as identified for Asia by Dransfield and Manokaran (1994), and for Africa by Tuley (1995) and Sunderland (1999)	230
21.5	The growth rates of some commercial rattans in cultivation	235
21.6	Commercial-scale rattan trials and plantations	237
22.1	Estimated fruit production of amla from a south Indian forest	241
22.2	The many uses of *Phyllanthus emblica*	243
28.1	Motivational factors in informal and formal economies	304
28.2	Multiple uses of Michigan NTFPs	306
28.3	Medicinal tree species extracted as timber, Pará, Brazil	316
28.4	Fifteen of the most useful tree species (> 10cm dbh) to caboclos of the Capim River, Brazil, in a 1ha forest plot (200m x 50m)	317

29.1 Markets for selected NTFPs and examples of marketing limitations and
      opportunities afforded by certification   334

Boxes

1.1   A perspective on NTFP certification from the organic sector   12
1.2   Lessons learned from fairtrade   14
17.1 The Strofilia (*Pinus pinea*) forest in south-western Greece   191
26.1 Irresponsible marketing of Amazonian Viagra   269
26.2 Bows and arrows: tools for palm heart management?   273
26.3 Marketing success: ecological and social failure   279
26.4 Borneo camphor: decline of a historically important NTFP   281
27.1 Ethical and legal obligations of commercializing traditional knowledge
      and resources   287
27.2 Ayahuasca (*Banisteriopsis* spp. and admixtures): appropriation and
      globalization of a sacred NTFP   297
29.1 An industry perspective: Shaman Botanicals' view on the certification of
      NTFPs   332
30.1 Management planning requirements for certification of NTFPs   339
30.2 Steps to establish production systems for NTFPs   340

About the contributors

Peter W Alcorn is president of Wild Things, Inc, a chewing gum manufacturer based in Gainesville, Florida.

Miguel N Alexiades, PhD, is Nuffield Fellow in Ethnobotany at the Department of Anthropology, University of Kent at Canterbury, UK.

Jean Allan is director of the Falls Brook Centre, an environmental organization promoting sustainable agriculture and forestry in New Brunswick, Canada.

Ganesan Balachander works in the Center for Compatible Economic Development at The Nature Conservancy in Leesburg, Virginia.

Beto Borges is programme executive for the Goldman Environmental Prize and was formerly the manager of Sustainable Harvesting, Ethnobotany and Conservation at Shaman Pharmaceuticals in San Francisco, California.

Bruce Campbell, PhD, works at the Center for International Forestry Research (CIFOR) in Bogor, Indonesia.

Anthony (Tony) B Cunningham, PhD, is WWF/UNESCO/Kew People and Plants regional coordinator for Africa.

Margaret Cymerys, MES, is a wildlife biologist with six years' experience working in the Brazilian Amazon.

John Dransfield is the senior principal scientific officer in charge of palm research at the Royal Botanic Gardens, Kew, in the UK. He has worked on the taxonomy, ecology and silviculture of rattans since 1970, is author of several books and two interactive CD-ROMs on rattans, and is co-author of *Genera Palmarum*.

Marla R Emery, PhD, is a research geographer with the United States Department of Agriculture's Forest Service, Northeastern Research Station, Burlington, Vermont.

Jamison B Ervin is an independent consultant in ecological research and policy analysis.

Carmen García, PhD, is an ecologist researching the ecology and value of non-timber forest products (NTFPs) at CIFOR's regional office in Belém, Brazil.

Kodzo Gbewonyo, who holds ScD and MBA degrees, has several years of industrial experience in pharmaceutical R&D, and is currently president of BioResources International Inc, a company engaged in commercial development of natural products from West African biodiversity.

Marina Goloubinoff is an anthropologist who has worked as a consultant for several French and international research centres including CIFOR and the International Centre for Research in Agroforestry (ICRAF).

Isla Grundy, PhD, is a faculty member of the Forestry Department at the University of Stellenbosch in Matieland, South Africa.

Bee Gunn works at the New York Botanical Garden (NYBG).

Dennis Johnson, PhD, is a geographer who has maintained a research interest in palm utilization and conservation for 30 years, while working in international development and teaching.

Esther Katz is an ethnobotanist at the French Institute of Research for Development (IRD) with fieldwork experience in Mexico, the Congo and Indonesia. She has collaborated for four years with the Forest People and Plants team at CIFOR.

Steven R King, PhD, is senior vice president for Ethnobotany and Conservation at Shaman Pharmaceuticals.

Cornelis (Kees) J F Konings, MSc, is a forest ecologist currently studying epiphytes in Mexico.

Leda Luz is a forester working in the threatened Atlantic Forest of Brazil.

Patrick Mallet is an environmental consultant who is focused on improving community-based resource stewardship in agriculture, agroforestry and forestry through ecological and social certification and marketing initiatives.

Daniel Marmillod works at the Centro Agronómico Tropical de Investigación y Enseñanza (CATIE) in Turrialba, Costa Rica.

Yorgos Moussouris holds degrees in engineering, geology and planning, and currently works with Alcyon, an Athens-based environmental consulting firm dealing with development projects.

Marie-Laure Ngo-Mpeck works with the International Centre for Research in Agroforestry (ICRAF) in Yaounde, Cameroon.

Enrique G Ortiz is senior programme officer for the Gordon and Betty Moore Foundation.

Maria Constanza von der Pahlen, MES, is an independent consultant in conservation science based in Massachusetts.

Julie Pereira is a former employee of FairTrade International in Alsemberg, Belgium.

Campbell Plowden, PhD, is acting head of Pennsylvania State University Graduate Ecology Program in College Park, Pennsylvania.

Pedro Regato, PhD, is a forest ecologist and currently serves as coordinator of the Forest Unit at WWF's Mediterranean Programme Office in Rome, Italy.

Claudia Romero is a tropical ecologist and PhD candidate in the Botany Department at the University of Florida in Gainesville.

Gunar Rundgren is an organic agriculture specialist working in Höje, Sweden.

Susanne F Schmitt, PhD, is International Plants Conservation Officer and Assistant Co-ordinator of the People and Plants initiative based at the WWF United Kingdom (WWF-UK) office in Godalming, UK.

Terry C H Sunderland, PhD, works with the African Rattan Research Programme, a project of the Royal Botanic Gardens, Kew (RBG), UK.

Zacharie Tchoundjeu works with the International Centre for Research in Agroforestry (ICRAF) in Yaounde, Cameroon.

Antonio Valente da Silva is an illustrator living in Corte Madera, California.

Róger Villalobos works at the Centro Agronómico Tropical de Investigación y Enseñanza (CATIE) in Turrialba, Costa Rica.

Jan H D Wolf, PhD, University of Amsterdam, is a tropical ecologist specializing in the ecology of epiphytes and epiphyte communities.

The NTFP certification project team

Patricia Shanley has worked with forest-based communities in the eastern Amazon over the past decade, concentrating on the impacts of logging on locally valued fruit and medicinals and the comparative economic value of timber and non-timber species. Shanley has co-authored two non-timber forest product (NTFP) manuals focusing on the use and marketing of significant NTFPs in eastern Amazonia: *Forest Fruit Trees in the Life of Amazonians* (1998) and *Recipes without Words: Medicinal Plants of Amazonia* (1995), both published in Portuguese. Shanley received her PhD from the University of Kent, UK, and is currently a research scientist for the Center for International Forestry Research (CIFOR) in Bogor, Indonesia.

Richard Z Donovan served as director of SmartWood, a forest management certification programme of the Rainforest Alliance, from 1992 to 2000 and is currently chief of forestry at the Rainforest Alliance. During 1987 to June 1991 he was senior fellow with World Wildlife Fund, US, coordinating the grassroots Osa Peninsula Forest Conservation and Management Project (BOSCOSA) in Costa Rica. He received an MSc in natural resource management from Antioch College.

Abraham Guillén worked for three years as the product and market development coordinator for the Bolivia Sustainable Forestry Management Project (BOLFOR), a US Agency for International Development (USAID) project. A Honduran native, he also worked for four years as associate regional forester for USAID in Central America. He holds an MA in international marketing from the Universidad Nur, in Santa Cruz, Bolivia, an MEd from Framingham State College in Massachusetts and an MBA from the Universidad Nacional Autónoma de Honduras. He is currently the international marketing and programme manager for the Rainforest Alliance's SmartWood programme.

Sarah A Laird works on the commercial and cultural context of biodiversity and forest conservation, including NTFPs. Her work is primarily based in Cameroon, although in recent years it has also included South Africa and Malaysia. She is co-author of *Biodiversity Prospecting* (1993), *An Introductory Handbook to Cocoa Certification* (1996) and *The Commercial Use of Biodiversity* (1999), and editor of *Biodiversity and Traditional Knowledge* (2002). She received an MSc in forestry from Oxford University.

Sergio Madrid is the executive director of the Consejo Civil Mexicano para la Silvicultura Sostenible (CCMSS), located in Mexico City. He has served on several national committees for forestry and certification issues. He holds a BSc in agronomy and is an MSc candidate in the Rural Development Programme at the Universidad Autónoma Metropolitana in Mexico City.

Alan R Pierce is an independent consultant specializing in ecological research and policy analysis. He previously worked with the Forest Stewardship Council. He received an MSc in forestry from the University of Vermont.

Tasso Rezende de Azevedo is the Manaus regional director of the Instituto de Manejo e Certificação Florestal e Agrícola (IMAFLORA), located in Piracicaba, Brazil. He has worked in the field of certification for more than seven years and is former co-chair of the Forest Stewardship Council's NTFP working group. He received a BSc in forestry from the University of São Paulo.

The People and Plants initiative

There has been great emphasis on timber extraction and its effects on plant conservation, but non-timber forest products (NTFPs) are increasingly recognized as being of major importance. The harvesting of such products can have lower impacts on forest ecosystems than other uses, provide a range of social and economic benefits to local groups, and is potentially compatible with efforts to integrate the use and conservation of biodiversity.

Some products, such as Brazil nut, rattan, palm heart, pine resin, maple syrup, mushrooms and chicle, are internationally traded. These are important revenue earners for regional and national economies, but they also provide communities with key resources and a valuable means of generating income. However, there is relatively little documentation about the ecology, use and management of even the most widely utilized non-timber species.

Non-timber forest resources are a more difficult group of products to certify than timber, partly because of their diverse nature and social and ecological complexity. However, in spite of these challenges, opportunities exist to promote sound ecological and social practices in NTFP management and trade through market tools such as certification, and their potential realization in practice is the subject of this book.

People and Plants is an initiative of WWF, the United Nations Educational, Scientific and Cultural Organization (UNESCO) and the Royal Botanic Gardens, Kew (RBG). It aims to increase the capacity for community-based plant conservation worldwide. Training is undertaken at field sites in selected countries, with case studies and other information made available to a wide audience through various publications, training videos and the internet. Publications include working papers, issues developed through a handbook and discussion papers, in addition to the People and Plants conservation series, to which the present work contributes.

The People and Plants website can be visited at www.rbgkew.org.uk/peopleplants. It contains full versions of the smaller People and Plants publications, as well as contact information for organizations involved in applied ethnobotany and news about field projects and other activities.

Alan Hamilton
Head, International Plants Conservation Unit
WWF-UK

PEOPLE AND PLANTS WEBSITE:

www.rbgkew.org.uk/peopleplants

People and Plants partners

WWF

WWF (formerly the World Wide Fund For Nature), founded in 1961, is the world's largest private nature conservation organization. It consists of 29 national organizations and associates, and works in more than 100 countries. The coordinating headquarters are in Gland, Switzerland. The WWF mission is to conserve biodiversity, to ensure that the use of renewable natural resources is sustainable and to promote actions to reduce pollution and wasteful consumption.

UNESCO

The United Nations Educational, Scientific and Cultural Organization (UNESCO) is the only UN agency with a mandate spanning the fields of science (including social sciences), education, culture and communication. UNESCO has over 40 years of experience in testing interdisciplinary approaches to solving environmental and development problems in programmes such as that on Man and the Biosphere (MAB). An international network of biosphere reserves provides sites for conservation of biological diversity, long-term ecological research and testing and demonstrating approaches to the sustainable use of natural resources.

ROYAL BOTANIC GARDENS, KEW

The Royal Botanic Gardens (RBG), Kew, has 150 professional staff and associated researchers and works with partners in over 42 countries. Research focuses on taxonomy, preparation of floras, economic botany, plant biochemistry and many other specialized fields. The Royal Botanic Gardens has one of the largest herbaria in the world and an excellent botanic library.

The People and Plants initiative is supported financially by the Darwin Initiative, the National Lottery Charities Board and the Department for International Development (DFID) in the UK, the European Union (EU) and the Norwegian Funds in Trust.

Disclaimer

Acknowledgements

This project, and the resulting manual, were made possible through a range of collaborations and reflect the diverse and multidisciplinary nature of NTFP use and management. Invaluable collaboration in the field-testing of guidelines was provided by a number of experts. We wish to thank team leader Sergio Madrid, ecologist Aliza Mizrachi, forester Xavier García, Fair Trade eV representative Margit Schlagenhauf and Peter Alcorn of Wild Things Chewing Gum Company for their help with the Noh Bec chicle assessment in Mexico. The Bolivian field assessment team was made possible through the efforts of team leader Sergio Madrid, biologist Damián Rumiz, anthropologist Ruth Silva and foresters Jeffrey Hayward and Pedro Savavia. Geographer and ecologist Dennis Johnson, agronomists Westphalen Nunes and Manuel Vital, anthropologist Rui Murrieta and forester Tasso Rezende de Azevedo provided assistance in the Brazilian field trials. The NTFP certification project is particularly grateful to the in-country support supplied by: Sergio Madrid and the staff of the Consejo Civil Mexicano para la Silvicultura Sostenible (CCMSS) for the Mexican field trial; Pedro Saravia (CIMAR), Fernando Aguilar (Consejo Boliviano para la Certificación Forestal Voluntaria), John Nittler and Roberto Sainz (BOLFOR/USAID, Bolivia) for the Bolivian field trial; and Tasso Rezende de Azevedo and the staff of the Instituto de Manejo e Certificação Florestal e Agrícola for the Brazilian field trials.

Of enormous assistance throughout was the Project Advisory Committee, which not only helped to ground the draft guidelines in its many areas of expertise, but also provided insight and comments, including review of the chapters presented in this book. Individuals in the committee include: Mike Arnold, Center for International Forestry Research (CIFOR)/Oxford/Overseas Development Institute (ODI); Jason Clay, WWF; Carol Colfer, CIFOR; Tony Cunningham, People and Plants; Ousseynou Ndoye, CIFOR; Alicia Grimes, US Agency for International Development (USAID); Nickie Irvine, Stanford University; Edward Millard, Conservation International (CI); William Milliken, Royal Botanic Garden, Edinburgh; Charles Peters, New York Botanical Garden (NYBG); Manuel Ruiz-Perez, Universidad Autónoma de Madrid; Terry Sunderland, African Rattan Research Programme, Royal Botanic Gardens (RBG), Kew; and Yorgos Moussouris, independent consultant to the NTFP Project of the WWF Mediterranean Programme.

The manual benefited greatly from the contributions and comments of a variety of individuals, including: Jamison Ervin, Patrick Mallet, Dennis Johnson, Tasso Rezende, Marla Emery, Trish Flaster, Conrad Reining, Julie Pereira and Gunnar Rundgren. A special thanks is owed to Dawn Ward for her assistance in coordinating various aspects of the NTFP certification project from its inception. The authors are very grateful to Antonio Valente da Silva, Bee Gunn and Jamison Ervin for contributing their beautiful illustrations. We would also like to thank Kees Konings for the use of Antonio Rodríguez's bromeliad sketch in Chapter 24.

The contents of this book stem from the Rainforest Alliance's NTFP Marketing and Management Project which received support from the United States Agency for International Development (USAID). The mission of the Rainforest Alliance is to protect ecosystems and the people and wildlife that live within them by implementing better business practices for biodiversity conservation and sustainability. Technical and logistical support was provided by the staff of the Rainforest Alliance and its SmartWood programme, including Daniel Katz, Karin Kreider, Elizabeth Skinner and G P Varshneya.

We wish to thank the Ford Foundation for its generous financial assistance in publishing this volume and the Center for International Forestry Research (CIFOR), the Rainforest Alliance and the People and Plants initiative for supporting the distributing of the book in developing countries.

And, finally, many thanks are due to USAID – in particular, John McMahon and Alicia Grimes, who made this project possible and were a source of great encouragement and support throughout.

While the invaluable assistance of all the above is greatly appreciated, any errors or omissions are, of course, the responsibility of the authors alone.

Section I

OVERVIEW

Introduction

Patricia Shanley, Sarah A Laird, Alan R Pierce and Abraham Guillén

NTFPs and certification

Non-timber forest products (NTFPs) are critical to rural subsistence livelihoods in both tropical and temperate forested areas and make up significant local, regional and international markets. They provide communities with key subsistence resources and with a valuable means of generating cash income. Some high-value, internationally traded products, such as Brazil nut, rattan, palm heart, pine resin, maple syrup, mushrooms and chicle, are also important revenue earners for regional and national economies.

In the tropical Americas and elsewhere, however, NTFPs have long been 'invisible' to, or undervalued by, many government policy-makers, non-governmental organizations (NGOs) and scientific researchers, most of whom have directed the bulk of their attention toward wood-based forest products. As a result, the economic significance of NTFPs is

Illustration by Antônio Valente da Silva

*Piquiá (*Caryocar villosum*)*

poorly documented and relatively little information exists concerning the ecology, use and management of even the most widely utilized non-timber species. This paucity of data stems from the difficulty of valuing NTFPs, as they are primarily used and exchanged in informal economies by local communities.

There is, however, growing recognition of the important economic, social and ecological values of NTFPs, and the complementary roles they can play to timber, agriculture and other land uses. NTFP harvests can have lower impacts on forest ecosystems than other uses, provide a range of social and economic benefits to local groups, and are potentially compatible with efforts to integrate the use and conservation of biodiversity.

In addition, the liberalization of international trade regimes has created significant opportunities for, as well as challenges to, the sustainable use and conservation of forest resources. Deregulation has the capacity to expand the commercialization of NTFPs that already play a significant role in the agricultural, pharmaceutical and personal care industries. However, initiatives to liberalize international trade may also threaten to escalate logging and overharvest of NTFP resources, which are likely to have direct and, in many places, detrimental consequences for rural communities and forest habitats.

Certification is a relatively new forest policy tool that attempts to foster responsible resource stewardship through the labelling of consumer products. The premise is that consumers will seek out and support products that are reputably certified as hailing from well-managed sources. To date, forest management certification has focused on timber products, although some attention is now being given to NTFPs.

While many lessons can be drawn from timber certification, transfer of existing timber-based guidelines and procedures to NTFPs is inappropriate. Non-timber forest resources are a more difficult group of products to certify than timber due to a multitude of factors, including their exceedingly diverse and idiosyncratic nature and social and ecological complexity. However, in spite of these challenges, opportunities exist to promote sound ecological and social practices in NTFP management and trade through market tools such as certification, and their potential realization in practice is the subject of this manual.

Demand from international consumers for 'green' or 'fairtrade' forest products is significant and on the rise. In addition to products with established markets, such as Brazil nuts (*Bertholletia excelsa*), palm heart (*Euterpe oleracea*), rattan (various species), maple syrup

(from *Acer saccharum*), ginseng (*Panax* spp.) and yohimbe (*Pausinystalia johimbe*), there is growing demand for new and varied products. These include medicinals such as cat's claw (*Uncaria* spp.), *Croton* spp., pau d'arco (*Tabebuia* spp.) and kava (*Piper methysticum*), natural sources of currently synthetic ingredients such as chicle (*Manilkara zapota* latex used as a base for chewing gum), and expanded markets for 'wild' foods such as fiddlehead ferns (*Matteucia struthiopteris*), various mushrooms and wild leeks (*Allium tricoccum*).

Certification may be able to create incentives for improved management and beneficial social practices associated with existing products, and might help ensure that products new to international markets meet standards for ecological sustainability and social responsibility. Certification can also help to differentiate sustainable and fairtrade products in the marketplace. Increasing numbers of companies are seeking certified sources of raw materials as part of wider efforts to position themselves as socially and environmentally responsible, to secure reliable sources of well-managed raw materials or as a means of tapping into new markets. A few local producers have found that certification can help them sell products and gain access to new markets.

Certification is a market-based tool for social and environmental change and is dependent upon companies and consumers sharing the common values and goals articulated in certification standards and guidelines. In some cases, this means companies and consumers will need to pay more, and in others they will need to make the additional effort to seek out certified products. European consumers and companies have proved most committed to creating change through the consumption of products certified 'organic', 'fairtrade' or 'eco'; but consumers around the world are increasingly receptive to certified products. The least receptive appear to be consumers in countries with widespread poverty, where certified products and concerns cannot be considered a priority. As a result, certification of NTFPs will work best for those products with significant markets in countries with the necessary corporate and consumer base, which rules out most of the NTFPs consumed around the world.

Certification requires a high level of organization and technical sophistication from producers, especially with regard to management planning, monitoring, product tracing and marketing. Many NTFPs are gathered by individuals or families with little thought toward the formal economic sector. The level of organization and sophistication required by certification programmes, not to mention their costs, will prevent most NTFP harvesters around the world from participating in such initiatives unless they have access to sustained technical and financial assistance. Many NTFP markets are small in scope and value, and attract limited attention or investment. The scope for certification to promote sustainable and socially responsible practices is thus limited to a select, small number of formalized, internationally traded NTFP species; however, in these cases it may be a potentially useful tool. Whether or not certification is the end goal, certification criteria and methods might also benefit forest managers, companies and donor agencies by providing reputable standards of sustainability against which local performance can be measured.

The NTFP marketing and management project

This manual is a product of the Rainforest Alliance's NTFP Marketing and Management Project (more commonly referred to as the NTFP certification project), which was supported by the United States Agency for International Development (USAID). The purpose of the project was to explore the feasibility of NTFP certification, with a principal geographic focus on Latin America. The project team worked with an extensive network of collaborators in Mexico and Central and South America to evaluate the impact of certification on the management, harvest and sale of several different NTFPs from distinct settings. The NTFP certification project and manual are a collaborative effort that grew in response to the interests of non-governmental organizations working with producer groups throughout Latin America, including the following: in Brazil, the Instituto de Manejo e Certificação Florestal e Agrícola (IMAFLORA); in Bolivia, the Centro de Investigación y Manejo de Recursos Naturales Renovables (CIMAR); and in Mexico, the Consejo Civil Mexicano para la Silvicultura Sostenible (CCMSS). Some of these groups had already begun to draft certification guidelines for high-value products such as Brazil nut, palm heart, pine resin and chicle, and many were familiar with timber certification through membership of the forest management network, Certificación Integral de Bosques Americanos (CEIBA), coordinated by SmartWood, the Rainforest Alliance's programme for forest management certification. The project strove to learn from and expand upon existing guidelines while promoting complementarity and consistency between geographically scattered and conceptually distinct efforts.

The first phase of the project involved drafting generic guidelines and indicators for NTFP certification, drawing upon the work of these groups and others. Guidelines, indicators and verifiers were developed by plant class or part and then field-tested in three sites – Brazil (palm hearts), Bolivia (Brazil nuts) and Mexico (chicle). Additional NTFP field tests were undertaken by the WWF Mediterranean Programme Office in Greece (for chestnut production) and Spain (cork). Based on these experiences, guidelines were modified, and information on the strengths of and limitations to NTFP certification was recorded. Species profiles for both temperate and tropical NTFPs from around the world were collected in order to expand our understanding of the social, ecological, marketing and technical aspects of certification and to test the desirability and feasibility of certification for a broad range of species. This book includes the final draft guidelines, indicators and verifiers and species profiles, as well as insights and practical guidance resulting from this process. It is not intended as the definitive word on the subject, but as the basis for further development of the concept and practice of NTFP management and certification.

Structure of the book

The book is organized into four sections. Section I provides an introduction to certification systems, tracing the evolution of timber certification and drawing out relevant lessons for NTFP certification. This section also introduces the guideline development process (readers can find the final generic guidelines, indicators and verifiers by plant class in Appendix I). Section I concludes by relating experiences from field-testing of the guidelines in Mexico, Bolivia and Brazil.

Section II expands the focus of the manual to incorporate a range of temperate as well as tropical NTFP species profiles. The species profiles examine unique ecological, social, cultural and marketing elements – and in so doing, portray the enormous diversity in NTFPs – as well as the potential, or incompatibility, of certification to act as a tool for the promotion of environmental and social objectives in each case. The species represent not only geographical diversity, but different classes (resins, roots, bark, herbs, fibres), markets (subsistence, local, regional, international), uses (eg medicinal, edible, craft, fibre) and sources (primary forest, secondary forest, fallow).

Section III examines the 'core elements' of NTFP certification, with chapters covering ecological, social, marketing and technical issues. An additional chapter on subsistence issues highlights the importance of NTFPs to subsistence livelihoods in both the North and the South.

Section IV concludes with a review of the central lessons learned, summarizing some of the opportunities and challenges afforded by NTFP certification.

Guidelines for assessing the management of NTFPs, incuding verifiers and indicators for sustainable harvest of vegetative structures (apical bud, bark, root, leaves), reproductive propagules (fruits, seeds) and exudates, are set out in Appendix I. Appendix II provides an example of species-specific guideline for maple syrup. Appendix III presents a list of valuable resources.

Chapter 1

The rise of certification, the current state of the playing field for NTFP certification programmes and future prospects

Jamison B Ervin and Patrick Mallet

Certification in context

As early as 1906, with the Food and Drug Act, labelling has been an important quality assurance tool for consumers (Hadden, 1986). Since then, the notion of quality, first used to describe food purity, has greatly expanded to cover health, nutrition, safety and social and environmental responsibility. Such programmes include dolphin-safe tuna, kosher-certified foods, sweatshop-free clothing, bird-friendly coffee, fairtrade coffee, environmentally safe electricity and cruelty-free cosmetics. Such labels empower consumers to voice their concerns directly through their purchases, instead of indirectly through their votes. While over half of all Americans consider the environmental attributes of a product (EPA, 1993), savvy consumer-citizens are

Illustration by Antônio Valente da Silva

*Brazil nut (*Bertholletia excelsa*)*

increasingly distrustful of industry claims and corporate green-washing and have begun seeking out third-party assurances regarding the products they purchase.

In many cases their distrust is warranted. A UK survey found 626 environmental claims on wood products from selected stores. Of the labelled tropical wood products, less than half were able to provide any kind of assurances whatsoever, and only three companies were able to document that their products came from well-managed forests (WWF-UK, 1995). 'For some companies', concluded WWF, 'establishing an environmental policy is primarily a public relations exercise' (WWF-UK, 1995).

At about the same time as the labelling proliferation of the early 1990s, forestry underwent its own transformation. The concept of 'sustained yield forestry' had gained currency among foresters during the mid-1900s. This approach viewed timber as the primary objective of forest management, and gave scant recognition to other forest products, benefits or services. In the 1980s and 1990s, public pressures for the protection of a host of forest attributes – clean water, wildlife habitat, old-growth protection – forced forest policy-makers to reconsider the sustained yield approach. Ecosystem management, a philosophy that sought to sustain healthy, diverse ecosystems by balancing human needs with environmental values (Robertson, 1992; in Salwasser et al, 1993) emerged as a new paradigm. This confluence of ecological and socio-economic values provided a backdrop in which forest product certification's goal of encouraging 'ecologically sound, socially beneficial and economically viable forestry' (FSC, 1999) seemed to be not a radical departure from existing norms, but a natural extension of prevailing attitudes.

The past decade has given rise to numerous principles, guidelines and standards for forest management at the international level, including the Pan-European Criteria, the Montreal Process, the International Tropical Timber Agreement, the Amazonian Treaty, the United Nations Conference on Environment and Development (UNCED) Forest Principles and the Forest Stewardship Council's Principles and Criteria (Elliott, 1999). The variety of actors involved, the abundance of approaches to defining sustainable forestry and the different purposes of the standards underscore the depth and breadth of the movement toward standardization and regulation of forest management worldwide.

The notion of corporate citizenship and environmental responsibility has become as fundamental to businesses in the 1990s as growth and corporate takeovers were in the 1980s. By the early 1990s, nearly half of all Fortune 500 companies had board-level committees for environmental affairs (Tibor, 1996) and over 70,000 companies were committed to some form of environmentally responsible commerce in the US alone (Hawken, 1993).

Environmental responsibility entails what author Paul Hawken calls a 'restorative economy', in which there is 'a predictable and consistent market that recognizes the true, full costs of doing business and reassigns them to the marketplace where they belong' (Hawken, 1993). Hawken cites companies such as The Body Shop, Ben and Jerry's and Tom's of Maine as exemplars of the new movement toward corporate responsibility.

The growing recognition of corporations' environmental responsibility to society at large, the need to manage for long-term intergenerational needs and the importance of the marketplace in achieving those goals afforded certification with a ready cadre of businesses willing to seriously consider third-party certification.

In short, the following conditions have created a climate that has enabled the rise of third-party certification:

- the proliferation of labels and the emergence of savvy consumer-citizens;
- increasingly complex expectations for forest management and the inadequacy of traditional assessments to measure that management;
- the failure of public policy to stem the rising tide of deforestation and the subsequent search for other models, including market mechanisms;
- the renaissance of standardization and the proliferation of attempts to quantify sustainable forestry; and
- the rise of corporate environmental responsibility.

Overview of NTFP certification programmes

Third-party certification includes both an independent assessment of the forest management practices of an operation, according to pre-defined standards and criteria, and a verification of the product origin through chain-of-custody monitoring and product labelling. The goal of certification is to improve environmental, social and economic aspects of forest management by ensuring market access for responsibly produced products (Elliott, 1999). Accreditation is a process whereby certifiers are evaluated to ensure consumers that the product labels they see in the marketplace are consistent, reliable and credible (Ervin et al, 1996).

Certification of natural products, including NTFPs, is a rapidly evolving field, as evinced by the emergence of a wide variety of new certification systems over the past 15 years. Each of these systems focuses on specific objectives, ranging from promoting the well-being of producers to reducing the environmental impact of a forest operation. While each certification programme has its own priorities and objectives, the general aim of most is to move production systems toward more sustainable practices. In the case of NTFP management, 'sustainable production' means practices that work within ecological constraints, provide socio-economic benefits to harvesters, producers and local communities, and are in alignment with prevailing cultural norms. The criteria within each certification system reflect these three cornerstones of sustainability.

The systems directly relevant to NTFP certification include:

- the Forest Stewardship Council (FSC), which promotes forest stewardship practices worldwide through an accreditation programme of forest product certifiers;
- the International Federation of Organic Agriculture Movements (IFOAM), which promotes sustainable agriculture through an international accreditation programme of organic agriculture certifiers; and
- the Fairtrade Labelling Organizations International (FLO), which promotes equitable trade relations between producers and consumers by coordinating national fairtrade labelling initiatives in 17 countries.

Forest Stewardship Council (FSC)

First conceived in 1989 by a handful of timber traders, woodworkers and representatives of environmental and human rights groups, the FSC is a relative newcomer to the accreditation scene. Propelled by the forces and trends described earlier, the FSC grew to include a broad spectrum of stakeholders, ranging from Brazilian rubber tappers to international labour leaders from local watershed advocacy groups to internationally recognized environmental groups; and from tiny community-managed operations to some of the largest timber producers in the world. Today, the FSC system has grown to cover more than 16.5 million hectares of forest in over 30 countries, and represents hundreds of diverse interests worldwide.

FSC's mission is to promote environmentally responsible forestry practices that ensure the maintenance of a forest's biodiversity, productivity and ecological processes; socially beneficial practices that provide local communities and society at large with an array of benefits; and economically viable management that provides adequate financial incentives to adhere to long-term stewardship practices. These objectives are further defined by a set of broad principles and criteria that apply to all forests worldwide. The FSC's principles and criteria, along with an accompanying set of more specific, regional standards tailored to local ecological and socio-economic conditions, allow for a fairly comprehensive yet flexible platform for developing NTFP standards and guidelines on an ad hoc basis.

FSC's current policy of allowing NTFP certification on a case-by-case basis, and the mandate from its recent strategic plan to 'provide an enabling environment for NTFP certification and labelling' (FSC, 1998), has resulted in a flurry of NTFP activities. Chicle gum is the first non-timber product to be certified and labelled under the FSC. Ongoing case studies and field tests on products include Brazil nut, palm heart and maple syrup. In addition, certifiers such as SmartWood are incorporating NTFP standards into their generic certification standards.

International Federation of Organic Agricultural Movements (IFOAM)

Founded in 1972 as a non-profit federation of organic agricultural interests, IFOAM is the oldest of the international programmes discussed in this chapter. Many of the initial members were European farmer organizations that were already certifying products as organic using their own locally developed standards. IFOAM has since grown steadily from its European roots to encompass over 650 members worldwide. The diverse membership has strongly influenced how IFOAM standards have been

and continue to be developed. While membership of IFOAM is open to any individual or organization with an interest in organic agriculture, voting rights are restricted to those organizations whose production systems are predominantly organic.

IFOAM's *Basic Standards for Organic Agriculture and Food Processing* were first published in 1980 as a means to standardize criteria within existing certification programmes. IFOAM members authorized the development of an international accreditation programme in 1990. This came as a result of its 15 years of experience in evaluating certification programmes (IOAS, 1998), and was built on the perceived need for an independent body to assess the compliance of organizations claiming to adhere to IFOAM standards (Courville, 1999). The accreditation programme was formally launched in 1992 and, in 1997, was transferred to the newly registered International Organic Accreditation Service, based in the US.

According to IFOAM (1998a), 'organic' is defined as:

> '...various systems for producing food and fibers according to specific standards that promote environmental, social and economic health. These systems take local soil fertility as a key to successful production. By respecting the natural capacity of plants, animals and the landscape, it aims to optimize quality in all aspects of agriculture and the environment. Organic agriculture practises sustainability by dramatically reducing external inputs such as chemical and genetically synthesized fertilizers, pesticides and pharmaceuticals.'

In contrast to the FSC, which depends upon a spare overarching framework, IFOAM's approach towards standards has been one of increasing detail and scope of the issues covered. Accredited certifiers are able to bring forward proposed criteria for new types of organic production that fall outside those covered by the basic standards. The result is a more detailed set of standards that certifiers and national certification programmes then adapt to fit local circumstances. Some examples of recently developed standards include aquaculture and textiles, while standards for NTFPs have been in effect for some time.

NTFPs fall within IFOAM's 'wild-harvested' section. The section specific to NTFPs, entitled 'Collection of Non-Cultivated Material of Plant Origin including Honey' includes a few sentences regarding protection from, and avoidance of, prohibited substances, pollution and contamination, and a brief reference to ecological processes (IFOAM, 1998b):

> '...wild-harvested products shall only be certified organic if derived from a stable and sustainable growing environment. Harvesting or gathering the product shall not exceed the sustainable yield of the ecosystem, or threaten the existence of plant or animal species'.

In addition to these standards, wild-harvested products must meet all other requirements as laid out in the basic standards document. Each certifier then has the option to develop specific additional standards related to wild-harvested products. While many certifiers have done so (NTFPs certified as wild harvested include berries, tea, honey, coffee, mushrooms and ginseng, among others), the percentage of total certified organic products that are wild-harvested is very small.

In the basic standards document, certifiers have the option to develop their own forestry standards based on IFOAM's 'Principle Aims for Organic Agriculture' and on the 'Standards for Social Justice'. While IFOAM has refrained somewhat from making further headway in developing its own forestry standards due to the obvious overlap with the work of the FSC, it has formed a subcommittee to explore the possible development of forestry standards in the future (see Box 1.1 for an organic perspective on NTFP certification).

Fairtrade Labelling Organizations International (FLO)

Fairtrade labelling emerged from a long history of alternative trade movements that date back to the 1960s. These 'alternative trade organizations' emphasized direct trading relationships with developing world producers and dealt mainly in craft products. Max Havelaar Coffee launched the first fairtrade product based on standardized criteria in the Netherlands in 1988. Numerous other initiatives, including the Transfair Network and the Fairtrade Foundation, quickly followed. In 1997, these initiatives coalesced under the umbrella Fairtrade Labelling Organizations in order to harmonize and standardize fairtrade labelling worldwide (Waridel, 1999).

FLO does not accredit its 17 national members, but rather plays a coordinating role between them. Its goal is to promote sustainable development through fairtrade by creating export opportunities for disadvantaged producers and increasing the volume and market share of fairtrade-labelled goods around the world. Like organic and forest product labels, fairtrade labels provide a means by which consumers can positively contribute to sustainable practices. Current trade in FLO

BOX 1.1 A PERSPECTIVE ON NTFP CERTIFICATION FROM THE ORGANIC SECTOR

Gunnar Rundgren

Organic agriculture certification relates to non-timber forest product (NTFP) certification in several different ways. Organic production standards cover agroforestry, forest garden and permaculture production systems fairly well. The International Federation of Organic Agriculture Movements (IFOAM) does not define products from such systems as NTFPs but rather as organic products.

Currently there are organic standards for 'wild' production of edible goods. These standards have been developed for the collection of herbs, berries, mushrooms, fruits and nuts, etc. The main reason for developing the 'wild' standard was to ensure that these products could be used as part of an organic food product. Having organic standards for wild products allows products with mixed or multiple contents to qualify for the organic label. Many organic consumers likely view wild products as being the most organic products available. Thus, use of the term wild may be somewhat confusing and contradictory, and should be understood as relating to the products and not to the production system. The wild standards normally regulate:

- non-cultivation of the actual product (the harvested/collected product will not be subject to any direct cultivation measures such as pruning, planting, etc);
- non-contamination (no use of chemicals, distance from points of pollution, etc);
- identification of the areas of harvesting/collection;
- sustainable harvesting/collection of the actual product (not necessarily the entire forest where the product grows).

The organic wild production standards therefore cannot be seen as standards for sustainable forestry, and organic wild products are not defined as sustainable forestry NTFPs.

The point of FSC certification for NTFPs is that the product originates from sustainable forestry. For the organic movement, including some products in sustainable forestry, NTFP certification makes little or no sense. Take the examples of typical agricultural crops such as oil palm and coffee. To define coffee as a forest product will not provide sustainable forestry NTFP certification with any improved credibility. It is true that coffee often grows under forest shade, but it is also clear that if coffee production is the principal goal of the farmer, he will tend to direct his forest management toward optimization of coffee production. In such a case, timber output will be extremely low and the rationale for the farmer to have his forest certified is small. If forestry is the farmer's main concern, any coffee that is grown will most likely be very low-yielding and neglected.

Organic coffee is grown under shade. (The IFOAM standards are general and do not specifically require natural shade; however, some IFOAM members' standards are more detailed in this area.) In this way, organic certification contributes to the maintenance of forests. In the marketplace, the certification of coffee under both FSC and organic standards will not be helpful and has the potential to confuse consumers and retailers – possibly resulting in less shade-grown coffee being marketed. There is thus a need for closer dialogue between IFOAM and the Forest Stewardship Council (FSC) to clarify these issues.

products exceeds US$200 million per year worldwide (Pereira, pers comm, 2000).

Producers interested in obtaining the fairtrade label must apply for registration with FLO's 'product registers', for which FLO currently has seven: coffee, tea, sugar, honey, bananas, cocoa and orange juice. Producers have to comply with product-specific fairtrade criteria that cover such areas as transparent and democratic decision-making about the use of extra premiums generated through fairtrade sales. Similarly, interested importers must meet a number of conditions to participate in the fairtrade chain, including paying a fair price and favouring a long-term and direct-trading relationship.

Fairtrade standards have so far been developed on a product-by-product basis. All criteria comprise generic concepts, including decent working conditions, setting prices to cover the costs of production and sustainable farming practices. In addition, product-specific criteria include references relevant to the unique aspects of production and trade for each product. As a young umbrella organization, FLO has harmonized its criteria and reviewed its current structure based on prior experiences. It is also deepening a dialogue with the organic movement, and is launching a common fairtrade certification mark to be used on all fairtrade products in all national markets (see Box 1.2 for lessons learned from fairtrade to date).

Given the level of overlap in criteria and the common interest in NTFP certification, it is not surprising that there have been a number of collaborative activities between certification and accreditation organizations over the past few years. These activities have included attempts at harmonizing criteria, joint assessment trials, discussions on logos and labelling strategies, common marketing and promotion activities and mutual recognition between accreditation systems. FLO, IFOAM and FSC have all held meetings with each other within the last three years to discuss ways to better collaborate in the future.

The most significant progress to date has been made on the ground through joint certification assessments. When assessors representing different certification programmes are brought together with producers to undertake trial assessments, there is the potential to share a wealth of information about different approaches. Joint certification assessments have taken place for chicle and shade coffee in Mexico and palm heart in Brazil (see Chapter 3 for summaries of chicle and palm heart certification tests). Lessons learned from these assessments will enable participants to identify gaps and areas of overlap. The eventual aim is to minimize redundancy and to have assessors who are qualified to certify under more than one programme, thus reducing the time and cost burdens to those producers seeking more than one certificate.

Lessons learned in marketing certified timber products

When forest product certification first began in the early 1990s, published material about the topic was scant to non-existent. In the past decade, however, certification has gained momentum and numerous books, scores of conference proceedings and entire issues of popular journals have been published on the sub-

Box 1.2 Lessons learned from fairtrade

Julie Pereira

Fairtrade is a *necessary* but not necessarily *sufficient* condition for sustainable development. Fairtrade facilitates access to markets for disadvantaged producers and ensures benefit-sharing and safe working conditions. Fairtrade is about establishing long-term trading relationships, enabling producers to invest in their futures with confidence and assisting the development of decision-making and negotiating skills. Simply put, fairtrade is about *empowerment* through trade. But implementing fairtrade can be challenging. Producer cooperatives can be fragile – as they grow, institutional investment is often necessary, just as in any other businesses. Recognizing the need to invest, and possibly to reorganize, in order to become more 'business friendly' may take time and political will. Finding the funds and support to transform cooperative business practices can be even harder.

In response, Fairtrade Labelling Organizations International (FLO) has recently set up the fairtrade producers' support network. The network will actively use the information that we gather from our regular inspection visits, beyond assessing eligibility for certification as fairtrade producers. The network will enable the exchange of information about difficulties encountered during assessment visits (such as with decision-taking or communication within an organization, restructuring finances and lack of marketing expertise), resulting in linkages with potential sources of support in the North and South. Such support could be in the form of a grant from a donor for specific resource persons to offer assistance, or could involve nearby cooperatives sharing their successful experiences.

Fairtrade is a process and the results and impacts of fairtrade certification will not be felt overnight. We recognize that it takes time for some of the most marginalized producer groups to meet all fairtrade criteria; yet, it is these groups that need the benefits of fairtrade sales the most. In order to make fairtrade more accessible, we divided our criteria between what we call 'minimum fairtrade criteria' for entry/inscription as a fairtrade producer, and 'process criteria', against which we hope producers will demonstrate improvements over time. We will be asking producers to prepare a yearly work plan (against which they will be assessed) to demonstrate how they intend to tackle difficult areas. One such area would be gender. For example, what measures will they be taking to improve the gender situation in their organization? Against which indicators would they expect monitors to assess progress?

FLO has a lobbying role to improve trading conditions and to promote sustainable development; it also has an educational role to inform people all over the world of existing unfair trading relations and to offer a sustainable and successful alternative. Trade can be a very valuable development tool, and it is possible to trade fairly and for all to profit.

ject. As a result, the failures, successes, limitations and potential of forest product certification are beginning to emerge. This section summarizes some of the lessons learned from timber certification and speculates about their implications for NTFPs.

Certification can help market value-added products

In the low-margin, commodity-driven world, volume is king. However, one of the emerging success stories for certified

Table 1.1 *Comparison of NTFP certification programmes*

	Forest Stewardship Council (FSC)	International Federation of Organic Agriculture Movements (IFOAM)	Fairtrade Labelling Organizations International (FLO)
NTFPs certified or in process	Chicle, maple syrup, baskets, palm hearts	Berries, tea, honey, coffee, mushrooms, ginseng and others	Coffee, tea, honey, bananas, cocoa
Other products certified	Timber	Organic produce, fish, meats, dairy	Sugar, orange juice
Main historical drivers	Timber users, environmental advocacy groups in late 1980s; concern over deforestation	Organic farmers and organic certification organizations in the 1960s; consumer concern about health	Producers (seeking market access) and consumers; concern about equity issues in the 1960s
Approach to NTFP standards	General principles and criteria, with region-specific detailed standards; NTFP guidelines developed by class on a case-by-case basis	Basic standards with additional section for 'wild-harvested products'	Product-by-product standards
Current issues	Developing a consistent framework for NTFP certification	Clarifying boundaries with FSC regarding forest product certification, expanding social criteria	Harmonizing criteria and refining certification process; investigating new products for certification
Primary focus for NTFP certification	Ecologically sustainable and socially responsible forestry	Avoidance of exposure to, and contamination by, chemical pesticides and fertilizers	Fair and equitable distribution of benefits to producers
Weaknesses	No requirements that NTFP food products are chemical free	Few ecological criteria for treating harvesting areas as functioning ecosystems	Narrow focus on trade equity and community well-being

companies is that they can improve their market position by increasing *value*, not *volume* (Mater, 1998a). For many producers, whether a small cooperative in Mexico or an industrial forest in Sweden, the prospect of increasing value from a green premium is a major motivator to obtain certification. While there may very well be certain products and certain niches that can potentially capture green premiums as a direct result of certification, it is more likely that certification can be a tool for the better marketing of already high-value products.

For example, a forest operation in Vernon, British Columbia, was able to market its certified logs by first sorting the logs according to species and by grade, resulting in a much higher price for the most desirable logs than would otherwise be paid (Mater and Mater, 1998). Similarly, California company Collins Pine found relative success marketing certified finished products, such as pine shelving and hardwood flooring. Once certified, these already high-value products found a consumer audience willing to pay a higher price (Hansen and Punches, 1998).

Adding value to certified products is not limited to forest operations. Portico, S A, a vertically integrated door manufacturer in Costa Rica, found that the cost of certification amounted to approximately US$1 per door. These high-end doors were marketed for hundreds and even thousands of dollars (Diener, 1998).

For NTFPs, opportunities to add value can occur both at the certified production site as well as along the supply chain. For example, certified Brazil nuts, shelled and processed locally, marketed directly to retailers instead of intermediaries and sold with even a modest green premium, could result in significant increases in profit margins to local communities (see Clay, 1992; Plotkin and Famolare, 1992).

Whether the product is fancy-grade maple syrup, high-end rattan furniture or dried gourmet mushrooms, certification can be not only an added value itself, but also a useful tool in marketing already high-value products to motivated, discerning buyers.

Certification can appeal to certain niche markets

Certification, like other forms of marketing, will appeal to some people more than others. Those forest product companies that have realized market benefits from certification have often targeted specific demographic niches such as progressive cities where consumers are likely to purchase environmentally responsible products (Hansen and Punches, 1998). Initial research on consumer willingness to pay for certified products indicates that women, in general, and urban women, in particular, are more likely to buy and pay more for environmentally responsible products (Forsyth, 1999; Ozanne and Vlosky, 1998).

The successful marketing of certified NTFPs is likely to entail the identification of markets, communities, companies and consumer groups willing to purchase (and

pay more for) environmental products. For example, producers of certified ginseng may do well to seek out retailers of high-end herbal products whose customers prefer 'natural products'. Certified Brazil nut producers may find they have a better chance of selling to Ben and Jerry's than to Breyers Ice Cream. Basket-makers with certified baskets may look to high-end mail order outlets whose customers are already willing to pay high prices for products they perceive to be in alignment with their personal values. By carefully identifying and targeting appropriate niche markets, producers of certified NTFPs may enjoy increased market access, market share and possible market premiums.

Diversified products and strategies can mean stability

Some producers of certified products are finding that a diversified product base means not only more opportunities to market different products, but also more stability should any one of those products fail. Collins Pine, for example, sells certified pine shelving, various grades of hardwood flooring, veneer quality logs and dimensional lumber (Hansen and Punches, 1998), while Seven Islands in Maine sells several different grades of flooring, dimensional lumber, studs and cedar shingles.

Certified NTFP producers may want to consider a management strategy for an array of products, based on the capacity of the forest and the management feasibility. Clay, for example, recommends marketing the following products from some types of Brazilian forests: Brazil nuts, rubber, babassu, acai, cupuassu, copaiba, andiroba, urucrum and cashews (Clay, 1992). Similarly, some forests in New England may yield a bounty of products, including maple syrup, ginseng and other medicinals, wild leeks and Christmas wreaths, while those in South-East Asia may yield mushrooms, rattan and fruits.

Opportunities may lie within existing markets and products

The cornerstone of an effective marketing strategy is not only an assessment of possible new products and market niches, but also an analysis of existing products, customers and suppliers. For example, Menominee Tribal Enterprises (MTE), a community-run tribal cooperative in Wisconsin, discovered through a market analysis of their supply chain that Gibson Guitar was one of their end users. Gibson was unaware that they were using certified wood, and had been exploring the possibility of developing a line of certified guitars. Once MTE discovered this, they were able to convince the intermediaries to obtain chain-of-custody certification, and within two years, Gibson had developed a line of certified guitars (Mater, 1998b).

Certified NTFP producers, especially those whose products ultimately reach environmentally conscious consumers, may consider tracing their supply chain to the end user, in order to identify possible marketing opportunities. In some cases, end users may even be willing to pay the costs of chain-of-custody certification.

A variety of models may be needed to suit different circumstances

A wide array of forest producers have been certified to date, ranging in size from less than 10 hectares to more than 1.8 million hectares. Ownership varies from individuals to large intergenerational families, forest companies, non-profits, cooperatives and whole communities. Each of these situations has faced a different challenge in the certification process. Very small operations often lack resources to conduct inventories, develop a management plan, monitor environmental impacts, or even cover the costs of certification. Very large operations face challenges in information management, staff training and supervision in certification, increased public scrutiny and expectations, external decision-making pressures such as boards of directors or shareholders, and political tensions within the organization and from peers within a recalcitrant industry. Certified cooperative organizations (such as those certified under 'resource manager' programmes), may face communication challenges with individual members, inconsistent management practices from owner to owner, and complex chain-of-custody issues. A community operation may face issues regarding equitable distribution of benefits, perceived imbalances from community to community, and cultural tensions resulting from the introduction or strengthening of a market-based economy.

NTFP producers interested in certification will first need to realistically assess whether any benefits may result from seeking certification or whether the costs will exceed the potential benefits. Secondly, producers seeking certification need to carefully evaluate the strengths, weaknesses and potential impacts of adopting any particular model.

Volume matters

One of the barriers to timber certification has often been the mismatch between the supply and demand of any one product. For example, Collins Pine attributes the discontinuation of its pine shelving line from Home Depot stores to its inability to meet the exponential supply demands of the company (Landis, 1997). Customers' adherence to exact specifications, such as grade, thickness and species, along with a limited number of certified distribution channels, can provide significant barriers to marketing of certified products (Hansen and Punches, 1998).

Clay emphasizes the importance of volume to NTFP marketing, stating that no single Amazonian producer can provide enough commodities to meet the needs of even a small company in North America or Europe (Clay, 1992). NTFP producers exploring potential certified markets would do well not to underestimate the importance of an even balance between supply and demand and the strength of market cooperatives in providing adequate supplies of NTFPs to major markets.

Being a pioneer has its price

The benefits of being one of the first certified producers of a particular product are clear: strong company positioning, improved or secured access to forest and other resources, improved market access and product differentiation (Propper et al, 1998). However, being a pioneer has its price. The development of a new product for marketing and certification can require significant investments of time and resources. Clay claims that product development requires at least five to ten years (Clay, 1992). In addition, such efforts are often small scale and experimental, with many expensive mistakes along the way. Once the product is developed, larger operations can easily duplicate the process for less cost, in less time, and with more efficiency of scale.

Nonetheless, the importance of a few pioneers on an entire industry has been well documented (Rogers, 1995), and producers of NTFPs may well consider the benefits of transforming an industry and establishing an early market presence worth the initial costs of product development.

Future scenarios for NTFP certification

Based on the past decade, it seems likely that, at least in the near future, certification will continue to be a growing trend in the forest products industry. It would also seem likely, given the increasing recognition of the importance of NTFPs to rural communities, and the growing consumer market for natural products, that the swell of interest in certified timber may carry over to NTFPs. What is not clear is how NTFP certification will evolve.

Already there are numerous first-party self-certification schemes, industry and trade association certification programmes, government certification initiatives, and environmental non-governmental organization (NGO) certification programmes, in addition to the third-party certification programmes described earlier. NTFP certification systems are rapidly emerging within the programmes of FSC, IFOAM and FLO – systems that potentially overlap and duplicate each other. As a result, the environment for NTFP certification is highly uncertain, and the future may hold several different scenarios.

The first scenario is one in which NTFP certification remains primarily third party, but there is no single framework for assessing and certifying NTFPs. In this case, different certifiers under each system would use their own standards for NTFP certification. Development of standards would be limited to particular regions where NTFPs were considered significant, and would vary considerably from region to region. Certification programmes could compete or collaborate with other organizations, depending upon the nature of their programmes.

The second scenario is one in which there is a coordinated system of primarily third-party schemes, with a common framework for NTFP certification, either through an NTFP principle and criteria or other guidelines. This framework could be used by the FSC as well as by other certification schemes, and could allow for the mutual recognition of certificates between collaborative certification programmes. In this scenario, there would be general agreement about the boundaries and scope of each organization in order to avoid redundancy and confusion.

The third scenario is one in which there is a broad proliferation of first-, second- and third-party certification programmes for NTFPs, run by governments, forest product companies, pharmaceutical companies, certifiers, environmental groups and harvesters themselves. There would be little or no consistency from programme to programme or even from product to product. Integrity and credibility would be left for the consumer to decide.

Chapter 2

The process of drafting and revising guidelines for NTFP certification

Patricia Shanley and Sarah A Laird

Introduction

Certification provides a useful framework in which to address a variety of issues relating to NTFP sustainability because it requires a grounding in management, as well as in broader environmental, social and marketing issues. Before the genesis of this project, non-timber forest products (NTFPs) received scant attention under the forest management guidelines of the Forest Stewardship Council (FSC) and its accredited certifiers. Working from momentum created by the FSC NTFP working group and various other NTFP certification initiatives, the United States Agency for International Development (USAID) grant to the Rainforest Alliance allowed for the creation of practical NTFP criteria, indicators and verifiers, and their subsequent field-testing.[1]

Illustration by Antônio Valente da Silva

*Uxi (*Endopleura uchi*)*

The process of creating the NTFP guidelines involved numerous experts and collaborators across the globe, with a particular emphasis on Latin America. The guidelines were drafted between 1997 and 1998, with input from the NTFP certification advisory committee, certification experts and other forestry and NTFP specialists. Field-testing took place in three countries: Mexico (chicle), Bolivia (Brazil nut and palm heart) and Brazil (palm heart), during the first half of 1998. Summaries of the three field trial experiences are reported in Chapter 3.

The guidelines were developed through a multistage process. Initially, it was decided that the guidelines should be inclusive – even to the point of being cumbersome – in order to reflect the broad range of social, ecological and commercial issues raised by sustainable NTFP management. The intention was to provide a document reflecting the current state of knowledge and experience, which might be whittled down and modified through field-testing. Modifications resulted primarily and importantly from practical experience, rather than from considerations hundreds or thousands of kilometres away from field sites.

Broad generic guidelines were drafted, drawing upon the FSC 'Principles and Criteria for Forest Management', including draft principle and criteria number 11 on NTFPs, and a range of certifier guidelines, including: NTFP guidelines developed by non-governmental organization (NGO) collaborators throughout Latin America, including Consejo Civil Mexicano para la Silvicultura Sostenible (CCMSS), Centro de Investigacion y Manejo de Recursos Naturales Renovables (CIMAR), Instituto de Manejo e Certificacão Florestral e Agrícola (IMA-FLORA); timber guidelines drafted by certifiers such as SmartWood, Scientific Certification Systems, SGS Silviconsult and the Soil Association; organic guidelines from groups such as the International Federation of Organic Agriculture Movements (IFOAM), the Soil Association, Organic Crop Improvement Association (OCIA), the Northeast Organic Farmers Association (for maple syrup) and Naturland; agricultural guidelines issued by the ECO-OK programme; and fairtrade guidelines from the Fairtrade Foundation, Max Havelaar and Goods & News. The work of the Tropenbos Foundation and the Center for International Forestry Research (CIFOR) on criteria and indicators for sustainability also proved invaluable, in particular CIFOR's project on Testing Criteria and Indicators for Sustainable Forest Management and subsequent *Guidelines for Developing, Testing and Selecting Criteria and Indicators for Sustainable Forest Management* (Prabhu et al, 1999) (the first manual in CIFOR's Criteria & Indicators Toolbox Series), and Tropenbos's *Hierarchical Framework for the Formulation of Sustainable Forest Management Standards: Principles, Criteria and Indicators* (Lammerts van Bueren and Blom, 1997).

The intention was to address a broad spectrum of issues within the generic guidelines, incorporating elements of organic, fairtrade and ecological/sustainability (FSC) criteria. The complex web of social, ecological and marketing issues raised by NTFPs requires an approach that integrates the concerns of these different types of certification. In addition, since NTFPs are often relatively low-value, low-density products with complex chain-of-custody issues, it was felt that experience from fairtrade, organic and FSC/ecological certification would complement and strengthen the assessment and monitoring operation.

Because NTFPs encompass such a wide range of plant forms, performance indicators and verifiers were drafted according to plant part harvested, including exudates, vegetative structures (apical bud, bark, root and leaves) and reproductive propagules (fruit, seed). This process involved the close consultation of scientific literature published on the ecology and sustainable management of NTFP species (eg Peters, 1994; 1996), and benefited from contributions by experts on particular species, some of whom are members of the advisory committee.

The performance indicators and verifiers for plant parts harvested provide the ecological detail necessary for an understanding of 'sustainability' for individual NTFP species (see Appendix I). The generic guidelines tackle broader social, environmental and legal issues. Additional species-specific NTFP guidelines, or

21

checklists, may be developed within the framework of the generic guidelines and plant class indicators and verifiers, as was done in the case of maple syrup (see Appendix II). Such species-specific checklists may be warranted in a variety of circumstances, including cases in which:

- existing expertise and detailed scientific knowledge is available;
- there is high demand for certification of a particular species;
- funding or human resources are available to invest in research and the development of guidelines;
- markets are expanding for a particular species;
- unique aspects of a product's management, harvest, processing or marketing require highly specialized indicators and verifiers.

In the case of palm heart, for example, class indicators and verifiers were adapted prior to, and during, field-testing by Dennis Johnson, a researcher expert in this area, for various species of harvestable palm (*Euterpe* spp.). A number of requests for maple sugar assessment by landholders in North America also necessitated further elaboration on the exudates section for maple sap production (see Appendix II). In Indonesia, NGOs and researchers are discussing the development of species-specific guidelines for rattan.

While social and cultural issues are addressed in the generic guidelines, given the complexity of this aspect of NTFP use, management and marketing, additional social performance indicators and verifiers should be developed. This was not possible within the scope of this project; but through field-testing of generic guidelines, a great deal was learned about the core elements of social standards for NTFPs. Critical social elements that must be addressed include: rights to land and resources; safe working conditions and adequate compensation; open participation and consultation; institutional capacity-building; and the nature and extent of benefit-sharing with local communities.

The NTFP guidelines were designed for areas where NTFPs are the primary products assessed for certification. However, in two of the assessment sites (Mexico and Bolivia) timber was also harvested, providing an opportunity to test combined assessments with both NTFP and timber guidelines. To avoid the cumbersome and repetitive work entailed in administering two separate sets of guidelines, discussions ensued among each assessment team as to the most effective way of tackling forests in which both timber and non-timber products are harvested. Assessors agreed on the need for a single field document that includes both timber and NTFP criteria, but could not reach consensus on how such a document should be formatted (ie by modifying the timber guidelines to be more holistic; by adding additional NTFP criteria to the timber guidelines as an appendix; or by nesting NTFP criteria under relevant subject areas within the existing timber guidelines sections).

Initial revision of guidelines

Initial draft guidelines were circulated to the advisory committee for comment. Resulting comments helped to focus and streamline the document prior to field-testing. Issues raised by the advisory committee, and subsequently by field assessment teams, fell into roughly six subject areas: general observations on both approach and guidelines, technical requirements of certification, social issues, ecological issues and economic issues. These are summarized below.

General observations and comments on approach

- Is certification practical, relevant, feasible or desirable for NTFPs?
- Will certification of NTFP management be considered by land area or by species?
- The study should not only look at NTFPs from natural forests, but also consider NTFPs from enrichment plantings, agroforestry systems and plantations.
- Excluding game and fish from the NTFP guidelines development process is problematic, as such forest resources are of great importance to rural communities.

General observations and comments on the guidelines

- The document too closely resembles timber management guidelines.
- The document should be simple – delete unnecessary rules and requirements.
- The document needs to address NTFPs and timber together in a holistic fashion.

- The complex, abstract, intimidating language makes it appear as if directed principally at large-scale operations and may render it incomprehensible to community-based operations.
- Who is the principal audience – companies, communities, NGOs?

Technical requirements of certification

- Information requirements of certification can be onerous, bureaucratic and costly, factors that will ultimately discourage small producers and favour large-scale, capital-intensive operations.
- Communities may not have the skills needed to record data in a way that is required by certification, despite having the requisite knowledge.
- Requiring separate plans for every harvested NTFP species will be difficult, time consuming and expensive.
- Tracking well-managed NTFPs from forest to marketplace (the chain of custody) is very challenging, likely very costly and impossible in some cases.

Social issues

- NTFP harvesters frequently operate on a system of minimizing risk as opposed to maximizing gain, the latter being the primary objective of certification.
- International Labour Organization (ILO) and International Tropical Timber Agreement (ITTA) standards are unknown, unrealistic and inapplicable to many NTFP harvesting operations.

- The certification process needs to specify a mechanism for increasing the likelihood of equitable distribution of benefits from NTFPs to women and marginalized groups who are typically not represented in traditional governing bodies.
- Completely resolving land tenure issues is a near impossibility, and will remain a blanket barrier for most harvesters wishing to enter the certification process.
- Certification needs to more effectively address community-based resource management.

Ecological issues

- There is a lack of documentation and often the knowledge necessary for determining sustainable-yield levels and management regimes for many NTFPs.
- Species sensitive to overharvest as a result of commercialization should be cautiously considered for certification.
- How does one determine when felling or destructive harvesting is permissible?
- Should naturalized, exotic species be certified?

Economic issues

- Small producers with small volumes are unlikely to generate sufficient earnings to cover the cost of certification, much less to comply with many of the regulations established to ensure acceptable conditions and practices in the formal sector.
- In the absence of external support, NTFP certification is likely to be more suitable for companies and well-organized, well-connected and skilled participants. Successful operations that merit certification will require access to management skills, capital and entrepreneurial skills that are difficult to access for most NTFP gatherers.
- Forest management plans need to better reflect the social and economic interests of local communities and should not be so onerous as to dwarf the value of the product(s).
- The need for income may drive people to divert labour and goods to the market that were previously allocated to subsistence, to the detriment of their health and nutrition (although added income might also improve livelihoods).
- History shows that increased value is often captured by outsiders, traders and the wealthy, not NTFP harvesters themselves.

Field revision of guidelines

In the field, assessment teams in Mexico, Bolivia and Brazil streamlined the guidelines, deleted repetitive criteria or indicators, and removed language and phrases drawn from timber guidelines and directed at large-scale operations which were inappropriate. For example, timber extraction criteria specific to road construction were amended to include paths or trails. The teams also changed the ordering of the guidelines and checked indicators for ease of use in assessments (eg the ability to assign a numeric grade to each indicator in the field).

Examples of language amended to make the requirements more accessible to small producers, and more effective in the field, include the following:

- 'Land tenure is secure' was amended to read: 'The rights to use of the property and access to resources is secured for the long term' (criterion 2.1).
- 'Resource conflicts with adjoining landholders or other resource users are resolved or are being addressed in a systematic and "legal" manner' was amended by inserting 'effective' in lieu of 'legal' (criterion 2.4).
- 'The forest management plan is comprehensive, site specific and detailed' was amended by adding: 'and appropriate to the scale and intensity of the forest operations' (criterion 3.2).

The diverse composition of the assessment teams assisted the field-testing process by offering views from anthropological, social, business and ecological perspectives. For example, botanists clarified the definition of 'naturalized' in criterion 5.18 to read 'exotic species that are reproducing on their own over a long time frame'. Members of the assessment teams with timber certification experience brought with them a wealth of knowledge about FSC requirements for certification that benefited NTFP experts new to the certification process.

Social scientists emphasized the importance of adding to, and strengthening, existing social criteria. During the Brazilian assessment, the attending social scientist made reference to the need for annual reviews to study the impact of palm heart harvesting on 'cultural capital' over time (ie the impact of palm heart commercialization on traditional gardening, marketing and labour division patterns and processes). An example of a social indicator added to the NTFP guidelines from the field-testing experience is: 'In the case of externally supported operations, a plan exists to reduce the level of dependency on external support (technical, financial) to maximize the level of self-sufficiency and control' (criterion 8.6). Field researchers felt such a criterion was needed in order to assure long-term economic and political self-sufficiency on the part of NTFP operations if they were to be viewed as truly sustainable.

In spite of significant modifications from the original draft, the guidelines remain formal and follow roughly the same framework of most timber certification guidelines. The resemblance to timber certification guidelines was unavoidable because the project sought certification under the FSC umbrella, which has standard principles and criteria for management of forest units.

Three key questions that arose during field-testing, and which remain partly unanswered after the assessments, are:

1 What is the most effective form for NTFP guidelines? Are they most effective as a stand-alone document, an addendum to timber certification guidelines or integrated directly into timber guidelines?

Most NTFP specialists felt that an addendum would not be sufficient to adequately cover NTFPs, believing that such a document would diminish the value and role of NTFPs in forests relative to timber. By contrast, timber certifiers tended to like the idea of an addendum, viewing it as a quick and easy way of including NTFPs into an already verifiable and working system. Two separate documents – as employed in the field assessments – were considered to be cumbersome and repetitive. It is likely that a multi-pronged strategy will be necessary, depending upon the case. In cases where an area is managed primarily for one or more NTFPs, a separate, stand-alone set of guidelines will be necessary that addresses the unique issues raised by particular NTFP species and NTFPs, in general. Where a forest is managed primarily for timber, and NTFPs will not be certified, it is necessary to include in the guidelines more effective criteria to ensure timber harvests only minimally impact NTFPs of local importance. And in cases where forests are managed primarily for timber, but where NTFPs will also be certified, a species-specific addendum (eg maple syrup) or plant class indicators would prove most effective.

2   How can social and ecological verifiers and indicators be most effectively incorporated within guidelines? Are they best integrated into the generic guidelines (as are some social criteria) or annexed, as for the ecological verifiers and indicators?

In general, the ecological indicators and verifiers were very well received by assessment teams, and were found to be the most useful part of the document because they provide concrete and field-specific guidance. However, since the ecological indicators and verifiers comprise many pages, of which only a few are applicable for any particular NTFP, they were annexed to the main generic guidelines. As an alternative, in the final version of the guidelines, reference is made to where ecological indicators might be placed within the body of the generic guidelines, should that be preferable.

The social indicators are nested within the body of the generic guidelines, following the format and layout of the FSC principles and criteria. Overall, assessment teams felt that social criteria could be strengthened, as has already been accomplished with the ecological indicators, by including more specific social verifiers throughout the text or by including a separate annex, as was done in the case of ecological verifiers and indicators.

3   How can the guidelines be accessible, fair and effective for both community-scale and industrial-scale operations? Is it possible to have a 'sliding scale' of scoring, taking into account the different scales of operations and contrasting access to technical resources?

Industrial NTFP operations generally possess financial and technical resources unavailable to community-based forest operations. In the cases assessed, external support permitted communities to map and inventory their forests and to develop forest management plans. However, in the cases of communities who have little or no external support, development of a detailed forest management plan is highly unlikely.

Timber certification assessors tackle this same problem when assessing large- and small-scale forest management units. Certifiers of community-based operations train their assessors to see that guidelines are met, but allow some latitude to employ discretion in the face of contextual issues such as the size, scale and access to resources (technical and financial) of a particular operation. In developing and applying NTFP guidelines, there is much that can be learned from the 'cross-pollination' of timber, organic and fairtrade guidelines, expertise and hard-earned know-how developed over many years of tackling a range of related issues.

Outlook

Development of the NTFP guidelines and their subsequent field-testing has generated a good deal of information and interest. Subsequent certification field trials for other NTFPs have been scheduled in Peru, Chile and North America as a result of the project. The guidelines remain a living document, open to further revision and fine-tuning as knowledge and experience warrant.

The guideline development process demonstrated that certification agencies (forestry, organic and fairtrade) still have a great deal to learn about NTFP management, harvesting and marketing. Certification institutions will require more specialized personnel to tackle the idiosyncrasies of NTFP certification, where and when certification is appropriate. It is hoped that the development and field-testing of NTFP certification guidelines will contribute to a better understanding of the complexities of NTFP management, regardless of whether certification is deemed appropriate in particular cases or not. The following chapters relating field test results, species profiles and analysis of ecological, social, technical and marketing issues provide more detailed findings and observations resulting from the NTFP certification project that are relevant to further efforts to develop and refine NTFP guidelines.

In August 2001, the NTFP Exchange Programme of PROFOUND and the NeoSynthesis Research Institute in Sri Lanka held a meeting on certification and community-based resource management. Participants from throughout South-East Asia felt that, while useful, the NTFP guidelines were too timber-based in orientation. The participants recommended that more attention be paid to community-based resource management and stressed the need for more simplified guidelines and certification processes.

Note

1   Appendix I includes the generic guidelines for assessing the management of NTFPs. This document contains the original guidelines that were field-tested in Latin America and has specific reference sections on class indicators and verifiers for sustainable harvest of exudates, vegetative structures and reproductive propagules. Appendix II provides an example of species-specific guidelines for maple-sugaring operations. It is formatted as an addendum to existing timber certification guidelines.

Chapter 3

Summaries of the field-testing results in Mexico, Bolivia and Brazil

Abraham Guillén

Introduction

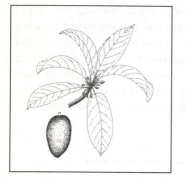

Illustrations by Antônio Valente da Silva

Chicle
*(*Manilkara zapota*);*

Brazil nut
*(*Bertholletia excelsa*);*

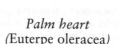

Palm heart
*(*Euterpe oleracea*)*

The NTFP certification project team selected three field sites for testing the guidelines based upon several criteria, including: potential marketing links; maturity of the production system; ability of the production system to produce commercially viable quantity and quality; forest conservation impact; and institutional capacity to collaborate. In addition, NTFPs for potential field-testing were chosen on the basis of their commercial value, use, export potential, eco-logical status, and local and regional economic importance. In the end, three cases were chosen: a chicle operation in Mexico, a Brazil nut-producing forest in Bolivia and two palm heart operations in Brazil – one an industrial operation and the other a community-run operation.

The NTFP guidelines (see Appendix I) were tested in the field in 1998 by teams of practitioners with local, regional and international expertise. The following summaries briefly describe the various settings and results of the field tests. Additional analysis of the field trials can be found in Chapters 26–30 (Section III) of this book, which describe the core elements of certification (ecological, social, marketing and technical issues).

Summary of the Mexican NTFP field test (chicle)

Background

Chewing gum has its origin in the Yucatan, where it has been used since Mayan times. The original Chiclets brand (whose name is derived from the chicle tree) was developed by an American who observed the Yucatan tradition of chewing natural gum and later turned that tradition into an entire industry. At first, natural base gum was used for manufacturing chewing gum. Today, most commercial chewing gum manufacturers use petroleum-based gums instead of natural base gums. Certification provides a way to reintroduce naturally based chewing gum to consumers while supporting the protection of the forests where chewing gum originated.

As a result of the certification field-testing process, the Noh Bec *ejido* (*ejidos* are communally owned lands whose tenure is granted by the Mexican government) is now certified by SmartWood and its affiliate, the Consejo Civil Mexicano para la Silvicultura Sostenible (CCMSS), under the rules of the Forest Stewardship Council (FSC). The Noh Bec *ejido* is one of the few forestry operations in the world to be certified for both timber and non-timber products (gum latex).

General description

The Noh Bec *ejido* has legal ownership of 23,100 hectares. Of this area, 18,000 hectares are dedicated to permanent forest management. Timber is managed according to a 25-year management plan that focuses on the harvesting of mahogany (*Swietenia macrophylla*) and Spanish cedar (*Cedrela odorata*), with a 75-year rotation, 25-year cutting cycle and an authorized annual allowable cut of 6708 cubic metres (m^3). The chicle tree (*Manilkara zapota*) is harvested in accordance with government regulations. The authorized harvest of dry gum latex is 59 tonnes per year, with a minimum tree diameter of 25 centimetres (cm), and an 8-year cycle between harvests. The traditional harvesting method of making zigzag incisions on the bole of the tree to extract the latex has not changed in generations.

The forest

The Noh Bec lands are classified as tropical semi-humid forest and receive approximately 1200 millimetres (mm) of precipitation per annum. Within Noh Bec's forests, over 70 tree species per hectare are found, with an abundance of 200 to 400 trees per hectare above 15cm in diameter. The land is relatively flat and has poor soils for which forests are its best land use. The most abundant tree species are chicozapote (*Manilkara zapota*) and ramon (*Brosimum alicastrum*). Both species have been used since the Mayan civilization. Chicozapote was used for construction and gum while the seeds of ramon served as a source of fodder. Fire is frequent in this forest type, and the two principal species (chicle and ramon) are fire-resistant/fire-adapted species. Hence, the cultural importance and ecological characteristics of the two species have led to their current dominance in this forest type. Chicozapote is also shade tolerant and has good natural regeneration. Its wood is very dense and was once considered undesirable by the timber industry; however, current demand for chicozapote wood appears to be growing. Chicle gum extraction has supplied a yearly source of income for local communities for decades.

The *ejido* system

The *ejido* system is the main legal mechanism under which Mexico has granted land and resource utilization rights to communities since 1942. One of the greatest benefits of the *ejido* system is that it has allowed communities to organize, become legally empowered and learn how to manage large forest areas. Under the *ejido* system, land areas are to be managed collectively. In the Yucatan peninsula, 51 *ejido*s own 489,000 hectares of permanent tropical forests. These *ejido*s are located between the biosphere reserves of Sian Ka'an and Calakmul. Between both land management systems, the total area comprises 1.7 million hectares of tropical forests and wetlands. The history of resource utilization in the Yucatan is long, stretching back to the time when the Maya first settled along the peninsula. The Yucatan was considered the last Mexican frontier, which resulted in politically induced massive deforestation during the 1960s. During 1957 to 1983, the Mexican government awarded a timber concession to MIQRO S A, after which the communities were granted the rights to manage the forests in their legally owned land. Deforestation has significantly diminished under *ejido* management practices and as a result of the establishment of the two biosphere reserves. Communities use the forests as their main source of revenue.

Timber certification

The Noh Bec *ejido* was one of the first community forestry operations to be certified in the world. The *ejido*s of Noh Bec, Tres Garantías and Caobas y Petcacab, organized under the Sociedad de Productores y *ejido*s Forestales de Quintana Roo (SPEFQR), have been certified under FSC standards since 1994.

FSC NTFP certification

Following the 1999 field trials, Noh Bec became the first forest operation in the world to be awarded certification for NTFPs under the FSC system. The Noh Bec *ejido* sought certification of its chicle resource independently from the SPEFQR organization, and is now assisted by the Plan Piloto Chiclero.

Fair Trade eV endorsement

Chicle production in the Noh Bec *ejido* was also evaluated by Fair Trade eV during the same time as the FSC certification assessment. Noh Bec is now endorsed as a producer that meets Fair Trade eV's social and business practices criteria. Fair Trade eV is helping to introduce the certified gum to the European market in coordination with the gum manufacturer (Wild Things) and the Plan Piloto Chiclero.

Fair Trade eV and FSC assessments are considered complementary given that Fair Trade eV emphasizes social and economic fairness, and FSC emphasizes the environmental, social and economic sustainability of the operation. The assessment was jointly conducted in order to reduce field assessment costs and share criteria to enhance both certification systems.

Wild Things

Wild Things, a manufacturer of natural (chicle)-based chewing gum, helped catalyse Noh Bec's certification. More than ten years in the making, Jungle Gum, the trade name of Wild Things' chewing gum product line, is the only existing chewing gum that fully meets FSC, fairtrade and organic certification standards. Wild Things purchases chicle from the Noh Bec *ejido* in Mexico, manufactures the final product in the US and markets the gum through retailers and via the world wide web. Wild Things hopes that consumers will differentiate their brand from other products that copy some of its attributes but do not fulfil the high ecological, social and economic standards and values that Jungle Gum represents.

Florida Growers Association endorsement

The Florida Growers Association has certified Jungle Gum as an organic product. Organic certification is considered critical for marketing edible NTFP products. The organic seal of the Florida Growers Association, combined with Fair Trade eV endorsement, have given Jungle Gum the marketing edge necessary for promoting responsibly produced edible products in an arena where the FSC label is unknown. Complementary branding, as demonstrated by this case, provides the producer with a stronger marketing 'mix' that enhances product attributes.

Reasons for pursuing chicle certification

- Lack of markets for natural gum base: during the 1999 season, chicle was not harvested due to low demand from traditional buyers – namely, Japanese chewing gum companies. The drop in demand has had significant economic repercussions for the *ejido* economy since the main sources of revenue are timber extraction (harvested during the dry season) and gum extraction (harvested during the rainy season). Agricultural production within the *ejido* is mainly for family consumption. It has been postulated that a closing of gum markets will drive further exploitation of the timber resource, principally to provide needed income, which in turn could result in overextraction of the most valuable species, lack of management for lesser-known species and eventual degradation of the forest ecosystem.

The Plan Piloto Chiclero is actively looking for new markets for chicle gum, an effort that requires additional international support mainly from the US and Europe.

- Motivated buyer: as society becomes more aware of environmental issues and socially and ecologically responsible industry practices, a new generation of environmentally sensitive companies is emerging. Wild Things' Jungle Gum is the first triple-certified NTFP available in the world. Jungle Gum was designed to use only certified gum base, thereby creating an incentive for its suppliers to request certification. Wild Things implemented a marketing strategy to utilize certification as a differentiating factor in a highly competitive industry. It made the first purchases of certified base gum from Noh Bec in 1999 and is now seeking to capture an environmentally sensitive market segment. Jungle Gum was first introduced at the FSC Product Fair in Germany, and is now being marketed in Europe and in the US.

- Fair Trade eV endorsement: this is expected to help find new gum markets in Europe for all the chicle producers in the Yucatan region. Fair Trade eV endorsement is strongly supported by the Plan Piloto Chiclero and was specifically requested by Wild Things.
- Diversification of income sources: because the Yucatan *ejidos* are basically dependent upon timber and chicle gum, additional sources of income are always welcome in the region. The Plan Piloto Chiclero aims to add value to its gum base by producing ready-to-chew gum in the Yucatan if demand for naturally based gum is realized.
- External organizations driving new alternatives: several organizations are trying to help the Yucatan *ejidos* capture new sources of income. It may be perceived that these external organizations are moving quickly to capture new opportunities without the full understanding of the situation by the *ejidos*.

Lessons learned from the field test

The following is a summary, organized by subject area, of some issues raised by the NTFP certification experience in Mexico.

Technical issues

- Timber and NTFPs need to be better integrated in management plans.
- The operation needs to implement a low-cost and scale-appropriate monitoring programme capable of answering questions about critical variables that are needed to manage the forest better. It is perceived that specialized research organizations should conduct the monitoring to allow for economies of scale and standardization of practices, particularly given the low availability of funds within the *ejidos*.
- Cost-effective forest inventory techniques for products other than timber species that are not normally included in forest management plans (eg palms, nuts, seeds, etc) are needed.

- Chain-of-custody controls are difficult to implement, especially with regard to avoiding the mixture (contamination) of certified products with non-certified products; to proper record-keeping (paper trails) of products as they move from the forest to storage areas through manufacturing processes and sales; and to implementing good physical inspection controls.
- Permanent training, technical assistance and transfer of technical know-how within and between communities is needed.

Ecological issues

- There is a need to strengthen the scientific rationale justifying the frequency of harvest according to prescription and practice, minimum diameter size, number of taps, and other critical variables.
- There is a need to understand more fully the long-term forest dynamics,

and changes in woodland structure and composition induced by forestry practices.

- Baseline data, from which to guide the management of wild fauna, is insufficient (this needs to be approached at a regional scale).
- The trend towards felling chicle trees that are considered 'dead or not productive' has no proper ecological justification since there is insufficient technical understanding of the impacts of such practices on fauna and the ecosystem.
- Unsustainable collection of other NTFPs (such as medicinal plants, seeds, fruits, etc) by *ejido* members goes unrecorded and may have negative ecological consequences.

Economic issues

- Prices for artificial (petroleum)-based gum are a fraction of the cost of natural-based gum; therefore, natural-based gum is not competitive for the same market segment.
- Markets for natural gum base are very small. Reintroduction of natural-based gum requires the development of a market where producers, manufacturers and buyers work together in product and market development.
- The *ejido* currently lacks a marketing strategy to promote certified timber and natural gum base.
- The European market seems to be more open to certified chewing gum and is more willing to pay higher prices for natural-based gum than the US market. The US market seems to be more price conscious than environmentally sensitive. A different marketing strategy may need to be developed for each market.
- Income from NTFPs alone is insufficient to cover all forest management

costs when compared to timber. NTFP revenues are considered part of the whole 'basket' of forest products that justify its maintenance.

- There is increasing market pressure to use the chicle tree as structural wood and flooring given its long-lasting wood characteristics.

Social issues

- There is very strong social participation in managing chicle in the Noh Bec *ejido*. The *ejido* holds annual assemblies where every major forest activity is approved, including the management of chicle. Chicle harvesting is organized under a committee that is responsible for its planning, control and payments to participants. Only members from the committee are allowed to harvest chicle and at the end of the annual harvest, the committee shares the profits (if they exist) with the rest of the *ejido*.
- Community operations seeking certification need to be sufficiently strong and organized to successfully acquire and maintain a certificate. Open, democratic and participatory processes, community participation in forest planning, good organization, strong financial controls and strong family participation, as seen in Noh Bec, greatly facilitate the certification process.
- There is a need for strong leadership within the organization in order to orchestrate the required balance between satisfying internal needs, managing outside pressures from assisting organizations (non-governmental organizations (NGOs), government, buyers, etc) and finding a path to successful business.
- There needs to be significant outside technical and marketing assistance in

order for communities to be competitive in the international marketplace.

- Initially, communities seem to be more competitive in supplying primary products (raw gum, logs, lumber, etc); but if they are to capture higher prices for their products, they should eventually try to integrate vertically or form joint ventures with socially sensitive entrepreneurs willing to participate in their development process.

- Communities who aspire to gain certification need to have a viable business that is acceptably run, have a positive cash flow, exhibit strong internal financial controls and have strong leadership.

Summary of the Bolivian NTFP field test (Brazil nuts)

Background

The Pando region in north-east Bolivia, about the size of Costa Rica, has a long history of commercial NTFP utilization. The region is one of the few large-scale cases where a forest product other than timber provides commercial justification for maintaining natural forests. Since the turn of the century, extraction of latex (rubber or *goma*) from the *siringa* tree (*Hevea brasiliensis*) brought labourers into the region's forests. In the 1950s, the harvest of *goma* reached its peak, employing nearly 3000 workers. The *goma* harvest declined due to competition from South-East Asian rubber plantations and improvements in the production of synthetic rubber made from oil; it finally collapsed in the early 1980s. Since the rubber boom and bust, forest product production in the region shifted in greater quantity to Brazil nut (*Bertholletia excelsa*) harvesting, which has not compensated for the economic loss from the rubber boom heydays.

The second NTFP field test was implemented on a quarter-million-hectare management unit owned by a company (which cannot be named here) that produces Brazil nuts and palm hearts (*Euterpe precatoria*). Emphasis was placed on Brazil nuts because they are the main products harvested and are the principal focus of the Bolivian government-approved management plan for the area. The palm heart (*asai*) harvest is covered under a 'sub-management plan'. The main certification challenges found include weak social conditions for direct workers and workers contracted through third parties, as well as the long-term financial viability of the forest operation.

General description

The property where the field test was conducted is located in the departments of Pando and La Paz in north-eastern Bolivia. The forest is predominantly contiguous low, medium and high rainforest, with an abundance of dominant Brazil nut trees. It seems likely that the only humans to make use of this forest in this century have been seasonal workers who came to the region first to harvest *goma*, and then later Brazil nuts (*castaña*) and *asai*. The limited seasonal work related to the *castaña* harvest has meant a continual reduction in the number of people who live year round in the collection centres (small forest settlements). Today, the permanent population of families who live in the forest settlements are three generations removed from the original *goma* labourers. In addition, over 500 seasonal workers migrate to the area during the *castaña* harvest season (the rainy season of January to March) and during the *asai* harvesting season (the dry period from July to November).

The forest

The total area comprises approximately 250,000 hectares, of which about 190,000 hectares are covered by forest. The region is classified as sub-tropical humid forest, with an annual precipitation of 1800mm, mean temperature of 26° Celsius (C), gentle, flat topography and an altitude of 160 to 200 metres above sea level. The topographical gradient influences the diversity in forest types. The high forests are dominated by *castaña* (*Bertholletia excelsa*), the middle forests are richer in timber species such as *roble* (*Amburana cearensis*), *cedro* (*Cedrela fissilis*) and *mururé* (*Clarisia*

spp.), while chaparral or the abundance of *asai* (*Euterpe precatoria*) and *goma* (*Hevea brasiliensis*) characterize the low forests. There also exist extensive pampas, riparian forests, periodically flooded areas and secondary forests growing on previously cultivated sites.

The region has historically possessed some of the greatest plant and animal diversity in Bolivia. However, today, as a result of uncontrolled hunting, most vertebrate species have diminished. International markets for hides and pets, as well as domestic (mainly subsistence) consumption of game, have resulted in many species being listed as threatened or endangered. These include caimans (*Melanosuchus niger*), giant otter (*Pteronura brasiliensis*), neotropical river otter (*Lutra longicaudis*), jaguar (*Panthera onca*), monkeys (families *Cebidae* and *Callithricidae*), and parrots and macaws (family *Psittacidae*).

Reasons for pursuing certification

The company's motives for seeking certification were largely driven by hopes of enticing investment and gaining business visibility and/or credibility. Certification appeared to be one of many strategies for making the company attractive to external investors. In addition, this operation was interested in receiving technical assistance from international projects that promote better forest management practices and improved production systems, for which certification was a requirement.

Lessons learned from the Bolivian field test

The Bolivian field test provided a number of issues and lessons, as presented below by subject area.

Technical issues

- A problem posed by Bolivian law is

that it does not explicitly require timber harvest plans to be integrated with NTFP plans.
- Treatments prescribed in the management plan had not been implemented in the field.
- Pressure for harvesting timber from

outsiders is increasing – in particular, for commercially valuable species and in marginal areas where the company has less control.

- There is no financial incentive and very little training given to gatherers to execute sanitary measures in order to prevent spoilage, aflatoxin (a mycotoxin) contamination and loss of product.
- The workers' conditions for handling food products require serious improvements.
- The characteristics of how the product is harvested from the wild make it difficult to prevent illegal extraction given the size of the area and the difficulty of controlling access.
- The harvesting method has not changed in generations, and basically the same principles and technology base are used to manufacture the 'final' product (simple drying of the Brazil nuts).
- Harvesting of *asai* is considered not sustainable given perceived over-harvesting and the required long harvesting cycles.
- Agroforestry systems are not incorporated into the management plan.
- A monitoring system (ie permanent plots) has not been established, either prior to or after harvest.
- Other land uses, additional to NTFP extraction, are being granted by the government to natural resource concessions (mining, oil exploration), which puts the long-term management of the forest at risk.

Ecological issues

- Uncontrolled hunting, and company tolerance of hunting by sub-contractors, are causing serious depletion of certain species such as monkeys, wild pigs, birds and endangered species.

- The operation does not have a plan or fauna study to guide its fauna management.
- Basic ecological baseline data is lacking.
- The Brazil nut harvest rates are well documented, but justification of harvest rates and predictive analysis regarding the implications of different harvest rates were weak. There is a lack of research data regarding growth and yield for Brazil nuts from the property.
- Some illegal logging is occurring, although the difficulty of accessing the area is preventing intensive timber extraction.
- The forest is relatively undisturbed because the main product harvested is the Brazil nut fruit. The *asai* harvest is recent and has been concentrated on only one third of the property (in the lower forests).
- Harvesting of *castaña* and *asai* is very labour intensive and uses traditional, non-mechanized techniques that cause minimal damage to the forest and require few access roads.
- The neighbouring Brazilian states have promoted deforestation through 'live' international boundaries. There is a threat that if transportation is improved in the region, deforestation may result from an influx of farmers and hungry industries looking for fast cash and/or land.

Economic issues

- There are strict European import restrictions on the aflatoxin allowance for Brazil nuts. This is threatening the entire industry, given their lack of proper technology and funds to meet the requirements.
- The final product is a small nut that poses serious challenges in terms

of implementing chain-of-custody requirements for production control, verification and monitoring. Differentiating non-certified nuts from certified Brazil nuts is perceived as the biggest challenge for chain-of-custody certification.

- Brazil nut producers from Peru and Brazil believe that Bolivian nut producers compete unfairly; Bolivian *castaña* sells for lower prices than nuts from other countries because Bolivian companies pay lower wages and offer fewer benefits to their workers.

Social limitations to sustainable-use issues

- Land tenure is still not completely defined, affecting the long-term stability and viability of the operation.
- The company has not granted land tenure or forest resource-use rights to the families who have lived in the forest settlements for several generations. These families do not feel that they have a recognized claim to any part of the concession area, and consequently their participation in securing the forest resources is weak.

- The government does not favour a policy for granting land rights to residents of the forest settlements or other long-term traditional land users.
- For the forest settlers, there are few income alternatives other than working as NTFP harvesters for companies in the region; their salaries and benefits are at subsistence levels and completely dependent upon company largesse. Such a situation leads to the creation of a cycle of poverty from which it is difficult for the families to escape. There is little incentive for the forest workers to apply better management practices.
- The company does not formally recognize the forest settler community and its use of the forest resource, fails to include the NTFP harvesters in management planning and does not provide guarantees against failing to renew housing leases or job opportunities.
- The working and living conditions are generally poor, with respect to medical care, education, sanitation and basic amenities, and are exacerbated by the company's current cash problems.

Summary of the Brazilian field test: industrial operation (palm heart)

Background

Euterpe oleracea or *açaí* is one of the key palm species in the *várzea* (seasonally inundated) forests of the lower Amazon. Its resprouting capacity gives this species a high potential for sustainable harvest. *Açaí* is a pioneer species and is a clear indicator of existing soil and moisture conditions. The *várzea* forests of the lower Amazon have a long history of

exploitation for agriculture, timber and NTFPs such as rubber and palm fruits. However, commercial harvesting of palm heart only began in the region in the late 1960s, after the industry relocated from the decimated Atlantic coastal forests to the Amazonian region.

Açaí is a very important species for the local population, providing two main products: palm heart for the Brazilian and international markets (a source of cash) and *açaí* 'milk' from its seed pulp. This reddish-coloured juice is very nutritious and used by Amazonian families as a refreshing drink. It is particularly important for children living in the rural areas (a kind of 'Amazonian milk'). About 65 tonnes of *açaí* juice are consumed per day in the city of Belem alone.

General description

This field test was conducted at the request of a company that manages approximately 3300 hectares of *várzea* forest and produces palm heart and *açaí* juice. Emphasis was placed on palm heart management, given that it is the main product being produced. The harvesting of palm heart is prescribed under a management plan approved by the Brazilian environmental protection agency (Instituto Brasileiro do Meio Ambiente e dos Recursos Naturais Renováveis – IBAMA). The economic importance of this species is inducing several companies and local users in the region to introduce enrichment planting and/or to favour *açaí* natural regeneration, at a potential hidden cost of forest simplification and a reduction in biodiversity. This situation, if not prevented, may be an impediment to achieving sustainable management, and therefore certification.

The forest

The *várzea* forest is one of the most important forest types along the Amazon River. *Várzea* forests are found in Brazil, Peru, Bolivia and Ecuador. In the lower Amazon, *várzea* forest is not a climax forest. Given the seasonal flooding and daily tides, the *várzea* forest type favours pioneer species that can tolerate flooding and saturated soils. *Açaí* is a pioneer species and is not found in *terra firme* forests. It competes very well in the *várzea* forest habitat.

There are several differences between *várzea* and *terra firme* forests:

- *Várzea* forests have, in general, fewer plant species than *terra firme* forests.
- *Várzea* forests have a greater abundance of species adapted to conditions of high humidity.
- The canopy of *várzea* forests is lower and more open than *terra firme* forests.
- Tree growth in *várzea* forests is relatively fast.
- The underbrush of the *várzea* forest is more open than *terra firme* forests.
- The *várzea* soils are relatively rich due to flooding and subsequent deposition of sediments.

Reasons for pursuing certification

The main motivation for seeking Forest Stewardship Council (FSC) certification by this operation is to comply with the environmental policies of financial investors, which require third-party verification of the company's forest practices. Furthermore, certification is to be used as a technical reference to introduce better management practices in order to ensure long-term supply for the production of palm heart and *açaí* juice.

Organic certification

Most of the palm heart products sold by this operation are destined for the

Brazilian market, which accounts for about 85 per cent of the world's market. Given that palm heart is an edible product, this operation also pursued organic certification as a marketing tool to differentiate its products from lower-quality processed *açaí* supplied by many small producers. At the time of the assessment, a recent death attributed to ingestion of canned palm heart imported from Bolivia had temporarily depressed the market and induced the government to impose stronger sanitary controls. The organic certification assessment was executed in combination with the forestry assessment, which resulted in lower costs and the sharing of technical criteria. This operation is also planning to pursue International Organization for Standardization (ISO) 9000 certification.

Lessons learned

The following issues, grouped by subject matter, were brought to light by this field trial.

Ecological issues

- There is insufficient information about the different harvesting rates to better define the sustainable harvesting level.
- The practice of underbrush elimination to favour the growth of palm trees still needs to be justified as a technical prescription and should be incorporated as part of the management plan. Underbrush clearing seems to promote forest simplification, which could lead to a loss of biodiversity.
- A monitoring system for better management needs to be established in order to evaluate the conditions of the forest, management operations and environmental issues.
- Forest protection and reserve areas need to be included in the management plan and clearly demarcated in the field. The protection prescriptions for areas along rivers and waterways need to be improved.

Technical issues

- The palm heart management plans approved by the government are mainly short-term harvesting plans. Technical information and forest management-plan models for palm heart exist, but they are not utilized.
- There is a need to develop an integrated management approach that is reflected in the overall management plan and that includes all commercial forest products being harvested (eg palm heart, fruits and firewood). The management plans also need to be tailored to address differences in the sizes of parcels managed – this holds particularly true for small-land managers and community operations.
- Financial targets instead of biological and ecological factors mainly drive palm heart harvesting levels.
- The forest management plan should address the issue of sourcing from different forest areas, which is typical for palm heart harvesting. Many communities are supplying palm heart to the company. Many have a harvesting permit, but few have a management plan.
- A clear chain-of-custody system to track all raw and processed palm heart bought by the processing plant

needs to be in place to control and monitor where the product comes from.

- Forest protection plans need to be expanded from a primary focus on fire control and illegal extraction in order to encompass wider issues. Given that the forest areas are of free traditional access, free harvesting of palm heart is frequent and difficult to control.

- Distance to the processing centre is a key factor given that palm heart is highly perishable (it quickly deteriorates three days after harvest). Processing by communities in remote areas seems to be an alternative to preventing deterioration. This 'satellite' processing would need to have acceptable processing quality control, technical assistance and training. Processing adds value to the product for small producers, increasing profits.

Economic issues

- Within the company's management areas, demand for palm heart seems to be greater than the forest can yield. The company may need to buy from additional outside sources. Paying harvesters by volume, even though practical, creates an economic incentive to overharvest the palm heart resource base.

- Payment to palm heart collectors was reported as frequently delayed by community members. In addition, the community considers grading for quality control by the company inconsistent. Grading is critical because it forms the basis for the payment rate.

- The economic viability of the processing plant is directly related to three factors that are driving prices down in Brazil: lower-priced imported palm heart from Bolivia and Peru; relatively

high production costs of the Brazilian factories; and relatively saturated traditional international markets, resulting in depressed prices. Palm heart collectors are affected by the economic viability of the factory.

- There is a need to develop a marketing plan that identifies new markets for palm heart. The Brazilian market, although the largest, is relatively saturated by low-priced palm heart. New international markets must be identified, given that traditional markets are being saturated by plantation-grown palm heart.

- In order to capture environmentally sensitive markets in Europe, a product differentiation strategy may need to be implemented. Such a marketing programme should emphasize the importance of supplying a product from well-managed and natural forests.

Social issues

- There are few to no labour opportunities in the region besides supplying palm heart to the processing industry. Additional activities are subsistence fishing and agricultural production. The processing factory is the main source of employment in the region. The interdependence between the factory and surrounding population is very significant.

- The company's recent purchase and management of land previously occupied by small landholders, some of whom have been relocated, have created land-use and resource-access conflicts.

- Workers' rights need to be revised in order to guarantee compliance with existing regulations. Work contracts should be available for all workers.

- Minimum conditions for work safety should be met and maintained in all operations, especially for fieldwork.

- Basic medical coverage needs to be made available not only for the workers in the processing plant, but for fieldworkers as well.
- Participation of the local population in developing the forest management plan should be fostered in order to

prevent social conflicts and improve compliance with good management practices at all levels.

- A training programme is needed to introduce and maintain good harvesting practices. This programme should cover workers, contractors and independent raw-material suppliers.

Summary of the Brazilian field test: community operation (palm heart)

Background

Palm heart (from *Euterpe oleracea*) is not a traditionally consumed product in the Lower Amazon, although residents of the area have consumed the fruit pulp of *açaí* for centuries. As noted in the previous section, *açaí* juice is extremely nutritious and calorific, and is a very important subsistence comestible in the nutritionally poor local diet. The soft, fleshy palm heart of *E. oleracea* is eaten principally as a salad ingredient, and has a large international and domestic market. As stands of palm heart were devastated in southern Brazil during the 1950s and 1960s, production of palm heart moved north to the *várzea* (seasonally flooded/wet) forests of Lower Amazonia.

Much of the *várzea* forests in the area of the certification trial have long been exploited for agriculture and timber. During the 19th century, relative prosperity came to the region with the boom in rubber extraction. Wealthy merchants and landowners (patrons) dominated the economic and social system, keeping most local farmers and rubber tappers landless or in states of continual debt through loans and overcharging of goods (known as the *aviamento* system). The *aviamento* system persisted in the region during the 20th-century boom and bust of the rubber

trade, followed by brief experiments in marketing Brazil nuts and hides of poached big cats, and cultivation of cacao and other crops. In recent years, local farmers banded together to manage *açaí*, leading to the formation of a local association and the construction of a palm heart canning factory. This case study of a community-organized palm heart association provides an interesting example of a populist movement to obtain tenure for local residents, to assert the rights of rural worker unions and to gain social and economic independence for local landowners.

General description

This field test took place in a community-managed forest, approximately 300 hectares in size, principally dominated by *várzea* forest with small patches of *terra firme* forest. The operation is an association of families, organized as a cooperative to produce palm heart and palm fruits, the former principally for external trade, the later for consumption and trade to local metropolises. Women in the cooperative also produce *açaí* juice and can *açaí* fruit jam. Farmers in the association have been managing their forestlands for more than half a century, with a particular focus on palm heart production in the last 20 to 30 years. In the early years, palm heart extraction was quite destructive and decimated the resource. Local residents, concerned about the depletion of an important subsistence product (the *açaí* fruit), began implementing more sensitive management practices in the 1980s. Families take primary responsibility for managing their own lands (for palm heart and other timber and non-timber products) within the context of a collective forest plan. Association members are also available to work as teams who clear new areas and participate in communal harvesting brigades. The community association is democratic, holds periodic meetings to discuss management of the resource base and the factory, and has regular elections of community representatives. The community receives technical and financial support from a local NGO and an overseas donor agency.

The forest

The site is classified as *várzea* forest habitat, as previously described on page 38.

The management system

Participating families manage at least one hectare of palm hearts to be supplied to the local factory. The palm hearts under management, *E. oleracea*, are multi-stemmed palms capable of sustainable management. The community management plan calls for intensive palm heart management (up to 1000 clusters of palms per hectare), with each palm cluster optimally containing six stems per cluster in three different age classes (the middle age producing palm fruits before they are harvested). One or two tall, older palms are kept as seed sources within plots. Desired forest conditions are met through thinnings, girdling, underbrush removal of competing trees and shrubs, and enrichment planting. Palm hearts are harvested on a three-year rotation. Economically valuable trees are also retained in forest areas, particularly *Virola surinamensis*, *Carapa guianensis*, *Ceiba pentandra* and *Parkia pendula*. Perhaps the greatest benefit of intensive management for *E. oleracea* to the community has been the increase in quantity of palm fruits available for harvest as well as the extension of the temporal availability of these fruits.

Reasons for pursuing certification

The community association sought certification for a number of reasons. Firstly, they desired a confirmation that their association was meeting the highest standards for palm heart management. A number of secondary motivations also made certification an attractive option. For example, certification was seen as a way of legitimizing progress to date and reinforcing steps taken to secure land tenure firmly to the production area. The association believed that certification could bring the operation higher visibility, both locally and internationally, and potentially increase market access, palm heart prices, community reputation and future ability to secure donor funds. In short, certification was valued not only as a tool to improve and validate good forest management practices, but also for its ability to bolster social, economic and political progress made to date.

Lessons learned

The following issues, grouped by subject matter, were brought to light by this field trial.

Technical and ecological issues

- The association's current management plan lacks policies and control measures governing the harvest of timber, game and other NTFPs on community members' land (ie the plan does not integrate management of the *várzea* forest for palm hearts and palm fruits with subsistence use of timber, game and other NTFPs and services).
- The community requires further technical assistance with regard to mapping its resources and conducting adequate monitoring of the resource base and its response to harvest.
- Differing practices in family management blocks have not been systematically monitored or recorded into the management plan, nor have differing practices been examined to determine which harvesting regime maximizes *açaí* fruit production.
- The community has not clearly demarcated conservation zones and protected areas in the management plan, in the field or on maps.
- Production capacity of individual producers' plots and a control system for tracing sales of product from individual plots to the association's factory or to other outside buyers are currently lacking.

Economic issues

- The community has no clear sales plan for palm fruits and canned palm hearts.

- To widen economic opportunities, the community needs to improve access to local markets and centres of processing beyond the scope of the association project.
- Long-term training in product management and product marketing is lacking.
- The canning factory and the factory store are currently closed. Prior to resuming operation they need to pass sanitary inspections.
- Management costs are currently subsidized by outside resources that could eventually be lost.
- The palm heart business is highly competitive, and the association may need to place great emphasis on the development of overseas specialty markets in order to ensure that it has a good, well-paying outlet for its products.

Social issues

- The association's dependency upon external assistance (technical and financial) makes its long-term solvency and stability questionable.
- Secure, legal tenure has still not been obtained from the relevant government agencies (a difficult undertaking in Brazil, although the process appears close to being finalized).
- Internal conflict resolution mechanisms need to be established for the long-term stability of the association.
- Baseline data on past and present subsistence use of the forest is lacking, as is an assessment of the operation's possible impact on the depletion of cultural capital (eg since pursuing commercial palm heart production, varieties and numbers of cultivated

crops in the area have dropped dramatically, knowledge of other forest resources has declined, dependency on the income from the project has increased, etc).

- The community needs to spell out rights, roles and responsibilities of its associates and determine penalties in cases of bad-faith practices.
- Gender equity in decision-making processes requires further attention.

Section II

NTFP SPECIES PROFILES FROM AROUND THE WORLD

Introduction

Patricia Shanley, Alan R Pierce, Sarah A Laird and Abraham Guillén

NTFPs and certification

Illustration by Jamison Ervin

*Argan (*Argania spinosa*)*

The following species profiles were gathered from non-timber forest product (NTFP) researchers around the globe. While not exhaustive, the profiles, taken as a whole, provide a glimpse into the diverse, complex and idiosyncratic universe that is encompassed by the term 'NTFP'. Like the diversity of the forest products they describe, the profiles vary widely in content and style and reflect the views of the individual researchers, the state of information regarding the species and the historic and present use and management of the plant.

The species profiles illustrate the range of product classes that characterize NTFPs and which are found in the indicators and verifiers section of the NTFP certification guidelines (see Appendix I), including exudates, whole plants, vegetative structures, bark, roots and reproductive propagules. Species profiled include:

- *exudates*: chicle gum, breu resin, *amapá* latex, *copaíba* oil, croton latex, maple syrup, mastic gum, pine resin and benzoin resin;

- *whole plants*: palm heart, rattan;
- *vegetative structures*: fiddlehead fern croziers, cat's claw leaves;
- *bark*: pau d'arco, cat's claw bark, cork oak, yohimbe, baobab;
- *roots*: titica, American ginseng;
- *reproductive propagules*: Brazil nuts, argan fruits, pine nuts, chestnuts, griffonia seeds and amla ('emblica') fruits.

Profiles were selected to not only illustrate issues raised by particular classes of products, but also diversity in plant forms (ie trees, vines, herbs), sources (eg primary forest, secondary forest, fallow), uses (eg medicinal, food, incense, construction, handicrafts) and markets (subsistence, local, regional, international).

Many products bridge a number of markets and use categories. For example, while argan, fiddlehead ferns and amla are subsistence goods of local importance, they also have regional markets. Brazil nuts, palm hearts, pine nuts, rattan, cork, pine resin, maple syrup, chestnuts, yohimbe, cat's claw, griffonia, ginseng and chicle have significant regional and international markets, but are also important locally as food or medicine. A few products with small or neglible international markets, but of significant local importance, were also included to illustrate the relationship of certification to the majority of NTFPs that are consumed or traded locally. Examples include *amapá*, *copaíba*, mastic gum, amla, benzoin, baobab bark, titica and breu. In addition, woodcarving and bromeliad case studies are included at the end of this section to provide insight into instances where certification and sustainable management regimes could be developed for non-wood products entering the handicraft and ornamental plant markets.

The profiled species come from a variety of habitats, including primary forests (Brazil nut, titica, pau d'arco), secondary forests (amla, maple), forest gardens (benzoin), riverine forests or seasonally inundated forests (fiddlehead fern, palm heart), lowveld forests (baobab) and agroforestry/silvo-pastoral systems (cork, argan). More than a few products demonstrate an ability to thrive in a variety of sites and conditions.

The NTFP profiles were drawn from both temperate and tropical regions in order to portray the diversity of products, markets and habitats from which NTFPs are sourced, as well as to underline the importance of NTFPs to populations living in both the North and South. There is a preponderance of species profiles from Latin America due to the geographical focus of the NTFP certification project. NTFPs from boreal forests and oceania are notably absent, while other regions are admittedly underrepresented when compared to Latin America.

Certain classes of critical NTFPs are also prominently missing. Products such as game, fuelwood, fodder and fungi were not purposefully neglected, but rather fell outside of the original plant-oriented focus of the project. Such products present a host of additional issues and sub-texts not covered in the following pages, and have unique economic, management and social/cultural characteristics that will impact their certification.

Despite obvious gaps, the profiles contained herein represent a unique blend of temperate and tropical NTFPs. Together, the profiles paint a portrait of complexity that is intended to further our understanding not only of certification, but also of broader NTFP management, harvest and marketing issues.

Chapter 4

Chicle (*Manilkara zapota*)

Peter W Alcorn

Botany and ecology of chicle

'Chicle' is a common name that refers to a number of different species of plants, found from Argentina all the way to Florida. These plants either exude a sticky white latex, produce a fleshy brown and very sweet fruit, or were once used in the manufacture of chewing gum. However, only one species can legitimately be referred to as the first-class chicle of chewing gum fame, and that is *Manilkara zapota* (L.) Van Royen in the family Sapotaceae. Even within its native range, two additional species are often mistakenly referred to as chicle. Both of these species have also, at one time, been used in the manufacture of chewing gum. *Manilkara chicle* and *Pouteria reticulata* are clearly distinct from *M. zapota*, and are referred to by those who know chicle as second- and third-class chicle, respectively.

Manilkara zapota is a tree that can reach over 45 metres (m) in height

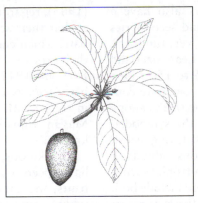

Illustration by Antônio Valente da Silva

*Chicle (*Manilkara zapota*)*

(Lundell, 1933a) and over 125 centimetres (cm) in diameter (Pennington, 1990). Mature trees are evergreen or semi-deciduous, show pronounced sympodial branching and have spirally arranged, simple leaves clustered at branch tips (Pennington, 1990). The cream-coloured flowers are bisexual and sympetalous, with petals alternating with petal-like staminodia. They are axillary, solitary and occur densely packed at branch terminals. The brown, scaly, rough-skinned fruit is about 4cm in diameter and is extremely sweet. The fruit usually contains two to five flat, shiny, dark-brown seeds (personal observation by the author suggests that seeds are, on average, 1.72cm long) with a long basiventral hilum scar and thick testa.

In the field, older trees are immediately recognized due to the omnipresent diagonal slashes – testament to the great economic importance of this species and the diligence of chicle harvesters (chicleros) to locate every tappable tree – extending the length of the bole and often well into the lower branches. Trees of 25cm diameter at breast height (dbh) or more are usually conspicuously scarred with this pattern. The bark is usually grey and furrowed on younger trees, becoming very thick, deeply fissured or checked with age. The slash (inner bark) is distinctly pink or occasionally white. The leaves, especially on younger plants, are distinguished from co-occurring species by their coriaceous leaves, thick and abundant white latex, the presence of epiphylls on the upper dark-green surface, and lack of such plants on the lower yellowish surface. The leaves also have a distinct yellow mid-vein and secondaries that join the mid-vein at very uniform, nearly-90-degree angles. Leaf size and shape vary considerably (5 to 15cm long and 3 to 8cm wide) and cause more confusion than elucidation. The tree's canopy is usually very dense and the sympodial branch form is immediately distinguished.

Chicle is found in various habitats of sub-tropical moist and sub-tropical semideciduous forest types. These include both upland and scrub swamp forest types of Belize, both high- and low-stature semievergreen forests of Quintana Roo and Campeche, Mexico, and the primary forests of much of the Petén Basin of Guatemala. The species also does quite well, throughout its range, in late secondary forest types.

Chicle is a dominant species in the forests where it occurs, often reaching densities of as high as 85 stems per hectare (>10cm dbh), and is almost always found within the top ten dominant species, in terms of number of stems and total basal area. The species is important to a host of animals that count on its sweet fruit throughout the dry season (though fruiting seems to peak at the end of the dry season, from March to May). Among those animals observed consuming the fruit are howler (*Alouatta pigra*) and spider (*Ateles geoffroyi*) monkeys, various parrots (*Amazona* spp.), kinkajous (*Potos flavus*), tapir, peccary and various species of bats.

The other disperser that may actually carry chicle seeds from the source habitat to a different habitat is the bat. The potential importance of bats cannot be overstated. In fact, the activities of the bat may have a great deal to do with the present distribution of *M. zapota*. One possible explanation for the high incidence of chicle trees around Mayan ruins – following the conclusions of Peters (1983), regarding *Brosimum alicastrum* – is that their seeds are dispersed there by bats, which carry the entire fruits back to their roosts (Hall and Kelson, 1959). Barbour (1945) has also observed that the bat *Artibeus jamaicensis parvipes* roosts in trees of *M. zapota*. The popularity of Mayan ruins to roosting bats is well known.

Kinkajous, related to the raccoon, have been observed feeding on chicle fruits, and bats have been observed either taking fruit or visiting the flowers. Heithaus et al (1975) observed entire flowers being consumed by three species of bats (*Carollia perspicillata*, *Artibeus jamaicensis* and *A. lituratus*), all of which are native to the chicle region. Heithaus et al (1975) also mention that it is rare for a plant species to exhibit both bat-pollinated and bat-dispersed syndromes: 'Only *Manilkara zapota* had both bat-dispersed pollen and seeds' (p843). These authors also found that one bat species (*Glossophaga soricina*), observed in Costa Rica, carried chicle pollen on its fur in 60 per cent of their captures, and that chicle was one of the six plant species most commonly represented by pollen on these bats. Furthermore, Pennington (pers comm) suspects that species of *Artibeus* bats are the principal pollinators of chicle.

The species has a substantial native range. *Manilkara zapota* is found in part or all of the Mexican states of Tamaulipas, Mexico (Martinez, 1959), Veracruz (Schwartz, 1990), Oaxaca (Martinez, 1959), Chiapas, Tabasco, Campeche, Yucatan and Quintana Roo (Pennington, 1990). It occurs nearly throughout Belize and the Petén of Guatemala, and has been recorded from isolated locations along the Atlantic coast of Nicaragua (Pennington, 1990). As a result of this broad distribution, chicle is recognized to have been a significant part of both the Aztec and the Maya cultures (Roys, 1931). And yet, almost no information regarding how the plant was used by these peoples is documented.

In the more recent past, chicle has had the distinction of being probably the single most economically (and politically) important plant species in Central America (Schwartz, 1990; Lundell, 1933a, 1933b, 1934). What is known about the species is a direct result of this economic importance. However, only very basic information about productivity, growth rates, distribution, seed germination requirements, etc has been published. The most complete data have been gathered by various *ejidos* (indigenous forest communities) in Mexico that depend upon the revenues from the harvest of chicle, and these data are not published. Data gathered from various sources (Lundell, 1937; Jorgenson, 1993; Schwartz, 1990) have recorded chicle yield figures of from 0.7 kilograms (kg) per tree in Mexico, to an average of between 1kg and 1.8kg per tree in the Petén. Yield is dependent upon many factors, however, including the size of the tree, how many times it was tapped in the past, how intensively it was tapped,

the weather at the time of the previous tapping, and probably many other factors, none of which have been documented. One thing is dramatically clear – yields of 14kg per tree recorded in the early days of the industry are unheard of today.

In a small study in Belize, Alcorn (1994) reported that spacial distribution of chicle trees appeared clumped. Structure of the seedling and sapling population was representative of a healthy and reproductive population. Distribution of seedlings and saplings also appeared to be clumped and indicated that most seeds germinate within the 7m 'canopy shadow' of the parent tree. This study also revealed that the highest levels of seedling mortality occur beneath the parent trees, showing only a simple pattern of density-dependent mortality. Probably the most significant information about chicle population dynamics generated from this study is that chicle is likely a gap-dependent species. In other words, its seedlings maintain a slow growth rate on the forest floor until a gap in the canopy opens, at which point the growth rate increases exponentially as the tree grows to reach the top of the canopy. This is a classic primary-species canopy strategy (Hartshorn, 1980), but indicates one of the most important reasons chicle has never been successful in plantations – it simply will not grow tall enough in clearings. The only thorough study of growth rates of mature trees was conducted by Karling in 1934. Karling documented an annual growth rate of approximately 0.5cm dbh per year for trees in the 20 to 30cm dbh size class. However, his study does not indicate sample size and Karling himself notes that huge variations (of up to 1.7cm) were documented.

Economic background of the chicle extraction industry

Despite the extensive distribution, vast anthropological and economic importance, dominance in forests and exceptional value as a food resource, relatively little is known of the ecology and natural history of chicle (Pennington, pers comm; Egler, 1947). The chewing gum habit, and the industry that feeds it, may never have developed had it not been for the discovery of natural chicle latex. The discovery of chicle at a time when the invention of modern chewing gum was in its infancy meant that the two would become inextricably linked forever. Some of the most incredible fortunes amassed in the United States were chewing gum riches in the early 1900s. These fortunes were almost as quickly lost as they were gained in the high-flying world of chewing gum marketing.

While chicle is most widely known by its latex, which is used in the manufacture of chewing gum – hence the brand name Chiclets – chicle has endured a long history of exploitation by human cultures. Beginning with the Aztecs and Maya indians, the fruit was popular because of its sweetness, and the latex (gum) was chewed by women and children (Roys, 1931). As the last stronghold of the Maya culture fell and European cultures took root in Central America, chicle was still an important culinary species. The Europeans considered the chicle fruit a delicacy for its subtle flavour and high sugar content. Despite their appreciation of the fruit, no evidence exists to indicate that the Spanish cultivated or favoured the species. It was not until the development of chewing gum that evidence for changes in the structure of the chicle population became important. Even that evidence, however, is anecdotal. The economics of chicle extraction have historically been dictated by the buyers of the resource: American companies such as Wrigley's and American Chicle (now Warner Lambert). The primary motivation of these companies was to acquire as much chicle as they could, and pay as low a price for it as the sellers would stand. Consequently, there was never any regard from the buyers for the long-term well-being of the resource or the chicleros. This tradition has continued under the present chicle buyers: Mexico, Japan, Italy and South Korea.

The chewing gum industry began in the late 1800s when chicle was tested as a cheap substitute for rubber. A New Yorker named Adams rediscovered its attributes as a chewing gum and began marketing the product with nearly instant success (see Hendrickson, 1976, for a complete review of this event). Several other companies got on the bandwagon and developed their own brands as gum chewing became a national craze. By the mid-1900s, the tapping and export of chicle for chewing gum was the most important industry in the Yucatan and the Petén (Schwartz, 1990). It was during this time that much of the three-nation area Mexico–Belize–Guatemala was mapped and most thoroughly explored. Most of this exploration, including the discovery of archaeological sites, was done by chicleros. During peak years of chicle production (1930–1950), as much as 10,800 tonnes of chicle was exported from the three-country region (Belize Customs Report, 1942–1952; Jorgenson, 1993; Schwartz, 1990).

Gum was very popular among soldiers in both world wars, particularly among American World War II soldiers who spread the popularity of gum to the far reaches of the world. The resulting increase in gum consumption (see Jorgenson, 1993; Salafsky et al, 1993; Reining et al, 1991; Ashcraft, 1973; Olizar and Olizar, 1968; Belize Customs Report, 1949; Egler, 1947; Hill, 1937; Standley, 1925; and Heyder, 1930, for a more complete description of the economic trends of the chicle industry) led to excessive demands on the chicle resource (Schwartz, 1990; Bartlett, 1935; Lundell, 1934) and ultimately to the development of more dependable and cheaper synthetic substitutes. By 1960 the chicle boom was over, and by 1980 the industry came to a comparative standstill.

While the chicle industry declined, the gum industry not merely survived but thrived. The chewing gum industry did a total retail business of US$140 million in 1942 (Egler, 1947) and over US$1.5 billion in 1986 (Warner Lambert, 1986). This transformation was largely due to the fact that at about the time that natural chicle was becoming depleted, chemists determined how to manufacture a petroleum-based gum that was cheaper, of more consistent quality and of apparently limitless supply (Hendrickson, 1976; Schwartz, 1990). Not all gum manufacturers switched entirely to synthetics, however, and for the last 40 years, meagre purchases by these companies have kept the chicle industry alive, although at a scale that is only vaguely reminiscent of the chicle boom of the previous century.

The effect of land-use change on the chicle population

While changes in land use most assuredly affect the chicle population throughout the region, how the effects are manifested is largely unknown. At the same time, it is quite clear that in spite of massive environmental and ecological changes in the region, chicle has survived. Whether the dominance of the species in the forests it inhabits is a result of the land-use changes of the past is as valid a question as whether there has been a negative effect on the population.

Even though the Yucatan plateau is of late Tertiary age, according to Graham (1977), much of the Yucatan's forests are of recent origin, developing their present characteristics only about 11,000 years ago. Climatic factors have contributed to the forest structure, most notably hurricanes (which have been shown to dramatically influence the patterns of regeneration for chicle; You and Petty,

1991) and fires. And although there is scant pre-human evidence for hurricane activity, events such as that of 1931, where vast tracks of forest were destroyed, were probably relatively common.

Following the arrival of human beings to the region, additional influences on forest structure and composition have developed. The Maya civilization is known to have flourished from about 2000 BC to AD 1000, although their ancestral characteristics and eventual demise are not well understood (see Hammond, 1982, for a review).

The influence of the Maya on the structure of present-day forests of the Yucatan Peninsula and Petén Basin are not entirely known. However, it is well documented that population levels were much higher for the region than they were when the colonists arrived, and that probably vast areas of forest were cleared in order to cultivate land for the production of food (Rice, 1991; Hammond, 1982). The effect of this clearing on the regeneration of forest tree species had to be substantial. In fact, it is hard to believe that after only perhaps 10 to 20 generations of trees, the effects of Mayan agricultural and forestry practices would not still be highly evident in present-day forests. Furthermore, if the Maya actually favoured the species (by not cutting it down) when they cleared areas or built living structures, the trees would have had a tremendous advantage over other species following the collapse of the Maya civilization and the natural regeneration of the forest vegetation.

Following the decline of the Maya, and their eventual conquest by Spaniards, various forms of forest resource extraction took place, gradually increasing in intensity to the present. Most economically important of these activities are the extraction of logwood (*Haematoxylon campechianum* – used as a source of dye in Europe; see Joseph, 1987), timber and chicle, and both widespread and localized slash-and-burn agriculture. Each of these industries and their associated activities has had some impact on the structure and composition of the forest.

Although timber harvesting has been taking place in the region for over 250 years (see Edwards, 1986; Napier, 1973, for a summary), systematic harvesting has only been in practice for the last 150 years (Standley and Record, 1936; Edwards, 1986). Logging of mahogany (*Swietenia macrophylla*), and to a lesser degree Spanish cedar (*Cedrela mexicana*), gradually replaced the extraction of logwood as the primary export commodity of the region and was a fundamentally different extractive industry. This transition occurred over a period of about 100 years, from the late 1700s to the late 1800s. Unlike logwood, the cutting of mahogany required gangs of 10 to 50 individuals and the use of teams of cattle, and caused marked damage to surrounding vegetation as a result of tree-felling, *barquadiers* (yarding areas), roads, railroads and access to water for transport.

The practice of mahogany cutting probably influenced the overall composition and structure of the Belizean forests (Brokaw and Mallory, 1993) as well as forests of Mexico and Guatemala. However, specific effects of logging on species other than mahogany have not been documented for the area. General effects of selective logging from other areas (Ganzhorn et al, 1990; Johns, 1988; Uhl and Vieira, 1989) include the decline of overstorey tree size; a decline in the number of seedlings of woody species (and an increase in the number of herbaceous plants); reduced thickness of litter layer; and a dramatic increase in the number of trails, roads and *barquadiers* and other small artificial clearings.

Several researchers from the early 1900s have suggested that the increased demand for chicle resulted in extensive overharvesting of the resource (Heyder, 1930; Lundell, 1933a; Karling, 1942a; Gilly, 1943; Egler, 1947). These authors provide anecdotal evidence of a 5–15 per cent mortality rate for tapped chicle trees, and some (eg Lundell, 1933a) suggested that the industry would not survive at peak production without periodic breaks in all tapping activity for several years. Despite forecasts of high mortality, the resource still appears to be rather abundant. However, a human-influenced mortality rate of even a low level, acting on a single species, could have a pronounced effect on the population structure of that species.

The chicle resource

The chicle-tapping season begins with the arrival of the winter rains around July and is usually over by the end of February when the rains abate. Trees at least 20cm in diameter are of tappable size. Trees are 'tapped' in a herring-bone pattern, with a central channel running vertically up the tree and lateral slashes intersecting the vertical about every 40cm. Slashes are made up the bole of the tree and into the upper branches, as high as 30 metres, by agile men (chicleros) wielding razor sharp machetes and slashing through the bark to the sap-filled phloem tissue. Because of the potential damage and limited yield produced through this tapping method, other tapping methods have been attempted but have failed to increase yield or reduce damage (including the Ibidem method used for rubber trees, *Havea brasiliensis* – Karling, 1942c – and extraction of latex from leaves and fruit – Morton, 1987). After tapping, the tree needs from three to eight years to heal, at which point it can be tapped again. As many as five sets of tappings have been observed on some trees, indicating that a tree may be tappable for 15 to 40 years.

Within 24 hours of tapping, the latex drains and collects in a cloth bag (often coated with natural rubber from *Castilla elastica*) at the base of the tree. Chicleros store daily yields in large cloth bags until the end of the work week, at which point the camp begins the chicle-cooking process. In order to reduce the total moisture content of the latex to about 30 per cent, the chicle is cooked in a large (about 136 litres) cauldron over a wood fire for about three hours and is stirred constantly. When the desired moisture content is reached (determined by observing the clarity of the bubbles rising to the surface during boiling), the pot is removed from the fire to cool. When cool enough to handle, a chiclero will soap his hands and set up a working surface, such as a spread of leaves (usually *Sabal morrisiana*) or a plastic tarp, and produce a four-sided wooden box to shape the chicle into a block or *marqueta*. He then reaches into the pot and pulls out a sizeable wad of the hot latex and kneeds it into the box, repeating the process until the box is suitably full (about 12kg).

When a block has been suitably formed, the chiclero presses into the hot surface a small block of wood with his initials carved in it, thus identifying the *marqueta* as of his making. The camp supervisor applies his initials and the chicle contractor's as well. This system of marking each block not only defines ownership, but also serves as a chain of responsibility, should the block be found unacceptable for one reason or another. *Marquetas* are stacked in a cool warehouse until a contract is filled and the chicle is ready for export.

In the past, the quality of chicle delivered to the buyer, and the quantity of chicle available from the forest, have been issues of primary concern in the industry. The advent of synthetics has meant that the price of raw chicle is compared not only seasonally to other chicle on the market, but also to the going rate of synthetic gum bases. Whether sustainability will also become an issue of concern in the industry is yet to be determined.

One of the most troublesome problems Wrigley's and other gum companies encountered at the peak of production (before switching to synthetics) was that the chicle received in the US was frequently contaminated with latex from other species of trees (at least one of them was the toxic *Metopium browneii*). Chicleros would even put rocks in the centre of a block of chicle in order to increase the weight (Karling, 1942b). Different latexes have different chemical properties; thus, impurities caused irregularities in the processing.

Today, impurities are no longer a problem for two reasons. Firstly, the current demand for chicle is far less than it was when large-scale tapping was practiced, so it is not difficult to find the contracted amount of 'first-class' chicle (*M. zapota*). Secondly, there are only a few buyers of natural chicle and they pay a high price for the material; consequently, middle-men have had to guarantee that no impurities will be encountered (if they are, the entire contract will be nullified). At present, all chicle comes from one abundant forest species, the 'first-class chicle' tree *Manilkara zapota*. If demand increases to World War II levels, however, contractors may have to work in areas where first-class chicle is less abundant. When this happens, the probability that impurities are encountered will increase. In addition, other behaviours that resulted from high demands for chicle may also resurface, particularly overtapping. This results when trees are retapped before the tree has had adequate time to heal from the previous tap, or when small trees are tapped, or when trees are overzealously tapped (girdled) and killed (Karling, 1942b).

There are numerous sources that describe the history of chicle extraction, the value of the export and the annual amounts extracted, dating back to the early 1900s (eg Schwartz, 1990). The greatest historical peak occurred in the mid-1940s when a combined total of approximately 10,000 tonnes were exported from the three-country region. With the introduction of synthetics, chicle production has steadily declined to the point where less than 2000 tonnes have been harvested annually over the last ten years. Primary buyers have been the Japanese, and until the 1998–1999 season, these purchases have kept the industry alive. Following the severe downswing in the Japanese economy during the last two years, purchases for chicle last year all but disappeared. In fact, both Guatemalan and Mexican chicle warehouses were left with over 100 tonnes each of unsold chicle. There are currently no indications of a rekindling of the Japanese market for chicle, thus leaving producers in serious doubt about the future of their industry. In addition, the domestic use of chicle for chewing gum remains unreliable.

Over the last two years a growing interest in 'natural chewing gum' from potential buyers of chicle has sparked enthusiasm for a rebirth of the chicle industry among producers. The enthusiasm derives from the fact that the market is depressed, higher prices are envisioned and the notion of sustainable production is generally attractive to producers. What is commonly neglected by producers in considering the potential of this new outlet for their chicle is the micro-scale of the marketplace, the necessity to grow the market slowly, and the extra work involved in producing chicle on a 'sustainable' basis.

Managing the chicle resource

Historically, the chicle resource has never been managed. Rather, the current population of chicle trees in the forests of the Petén and Yucatan are a result of the interaction between once native forests and the past and ongoing human activity in the region. Today's chicle resource has been shaped by silvicultural and agricultural practices of the Maya, the disappearance of the Maya, the industry of timber extraction, the chicle extraction industry, and the ebb and flow of market demand for chicle. If the chicle population has been in a state of transition for the last several thousand years, what then should be the goal of a management plan? It is helpful in answering this question to understand that this species is not in a state of pristine native existence, but has been manipulated by humans to such a degree that its 'natural' level of importance in the forest is not now known. This knowledge should come as somewhat of a relief to potential managers, allowing them to determine goals based on the needs of the system as a whole, including the humans who depend upon the resource and the economic system within which they must live.

Recently, chicleros have begun to organize (SPFEQR, 1993), and already a substantial database on chicle productivity, tree size-class distribution, tree growth rates and chiclero performance/documentation has been established by the Plan Piloto Chiclero group in Quintana Roo, Mexico. This first attempt at developing standards for chicle monitoring is to be lauded, but much more needs to be done. Any management plan for chicle must approach the task as holistically as possible – including, in particular, consideration of the fact that without a market, there will be no point to management at all.

Furthermore, any management strategy must include a significant buffer contingent that will protect the chicle resource from overharvest or extremes in weather or other factors that produce severe negative impacts on the chicle resource.

Chicle management plan

A basic chicle management plan should seek to determine and/or monitor the following:

- yield of individual trees and the resource as a whole;
- growth rates of chicle trees;
- mortality rates of chicle trees;
- analysis of cause of death for tapped and untapped chicle trees;
- chicle pollination ecology;
- definition of chicle seasonality in terms of both meteorological and biological data;
- fruit and seed production, predation and survival;
- seedling survival, growth rates and recruitment;
- size-class distribution of chicle population;
- wildlife density/abundance.

Socio-economic aspects of chicle management

Socio-economic aspects of chicle management that require examination include:

- social costs of chicle harvesting, including a cost–benefit analysis;
- comparison of harvesting and management under different land tenure scenarios (Mexico versus Guatemala versus Belize);

- influence of the different marketing strategies (open market production versus managed production);
- marketing issues (eg what will make a more saleable chicle?);
- safety and hygiene in chicle camps; education and social security for chicleros and their families;
- economic analysis of chicle harvesting in order to establish market price minimums each year (there is currently no logical system).

Specific management practices

Specific management practices should include:
- mapping of the chicle resource, including trees, trails, water sources, etc;
- placement of permanent tags on chicle trees;
- data on tree yield, dbh, estimated number of previous taps, weather conditions, time of day, chiclero, amount of time for tapping;
- training of chicleros and other community members in data collection and analysis;
- collection of data by chicleros and/or other members of the community;
- establishment of appropriate number of permanent chicle research areas for work on seedling establishment, pollination ecology, etc;
- provision of access by all members of the community to all aspects of research and management of the chicle resource.

Chicle certification

Chicle extraction has taken place in Mexico, Belize and Guatemala at varying levels for well over 100 years. The fact that the industry is still functional suggests that extraction may have been conducted in a sustainable fashion. However, anecdotal evidence of overharvesting in the past, more intense pressure on contemporary forests for conversion, and a renewed enthusiasm to take part in the business of 'natural gum' could again lead to overharvesting. Adding value to a natural resource has generally positive effects. However, adding value on the production side, without adequate controls, could lead to overharvesting.

Of the many resources and extraction scenarios currently being evaluated for certification (eg timber, rattan, tagua, Brazil nut, palm heart, various types of tropical foliage, fibres, fruits and seeds), chicle certification offers perhaps the most compelling opportunity to fundamentally reshape an industry.

The strength of this conclusion rests on several observations:

- Chicle is a dominant species of tree in the forests of the Yucatan and Petén Basin and has shown a remarkable biological resilience in response to human manipulation.
- The chicle industry is firmly rooted in the region's culture and traditions.
- The chicle market is currently completely flat, with no pending orders for the purchase of large amounts of chicle.
- There is a developing trend for 'natural chewing gum'.

However, there are some very serious risks. Most of these risks are related to the fact that much is riding on the rebuilding or saving of the chicle industry in the face of a collapsed market. The opportunity exists to use certification to rebuild the chicle industry in a manner that protects not only the resource itself, but also the forests that produce chicle and the chicleros who depend upon the revenues from it. In addition, certification could be the vehicle that will bring to producers new forms of employment in the chicle industry, as well as greater control of the resource upon which they depend. Certification could also be effectively used to educate customers about higher levels of quality in chicle products. All of these elements are critical if a market for 'natural chewing gum' is to be given fertile ground in which to grow.

Already evident in this new market are products that offer a 'green-washed' version of what producers and astute customers hope to create. Two products that recently arrived on the market make false claims that work directly against the efforts of certification. One claims to be 'certified sustainably managed', and that 'tapping chicle gum from rainforest trees is non-detrimental to the life of the tree or to the environment'. Even though the first claim is flatly untrue, the customer has no way of knowing this. The second claim is unfounded and misleading. Tapping chicle trees in an unmonitored fashion can kill the trees. And there are many environmental issues that can be raised for discussion about tapping practices. As if these comments were not misleading enough, on a single pack of chewing gum, the authors also write: '6000 chiclero families farming 80 million chicle trees in the rainforest'. This comment serves only to misinform customers about how chicle is produced, as chicle is not farmed at all, but rather requires intact natural forest to produce adequate latex flow. The second new 'natural chewing gum' indicates that it is 'all natural gum'; the reality is that it is made from only partially natural gum base. The other portion of the base is a synthetic material, no different from commercial chewing gums.

These products are mentioned as examples of the types of obstacles that will need to be overcome if certification is to be successful. Certifying chicle is only part of the battle; a marketplace must also be created that will understand the difference between certified and uncertified 'natural chewing gum'. This point cannot be overemphasized. Should the marketplace not be adequately monitored and non-certified 'natural chewing gum' products end up being promoted to customers without a resounding and thorough response from the certification industry, the effects of certification will only serve to put certified producers at a strong disadvantage in the market. The short-term effect of this scenario would hurt producers of certified chicle. The long-term effect would be to confuse the consumer, and that would have the effect of turning 'natural chewing gum' into another rainforest fad, a result that could potentially destroy the industry. If, on the other hand, a strong effort is made early on to identify 'good natural chewing gum' as being gum produced from certified sources, customers will learn what to expect and what to demand from all 'natural chewing gums'.

Certification of chicle involves two important elements – chain of custody and the management and monitoring of forests. Once these two practices are employed in the chicle industry, a host of other benefits follow. The application of the concept of chain of custody allows not only the realization by producers that they control their resource, but also that they are linked to the end of that chain – the market. This is a new role for producers of chicle. Throughout the region, producers have traditionally been kept in the dark about all aspects of the final use of the product they create. Not only does this new role create numerous opportunities for producers; it also allows them to prepare for market fluctuations before it is too late. While the benefits of employing effective forest management have been discussed at length and are well known in certain areas, effective certification of chicle could bring the theory of certification to a whole new audience, at a whole new scale.

Chapter 5

Brazil nut (*Bertholletia excelsa*)

Enrique G Ortiz

'The noblest trees in the forests of Tauaú were the Bertholletia, *and one specimen was perhaps as large a tree as I have anywhere seen on the Amazon valley'* R Spruce (1853).

Brazil nut forests in a nutshell: an overview

Brazil nuts (*Bertholletia excelsa* Humb. and Bonp.), also known more recently as 'Amazonian nuts', are one of the only non-timber forest products (NTFPs) widely used in international markets that come strictly from natural forests and not from plantations. They are not only a tasty commodity but also a resource that plays an important social and environmental role. Their collection and marketing are responsible for the protection of millions of hectares of healthy forests in Brazil, Bolivia and Peru and represent a major source of income for hundreds of thousands of Amazonian residents. It is indeed a very important nut.

The seeds of the Brazil nut tree are the commercial product. The seeds are con-

Illustration by Antônio Valente da Silva

*Brazil nut (*Bertholletia excelsa*)*

tained in a hard coconut-like fruit that is opened in the forest by Brazil nut harvesters or *castañeros* (the tree is known as *castaña* in Bolivia and Peru, and *castanheira* in Brazil). The seeds (vernacularly called nuts) are then transported to a village where, after some initial processing, they are ready to start a long commercial and geographical journey that may take them as far away as a Christmas feast table in England (the 'Christmas nuts' mentioned in Sokolov, 1995).

The biology of the Brazil nut tree is one of the most remarkable and often-cited natural history stories that show the intricate relation between an ecologically healthy forest and low-impact human use. The reproductive success of the Brazil nut tree is dependent upon a handful of species that perform vital pollination and seed dispersal services, and is illustrative of a fragile system that is easily disrupted by unsustainable human interventions.

Analyses of the nutritional value of Brazil nuts have shown it to be rich in oil (approximately 65 per cent) and protein (approximately 17 per cent), with a high content of methionine, a type of protein named 'excelsina', as well as all the essential amino acids (Zucas et al, 1975; Mori and Prance, 1990). Due to its high content of selenium, it is also used for treating several types of cancer, and has lately been recommended as a treatment for prostate cancer.

The Brazil nut tree is one of the giants of the forest, reaching heights close to 60 metres (m), diameters of over 2m, and ages of over 1000 years. It may indeed be the longest-living tree known in the Amazon. Its canopy resembles a huge emerging umbrella, branching out only at the top and presenting its flowers and fruits mainly at the outer edges of its canopy. The trees occur in *castañales* (clumps of trees), separated from each other by distances of up to several kilometres. In these stands, *B. excelsa* undoubtedly holds the greatest biomass per hectare among all trees. With a variable number of fruits per tree, each fruit contains 15–25 seeds, arranged in segments much like the pieces of an orange. *B. excelsa* is the only species of its genus, belonging to the pan-tropical family Lecythidaceae (the family of the monkey pot and *Sapucaia* trees). This species naturally occurs mainly in Brazil, Bolivia and Peru; however, some smaller populations are found in the Guyanas, Colombia and Venezuela. Brazil nut trees occur naturally only in lowland rainforests, at elevations below 800m, on well-drained soils in high-ground forests or *terra firme*.

The famous explorers Humboldt and Bonpland were the first to describe this tree species scientifically in 1807, from samples collected in Venezuela – trees later thought to have been planted by missionaries from seeds brought from Brazil. Given the majestic size of the Brazil nut tree, it has been said that Humboldt offered an ounce of gold to whomever could climb the tree to procure a flower for its botanical description. The earliest historical reference to Brazil nuts dates back to 1569 and comes from an account of a Spanish explorer, Alvarez Maldonado, who claimed that he survived on these nuts after fleeing from an attack by Indians in south-eastern Peru. When the Spanish captured the English pirate Richard Hawkins in 1594, he was reportedly fed Brazil nuts while he languished in jail in Lima. Dutch merchants were the first to introduce Brazil nuts to Europe early in the 17th century. However, Brazil nuts came to be a regular export product only later in the 19th and 20th centuries, first entering the United States at the beginning of the 19th century (Rosengarten, 1984).

Amerindians have used Brazil nuts for thousands of years. In fact, based on the occurrence of human-related black organic earth – *terra preta do indio* – several researchers believe that the current geographical distribution of the Brazil nut tree is a direct result of indigenous practices. The Kayapó in Brazil, among other groups, currently carry and plant Brazil nut seeds on their journeys through the forest. I have encountered several 100-year-old trees connecting, in a line, two points from a lake to a river, suggesting an old trail that was probably widely used by ancient Toromona or Ese-eja Indians in Peru. However, the current distribution of the Brazil nut tree species may also have resulted from unintended practices by indigenous peoples and/or, to a greater extent, through 'natural' ecological processes (see the following section on Brazil nut tree ecology).

Brazil nut harvesting is a physically demanding and dangerous activity. Fruits are gathered from the ground, usually during the rainy season when the fruits ripen and fall. There have been several cases of reported deaths and serious injuries resulting from fruits or *cocos* falling on unlucky harvesters: a 1 to 2 kilogram (kg) fruit falling from a height of 50m is a potential killer. Although the risk is omnipresent, *castañeros* know when and how to collect fruits to reduce risk or injury. Harvesters in Brazil and parts of Bolivia use hand-woven baskets and a grabbing stick to gather fruits (in Peru, fruits are mainly gathered by hand). The fruits are then accumulated outside the canopy shadow of the Brazil nut tree to be opened with a machete. All the seeds are then poured into a standard-sized nylon sack that holds 70 to 75kg of nuts. It takes the nuts of approximately 400 *cocos* to fill up a sack or *barrica*, depending upon the size of the fruits. The sacks are then carried to a main camp or loading point (next to a river or a road) for a pre-transportation treatment of drying and cleaning. At the end of the harvesting season, the cargo is then transported to the nearest town to be sold to peeling factories (private or communal), or alternatively to be unshelled in households. Although there are variations depending upon the site, it should be noted that the described harvesting process mainly takes place in the forest, a wild forest, from widely scattered trees connected by narrow and muddy trails, and in camps often hundreds of kilometres from an urban centre.

Once the nuts are shipped to towns, the processing and commercialization of the product follows a few set patterns. Middlemen, often commissioned by transformation and commercialization companies, may buy the nuts. Alternatively, companies that paid earlier monetary advances to harvesters may directly receive pre-arranged nut shipments at ports. However, a few community-run enterprises in the three main Brazil nut producing countries are still active and carry out the initial stages of processing (ie the de-shelling and quality selection of the product). Strict quality control, dry packaging and transportation follow this process to the final destination, mainly the US and Europe. Although processing is still carried out traditionally, most of the nuts traded in the world market today likely come from sophisticated processing factories that are increasingly replacing hand labour with mechanization, a reality that arose in direct response to cost and quality standards imposed by buyers in the Northern hemisphere.

Brazil nut stands are not free land. In large part, they are portions of forests assigned by governments to communities or to individual caretakers that may take the form of private corporations, companies or individuals. A smaller portion of the world's *castañales* is found on private property. However, in most cases, the 'concessionaries' (or other forms of landholding) own the Brazil nut harvest. Brazil nut landholdings are of varying sizes, depending upon the country and on the region. For example, in south-eastern Peru, an extension of close to 1.2 million hectares in the Madre de Dios department has been granted as concessions to individual heads of families in units usually no larger than 1000 hectares. In Bolivia, in addition to small Brazil nut landholders, there are individuals and companies who control, hold resource rights or own medium to large areas, in some cases portions of land the size of Belgium. The tenure situation in Brazil is similar to that in Bolivia, with the additional exception of significant-sized areas being designated as 'extractive reserves' where small plots (300–400 hectares) are divided among community members.

Whatever the size of the land or social organization, the individuals in charge of Brazil nut harvesting operations depend upon hired-hand labour and a system of loans to finance the harvesting season. Thus, Brazil nut harvesting uses a large number of people directly in the forest activity. Although no one has ever assessed the number of people (and their dependants) involved in, and dependent upon, Brazil nut harvest and trade, its number may easily account for several hundred thousand people. The case of Puerto Maldonado in Madre de Dios, Peru, provides a glimpse of the magnitude of the industry's impact. In Puerto Maldonado, there are about 1200 concessions and concessionaries. Each requires an average of three workers for nut gathering in addition to the concessionary. The average family size in the area is of six individuals. Just counting the field operations, close to half of the population of the city is dependent upon this resource for their income. If the middlemen and factory workers (one of the few occupations for women and, in many cases, single mothers) are added, it can be extrapolated that the number of people employed by the Brazil nut industry would easily comprise two-thirds of the population of one of the most biologically rich areas of the world – an area where no other economically and environmentally sustainable alternatives exist.

The Brazil nut-rich forests of Peru represent less than 10 per cent of the total area of *castañales* in Amazonia, hence underscoring its regional and global socio-environmental importance. The labour figures in Brazil and Bolivia may be similar to those seen in Peru, although with a significant difference in social conditions (see the section on 'certification potential' at the end of this chapter). Recent studies show that even though it is an activity that takes place only seasonally (although the peeling and processing may extend for several months beyond the harvest season), Brazil nut extraction accounts for over 60 per cent of the yearly income for a large portion of the people involved (Agreda, 1999).

The position of the Brazil nut's place in the world nut market has dropped from 4 per cent in the 1970s to less than 2 per cent today (Clay, 1997b). Brazil nuts currently serve a 'filling role' in world nut trade, and their trade is linked to the availability or scarcity of other, more preferred nuts (eg peanuts, almonds, cashews, walnuts, pistachios and macadamia nuts). However, trade with the UK, the Netherlands, Germany and the US, the main buyers of Brazil nuts, still brings around US$40 million in export revenues per year to Bolivia, Brazil and Peru together (LaFleur, 1992; Clay, 1997b). Several researchers have attempted to explain the fluctuations in prices, and have analysed the various prices paid for nuts to actors in the trade – from the forest gatherer to the retailer – in order to understand the economic chain of revenue and to improve the social and environmental aspects of Brazil nut trade. What remains clear is that the Brazil nut industry is a sector that is facing a continuous drop in volume, which in turn is jeopardizing its social and environmental role.

However, recently developed Brazil nut forest management plans, as well as an increasing commercial potential due to its organic nature, bring hope for those wishing to re-establish the Brazil nut's previous position in the world nut market. Although agronomic techniques have been successfully developed, large-scale attempts at domestication have failed, and Brazil nut harvesting from wild groves remains the only viable commercial source of nuts. Brazil nut certification may play an important role in bolstering its continuity as an industry. Although several issues need to be resolved, the organic and environmentally friendly attributes of Brazil nuts may make the product readily certifiable for certain markets. However, the social aspects of the industry will require some modifications and close supervision.

Brazil nut tree ecology

The botanical description of the Brazil nut tree is as follows. Large trees to 60m tall, unbuttressed, the young branches glabrous, sparcely lenticellate. Bark with conspicuous longitudinal fissures. Leaves simple, alternate, the blades oblong, 17–36cm x 6.5–15.5cm, coriaceous, glabrous on both surfaces, longitudinally striate, with 29 to 45 pairs of lateral veins prominulous on both surfaces. Inflorescence of axillary spikes or of terminal, paniculate arrangements of spikes with one or two orders of branching, the latter with two 2–7 lateral branches. The bracts and bracteoles are lanceolate. Flowers approximately 3cm diameter at anthesis, calyx with two lobes. Petals six, pale yellow to white oblong-ovate to 30mm long, androecial hood white to yellow, the inside of hood with depression into which fits the staminal ring, the inside of ligule often tinged with pink. Staminal rings asymmetrical with 80–135 stamens; ovary (3–) 4 (–6) locular, the 16–25 ovules inserted at the base of septum. Fruits round, usually 10–12.5cm x 10–12.5cm but up to 16cm x 14cm, often of varied shape and size even within same tree. Seeds 10–25 per fruit, approximately 3.5–5cm x 2cm, the embryo undifferentiated (adapted from Mori and Prance, 1990).

Brazil nut trees are found in non-flooded Amazonian forests at lower elevations, in areas with a mean annual temperature of between 24 and 27° Celsius (C) and annual rainfall between 1400 to 2800 millimetres (mm). It is thought that two to seven months of reduced rainfall are required for this tree species to develop properly. Trees are usually found in stands called *manchales* or *manchais* of 50 to 100 trees, each clump separated by distances that may extend up to several kilometres. There are some records of 10 to 25 Brazil nut trees in a hectare; however, these are exceptions. Typically, when larger areas are considered – including those between *manchales* – tree densities fluctuate between 2.5 to 3 adult trees per hectare. No one knows what is the total area covered by Brazil nut forests in Amazonia. Some conservative estimates place it at around 20 million hectares (Clay, 1997b), an estimate that may fall far short when the wide geographical range of the species is considered.

The age structure of *Bertholletia* populations does not show the reversed J-shaped curve characteristic of self-maintaining tree species, with most plants being mid-age reproductive individuals of basal diameters between 1 and 2m. Seedlings at the earliest stages of development are rarely found, suggesting that a major recruitment bottleneck occurs at the seed dispersal stage or during seed establishment (Ortiz, 1991). Brazil nut trees are long lived, a factor that may explain its persistence as a species through time (based on radiocarbon analyses and allometric measurements, some trees are estimated to be well over 1000 years old; Camargo et al, 1974; Salomao, 1991). Nursery as well as field studies have shown that Brazil nut tree seedlings and saplings require intermediate to high levels of light for their initial development, growing faster and shedding more leaves under those conditions. However, desiccation of leaves has been reported in seedlings growing in open nurseries. Their gap dependence may explain in part their occurrence in stands, whether these gaps are a result of natural or human disturbance. Once a seedling reaches a gap, it grows relatively quickly to access available sunlight. Reproductive maturity (ie flower and nut production) is reached at a basal trunk diameter of >40cm in the forest, or at 15 to 20 years of age for a tree growing under good light conditions. In grafted trees, reproductive age can be reached in a third of that time.

Fruit production varies between trees, from no fruits at all to over 2000 per tree. When all fruit-bearing trees in a population are considered, productivity per tree averages close to, or slightly above, 20kg of raw or in-shell nuts, or around 100 fruits. However, this average figure is reduced by half when all of the *B. excelsa* plants are considered (seedlings as well as unproductive trees). *Castañeros* only keep account of, and harvest, productive trees (eg a 10–20-fruit tree would be ignored). Tree and fruit numbers may vary depending upon the specific area within a region. For instance, within the same region, locals usually know 'hotspot' areas where *manchales* are bigger, tree numbers per hectare are higher and fruit production is known to be exceptional. Explanations for these patterns remain speculative, and no correlations have been found between fruit numbers and tree diameters, tree heights or soil types. Fruit yields also vary between years, but it is frequently observed that productive trees often yield better crops in relation to average trees, independent of the year. It is still unclear what determines high-production years, as well as how often these occur. Extrapolations of yearly commercial yields indicate that only 20 to 30 per cent of the potential Brazil nut areas are currently under commercial management.

Flowering occurs mainly at the onset of the rainy season, reaching a peak in November and December. Changing weather patterns may vary the timing of this event, as well as the length of the flowering season. Flowers follow a relatively generalized leaf-drop cycle and are produced *en masse*. One can readily identify a Brazil nut-rich forest during flowering season by the profusion of pale yellow flowers carpeting the ground. Flowers last only a few hours, opening before sunrise and falling early in the afternoon. Thus, insect visitation and pollination take place early in the morning when flowers are receptive.

Large-bodied bees presumably pollinate the flowers of *Bertholletia excelsa*, particularly the colourful Euglossinae group. Due to the logistical constraint of flowers being at heights of over 30m, all research on pollination of Brazil nut trees has been carried out in plantations, where trees were grafted, and flowers were at no more than 8–10m above ground. Only recently have researchers in Peru looked at wild trees to investigate what species are the main visitors and pollinators. Bees of the genera *Xylocopa*, *Eulaema* and *Exaerete* appear to be among the main visitors; however, ongoing research will clarify their identities, importance and how specific visitors/pollinators are to this tree species.

It has long been believed that the lower production of Brazil nuts is related to a pollination deficiency, mainly attributable to smoke resulting from increasing forest fires in the Amazon (ie smoke and forest fragmentation affecting bee abundance, and thus pollination). Recent observations of lower visitation rates and a reduced composition of the bee assemblage visiting Brazil nut flowers in Peru (Centeno and Ortiz, unpublished report) seems to support this hypothesis; however, confirmation of this relationship awaits further results. Other studies have shown the reluctance of some bee species – Euglossines, in particular – to visit fragmented or modified habitats (Powell and Powell, 1987), a fact that may help to explain, in part, the failure of Brazil nut plantations, which have shown good vegetative growth but poor fruit yield. In addition to these observations, several of these bee species show a tight seasonal specialization to flower species (as has been found for *B. excelsa*), some depending upon orchids that grow in Brazil nut tree canopies for odours essential to their reproductive rituals. Brazil nut trees are mainly allogamous (ie they require cross-fertilization or, in other words, need other genetically unrelated conspecific trees nearby and gamete carriers for fertilization). There is one lesson from this natural history that is highly relevant for Brazil nut-rich forest management: a productive Brazil nut forest requires a healthy forest.

After pollination, only a few flowers advance through the transition stages between immature and mature fruits, a process that may take up to 14 months on the canopy. For instance, before fruits fall in the middle of the rainy season, one can see two generations of fruits at the same time: developing fruits and mature fruits ready to fall. During this time, fruits endure attacks by insects, mammals and hungry birds, particularly parrots. Macaws are regular consumers of the still-soft, unripe fruits. Macaws visited close to 75 per cent of a monitored tree population in Peru and damaged close to 5 per cent of the fruit yield from those trees

(Ortiz, 1991). If shotgun shells were not so expensive, hunting of macaws by *castañeros* would be a more common practice.

Fruits begin falling in the middle of the rainy season (in Peru and Bolivia and parts of Brazil, by mid-December), at which time seed dispersers and seed predators commence their activities. A handful of mammals eat Brazil nuts, but only after three species of rodents gnaw open the fruits and liberate the seeds: the agouti, the paca and a squirrel. The agouti (*Dasyprocta* spp.) is responsible for most of this work – more than 80 per cent of the total (Ortiz, unpublished observation). After eating a share of the nuts from a fruit, only agoutis, squirrels and acouchis (*Myoprocta* spp.) bury and rebury the rest of the seeds, at depths of 1 to 2cm, for later consumption when food becomes scarce (a behaviour called 'scatter-hoarding'). Unfortunately for the scatter-hoarders, other mammals (mainly peccaries, rodents and others), knowing of the seed burial patterns of agoutis, specialize in seeking out their caches. Without the agouti, virtually no natural regeneration of Brazil nuts would occur. Agoutis often remove originally cached seeds and subsequently rebury them at further distances, a fact that may help explain how Brazil nut stands are formed. Although home ranges of adult agoutis are small, juvenile agoutis wander widely, taking seeds or whole fruits with them for distances greater than 1 kilometre (km), thus offering another explanation for the formation of new Brazil nut stands.

Due to the death or poor memory of the seed disperser, some of the buried seeds may escape predation. It is important to keep in mind that agoutis are not only seed dispersers but also seed predators. In order for natural regeneration to occur, a portion of the seeds liberated from the fruits needs to survive. How does seed harvesting by *castañeros* affect this natural process? Some researchers have proposed that harvesters should leave a minimum of 20 per cent of the seed yield in the forest in order to facilitate the regeneration process (eg Peters, 1990). This recommendation assumes that intensive harvest adversely impacts *B. excelsa* recruitment. Research of varying harvest intensities (normal and purposely intensive) in Peru and Brazil showed that close to 40 per cent of the total fruit production in the forest, including all trees in the research population, were left in the ground or were taken by mammalian seed dispersers before fruit gatherers arrived (Miller, 1990; Ortiz, 1991; Ortiz, unpublished report). In addition, empirical evidence shows that natural seed regeneration (number of naturally occurring seedlings) is greater in areas where harvesting takes place than in areas not harvested. This fact may be explained by the indirect seed dispersal accomplished by harvesters (seeds dropping from sacks), combined with hunting practices and a subsequently larger agouti population that retrieves a greater number of seeds to cache. In areas that are not harvested, seed mortality may be greater due to less-disturbed agouti populations that have an easier time retrieving their caches, as well as greater levels of seed predation by healthier populations of other seed consumers, such as spiny rats.

Some levels of seasonal hunting pressure often accompany Brazil nut gathering. I have visited several Brazil nut areas in both Bolivia and Peru where large monkeys and other medium-sized animals are now rare or absent due to hunting pressure. Hunting is often promoted by *patrones* who refuse to provide animal protein to their workers. Interestingly, in all of these areas, agoutis are one of the few animals that have resisted low, medium and moderately high levels of

hunting. Moreover, and counterintuitively, in most cases agoutis are even more abundant in harvested areas than in areas that experience little or no hunting (ie nut harvesting per se has not affected their populations). This observation has already been quantified in several countries (eg Dirzo and Miranda, 1991; Emmons, 1984) and probably is due to a populational release from their main demographic regulators: large cats (jaguar and puma). Big cats are often the first to flee or be hunted out when hunters arrive. This intriguing observation opens the possibility for Brazil nut-rich forest management where this rodent species could become part of a management plan.

Once a seed escapes predation, it needs to be buried in a spot that is not seasonally flooded and receives some level of direct sunlight in its first years, if it is to have a chance of developing into a seedling. The energy stored in the nut serves as food for the developing plant and is slowly consumed over the first year of growth. After that period, the seedling will survive only if it is able to photosynthesize and escape from its new predators, the herbivores. During the seedling's first year of growth, seed predators will often seek out, unearth and consume the buried nut, thereby killing the seedling. Observations on seedlings closely monitored over time in Peru have shown that other rodents, and tapirs in particular, are responsible for the mortality of a large portion of Brazil nut seedlings, mainly during the dry season. If conditions allow, it may take several years, or even decades, for a seedling to capitalize on the creation of a forest gap and grow to reach the canopy. Chances are high that an established sapling will become a mature Brazil nut tree. Once an adult, the main causes of Brazil nut mortality in natural forests are strong winds after heavy rains (or unusually rainy seasons that loosen soil and facilitate windthrow), fungal infections and lightning. In 1991, this author witnessed a massive blow-down (caused by hurricane-like winds following several days of rain) that felled close to 400 Brazil nut trees in an area of several hundred hectares where *B. excelsa* alone accounted for more than half of all fallen trees.

Apart from the species closely linked to the Brazil nut tree described above, there are several other animals that in one way or another depend upon this tree species for their survival. In fact, there are several species that are exclusively found in association with *B. excelsa*. For example, there is a poison arrow frog (*Dendrobates castaneoticus*) and a toad (*Bufo castaneoticus*) that breed almost exclusively in empty, rain-filled Brazil nut shells that have been opened by agoutis. No one has ever looked at the soil microorganisms associated with this tree species, a field that undoubtedly will yield surprises. For the reasons mentioned above, it is perhaps appropriate to distinguish Brazil nut-rich forests as a distinct forest type. Ongoing studies are showing that biodiversity levels found in Brazil nut

forests under seasonal and exclusive use by nut harvesters are not much different from other pristine forests. It could be expected that – given a slightly increased habitat heterogeneity – they may be even richer in populations of some types of organisms, although this latter point is speculative and awaits further evaluation.

Mammal, tree and Scarabeid beetle species richness have been evaluated in Brazil nut-rich forests in Peru, comparing sites with different levels of use intensity. Sites managed under seasonal and exclusive use for nut harvesting showed high diversity levels, similar to what would be found in pristine forests. Areas with greater disturbance levels due to associated logging and year-round hunting showed a noticeable difference in species richness and abundance. Interestingly, the low-disturbance Brazil nut forests harboured several endangered species rarely seen in any other areas, such as short-eared bush dogs and big cats (J Mena; K Kirkby; T Larsen, unpublished reports). Thus, Brazil nut forest management has the potential to help keep species richness levels high.

Land-use impacts

As seen in the previous section, land-use intensity affects biodiversity levels and, potentially, nut yields. However, this is a minor problem when compared to what is happening to Brazil nut areas at a larger scale. Although Brazil nut tree logging is illegal in all producing countries, potentially productive Brazil nut forest areas are increasingly being reduced, mainly through forest degradation caused by opening areas for cattle ranching, agriculture and intensive logging.

Felling a standing Brazil nut tree is punishable by prison and heavy fines in

Brazil, Bolivia and Peru. Although the law, as written, has been respected to some extent, it has been totally ineffective in protecting its target. Large prime Brazil nut areas, on the order of hundreds of thousands of hectares, have been cleared for cattle ranching, leaving only standing Brazil nut trees. It is common in areas such as those between Cobija in Bolivia and Rio Branco in Brazil to see kilometre after kilometre of lone, white, bone-looking, dead Brazil nut trees standing in solitude amid great extensions of decaying pasture. Studies carried out in Acre,

Brazil, have shown that 20 years after grassland establishment, 80 per cent of the standing Brazil nut trees were dead and no regeneration was present (Viana et al, 1998). In other areas, landless peasants with no Brazil nut-related traditions have migrated to Brazil nut stands to establish ephemeral agricultural plots, with similar results. More recently, some levels of logging are being permitted in Brazil nut-rich extractive reserves in Brazil. Although low-intensity/selective logging may not necessarily be pernicious to Brazil nut forests, it opens them up to other non-sustainable uses. The total area of Brazil nut forests is still very large, and recent events taking place in Brazil, Bolivia and Peru are promising for their future protection. Prime Brazil nut areas are being recognized, zoned and protected for exclusive traditional use. Brazil nut forest management is also increasingly being considered and implemented in some areas, as well.

Although Brazil nut wood is not attractive for logging due to its hardness, it is widely used for construction and ranch fences. Once a tree dies, it is legal to obtain permission to use its wood, a provision that may encourage the killing of Brazil nut trees.

As reported above, traditional Brazil nut harvesting does not appear to be harmful to the forest, even when intensively practised. However, other forest uses that could accompany harvesting might be detrimental to forest health. For example, palm fruit harvesting is often accomplished by felling palm trees; hunting pressures that accompany Brazil nut harvest may be intensive enough to wipe out mammal and birds that are important to ecological processes, and logging and thinning may affect forest characteristics necessary for Brazil nut seedling regeneration. Brazil forest management should incorporate current knowledge about the structure and functioning of Brazil nut forests in order to assure its continuity. Brazil nut forest certification may play an important role as a driver for the application of sound management techniques.

Brazil nut management and best practices

Native populations have managed Brazil nut forests for thousands of years. Deliberate planting and protection of seedlings, together with low-impact harvesting practices (narrow trails and other practices for non-commercial use), have probably resulted in the 'rich' *castañales* that are still found today. However, Brazil nut commercialization has driven producers to seek greater efficiency and better yields (in quality and quantities). 'There are many ways to harvest a Brazil nut tree,' it could be said, and indeed there are.

Current management techniques are, to a great extent, the application of traditional methodologies together with new developments arising from biological research on *Bertholletia*. One issue that researchers had to solve was that there were several variants on methodologies carried out by indigenous peoples and *caboclos* (rural peasant farmers of mixed descent), and that those techniques differed substantially, although one of them had to be more efficient. For example, in Peru and parts of Bolivia, fruits are gathered from the ground by bare hand, while in Brazil harvesters use a basket and a grabbing stick. Practitioners of both techniques claim their collection method is faster and easier. When compared, fruit-picking time proved to be twice as effective and safer with the use of baskets. Other techniques have to be developed from scratch.

As for management techniques, this chapter includes those practices that take place in the field with an aim of improving productivity of Brazil nut stands and yield per tree. These are practices that reduce the negative impacts of harvesting and improve harvesting techniques, thereby increasing efficiency, quality and cost effectiveness. Several of the techniques mentioned here have been systematically quantified and evaluated for their cost benefits, while other practices are currently under evaluation but are showing promising results. It has to be kept in mind that some of these techniques may only make economic sense in some areas and may not apply to other regions.

Brazil nut stand productivity may be enhanced in the short term, as well as in the long term. In the shorter term, the elaboration of a map base that identifies individual trees and their production patterns could enhance productivity. Such a map helps to redesign and maintain a more functional harvesting trail system that emphasizes harvesting efforts in more productive sections of a *castañal*, and at the same time reduces walking distances, thus making the harvest more efficient and economic. These maps also help hired harvesters (who are often unfamiliar with an area) locate trees and facilitate the planning of systematic searches for new trees within a concession (in general, almost a third of the Brazil nut trees within an area may not be known to exist).

Current evaluations of double-harvesting regimes (ie early and late in the harvesting season) are showing that more fruits may be gathered overall, due to reductions in losses of fruits taken by agoutis as well as increases in untaken fruits that fall after the regular harvesting dates. In the longer term, stand production can be improved through forest enrichment techniques, where genetically selected seeds are planted after careful identification of sites with the best lighting, soil and other competitive conditions (generally in natural gaps), followed by some level of care provided for the planted seedlings. Studies are showing that it is a better investment of time and money to place efforts on forest enrichment than on the care of naturally regenerating seedlings. Liberation thinning techniques have been shown to be efficient in helping the growth of medium-sized saplings, especially in cases where competition with other plants and vines prevents their development. Overall, however, it is important to note that probably the most effective way to maintain the productivity of a Brazil nut stand is to keep the surrounding forest as healthy as possible and allow the ecological processes of pollination and regeneration to occur without negatively affecting their biological vectors.

Fruit yields per tree could be improved by agroforestry techniques that include liberation thinning, mainly in juvenile and young trees where competition from other trees may limit their growth and production. Along the same lines, removal of lianas and vines that compete with Brazil nut trees in the canopy for light and increase branch weight (which may provoke branch breakage) is believed to increase fruit yield. Quantitative evaluation of the benefits of liana removal is still unproven, although research is underway. Some researchers suggest the use of fertilizers (also useful for seedling growth), but their effectiveness has yet to be tested.

Apart from the use of baskets for picking fruits and the improved trail system (examples mentioned earlier), there are other techniques that may help to improve the efficiency of Brazil nut harvesting. The use of oxen for transportation of Brazil nut sacks in the forest (making harvesting less physically demanding) and clearing of the undergrowth under the Brazil nut tree canopy have been described as cost effective in some areas of Brazil and Peru. Overall, quality of seed production – lately a more important issue due to the hardening of exportation standards – may be enhanced by double-harvesting regimes and by protecting unopened fruits from excessive humidity. For example, nuts may be covered with palm leaves or placed in appropriate, predetermined collection sites after gathering. Cleaning and drying of nuts in harvesting camps have also been reported as cost effective. Related to this, it is important to build appropriate infrastructures at harvesting camps that will help to reduce losses to rodents (such losses account for 20 per cent of all nuts in some production areas; Empresa Hecker Hermanos, S A, 1998).

Environmental damage from activities related to Brazil nut harvesting can also be reduced under specific management regimes or through the introduction of appropriate technologies. For example, where hunting is difficult to eliminate, controlled culling of certain species may be a solution. Tree-injuring bark extraction (for raw materials used to fashion straps for carrying loads of nuts) may be halted by introducing synthetic belts, as is successfully done by some harvesters in Peru.

Use and applications

Brazil nut trees are widely known because of their nuts. However, for traditional dwellers in Brazil nut forests (indigenous people and *colonos/caboclos*), nut consumption is not the only use of this tree, as virtually all the accessible parts of the species have a local application.

Internationally, nuts are commercialized under three modalities: in-shell, unshelled or as a processed part or derivate. In-shell nuts are sold mainly to the US and UK and have become part of the traditional Christmas feast. The main use of unshelled nuts is in nut mixes, but they are also consumed raw, roasted, salted or used as ingredients in ice creams and desserts. Brazil nut oils, due to their chemical properties, are increasingly being used in the personal care industry. Products such as Brazil nut soaps, shampoo and skin care lotions can be easily found in any organic goods shop. Brazil nut pods are now being exported as containers for aromatic candles. A variety of medicinal properties have been attributed to *Bertholletia*. For example, rubber tappers in Brazil use it for treating diarrhoea, while in Peru it is used to treat leishmaniasis. It is also recommended for treating patients with certain types of cancer (eg prostate cancer) due to its high selenium content (Ip and Lisk, 1994).

At a local level, Brazil nuts are mainly used raw as a food source, but also have a number of other uses. For example, the nuts may be smashed and consumed as vegetal milk, converted into flour for baking bread or mixed with other products such as cassava. Brazil nuts also have an extensive variety of local uses that are often restricted to certain areas. For example, in Puerto Maldonado, Brazil nut hot sauce and Brazil nut bread are local delicacies. Similarly, residual or broken Brazil nuts are often pressed for oil that is widely used for cooking, soap, as a hair care product, as lamp fuel and as feed for domestic animals.

Brazil nut wood is used for the construction of houses and fences as well as for boat-building. Processed bark is employed by indigenous peoples to fabricate rudimentary clothing. Gum exudates from the trunk are used for boat repairs.

Empty Brazil nut capsules are used as multipurpose containers (eg tappers use it for collecting rubber), made into handicrafts, burned as fuel and, more recently, are being investigated for their use as an abrasive as well as for activated carbon (for international markets). Nut-processing factories produce large amounts of husks. This residual material has special thermal properties that render it a good burning material in ovens used to dry nuts prior to packing in some areas. In towns such as Riberalta in Bolivia, Brazil nut husks are used as fuel to provide electricity for the city (until a few years ago, half of the town's electricity was produced this way).

The US, UK, Germany, Italy and other European nations are the main importers of Brazil nuts, accounting for close to 90 per cent of the total volumes processed by exporting companies, with probably less than 5 per cent consumed in producing countries (LaFleur, 1992). During the last decade, lower production costs and an aggressive marketing strategy have given Bolivia a competitive economic advantage over neighbouring Brazil, making Bolivia the world's leading Brazil nut-producing country. The industry has flourished in towns such as Cobija and Riberalta, where most of the Brazil nut production is being processed and sent ready for exportation. Total export volumes of Brazil nuts fluctuate according to the year and demand, ranging from 30 to 60 (metric) tonnes with exportation values around US$40 to US$70 million (Clay, 1997b). Thorough analysis of the price dynamics and the market potential for Brazil nuts (see LaFleur, 1992; Clay, 1997b) has concluded that the characteristics of the Brazil nut supply and marketplace (high degree of product substitution and the relative scarcity, respectively) offer opportunities to expand market share by increasing production without a proportional decrease in price. Effective protection and management of existing Brazil nut stands, combined with innovative approaches such as certification, could help to provide a sustainable future for large forested areas as well as for a large population of people, who depend upon them.

Certification potential

Brazil nuts provide a good fit for the core subject areas of certification programmes. Environmentally, they are traditionally harvested mainly from primary tropical forests and not from plantations. Brazil nut trees probably live in the most biologically rich areas of the world, coexisting with populations of a number of endangered species in certain areas. As far as studies have determined, traditional harvesting does not negatively affect regeneration, nor does it degrade the forest ecosystem, unduly threaten biodiversity or diminish many ecological processes associated with such forests. Brazil nut utilization (through concessions) 'unintentionally' protects several million hectares throughout Amazonia, a territory larger than the size of all formally protected areas taken together in the region. Brazil nut harvest promotes conservation because the species requires a healthy forest ecosystem in order to thrive and be productive. Brazil nuts are gathered from the forest floor, and as such are completely organic and require no fertilizers or genetic manipulation.

From a socio-economic perspective, Brazil nut harvest often represents a highly significant, if not the primary, source of yearly income for close to half of the human population in Brazil nut areas (numbering several hundred thousand individuals). The benefits of the Brazil nut industry are spread across a wider social base than most other activities. Brazil nuts offer an empowering mechanism for women: apart from those who are directly involved in the harvesting (30 per cent of concessions in Peru are owned by women), women are the primary workforce in Brazil nut factories in semi-urban areas where processing takes place (60–80 per cent of the total; Agreda, 1999; Assies 1997). Such employment often represents the only source of family income. Brazil nut harvest plays a number of roles in the 'dynamics' of families living in rural areas (for example, due to their long storage capacity, Brazil nuts serve as instant cash for emergencies; Ortiz, 1995).

Although the above information is true for traditional harvesting of Brazil nuts, not all of the elements intersect in all areas or cases. In some areas, forest degradation is rampant; *Bertholletia* stands are becoming patchier due to habitat conversion; fauna is being depleted due to excessive hunting; and a number of other unsustainable activities are taking place. In large areas in Brazil and Bolivia, Brazil nut concessions are controlled by landlords or *patrones* who enslave workers through advances of supplies or the *habilito* system. In most areas, prices are unjust when compared to the work and the risks involved in the harvesting activity (as typical of many rural production systems). Factories often do not provide basic labour rights and safe conditions for their employees. However, ideal Brazil nut-use conditions (where environmental and basic socio-economic conditions can be met) do exist, and obstacles to certification are not insurmountable – there are a few examples of good operations.

Brazil nut certification should ensure that nuts come from natural forests and that their harvest is not affecting the ecological viability of the forest. Certification should not only protect the continuity of Brazil nut tree populations but also maintain other species and biological processes within the Brazil nut forest. Moreover, certification can ensure that no other unsustainable activities are taking place in the same forest. In cases where other uses of the forests are taking place, these should also be required to meet certification criteria (eg logging). Land tenure issues that benefit producers should be required in order to promote sound management, as well as to support a better and more equitable sharing of profits.

Labour conditions should be in compliance with international conventions and promote greater benefit-sharing with rural producers. The low prices paid to producers, in combination with established middlemen systems, act to the detriment of this objective. In addition to forest management and forest-gathering activities, attention should be given to other parts of the Brazil nut production chain, such as processing factories, where labour conditions are often poor. However, some flexibility should be allowed, according to regional conditions and traditions (eg supervised under-age labour). In summary, the principles laid out by the Forest Stewardship Council (FSC) could be met and readily verified. Under the FSC umbrella, efforts to develop national and regional standards for Brazil nut certification in the three main producing countries are currently taking place. By the beginning of the 21st century, the world should be able to enjoy certified Brazil nuts (or Amazonian nuts), and at the same time protect large tracts of tropical forests and the traditional activities of the people who depend upon those forests.

Chapter 6

Palm heart (*Euterpe* spp.)

Dennis Johnson

Introduction

Commercial palm heart production in South America from the wild involves exploitation of three major species: açaí (*Euterpe oleracea*) asai (*E. precatoria* var. *precatoria*) and juçara (*E. edulis*), in approximate order of their current economic importance (see Table 6.1). Details about the other non-commercial *Euterpe* species are given in Table 6.2.

The three commercial species of *Euterpe* differ in growth form and in habitat. *E. oleracea* is a clustering palm that occurs in periodically flooded open forest areas in dense stands. *E. precatoria* and *E. edulis* are solitary palms found in more elevated, better-drained closed forests not subject to flooding. *E. precatoria* has a scattered distribution in the forest, whereas *E. edulis* may form large stands. The geographic range of *E. oleracea* is in north-eastern and north-western South America. *E. precatoria* occurs in the Western Amazon Basin

Illustration by Antônio Valente da Silva

*Palm heart (*Euterpe oleracea*)*

and Central America and *E. edulis* is found along Brazil's Atlantic coast and inland.

As many as nine South American countries have palm heart industries with raw material derived from wild *Euterpe* palms. The country of Brazil and *E. oleracea* production in particular predominate in the industry at large. In most countries, palmito production is largely for export markets in Europe and the United States, although Brazil has significant domestic consumption.

Harvesting, transporting and processing wild palm hearts is labour intensive and provides employment in typically remote areas where job opportunities are limited. In large measure, the commercialization of palm hearts is profitable because the wild resource is nearly free and the labour costs are low.

The *Euterpe* palm species is also a local source of other commercial and subsistence products. In the Lower Amazon, fruits of *E. oleracea* are gathered and used to make a beverage and to flavour ice cream. The palms are likewise sources of leaves for thatching and to make various objects such as baskets and brooms. The palm stems can be used to make house frames and flooring. Roots of *E. precatoria* have reputed medicinal properties. The palms are also popular as ornamental trees because of their graceful leaves and overall attractive appearance.

Palmito is one of the traditional NTFPs of the Latin American region. Palm hearts are being investigated as one of several products that could support the establishment of extractive reserves, the aims of which are to maintain forest cover and to discourage more deforestation. Thus, palm heart harvest can play an important conservation role and has the potential to contribute to both economic and biological sustainability of select forest management units in the tropics.

Ecology

In most instances, there is insufficient knowledge concerning the ecology of individual Latin American palm species. The genus *Euterpe* is in a somewhat favourable position because of the recent monograph by Henderson and Galeano (1996) and because *E. precatoria* and *E. oleracea* were among the palms included by Kahn and de Granville (1992) in their study of palm ecology in Amazonia. The following information on *Euterpe* ecology is based on the two foregoing sources.

Euterpe edulis is a solitary rainforest palm of well-drained soils occurring from 0–1000 metres (m) and may form large stands. It can colonize areas of forest disturbance. *Euterpe oleracea* is a clustering rainforest palm of low elevations in areas of periodic flooding and occurs in large, high-density stands. It too is an aggressive colonizer of disturbed areas of swamp forest. *Euterpe precatoria* is a solitary rainforest palm of the well-drained and periodically flooded lowlands.

The density and distribution patterns of *Euterpe* palms cannot be easily generalized because they appear to be influenced by soil conditions, hydrology and associated vegetation. Population surveys of six sites of *E. oleracea* in the Amazon Basin found averages of 775 juvenile and 267 adult palms per hectare. A study of species richness, density and vertical distribution of palms in a 0.4 hectare plot in the Peruvian Amazon found *E. precatoria* to be the second most common palm, after *Astrocaryum carnosum*. A total of 244 *E. precatoria* were enumerated in this study, with tree height classes as follows: 176 individuals in the 0–1m size class; 67 in the 1–10m size class; and 1 in the >10m size class. Results of other research in Acre, Brazil, determined that there were 40 adult *E. precatoria* palms per hectare.

Little information exists on the reproductive biology of *Euterpe* palms. Natural reproduction of all three commercialized species is by seed. In addition, *E. oleracea* produces basal shoots to maintain a cluster of stems of different ages and heights. *Euterpe* palms are monoecious and inflorescences are intrafoliar. The age of sexual maturity of *Euterpe* palms is not known precisely and may vary considerably depending upon soil conditions, growth rate, competition and light availability.

Under ideal conditions, *E. oleracea* may flower when only three years of age, although full fruit production may not be achieved until five to six years of age. It has been observed that *E. precatoria* in Bolivia begins to flower when the tree reaches 12m in height, producing one to four inflorescences. The average age of a tree of that height is thought to be 10 to 15 years, but this is anecdotal information.

Male and female flowers of *Euterpe* species are small, some 2–3 millimetres (mm) in width. The male flowers of *E. edulis* and *E. oleracea* are purplish in colour. Field studies of *E. oleracea* revealed that female flowers produce nectar and that bees appear to be the major group of pollinators. In Peru, a study of a population of *E. precatoria* showed that palms produced two to six inflorescences each year, flowering commencing with the dry season in May and fruits maturing over seven to eight months, during December to January. The fruiting period

of *E. oleracea* in Eastern and Central Amazonia extends throughout the calendar year, but fruit is most abundant in the drier season from July to December. Reportedly, *E. oleracea* fruits from February to April in the Orinoco Delta. Fruiting of *E. edulis* in southern Brazil occurs from April to November. Fruits of these three commercial species are similar in size (1–2cm in diameter) and purple to black when ripe.

The fruit of *E. oleracea* is dispersed by water during seasonal flooding, and fishes are reported to eat the fleshy fruit and aid in its dispersal. Birds, rodents and monkeys consume the fruit of several species of *Euterpe*; birds are most often mentioned, but that could be because they are more readily observed.

Seeds of *E. oleracea* and *E. precatoria* have been tested and both germinate in about one month. Germination of *E. edulis* seeds was found to occur in three weeks.

Impact of land-use changes

An estimated 90 per cent of all palms in South America occur in forests, and this includes all species of *Euterpe*. In general, forest clearing for agriculture and pasture, and degradation as a result of timber harvest, represent the primary threats to palm conservation. Forest palm species fall into two groups with regard to disturbance. The largest group is composed of palms that are very sensitive to clearing and disturbance. These species almost immediately die off in impacted areas or their numbers and distribution become severely reduced, putting their local survival in peril. The second (smaller) group of palms appears to comprise pioneer species that are adapted, in varying degrees, to forest

disturbance and are able to regenerate and persist on cleared sites and in degraded areas of forest. Sufficient scientific information is known about the three commercial species of *Euterpe* to place them into this second group.

The clustering of *E. oleracea* occurs in seasonally inundated areas where it can be found in large stands of high density. In locations where forest disturbance has taken place, *E. oleracea* can be an aggressive colonizing pioneer species. Partial forest clearing and degradation may therefore actually be beneficial to the populations of *E. oleracea*. However, the *E. oleracea* habitat is suitable for the development of rice cultivation and shrimp farming, both of which result in elimination of the palm when developed.

Euterpe precatoria is a climax forest species and ecological studies have shown that the palm is well represented in all height classes. This solitary palm is described as being a dominant palm species in some portions of its range – as, for example, in the Beni region of the Bolivian Amazon. *E. precatoria* regeneration benefits from minor natural disturbances that allow a greater amount of light to penetrate through the forest canopy. However, it appears that *E. precatoria* seedlings require a shaded environment in their early growth stages. Hence, major disturbance would adversely affect germination and seedling growth and result in a decline of the palm population over time in a given area if the degraded forest conditions persist. Clearly, *E. precatoria* needs a forest habitat in which to survive naturally. *E. precatoria* appears to be compatible with logging, although logging activities destroy palms when timber trees are felled and skidded and when logging roads are constructed. *E. precatoria* populations would not be impacted by gathering other forest products, such as latex and Brazil nuts.

Euterpe edulis, like *E. precatoria*, is a climax species that requires forest habitat to survive. However, *E. edulis* is a smaller solitary palm that can form large stands and is described as being able to colonize disturbed areas of forest.

Harvesting of mature *E. precatoria* and *E. edulis* for palmito poses a potential threat to the vigour and survival of the populations of these species if the harvest practices and cycles significantly reduce seed sources for natural regeneration. But no matter how intensive the harvesting, it would not lead to extinction of either *E. precatoria* or *E. edulis* because palmito harvest would become self-limiting when the population density of harvestable trees was reduced to low levels. This is exemplified by the shift of Brazil's palmito industry in the 1960s from reliance on *E. edulis* in the Atlantic Forest to *E. oleracea* in the Amazon, a move which relieved most of the commercial harvesting pressures on the wild populations of *E. edulis*. Forest clearing represents the greatest threat to both *E. edulis* and *E. precatoria*.

Management

Examples of traditional/indigenous management systems of *E. oleracea* for palm heart and fruit production are found in the Lower Amazon. This management probably derives originally from leaving the palms in place when clearing a shifting cultivation plot, and likely eventually led to the palm's cultivation. It could be argued that this represents a form of agroforestry. Other *Euterpe* species of palms are not cultivated except for their occasional ornamental use.

Over the approximately 50 years that palm hearts have been commercialized, the industry has operated by following what may be referred to as 'extractive practices', with little if any regard for direct management of the wild resource. One regulation that is codified for the industry (but not always followed) is the minimum diameter size of the palm heart that will be purchased from harvesters. Experienced cutters are able to select trees for felling that will yield legal-sized processed palmito (ie 2cm in diameter in Brazil). Brazil has legislation that requires the planting of three *E. edulis* for each cut, and the planting of one *E. oleracea* for each individual harvested. Whether these regulations are being followed is difficult to tell, but they probably are not. Concession agreements for palm heart harvesting have been modelled after timber harvesting concessions so that the way in which the industry has operated is not a surprise. When a palm heart factory becomes unprofitable because local raw material resources have been depleted, the practice has been to move to another area and begin anew.

The annual allowable cutting of palms and harvest rotation cycles are difficult to determine in the absence of reliable regeneration data. Cutting cycles discussed range from as short as three to four years for *E. oleracea*, to as many as 30 years or more for *E. precatoria*. The correlation between the minimum diameter at breast height (dbh) of the peeled palm heart and the dbh of the stem has been calculated. A 2cm palm heart is equivalent to a stem with a dbh of 8.5cm.

Various management techniques have been suggested to sustain palm heart production from the wild, most of them aimed at enhancing regeneration. Recommended silvicultural treatments include weeding around naturally occurring seedlings to reduce light and nutrient competition. Enrichment plantings are also an option, using either direct seeding or the transplanting of seedlings, coupled with the above-mentioned silvicultural treatments. *Euterpe* palms could be cultivated within an agroforestry system, or such a system could be implemented in areas of natural palm stands.

Management of wild palm heart resources for sustainable production poses several challenges. Most prominent is the lack of sufficient detailed botanical and ecological information about the palms exploited and the longer-term results of harvesting on the palm species and on the surrounding forest. Thus, any adopted management practices must be monitored closely and refined through information gleaned from data collection and field observation. Of equal importance is monitoring the general health of the forest itself from which the palms are harvested. At the same time, it is essential that test plots are established to provide scientific baseline data about subjects such as growth rate, age of sexual maturity, natural regeneration and soil and habitat variations. Results of test plot studies also must be incorporated into refinement of the management plan.

Another challenge is that a different set of general management practices must be developed for solitary palms and clustering palms. Moreover, all management practices must be site-specific to particular forest management units. Inventory data on palms by age class is essential.

Use

Eating fresh palm hearts is mentioned in the anthropological literature as a practice of various cultural groups in Latin America, but it is not a staple food since it is a poor source of calories and nutrients.

In traditional, largely subsistence food systems, palmito simply represents an occasional food from the forest, often obtained in association with felling a palm for another purpose, such as its stem wood. Fresh palm heart spoils quickly in the tropics; unpeeled, it deteriorates in just a few days. Palm hearts only became a commercial product when canning industries were developed to preserve the palmito. Currently, in almost every location where palm hearts are commercialized, only the canned product is obtainable. The exception is Iquitos, Peru, where there is a tradition of consuming fresh palm heart salad.

Euterpe palms are a source of several other products in addition to palmito. Fruit is the most important and is itself commercialized in the Lower Amazon to make a sweet beverage and to flavour ice cream. *Euterpe* leaves are used for thatching and to make woven objects such as baskets, while its stem wood is used for framing thatched houses and as flooring. The roots of *E. precatoria* are used in traditional medicine. The trees are occasionally planted as ornamentals, especially *E. oleracea*.

Palm heart harvest kills the tree of a solitary species, or the stem of the clustering *E. oleracea*. When the tree is cut down and the heart extracted, the trunk, leaves and fruit could potentially be used, but they are not worth transporting any distance. Hence, only the palm heart leaves the forest. Apart from diminishing its population numbers and reducing species diversity to a degree, cutting palm hearts has little impact on a mature forest. Small gaps may be opened up, but these will rapidly be filled in by other species in the case of harvesting *E. precatoria*.

Factories, most often located in the forest, are established and continue to operate until the stands of accessible wild palms are depleted. Typically, harvesting and processing are separate activities. The factory purchases cut palm hearts, sometimes through a middleman, from harvesters who are paid per stem. Factory operators pay little attention to the sus-

tainability of their raw material supplies, except for some form of sequential harvesting of blocks within their forest concession.

Felling palms, transporting palm hearts to the factory and processing and canning the finished product provides employment in remote areas where opportunities for earning a cash wage are generally limited. The industry is labour intensive, including the factories. The factories are quite simple in their operations and machine use is typically limited to closing tins and heating the contents. Capital investment in processing facilities is minimal. Men typically work at felling trees and transporting the palm hearts, while women mainly work in the factories.

Palm heart industries that rely upon wild species of *Euterpe* are known to operate in Argentina, Bolivia, Brazil, Colombia, Ecuador, Guyana, Peru, Venezuela and, if still active, in French Guyana. Paraguay also has an industry that exploits another palm, the caranday (*Copernicia alba*).

Overall production in Latin America of wild-collected palmito is difficult to ascertain because reporting varies from country to country, and in some cases wild and cultivated products are aggregated. The following production and export data are from official national sources. Brazil has the best statistical data on palmito. A total of 20,653 tonnes of canned palm heart were reportedly produced in 1995, with the states of Pará and Amapá accounting for nearly all production. Canned palm heart is produced primarily for the international market, although in Brazil the highest grade is canned for export while medium grade is canned for domestic sale. Bolivia valued its exports of palm heart at US$12,355,420 in 1997. Paraguayan exports of palm heart in 1993 were valued at US$2,914,000. The quantities represented by these monetary amounts are not available. France and the US are the two major importing nations, together accounting for about 90 per cent of all palm heart entering international commerce.

Certification potential

There is potential for certification of wild sources of palm heart, but at least three obstacles need to be overcome. One is sustainability in terms of replenishing the standing stock of the resource through natural means or through silvicultural treatments to enhance regeneration. This issue is most problematic with solitary palms because sustainable harvesting cycles may be so lengthy as to be uneconomic. There is general consensus that *E. oleracea* has the greater biological potential for sustainable management and certification.

A second obstacle relates to the adoption of, and adherence to, management plans. Under general harvesting practices in place, palm cutters function as independent contractors who are paid by the piece; their incentive, therefore, is to maximize production. Field supervision of harvesting by factory personnel would probably be prohibitively expensive, so some other means of ensuring proper harvest must be sought. One option would be for the palm cutters to become direct factory employees paid on the basis of their following good management practices rather than simply the number of palm hearts harvested. Full vertical integration of the industry would certainly have advantages for the harvesters in terms of employee benefits.

The third obstacle relates to compliance with regulations regarding the minimum diameter of palm hearts. In recent years in the Lower Amazon, an increasing percentage of processed palm hearts are below the legal diameter limit, a clear indication that smaller and smaller diameter stems are being cut. Factories have the means to rectify this situation by refusing to purchase palm hearts that are not of minimum legal size.

In conjunction with attempts to certify wild-collected palm hearts, there should be a parallel effort to do the same for cultivated palm hearts as a 'green' product. In Latin America, the pejibaye palm (*Bactris gasipaes*) is a source of cultivated palm hearts, which have been traded in international markets since the late 1970s. Costa Rica currently is the major producer, but this could change dramatically if cultivation of the palm in Brazil and elsewhere is successful and able to compete commercially with wild palm hearts. In 1995, the Brazilian state of Espírito Santo reportedly had 200 hectares of palms under cultivation for palmito production; what species this represents is not certain, but it is likely to be *Bactris gasipaes*.

Bactris gasipaes has a comparative advantage over the *Euterpe* species for cultivated palm hearts because it is a fully domesticated palm and its biology, ecology and agronomy are known in detail. There are at least three good reasons to pursue certification of wild and cultivated sources of palm heart. Firstly, it is likely that cultivated sources will replace wild sources in the early decades of the 21st century. Secondly, the entire palm heart industry of the region, wild and cultivated, could potentially be certified. Thirdly, there is the opportunity for a useful exchange of ideas and information between the parallel efforts.

Table 6.1 *Commercialized* Euterpe *species*

Species, synonyms and common names	Description and reported other uses	Natural distribution	Habitat
E. edulis (*E. espiritosantensis*) **Argentina**: *yayih*; **Brazil**: *coco de palmito, coco de jissara, coco de usara, ensarova, içara, inçara, iuçara, jiçara, jocara, jucoara, juçara, juçara vermelho, juçara branca, junça, palmiteiro, palmeteiro branco, palmeteiro encapado, palmeteiro macho, palmeteiro vermelho, palmeteiro doce, palmito, palmito doce, palmito juçara, palmito amarelo, palmito vermelho, ripa, ripeira*; **Paraguay**: *palmito, yayi*.	Solitary or rarely clustering and then with few stems; usually grey with lichens, with a dense cone of reddish-brown roots at base; 5–12m tall; 10–15cm dbh. **Other uses**: stems in construction, leaves for thatching and fruits made into a drink.	Atlantic coast of **Brazil** and adjacent areas (Alagoas, Bahia, Distrito Federal, Espírito Santo, Goiás, Minas Gerais, Paraíba, Paraná, Pernambuco, Rio de Janeiro, Rio Grande do Norte, Rio Grande do Sul, Santa Catarina, São Paulo, Sergipe); **Argentina** (Misiones); **Paraguay** (Alto Paraná).	Rainforest on steep slopes, rarely in inundated areas, at 0–1000m. Can form large stands on ridges and valley slopes, especially on quartzite and sandy soils; also colonizes areas of forest disturbance.
E. oleracea (*E. badiocarpa, E. beardii, E. cuatrecasana*) **Brazil**: *açaí, açaí branco, açaí do Pará, açaizeiro*; **Colombia**: *chapil, maquenque, murrapo, naidí, palmicha*; **Ecuador**: *bambil, palmiche*; **French Guyana**: *pinot*; **Surinam**: *baboenpina, kiskis, pina, manaka, pina, prasara, wapoe, wapu, wasei*; **Trinidad**: *manac*.	Clustering with up to 25 stems or occasionally solitary with shoots at base; 3–20m tall; 7–18cm dbh; usually grey with lichens, with cone of red basal roots and pneumatophores. **Other uses**: fruit mesocarp made into a drink and as ice cream flavour, stems used in construction and palm grown as an ornamental.	**Panama** (San Blas); **Colombia** (Cauca, Chocó, Córdoba, Nariño, Valle and some areas of Río Sinú and middle Magdalena valley in Antioquia, Córdoba, Santander); **Trinidad**; **Venezuela** (Bolívar, Delta Amacuro, Sucre); **Guyanas**; **Brazil** (Amapá, Maranhão, Pará, Tocantins).	Occurs in large stands of high density in low-lying tidal areas near the sea and in wet places near rivers, seldom occurring inland and then in wet places near streams or rivers. In Eastern Amazon Basin it replaces E. precatoria in these habitats. In Pacific coastal region of Colombia and Ecuador, the two species are sympatric, but with E. oleracea in inundated places and E. precatoria on non-inundated soils. E. oleracea can be an aggressive colonizer of disturbed swampy areas.
E. precatoria var. precatoria (*E. confertiflora, E. jatapuensis, E. stenophylla*) **Bolivia**: *asai*; **Brazil**: *açaí, açaí da mata, açaí de terra firme, juçara*;	Solitary; 3–20m tall, grey with cone of roots visible at base and pneumatophores; 4–23cm dbh. **Other uses**: fruits used to make a drink, stems for house construction, roots for medicine,	**Colombia** (Amazonas, Caquetá, Guainía, Guaviare, Meta, Norte de Santander, Putumayo, Vaupés, Vichada); **Venezuela** (Amazonas, Anzoátegui, Apure,	Lowland rainforest, commonly along rivers in periodically inundated areas, below 350m, occasionally reaching 600m in Andes and Guyana Highlands.

Colombia: *asaí, guasai, guypani, manaca*; **Ecuador**: *palmito*; **Guyana**: *manicole*; **Peru**: *huasai*; **Surinam**: *nomkie muruku pina*; **Venezuela**: *manaca, mapora, palmito manaca*; **Trinidad**: *manac*.	leaves to make brooms and as temporary thatching.	Bolívar, Monagas); **Trinidad**; **Guyanas**; **Ecuador** (Morona Santiago, Napo); **Peru** (Amazonas, Cuzco, Loreto, Madres de Dios, Pasco, San Martín); **Brazil** (Acre, Amazonas, Pará, Rondônia); **Bolivia** (Beni, Pando, Santa Cruz).

Source: Henderson and Galeano, 1996

Table 6.2 *Non-commercialized* Euterpe *species*

Species, synonyms and common names	Description and reported other uses	Natural distribution	Habitat
E. broadwayi **Dominica**: *manicol*; **Lesser Antilles**: *mountain cabbage, palmiste*; **Trinidad**: *manac*.	Clustering with two to three stems or seldom solitary; 8–20m tall; 20–25cm dbh; grey with root cone at base. **Uses**: palm heart eaten.	**Lesser Antilles** (Dominica, Grenada, St Vincent); **Trinidad and Tobago**.	Exposed, windswept places on forested mountain ridges or steep river valleys, at 600–1000m.
E. catinga* var. *catinga **Brazil**: *açaizinho, açaí da caatinga, açaí chumbinho, açaí cubinha*; **Colombia**: *asaí de sabana, asaí paso, guasaí pequeño*; **Peru**: *huasaí de varillal*; **Venezuela**: *manaca*.	Clustering with a few stems, or only one stem developed with basal shoots, or solitary; 5–16m tall; 3.5–9cm dbh. **Uses**: stems used in house construction, leaves for thatching temporary shelters, and mature fruits occasionally used to make a drink.	Western Amazonia in **Colombia** (Amazonas, Caquetá, Guainía, Guaviare, Vaupés); **Venezuela** (Amazonas, Bolívar); **Peru** (Loreto); **Brazil** (Amazonas).	Open or dwarf forest in wet, poorly drained areas on white-sand soil and black-water drainage areas below 350m; also in similar habitats in south-western Guyana Highlands of Venezuela (Amazonas, Bolívar), in open-cloud forest at 1100–1500m.
E. catinga* var. *roraimae **Venezuela**: *manaca*.	Solitary or clustering with two to six (up to ten) stems per clump; 4–15m tall; 7–15cm dbh. **Uses**: palm heart occasionally eaten and fruits made into a drink.	**Venezuela** (Amazonas, Bolívar); **Guyana**; **Ecuador** (Pastaza); **Brazil** (Amazonas).	White-sand soils in wet or swampy areas in low forest, cloud forest or dwarf forest on tepui summits in Guyana Highlands (or rarely on Andean slopes), at 900–2100m. In some areas forms large dominant stands. Andean population is geographically isolated and occurs on different soils.

Table 6.2 *continued*

Species, synonyms and common names	Description and reported other uses	Natural distribution	Habitat
E. longibracteata **Brazil**: *açaí chumbo, açaí da mata, assay da terra firme.*	Solitary or occasionally clustering, with cone of orange or red roots at base; 5–15m tall (up to 20m); 5–8cm dbh. **Uses**: none reported.	**Venezuela** (Amazonas, Bolívar, Delta Amacuro); **Guyana**; **Brazil** (Amazonas, Mato Grosso, Pará).	Lowland rainforest, usually on *terra firme* but also in inundated areas, at low elevations.
E. luminosa **Peru**: *guayaquil, palma palanca.*	Clustering but generally only one developed with suckers at base; 5–11m tall; 5–7cm dbh; greyish. **Uses**: stems used as poles.	**Peru** (Pasco).	Understorey of moist cloud forest bordering pajonal vegetation, characterized by its shrubby, xeromorphic compositions, at 2000–2500m.
E. precatoria* var. *longevaginata **Belize**: *mountain cabbage;* **Colombia**: *hicara, manaca, palmicho;* **Costa Rica**: *caña lucia;* **Ecuador**: *palmbil;* **Panama**: *palmita.*	Solitary or clustering; 3–20m tall, grey with cone of roots visible at base; 4–23cm dbh. **Uses**: palm heart occasionally eaten.	**Central America** in Belize, Costa Rica, Guatemala, Nicaragua, Panama; **Colombia** (Antioquia, Boyaca, Chocó, La Guajira, Santander del Sur, Tolima, Valle); **Venezuela** (Barinas, Carobobo, Falcón, Lara, Miranda, Monagas, Táchira, Yaracuy, Zulia); **Ecuador** (El Oro, Esmeraldas, Zamora-Chinchipe); **Peru** (Amazonas, Huánuco, Madre de Dios, San Martín); **Brazil** (Acre); **Bolivia** (Cochabamba, La Paz).	Forested areas on mountain slopes and ridges or in lowland areas, at 0–2000m.

Source: Henderson and Galeano, 1996

Chapter 7

Pau d'arco (*Tabebuia* spp.)

M Constanza von der Pahlen

Introduction

Pau d'arco, meaning 'bow stick', was traditionally used by aboriginal communities of the Amazon to make hunting bows, as well as for the treatment of various ailments. Today, various species of pau d'arco are widely used as ornamental trees and are highly prized for their beautiful and hardy timber, as well as for the medicinal properties of the bark.

Pau d'arco is the common name of at least six different species of the genus *Tabebuia*, most of which are closely related and have similar medicinal properties. Some of these include *Tabebuia impetiginosa* (Martius ex DC) Standley, *T. barbata* (E Meyer) Sandwith, *T. capitata*, *T. heptaphylla* (Vellozo) Toledo, *T. incana* A Gentry, *T. selachidentata* A Gentry and *T. serratifolia* (Vahl) Nichols. The ones addressed here are among the most commonly used in

Illustration by Bee Gunn

Pau d'arco
*(*Tabebuia impetiginosa*)*

the international herbal markets, although not exclusively; nor are they the only ones of medicinal value. These are *Tabebuia impetiginosa* (Martius ex DC) Standley, *T. serratifolia* (Vahl) Nicholson and *T. heptaphylla* (Vellozo) Toledo.

Tabebuia is the largest neo-tropical genus, comprising at least 100 species. It ranges from northern Mexico to south-western Argentina, with its highest diversity concentrated in Cuba and Hispaniola (Gentry, 1992). *T. impetiginosa* and *T. heptaphylla* have showy purple flowers, while *T. serratifolia* has yellow ones. These trees can reach heights of up to 30 metres (m) and are widely dispersed in both dry and wet forest communities (Gentry, 1992).

These trees are considered among the most beautiful flowering ornamental trees. Several countries have nominated regional *Tabebuia* species as their national tree, including *T. serratifolia* in Brazil, *T. rosea* in El Salvador, *T. Chrysantha* in Ecuador, *T. heptaphylla* in Paraguay and *T. billgergii* in Venezuela (Gentry, 1992a). Furthermore, they are found in streets and arboretums all around the world.

The timber of various *Tabebuia* species is greatly valued for construction because it is one of the hardest, heaviest and most durable woods. During World War II, the US Navy experimented with *Tabebuia* species for the construction of ball bearings (Sheldon et al, 1997). It is also valued for the production of furniture and crafts, such as bowls, spoons and carved statues, due to the aesthetically appealing contrast of the dark heartwood against the light sapwood (Gentry, 1992a).

The inner bark of several *Tabebuia* species has been widely used by aboriginal communities and local populations in South and Central America for the treatment of various conditions, including cancer, candidiasis-type fungal infections, pain, leukaemia, diabetes, allergies, dysentery, malaria, herpes, overall health, baldness and acne. Recently, teas made from the bark of pau d'arco, and pau d'arco medicinal capsules, can be found on the shelves of health food stores, drugstores, co-ops and supermarkets in Europe and the United States.

Ecology

The three pau d'arco species addressed here, *Tabebuia serratifolia*, *T. impetiginosa* and *T. heptaphylla*, from the Bignoniaceae family, share several common characteristics. They all have dehiscent fruits perpendicular to the septum and wind-dispersed seeds. Several *Tabebuia* species are pollinated by small- (*Trigona*) and medium-sized bees (*Apis*) that can be frequently observed visiting the flowers of these trees (Piña-Rodrigues, pers comm). *Tabebuia* species are generally considered slow-growing, secondary-forest community trees. Some *Tabebuia* species growing in floodplain areas are capable of producing root sprouts; however, vegetative propagation of most tropical trees is poorly understood (Piña-Rodrigues, pers comm).

T. impetiginosa and *T. heptaphylla* are closely related, often confused and are used interchangeably. However, they are usually distributed in ecologically different areas.

Tabebuia impetiginosa

Tabebuia impetiginosa (Martius ex DC) Standley is commonly known as pau d'arco, ipê-roxo, lapacho and tayi. It is also referred to as *Tabebuia avellanedae* (Lorentz ex Grisebach), *T. nicaraguensis*, *Tecoma ipe* and *T. palmieri*, among others (Gentry, 1992). It reaches 30m in height and 70 centimetres (cm) diameter at breast height (dbh). It has a straight trunk, with smooth grey bark and a dark dense inner bark, containing a yellow powder (lapachol) in the vessels. The pink-purple tubular flowers are 4–7.5cm long (Gentry, 1992), flowering between July and October (IPEF, 1999). In Argentina there is a white-flowered variety, called var. *alba*, which Gentry (1992) believes to be an occasional variant of the purple-flowered *T. impetiginosa*. The dark green leaves are palmately 5 (–7) foliate, ovate to elliptic and irregularly serrate in the upper half. They are 5–19cm long. The fruits are elongate cylindrical, 12–56cm long, with thin wind-dispersed seeds (Gentry, 1992), and ripen between August and November (IPEF, 1999).

T. impetiginosa is widely spread from north-western Mexico to north-western Argentina, between sea level and 1400m, a distribution which explains the numerous common names given to it. In Brazil it occurs in the Amazon, in the Atlantic Forest, in the riverine forests of the West–Central Amazon regions and also in the mountainous areas of the north-east. *T. impetiginosa* is mainly found in dry, rocky areas (Gentry, 1992).

Tabebuia serratifolia

Tabebuia serratifolia (Vahl) Nicholson is commonly known as pau d'arco amarelo, ipê amarelo, ipê do cerrado, piúva amarela, vero, flor amarillo and araguaney pui. It is also referred to as *Bignonia serratifolia*, *Tecoma serratifolia*, *Tecoma araliaceae* and *Tabebuia araliaceae*. This deciduous tree is best known for its bright tubular yellow flowers, 8–12cm long, flowering between August and November while completely bare of leaves. It has a straight trunk, with dark rough bark, and can reach 30m in height and 90cm dbh. The leaves have five oblong to lanceolate or ovate serrated leaflets. The fruits are (8–) 12–60cm long, more or less glabrate, maturing in October and December. Its rectangular seeds are winged and wind dispersed (Gentry, 1992).

T. serratifolia is found between Colombia and Bolivia, and from the Guyanas to south-eastern Brazil. It grows in ecologically diverse areas, except in the Amazon, where it occurs most frequently in more or less seasonal forests with well-drained lateritic soils. However, in sub-Amazonian regions it also occurs in richer or sandy soils, between sea level and 1200m in elevation (Gentry, 1992). In the Brazilian Savanna (Cerrado) region, *T. serratifolia* is fairly common, with a density of 250–300 trees per hectare and an average distance of 15m between neighbouring trees (Piña-Rodrigues, pers comm).

Tabebuia heptaphylla

Tabebuia heptaphylla (Vellozo) Toledo, known as pau d'arco, ipê-roxo, lapacho negro/morado, ipe and taiiy zaiyú, is also known as *Bignonia heptaphylla*, *Tecoma ipe*, *T. exilia*, *T. curialis* and *Tabebuia impetiginosa* var. *paulensis/lepidota* (Gentry, 1992). It is a deciduous tree up to 30m tall and with a 65–90cm dbh. The straight trunk has a broad canopy and deeply furrowed bark. The leaves are palmately five to seven foliolate, lanceolate ovate. Flowers are tubular rose purple, 4–6.5cm long, and they flower between May and September (IPEF, 1999) when the tree is bare of leaves. The black fruits, up to 50cm long, ripen in September and October and contain numerous winged seeds (Gentry, 1992).

T. heptaphylla is found in moist areas, below 1000m elevation, along the Brazilian coast, in the Atlantic Forest, from Bahia to Rio Grande do Sul, in the Pantanal, along the Paraná and Paraguay rivers, in Paraguay and Argentina, and also in Peru (Gentry, 1992). It is usually found scattered in primary forests in the Atlantic Forest region, but also in open areas and secondary forests (May, pers comm).

Use

Tabebuia species are popularly used as ornamental trees, for construction, furniture and crafts, and as a medicinal. The utilization of Pau d'arco for medicinal purposes is widespread throughout Central and South America, and more recently the US and Europe. The use of its bark and leaves as a medicinal goes back to indigenous populations, including the Campas in Peru, the Incas and the Guaraní and Tupí tribes (Raintree, 1999). In Argentinian gaucho folklore, the Lapacho (*Tabebuia avellanedae, T. impetiginosa*) is considered the tea of horse tamers, since it is extensively used in cuts and fissures when gauchos fall off of their horses (Alonso, 1988). Indigenous populations in the Amazon extensively use the bark of this tree to treat internal inflammations, tumours, cancer, skin ailments and to alleviate pain.

In Argentina, a tincture made with the leaves and bark of *T. avellanedae* is used as an antiseptic for external ulcers (Alonso, 1998). Indigenous populations in Brazil also used the leaves to treat scabies. A dye made from the bark of *T. avellanedae* has been used to add a yellow-reddish colouration to clothes and leather (Alonso, 1988). In addition to its use as a popular treatment for various ailments (Bianco, 1983), the bark of *T. heptaphylla* is also used to add colouration to cotton and silk (IPEF, 1999).

Pau d'arco is growing in importance as a herbal medicine in both Europe and the US. IBAMA (Instituto Brasileiro do Meio Ambiente e dos Recursos Naturais Renováveis), the Brazilian environmental agency, calculated that one major airport in São Paulo was exporting 80 tonnes of pau d'arco in 1993 alone (Danusa, pers comm). During the ensuing six years, the demand for pau d'arco bark for the global phytochemical industry has grown substantially.

Popular literature credits the inner bark of pau d'arco with potent anti-inflammatory, anti-microbial, anti-allergic, anti-fungal, anti-cancer, diuretic and astringent activities. It is also used in the treatment of malaria, syphilis, Hodgkins disease, leukaemia, dysentery, ulcers, warts, wounds, pain, herpes, rabies, acne and baldness. However, not all of these treatments apply to every *Tabebuia* species. In the US and Europe, where the use of pau d'arco bark as a herbal medicine is growing in popularity, preferred barks include the bark of *Tabebuia impetiginosa* (also known as *T. avellanedae*), *T. heptaphylla* and *T. serratifolia*.

Medical research has determined that lapachol, alpha- and beta-lapachone, and other naphthoquinones found in the bark of several *Tabebuia* species (*T. avellanedae/impetiginosa, T. barbata, T. cassinoides, T. chrysantha, T. caraiba, T. heptaphylla, T. rosea, T. serratifolia* and *T. incana*) have anti-tumour properties (Rao and Kingston, 1982; Grazziotin et al, 1992), anti-microbial properties (*T. impetiginosa*; Anesini and Perez, 1993; Lewis and Elvin-Lewis, 1977), diuretic and astringent properties (*T. impetiginosa*; Ueda et al, 1994) and immuno-stimulating properties when applied in small doses (*T. avellanedae*; Arnason et al, 1994). Effectiveness against *Brucella* and *Candida* has been attributed to xyloidone, another component in the bark of *Tabebuia avellanedae* (Lewis and Elvin-Lewis, 1977). Other components found in pau d'arco include tannins, resins, calcium, iron, cobalt and additional minerals and vitamins.

While some research has indicated that the potential use of pau d'arco in treating cancer is promising, there is a need to further evaluate its mechanisms of action and toxicity. In 1974, the National Cancer Institute (NCI) in the US conducted tests on pau d'arco for anti-tumoural properties and toxicity. NCI soon dropped the research due to high levels of toxicity found in the treatment; when given in sufficiently high doses for the active ingredient lapachol to have any anti-tumoural benefit, side effects included nausea, vomiting, anaemia and internal bleeding (Raintree, 1999). Already during the 1960s, Osvaldo Riveiro de Lima from the Intituto de Antibióticos do Recife (Antibiotics Institute of Recife) in Brazil reached the conclusion that lapachol was improper for human consumption (Mara Danusa, pers comm). Recently, the American Pharmaceutical Association (APHA) published the *Practical Guide to Natural Medicines*, which specifically warns against taking pau d'arco because of its toxic side effects (Peirce, 1999). Less conservative recommendations indicate that pregnant women and children should abstain from taking pau d'arco.

While its use in cancer treatment may prove toxic, other uses that do not require such high doses may prove effective for a number of conditions. External use of pau d'arco for inflammations on the skin, ears, vagina or uterus may be harmless, as well as its use as a mouth wash. However, further studies are needed to understand the medicinal value of pau d'arco bark in crude extracts, to determine the specific effects of lapachol and to prevent toxic side effects from lapachol ingestion.

Herbal companies and consumers need to be wary of ascribing all the claimed medicinal values for pau d'arco to any one species. While most *Tabebuia* species contain the active ingredient lapachol, they can still differ in their medicinal properties. For instance, *T. impetiginosa* has anti-microbial properties, while *T. heptaphylla* does not (Anesini and Perez, 1993).

Pau d'arco is widely available for sale in local health-food stores, large supermarkets and directly from companies by phone and through the internet. Its most popular form in the US is as a tea, but it is also found as loose powder, capsules and as a tincture (alcohol extract). It is both taken orally and applied locally.

Quality control is still an issue in the marketing of pau d'arco. The reliability of the resource seems to be questionable. In 1987, a lab analysis of 12 commercial pau d'arco products found only one to have measurable amounts of lapachol in the bark. This was attributed to the active ingredient being lost during transportation and processing, or due to the substitution of another similar-looking bark for pau d'arco (Raintree, 1999).

Impact of land-use change and management

The popular use of pau d'arco bark as a folklore medicine and the use of *Tabebuia* wood in construction has led to the overharvesting of these trees in several Latin American countries (Gentry, 1980; Sheldon et al, 1997; Kinghorn, 1993). Because of the high timber value of *Tabebuia* species, loggers have often been willing to travel farther to harvest this species. In Brazil, the wood of pau d'arco is sold for US$300 per cubic metre (m^3) cut (Barreto, pers comm). Pau d'arco bark is frequently collected in sawmills for herbal markets, as a by-product of the timber industry. The majority of pau d'arco bark is claimed to be harvested from live trees in the forest, because freshly harvested bark is most highly prized by herbalists. However, due to declining abundance and overharvesting for timber, it is increasingly difficult to find pau d'arco in the wild or in Brazilian sawmills.

Due to this increasing scarcity, pau d'arco bark has frequently been substituted with bark from unrelated trees with similar colour characteristics. In Argentina, bark from *Piptadenia* trees, from the Leguminosae family, has been sold as pau d'arco in markets. In Peru, pau d'arco has been swapped with bark from *Cariniana* trees, from the Lecythidaceae family (Sheldon et al, 1997), while in Brazil, mahogany sawdust (*Swietania macrophylla*, from the Meliaceae family) has been collected in sawmills and sold as pau d'arco in herbal markets.

It is not clear how the ecology and sustainability of the various *Tabebuia* species is affected by the ongoing land-use changes in Central and South American countries. In the Amazon region, the principal agents of land conversion are fires, logging, ranching and agriculture. None of these factors are easily isolated from each other, nor are there sufficient studies to evaluate species regeneration after each of these very different land conversion events. Uhl et al (1998) studied succession on abandoned pastures in the Amazon and found that within eight years of abandonment, *T. serratifolia* regenerated well in pastures that had been logged, burned every two to three years, seeded and weeded with machetes. However, there was a loss in species diversity, and more heavily used areas that were also mechanically cleared and mowed showed less successful re-establishment by trees.

Enrichment planting experiments in southern Brazil showed that several *Tabebuia* species grew best under medium light conditions (50–60 per cent full sun). Those planted in open areas contracted a disease that caused leaf fall. However, trees recovered after a period of precipitation (Piña-Rodrigues, pers comm). *T. serratifolia* has been planted in Rio de Janeiro, Brazil, intermixed with more rapidly growing pioneer species for the restoration of degraded areas (Correia Lopez et al, 1994).

Seed collection and preparation for cultivation has been studied for all three *Tabebuia* species mentioned in this chapter. The seeds of *Tabebuia* species are short lived and require initial sowing in a nursery environment, followed by transplanting (Piña-Rodrigues, pers comm). To create seedling stock, the fruits of *T. impetiginosa* must be collected from the tree before falling, when the fruits are turning dark, and allowed to dry in the sun (May, pers comm). The seeds must be placed in small bags, where they take 10 to 12 days to germinate. They reach approximately 3m in two years. When the seeds are stored in a dry or cold chamber, they remain viable for up to nine months (IPEF, 1999).

The seeds of *T. heptaphylla* can be collected from the tree when the fruits open spontaneously (May, pers comm), or when the fruits are still green, but turning black, to avoid losing any seeds (IPEF, 1999). To produce seedling stock, the seeds can be germinated immediately after collection or left in a dry or cold chamber for up to 15 months (IPEF, 1999). They reach 2–3m in two years (May, pers comm).

Cultivated at a spacing of 4m x 4m, the maximum production obtained for both *T. impetiginosa* and *T. heptaphylla* was 6.6m^3 per hectare per year, with an 85 per cent survival rate (IPEF, 1999). Information on seed collection, storage and germination for *T. serratifolia* can be obtained from the Companhia Vale do Rio Doce (CVRD) Linhares Reserve, in Espíritu Santo, Brazil.

Due to the increasing international demand for *Tabebuia* products, the species is under severe pressure. Thus, there is a clear need to better understand *Tabebuia* ecology as well as the sustain-able management strategies for the species and/or the feasibility of agroforestry plantations that would permit a sustainable long-term yield of desired products. Otherwise, current international and national market demand could decimate the preferred *Tabebuia* species of the medicinal and timber trades and limit access to a traditional medicine used by indigenous peoples of South America for centuries.

Certification potential

Today, the harvesting of *Tabebuia* for the timber and herbal industries may be threatening the sustainability of this species in the wild. There is a need to bring together ecological, management and marketing information regarding the various *Tabebuia* species.

There are medical, quality-control and resource-management issues that need to be resolved before pau d'arco can be recommended for certification. From a medical point of view, there is a need to further research specific medicinal properties, mechanisms of action and toxicity. Furthermore, the chain-of-custody process for pau d'arco would need to assure consumers that the bark used does, indeed, come from certified, well-managed forests and that it has not been adulterated with other ingredients. Scrupulous members of the herbal industry would also need to have the forest management operation identify the specific species of *Tabebuia* provided, with accompanying samples, in order to inform consumers about the active ingredients in, and proper use of, their products.

From a conservation standpoint, there is a need to find cases of sustainable forest management that guarantee sustainable harvesting of *Tabebuia* species, potentially through green-certified sawmills. At present, there is a very small amount of certified *Tabebuia* that is marketed from one Brazilian forest operation as a timber species. A European buyer expressed interest in obtaining certified pau d'arco bark as a by-product of the forest operation. However, the amount of bark requested was far in excess of what the operation could sustainably produce (Rezende, pers comm, 1999).

Forests managed for multiple purposes, including for non-timber forest products, could benefit from the sustainable extraction of pau d'arco bark for medicinal markets. However, the economic and ecological viability of this still needs to be evaluated. Intensive cultivation of *Tabebuia* is still questionable, although plantations established for restoration purposes, intermixed with pioneer species, have shown excellent tree survival rates. Successful cultivation and certification of pau d'arco plantations or agroforestry systems could theoretically alleviate some pressures on natural forest sources of *Tabebuia* species.

One interesting possibility may be to harvest pau d'arco bark from branches, rather than cutting the entire tree. According to Ueda et al (1994), trees must be at least 20 years old before harvesting their bark for medicinal purposes. This would require a better understanding of the content of lapachol and other naphthoquinones in the branches, their medicinal effectiveness, age of trees when active components are effective, and the response of the various pau d'arco species to pruning. Finally, another potential non-timber forest product value is the marketing of pau d'arco seeds, collected in natural forests, for ornamental purposes.

Chapter 8

Cat's claw (*Uncaria guianensis* and *U. tomentosa*)

*Miguel N Alexiades**

Introduction

Uña de gato (cat's claw) is a widely used medicinal plant native to much of tropical Central and South America. This climbing, twining woody vine belongs to the genus *Uncaria*, a member of the madder family (Rubiaceae), which includes such important economic species as quinine (*Cinchona*), ipecac (*Cephaelis ipecacuanha* (Brot.) Tussac) and coffee (*Coffea arabica* L.). Despite its broad distribution, extending as far north as Belize, south to Paraguay and east to Marañao, Brazil, as a commercial medicinal, uña de gato is almost exclusively associated with Peru. Although some of these other countries are now showing interest in the plant, most of the commer-

Illustration by Bee Gunn

*Cat's claw (*Uncaria tomentosa*)

cial supply of cat's claw comes from Peru (Hughes and Worth, 1999). The fame and demand for Peruvian *Uncaria* is at least in part related to the particular historical circumstances through which this medicinal captured the attention of researchers, entrepreneurs, the media and the international alternative health community.

Though uña de gato has 'traditionally' been used as a medicinal by certain ethnic groups, the plant's medicinal uses were unknown to many rural Amazonians, who nonetheless were familiar with the species as a swidden weed and as a source of potable stem water. Uña de gato began to be more widely known and

* Kerry Hughes and Wil de Jong provided valuable comments on earlier drafts of this chapter and assistance in locating some of the references on cat's claw. The author is also grateful to Joaquina Albán Castillo, Miguel Pinedo-Vásquez and Didier Lacaze for providing additional assistance with the literature.

used in Peru a few decades ago, and may be an interesting example of a plant whose local ethnobotanical importance followed from its commercialization – a curious inversion of the usual sequence of events. By the 1980s, uña de gato was a popular medicinal in the local markets of such Amazonian urban centres as Pucallpa and Iquitos. Media reports, including articles in the Peruvian national newspaper *El Comercio*, helped focus national attention on the plant. By the early 1990s, uña de gato was widely commercialized within Peru, but still largely unknown internationally. In 1993, for example, only 0.2 (metric) tonnes were exported from Peru, and then only to the US (de Jong et al, 1999). Exports increased to over 20 tonnes and eight countries in the following year, sky-rocketing to over 726 tonnes in 24 countries in 1995. The 'free on board' (FOB) value of exports that year was US$3.3 million (de Jong et al, 1999). In the following years, exports levelled off at about 300 tonnes per year (Hughes and Worth, 1999), though according to one source, 1999 exports reached 800 tonnes (Lama, 2000).

A number of factors contributed to the sudden 'discovery' of *Uncaria* by the international community. Austrian, German, Italian and Peruvian researchers began studying the plant in the 1950s, and many of these studies included clinical trials and experimental treatment patients – particularly patients with cancer. The year 1994 saw two widely publicized cases involving Latin American public personalities who claimed rapid recovery from cancer following their use of *Uncaria*. That same year the World Health Organization (WHO) sponsored the first international conference on uña de gato in Peru, where the vine received official recognition as a medicinal plant.

The Peruvian government's interest in uña de gato is encouraged by ongoing anti-drug efforts, which seek to identify economic alternatives for coca growers (eg Efe News Services Inc, 1999a). By 1997 there were 12 manufacturing laboratories in the US processing uña de gato, and these products were distributed inside the country by over 39 companies (de Jong et al, 2000). The international market for *Uncaria* has spread from the US to Europe, Latin America and, more recently, Asia. In 1999, for example, an agreement was reached between Liofilizadora del Pacífico, the maker of one of Peru's best-selling cat's claw capsules, and the largest Chinese manufacturer of herbal products to form a consortium and sell cat's claw in China (Efe News Services Inc, 23 October 1999). A recent change in cat's claw importation and medical status in Spain has been read by some industry analysts as a sign of an impending growth in demand among other member states of the European Union (EU) (Efe News Services Inc, 16 January 1999).

Despite the promising future of the international cat's claw market, as with other herbal supplements, the demand is ultimately uncertain (K Hughes, pers comm, 16 November 1999). The unpredictability of the cat's claw market is exemplified by the 1995 spike in exports, interpreted by some as an attempt to stockpile *Uncaria* following rumours of an export ban, and/or a contraction of the market due to poor or variable bark quality (de Jong et al, 2000). This may particularly be the case given concerns that 'the marketing of [uña de gato] is ahead of science' (Mark Blumenthal, cited in Romell, 1996). Other medicinal plant experts, including James Duke and Varro Tyler, have likewise cautioned in the past that the scientific evidence for the efficacy of uña de gato does not support many of the statements made by some of the companies that commercialize the plant (Mark Blumenthal, cited in Romell, 1996).

The importance of uña de gato to the local economy varies. In most cases, it provides complementary income to local farmers and other local producers who participate in local extractive industries, and who up to now are the major suppliers of commercial cat's claw bark. The price paid by middlemen for the bark in Pucallpa ranges between US$0.50 and US$1 per kilogram (kg) (D Lacaze, pers comm, May 1999). Middlemen, in turn, receive about US$1.5 per kg from export companies, while the price of the finished, processed product is around US$6.60 per kg (de Jong et al, 1999, p8). Retail prices for uña de gato vary; but in 1999 in the US, bark sold for about US$50 per kg, capsules for about US$200 per kg, concentrated tablets for about US$500 per kg, and extracts for about US$600 per litre.

The sudden and high demand for *Uncaria* has raised concerns relating to the ecological viability of the species, also highlighting many of the biological, social and ethical issues associated with the commercial development of non-timber forest products (NTFPs). A realistic assessment of the pharmacological value, ecological status and potential of *Uncaria* as a sustainable income source is hampered by the severe lack of baseline data. This limitation has recently begun to be redressed by a number of monographs presenting known aspects of the plant's biology, pharmacology, ecology and management (eg de Jong et al, 2000; Domínguez, 1997; Hughes and Worth, 1999; Obregón, 1997; Ocampo, 1994; Zavala and Zevallos, 1996). Study and management of uña de gato is complicated by the fact that this name is used interchangeably for two species: *Uncaria guianensis* (Aublet) Gmelin, and *U. tomentosa* (Willdenow ex Roemer and Schultes) DC. Though these species have largely overlapping distributions and are often used interchangeably as herbal medicines, they do differ in their habit, ecology and chemistry (see 'Use' later in this chapter and Table 8.1). These differences have important and unique implications for the commercialization, management and conservation each species and for the resource as a whole.[1]

Biology and distribution

Uncaria species are all coarse, scandent shrubs or lianas that climb through and over other vegetation by means of characteristic accrescent 1–3 centimetre (cm) clasping hooks or spines (hence the plant's name cat's claw). These paired, recurved spines, which emerge from the nodes beneath the leaves, are the most diagnostic characteristic for the genus. Though the genus, which totals about 60 species, is pan-tropical, it is mostly centred in South-East Asia. Although *U. tomentosa* and *U. guianensis* are the only species found in the neo-tropics, they have a very wide distribution: their range extends between Panama to the north, Paraguay to the south, Trinidad and Tobago, Guyana and north-eastern Brazil to the east, and the lower foothills of the Andes to the west (Domínguez, 1997; de Jong et al, 1999).

While both species overlap in their habitat range – tropical forest at altitudes ranging from 100 metres (m) to about 1000m above sea level – *U. tomentosa* prefers the moister, more elevated regions,

Table 8.1 *Differences between* U. tomentosa *and* U. guianensis

	U. tomentosa	U. guianensis
Habit	Tends to grow as climber, liana diameter 20–30cm	Tends to grow as creeper, liana diameter 4–15cm
Leaves	Oblong shaped; 7.5–17cm long, 5–12cm wide	Ovate or elliptic shaped;. 8–19cm long, 6–9.5cm wide
Leaf-secondary veins	Eight to ten pairs	Six to seven pairs
Pubescence	Characteristic white pubescence in leaf undersides, particularly along veins	No pubescence
Spines	Spines generally more recurved, slimmer and with sharper tips	Spines generally straighter, shorter and stouter
Inner bark	Yellowish	Reddish
Inflorescence	10–20cm long and 1.5–4cm wide	1.5–3.5cm long and 0.1–0.15cm wide
Flowers	Sessile (no flower stalks) yellowish	Pedicellate (flower stalks present) reddish
Capsules (fruits)	6–17mm long	12–25mm long
Seeds	2–4mm long	5–8mm long
Elevation	Most abundant at circa 400–800m	Most abundant at circa 200m
Climate	Prefers moister regions with smaller seasonal temperature and rainfall changes	Greater resistance to dry conditions and to greater fluctuations in temperature and rainfall
Soil	More common on well-drained hills with high organic soil content	More common on lower, flatter and poorly drained regions
Habitat	More common in closed, mature forest	More common in open, disturbed vegetation or secondary forest
Phenology	Flowers February–June; fruits April–August	Flowers September–November; fruits in September–January

Sources: Albán, 1996; Andersson and Taylor, 1994; de Jong et al, 1999; Domínguez, 1997; MacBride, 1936; Quevedo, 1995; Zavala and Zevallos, 1996

while *U. guianensis* is more abundant at lower altitudes.[2] The minimum and maximum mean annual temperatures for *U. tomentosa* in Peru are 17° Celsius (C) and 25.7° C, with minimum and maximum rainfall of 1200 millimetres (mm) and 6000mm respectively. *U. guianensis* has smaller minimum figures. Both species occur in tropical, pre-montane tropical and sub-tropical forests. *U. tomentosa* favours hilly, well-drained conditions with rich soils, as well as interfluvial levees and *terra firme*. *U. guianensis*, on the other hand, is associated with flatter terrain, *várzea*, poor drainage and more acidic or depleted soils. Consequently, *U. tomentosa* is more commonly found in mature forest, associated with light disturbances or forest gaps, while *U. guianensis* is found mostly in fallows, other secondary forests, river margins and/or intensely disturbed areas (Quevedo, 1995; Zavala and Zevallos, 1996). Both species favour Ortic Acrisols, District Cambisols and Fluvisols.

In open areas, *Uncaria* grows as a scandent shrub, forming a dense tangle of leaves and thin stems. In old secondary forests, it develops into a thick liana that climbs 20m or more into the canopy before branching into leaf-bearing stems. Again, there appear to be differences between species. *U. tomentosa* grows taller, has thicker stems and develops more as a climber, whereas *U. guianensis*, whose spines are shorter, is more of a scandent creeper. Adult lianas of *U. tomentosa* are between 10–30m long, reaching a base diameter of 5–40cm, in contrast with *U. guianensis*, which has a base diameter range of 4–15cm and reaches lengths of 4–10m (Quevedo, 1995).

The plant's primary root can be several metres long, ranging in thickness from about 2 to 10cm. Root bark is selected over stalk bark by a number of treatment or herbal specialists, although as Cabieses (undated) points out, the folk definition of root often encompasses parts of the stem.

The variability and flexibility of *Uncaria* growth habit has important implications for its management. Although more abundant in fallows and young secondary vegetation, *Uncaria* biomass in these environments consists mostly of leaf matter or thin stems, with relatively little harvestable stalk and root bark. In contrast, the larger vines found in closed forests, though scarcer and less easily accessible, have more bark and hence are the targets of most commercial harvesting.

Over 50 secondary compounds have been identified in *U. tomentosa*, including indole and oxindole alkaloids, quinovic acid glycosides, triterpines, polyphenols, proanthocyanidins and sterols (Hughes and Worth, 1999). There appear to be qualitative and quantitative differences in the chemical composition of both species, though much research still needs to be done. Some have suggested that *U. guianensis* has lower levels of alkaloids than *U. tomentosa*, to the extent that its bark and leaves occasionally lack these altogether (Cáceres, 1995). Though widespread in the marketplace, the notion that *U. tomentosa* has a more favourable alkaloid profile than *U. guianensis* is not backed up by experimental data (Hughes and Worth, 1999). According to Keplinger and his associates, *U. guianensis* from Peru exhibits alkaloid patterns that are quite different from *U. tomentosa* (Keplinger et al, 1999). These and other differences lead the authors to suspect that the two species are not closely related. There is considerable intra-specific variation in chemical composition, as well. In addition, quantitative and/or qualitative differences occur seasonally between different populations, between different plant tissues and possibly between different stages of development and age of the plant (Jones, 1995; Kam et al, 1992; Laus et al, 1997; Keplinger et al, 1999).

Two chemotypes of *U. tomentosa* have been identified (Reinhard, 1999). One of these contains pentacyclic, the other tetracyclic indole and oxindole alkaloids (Laus et al, 1997). Tetracyclic alkaloids are immunosuppressing while pentacyclic alkaloids are immunopotentiating (Hughes and Worth, 1999). The fact that tetracyclic alkaloids act antagonistically to pentacyclic alkaloids has critical implications for the use and management of different *Uncaria* chemotypes (Keplinger et al, 1999). The existence of these chemotypes is ignored in industry sourcing, not least because there are no known means to distinguish chemotypes on the basis of appearance (Hughes and Worth, 1999).

Ecology

Both species of *Uncaria* are heliophytes, though *U. tomentosa* is associated with gaps in mature forests, while *U. guianensis* is more restricted to secondary growth and disturbed areas such as swidden fallows. In young secondary forests, *Uncaria* is often found in dense clumps. In these areas it is difficult to inventory individual plants, as the stems frequently send out roots when they touch the ground. In these areas, *Uncaria* is commonly associated with such species as *Cecropia*, *Ficus*, *Heliocarpus*, *Ochroma*, *Vernonia*, *Inga* and *Himathantus* (Domínguez, 1997). In more mature forests, *Uncaria* is found as individual lianas, although even here distribution may be patchy. In closed forests, *Uncaria* is commonly associated with *Cedrela*, *Chorisia*, *Iryanthera*, *Swietania*, *Terminalia*, *Cedrelinga*, *Callicophyllum* and *Pouteria*.

Under the right conditions *Uncaria* may grow rather aggressively. In Central America, for example, it is reported as a weed in banana plantations (Standley, 1930, p1379), and farmers in Amazonian Peru are familiar with the plant as a swidden weed. Moreover, the plant is very resistant to fire and other disturbances, growing back after forest is cleared and burned for agriculture. The aggressive growth and rapid recovery of *Uncaria* following burning is partly enabled by the capacity of stems to root whenever they touch the ground. Though opportunistic and quite resistant, however, *Uncaria* prefers richer soils.

There is very little baseline data on the population biology and ecology of *Uncaria*. One study conducted on 60 hectares of forest in a native community on the Palcazu estimated about 17 *Uncaria* individuals per hectare (Arce, 1996, cited in Domínguez, 1997, p35). Data from another survey in Ucayali indicates densities ranging from 2 to 15 individuals per hectare (Quevedo, 1995). Cabieses (undated, p113) mentions an unidentified source reporting up to 80 plants per hectare in secondary forests in Manu, though such figures, if correct, are by no means usual. Domínguez (1997, p34) estimates about two adult plants per hectare based on inventories from different sites. Differences in population densities may reflect bioedaphic variations or different intensities of destructive harvesting. Densities in natural forest are lower, from two to eight individuals per hectare, than in managed forests (Hughes and Worth, 1999). Moreover, some sites do have patches of adult lianas (*manchales*) where densities are obviously higher, but these are not very common.

A five-year-old liana will have a base diameter (dbh) of about 5cm, though growth rates depend upon bioedaphic conditions. There are no data on growth rates for bark, though different field estimates suggest periods ranging between five and ten years before harvestable stalk bark is produced (Quevedo, 1995; Zavala and Zevallos, 1996). The required growth period for root bark may be longer, while that for leaves is obviously much shorter.

Carrasco (1996, cited in Domínguez, 1997, p34) estimates that about 0.5kg of the bark may be harvested per metre from a 10cm-wide liana. Destructive harvesting of such an individual would thus yield about 30kg of dry bark. Other estimates of 8–10kg for a 5cm-wide liana roughly agree with this figure (D Lacaze, pers comm, May 1999). Based on these figures, Carrasco estimates an approximate harvest rate of 60kg of dry bark per hectare in mature forests, or 17 hectares for 1 tonne, based on an average of two lianas per hectare. In the case study in Palcazu, Arce (1996, p35) estimates a yield of 306kg of dry bark per hectare, based on 17 lianas per hectare.

Uncaria regenerates both by seed and by sprouting. Very little is known about the reproductive biology of *Uncaria*. The presence of yellow and red blossoms and a sweet odour suggest pollination by bees, though red colours are often associated with pollination by hummingbirds, as well. The presence of winged seed testa suggests wind dispersal. Phenological observations in Ucayali, Peru, report a longer reproductive period for *U. guianensis*, with flowering taking place between February and June (mid-rainy season to early dry season), fruiting between April and August (end of rainy season to mid-dry season), and dispersal between June and October (early to late dry season). In contrast, *U. tomentosa* phenology is later and much shorter: flowering takes place from September to November, fruiting from October to January and dispersal from January to March (Domínguez, 1997; Quevedo, 1995).

Impact of land-use change, trade and legislative initiatives

As a heliophyte and secondary growth species, the distribution of *Uncaria* is clearly related to patterns of anthropogenic disturbance. While cat's claw has not been subject to intentional management as a medicinal, at least until recently, it is definitely a plant whose distribution and abundance is related to patterns of human management and disturbance. The plant's aggressive growth, its ability to sprout from stem sections and to recover after cutting and burning, and its close association with anthropogenic landscapes all indicate a high potential for management.

Past use of *Uncaria* is not likely to have created much of an impact on its population ecology given the relatively small amounts harvested and the species' relative abundance. Moreover, this type of extraction is not always destructive:[3] people may also strip off pieces of bark from the living liana. As long as the liana is not girdled, many individuals are likely to regrow bark and survive.

Commercial harvesting, on the other hand, is almost always destructive and frequently involves 'natural' populations from closed forests. The plant is usually cut at the base, pulling down as much of the vine as possible. At times this may require climbing up a tree trunk and pulling down tangled upper sections.

Often, collectors simply cut down the whole tree, the fall of which frequently downs several others growing around it (Kerry Hughes, pers comm, 19 November 1999). The environmental impact of destructive harvesting is thus not limited to the vine itself. 1m-long sections are then cut off and pounded, allowing the outer bark to be easily peeled away. The reddish inner bark is stripped away from the stem and tied into 40–50kg bundles. Leaves and branches are usually wasted, given the limited demand for these materials. Bark bundles are carried back to a camp or village, where the bark strips are laid out to dry on a tarp in the sun. In the dry season, the bark dries in three to five days, longer in the rainy season.

Smallholders, farmers and native people, who sell the bark to middlemen, carry out most commercial extraction. There is often a chain of intermediaries between the harvester and the buyer. Middlemen pay between US$0.50 and US$1 per kg. De Jong et al (1999) calculate that 1995's exports from Peru required 24,000 labour days of work. For intermediaries, profit margins are ultimately determined by the international price. High export prices in 1995 and 1996 made trading of uña de gato profitable; but a drop in prices after 1996 drastically cut into profits (de Jong et al, 2000). A number of Peruvian intermediaries interviewed in 1997 had left-over stock that they could not sell profitably (de Jong et al, 2000). According to another study in Peru, in 1996 it was more profitable for collectors to be hired by intermediaries than to collect independently and sell directly to buyers (Carrasco, 1996, cited in de Jong et al, 2000).

In Peru, commercial extraction is subject to certain legal restrictions and procedures. In theory, harvesters require a permit (*contrato de extracción*), which allows the extraction of a predetermined amount of *Uncaria* from a delimited area over a specific period of time, ranging from one to ten years (de Jong et al, 2000). In practice, such permits are obtained by middlemen who sub-contract to a number of different harvesters. As a result, *Uncaria* is often harvested from areas not included in the permit.

Uña de gato has been commercially available within Peru for several decades at least, and this demand has always been satisfied by destructively harvesting mature individuals in closed forest. The sudden increase in international demand for uña de gato in recent years has placed an entirely new level of pressure on this resource, particularly in Peru, the main commercial source country. In 1995, Peru exported over 700 tonnes of bark, mostly from the regions of Ucayali, Huánuco, Pasco and Junín. Based on estimates of yields and productivity derived from *Uncaria* in mature forests, Domínguez (1997) extrapolates that exports for 1995 alone entailed destructive harvesting of *Uncaria* in 20,000 hectares of forest.

Uncaria is officially considered to be 'vulnerable' in some parts of its range. One source indicates that wild stocks of cat's claw have been almost eradicated from parts of Huánuco and Tingo María due to overharvesting, and that collectors are currently targeting areas such as Contamana and Rioja, in the departments of Loreto and San Martin, Peru, respectively (Efe News Service Inc, October 1999). Likewise, the Centro de Datos para la Conservación (CDC) categorizes it as 'N2', suggesting it is under threat and that, though fairly abundant, the viability of its natural populations is not guaranteed (Zavala, 1996). Moreover, although technically not illegal, the Instituto Nacional de Recursos Naturales (INRENA) does not issue permits for the harvesting of roots, in an attempt to curtail a type of harvesting seen to be more ecologically damaging than that involving bark (de Jong et al, 2000).

Environmental concerns were part of the motivation that prompted the Peruvian government to issue a presidential decree (*Decreto Supremo*) in 1999, which prohibits the export of unprocesssed or mechanically processed cat's claw unless it is obtained from managed natural stocks or plantations (de Jong et al, 2000). The rationale behind this ban is that it will increase profits accrued by Peruvians and assist in the conservation of the species. If *Uncaria* populations continue to be destructively harvested, the species may also end up listed under the Convention on International Trade in Endangered Species of Wild Fauna and Flora (CITES), further complicating its commercialization.

As de Jong et al (2000) note, the social, economic and ecological effects of such legislative initiatives are complex, ambivalent and potentially counterproductive to the cat's claw industry in Peru, and particularly to the small producers who are evident stakeholders in the market. While current levels of commercial extraction are clearly having an impact on *Uncaria*, particularly on more accessible populations and/or on species demographics, the level or significance of this impact is not fully understood. De Jong et al (2000) suggest that current trends, though poorly documented, indicate that there is little threat to the species as a whole at current exploitation levels. Ultimately, concerns that the species is threatened might be exaggerated, particularly given *Uncaria*'s abundance, growth habit and distribution. This does not mean that continued increasing demands on *Uncaria* could not pose additional threats to the species but, rather, that the presidential decree may be, at the very least, premature (de Jong et al, 2000).

Likewise, de Jong et al (2000) suggest that the practice of discouraging harvesting of root bark should be more closely examined, given the lack of ecological evidence to show the effect of such practices. If, as some have argued, root bark contains higher alkaloid content, an argument could be made to support the use of root bark as a less destructive process (de Jong et al, 2000).

Though intended to favour the cat's claw industry, the ongoing Peruvian legislation may ultimately harm it, particularly if it encourages buyers to seek alternative sources. In addition, such legislation could favour large producers who have the means to process cat's claw, develop 'formal' management programmes and plantations, and deal with central bureaucratic agencies. There are powerful historical precedents that suggest that as non-timber forests become significant commodities, economically and politically more powerful actors take control over the production process, displacing local stakeholders (eg Dove, 1996; Homma, 1992). Frequently, this shift entails a geographical as well as socio-economic transfer in the production of the commercial resource, as the plants are grown in different regions or countries. One danger of legislative, as well as certification efforts, is that they will thus assist in this process, to the detriment of the very local stakeholders who traditionally managed the resource, and perhaps even to national stakeholders as well.

Moreover, a shift towards commercial plantations or alternative modes of production, and away from local farmers, could undermine cat's claw's potential to support economically viable uses of secondary forests and promote socially and ecologically viable tropical forest management strategies.

Management

Besides its effect on legislation, concern over the status and future of *Uncaria* has also had an effect on the marketing, research and development of cat's claw as an economic resource, and these efforts are important factors in determining both supply and demand.

A number of Euro-American suppliers of *Uncaria*, addressing an ecologically conscious market, claim that their supplies are harvested 'in a sustainable, ecological friendly manner'. In many cases, however, the label of 'sustainable' is applied rather loosely, as in cases where stalk bark, as opposed to root bark, is harvested. While harvesting stalk bark is less destructive than harvesting root bark, such practice offers no guarantee of ecological sustainability. There are also some reports of techniques that minimize damage or individual mortality. One commercial firm, for example, maintains that it has developed a means of harvesting the root without disrupting the growth of the vine, removing a portion of the main root and allowing the rest to grow (Jones,

1995, p105).

A few programmes have sought to work closely with local communities to develop controlled or managed harvesting practices. The Peruvian non-governmental organization (NGO) Pro-Naturaleza, for example, has developed a cat's claw management project with a Yanesha community. The community has set aside 170 hectares of forest for harvesting of non-timber forest products (NTFPs). Only 60 per cent of uña de gato individuals are harvested from this area, on a ten-year rotation basis. Thus, 40 per cent of the *Uncaria* stock is left to regenerate naturally. Individuals are cut 1m from the base in order to increase their chances of survival, and competing vines are removed at regular intervals to assist regrowth (de Jong et al, 1997; Domínguez, 1997).

Another project involves the Asháninka of the Ene River Valley and the NGO Asociación para la Conservación del Patrimonio Cutiriveni (ACPC). Vines are harvested about 20cm above ground, in order to allow the stem to grow back. Two 20-cm sections are cut from each harvested vine; one for replanting and one for analysis. Harvesting is conducted during the dry season. Technicians also supervise and advise the Asháninka on processing of the harvested bark. *Uncaria* reportedly provides an important source of income for this group (Domínguez, 1997). The Peruvian company Liofilizadora del Pacífico/Omniagro has an agreement with a community in the Ucayali to conduct controlled harvesting of natural *Uncaria* populations (de Jong et al, 1999).

Many other efforts are also underway for cultivating *Uncaria*. One major commercial supplier of *Uncaria* has reportedly been cultivating the vine for ten years. 'Cultivars are contracted out to Asháninka Indians who raise them and are paid for their service through the purchase of the plants at the time of harvesting' (Jones, 1995, p105). Other farmers have spontaneously started planting it in their swiddens and fallows. Studies in Peru suggest that *Uncaria* can successfully be intercropped with other secondary-forest economic species, such as *Croton* (see Chapter 13), or with such cultigens as plantains, beans, manioc, papaya, pineapples, sweet potatoes, watermelons and fruit trees (Quevedo, 1995). Government-sponsored reforestation committees in Iquitos and Pucallpa have encouraged the planting of thousands of uña de gato seedlings (de Jong et al, 2000).

One potential problem of such reforestation and management initiatives is that their success will ultimately depend upon a mid- and long-term commitment, both in terms of financial support and follow-up, that ensures the plants are being adequately managed and successfully articulated with market demands. For example, uña de gato planted in open areas is unlikely to produce much marketable bark, instead spreading as tangled shrubs, which may ultimately also compete with other crops. Hence, the problem is not so much cultivating *Uncaria*, but cultivating it in such a way as to produce bark. Indeed, *Uncaria gambir* (Hunter) Roxb. is cultivated in South-East Asia as a commercial source of tannin, an appropriate management regime given that it is the leaves that are used.

Efforts at propagating *Uncaria* have been most successful with seeds. Though preliminary, there are some studies on germination and propagation techniques for planting and cultivating *Uncaria* (eg Flores, 1995, cited in Domínguez, 1997, p130). Like many rubiaceous species, *Uncaria* may have intermittent dispersal, meaning that not all seeds mature (or capsules open) simultaneously. Seeds germinate in 5 to 20 days and may be transplanted 6 months to 2 years later

(Didier Lacaze, pers comm, May 1999; Quevedo, 1995). Highest germination rates are obtained in the first month, a large percentage of seeds losing their viability within months (Domínguez, 1997). Overall germination rates of 65–84 per cent are reported for *U. tomentosa* (Flores, 1995, cited in Domínguez, 1997). Lower germination rates may be due to the seed's vulnerability to fungal attack (Quevedo, 1995).[4]

Quevedo (1995) reports that natural regeneration can be managed by opening belt clearings 1m wide, 5m long, spaced at every 4m, around fruiting vines. Seedlings may then be transplanted to other areas. While feasible, techniques for vegetative reproduction are not as effective as those involving seeds. Even so, Quevedo (1995) reports 98 per cent and 80 per cent success rates with *U. guianensis* and *U. tomentosa*, respectively. Under appropriate conditions, *U. guianensis* roots in 9 days, while *U. tomentosa* takes 15 to 20 days (Piñán, 1995, cited in Domínguez, 1997, p117). Stakes that are 20–30cm long, 3–5cm wide, should be cut from side branches and not the main stem, as these have more vigorous buds (Quevedo, 1995). The most favourable time for planting is October to December, so that the three-month rooting period coincides with the rainy season. Because vegetative propagation eliminates genetic variability in alkaloid content, this form of propagation is most promising, once plants with desirable qualities are identified. Vegetative propagation techniques require improvement since appropriate protocols need to be defined for identifying donor plants, selecting sections of stems, determining the type of cut, timing the collection and selecting an ideal substrate for rooting (see Cuéllar, 1996; Quevedo, 1995).

Researchers at the Universidad Nacional Agraria 'La Molina' have produced in-vitro *Uncaria* seedlings from leaves and buds. Another group of researchers at the chemistry department at the Pontificia Universidad Católica del Peru is looking at in-vitro culturing of roots. Such technology holds some promise in producing clones with desirable and standardized qualities. In-vitro technologies also allow the use of genetic material from older individuals, which often lose their regenerative capacity, permitting the selection of favourable genetic traits faster and more economically than through traditional means. If effective and economically viable, such technology could have a dramatic impact on the cat's claw industry and the management of wild populations. For one thing, such technology could, in principle, allow international buyers to move their operations away from source regions and countries.

Use

During the 1930s, a Bavarian by the name of Arthur Brell travelled to the German community of Pozuzo in Chanchamayo, Peru, to work as a schoolteacher. His interest in medicinal plants led him to *Uncaria*, which was used as a medicinal and a female contraceptive by the native population of the region. Over time, Brell began experimenting with *Uncaria* as a medicinal and cancer cure, treating many people with his own herbal formula and eventually opening a small clinic northeast of Lima (Jones, 1995).

One of the cancer patients successfully treated by Brell with *Uncaria* was Peruvian–German Luis Schuler, who recovered in the late 1960s from what was diagnosed as advanced lung cancer.[5] Word of this incident reached Austrian journalist and self-taught ethnologist Klaus Keplinger, who had a personal interest in ethnobotany and cancer. Keplinger travelled to Oxapampa in 1979 and 1981, collecting samples of *Uncaria tomentosa* and initiating a long series of activity studies based on root material collected in the Chanchamayo region. Keplinger worked closely with Asháninka informants, eventually writing on different aspects of Asháninka folklore and culture (Jones, 1995). Both Schuler's descendents and Keplinger developed *Uncaria* commercially, the former as suppliers of capsules and the latter as director of the Immodel laboratory in Austria. Immodel has developed the pharmaceutical 'Krallendorn', based on an extract of the root of *Uncaria tomentosa*, filing two patents for the extraction process.

The early work of Brell, Schuler and Keplinger profoundly shaped popular perceptions of cat's claw, including the current association between uña de gato, Peru, the Selva Central and the Asháninka. It is quite remarkable that a plant as widely distributed and utilized as *Uncaria* is so strongly associated with one particular region. International attention to Peruvian *Uncaria* was also fostered by the popular writer and ethnobotanist Nicole Maxwell (1990), who reported that the National Cancer Institute (NCI) had obtained encouraging preliminary results in the use of *Uncaria* as a tumour-inhibiting agent.

Over the last few decades, uña de gato has become an increasingly popular folk remedy in urban areas in Amazonia, as well as in the Andes and Pacific coast. In Peru, uña de gato, together with copaíba and sangre de drago, are the most popular Amazonian medicinal plants sold by street vendors. In recent years the socio-eco-nomic profile of the plant's consumers has undergone a dramatic change. Once used almost exclusively by the economic underclass, uña de gato and other medicinals have begun to be widely sought after and used by middle and upper classes, who clearly have a much greater purchasing power and who can afford more highly processed preparations, with higher added values.

While uña de gato, or garabato, as it is more commonly known in parts of Peru (Quevedo, 1995), is reported as a traditional medicinal among several indigenous groups, including the Aguaruna, Asháninka, Bora, Cashibo, Conibo, Ka'apor, Shipibo and Yánesha (Balée, 1994; Oregón, 1997), it is quite clear that the publicity generated during recent decades and its demand by urban consumers have increased its ethnobotanical importance among many local communities. Its use among several indigenous groups in Madre de Dios, for example, is clearly the result of the explosion in its popularity in urban areas.

Irrespective of how *Uncaria* acquired its ethnobotanical salience and popularity, the fact is that today the tea of the stem, stem bark, root bark and leaves are widely used throughout Latin America in the treatment of numerous ailments, including fever, rheumatism, arthritis, wounds, haemorrhages, peptic ulcers, diverse gastro-intestinal ailments (diarrhoea, dysentery, parasites), prostate problems, kidney problems, urinary tract infections and tumours. The tea is also used in the recovery from chemotherapy side effects, as an anti-infective, as a tonic, an aphrodisiac, a female contraceptive, in post-partum recovery, for disease prevention and as a panacea.

The medicinal value of uña de gato is confirmed by reports of use for other *Uncaria* species worldwide. The Chinese species *U. hirsuta* and *U. rhynchophylla*, for example, are used as anti-inflammatories and for liver ailments, while in Taiwan *U. formosana* is used as an anti-hypertensive and *U. kawakamii* is used for kidney stones. *Uncaria gambir* (Bengal gambir) is used for diarrhoea (Lewis and Elvin-Lewis, 1977) and for urinary tract problems, and *U. africana* is used to treat coughs, stomach pains and syphilis (Phillips, 1991). The flavonoids in some *Uncaria* species are already in use by the pharmaceutical industry. Rutin and its derivatives from *U. elliptica* R.Br. ex G Don, for example, have been marketed as the drugs Venoruton™ and Paroven™ for the treatment of vascular disease, as well as the drugs Catergen™ and Cianindol-3™ (Law and Das, 1990).

Uña de gato is also touted as bolstering the immune system, helping in the treatment of AIDS, allergies, bursitis, cancer, candidiasis, colitis, conjunctivitis, diabetes, diverticulitis, flu, gastritis, haemorrhoids, herpes, hypertension, menstrual irregularities, lupus and for post-partum care. *Uncaria* sales in Euro-American markets are largely based on its purported immune-supporting, anti-inflammatory, anti-bacterial, anti-viral, anti-mutagenic, anti-oxidant, diuretic and hypotensive properties. A New Jersey-based company, MW International, for example, launched a product called C-MED-100™ containing a proprietary extract of cat's claw bark that is used to maintain a responsive immune system (Anonymous, 1999). Another company, Rexal Sundown, has a product for Alzheimer's disease that includes cat's claw (Kerry Hughes, pers comm, 16 November 1999).

Its wide range of uses originates from its immuno-stimulant properties. Pharmacological testing certainly suggests specific immuno-stimulant effects (Cabieses, undated; Jones, 1995, p38). In addition, extracts of *U. tomentosa* have shown in-vitro anti-mutagenic effects (Rizzi et al, 1993), as well as anti-viral (Aquino et al, 1989), anti-inflammatory (Aquino et al, 1991) and anti-leukaemic activity (Keplinger et al, 1999). Though promising, most of these results come from pharmacological and in-vitro tests. Controlled clinical studies are being undertaken in Europe with a number of proprietary extracts for the treatment of leukaemia, rheumatoid arthritis, allergic respiratory diseases, ulcers, gastritis and viral diseases including AIDS and herpes; however, the results of these studies remain largely unpublished and/or unfinished (Jones, 1995). The results of these and other trials will have an important effect in shaping future demands for *Uncaria*.

The presence of numerous bioactive compounds (some of which appear to interact synergistically, others antagonistically), together with observed variations in levels and presence of different compounds between different species, plant parts and seasons, complicate attempts to formally evaluate the benefits and activity of *Uncaria*. This chapter has already outlined the existence of two chemotypes of *U. tomentosa*, the roots of which contain alkaloids with different and antagonistic effects (Reinhard, 1999). In addition, while Keplinger and associates attribute cat's claw's properties to its indole alkaloids, other industry-backed research suggests that other compounds, including carboxy alkyl esters, may also be involved (Kerry Hughes, pers comm, 19 November 1999).

While root and, more commonly, stalk bark have been the most common locally utilized plant parts, many medicinal recipes use leaves and whole stems, too. The commercial market for *Uncaria* is almost entirely based on stem bark, even though many of the evaluations of pharmacological activity have been conducted with root-bark extracts. It is widely believed that there is a greater demand for *U. tomentosa* and that the US imports mostly *U. tomentosa*, while the European market favours *U. guianensis* (eg Duke and Vásquez, 1994). Some industry analysts have questioned both of these statements, indicating that the latter species is already playing an important role in satisfying the international, including US, demand for cat's claw (Kerry Hughes, pers comm, 16 November 1999). In any event, there are very likely additional, as yet undeveloped, markets for other plant parts and/or for *U. guianensis*.

Locally, *Uncaria* is most commonly commercialized as chopped, shredded or ground bark, powdered leaves, or as a beverage made with the bark steeped in spirits. Local applications involve both internal and external treatments, using decoction of the stems, bark roots or leaves or an infusion of leaves. The powdered bark or leaves are also used in some external applications. Nationally and internationally, uña de gato is commercialized as milled bark, tea bags from pulverized bark, extracts and tinctures, capsules, pills and creams. In Europe and the US a number of techniques is also used to enhance or standardize alkaloid content or activity, such as removing phenolic tannins and standardizing alkaloid content. In addition to its medicinal use, there is local commercial demand for the liana in Peru as a raw material for furniture manufacturers (Hughes and Worth, 1999).

Certification potential

A number of factors favour a certification programme for *Uncaria*:

- *Uncaria* has a significant international market, some of which is sensitive to social and ecological issues. The publicity and high profile of this medicinal, together with its association with tropical forests, would all help to encourage certification as a marketing strategy in the US and Europe. Moreover, many manufacturers are concerned about the viability, reliability and quality of supplies, issues that certification could address.

- There are a number of biological and ecological features that render *Uncaria* amenable to management. It is a heliophyte, rapidly growing, easily propagated and a common species, associated with natural and anthropomorphic disturbances.

- Uña de gato is ideally suited to the swidden cultivation systems practised by Amazonian farmers, who are currently also the principal harvesters of this forest product. Uña de gato could serve as an additional resource to increase the value of such forests and promote their important role in biodiversity conservation.

- The fact that most harvesters of the bark are local inhabitants would also favour a certification programme, given their extensive background knowledge and vested interest in the sustainability of the resources in the region.

On the other hand, the following limitations and difficulties confront a certification programme:

- There is a lack of ecological baseline data to develop suitable guidelines, particularly for mature forests (see below).

- Future international demand, upon which economic and management expectations are largely based, is uncertain. Important factors that may determine the direction and characteristics of the market include results of pharmacological and clinical testing of such experimental technology as tissue culture, and national and international legislation.

- Supply levels are also uncertain. As de Jong et al (2000) point out, cultivation of cat's claw could lead to overproduction and a decrease in prices. Other countries are now embarking on cat's claw production and marketing, and this may also lead to an increase in supply.

- Like legislative measures, certification initiatives may inadvertently help strong economic and political actors to wrestle control of cat's claw production away from local stakeholders, ultimately undermining their purpose. Certification efforts need to be established with a clear understanding of the social, political and economic ramifications of external interventions.

- Carrasco (1996, cited in de Jong et al, 1999) estimates that for collectors it is more profitable to work for intermediaries than to collect independently. The role of intermediaries and the legal protocols that regulate extraction of forest products need to be incorporated and assessed in a certification programme.

- The two species of *Uncaria* have different characteristics in terms of their ecology, management, pharmacology and market potential. *U. tomentosa* is clearly in an advantageous position and is presumably under much greater pressure from harvesting.

- Ecotypic, genotypic and seasonal variability in chemical composition complicate the selection, management and quality standardization of the species, particularly among natural populations. The identification of two chemotypes of *U. tomentosa* with quite different pharmacological properties is particularly significant, as are variations in chemical composition between different tissues, and between the same tissues at different stages of development. Chemical variations need to be understood and integrated into the management of the species.

Certification could, and perhaps even should, encompass a number of legislative, political, socio-economic, ecological, marketing, sourcing and quality aspects relating to cat's claw production.

Marketing, product development and quality control

A certification programme could be tied to a programme that develops new markets for *Uncaria*. Leaves of *U. tomentosa* appear to be quite rich in certain alkaloids, for example. A market for *Uncaria* leaves would open many alternative possibilities for managing *Uncaria* as a sustainable NTFP and integrating it within agroforestry systems. Production of leaves, and particularly young leaves, creates management options, limitations and requirements that are very different to the production of inner bark. While this makes management and certification a more complex process, it also increases the number of possibilities and options, and thus constitutes an asset as well as a problem.

Factors relating to variability in chemical composition are particularly important for the marketing of raw plant material. A manufacturer of extracts seeking to target certain compounds can utilize tissues with lower levels of compounds as long as these are easier or more economical to obtain.

Aside from the importance of product development, market expansion and quality control – factors that ultimately shape demand – there are also important factors that determine supply and its economic impact. Increases in supply relative to demand could lead to price decreases, which would have detrimental effects on the industry as a whole, particularly for local stakeholders and low-level intermediaries whose profit margins are already small. Such increases in supply could be effected through an increase in the number of producers, nationally and internationally, and in the increased production of cat's claw following cultivation and reforestation (de Jong et al, 2000).

Legislative and ethical issues

Another important issue concerns the question of intellectual property rights (IPRs). Patents for oxindole alkaloids of *U. tomentosa* were filed in the US during 1989 and 1994 (Blumenthal, 1995). There is at least one other patent involving a standardized extract with high levels of carboxyl alkyl esters (Hughes and Worth, 1999). Some of the researchers who filed patents for *Uncaria tomentosa* have explicitly acknowledged the contribution of Asháninka medical specialists in these discoveries (Keplinger et al, 1999).[6] Even though the patents apply to the extraction process, as opposed to the substances themselves, it is interesting that the *Uncaria* patents have not drawn the public attention surrounding other similar patents, such as that of *Croton* (Chapter 13). Questions of compensation and controversies relating to commercialization of uña de gato are very likely to emerge in the future, particularly if a producer seeks

certification as a marketing tool to reach socially and ecologically aware consumers. The IPR issue will be facilitated by ongoing legislative initiatives in countries who signed the Cartagena agreements and the Convention on Biological Diversity (CBD).

As acts of intervention, legislative and certification initiatives raise troubling questions regarding their effects on power relations between different stakeholders. As Miguel Pinedo-Vásquez has noted (pers comm, May 1999), 'uña de gato is a political, and not only a commercial or pharmacological resource', a factor that needs to be carefully taken into account, particularly given the historical precedents involving other commercial non-timber forest products.

Ecological issues

A certification programme would need to differentiate between different types of managed environments, as each raises different issues:

Mature or closed forest

These environments are important elements of a certification programme given that they are the primary targets for ongoing commercial harvest operations. Closed forests support older *Uncaria* plants, which have the largest amount of bark. Equally important, mature forests are important repositories of *Uncaria* germplasm, the conservation of which would have important implications for propagating *Uncaria* in more intensely managed environments.

Following the model established among Yanesha and Asháninka communities, a certification programme might establish criteria to limit the type and intensity of use pressure. The effectiveness and viability of different management practices, such as harvesting the lianas at heights of 1m or eliminating competing vines, need to be evaluated and modified accordingly. Lack of long-term ecological data supporting the merit of these management regimes is problematic. Propagating and managing *Uncaria* in closed forest are technically complex activities.

Secondary forests and fallows

Uncaria has a very high, and unfortunately rather unrealized, potential for management in secondary forests. Firstly, secondary vegetation does not present the technical challenges of closed mature forest as far as propagating *Uncaria* is concerned. Secondly, productivity is much higher than in closed forests. Thirdly, many local farmers already have sophisticated and flexible management systems for fallows, into which *Uncaria* could easily be integrated. The growth period of six to ten years for *Uncaria* is quite compatible with the fallow periods used by farmers in many regions. Cultivation of *Uncaria* in secondary forests and the integration of such practices into traditional swidden fallow management practices seem to be the most promising options for the medium- to long-term management of this medicinal.

Swiddens and cultivated fields

Intensive cultivation of *Uncaria* appears problematic for many different reasons, most of which have already been discussed: technical problems in obtaining bark tissue, pest problems and unpredictable markets in relation to labour investment all require evaluation.

Notes

1   In addition to referring to two species of *Uncaria*, the name uña de gato is also used in different parts of Latin America for at least 20 taxonomically and often ethnobotanically unrelated plants, including *Macfadyena*, *Caesalpinia*, *Bytneria*, *Mimosa*, *Piptadenia* and *Zanthoxylum* (Albán, 1996), from a total of 12 different plant families (Duke, 1994). This creates additional sourcing and quality problems, especially for uña de gato sold in local markets in Latin America.
2   According to one source, however, *U. guianensis* grows up to 1000m, while *U. tomentosa* only reaches 500m (Quevedo, 1995).
3   The term 'destructive harvesting' needs to be qualified since some individuals are able to recover as long as the base and roots are left largely intact.
4   See Quevedo (1995) for guidelines on propagating *Uncaria* by seed.
5   An alternative or parallel version offered by descendents of the Schuler family is that Schuler was also treated by an Asháninka shaman with *Uncaria*. Cabieses (undated) suggests this version seems to weaken Brell's contribution, given Schuler's vested economic interests in *Uncaria*. This raises an important point – namely, that knowledge of these commodities, whether historical or pharmacological, is frequently produced by actors with vested financial interests, raising potential conflicts of interest.
6   Keplinger et al (1999, p31) not only acknowledge the ethnobotanical importance of *Uncaria* among the Asháninka, but also indicate that their specialists are able to distinguish between the two chemotypes, suggesting that the Asháninka have a body of highly specialized technical knowledge of the species.

Chapter 9

Breu resin (*Protium* spp.)

Campbell Plowden

Introduction

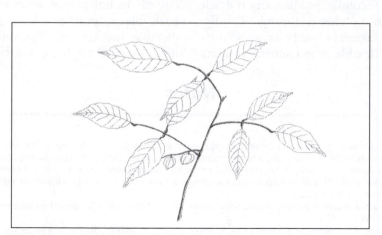

Illustration by Antônio Valente da Silva

*Breu (*Protium *spp.)*

The tropical plant family Burseraceae has several genera and hundreds of species whose bark contains resin-producing cells. These resins exude from the tree naturally or in response to various types of wounds. In some species of the genus *Protium*, insect attack provokes resin flow that subsequently accumulates and dries on the tree's trunk. Indigenous people collect and use such exuded lumps of breu resins for a variety of purposes. There is a fairly robust local market for various breu resins as a commercial wooden-boat caulking material, incense and folk medicine.

Ecology

The family Burseraceae is pan-tropical, but most species are found in the neo-tropics. The family has characteristic pinnately compound leaves, which are often aromatic. The three main genera that produce harvestable resins in the neo-tropics include *Protium, Tetragastris* and *Trattinnickia*. Gentry (1993) provides more detailed taxonomic descriptions of these groups. Balée (1994) found 20 species from these genera in his study areas in the eastern Brazilian Amazon. In a study area in the Tembé Indian Reserve, our research team found that in relatively undisturbed forest areas, the combined density of species that produce harvestable resin reaches ten trees (>10 centimetres' (cm) diameter at breast height – dbh) per hectare; but the average density at a larger scale is about one tree per hectare. Larger trees have a greater likelihood of having resin on them. The white (*P. heptaphyllum* and *Protium* spp.)

and breu amescla (*Trattinnickia* spp.) species are more common in drier *terra firme* forest, although the amescla type is inherently rare. The *sarara* (*Protium* spp.) group of breu species (according to Tembé Indian designation) is more common in wetter forest areas. The density of these harvestable species was much lower in areas that had been affected by a forest fire 18 years before.

Protium fruits are generally red with one or two seeds covered with a white succulent aril (Gentry, 1993). This scent-rich fruit is very attractive to a wide variety of forest wildlife, including agoutis, pacas, peccaries and land turtles (Balée, 1994). It may, therefore, be assumed that these animals all play some role in dispersing breu seeds throughout the forest. The popularity of its fruit to game animals makes breu one of the types of trees that Indians are fond of using as a stakeout point for night-time hunting.

Resin formation

The two major classes of breu are distin-guished by their different origins of resin formation. While many species in the Burseraceae family produce aromatic resins in their leaves, twigs and trunk, only a limited number produces enough resin to permit its collection. In some cases, the material exudes from a wound made by a tree fall or a man-made incision (Mors and Rizzini, 1966). In the eastern Brazilian Amazon, however, those species that are attacked by several types of bark-boring insects produce the largest quantities of breu resin.

In the case of 'white' and *sarara* breu, the principal resin-stimulating agent is a bark-boring beetle in the genus *Sternocoelus* (formerly *Coelosternus*), of the weevil (Curculionidae) family. It is not unusual for a few species of specialized insect pests to evolve ways of overcoming potent chemical defences in their plant hosts. But in spite of frequent attacks of the Sitka spruce by the white pine weevil, the spruce resin is still toxic to weevil eggs and larvae (Tomlin et al, 1996). The breu beetle has gone several steps farther. Not only has the weevil overcome any detrimental effects from chemicals contained in the resin, its larvae have apparently become dependent upon stimulation of resin chunks for development. An adult female beetle apparently deposits her eggs in the bark of a susceptible breu tree. Research so far indicates that these 'pests' do not attack very young breu trees. Beyond this age-size threshold, there is no close relationship between tree size and degree of infestation, although a few old and rotting trees do have large amounts of accumulated resin on their trunks.

As a larva develops, it uses its own sharp mandible to chew into the bark to tap the resin ducts. As the larva grows over the succeeding months, it digs deeper into the same hole and eventually bores new holes until many thin layers have formed a large lump of semi-hard resin around it. Inside, the larva has carved out a little cavern, which gives it room to move until it is ready to pupate. When this phase is complete, it bores its way out. Preliminary studies indicate that several hundred grams of resin accumulate during the developmental process for each single larva that reaches maturity. Such lumps are often found alone on a trunk; but multiple generations of larvae also leave their mark on a trunk, leading to the formation of breu lumps that weigh several kilograms. The resin lumps clearly provide protection for the larvae. It is not yet known if the larvae ingest the resin to receive chemical or nutritional benefits. Once the young adult weevils leave the resin lumps, their association with the breu trees seems to continue since large adults have been found in the bark of rotting sections of these trees.

There are several other invertebrates that profit from the resin-producing efforts of the breu beetle. At least one type of ant raises its larvae in the cavities of dried resin lumps vacated by the beetles. Several species of stingless bees collect fresh resin on their legs and carry it back to their nests, where it is presumably used as a construction material or as a source of scent (Plowden, unpublished data).

In *sarara* breu, the larvae from at least two species of flies are also often found in the resin. Since their hard parts in front are more like hooks than the sharp-edged mandibles of the beetles, it seems highly unlikely that the fly larvae contribute to resin flow. Another difference between fly and beetle larvae use of resin is that resin lumps with flies can have dozens of tiny juveniles, whereas a resin lump will rarely contain more than one beetle larva. Beetle-stimulated resin tends to retain its original white or off-white colour and dries to show a series of layers laid down over time. Fly-manipulated resin is very distinct since these larvae transform it into a brown, caramel-like consistency. When it hardens, a myriad of tiny tunnels is left behind.

Management

Indigenous people in the eastern Brazilian Amazon harvest breu for both personal and commercial purposes. If someone is going to use a small amount of breu around the village, it is usually harvested opportunistically. In other words, a man who encounters some resin on a breu tree while he is out in the forest hunting or collecting other forest products will simply pick a few chunks off a tree by hand or with a machete and wrap them in leaves for transport home. When someone is seeking to collect breu for sale, he will generally go to an area of forest farther from the village where breu has not been intensively harvested, bringing along a machete and a sturdy sack (usually the type used to carry sugar or farinha). He may spend several days devoted solely to gathering an entire sack full of breu that weighs 30 kilograms (kg). Since most trees yield well under 1kg of resin, filling a sack usually requires many hours of walking. If he is lucky, the breu collector will encounter a tree that has not been harvested for many years and is capable of yielding enough resin to fill an entire sack. Most resin is easily collected within 2 metres (m) of the ground. Occasionally, large chunks of resin form higher up on the trunk; these can often be dislodged with prodding from a long, sharpened pole. When the resin is brought back to the village, it is laid out on bags in the sun to dry. The 'drying' process is not so much a process of driving off water as driving off volatile chemicals. Depending upon how long it has been drying in the forest, the resin loses about 20 per cent of its initial weight after a week in the sun.

Use

Indigenous people and other Brazilians have used the resins of *Protium* and other Burseraceae genera for many centuries. The principal functional use is for caulking wooden boats. Indians use it for caulking both dugout canoes and motor launches. The resin is burned on torches as a direct source of illumination, and simmering chunks can start a wood or charcoal cooking fire. Many breu varieties are popular as incense in both churches and Indian shaman ceremonies. Indians from the Colombian Amazon have used 'white' breu resin to flavour coca powder. Breu resin is also used as a medicine for treating a variety of ailments, including external infections, skin parasites, nasal congestion, hernias and poor vision (Mors and Rizzini, 1966; Reitz, 1981; Plowman, 1984; van den Berg, 1984; Schultes and Raffauf, 1990; Balée, 1994; Boom, 1996).

The main commercial use of breu resin is for caulking wooden boats, including tugboats, launches and fishing boats. The dried breu is first heated up and sieved to remove dirt, wood and other plant material. The liquefied resin is then mixed with another oil, usually linseed or diesel. When cotton or other fibres have been wedged into the spaces between boards on the sides of the vessel, the breu mixture is pasted on top of it. This provides effective waterproofing of the craft as well as protection from attack by wood-boring parasites. Preparing a medium-sized boat consumes 20–40kg of breu resin, so quite a few tonnes of the material are likely traded each year. Since other synthetic materials are used for the same purpose, however, the price for breu is relatively low. Indians typically receive well under US$1 per kg for dried resin.

Beyond the use of this sticky balsam-type breu, boat caulkers also use an amber translucent material, which dries to a very brittle state. It is variously referred to as *breu amescla*, *breu americano*, *pes* and *jutaicica*. It has not yet been verified whether this material comes from one or more varieties of true breu trees (possibly *Trattinnickia burserifolia*) or is the hardened exudate of the jatobá (*Hymenea courbaril*) tree.

The chemistry of breu resins has only been sparsely studied (Schultes and Raffauf, 1990; Zoghbi et al, 1994). Its aromatic features, however, make it a natural candidate for commercial applications such as perfume. A plant chemist researching Amazonian plant's essential oils has begun to explore this potential more closely. If this work produces promising results, it is possible that a new market for breu resin could develop in the future.

Breu timber is used to a certain extent in civil construction and other applications, presumably because its high resin content gives it good resistance against various insects and pathogens. It does not command a high price, however, so pressure by the logging industry on the various breu species is only considered moderate (Reitz, 1981; Martini et al, 1994).

Certification potential

One would be tempted to assume that collecting a resin that has accumulated on the outside of a tree's bark poses no risk to the health of the target population, thus making the task of determining sustainability a relatively simple one. Attempting to evaluate the impact of resin harvesting on breu trees and the forest, however, may not be such a straightforward task.

In the case of *Protium* species, the amount of resin that can be harvested sustainably will depend upon:

- the susceptibility of the individual tree to attack by specific bark-boring beetles and flies;
- the amount of resin produced during the maturation of these organisms; and
- the rate of reinfestation by these organisms following resin harvest.

Learning more about these breu–insect interactions is fundamental to a better systematic management of breu harvest since our research demonstrates that experimental drilling is an ineffective means of stimulating appreciable flows of resin.

It is clear that different species of breu trees produce vastly different amounts of resin. It is not known whether this is because species such as 'white' breu have inherently greater resin-producing capacity or whether certain insects that attack them have simply been more successful in adapting to their defensive chemistry than other species. The closely related 'red' breu (*Protium decandrum*), for example, is apparently uninfested and produces no collectable resin. Within the main resin-producing species, there are undoubtedly genetic differences and possibly environmental site differences from tree to tree that make them more or less attractive to the resin-flow-inducing insects.

It appears to take at least eight months, and possibly a year, for a breu bark-boring beetle to develop within a resin lump on the side of a breu tree. Once the larva reaches the pupa stage, it stops boring into the trunk so that no more exudate is added onto its resinous cocoon. Some trees have only one resin lump; others have 50 or more such lumps at different stages of development. While it is not known whether beetles that emerge from resin lumps remain in the vicinity of their nursery tree, it does appear that already infested trees attract greater numbers of beetles than uninfested trees. Since standard resin harvesting removes all resin from a tree, the practice removes dried resin lumps that have been vacated by beetles, as well as lumps that are still expanding due to larval activity. Our experiments in the eastern Brazilian Amazon have shown that the rate of reinfestation of harvested trees is very uneven. It therefore seems worth investigating whether or not leaving some resin (and their developing larvae) on the tree might reduce the time required between harvesting events on particular trees.

Looking at harvesting impact from a broader perspective, one must also ask whether or not overly aggressive breu-resin harvesting would threaten populations of bark-boring beetles and other invertebrates that utilize the resin in various ways. In the case of the main species of beetle and fly, their progeny are killed in the process of resin harvest. With at least one other variety of ant, resin cavities are occupied for tending their young. Several types of stingless bees and a Reduviidae bug routinely gather fresh resin for their own purposes. While the breu trees might arguably benefit from resin harvesting by removal of at least two 'pest' species, it is not far-fetched to imagine that one or more of the creatures that use its 'pest'-induced resin play an important role as pollinators to the breu or some other tree in the forest. Clearly, too little is known about the ecology of breu to determine sustainable harvesting regimes needed for the purposes of certification. Although fully evaluating these relationships is beyond the scope of a conventional certification process, an ecological approach demands that these questions be considered.

Chapter 10
Titica vine (*Heteropsis* spp.)

Campbell Plowden

Introduction

Titica is a hemi-epiphytic vine from the genus *Heteropsis* (family Araceae) that grows in the Brazilian Amazon. This type of plant germinates on the forest floor and seedlings climb a host tree into the lower canopy. Once the stem is established, aerial roots descend, and eventually mature and spread out in the ground (Hoffman, 1997).

Indigenous people have traditionally used the strong and flexible roots of this vine as a lashing material in house construction and for weaving baskets and hats (Bown, 1988; Balée, 1994). In recent decades, large amounts of titica have been harvested in northern Brazil as a raw material for making wicker furniture. However, its commercial importance is

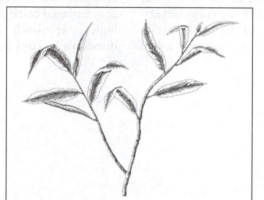

Illustration by Antônio Valente da Silva

Titica vine (Heteropsis *spp.*)

declining due to reduced supply (Troy and Harte, 1998), presumably a result of Amazonian deforestation and overharvesting.

Unfortunately, little is known about the regeneration of this vine. Many Amazonian indigenous groups believe that titica and the roots of related vines descend the trunk of a tree through the extension of the legs of certain dead ants (Lenko and Papavero, 1996). Learning more about this plant, developing effective management schemes and improving enforcement of forestry laws that govern its harvest are all necessary to preserve an important subsistence and economic resource for many forest peoples throughout the Amazon.

Ecology

The genus *Heteropsis* contains 12 or 13 species. All are herbaceous hemi-epiphytic vines that are found in South American tropical forests. The common names titica and junco refer primarily to the species *H. spruceana* Schott, *H. flexuosa* (Kunth) Bunting, *H. jenmani* Oliver (synonym for *H. flexuosa*) and *H. longispathacea* Engl that are used and sold by forest peoples in the Brazilian Amazon (Bown, 1988; Gentry, 1993; Balée, 1994; Troy and Harte, 1988). Plants have slender, rather woody stems and adventitious roots. Titica vines have alternate elliptic leaves that are sub-sessile on short petioles. The leaves have parallel secondary veins with a strong marginal collecting vein. Fertile plants contain a uniform spadix and a caducous spathe, which drops off during flowering (Bown, 1988; Gentry, 1993). The exposed spadix is apparently pollinated by bees and Hemipteran bugs. Berries hang at the end of stems. In at least one species (*H. integerrima*), these give off a fermenting smell common to other fruits consumed by bats (Bown, 1988).

Titica vines are found almost exclusively in intact primary forests. Their preferred habitat seems to be drier *terra firme* forest rather than areas subject to flooding. Titica does not appear to have preferred host trees. It is, however, apparently sensitive to high-light conditions. In a study area in the eastern Brazilian Amazon, titica was absent from forest patches that had burned almost 20 years before, even though it was common in adjacent unburned areas (Plowden, 2001).

Management

The most common method of harvesting titica roots is for the collector to pull hard on one root at a time until it breaks. Each root originates from the bottom of a branch off of the main vegetative stem, commonly called the *mae* (mother). The *mae* is attached to the trunk of the host tree anywhere from several metres above the ground on up to the full height of the tree. These roots bifurcate as they descend from their attachment point; but usually one side atrophies, leaving a hard node behind. When a root is pulled, it generally breaks off near one of these nodes. Pulling on a root will occasionally dislodge part of the *mae* from the trunk or pull it all the way down.

Collectors generally harvest all commercially viable titica roots from a host tree. Marketable roots must be mature and thick (minimum of about 0.4 millimetres (mm) in diameter). Mature roots have generally been rooted in the ground for a time. With roots of questionable age, indigenous collectors scrape their fingernail across the bark to test its toughness. Roots that are still green are not extracted since they are not considered strong enough for most weaving and construction applications. Likewise, dead roots are not collected because they also break too easily. Harvest of root sections with many closely spaced nodes is also avoided. While the number of harvestable stems per tree can be as high as 40, the average is about 3. Our study in eastern Amazonia indicates that about 28 per cent of roots were harvestable for commercial purposes (Plowden, 2001).

Extracting roots is hard, dirty work. When a vine breaks the long root whips down toward the collector, accompanied by a shower of grit, leaves, bugs and branches dislodged from the host tree. Once titica roots are pulled down, the collector breaks or cuts the root into sections that have no more than one node at an end. Nodes are eliminated since pieces with nodes in the middle are weaker, lack flexibility and, therefore, cannot be sold. The spacing of nodes throughout roots is quite variable. One section may have many nodes per metre (m) while another may have 6m free of them. Generally, saleable sections must be at least 1m long, although shorter pieces are often included in batches sold to dealers. Each collector carries his vine sections from one tree to the next, tying them together in small bundles every five trees or so. Collectors generally enter the forest in the morning and work until they have a bundle of marketable vines weighing 25 to 35 kilograms (kg). Collecting this quantity of vine involves substantial meandering through the forest, harvesting vines from 30 to 50 trees.

If they are gathering the product for personal use, vine collectors usually operate alone. Titica gathering for commercial purposes, however, is usually done in teams. A group of 6 to 30 people will set up a base camp near an area of forest that has not been harvested for at least several years (Troy and Harte, 1998; Plowden, 2001). Collecting trips generally last two to seven days. Each day, team members will split up and harvest vines in a different section of forest. While collectors usually work alone, sometimes two or three men will join efforts.

Studies of titica vines in the eastern Brazilian Amazon revealed that medium to lightly used sites had an average of 369 host trees per hectare with aerial roots reaching the ground. These vines had a range of 351 harvestable stems per hectare with a raw weight of 46kg. The actual amount of vines pulled by one harvester per unit area of forest is less, however, since he cruises the forest quite rapidly. Once the nodes and bark are removed and the stems have lost most of their water, only 20 per cent of the initial weight remains as saleable vines (Plowden, 2001).

When vines are brought back to a collector's camp or village, the next stage of processing involves removal of the bark (cortex) from the roots. Among Indian groups, both collectors and their families carry out this activity. Fingernails, knives and machetes are used to strip or scrape off the root bark to expose the inner whitish, woody stems. This is also hard work, taking much if not more time than the initial harvesting of the vines. Debarked vines are then retied in bundles of approximately 30kg each in preparation for transport to a buyer.

The principal questions concerning management of this species are the rate of regrowth under current harvesting techniques and whether or not alternative harvesting techniques can reduce the waiting time between successive harvests. Two experiments conducted in Brazil and Guyana showed that 17–33 per cent of mature titica roots started growing again 6–7 months after they were cut in simulated harvest, while 17–63 per cent of the roots had died. More favourable results were found in Guyana where an average of 25 per cent of a plant's roots were cut, compared to the Brazil study where 50–100 per cent of roots were cut (Hoffman, 1997; Plowden, 2001). Hoffman estimated that harvested plants that survived would take 20–50 years to grow back to harvestable condition.

Given its slow regrowth, there is a clear need to explore other means to enhance titica production. The major material used for wicker furniture manufacture in southern Brazil is vime (*Salix viminalis*), which is very successfully cultivated. Some effort has been devoted to cultivating titica, but no results have yet been published (Troy and Harte, 1998). Given the lack of scientific understanding of titica reproduction and the regional belief that titica roots are created via the extension of the legs of certain ants that die on the tree (Lenko and Papavero, 1996), concerted effort needs to be directed at this problem before titica can be cultivated or intensively managed.

Use

Indigenous and other forest peoples in the Amazon use sections of titica with the cortex intact as a lashing material in various contexts such as connecting poles, mending tools and attaching leaves to cross pieces in thatch roofs. Stripped vines are also used for making durable baskets, brooms and hats (Bown, 1988; Balée, 1994). In Amazonia, *Heteropsis* spp. form an indispensable part of rural peoples' livelihoods. Since there are few forest substitutes with the resilience and flexibility of titica, it is the preferred forest fibre utilized in almost every aspect of life. Thus, the most numerous consumers of titica are the millions of Amazonians who construct their homes, build their fences and carry their game, forest and agricultural produce home each day in containers made of titica. Tembé peoples also commonly use aerial roots of timbo-açu (*Evodianthus guiansis*), another hemi-epiphytic vine, as a lashing material in house construction and to construct crude baskets.

While it is widely used throughout Amazonia in the support of local livelihoods, the main commercial use of titica is for making wicker furniture. Half a dozen wicker furniture shops are located in one neighbourhood in the city of Belém. In the smallest shop, the owner does most of the work. The largest enterprise has 5 regular employees, but up to 60 people are hired on a temporary basis when a large job is landed. All stores have ready-made items for sale, but most of the businesses seem to depend upon custom orders. Clients typically provide a drawing or photo of a design they like, and the shop copies it for them.

The mainstay of these businesses is making vine furniture; but to varying extents all of the shops also make wooden or metal furniture where vines are either a marginal component or absent. Titica vine is the principal vine used in these enterprises and is the dominant material in many types of chairs and sofas. A small to medium chair consumes 3–4kg of titica, with a large one using 5–8kg. One kilogram of titica is used to make a large basket while leftover vines are used to make small baskets. Most of these items use whole titica and are commonly sold in their natural colour. This vine is also used in wrapping joints in furniture made with other principal materials. Titica can be split and soaked in caustic soda to make it extra pliable. It is also sometimes painted or stained (Plowden, unpublished data).

Most of the furniture-makers buy titica from three or four regular suppliers who come by with the material in hand, since deals are rarely brokered in advance. These suppliers come from both Pará and the adjoining state of Amapá. A few purchase material directly from Indian collectors. The smallest shops use

50–100kg of titica per month; the larger ones use 100–200kg per month. A few buy only a month's supply at a time, while others lay in a stock of 500–1000kg. Shop owners typically pay US$0.80 to US$3.00 per kilogram of debarked titica (Plowden, 2001). Dealers in cities outside of Belém, such as Fortaleza and São Paulo, pay up to US$5.00 per kilogram for this material (Troy and Harte, 1998).

Other types of wild-harvested vines used in these shops are graxama (*Aribadeae* spp.; also called guela de jacu from *várzea* forests), apui or cebolão (*Clusia grandiflora*), timbo-í (*Derris floribunda*), timbo-açu (*Evodianthus guiansis*), umbe, murure and berrega. Vime and rattan are cultivated plants purchased from Paraná and other parts of southern Brazil. Some bamboo is also bought from Goias and São Paulo (Troy and Harte, 1998; Plowden, unpublished data). Vime is a functionally similar material to titica, but the latter is used more commonly around Belém because vime costs about US$3 per kilogram to buy from the south.

Making vine furniture is a labour-intensive enterprise. A large chair generally takes an experienced person one and a half to two days to complete; a complicated piece may take three days. Since Brazilian workers are paid about two minimum salaries (US$12 per day), the cost inputs for a large chair are about US$10 for material and US$24 for labour, for a total of US$34. A regular large chair usually sells for US$100 to US$180. A fancy piece may fetch US$500 to US$1000, but such sales are rare. Belém dealers sell all or most of their products to local customers. Larger dealers do some business with buyers in São Paulo or outside Brazil (US, Japan, France and Belgium). One large Belém dealer lamented that business was not as good as it had been in the past. He used to have 20 to 25 regular employees and now only has 5. Because it takes several years to learn the craft well, the owner has discontinued training (Plowden, 2001).

Considering the high markup between the cost of the raw material and the finished product, it is tempting to contemplate the potential advantages for some collectors such as Indians to make and sell titica-based furniture themselves, since they possess a natural aptitude for working with this material. There are several challenges, however, that could make this a problematic venture. Firstly, it is much easier to transport large batches of straight vines than bulky furniture from remote areas that are frequently only accessible by small boats or poor roads. Secondly, the furniture dealers in Belém only buy vines – not finished product. The Indians would need to make a considerable investment in order to acquire a space suitable for displaying such materials for sale. Since much of the local business is based on custom orders, there would also need to be an effective means to link customers with artisans to discuss customer needs. Current communication systems based upon 'ham' radio communication do not favour this. One option for expanding the profitability of Indian sale of vines is to explore titica markets in more distant cities where furniture-making is prominent. It is possible that the higher prices paid for delivery of debarked vines to these cities would justify the extra cost and logistics of transporting them beyond Belém.

Certification potential

As is the case with many locally and regionally used species, a 'green seal' is an unknown and unnecessary concept to most consumers of titica. Lack of relevance to, or knowledge of, certification for the majority of producers and consumers is thus a fundamental flaw in considering certification for titica. However, in the case of titica, as with many non-timber forest products (NTFPs), the process leading to certification – that of identifying ecological requirements and sustainable management regimes – could be extremely beneficial.

This is especially the case due to the vulnerable status of titica. As ranching, logging, fire and colonization steadily degrade primary forest in the eastern Brazilian Amazon, indigenous areas are being increasingly invaded by non-Indian collectors for timber as well as forest products such as titica. In the case of titica depletion, environmental and social degradation are inextricably linked. Resource theft has a direct economic consequence on tribes in 'protected' areas since, in some regions, titica is a principal source of cash income.

In addition to considerable social and economic obstacles to certification, there exists a fundamental gap in knowledge regarding the ecology and management of *Heteropsis* spp. that needs to be filled in order to determine sustainable harvesting and management strategies. Key technical challenges regarding management of titica include:

- research and education concerning the effect of different harvesting regimes on individual plants;
- setting norms for how often individual plants or titica-rich areas can be harvested;
- definition and security of resource ownership in titica-rich areas;
- creating mechanisms to track the flow of vines from forest collectors to furniture-makers; and
- effective enforcement of laws that prohibit unauthorized collection of forest products from protected areas.

Given the rapid rate at which the social and ecological landscape has changed, management strategies have not yet been developed to counter the deleterious effects of fire, logging and overexploitation. As discussed above, current harvesting practices involve pulling down all commercially viable vines from a tree. However, vines may regenerate faster if some portion of a large vine is left to continue transporting the flow of water and nutrients from the ground to the upper vegetative parts of the vine. If this is the case, it will be important to disseminate this information to vine collectors. Likewise, information regarding the effect of different harvesting cycles on vine productivity in a given area should be made widely available to collectors.

Even if such information becomes available, however, it is unlikely that people who lack secure ownership and control over potential titica-harvesting areas will implement any management protocols that recommend more restrained harvest. This is especially true of collectors who invade indigenous areas in clandestine hit-and-run collecting trips. Even legitimate resource owners such as Indians, however, would be unlikely to modify their methods if they sense that what is not harvested today will be extracted by someone else tomorrow. Even among Indians, though, there is a need to regulate titica harvest, area by area. Reserves with intact forest may be large, but the areas of accessible forest away from navigable rivers or roads are limited. Even strong collectors can only carry 30kg bundles of vines so far. Harvesting in prime and accessible areas, therefore, should ideally be apportioned among villages on a sustainable and equitable basis.

Assuming best-practice management schemes could be implemented at the local level, there would be a need to track the flow of vines to the market. Tracking is important so that certifiable collecting operations and their buyers can be properly identified and compensated. In addition to management criteria, certification of communities must also include quality control over the products they sell. Dealers justifiably complain that vine sellers often try to increase the weight of their product by including unusable pieces of vines, rocks and other debris in the midst of their vine bundles (Troy and Harte, 1998; Plowden, unpublished data).

The Brazilian environmental agency responsible for enforcement of forestry laws, the Instituto Brasileiro do Meio Ambiente e dos Recursos Naturais Renováveis (IBAMA), requires that logging trucks carry documentation showing that their products came from an approved management area. While such documentation is subject to considerable fraud, it provides at least some measure of control against improper extraction. Little to no implementation of such laws occurs for NTFPs in Eastern Amazonia. In spite of repeated invasion of the Alto Rio Guamá Indigenous Reserve in the Eastern Amazon by non-Indian vine collectors, IBAMA has issued only one citation for illegal extraction of titica in the past several years.

Theoretically, certification could serve as a positive incentive for communities who control forest resources to manage titica harvests well. Vine resources will soon be exhausted, however, unless there is some effective means to curb the activities of harvesters who have no intention of being guided by any criteria other than the fastest possible harvest and sale of the vines. Three important steps to shifting the extraction of titica vine towards sustainability would be encouraging government authorities to conduct more stringent enforcement activities; recognizing the significant domestic economic benefit of titica to subsistence livelihoods; and educating the public about ecological and social concerns related to their purchase of wicker furniture.

Chapter 11

Amapá (*Parahancornia* spp. and *Brosimum* spp.)

Campbell Plowden

Introduction

There are two groups of Amazonian trees with non-elastic edible latex whose common name is amapá. One group includes several species in the family Apocynaceae. The most common species is *Parahancornia amapa*. Some eastern Amazonian indigenous groups also refer to the latex-producing tree *Couma guianensis*

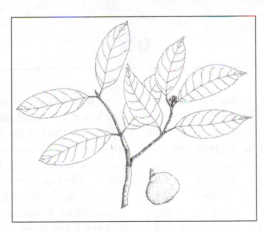

Illustration by Antônio Valente da Silva

*Amapá (*Parahancornia *spp.)*

(also Apocynaceae) as another variety of amapá. This chapter focuses on the latex of these trees, which is often called amapá amargosa. Two species in the genus *Brosimum* (family Moraceae), which produce a sweeter latex, are often called amapá doce (Mors and Rizzini, 1966).

The *Parahancornia* genus has eight species of trees native to tropical South America. The species whose latex has been collected for medicinal purposes by indigenous people in the Amazon region include *P. amapa*, *P. krukovii* and *P. fasciculata* (Schultes and Raffauf, 1990; Balée, 1994). In outdoor markets of Belém, the thick white latex is stored and sold in recycled glass bottles. Lacking additional botanical material such as leaves, flowers or fruit, it is not possible to identify the source of the latex to genus or species. However, it is widely claimed that *P. amapa* is the species most often commercialized in places such as the Ver-o-Peso public market in Belém, Brazil (van den Berg, 1984).

Ecology

Amapá trees are most commonly found on poor soils in seasonally flooded (*igapó*)-type forests, but they also occur in drier upland forests. Trees often reach heights of 30 metres (m) and can grow as high as 50m. Leaves are obovate-oblong; fruits are large, with a thick skin and two indehiscent mericarps. Monkeys and other animals that live in the forest canopy consume the fruits (Gentry, 1993; Morais et al, 1995a).

Like many Amazonian species of non-timber forest products (NTFPs) that are commonly used and sold, very little infor-mation has been quantified concerning amapá's ecology and associated harvest-ing practices. The only scientific papers published to date on the species concern the consumption and infection of fallen fruit by drosophilid flies and *Candida* yeast (Morais et al, 1995a; 1995b). While many members of the Apocynaceae family contain a great diversity of alkaloids (Goutarel, 1964; Raffauf, 1970), the chemistry of the *Parahancornia* genus remains unknown (Schultes and Raffauf, 1990).

Use

In spite of scant study, many Amazonians have used amapá latex for centuries and continue to swear by it as a potent tonic for weakness, to soothe respiratory dis-eases, as an anti-emetic, cicatrizant and poultice (Schultes and Raffauf, 1990; Balée, 1994). Among Indian tribes in east-ern Amazonia, the product is most often gathered and used by women (this is qual-ified by the fact that in the author's region it was collected and used by men). The most common method of harvest is cut-ting one or two diagonal furrows in the bark with a machete and then collecting the latex that drips out in a cup or other vessel. Indigenous women may drink the latex directly, but the bitter variety is often diluted with water or mixed into coffee. Both Tembé Indian women and Ver-o-Peso vendors warn against collect-ing the latex from fruiting trees during the dry season in July, since it is widely claimed to be poisonous at such times.

Management

A study of amapá production in the east-ern Amazon shows that regular tapping has different effects on the two species that produce the bitter latex. With amapá preta (black – *Couma guianensis*), the first cut produces the most latex: frequently 50 to 200 millilitres (ml) for an adult tree. Latex flow progressively declines with successive cuts, most often made above the first wound several days later. Production increases temporarily when a new series of cuts is made on the opposite side of the trunk. By contrast, latex flow for amapá branca and vermelha (white and red – *Parahancornia amapa*) is initially less than the black variety, but successive cuts appear to stimulate slightly higher latex flow. Short-term variation in rainfall does not affect latex production; but, thus far, this has only been examined during one rainy season. Contrary to Indian speculation, latex production over a six-week period did not appear to shift in relation to changing phases of the moon.

The most important variable affecting the economic viability of amapá appears to be the tree's density. The study area in the eastern Brazilian Amazon had an average density of three mature trees per hectare in undisturbed (or intact) forest and one tree per hectare in burned forest. At these densities, a pair of collectors can tap from 20 to 30 trees per day. A tapping regime of two visits to each tree per week can yield 2–3 litres of latex. Since the average price received by producers is approximately US$2 per litre, collection of amapá does not appear particularly lucrative. However, in certain areas of flooded forest, amapá trees are reportedly much more abundant. Therefore, commercial harvest of amapá would likely be more viable in such areas.

Outlook

Like copaíba (see Chapter 12), amapá is an example of a regionally and locally valuable non-timber forest species that is also highly valued and readily extracted by the timber industry (Martini et al, 1994). However, due to paltry logging fees currently offered in the region, an entire tree often yields less than US$2, hardly compensation for the loss of a valuable forest medicinal.

The cultural, social and medical importance of amapá to urban and rural Amazonians is not easily measured in dollars. Distant from any health clinic, lacking transportation and commonly infected with a wide range of chronic health ailments, local forest pharmaceuticals are often the only option to improve health. Because it is an important subsistence, trade and medicinal resource for many rural and urban Amazonians, efforts are needed to protect the various species of amapá trees from overharvesting. While amapá latex will not likely warrant certification on its own, this locally valued forest resource could be conserved if timber certification teams implement standards that specifically recognize and protect amapá populations.

Chapter 12

Copaíba (*Copaifera* spp.)

Campbell Plowden

Introduction

Among the wide range of non-timber forest products (NTFPs) that are routinely harvested in the Amazon region, few are as well known and as little understood as copaíba. Copaíba not only is the common name of the tree but also refers to oleoresin that flows in tiny vessels and sometimes accumulates in large cavities in the middle of this large tropical forest tree. Its medicinal value has long been recognized by indigenous societies of the region. Westerners, beginning with the first Portuguese who came to Brazil, were quick to learn that this material's potent chemicals could aid in the treatment of conditions as diverse as venereal disease, bronchitis and a whole host of inflammations.

In the early part of this century, demand for the product probably in-

Illustration by Antônio Valente da Silva

Copaíba (Copaifera *spp.*)

duced a reduction in copaíba populations in some areas because the most common harvesting method was to cut a large hole into the tree's heartwood to reach the oleoresin. Today most copaíba oil is obtained by drilling into the trunk and then plugging the hole for reharvest about one year later. It continues to be a very popular 'natural' medicine in Brazil and is exported to a limited extent as an ingredient in cosmetics. While the chemistry of its volatile oils has been documented, the mechanism that leads some trees to yield buckets full of oil and others to produce no more than a trickle remains a mystery. This unpredictability regarding collection of its precious liquid had led to popular lore that warns any would-be harvester to avoid looking up in the canopy of a tree before attempting to collect the oil. Scientists have yet to come up with any more academic recommendations for improving a harvester's chances of success.

Copaíba trees belong to the genus *Copaifera*. It is a member of the Caesalpinoideae sub-family of the Fabaceae (Leguminosae). The genus name is derived from a combination of the Tupi Indian word for the resin from the copaíba tree, *copai*, and the Latin verb *fero*, meaning 'to bear or produce' (Allen and Allen, 1981). There are at least 30 species in this genus in the neo-tropics and another four to five in Africa (Dwyer, 1951). Most species are found in wet tropical forests; a few are also found in drier *cerrado* areas. Some 16 species from South America are known to be oleoresin producers. The main commercialized species are *C. guianensis* Desf., *C. langsdorfii* Desf., *C. martii* Hayne, *C. multijuga* Hayne, *C. officinalis* L. and *C. reticulata* Ducke (Clay and Clement, 1993).

Depending upon the species, the tree can grow from 20 to 35 metres (m) in height. The leaves are simply pinnate with one to many pairs of leaflets that are more or less falcate, commonly glabrous, reticulate, frequently punctate, and short-petiolulate. The inflorescence is a terminal or sub-terminal panicle of multiflowered spikes. The flowers are small, apetalous and yellow or white. The legume is short and somewhat oblique. It has one large arillate seed.

Ecology

In South America, one or more varieties of copaíba are found in almost every tropical country. *C. langsdorfii* primarily occurs in woodland habitats of southern Brazil and northern Argentina. It may be found in climate zones classified as sub-tropical dry, tropical dry and wet forest zones. (Figliuolo et al, 1987; Duke and Cellier, 1993). Farther to the north, *C. officinalis* and *C. multijuga* likewise tolerate a variety of dry and wet conditions. *C. multijuga* can be found in *terra firme* (non-flooded rainforest), *várzea* (flooded forests), sandy margins near lakes and streams and even the *cerrado* (savanna) of central Brazil (Clay and Clement, 1993). It is most often found, however, on extremely nutrient-poor soils (Figliuolo et al, 1987). While sometimes found in flooded areas, *C. reticulata* does better in more upland forests on firm, preferably sandy, soils. Although some members of the Fabaceae are known for their ability to fix nitrogen through root nodules, *Copaifera* species apparently do not possess this capability, yet still persist in nutrient-poor soils (Figliuolo et al, 1987).

Like many rainforest trees, *Copaifera* tends to have rather sparse distribution even in areas where it is most common. Various published surveys in the Brazilian Amazon indicate natural abundances of *C. multijuga* that range from one to two trees per hectare in size classes that ranged from minimum diameters of 20 to 35 centimetres (cm) (Clay and Clement, 1993). In eastern Pará State, densities can be well below one tree per hectare over a large tract of forest; but clumped distribution does create small areas where three to four trees can be found in relative proximity (Plowden, unpublished data).

Adult trees do not tolerate shade, so survivors generally occupy the upper canopy and may be emergent (Clay and Clement, 1993; Duke and Cellier, 1993). Copaíba seedlings appear to perform best in forest gaps with abundant light

(Alencar, 1981; 1984; Plowden, unpublished data). The tree produces sprouts, but regeneration seems to occur primarily through production and dispersal of seeds. In the northern Amazon, flowering occurs during the local rainy season (usually between January and April) and fruiting between March and August (Clay and Clement, 1993; Plowden, unpublished data). Prominent seed dispersers appear to be toucans, who consume the pulpy aril and pass the seeds through unharmed (Plowden, unpublished data).

Formation and chemistry of the oleoresin

Phenolic compounds are often considered important defences against plant predators, but plants may produce other classes of chemicals that may also be important in protecting their leaf tissues (Figliuolo et al, 1987). Many species in *Copaifera* and the closely related genus *Hymenaea* produce a similar array of sesquiterpene hydrocarbons that can be found in their trunk, stems and leaves. The compounds are constituents of oleoresins that are synthesized in parenchyma cells that line elongated canals, rounded pockets or cysts. The resin is secreted into these spaces, which are formed by schizogeny and/or lysigeny. Schizogeny leads to the separation of cells, which increases their intercellular space to create thin capillaries that may extend from the bottom to the top of the trees. In *Copaifera*, these canals are located in concentric circles in the secondary wood (Langenheim, 1973).

In addition to its presence in these ducts, the oleoresin accumulates in lysigenous cavities formed by the breakdown of secretory cells. In the main trunk these cavities may enlarge to the point where they can contain several litres of oleoresin. Pockets of resin are also found in the pith of young stems, bark and parenchyma cells of leaves and flower buds (Youngken, 1943; Osol and Farrar, 1947; Poucher, 1950; Langenheim, 1973). The oleoresin consists of large but varying amounts of volatile oils that are primarily composed of sesquiterpene hydrocarbons, resinous substances and small quantities of acids.

Impact of land-use change

As with most rainforest trees, deforestation has a heavy impact on copaíba trees. While it is a light-loving tree, it does not regenerate as rapidly as typical pioneer species. In areas where forest fires have burned but not killed the tree, one can see fully leafed and seed-producing trees that nonetheless no longer yield oil from the trunk because fire damage has permitted the destruction of the heartwood by termites and various pathogens (Plowden, unpublished data).

Apart from escalating deforestation, there is also considerable pressure on the species from the logging industry. The timber has heavy wood with a grain and texture similar to cedar (the Latin American variety *Cedrella odorata*, Meliaceae). Like the oil, the wood emits the odour of coumarin when cut. The wood of the major oleoresin-producing species is fairly similar with some timber being heavier than others. The timber is processed for both plywood and sawnwood to be used in carpentry and construction (Le Cointe, 1947; Duke and Vásquez, 1994).

Heavier types of *Copaifera* wood may be rough cut into railway sleepers. The lighter woods may be peeled to make medium-quality veneer; heavier woods may be sliced to make higher-quality veneer sheets. Most of the timber is consumed domestically. A negligible amount of sawnwood is exported, and only a small amount of peeled veneers are sold abroad. The International Tropical Timber Organization (ITTO), however, included copaíba in its *Tropical Timber Atlas of Latin America* (Chichignoud et al, 1990) and a collection of brochures on lesser-known species. ITTO's publications add to efforts of the past that have attempted to boost the foreign market for this and other tropical timber species (eg Record and Mell, 1924; Le Cointe, 1947; Chichignoud et al, 1990; Clay and Clement, 1993).

A serious drawback to increased commercialization of copaíba and other low-density species is that logging in the Amazon Basin is virtually unregulated. The most highly sought-after species are simply extracted until no more can be found, with no regard to population densities or regeneration rates. One study examining the vulnerability of individual tree species to logging based on their ecological characteristics found the most heavily harvested *Copaifera* species in Pará (*C. reticulata*) to be moderately vulnerable (Martini et al, 1994).

Apart from commercial logging, copaíba trees are also lost in the wake of creating farm and pastureland from primary forest. This occurs with colonist as well as indigenous populations. Even though the copaíba trees may be valued as a source of medicinal oil, trees are either felled intentionally or unguarded against fires used in the process of creating fields to grow manioc and other crops.

Management

The oleoresin in copaíba generally stays inside the tree. However, oil occasionally collects in large cavities where sufficient pressure can build and cause the oil to burst out of the trunk. While it may be inferred that the first people to use copaíba took advantage of naturally exuded oil, all accounts of its use reference two principal types of methods to harvest the oleoresin. The first technique generally involves chopping a large hole near the base of the tree with an axe. This creates a drainage reservoir into which the oleoresin ducts will eventually drain their fluid (Duke and Cellier, 1993; Furnemore, 1926). This method has the advantage of yielding a relatively large amount of resin

at one time – perhaps from 45 to 53 litres (Duke and Cellier, 1993; Poucher, 1950). While several harvests are possible with this technique, it commonly has the effect of killing the tree (Pittier, 1926). Even where trees survive axe harvesting, such trees tend to become hollow following infestation by termites and pathogens, which renders them unusable for future oleoresin harvests.

The second, more common, method of harvesting copaíba is to drill a hole towards the centre of the tree and then use a bottle, can or other container to collect the resin that flows out. Once a session of tapping is concluded, the hole is tightly plugged with a piece of wood. Duke and

Cellier (1993) report that trees yield the most oleoresin if tapped during the dry season and may be tapped more than once during this time.

Harvesters sometimes bore two holes into the trunk – one less than 1m above the ground and the second hole placed 3–7m higher. In place of a plug, a bamboo tube with a stopcock may be driven into the lower hole (Duke and Cellier, 1993). Another alternative method of harvesting the resin involves use of a pump (Pittier, 1926). A complement to the drilling technique involves breaking off a large branch from the tree. This seems to break the pressure tension of the oleoresin in canals, allowing gravity to carry the resin down toward the collection point.

In parts of Brazil, the prime season for harvesting oleoresin from *C. officinalis* is between July and November. If a tree has not been tapped for several years, the initial copaíba gathered is thin and clear. If it is retapped in the same season, subsequent oleoresin becomes thicker and yellowish. If the resin is not flowing, a fire is sometimes built at the base of the tree to make the oil flow more easily due to the higher temperature. In Venezuela, the dry summer season occurs between December and April. Here, the first liquid to emerge from *C. langsdorfii* is thick and dark, the second one is clearer, and the third is thin, red and translucent. It is not clear from this case, however, whether the author is referring to different consistencies of oil obtained during one round of tapping or a progression of types obtained over a season (Pittier, 1926).

A systematic study of oleoresin yield from *C. multijuga* was conducted by Alencar (1982) near Manaus, Brazil (Clay and Clement, 1993). In this case, two holes were drilled on opposite sides of a tree. The oleoresin was collected at different intervals and during different seasons to quantify these variables. Many trees did not yield any oil during the first collection, and very few produced more than a few litres. By the time of the fifth collection, the yield had dropped to a low average of 34 millilitres (ml) per tree. These results may be modest because they were obtained from younger trees planted in dense concentration in an experimental plantation. A study of some 50 older copaíba trees of three different species in eastern Pará State, however, had similarly poor results, with the most prolific tree yielding 1 or 2 litres per year, but most tapped trees producing little or no oil (Plowden, unpublished data).

It seems possible that *C. reticulata* is a more prolific oleoresin producer either due to its nature or growing conditions, since Duke (1986) reports that an average tree yields 17 to 18 kilograms (kg) per year. It is assumed this yield is associated with tapping a tree. Assuming that 4 litres of copaíba weighs approximately 3.5kg (based on 0.9 specific gravity at 30° Celsius), a rough calculation would indicate that a one-time harvest of 45–53 litres from a good tree using the hole-chopping methods would yield 40–47kg of oleoresin.

Uncertainty surrounding the harvesting of copaíba oil has led to a variety of forest peoples' beliefs connected with the practice. The most common edict is that a harvester should not look up into the canopy before drilling or chopping into a tree. If he does, the oil will supposedly be sucked up into the canopy. The second stipulation is that a harvester (presumably a man) should not have sexual relations with his wife for several days before setting out to collect copaíba oil. Local lore also suggests that oil will not leave the tree if a pregnant woman is present beneath it (Shanley et al, 1998). Presumed violations of these prohibitions is the most common explanation for a harvester's failure to obtain large quantities of oil.

Use

Given the chemical potency of the exudate from copaíba trees throughout the Amazon, it is not surprising that indigenous peoples of the region were the first people to discover its value as a medicine. Medicinal uses have been noted for the Puinaves and the Makunas of the Vaupés (Schultes and Raffauf, 1990). As mentioned earlier, the prefix of the name *Copaifera* was derived from the Tupi Indian word *copai* for the tree's resin (Allen and Allen, 1981). Beyond medicinal use, native peoples also rubbed the oil on their bodies and hair (Record and Mell, 1924).

The first Western record of trees yielding copaíba comes from a report written by Petrus Martys to Pope Leo X, published in 1534, where they are referred to as *copei*. A Portuguese monk writing about the natural products of Brazil in 1625 mentioned a drug called *cupayba*. A tree yielding the substance was first described and illustrated in 1648. The London Pharmacopoeia listed the drug in 1677, and it was included in the United States Pharmacopoeia during 1820–1940, and then admitted to the National Formulary (Youngken, 1943).

As the value of the commodity grew in foreign markets, Brazil and Venezuela became the major exporters. Particular varieties of the oleoresin took on the names of the ports from which they originated. Some of these varieties, which had different ranges of volatile oil content, specific gravity, optical rotation and refractive indices, could be reasonably linked to the product from particular species.

Early data on production in Brazil is not currently available, but one report cited that prior to 1883, an average of 15,400kg of copaíba was exported from Venezuela per year. Trade disruptions associated with World War I may have reduced exports from this country to around 10,000kg per year (Pittier, 1926). However, Furnemore (1926) reported that copaíba exports to the US from Maracaibo alone were 28,122 pounds (lbs) (12,783kg) in 1919 and 50,154lbs (22,797kg) in 1920. During the years preceding the beginning of World War II, US imports of copaíba rose considerably. Between 1938 and 1940, the US annually bought an average of 204,130lbs (92,787kg) of copaíba worth some US$33,409 per year (with the price increasing from US$0.07 per kilogram to US$0.08 per kilogram during the period; Duke and Cellier, 1993). By 1945, the US import of copaíba from South America had dropped to 145,412lbs (Osol and Farrar, 1947).

In more recent times, combined US imports of all natural 'balsams' (including copaíba, Peru and tolu) were about 250,000kg, worth US$1.5 million in 1984 (average price of US$6 per kilogram). The amount imported dropped to just over 100,000kg in 1990, but the average price had risen to almost US$17 per kilogram. Of the three major 'balsams', copaíba's price was the lowest at US$5.50 per kilogram (Duke, pers comm, 1999). Although the term balsam is often used in reference to copaíba oil, it should be noted that this oleoresin does not strictly fit the chemical definition of a balsam.

If the lowest point of combined production in Brazil and Venezuela was 20,000kg of copaíba per year, a rough estimate would indicate that either 500 trees were cut open or 1200 trees were tapped to produce this amount. During the highest known production years, circa 1938, it is possible that some 5000 trees were axe harvested or 12,000 trees were tapped each year to meet the demand for copaíba exports to the US. Clearly, prevalent use of the chopping method could take a drastic toll on the population of copaíba trees. Pires (1993), a Brazilian anthropologist, discussed a mid-century research report indicating that the destructive axe harvesting of copaíba oil had led to a reduction of these trees in various parts of the Amazon.

Before its use in cosmetics and various industrial products, copaíba was used primarily as a medicine in both internal and external applications. Copaíba was traditionally used in the Amazon region and abroad as a cicatrizant, applied to sores and used in treating psoriasis and chronic gonorrhoea (Uphof, 1968; Schultes and Raffauf, 1990). Other external uses of the oil are on wounds as an anti-inflammatory and on sores caused by herpes. Internal uses include treatment for a variety of ailments involving mucous membranes, such as sore throats, respiratory tract disorders, ulcers and various conditions of the genito-urinary tract (including gonorrhoea, leucorrhoea, syphilis and urinary incontinence). It is also used as an anti-rheumatic, antiseptic, anti-bacterial, diuretic, expectorant, hypotensive agent, laxative, purgative, vermifuge and vulnerary (Youngken, 1943; Berg, 1982; Duke, 1986; Basile et al, 1988; Duke and Vásquez, 1994; Viera, 1992).

The potential value of copaíba as a medicine stimulated its use in Europe several centuries ago for treating chronic cystitis and bronchitis. It was also used in treating haemorrhoids and chronic diarrhoea (Leung, 1980). Both *C. coriacea* and *C. multijuga* have all been noted for various medicinal properties. The species that are mentioned most consistently for

having the strongest effects in treating tough urinary tract, pulmonary and skin ailments, however, are *C. langsdorffii*, *C. officinalis* and *C. reticulata*. These trees produce oleoresins that are thicker than other *Copaifera* species and have a deep yellow or brownish colour, a disagreeable smell and an acrid, bitter taste (Le Cointe, 1947; Uphof, 1968; Clay and Clement, 1993). To cut the bitter taste in internal preparations, it is sometimes mixed with andiroba oil (from *Carapa guianensis* Aubl.), honey, santal oil and cubebs (Viera, 1992).

Even while the US was still importing considerable amounts of copaíba just after World War II, however, the efficacy of copaíba as a medicine was being questioned in some quarters. The 1947 edition of *The Dispensatory of the United States of America* (Osol and Farrar, 1947) cited a Norwegian literature survey and stated:

> '...the drug has no place in human therapy; in gonorrheal urethritis it has little or no curative effect, but its administration is associated with severe symptoms such as cutaneous eruptions, gastrointestinal attacks, and renal lesions. In excessive doses it may cause vomiting, painful purgation, strangury, bloody urine, and a general state of fever. Much more effective drugs are now available for whatever use has been made of copaiba.'

These views then came to typify the Western scientific view that copaíba oil lacked utility as a medicine and the post-war export market for it virtually disappeared. In 1987, however, a group of Brazilian researchers from the pharmacy department at the University of São Paulo conducted experiments with copaíba oleoresin and confirmed the folk medicine claim that it could be useful as an anti-inflammatory drug. They were conducting follow-up studies to see if the copalic acid or specific sesquiterpenes in the resin could be identified as the active anti-inflammatory agent (Basile et al, 1988). A study of medicinal plants in Surinam included a test of oleoresin from *C. guianensis* for its anti-microbial powers. Results indicated that the substance had some activity in combating the bacteria *Bacillus subtilis*. Today, copaíba oil is still commonly sold in folk medicine markets such as Ver-o-Peso in Belém. It is also sold in various commercial preparations such as gel caps and included in several Brazilian brands of 'natural' cough syrup. There is reportedly a small but growing market for the oil as a 'natural' medicine in Japan.

The range of products in which oleoresin of copaíba and its distilled oil have been used is quite extensive. While copaíba was first introduced to Europe as a medicine, its combination of essential oils and resinous compounds eventually made it useful in the preparation of various cosmetics, massage oils, lacquer, paints, varnishes and tracing paper (Youngken, 1943; Balsam and Sagarin, 1974; Leung, 1980; Duke, 1986).

The first category of cosmetic preparations includes soaps, detergents, creams, lotions, massage oils and perfumes. Copaíba acts as an odour fixative in scenting soaps. One author stated that its 'fresh, somewhat peppery odour blends well with geranium, cinnamon, clove, and cassia' (Poucher, 1950). Other favourable combinations are cedar wood oil and ionones. While reportedly used less extensively in perfumery, copaíba oil may be added to perfumes as a fixative and/or a fragrance component. The resin portion of copaíba has the primary fixative role in perfumes, while the essential oils provide the scent (Poucher, 1950; Leung, 1980;

Duke, 1986). Both copaíba oleoresin (referred to in the trade as copaíba balsam) and copaíba oil are currently being used by drug and cosmetic manufacturers; 11 different companies were listed as supplying these products in a 1992 industry trade journal directory of raw materials. All of these companies were located in New Jersey or the New York City metropolitan area (DCI, 1992).

Copals, rosin, damars and spirit-soluble resins are four types of natural resins produced in trees that are important in the paint and varnish industry. It is tempting to infer that copal and copai (the root of *Copaifera*) have the same origin since both words are attributed to New World indigenous names for a resin that exudes from a tree. The apparent similarity may be a coincidence, however, since copal was supposedly derived from a group in Mexico, while copai was a South American indigenous word (Allen and Allen, 1981).

While the resin and wood from copaíba can easily be burned as a simple source of fuel in fires, one of the most intriguing uses of the oleoresin is as an alternative fuel source in diesel engines. Various reports indicate that the liquid can be poured directly into the fuel tank of a diesel-powered car, and the vehicle will run normally with a bluish exhaust smoke being the only noticeable difference (Duke, 1986; Clay and Clement, 1993).

Experimental plantations were established in Brazil with *C. multijuga* to see if placing two taps in the trees could increase the yield of oleoresin. It was hoped that an acre (0.4 hectares) of 100 mature trees could produce 25 barrels of fuel per year (Maugh, 1979). However, modest yields of the oleoresin from these trials (Alencar, 1982) hold little promise that a plantation strategy will produce a viable alternative energy source (Clay and Clement, 1993). Recent studies in Acre,

Brazil, demonstrate highly variable production from less than 1 litre to over 30 litres per tree, with an average of 4 litres per tree, with one out of four tress productive (Leite et al, 2002).

Certification potential

For the purpose of conserving a valuable, low-density mature forest species with wide local and regional application, as well as international sales, certification could play a role. In timber certification assessments, it would be a species for teams to identify as vulnerable to overharvest and as having an economic worth for its oil that supersedes its timber value. However, in terms of certifying the oil, local consumers have little to no interest in how, or from where, copaíba is sourced; rather, they care most about whether it is pure and unadulterated. Therefore, issues that would need to be addressed regarding certification are its relevance to consumers, the forest of origin, the method of harvest and the quality of the product.

The first question to be answered regarding the source of the oil would be whether or not it was obtained from trees that are still part of a forest. In theory, the species could be managed in natural stands or in plantations for oil production until economics dictated it was appropriate to fell the tree for its timber. In current practice, however, such integration does not occur. It is rare that the person or group harvesting oil from copaíba trees is also the party responsible for timber harvesting. Therefore, unless the logging operation responsible for cutting copaíba trees is itself well enough managed to be certified, it seems inappropriate to consider that oil obtained from trees in logging areas might be sustainably produced. One experimental copaíba tree plantation was created to produce enough oil as an alternative to fossil fuels in diesel engines. While production potential fell far short of the amounts needed to justify investment in the plantations for energy purposes, an increase in demand for copaíba as a medicinal or cosmetic substance might make the endeavour viable. For the time being, however, copaíba certification should be limited to intact forest areas where control of the land rights are secure and the benefits of copaíba oil sale accrue to the owners. A further provision concerning land stewardship in an area where copaíba oil production is considered important is the protection of productive trees from fire. Moderate burns can lead to infestations that will seriously impair the tree's oil productive capacity.

Evaluation of oil harvesting methods will pose a dilemma. It is obvious that making one or two holes in a tree with a drill is much less destructive than chopping a large hole with an axe. It is also apparent, however, that the yield from drilling varies tremendously from tree to tree, species to species and perhaps area to area (Leite et al, 2002). Drilling trees may not produce enough oil for the operation to be financially viable. If a group of forest peoples are interested in maintaining a modest ongoing source of copaíba oil for their own use, however, restricting harvesting to drilling is a more sensible option. For commercial purposes, axe harvesting may be more lucrative in the short and long term if not too many trees are treated in this way. Given the natural low density of these trees, the potential to wipe out local populations in a short time is very high. If this method were used, the operation would need to be evaluated like a logging operation, since the risk of tree mortality in one harvesting event is so high. Even if a tree does not die, it is virtually certain that the tree will not produce any more harvestable oil. Use of techniques such as breaking off major branches to augment oil production should also be evaluated very critically, since this increases the risk of accelerating the onset of heartwood rot. The type and quality of plugs used in drill holes is also worthy of attention. Plugs that are not shaved carefully enough to fully fill tap holes, or which are made from a type of wood that rots within six months, allow for leakage and leave the tree more vulnerable to infestation by termites and pathogens.

Quality control of copaíba oil presents another certification challenge. Among the various species of oleoresin-producing trees, there is tremendous variety in the colour, viscosity and odour of copaíba oil. The material is routinely diluted when sold in folk markets. Even in packaged goods, the listing of particular species of copaíba is highly suspect. Most of the oil comes into the market via middlemen who travel around the Amazon buying small amounts from people living in the forest. It would take a lot of legwork to sort through these informal marketing channels to have any confidence in the type and purity of copaíba oil purchased. One cooperative based in Rondonia, Brazil, however, was able to carry out its harvesting and marketing of copaíba oil in an organized fashion, and some communities in Acre are forming links with industries to guarantee them a managed source for a quality product. With respect to foreign markets, the chemistry of the oil is paramount. One Canadian-based supplier to the cosmetics industry analyses samples of large lots prior to purchase. If a sample does not contain a minimum percentage of a particular sesquiterpene, sale is refused. Such testing may work for particular applications, but evaluating oil purity for medicinal purposes will require more thorough chemical screening.

It is possible that certification could provide some incentive to conserve *Copaifera* spp. in cases where production is targeted at international markets. It is unlikely, however, that domestic consumers would pay a premium for a sustainably harvested product. While axe harvesting of trees for the oleoresin is clearly unsustainable, little ecological or production information exists to indicate what level of sustainable harvesting is possible by tapping.

For industries that require a particular quality of oil, certification could play a role in standardizing supply. Among all consumers, there is justifiable concern in the marketplace about the quality of a chemically potent material taken internally. In these cases, certification could increase consumer confidence about the purity of copaíba oil for sale.

Direct certification of copaíba may be unrealistic because there is a paucity of ecological information needed to create guidelines for best management practices and little interest in certification by copaíba consumers or producers. The main value of certification for *Copaifera* spp. may not lie in its direct certification as an NTFP, but rather in the application of strict forestry certification guidelines that require logging concessions to become more knowledgeable and sensitive to locally valuable NTFPs. Copaíba provides a telling example of a species whose domestic, cultural and social capital far exceed its value as sawnwood.

Chapter 13

Sangre de drago (*Croton lechleri*)

Miguel N Alexiades[*]

Introduction

Sangre de drago – also known as sangre de dragón, sangre de grado or dragon's blood – are neo-tropical trees of the genus *Croton*, named after their striking red latex.[1] The use of sangre de drago to treat a wide range of health conditions is well established in much of tropical America. Users include not only the rural inhabitants who live and directly interact with the living resource, but also urban dwellers within and beyond the tropical forests where it grows. For many years, sangre de drago has been commercialized by an extensive, and until recently largely informal, network of suppliers and vendors. Until the

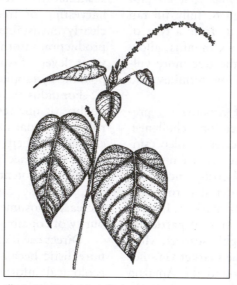

Illustration by Jamison Ervin

Sangre de drago (Croton lechleri)

recent emergence and widened popularity of uña de gato, sangre de drago was probably the most well known Amazonian medicinal in Latin American cities, particularly in Peru. Although not to the extent of uña de gato (see Chapter 8), sangre de drago has experienced a recent increase in media, public and government attention.

Like uña de gato, though at a much smaller scale, sangre de drago also became an international commodity during the 1990s. According to official records, *Croton* latex exports to the US in 1990 amounted to 320 kilograms (kg), increasing to about 1 tonne annually over the

* The author is very grateful to Beto Borges and to Steven King for providing copies of a multitude of unpublished reports and *Croton*-related literature, and for their helpful comments on earlier drafts of this chapter. Daniela Peluso helped with the compilation of literature. Kerry Hughes, Brian Smith and Manuel Ruiz provided additional, and very valuable, comments.

next two years. Between 1993 and 1996, annual exports varied between less than 1 tonne to over 4 tonnes. Exports tripled between 1996 and 1997, and doubled again in 1998, reaching over 26 tonnes that year. Beginning in 1996, other countries, including Chile, Italy, Lithuania, the Ukraine, Russia and Spain, started importing small amounts of latex – about 600kg up to 1998. Of these countries, Spain has been the main importer, accounting for about 500kg (INRENA, undated).

In the last decade, sangre de drago has undergone profound changes in terms of how it is perceived, produced, managed, commercialized and consumed. The publicity generated by Shaman Pharmaceuticals' involvement with *Croton* has undoubtedly helped to popularize sangre de drago and its use in source countries, and particularly in Peru, as well as internationally.

As with uña de gato, corporate, scientific, media and government interest in sangre de drago has led to its 'legitimization' among middle- and upper-class consumers. The upward social mobility of sangre de drago as a medicinal resource has been accompanied by a concomitant 'professionalization' in how it is managed as an ecological resource. Government and private initiatives involving foresters, extensionists and other professionals are, in effect, helping to shape how Amazonian swidden farmers interact with and manage *Croton* as an ecological and economic resource. This 'professionalization' of *Croton* can also be seen in the plant's role as commodity. Once commercialized in an unprocessed form and by agents operating within the informal economy, *Croton* latex is increasingly processed, packaged and distributed in more technologically sophisticated ways, with higher added values, and by actors who operate within formal economic structures.

Shaman Pharmaceuticals, ShamanBotanicals.com and *Croton*

The popularization of *Croton* and its emergence as an international commodity is clearly related to the well-publicized interest and activities of Shaman Pharmaceuticals and, more recently, ShamanBotanicals.com.[2] Shaman Pharmaceuticals, a US company launched in 1989, specializes in the development of drugs from tropical plants with a history of human use. A small company by industry standards, Shaman sought to demonstrate the effectiveness of the ethnobotanical route for drug development. Moreover, the company has sought to devise and implement a series of mechanisms whereby material benefits accrued from drug development can be shared with participating communities and local peoples (King and Tempesta, 1994).[3]

Shaman Pharmaceuticals filed a patent in 1992 for the production of SP-303, a large proanthocyanidin oligomer, obtained from the latex of *Croton lechleri* Müll. Arg.,[4] with demonstrated effect as an antidiarrhoeal and broad activity against a variety of DNA and RNA viruses. During that time, Shaman Pharmaceuticals began developing two drugs based on *Croton lechleri* latex, Provir™ and Virend™, used to treat diarrhoea and herpes, respectively. Clinical trials for Virend were subsequently suspended during Food and Drug Administration (FDA) level I and II trials in 1998 (*Wall Street Journal*, 2 February 1998), but Provir underwent level I, II and III clinical testing for the FDA.

Later that year, and following a request by the FDA for additional clinical trials, Shaman Pharmaceuticals reorganized, putting Provir and its drug development programmes on hold, and moving its assets and operations into the more loosely regulated nutritional supplement and herb industry. The privately held division ShamanBotanicals.com was launched in order to develop and market clinically tested botanical dietary and herbal supplements (Pollack, 1999). The first product released by Shaman-Botanicals.com, SB-Normal Stool™, entered the market in 1999. The product is being marketed for treatment of travellers' diarrhoea, HIV-associated diarrhoea (Koch et al, 1999) and, in the near future, for diarrhoea in infants and toddlers (Borges, pers comm, February 2000). Shaman also announced its hopes to release another *Croton*-based product, a salve to treat herpes, in the near future (Abate, 1999).

Shaman's influence over *Croton* extends well beyond its role as a patent owner, commercial buyer of latex and developer of *Croton*-derived pharmacodynamic commodities. Shaman has also been the primary force for developing baseline studies on *Croton*. As a result, the majority of ecological and market studies on *Croton* have either been conducted by Shaman associates or funded by Shaman (eg Aguirre et al, 1999; Ayala, 1993; Castanel et al, 1995; Catpo, 1998; Zak, 1991).[5] While leading to several important academic publications (eg Forero, 2000; Meza, 1999a) and a community manual (Meza et al, 1998), the bulk of these studies and data, particularly with regard to *Croton*'s management and ecology, remains unpublished and hence largely inaccessible.

In an attempt to guarantee the viability of the species and of its own supplies of latex, Shaman has also been actively encouraging the cultivation and management of *Croton* in parts of Colombia, Ecuador and Peru (Borges, pers comm, 21 December, 1999). These efforts have numerous socio-economic and ecological implications, both realized and anticipated.

Over the past ten years, Shaman has developed a series of contractual agreements with harvesters, either directly or, more commonly, through individuals, non-governmental organizations (NGOs) and private companies acting as intermediaries (eg Meza, 1998a; 1998c). In addition, a broad range of private and governmental agencies have been contacted in an attempt to identify latex sources and encourage interest in sangre de drago (eg Meza, 1998b; 1998d). Officials in most regions of the Peruvian Amazon, for example, received written notice and follow-up visits in the 1990s to communicate expected demands, and encourage harvesting and reforestation of *Croton* (eg Meza, 1998d; 1998e).[6] The response by some regional reforestation committees to include sangre de drago in the species distributed for reforestation, for example, may reflect these efforts (eg Oficina de Planificación Agraria, 1998).

Clearly, these activities have influenced the actions, perceptions and expectations of such stakeholder groups as swidden farmers, public officials, legislators and conservation groups with regard to *Croton*. Shaman's projected demands for latex generated a considerable amount of excitement and expectations – expectations which, following the company's reorganization, have not been met. In any event, Shaman has been, and will continue to be, a critical factor in shaping *Croton*'s role as an ecological, social and market resource, locally, regionally and even internationally.

Biology

The genus *Croton*, which includes about 800 tropical and temperate species, (Mabberley, 1987), is part of the large and diverse Euphorbiaceae family, a family that includes such economically important plants as manioc (*Manihot esculenta* Crantz.), rubber (*Hevea brasiliensis* (A Juss.) Muell. Arg.) and many poisonous or medicinal plants. Of the 800 species of *Croton*, only a handful have red latex, mostly in the section Cyclostigma of the genus. Clear-resin species of *Croton*, some of which are found growing together with the red latex-bearing species, are not referred to or used as sangre de drago.

There is as yet an undetermined number of red latex-bearing *Croton* species.[7] Species include *C. lechleri*, *C. palanostigma* Klotzsch, *C. perspeciosus* Croizat, *C. rimbachii* Croizat, *C. sampatik* Müll. Arg., and *C. erythrochilus* Müll. Arg. native to parts of Amazonia; *C. sordidus* Benth. and *C. gossypifolius* Vahl from the Andes; *C. urucurana* Baill. from Brazil and Paraguay; and *C. draco* Schltdl. and *C. xalapensis* Kunth from Mexico and Central America (Borges et al, 2000; Ubillas et al, 1994). *Croton lechleri* is by far the most common species in western South America, and is certainly the most widely used and studied. *C. urucurana*, on the other hand, is most common in Brazil (Brian Smith, pers comm, March 2000).

While *C. lechleri* is by far the most common sangre de drago species, at least at the lower and middle portions of its elevation range (Meza, 1999c; Meza and Pariona, 1999), there are other species that grow within and outside of the range of *C. lechleri* and that have been mistakenly identified as *C. lechleri* (Brian Smith, pers comm, February 2000). An ongoing

partial taxonomic revision of the genus *Croton* will hopefully address many of these problems (Smith, 1997, cited in Meza, 1999c; Webster, 1993).

Croton lechleri and related species are fast-growing pioneer trees, typically between 3 and 25 metres (m) tall, with diameters normally ranging between 15 to 55 centimetres (cm) and an estimated life cycle of 5 to 20 years (Forero et al, 2000).[8] The bark is smooth, about 1cm thick, with thicker barks reported for trees exposed to higher amounts of solar radiation (Meza, 1999b). A slash in the trunk produces a reddish latex, whose tone and viscosity varies with age and according to the degree of water stress suffered by the plant. The latex tends to be watery and reddish brown in younger trees, or right after periods of rain, becoming more viscous and deeper in colour as individuals age or at times of greater water shortage (Jordan, 1996). The leaves – quite variable in size – range from 5–25cm long and 3–19cm wide and are simple, alternate and heart shaped (Forero et al, 2000).

Minute unisexual cream-yellow flowers are arranged along a terminal bisexual inflorescence, 22–72cm long. The fruits, 7 millimetres (mm) long and 5mm wide, are schizocarps, which explode when mature, forcibly releasing three small seeds (Forero et al, 2000). In this way the seeds, about 3mm long (Jordan, 1996), are scattered around the tree. The seeds are also eaten by several species of birds, and these may be involved in their dispersal, as are gusts of wind and possibly streams and rivers as well (Meza, 1992a). Ant dispersal, suggested by the presence of seed elaiosomes and directly documented in *Croton priscus* Croizat (Passos and

Ferreira, 1996), is most likely an important dispersal method.

Germination takes anywhere between 8 to 22 days, most often 15 days (Aguirre et al, 1999; Meza et al, 1998). Natural regeneration is minimal in closed canopies and even in secondary forests with fairly closed canopies, where the ground is shaded. In these cases, reproduction is entirely contingent on seeds being dispersed to natural clearings or disturbed areas. Only in trees growing in open areas are seedlings found at the base of the tree (Meza, 1992a; 1995, p9).

Ecology

Habitat and distribution

Croton lechleri grows in the Western Amazonian forest region in low- and mid-elevation forests, between 100 to about 1800m, within temperature ranges of 18° Celsius (C) to 30° C and annual rainfall between 2000 and 4000mm, with a minimum of 1000mm (Forero et al, 2000). According to Meza (1999c), some related species, including *C. perspeciosus* and *C. rimbachii*, share the upper-elevation range of *C. lechleri*, extending beyond it to over 2000m. Others, such as *C. sampatik*, share the low- and mid-elevation range with *C. lechleri* (Meza, 1999c). There is some data to suggest that sangre de drago is more abundant at elevations between 700 and 1600m (Forero et al, 2000; Meza, 1991). Such correlations may be spurious to the extent that they reflect differences in the rates of anthropogenic disturbance. In this case, the reported lower densities in the lowlands could be due to the higher proportions of closed canopy forest in these areas, as opposed to the more deforested and intensely used piedmont region (Brian Smith, pers comm, February 2000). In contrast to South American sangre de drago species, Central American species appear to be more widely associated with moist tropical and sub-tropical forests, and those in Paraguay and southern Brazil with the drier *cerrado* vegetation.

Croton lechleri and related species are all pioneer, light-demanding species (King et al, 1997). *Croton* is commonly associated with non-flooded riparian habitats – in particular, with lower alluvial terraces – as well as with secondary vegetation in human-disturbed areas, both in *várzea* (floodplain) and *terra firme* (non-flooded land). Though present, *Croton* is found at much lower densities in mature forest and is associated with natural gaps (eg Pariona, 1997, cited in Meza, 1999c). Although the species cannot withstand waterlogged conditions, it grows in sandy riverbanks, in close association with *Tessaria*, *Gynerium* and *Cecropia*. In fallows and other disturbed areas, it is commonly associated with *Cecropia*, *Inga*, *Ochroma* and *Jacaranda*. Though growing in both sandy and clay soils, *Croton* prefers deeper, darker and moist, albeit well-drained, soils with a pH above 5.0 (Aguirre et al, 1999; Meza and Valencia, 1999). The preference for well-drained yet moist conditions may explain why *Croton* prefers areas with a slight inclination close to streams and rivers (Aguirre et al, 1999, p83).

Mycorrhizae are commonly associated with the *C. lechleri* root system, a fact that might partly explain *Croton*'s requirement for moist, well-aerated soils, conditions associated with mycorrhizal development. The fact that the same conditions favouring mycorrhizal development in *Croton* also favour high SP-303 levels in *Croton* latex may indicate a possible role for mycorrhizae in metabolic synthesis of biodynamic compounds (Meza and Calderón, 1999). No *Croton*-specific animal–plant interactions or specialized pollinators have been reported to date.

Croton's distribution tends to be patchy, both regionally and locally. For example, Meza (1992a; 1999c) found that in over half of visited sites from surveys in Alto Napo, Loreto and Puerto Bermudez, Peru, *Croton* was not present. Its absence has also been observed in other parts within its growing range in areas of Ecuador and Colombia (eg Aguirre et al, 1999, p122; Kircher and Meier, 1997). Meza (1999c) suggests that this localized distribution may reflect edaphic differences or may be due to dispersal patterns. Trees above 10cm in diameter (dbh) have been observed at densities ranging from less than 1 tree per hectare, as in parts of Madre de Dios, Peru, to over 190 trees per hectare, as in Napo, Ecuador (Catpo, 1998; Espinosa and Paspuel, 1993). Densities of 15 to 80 individuals per hectare in the 10cm-and-over dbh range are quite common (King et al, 1997). In the Colombian Putumayo, for example, Aguirre et al (1999) report densities ranging from 13 to 76 trees over 10cm dbh in plots where the species was encountered. Under appropriate conditions, seedling densities can also be very high: 3200 and 7000 per hectare in two 1-hectare plots in Peru, for example (Meza, pers comm, May 2000).

Individuals in the larger, commercially viable, size classes are reported to occur at natural densities ranging between 3 and 10 individuals per hectare (Borges et al, 2000). Forero (1992), for example, reports an average of about 15 trees per hectare in the 30–40cm diameter size range, in a sample involving 10-hectare plots in alluvial floodplain soils in the Putumayo, Colombia. Surveys in other areas reveal much lower densities, however. For example, in an inventory of close to 60,000 hectares in the Sucumbiós region of Ecuador, only about 10 per cent of the *Croton* population was estimated to be of commercial size. According to this data set, the overall density of mature *Croton* individuals amounts to about 1 tree per 5 hectares (INEFAN/GTZ, 1997, cited in Borges et al, 2000). Another survey in Oxapampa, Peru, revealed that only 4 per cent of inventoried *Croton* plants were over 30cm dbh (Meza, 1999c). In Madre de Dios, Peru, a census of 139 hectares along four different rivers likewise revealed about 0.3–0.5 trees per hectare in the dbh range of 30cm + (Catpo, 1998, p35). These data sets suggest that *Croton*'s distribution is localized, yet when found it is often common. The apparent lack of commercially viable trees within some of these sites may reflect considerable pressure from harvesters (eg Catpo, 1998; Meza, 1992a).

Growth rates

Typical of pioneer species, *Croton* has fast vertical and diameter growth rates. A study conducted in 40 sites by Shaman associates suggests a vertical growth rate of 25cm per month during the first year (King et al, 1997). Aguirre et al (1999) report a growth rate of 2.5m per year. According to one estimate, trees achieve a diameter of about 30cm after 7 to 8 years, at which time latex production is estimated to be commercially viable (Aguirre et al, 1999, p132). Other estimates are more conservative, suggesting 8 to 12 years for a tree to attain commercially ideal sizes of 30cm and over, and heights above 20m (Phillips, 1991, in Gudiño et al, 1991; Meza, 1999c). Latex production at this time is reportedly linked to the increased number and size of lati-cifers, the specialized latex-producing cells (Meza, 1999c, p103). Possibly, growth rates vary regionally, and perhaps locally as well, in response to genotypic or environmental variations.

Reproductive biology

Although flowering and fruiting season is not as clearly delimited in *Croton* as in other species, flowering tends to take place during the rainy season. Flowering has been reported to occur between October to February in Colombia, Ecuador and Peru, with some regional variations within and between countries (Aguirre et al, 1999; Flores and Revelo, 1993; Meza et al, 1998). In some areas there is another flowering peak around May and June (Meza 1992a; Meza et al, 1998). Trees at higher elevations may flower a little later than those at lower elevations (Flores and Revelo, 1993).

Typical of pioneer species, *Croton* achieves reproductive maturity early in its development, after four years (Meza et al, undated). The seeds, which are ant, bird and wind dispersed, are minute and are produced in massive quantities, up to 600,000 per individual mature tree (King et al, 1997). Though natural regeneration is through seeds, some individuals claim that *Croton* has the ability to sprout from cut stumps (Gudiño et al, 1991, p14).

The light-demanding nature of *Croton* means that natural regeneration is restricted to open areas, either in natural or anthropogenic clearings. While older fallows may have large trees, these have no seedlings growing below them. Large numbers of seedlings under mature trees are mostly found in open, more intensely used environments (Catpo, 1998). This has implications in terms of managing the species, particularly for the collection and transplanting of 'wild' seedlings.

Yields

Measured yields vary according to the harvesting technique employed. Tapping is much less efficient than felling, both in terms of rate of flow and total latex harvested. Tapping live trees yields only 12 per cent of the individuals' latex, 0.3 litres on average, as opposed to 80 per cent obtained through destructive harvesting (Jordan, 1996; Zak, 1991).

Felling also yields more latex than that obtained by repeated tapping of the same tree over time. Indeed, tapped trees do not yield as much latex as untapped trees when subsequently felled, even under the best environmental conditions (Meza, 1999b). The susceptibility of *Croton* to tapping is due to the morphology of its latex-producing cells, the laticifers. Unlike those of its relative, the rubber tree (*Hevea brasiliensis*), *Croton*'s laticifers are ramified, non-articulated, linked to a single cell and incapable of regenerating (Medina and Meza, 1999). This means that tapping in *Croton*, in contrast to such regularly tapped species as *Hevea*, irreversibly damages the plant's latex-producing tissues.

A monitoring study involving 77 trees suggests that tapping trees increases mortality rates dramatically, exposing *Croton* to disease and fungal infections. In this study, 44 per cent of tapped trees reportedly died within a year after tapping 300 cubic centimetres (cm^3) (Medina and Meza, 1999; Zak, 1991).[9] It is possible that if very small amounts of latex are tapped for subsistence use (ie if damage is relatively small), mortality is also less. The presence of *Croton* trees with multiple scars in Amazonian home gardens provides some anecdotal evidence to support this possibility. In any case, it appears that latex production is irreversibly limited by tapping (King et al, 1997).

Latex yields through felling vary according to the size of the tree, ranging from about 2 litres in a 20cm tree to 5 litres in a 60cm tree, with an average of 2 litres per tree (Aguirre et al, 1999; Zak, 1991). Other estimates are higher. Reports from Peru, for example, report yields of 3 to 4 litres of latex under optimal conditions for 30cm trees (Meza, 1999).

Some trees, particularly old or diseased ones, produce little or no latex (Meza, 1999b). Some apparently healthy trees may also yield little or no latex. Some harvesters refer to these latex-yielding and non-yielding trees as *lecheros* and *no-lecheros*, respectively (literally 'milk-producing' and 'non-milk-producing'), linking these traits to certain physiognomic and ecological features, such as bark colour (Meza, 1999b). If genetically determined, these differences have important implications for management, particularly in terms of selecting wild germplasm for cultivation.

Latex yields are also influenced by a number of environmental variables, most notably solar radiation and water availability. Trees exposed to higher solar radiation, either through aspect or because they are growing in open areas, tend to have lower yields. The importance of solar radiation may be related to its effect on moisture availability, which is known to affect latex quantity and viscosity. Access to moisture increases not only yields but also the speed of latex flow (Meza, 1999b). As a result, trees growing close to water or among closed vegetation tend to produce more latex and at higher flow rates than trees in high, drier ground, or in recently disturbed vegetation (Meza, 1999b; Zak, 1991). Again, this has some implications for management, as *Croton* planted in agricultural systems will have lower yields than those planted in agroforestry systems. These differences may be offset by the higher planting densities used in crop associations, however.

There is also some evidence (eg Meza and Valencia, 1999) that soil conditions have an effect on the chemical composition of the latex. For example, higher SP-303 levels in latex are found in plants growing in Ilder (Aquic dystropepts), Shivitashari (Typic distropepts) and Trocha (Typic distropepts) soils (Meza and Valencia, 1999).

In addition, there are daily and seasonal variations in the yields and consistency of latex. There is some data to suggest that more latex, perhaps as much as 30 per cent, is collected during the waxing, as opposed to waning, stages of the lunar cycle (Zak, 1991). Interviews conducted by Meza (1992b) among several indigenous groups in Peru further support the notion that greater yields are harvested during the full moon. In areas with seasonal variations in rainfall, tapping may yield less latex in the midst of the dry season, when plants are undergoing water stress (Meza, 1999b). Similarly, the latex flows less easily as ambient temperature increases during the day. As a result, harvesting is preferably carried out in the morning. Rainy days, on the other hand, produce a more watery and commercially less desirable latex (de Jong, 1992, cited in Borges, 2000). Some suggest that the day after rain is ideal for tapping, however (Meza, 1999b). From these reports, then, it seems that a number of environmental factors have qualitative and quantitative effects on latex yields, and these environmental factors vary both spatially and temporally.

Though not as important as latex, *Croton* bark is also harvested for subsistence and commercial use. Shaman, which used to import bark early on during its operations, ceased doing so in 1994 and now imports only latex (Borges, pers comm, February 2000). Trees in the 30cm dbh size range yield 10 to 15 kilograms (kg) of dry bark (Gudiño et al, 1991; Phillips, 1991, cited in Espinoza and Paspuel, 1993; Meza, 1999).

Impact of land-use change, harvest pressure and demand

Although there is very little quantitative data, field observations suggest that high collection pressures have had a considerable impact on this resource in the more accessible areas (eg Catpo, 1998; Meza, 1992a; Zak, 1991) and among larger trees (Meza, 1993a).[10] One preliminary census in Ecuador found fewer individuals in the seedling size class than in the intermediate size class, a pattern which runs contrary to the norm and which might be indicative of overharvesting (Peters, 1994).

A rough estimate of the impact on naturally growing *Croton* may be indirectly calculated from available export figures for latex, at least for Peru. According to official records, a little over 56 metric tonnes of latex were exported between 1991 and 1998 (INRENA, undated). Assuming an average of about 3kg of latex harvested per tree, this is equivalent to about 20,000 trees. The actual number of trees harvested is very much higher, given that these figures do not include latex exported without permits or latex harvested for national consumption.

Harvesting pressure is not distributed equally throughout *Croton*'s distribution range. More accessible areas and areas closest to the largest markets are clearly being targeted more intensely. Official, though very likely incomplete, harvest figures from Peru for 1992–1993 show the departments of Junin, Loreto and Pasco bearing the highest rates of harvesting (INRENA 1995, cited in Meza and Lara, 1997). On the other hand, large-scale conversion of Amazonian forest to agricultural land is clearly favouring *Croton*. One possibility, then, is that overall, *Croton*'s distribution has increased, but that within that expansion, certain populations are being intensely targeted and perhaps overharvested.

Demand for *Croton* appears to be increasing. Almost half of all Peruvian latex exports for the period of 1991–1998, for example, were for the last year. Imports from Shaman alone, the main international buyer, increased from a little under 17,000 litres in 1997 to almost 74,000 litres in 1998, and over 103,000 litres in 1999 (Borges, pers comm, 4 January 2000). Though much lower than the Provir-based estimates, Shaman still expects significant demand increases as ShamanBotanicals.com expands the markets for SB-Normal Stool formula and develops other *Croton* products (Borges, pers comm, 4 January 2000). Domestic markets are also expanding (Borges et al, 2000), even though the importance of these buyers, both in economic and ecological terms, is poorly known (see the sub-section 'Levels of use' in the section 'Use' later in the chapter).

Until now, almost the entire demand for *Croton* has been met by naturally growing *Croton*. Shaman obtains 95 per cent of its latex from non-cultivated trees, though the company aims to decrease this figure to 75 per cent over the next 7 years (Borges, pers comm, February 2000). Commercial harvesting is thus having a clear ecological impact on *Croton*, a fact that has been a source of concern for conservation groups and government agencies (eg Meza, 1998b, p14; 1998d).

The management of *Croton* as an ecological and economic resource

The abundance and distribution of *Croton* as a resource is strongly influenced by patterns of human management.

Swidden fallow agriculture, as a management technique, favours the *Croton* resource while excessive commercial harvesting threatens it. The successional cycle associated with swidden agriculture is particularly well suited for pioneer species such as *Croton*. Abandoned swiddens are ideal environments for the establishment of *Croton* seedlings, which are frequently allowed to grow to, and past, reproductive maturity in fallows before being cut down in order to plant a new swidden. The overabundance of *Croton* in relation to its subsistence use means that, traditionally, *Croton* was not particularly valued or tended, except perhaps in home gardens. Rather, as a pioneer species, farmers typically treated *Croton* as a weed.

The increased commercialization of *Croton* is changing how this resource is managed and perceived. While swidden agriculture continues to create environments suitable for *Croton*, increased harvesting is affecting its distribution and demographics. At the same time, *Croton* is increasingly perceived as a commercially valuable resource, both by farmers and policy-makers. As a result, management regimes have been implemented specifically to propagate and manage *Croton*. *Croton*, in sum, is becoming more intensely managed, both in terms of harvesting and propagation.

The changing role of *Croton* in Amazonian agroforestry systems is accompanied by a concomitant 'professionalization' of its management, as private companies, NGOs, conservation groups and government agencies implement programmes to propagate its management and reforestation (Ayala, 1993). *Croton*'s role as a pioneer species and its association with secondary forests make it an ideal candidate for increasing economic returns from fallow management.

On the basis of ecological assessment studies, Shaman has established a minimum ratio of 3:1, and an ideal ratio of 5:1, for replanting versus harvesting (Borges et al, 2000). This 3:1 planting-to-harvesting ratio is included in the contractual agreement with harvesters. Moreover, a value is added to the price of the purchased price of latex to ensure that the practice is followed (Borges, pers comm, February 2000). Although not stipulated in the contract, suppliers are encouraged to plant *Croton* in fallows, swiddens or pastures. Monocultures are strongly discouraged due to potential pest and environmental problems, particularly given the potential volumes involved (Borges, pers comm, 21 December 1999).

To date, Shaman has reforested with more than 300,000 trees in Peru and 50,000 trees in Colombia (Borges, pers comm, 21 December 1999). In Colombia, indigenous communities in the Putumayo and Cauca began reforesting with *C. lechleri* in 1993, merely in anticipation of the demand for the latex. Between 1993 and 1997, 711 hectares were reforested with 44,500 trees, in four communities (Aguirre et al, 1999, p136). A *Croton* management plan drafted by Shaman for the Putumayo was recently approved by the Colombian Ministry of the Environment.

Encouraging *Croton* latex production has also entailed training and transferring management practices. Shaman recently released a community manual to help farmers cultivate *Croton* in their swiddens, pastures and fallows (Meza et al, 1998). Extension work has been conducted in the form of technical workshops (eg Meza, 1996). One example of a *Croton* management programme is with the Ashaninka in Peru, where women in one community have set up a cooperative to grow and sell seedlings (Borges, pers comm, January 2000).

In order to mobilize the necessary labour, Shaman has developed agreements with intermediary suppliers and, occasionally, with producers (see the subsection 'The socio-economics of *Croton* harvesting' in the following section on 'Management'). Negotiations and preliminary contractual agreements were established with such national indigenous federations as the Asociación Interétnica de Desarollo de la Selva Peruvana (AIDESEP) and with regional indigenous federations, such as the Consejo Aguaruna-Huambisa (Meza, 1998a), Federación de Comunidades Nativas Yaneshas (FECONAYA) (Meza, 1998c) and Apatayawaca Nampitzi Ashaninka Pichis (ANAP) (Meza, 1992a). Indigenous groups approached by Shaman have included Yanesha, Ashaninka, Aguaruna Huambisa and Cacataibo in Peru (Meza, 1992a; 1992b; 1993a; 1995; 1998d; 1998f), Quichua and Shuar in Ecuador, as well as other groups in the Putumayo, Colombia, and Beni and Pando, Bolivia (Borges, pers comm, February 2000).

Increased national and international attention on *Croton* has also helped to attract interest from government, international organizations such as the International Tropical Timber Organization (ITTO) and conservation organizations (Meza, undated). The Ministry of Agriculture in Loreto, Peru, for example, has put in place a reforestation programme with *Croton* and other medicinals that has included the distribution of seedlings and the publication of written guides (eg Oficina de Planificación Agraria, 1998). Government officials distributed over 9000 seedlings in Madre de Dios and 200,000 seedlings in the Ucyali, Peru, between 1996 and 1998 (Lazarte, 1998; Meza, 1997a). The central government in Peru has established an official goal of planting two million *Croton* trees, of which 400,000 are to be planted in Loreto, Peru (Aguirre et al, 1999, p3).

While encouraging, the success of such initiatives will depend upon subsequent adequate management of reforested plants and, ultimately, upon the market and the price of latex. An emphasis on numbers planted can conceal lack of follow-up and post-planting management. It is not clear how many of the *Croton* seedlings distributed by government agencies were actually planted by farmers, how many have survived and how they are being managed. More importantly, there is practically no information on the economic and social impact of *Croton* and of *Croton* management programmes on, for example, income amounts and distribution, community dynamics and social structure, land tenure and resource rights (but see Meza, 1994; undated).

Management

Harvesting methods

Croton latex is harvested in a number of ways. The simplest method involves tapping the living tree by making straight or, more commonly, V-shaped incisions on the bark, the size and number depending upon the amounts of latex to be collected. While most farmers use a machete to make their incisions, more specialized harvesters use a *rasqueta*, a knife with a curve at the tip used for tapping rubber (Meza, 1999b). Because tapping only yields relatively small amounts of latex – up to 1 litre in large trees, much less in smaller trees (see Zak, 1991, p16) – its use is generally restricted to subsistence, or small-scale, opportunistic commercial harvesters.[11]

Subsistence tapping is usually carried out whenever the need arises, though some farmers store the latex in a bottle. This author's field observations in Peru suggest two different types of subsistence use, each employing slightly different management techniques. When small amounts of the latex are needed and/or when the latex is needed immediately – as in the spot treatment of a cut, for example – the person may tap a small amount of latex from a nearby tree, not uncommonly one in his or her garden. Indeed, the sight of a *Croton* tree covered in scars is a common sight in Amazonian back-yards. Subsistence uses that require larger amounts of latex and/or which involve more lengthy preparation may involve less accessible trees and more destructive harvesting (ie felling or stripping the bark as opposed to tapping).

Most commercial harvesters fell the tree, collecting the latex and/or stripping the bark, which in turn is sold in rolls, dried or soaked in alcohol to extract the latex. Harvesting by felling requires substantially more work than tapping but also yields considerably larger amounts of latex. Tree size becomes more important when larger amounts of latex are sought. Though some harvesters fell trees as small as 15cm dbh, only trees with diameters greater than 30cm produce optimal returns of latex (Meza et al, 1998). The felled tree often brings down with it other neighbouring trees. In order to maximize the collection of latex, some harvesters build a support for the felled tree trunk, directing the fall of the tree towards the support, so that the crown of the tree remains lower than the base. Elevating the bole above ground level also facilitates collection of latex and allows the har-

vester to cut concentric rings at 15cm intervals along the trunk, again leading to a more efficient collection of latex (Meza, 1999b).

The latex is gathered in a number of small vessels placed under each concentric ring or, alternatively, a canal is fashioned from one of several locally available plants and used to direct the dripping latex to one larger vessel (see Meza, 1999b). A timed observation involving harvest of two trees suggests investments of five and eight man-hours per tree in open areas and secondary forests, respectively. While trees harvested in secondary forest demand higher investments of time, they also yield larger amounts of latex, perhaps as much as double (Meza, 1997).

Bark is also harvested destructively. The tree is cut down and sections of the bark are cut and stripped off, an operation facilitated by the bark's tendency to peel off easily (Gudiño, 1991). Due to the ease with which bark becomes contaminated with fungi, harvesting is more appropriately conducted during the dry season (Meza, 1992a). Close to 14kg of dry bark are needed to extract 1 litre of latex (Espinosa and Paspuel, 1993, Appendix 9). Aside from the use of bark to extract latex, there is also a market for the bark itself, which is used in a number of medicinal preparations.

The socio-economics of *Croton* harvesting

Though some latex is harvested opportunistically, as in the clearing of fallows to prepare new swiddens, most latex is collected after surveying an area for harvestable trees (Meza, 1999). One study among 13 communities in the Ecuadorian lowlands suggests that about 10 per cent of farmers exploit *Croton* as a resource with some regularity (Alarcón et al, 1994). This author's observations in Peru and Bolivia likewise suggest that *Croton* harvesting is frequently practised by a small, yet significant, percentage of sub-sistence and local farmers who derive additional income from extractivism.

Opportunistic harvesters typically sell or trade the latex, by the gallon or even by the bottle, to travelling river merchants or to *regatones*: buyers who frequent the ports of Amazonian cities. Some interme-diaries specialize in purchasing *Croton* and other medicinal plants, often employ-ing a network of harvesters or other intermediaries. Not uncommonly, there are several small intermediaries between harvesters and large buyers in the cities. One study in Ecuador suggests that the majority of local intermediaries had over ten years' experience in the business, maintaining profit margins of about 33 per cent (Jordan, 1996).

About 90 per cent of the latex con-sumed by Shaman is bought from a handful of its own intermediaries – small local enterprises run by professionals. These intermediaries, in turn, seek out and make the necessary contractual arrangements with harvesters, also assist-ing in the transfer of technology from Shaman to communities. In the past, Shaman also purchased latex directly from indigenous federations, and it con-tinues to purchase latex directly from producers such as landowners, individual farmers and communities (Borges, pers comm, December 1999; pers comm February 2000; Shaman Pharmaceuticals, 1998). Two sets of contracts thus mediate the flow of latex from harvesters to Shaman: one between producers and intermediaries and another between inter-mediaries and Shaman. In its contract with intermediaries, Shaman stipulates certain conditions for contracts with har-vesters, such as a minimum price.

In Peru, at least, harvesters are theo-retically supposed to obtain a permit from the Ministry of Agriculture (*contrato de extracción*). Listed in this contract are the areas and amounts to be harvested. In practice, however, many harvesters avoid the costs and time that obtaining such per-mits entails, and/or collect from areas or in amounts not covered by the contract.

Propagation methods

Croton can be readily propagated by seed or by transplanting seedlings. Moreover, *Croton* has the ability to resprout from cut stumps, adding another option for its management (Flores and Revelo, 1993). Propagation by seed follows standard pro-tocols. Viable seeds are planted in plastic bags at 1cm depth, using a mix of forest soil, sand and manure, grown to a height of 25–35cm and transplanted. When transplanted to pastures, seedlings are left to grow for a year, due to their suscepti-bility to trampling and to pests associated with grasslands (Meza et al, 1998). Seedlings may also be gathered from underneath mature trees and transplanted directly after growing to 5–15cm.

King et al (1997) report rates of 90 per cent seedling germination. Slightly lower germination rates (80 per cent) are reported by others in Ecuador and Colombia (Castanel et al, 1995; Gudiño, 1991; Pasapuel, 1998). Disinfecting seeds and soil increases germination rates to 95 per cent (Flores and Revelo, 1993). However, seeds rapidly lose their viability over time and through refrigeration (Castanel et al, 1995; Flores and Revelo, 1993).

Germination takes place anywhere between 12 to 26 days, depending upon the site (Flores and Revelo, 1993, p71). Meza and Calderón (1999) recommend inoculating *Croton* seedlings with mycor-rhizae and keeping seedlings shaded as a way of encouraging healthy growth and development. The presence of mycorrhizae in *Croton* has additional implications for subsequent management – notably, avoiding the use of insecticides, fungicides, herbicides and fertilizers with soluble nitrogen and phosphorus, all of which can damage mycorrhizal development (Meza and Calderón, 1999). Instead, these authors speculate that the use of a natural mineral phosphate fertilizer may help *Croton* growth and latex production (Meza and Calderón, 1999). Alternatively, *Croton* can be planted together with nitrogen-fixing leguminous species (Meza et al, undated).

Gudiño et al (1991) and Hurtado (1998) report that vegetative propagation through the use of stakes or stem cuttings is not possible. However, Flores and Revelo (1993) report a success rate with these of 53 per cent. All of these authors report very high success rates when propagating *Croton* with false stakes.[12] Short-term survival following planting is high – 97 per cent in one study (Flores and Revelo, 1993). Preliminary data from two other localities also suggest high survival rates over time, about 70–80 per cent for trees up to nine years old (Shaman-Botanicals.com, unpublished data).

One reforestation trial in the Napo region, Ecuador, reports spacing intervals ranging from 5 to 10m, depending upon the associated species. Here, *Croton* was planted in association with coffee, cocoa, *naranjilla* (*Solanum quitoense* Lam.), manioc, and in pastures. Different combinations yielded different growth rates for *Croton* (Castanel et al, 1995). In some of these agroforestry systems, *Croton* may be used as a shade species (Meza et al, 1998). In one community in Pasco, Peru, for example, *Croton* was spaced at 4m and 5m intervals with manioc, rice and corn, and at 5m intervals in belts 15m apart, among several timber trees, including *Cedrela* and *Swietania* (Meza, 1997, p10).

Planted *Croton* trees need to be weeded during the first months and the side branches pruned during the first three years to ensure a straight bole. King et al (1997) mention the presence of pests in commercial plantations, but no details are given as to the scale of the problem and possible management strategies (Gudiño et al, 1991, p19). Meza (1992a) notes the sensitivity of *Croton* to ants, particularly in the seedling stage. Young saplings are vulnerable to being trampled by cattle and may be susceptible to attack by grasshoppers. Adequate control of these pests has been reportedly obtained by using chickens (Borges, pers comm, 21 December 1999).

Use

Parts utilized

Croton's most widely recognized use involves its wound-healing properties. The latex is also widely used in the treatment of mouth sores, and drunk in the treatment of a wide range of digestive and respiratory disorders. Other reports note its use as a haemostat, an analgesic for toothache, tooth-decay preventative, for burns, fractures, skin fungal infections, rheumatism and as a feminine douche for the treatment of venereal disease. There are also reports of its use as an anti-tumour agent (Marcelo and Meza, 1999; Zak, 1991).

Most pharmacological studies have been performed with *C. lechleri*, and so little is known on the chemistry of related species. SP-303 has been found in the latex of the other Peruvian species and so, from Shaman's standpoint, these are potential candidates for use and commercialization (Meza, 1999c). Again, with the exception of studies with SP-303, there is little data on intra-species chemical variation (Meza and Valencia, 1999).

The latex of *Croton lechleri* has been subjected to detailed chemical study, revealing a large number of secondary metabolites, including polyphenols, simple phenols and their derivatives, three steroids and one alkaloid (Chen et al, 1994). Marcelo and Meza (1999) report a study in which not one but two, an iso-quinoline and a phenanthrene alkaloid, were extracted from *Croton* bark.

The phenanthrene alkaloid taspine may be responsible for some of the reported anti-tumour, anti-inflammatory and wound-healing properties of the latex (Chen et al, 1994; Desmarchelier et al, 1997). Polyphenols such as proanthocyanidin, catechin, epicatechin, gallocatechin and epigallocatechin account for up to 90 per cent of dry weight of sangre de drago latex. Pharmacological studies have shown that these substances play an important role in the wound-healing properties of the latex, probably due to their oxygen free-radical scavenging activity (Chen et al, 1994; Desmarchelier et al, 1997). The wound-healing effects of *Croton* latex are supported by laboratory tests (eg Pieters et al, 1995). *Croton* latex has also a marked anti-bacterial effect (Marcelo and Meza, 1999). The anti-oxidant properties of *Croton* polyphenols may also be related to the latex's reputed anti-inflammatory and anti-carcinogenic properties (Marcelo and Meza, 1999). Taspine has an effect against certain viruses associated with cancer. Moreover, at low levels, taspine appears to act as an immuno-stimulant (Marcelo and Meza, 1999). At higher levels, this alkaloid is cytotoxic, and some have cautioned

against the use of latex with high taspine content (Marcelo and Meza, 1999). Anti-inflammatory and wound-healing properties have also been attributed to the lignan 3',4-0-dimethylcedrusin (Chen et al, 1994). The presence of tannins in the latex may also account for the latex's astringent properties.

In cell culture, SP-303 exhibits potent activity against isolates and laboratory strains of respiratory syncytial virus, some influenza and para-influenza viruses and herpes viruses. Acitivity has also been observed against some hepatitis viruses (Ubillas et al, 1994). Laboratory testing with mice suggests a broad-spectrum anti-diarrhoeal effect for *Croton* latex, indicating its possible use for secretory diarrhoea, which includes cholera (Gabriel et al, 1999).

Croton bark is also utilized and commercialized for local, regional and international consumption (see Lazarte, 1998). *Croton* bark is locally commercialized dry, in rolls or steeped in alcohol. The steeped bark is effectively used as a source of latex. The dry bark is used in a number of herbal preparations, either alone or mixed with other plants. Dry bark can also be processed industrially in order to extract the dry latex.

Both the latex and bark can be stored for long periods of time. Shaman reports extracting normal amounts of SP-303 from latex that is two and a half years old, with latex as old as ten years producing good concentrations of SP-303 (Borges, pers comm, February 2000). These observations contradict other reports suggesting much shorter shelf lives for latex (eg Jordan, 1996).

The soft *Croton* wood is used in Ecuador for making fruit crates, toothpicks, cellulose and firewood (Jordan, 1996). These products can potentially increase the commercial value of *Croton*, particularly if suitable markets are found.

Levels of use

Beyond its use by Amazonians, *Croton* has been known and utilized for many years by rural immigrants and the urban lower-middle to lower class in the Andes and along the Pacific coast as a household treatment for gastric ulcers and other ailments. Sangre de drago is also one of the Amazonian medicinals most widely used by Andean and coastal healers, or *curanderos*, in Peru. Its use in urban areas and the presence of an important regional and national market thus goes back 30 years or more.

Beginning in the early 1990s, the use and popularity of sangre de drago, as that of other medicinal plants, began to increase among socially and economically more privileged consumers, many of whom had previously scorned such plants as treatments of the underclass. Over the past ten years, sangre de drago has continued to experience a rise in social status. In a survey carried out in Lima, Peru, Meza and Lara (1997) found that about half of all respondents across income levels were familiar with *Croton* and had had previous experience with the plant, although knowledge and use of sangre de drago was more prevalent among lower-income respondents.

The growth in demand and the expansion of the market have resulted in a diversification of companies and entities commercializing the latex. Between 1992 and 1997, for example, the number of companies that sold bottled latex in Lima alone increased from 6 to 16 (Meza and Lara, 1997). The number of *Croton*-based products has also grown. Beyond the bottled latex and dry bark that were customarily available, it is now possible to purchase tinctures and extracts, creams, soaps and shampoos.

Companies selling *Croton* latex on small street stands and in popular markets are usually small, family-run businesses, operating largely within the informal sector of the economy and with little, if any, quality control. In some cases, these street merchants adulterate latex with water or with red exudates, such as that from *Iryanthera* or *Pterocarpus*. In recent years, and following the increased legitimization of sangre de drago and the expansion of its market, a number of larger firms with greater quality control have begun selling sangre de drago in such outlets as pharmacies, airports, vegetarian restaurants and natural products stores (Meza and Lara, 1997). Meza estimated the annual demand of sangre de drago in Lima, Peru, to be about 1400 litres in 1992, a figure that has now been clearly superseded (Meza, 1992c). More recently, Ayala (1997, p13) estimated the annual local demand in Iquitos to be close to 3000 litres. That same year Ayala (1997) reported exports of about 9000 litres annually from the Marañón River alone to markets on the coast of Peru. Annual demand for Ecuador was estimated at around 25,000 litres in the mid-1990s (Jordan, 1996). Probably underestimated at the time, this figure is likely to be much greater today, given the rise in popularity of sangre de drago.

During 1991 to 1997, latex was exported from Peru to six different countries the US, France, Russia, Italy, Lithuania and Chile – with an export value amounting to just over US$140,000 (Meza and Lara, 1997). Official harvest estimates for 1996 (about 1042 litres of latex and 1820kg of bark) seem to be very much below actual harvest rates. Indeed, export figures for that year from Iquitos alone are about 1060 litres of latex (Lazarte, 1998)![13] Unfortunately, precise export figures are difficult to obtain because export figures are cumulative for all plant products used as perfumes and medicinals. Moreover, much harvesting is conducted by small farmers who sell the bark to intermediaries and who do not obtain the necessary permits, or who exceed the quotas established by the permit. As a result, it is hard to evaluate the scale of supply.

According to an official publication of the Peruvian Ministry of Agriculture (Oficina de Planificación Agraria, 1998), the expected demand for *Croton* latex in the year 2002 is 400,000 gallons (1.8 million litres), increasing by 50,000 gallons (227,000 litres) over the next year and 100,000 gallons (454,000 litres) thereafter. This estimate, however, was calculated at a time when Shaman Pharmaceuticals was still planning to market *Croton*-based drugs such as Provir. Projected demands for SB-Normal Stool formula are much lower, although they are as yet unspecified (Borges, pers comm, February 2000).

Prices

Prices for latex are quite variable and depend upon quality, the number of intermediaries between producer and consumer, and the buyer. Moreover, prices frequently fluctuate throughout the year, probably in response to shifts in supply and demand.

The 1990 price for *Croton* in one region of Amazonian Ecuador ranged from between US$7 and US$10 per litre (Zak, 1991, p36). Local prices in Peru in 1997 varied seasonally and between regions. In Iquitos, for example, latex prices ranged from US$3 to over US$7 per litre. The lowest prices that year were consistently paid in Iquitos and Pucallpa, on average US$6 per litre – perhaps because the supply there is greater. Latex in Tarapoto and Puerto Maldonado, on the other hand, ranged around US$9 per litre, reaching as much as US$15 in Tarapoto (Lazarte, 1998). The highest prices were paid in Lima, with a more or less steady price of US$17 per kilogram (Lazarte, 1998). Meza and Lara (1997) report a much lower wholesale price in Lima, about US$8 per litre. Current market prices range from US$4 to US$14 per litre, with US$7.50 per litre being the usual maximum for commercial sale (Borges, pers comm, 21 December 1999). Shaman intermediaries pay harvesters between US$2.60 and US$3.20 per litre. Shaman, in turn, purchases the latex from intermediaries at US$7.90 to US$10.60 per litre (Borges, pers comm, 21 December 1999).

Retail prices for bottled latex in Lima ranges from US$14 to US$15 per litre. Latex sold in capsules in Lima has a much higher retail price: about US$5–US$10 for 100 capsules containing a total of 50 grams of latex (Meza and Lara, 1997). Internet companies sell *Croton* latex at about US$12 for a 62-gram bottle of latex, while a 20-count bottle of SB-Normal Stool containing 350 milligrams (mg) of latex extract sells over the internet for about US$20.

Certification potential

Biodiversity legislation and the commercialization of *Croton*

The signing of the Convention on Biological Diversity (CBD) in 1992 marked a milestone in how biological resources, and more specifically genetic resources, are viewed in today's global economy. By providing a broad legal framework to structure access and benefit-sharing (ABS) agreements, the CBD sought to address a central paradox in the early 21st century: the simultaneous commodification and destruction of the Earth's genetic resources.

Implementing the CBD raises difficult questions, as nation states seek to define genetic resources, establish proprietary rights over these resources, and develop legal and institutional frameworks to articulate these proprietary rights. One concrete example of such a challenge is the need to label different plants and plant products as either biological products or as genetic resources. While some plants – timber species, for example – are viewed as biological resources and may continue to be traded like any other natural resources, plants considered to be genetic resources are subject to entirely different legislative constraints.

Moreover, the CBD agenda has come into conflict with the intellectual property regimes espoused by the World Trade Organization (WTO) and its Agreement on Trade-Related Aspects of Intellectual Property Rights (TRIPS) and which the US has tried to implement through a number of bilateral agreements with countries such as Ecuador (eg Wateringen, 1997). These conflicts have become exacerbated and are epitomized by the strong outcry that cases such as the Ayahuasca patent elicited among Andean countries and indigenous peoples (see Box 27.2 in Chapter 27). The complex legal and political backdrop against which plants such as sangre de drago are commercialized may create considerable difficulties for companies, particularly if these have high public profiles.

Clearly, how the CBD is implemented nationally and regionally is critical to the development and certification of plants such as *Croton*, whose status as a biological or genetic resource is open to debate. Borges et al (2000), for example, note that Shaman's *Croton* imports from Ecuador

have been on hold since 1994 and the company is waiting for the government to finalize its legislature before resuming its activities there. Biodiversity legislation may turn out to be an important factor in shaping the medicinal plant industry, not only in terms of encouraging certain practices, but also by inadvertently encouraging companies to seek nations and regions offering more favourable conditions for purchasing plant products.

At the time of writing the Peruvian government was drafting a bill addressing some of the environmental, access and benefit issues raised by the CBD, effectively attempting to put into place mechanisms that will certify the commercial extraction and utilization of medicinal plants such as *Croton*. There is also a possibility that a presidential decree, such as that issued for uña de gato in Peru, will be issued for *Croton* (Chapter 8 discusses some of the complexities and risks that such legislative initiatives entail, particularly for local stakeholders). Certainly, any international certification effort will have to take into account this international and national legislative framework, possibly even working directly with some of the institutions set up by national governments in order to regulate the medicinal plant industry.

Croton and certification

There are a number of ecological and socio-economic aspects to *Croton* that would favour both its management and its inclusion in a certification programme. At the same time, a certification programme would have to address a number of problems and challenges, some of which have already been outlined.

While not imminently threatened, sangre de drago is clearly being subjected to fairly intense collection pressures in some areas, pressures that will continue to mount in the likely event that the market for latex continues to grow. With few exceptions, demand for *Croton* among buyers is not being met with any ecological accountability, even though several internet companies advertise that their latex is 'sustainably' gathered. Moreover, *Croton* has a high public profile and has successfully captured media attention, characteristics that can be successfully harnessed by a certification programme and awareness-raising initiatives. The same high media exposure and public profile make certification a more sensitive and complex process, however.

Croton's role as an ecological pioneer and its close association to disturbed environments makes it an ideal candidate for management in secondary forests and agroforestry systems as a shade plant, or planted in association with other timber, non-timber or agricultural species. Large-scale clearing of tropical forests clearly favours *Croton* and other pioneer species. As a result, even if harvesting pressures have increased, the total resource base may also be increasing.

Borges et al (2000) note that *Croton* has a higher per-kilogram commercial value than other non-timber forest products (NTFPs), including tagua and chicle, and a comparable value to Brazil nuts. However, a valuation of *Croton* in terms of returns on investment may be a more accurate way of establishing its value in relation to other extractive activities. This, in turn, points to a broader issue: the economics of *Croton*, in terms of subsistence and economic strategies by different stakeholders, needs to be understood and integrated within the certification process.

As the most important single buyer of *Croton* and a key player in the present and future *Croton* market, Shaman-Botanicals.com is an ideal candidate and stakeholder in the certification process (see Chapter 28). However, Shaman, as well as other buyers, obtains most of its latex from intermediaries, who in the end are the ones who need to conform to certification. Thus, certification would involve interfacing and incorporating multiple levels and actors involved in *Croton* production and commercialization.

It is uncertain how much interest a certification programme could elicit from minor commercial buyers, though several do profess a commitment to 'sustainable' harvesting (eg rain-tree.com). Clearly, this will depend, among other things, upon the direction the market takes and the number and scale of commercial stakeholder investments in the *Croton* industry. In terms of the national market, a certification programme might be able to successfully capitalize on the interest by source country governments and/or the host country conservation community to implement guidelines and protocols for domestic *Croton* buyers.

The uncertainty and unpredictability of the international market, a common problem among many other medicinal plants, is particularly noteworthy in *Croton*. The international demand for *Croton* latex is largely driven by Shaman, whose future, if promising, is nonetheless uncertain. Thus, while demand for latex is potentially considerable, its uncertainty poses risks to those committing themselves to production. This is particularly problematic given that trees take anywhere from seven to ten years to become productive.

Aside from ecological, social, economic and legal components, a certification programme would have to address sourcing and quality problems, as well as product-tracking from forest or fallow to market. Again, these are concerns of some host country government agencies, and certification initiatives might be able to interface with these, where they exist.

Notes

1   The names sangre de drago and dragon's blood are also used for other plants with red exudates, including *Jatropha dioica* Sessé ex Cerv. (Euphorbiaceae) from Mexico, *Pterocarpus* spp. (Fabaceae) from the East Indies and South America, *Dracaena* spp. (Agavaceae) from the Canary Islands and *Daemonorops* spp. (Arecaceae) from South-East Asia. With the exception of *Jatropha*, these other dragon's blood species are taxonomically unrelated to *Croton*, yet have similar ethnomedical uses, such as wound healing and treating diarrhoea. Several of the Old World dragon's blood species are also used in the manufacture of varnishes (Ubillas et al, 1994). This chapter is limited to those neo-tropical *Croton* species known as sangre de drago. Throughout the chapter, the names sangre de drago and *Croton* are used interchangeably.

2   For convenience, the abbreviation 'Shaman', in lieu of 'Shaman Pharmaceuticals' and/or its division, 'ShamanBotanicals.com' is used.

3   In the period between writing this chapter and early 2002, Shaman Pharmaceuticals underwent Chapter 11 bankruptcy. A new private company, PS Pharmaceuticals, is currently raising funds to put SP-303 back into Phase III pharmaceutical trials for HIV/AIDS diarrhoea and for irritable bowel syndrome (IBS) diarrhoea, as these are considered to be the largest markets for this product. PS Pharmaceuticals purchased all the plants, database, patents and all other materials related to PS-303. ShamanBotanicals.com, on the other hand, continues to sell dietary supplements through the internet and retailers.

4   Aside from Shaman's patent, another three US patents have been filed on *Croton*. The first two, filed during the 1970s and already expired, pertain to the anti-inflammatory effects of taspine and the use of *Croton lechleri* latex to treat cuts and abrasions. A third patent, relating to the use of several compounds as cicatrizants, was filed in 1990 by Walter Lewis and associates. All four *Croton* patents refer to specific procedures used to obtain particular compounds or desired effects, and not to the compounds themselves (Meza and Marcelo, 1999).

5   Most of these publications are in the form of unpublished manuscripts. The author is very grateful to ShamanBotanicals.com, and in particular to Beto Borges and Steven King, for providing copies of these valuable materials.

6   The amounts indicated in these estimates were based on the amounts needed to produce commercial amounts of Provir. The temporary shelving of Provir and subsequent release of SB-Normal Stool mean that these original figures are overestimates.

7   One *Croton* specialist estimates that there are at least 15 to 20 species. An exact number is particularly hard to obtain given that many collectors do not note latex colour (Brian Smith, pers comm, March 2000).

8   There are reports of larger *Croton lechleri* individuals, with heights of 35m and diameters close to 70cm (eg Aguirre et al, 1999). However, these individuals are rare and definitely represent the extreme upper size range.

9   This study was conducted at the upper range of *Croton*'s altitudinal distribution, between 1700 and 2200m. *Croton*'s response to tapping may possibly be different within its optimal elevation range.

10 Restricting harvesting to trees above 30cm dbh would presumably minimize the impact on *Croton*'s reproductive ecology, leaving individuals several years of reproductive life before being felled. Unfortunately, however, this is frequently not the case, except perhaps among Shaman harvesters, reportedly required to limit harvests to trees above this size class.

11 In one study among local commercial harvesters in Ecuador, almost 30 per cent of respondents claimed that they harvested the latex by tapping (Alarcón et al, 1994).

12 False stakes are seedlings whose leaves are stripped off before transplanting in order to cut transpirational loss.

13 Original figures are cited in kilograms. However, for the purpose of consistency, the author uses litres to refer to amounts of latex. There is approximately a 1:1 ratio of volume to weight for *Croton* latex (Borges, pers comm, February 2000).

Chapter 14

Fiddlehead ferns (*Matteucia struthiopteris*)

Alan R Pierce

Introduction

Each April, day-glo placards appear in the windows of a handful of shops and petrol stations slung out along the western reaches of Vermont's Winooski River Valley. 'Wanted,' they read, 'fiddlehead greens'. The signs divulge an offered price (recently US$0.50 to US$0.60 per pound), desired condition of goods ('fresh, dry, tightly curled, no more than one inch stems'), road-side purchase location, suitable hours for delivery and a telephone number. As sure as the sight of a chirping robin or a spring-beauty blossom, the posters announcing the commencement of fiddle-heading season are a northern New England harbinger of spring.

The young, curled growth or cro-zier of the ostrich fern's (*Matteucia struthiopteris*) sterile, vegetative fronds is

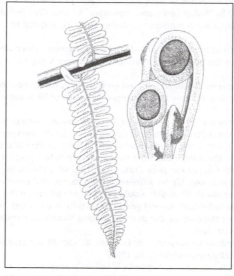

Illustration by Jamison Ervin

Fiddlehead fern
(Matteucia struthiopteris)

known as a fiddle-head because of its semblance to the neck-end of a violin. Although the fern is found in northern Europe and across the upper latitudes of North America, it is primarily collected as a seasonal edible green only in north-ern New England and the eastern pro-vinces of Canada. Von Aderkas (1984) notes that elsewhere across its range, ostrich fern has been little used, save as an ingredient for fern beer or as goat feed in Norway, and as a vermifuge in Russia.

Native Americans, including the Abenaki and Maliseet, used fiddleheads as a food source and a tonic. Among the Maliseet of New Brunswick, the fern's name and pictorial representation con-veyed magical associations. European colonists first encountered the fern as a starvation food in the spring, likely learning of the plant's palatability from the indigenous populations. A regionally restricted taste for the fern as a seasonal delicacy developed among the colonists that has persisted to the present day.

Biology and ecology

The ostrich fern is found in a number of wooded and non-wooded habitats, in full or partial shade, occasionally in full sun. The fern competes best in bottomlands and on rich alluvial soils bordering waterways such as Canada's St John, Miramichi, Restigouche and Matapedia rivers and, in the US, the Connecticut, Penobscot, Kennebec and Winooski rivers. In riverside forests, ostrich fern may dominate the understorey in pure carpets. Among densely populated stands on Gilbert Island in the St John River, the fern may yield up to 1400 pounds (lbs) per acre (approximately 1570kg per hectare) (von Aderkas, 1984).

Ostrich fern fronds are annual and dimorphic. The fern produces a stiff, erect, brown, fertile frond, approximately 0.5 metres (m) tall in mid-summer (June to July). Sterile vegetative fronds surround the fertile frond, growing to heights of 1m or more and occasionally exceeding 1.5m. Both the fertile and sterile fronds exhibit a distinctively grooved rachis. The fertile, spore-heavy frond often persists through the winter into the succeeding year. The sterile leaflets are deeply cut into forward-pointing, rounded, oblong, near-opposite sub-leaflets. The fern's spores are wind dispersed. In addition to sexual propagation, the fern also spreads clonally by means of runners (rhizomes). 'It is conceivable that the plants of a large stand may all have developed from a single plant', writes von Aderkas (1984).

The fern's young croziers overwinter in a dormant state. The croziers are covered with brown papery scales and surrounded by trichomes in the tough, fibrous root crown. The first croziers to appear in April and May are the ones harvested for consumption. As the fern leaves unfurl and mature, they amass silicon, making them unpalatable (for further information on silicon accumulation in ostrich fern, see von Aderkas et al, 1986).

Commercialization, markets and use

Over 400,000 kilograms (kg) of fiddleheads are gathered from the wild each year in eastern North America (Dykeman and Cumming, 1985). In the US, the leading commercial distributor of fiddleheads is the W S Wells and Son Company in Maine, which produces 12 to 15 tonnes of canned fiddleheads per annum under the Belle of Maine brand (von Aderkas, 1984). Roughly one third of the company's raw material originates from Vermont, bought by representatives who advertise with the aforementioned posters in the Winooski and Connnecticut River Valleys, and in Vermont's North-East Kingdom. The remainder of the Belle of

157

Maine fiddlehead crop is harvested in Maine. So ingrained is the consumption of fiddleheads to the citizenry of Maine that Blake (1942) hyperbolically described the green as all but indispensable:

'The outer world knew not of this delectable vegetable, and the native sons of Aroostook who wandered far from its borders grew thin and hollow-cheeked for want of their favorite provender, until in despair they abandoned lucrative positions elsewhere and returned to the potato fields of Aroostook and the there obtainable fiddleheads.'

In Canada, the McCain Company of New Brunswick is the largest commercial distributor of fiddleheads, selling 50 to 100 tonnes of frozen fiddleheads per year (von Aderkas, 1984). New Brunswick is the centre of fiddlehead consumption, and the passion for the fern within the province is rampant. So central is this wild edible to New Brunwick's identity that it has been featured on the province's official coat of arms since 1984. The recent Canadian postal service's 'Scenic Highways' series of stamps also prominently features fiddlehead fern croziers on the New Brunswick Province commemorative in the set.

Von Aderkas (1984) and Dykeman and Cumming (1985) note that demand for fiddlehead greens exceeds annual supply. The major market for the ferns is confined to north-eastern North America. Von Aderkas (1984) notes that access to fiddleheads and a shortage of seasonal labour account for the limited supply of the greens, citing a Canadian study that estimates a potential harvest of one million kilograms of ferns in New Brunswick alone. Curiously, other regions possessing ostrich fern have not attempted to supply the eastern North American market with fiddleheads or, for that matter, to encourage new markets for the fern within their own borders. Several company start-ups in Maine (Blake, 1942) and Vermont (personal observation) to increase supply of the greens in the north-east during the past century have notably failed. Recently, several small canneries have begun to offer pickled fiddlehead ferns as a Vermont gourmet product, and a Vermont company now offers high-priced buffalo milk mozzarella and fiddlehead fern pizzas for sale each spring (primarily aimed at buyers in Boston and New York).

The taste of the fiddlehead fern has been described as having 'the delicate qualities of asparagus and the artichoke, with an overtone of broccoli's brute strength' (Paddleford, reported in Blake, 1942). Fiddleheads are most often boiled and served as a side dish green, with the addition of lemon and butter. Additional recipes include their use in pasta dishes, soups and quiches. A number of recipes are available on the internet. Unlike bracken fern (*Pteridium aquilinum*), ostrich fern is reportedly not carcinogenic. However, some reports of food poisoning, perhaps due to poor preparation (eg insufficient boiling), have been attributed to ostrich fern (Morgan et al, 1994; Health Canada, 1997). The effects of water pollution on the edibility of the fern may need to be studied further.

Harvest and management

Fiddlehead ferns were traditionally gathered by Native Americans as a seasonal cash crop for trade with early settlers (von Aderkas, 1984). Over time, people of English and French ancestry have joined in the seasonal gathering of ferns. Today, according to von Aderkas (1984), the gathering of fiddleheads is largely a 'family occasion'. For many, gathering fiddleheads is a rite of spring, a chance to get outdoors after a long winter, and an opportunity to gather food for personal consumption or as a gift for neighbours and family. Other individuals and family groups gather fiddleheads as part of a livelihood strategy, working an area intensively for a week, or following the fiddleheads' emergence north with the advancing spring.

Harvesting fiddleheads requires frequent stooping, and often leads to a very sore back after a day's labour. Von Aderkas (1984) reports that harvesters may gather more than 54 kilograms (kg) (120 pounds) of ferns per person per day during the height of the season, making as much as US$60 each after expenses. However, as the season progresses, the daily return can drop to as low as US$25 per day. Harvesters may make greater profits by selling their harvest directly to speciality restaurants, local health-food stores or at roadside stands of their own construction. In the early 1990s, this author was able to obtain US$2 to US$4 per pound for fiddleheads from local chefs and health-food stores, roughly four to eight times the amount of money that would have been earned selling the harvest to local representatives of a large canning company in Maine. Several restaurants were found that already maintained long-term relationships with individual local gatherers for their seasonal supply of fiddleheads. Overall, the marketing of fiddleheads still remains a 'haphazard affair' as described by von Aderkas (1984) over a decade and a half ago.

Fiddleheads are treated as common property resources by gatherers. Within the boundaries of their reservation, the Passamoquoddy Indians of Maine control licensing of gatherers along the Penobscot River (von Aderkas, 1984). Across the rest of the US north-east and Canada, gatherers access the fern on private, state or federal land seemingly at will, with little to no restrictions or regulations. The number of fiddlehead gatherers in the region is unknown.

Ostrich ferns are wild, unmanaged resources. Harvesting pressure may adversely impact the viability of ostrich fern individuals and populations. Von Aderkas (1984) relates that overharvesting in the St John River Valley has led to a decline in the size and tenderness of harvested ferns. Repeated overharvesting of ostrich fern croziers in test plots in Maine caused eventual plant mortality (study reported in von Aderkas, 1984). Dykeman (1985) studied the effects of crozier removal on ostrich fern growth over four cycles and found that the fern 'showed a remarkable ability to adapt to regular harvesting'. Dykeman (1985) found considerable variability in response to harvesting within his test populations. He concluded that a removal rate of six croziers per crown would likely result in no loss to the viability or vigour of the plant. On the other hand, removal of 12 croziers per crown per cycle substantially reduced plant vigour (ie decreased the number of croziers produced, the size of croziers and the mean fresh weight of the harvest;

Dykeman, 1985). Personal observations of harvest areas in the Winooski River Valley of Vermont reveal a wide range of harvesting practices, varying from removal of three or fewer croziers per crown to complete stripping of all emergent croziers on a single fern.

Impact of land-use change

Ostrich fern is quite common in eastern North America. However, some prime ostrich fern habitat has been converted for housing and agriculture, particularly along rivers. Nevertheless, many areas where the ferns grow are free from conversion pressures because they occupy designated floodplain areas, small islands or wetlands and bottomlands that are either protected by local zoning or conservation laws or are considered undesirable for development.

Local environmentalists and sport fisherman are increasingly recognizing the importance of maintaining healthy riverine forests. For example, brook and brown trout (*Salvelinus frontinalis* and *Salmo trutta*, respectively) are prized river fish that serve as good indicator species of healthy rivers, requiring the cooling shade and erosion control services of riverside forests (Long, 1995). Dairy operations often clear riverine forests, allowing cows to graze to the edge of a river as well as to enter the river for refreshment. Phosphorus loading, erosion, sedimentation/siltation and other water pollution problems associated with dairy farm runoff have been identified as threats to water quality and aquatic diversity in the region. Conservation groups have begun restoring streamside forests in north-eastern North America and may begin to put increasing pressure on farms to fence cattle away from river edges. Such restoration measures could theoretically promote the return of riverside forests and their associated flora, including fiddlehead ferns, to areas where such forests have disappeared.

Certification potential

The potential for certification of ostrich fern is likely to be limited. Overstorey tree associates of prime ostrich fern habitat tend to be low-quality timber species with limited markets, such as red maple (*Acer rubrum*), silver maple (*Acer saccharinum*) and black willow (*Salix nigra*). Unless such riverine forests are part of a larger holding seeking certification, it is unlikely that certification alone will be financially justifiable or will provide an economic incentive for better management of the timber and non-timber resources within such forests. Nevertheless, the retention and proper management of such forests is paramount, as they provide valuable habitat for fish, birds, mammals and amphibians. If ecosystem benefits rather than economics spur the acquisition of certification for such forests, then ostrich fern populations may derive some benefit from certification standards.

Controlling access to the fern and monitoring its harvest over the long term will present difficult challenges. Gatherers are accustomed to open-access conditions and operate freely without the fetters of licences or harvesting regulations. Modifying or curtailing access to fiddle-heading areas may meet with social resistance or outright hostility. Involvement of gatherers in creating harvest guidelines and access criteria will be critical for social acceptance. Tracking fiddleheads through the informal market-place may also pose novel chain-of-custody challenges for certifiers.

It is unclear how the large producers of fiddleheads – Belle of Maine brand in the US and McCain's in Canada – would view certification. If the largest buyers of the ferns in the region are concerned about resource availability, harvest practices and the size and tenderness of ferns harvested from heavily used areas year after year, then fiddlehead certification may have the potential to become widely adopted. Likewise, if many gatherers of fiddleheads become concerned about the long-term viability of the resource, the concept of certification may also be embraced. For now, the haphazard nature of the fiddlehead market, the relatively low value of the product and the abundance of the species in the region may make certification an unattractive nuisance for harvesters and buyers alike. However, if movements toward embracing regional cuisine made from fresh, local, seasonal produce and unique food products – as espoused by the burgeoning Slow Food movement (see Orecklin, 1999) – continue to gain momentum, new niche markets for conscientiously gathered wild edibles may well emerge.

Chapter 15

Maple syrup (*Acer saccharum*)

Alan R Pierce

'A sap-run is the sweet good-by of winter. It is the fruit of the equal marriage of the sun and frost' John Burroughs (*Signs and Seasons*, 1886).

Introduction

The singular beauty of autumn in north-eastern North America must be seen first hand to be appreciated. As temperatures drop and the hours of daylight decrease, the green forest canopy erupts into incendiary yellows, oranges, reds and purples. The colours appear first on the highest mountains and hilltops and descend – wavelike, ineluctable as the coming winter itself – into the vales and hollows and onto the lowest valley floors. Unlike many natural wonders that appear singly or in small groups – an exquisite single flower or a herd of animals – the dazzling autumnal foliage spectacle occurs on a landscape-wide scale visible from space. It is a brief eruption of fire signalling the approach of a long season of ice.

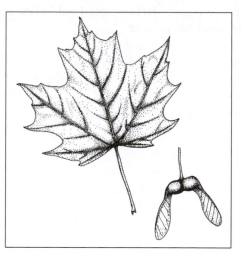

Illustration by Jamison Ervin

Sugar maple (Acer saccharum)

The principal tree species responsible for eastern North America's riotous foliage extravaganza, the lead actor in each year's colourful pageant, is the sugar maple (*Acer saccharum*).

Nearly half a year after foliage season, while the north-eastern North American landscape still lies dormant in the final grips of winter, there occurs within sugar maples a phenomenon as remarkable as its foliage display, although it is all but invisible to the eye. As temperatures rise above freezing on sunny days in February and March, the sugar maple's sap begins to run due to a complex suite of factors involving freezing, thawing and trapped gasses in sap-transporting vessels – a process still not fully explained by plant physiologists. The sap of the sugar maple is slightly sweet, as its Latin name *saccharum* implies, and the very sugars present in the tree's sap help to create the characteristic fiery hues of its leaves each autumn. When the sap of the sugar maple is extracted from the tree in early spring and concentrated through boiling, it produces a syrup or sugar known worldwide for its unique flavour.

Maple syrup may be made from a variety of *Acer* species, including red maple (*Acer rubrum*) and silver maple (*Acer saccharinum*). However, the sweetness and quality of those saps does not compare to that of the sugar maple. Black maple (*Acer nigrum*) also produces fine-quality maple sap, although there is some debate about whether it is a distinct species or merely a variety of sugar maple. For the purposes of this chapter, black maple will be considered analogous to sugar maple.

The sugar maple is a noble tree. It is the official state tree of New York, Vermont, West Virginia and Wisconsin, and its leaf is known worldwide as the symbol of Canada. In open fields, the tree develops a pleasing, many-branched, ovoid silhouette, while in dense forest sugar maple forms tall, straight boles that are highly prized in the wood trade, especially among furniture-makers. Sugar maple wood is strong and durable, earning it the common nicknames 'hard maple' and 'rock maple'. Indeed, Peattie (1948) reports that 'a marble floor in a Philadelphia store wore out before a Hard Maple flooring laid there at the same time'.

While its wood has always been prized, it was the tree's ability to produce sugar that gave it fame and respect among the first colonists of the Americas. Benjamin Rush, in a letter written to Thomas Jefferson in 1791, proclaimed: 'In contemplating the present opening prospects in human affairs, I am led to expect that a material part of the general happiness which heaven seems to have prepared for mankind will be derived from the manufacture and general use of Maple Sugar' (Nearing and Nearing, 1950). Jefferson, the third US president, fervently embraced maple sugaring, going so far as to plant a maple orchard at his home in Virginia (unfortunately for Jefferson, a climate too warm for producing consistent runs of sap). In an 1808 letter, Jefferson wrote, 'I have never seen a reason why every farmer should not have a sugar orchard, as well as an apple orchard. The supply of sugar for his family would require as little ground, and the process of making it as easy as that of cider' (Nearing and Nearing, 1950).

In time, maple sugaring came to be viewed as an American means of self-sufficiency and independence from the European-dominated sugar trade. By the beginning of the 19th century, abolitionists argued for the moral imperative of consuming maple sugar rather than cane sugar produced through slave labour. Almanacs of the time encouraged readers to 'prepare for making maple sugar, which is more pleasant and patriotic than that ground by the hand of slavery, and boiled down by the heat of misery' (Nearing and Nearing, 1950). Centuries later, the art of maple sugaring remains a symbol of independence and an icon of rural life in north-eastern North America. The social and cultural trappings associated with sugaring have become part of the very warp and woof of the rural north-eastern landscape and its people.

Biology and ecology

Acer saccharum is native to North America, ranging from south-eastern Manitoba east to Nova Scotia, south to Georgia, Louisiana and parts of Texas, and west as far as Iowa and eastern Kansas. Within its range, weather conditions permitting, reliable collections of sugar are generally found from Pennsylvania and Ohio northwards. The tree is found in 23 US forest cover types and is a major component in 6 (Harlow, Harrar and White, 1979). In Vermont, sugar maple accounts for 23 per cent of the growing stock (Frieswyk and Malley, 1985), while in New York, maple comprises 16 per cent of the tree cover on commercial forestlands (Lawrence and Martin, 1993). Across the US, sugar maple grows on 9 per cent of all hardwood-dominated lands, representing an estimated net volume of 130 million cubic metres (m^3), or 6 per cent of the sawtimber volume in the US (Godman et al, 1990).

Sugar maple is slow growing and shade tolerant. It is a climax forest species that may live up to 400 years or longer. It is found in rich mesic woods, but also tolerates drier uplands. The tree achieves its best growth on well-drained, fertile soils with a relatively high (for its range) pH (from 5.5 to 7.5). Its bark is variable, ranging in colour from light grey to brown, becoming deeply furrowed with age. Sugar maple grows up to 750m in the northern reaches of its range, and as high as 1650m at the southern edges of its range in the Appalachian Mountains (Godman et al, 1990).

Sugar-maple flowering commences after 22 years of growth, though occa-sionally later (Godman et al, 1990). The long-pedicelled (up to 6.5 centimetres (cm) long) yellow flowers appear in the spring, from late March to mid-May, depending upon location. The flowers are wind pollinated and bee pollinated (Godman et al, 1990; Gabriel, pers comm, 2000). The wishbone-shaped winged fruits are schizocarps, commonly referred to as samaras or double samaras. The papery wings of the fruits (each about 7–9 millimetres (mm) long) facilitate wind dispersal of seeds and fall in September and October just prior to the shedding of foliage. The tree is prolific. Harlow, Harrar and White (1979) report that maple 'seed traps indicate a fall of eight million per acre under some old-growth stands'.

Marks and Gardescu (1998) studied sugar maple seedlings in forest understories over 24 years and found that seedlings less than 1m in height could survive for decades (up to 30 years) and still retain the ability to grow rapidly to fill forest gaps once light availability increased. Their findings led Marks and Gardescu (1998) to classify sugar maple as a 'forest seedling bank species', as distinct from soil seed-bank species such as pin cherry (*Prunus pennsylvanica*) or fire-adapted canopy seed-bank species with serotinous cones such as Jack pine (*Pinus banksiana*). Marks and Gardescu (1998) hypothesize that the persistence of sugar maple seedlings in the forest understorey allows the species to survive despite periodic poor seed crop years and to compete well within the small gap disturbance regime typical of north-eastern American forests.

Syrup production

Many sources (eg Nearing and Nearing, 1950; Willits, 1965; Koelling and Heiligmann, 1996) credit the discovery of maple sap extraction and syrup production to Native Americans. European colonists subsequently learned the art of sugaring from the continent's original inhabitants. Some authors, however – notably Mason (1987) – dispute this claim (also see Lawrence and Martin, 1993, for a further discussion of the issue).

Historically, sap was gathered each spring by creating a V-shaped gash in the bark of a sugar maple with a hatchet and collecting the runoff, via a crude lip or spout, in birch-bark containers or wooden buckets. The sap was then boiled down to syrup, or more often in bygone days to granulated sugar, in large iron kettles set over open wood fires. While methods and equipment have greatly improved over the years, the general concept of sap collection and evaporation remains as it has been for hundreds of years.

Today, sugar-makers tap trees with special drill bits, 7/16 of an inch (1.1 centimetres (cm)) in diameter, to a depth of approximately 2–3 inches (5–7.6cm), at a slightly upright angle. Newer, 'small diameter' spouts, measuring 5/16 of an inch (0.8cm), have recently been introduced. These taps appear to cause less damage than traditional spouts, heal more quickly than 7/16-inch tap holes and produce nearly as much sap as 7/16-inch tap holes. Once maples reach 10–12 inches (25.4–30.5cm) in diameter at breast height (dbh), they can be tapped yearly until the tree senesces and is removed or dies. Overtapping hastens tree decline; thus, careful tapping techniques are imperative. A properly administered tap should heal within two to three years.

After a taphole is drilled, the sugar-maker inserts a metal or plastic spile that directs sap into waiting buckets or, in the case of most large-scale modern operations, a network of tubing. Sap is conducted by gravity-fed or vacuum-pumped tubing, or otherwise collected and transported, to a sugaring shed for processing. Inside the shed, a flat-pan evaporator resting over a wood-fired box, or arch, is used to concentrate the sap into maple syrup. Recently, oil-fired sugaring 'rigs' (evaporating systems) are common as well. Despite technological improvements, such as better evaporator design, improved tubing systems and the introduction of steam-aways and reverse osmosis machinery (technologies that remove some of the water from the sap on its journey to the evaporator pan), sugaring remains an extremely labour-intensive process.

At the height of the sugaring season, it is not uncommon for farmers to work all evening boiling sap, tending the fire and monitoring their evaporator pans. The length and intensity of each sugaring season is weather dependent, but usually lasts about three weeks. Sap runs are sporadic during sap season, but when large runs occur, sugar-makers must race to boil and package as much sap as possible to preserve the flavour and freshness of the product. Federal and state laws and regulations mandate a number of standards for syrup density, colour-grading, packing and labelling.

Maple management

Maple sugar orchards, or 'sugarbushes', are managed as modified natural forest or as a kind of plantation. Species other than sugar maples are generally culled from a prospective sugarbush. Saplings and understorey brush may be removed to allow unfettered movement within the sugarbush. The management of a sugarbush, in many ways, is antithetical to management for timber. In general, the amount of maple sap produced by a tree is positively correlated with the amount of foliage it bears. To maximize sap production, sugar-makers thin sugarbushes to encourage widely spaced, large-crowned trees – trees the exact opposite in growth form from the tall, straight boles prized by the timber industry. A sugarbush's basal area may be 30–40 square feet per acre (3–4 m² per 0.4 hectare) lower than recommended stocking levels for timber management, although some managers choose to retain higher levels of stocking, managing their stands for timber and sap production (though at a lower-than-optimal level of efficiency for both). Tapping also causes defects in maple wood, thus lowering its potential value as a sawtimber tree. And because sugaring is conducted during the spring thaw, operations that use tractors or heavy equipment to haul sap may experience rutting and some degree of road degradation.

According to Beattie, Thompson and Levine (1993), 'a well-managed sugarbush has between 70 and 90 taps per acre (0.4 hectares), which annually produce from 600 to 800 gallons (2730–3640 litres) of sap, or about 20 gallons (91 litres) of syrup'. The average sugar concentration of sugar maple sap is about 2.2 per cent.

Approximately 40 gallons (180 litres) of sap are needed to produce a single gallon (4.5 litres) of syrup. The sweetness of individual trees varies greatly, and certain trees produce sap with a sugar content of 5 per cent or more. Therefore, it is in the sugar-maker's interest to thin his or her sugarbush not only with a view toward an individual tree's vigour, but also with a mind toward considering the sweetness of its sap. A tool called a refractometer now allows sugar-makers to test the sweetness of the sap from individual trees, thereby assisting decision-making processes for retaining or culling trees.

Trees less than 10 inches (25.4cm) dbh should not be tapped, because of the potential harm to long-term tree health and vigour (Willits, 1965; Lawrence and Martin, 1993; Beattie, Thompson and Levine, 1993). However, maple specialists differ in their opinions about when to add a second, third or fourth tap, if at all. Traditional guidelines (eg Willits, 1965) recommend adding a second tap for trees between 15 and 19 inches (38–48cm) dbh, a third tap for trees ranging from 20 to 24 inches (51–61cm) in diameter and a fourth bucket on trees 25 inches (64cm) dbh and larger. Some new guidelines recommend commencement of tapping at 12 inches (30cm) dbh with the addition of a second tap only after a tree has reached 18 inches (46cm) dbh. The new conservative guidelines also caution sugar-makers to never drill more than two taps in a tree per season, regardless of the tree's size (see Koelling and Heiligmann, 1990). Caution may be warranted, as a single sugarbush, if well managed, can be used for the benefit of multiple generations.

Land-use change and other threats

Maple syrup has been produced on small-scale farms in north-eastern North America for centuries. The sugaring season comes at the end of winter, during a time when farmers have few other projects to occupy their time. Sugaring provides a temporal fit with the agricultural rhythms of farm life and provides a source of supplemental income. Over time, sugaring came to be viewed as a cherished socio-cultural event. Sugaring is a time of visiting and a time to celebrate the coming of spring. Side discussions during town-meeting day often turn to sugaring, and local sugaring festivals help brighten the last dreary days of winter for hardy New Englanders and Quebecois.

As the 21st century dawns, few north-eastern farmers can afford to compete economically with large-scale agriculture and dairy operations found in other regions of the globe. The farms of New England and Quebec are smaller and less fertile than their competitors, and costs for operating farms in the region are high. Farm jobs are some of the poorest-paying jobs within the region, and today many farmers cannot afford to hire additional labour to help milk cows or to sugar. Rural land prices have risen dramatically as urban residents from Montreal, Boston, New York and other eastern metropolises seek sites for second homes. As a result, the values and tax burdens of farms have risen. Many farmers have sold all or a portion of their land to developers, cashing in on the new real-estate boom. In combination, these complex economic factors are endangering the mix of agriculture, light industry and forestry that has sustained a working landscape in the region for hundreds of years.

Other forces have actually served to promote establishment of sugar maple in various parts of the country. Selective harvesting and high-grading (forest harvests that 'take the best and leave the rest') are common forestry practices in North America. Sugar maple is favoured by such harvesting practices because it is a shade-tolerant tree that can withstand the partial to full shade left after selective harvests. High-grading, fire suppression and succession to tolerant species have caused a decline in species diversity and a rise in the predominance of sugar maple in Great Lake states' stands, often at levels as high as 70–90 per cent (Niese and Strong, 1992). Fire suppression, in particular, is credited with the replacement of oak-dominated sites by sugar maple and other mesophytic species throughout the American Midwest. Iverson (1989, in Fralish et al, 1991) reports that 'In Illinois, from 1962 to 1985, there was a 4119 per cent increase in the area occupied by the beech-maple cover type'. Fralish et al (1991) speculate that oak forests and their complement of animals and understorey plants may be classified as a rare ecosystem in parts of the Midwest within the next 100 years.

There are some large-scale threats to sugar maple that lie beyond the ability of individual landowners, or certification, to address. For years, scientists have been concerned about observed maple decline in eastern North America. A variety of studies have not produced clear answers, but arguments can be made that airborne heavy metals and acidic pollutants, in combination with global warming and intermittent stresses of drought and pest outbreaks, are responsible for maple decline, which is manifested by crown die-back. For example, Likens et al (1996) estimated that calcium levels (a critical plant nutrient) in forest soils might have shrunk by nearly 50 per cent over the last 45 years as a result of acid deposition-induced leaching. DeHayes et al (1999) have provided evidence linking red spruce (*Picea rubens*) freezing injury and decline in eastern North America to acid rain-induced alteration of foliar calcium pools at the cellular level. DeHayes et al (1999) further note that while acid-induced foliar calcium leaching has been demonstrated in other US trees, including sugar maple, definitive studies have yet to be conducted.

Exotic pests may also pose a threat to the long-term survival of sugar maple. Of particular concern to entomologists is the Asian longhorn beetle (*Anoplophora glabripennis*), a voracious maple-boring insect recently found in the suburbs of New York and Chicago. Some entomologists worry that this insect could decimate the sugar maple, turning it into another sad ghost of the eastern forest, much like the sorely missed chestnut (*Castanea dentata*), elm (*Ulmus americana*) and butternut (*Juglans cinerea*) – trees all but extirpated by introduced pests and diseases.

Syrup markets and economics

'Pure maple sugar will always command a market abroad, if we choose to part with the article'
Walton's Vermont Register and Farmer's Almanac (1847).

During the 1800s, cane sugar was considered a luxury commodity in much of North America. Maple syrup and maple sugar were subsistence goods, a type of poor man's substitute for refined cane sugar (Koelling and Heiligmann, 1996). Today, the situation is reversed. Cane sugar is a plentiful, inexpensive, industrial commodity while maple syrup is considered a luxury product.

Agriculture Canada estimates that over 12,000 Canadians currently produce maple syrup. The state of Vermont estimates that over 2000 of its citizens sugar each year. Estimates for the remaining number of sugar-makers across maple syrup country have not been published, but the total number of sugar-makers worldwide probably does not exceed

20,000. For most producers, sugaring provides supplemental income, not a living. Many operations do not even meet minimum wage rates when the hours of chopping wood, hauling sap, monitoring and cleaning equipment, and packaging and selling syrup are calculated. Still, for many farmers who are land and labour rich (when the work of the entire family is calculated), but cash poor, sugaring offers an important source of legal tender. As Lawrence and Martin (1993) relate, sugaring provides 'money to buy seed, to pay the taxes, to square the accounts at the feed store. Many who grew up on farms remember that sugaring meant a new pair of boots or shoes for Easter.'

Maple syrup is one of the few temperate non-timber forest products (NTFPs) acknowledged to compete with, and even exceed, the value of timber on a hectare-per-hectare basis. 'The exception to the economic advantage of timber production over other forest uses may be sugarbush production, which is likely to yield more

Table 15.1 *Canadian and US production of maple syrup, 1997 and 1998*

	Canada (1000s of litres)	US (1000s of litres)	World (1000s of litres)
1997	22,603	4,913	27,516
1998	20,618	4,387	25,005

Sources: Agriculture Canada (2000), US Department of Agriculture (USDA) (2000), Quebec Maple Federation (2000)

net income per acre than timber. *This holds true only if sugarbush management began early in the life of the stand, and if the stand is of commercial size'* (emphasis by authors Beattie, Thompson and Levine, 1993).

Maple syrup commands a strong market in Canada and the US, and has small but respectable markets abroad in Europe and Asia. The province of Quebec leads all regions in the production of maple syrup, producing nearly 70 per cent of the world's total annual crop. Statistics for the 1997 and 1998 seasons are given in Table 15.1.

The value of the Canadian maple syrup crop in 1998 was about Cdn$115 million, down from an estimated 1997 farmgate value of Cdn$133.4 million (Agriculture Canada, 2000; Quebec Maple Federation, 2000). The value of US maple syrup production was estimated at about US$32 million in 1998, down about 10 per cent from the 1997 value of approximately US$35 million (USDA, 2000).

The total value of the maple industry as a sector has not been well documented. The state of Vermont, which produces one-third of the US's maple crop each year, estimates that the maple syrup industry (the value of all syrup produced plus the sales of the sugaring equipment-manufacturing industry, and maple-associated trucking, packing and mail-order businesses) contributes more than US$100 million per annum to the local economy (Chase, 1996). What makes the sugar maple even more interesting as an eco-

nomic case study is its value as a tourist attraction. Indeed, revenue generated by foliage tourists is thought to be the tree's greatest economic asset.

While maple syrup markets are fairly robust, some experts worry that the product may become irrelevant in the modern marketplace. Former Vermont Senator George Aiken's famous quip, 'You can bribe anyone in Washington with a quart of maple syrup', may no longer hold. A marketing specialist warned a recent conference of sugar-makers that they could no longer expect easy sales of maple syrup in today's marketplace:

'What we are selling is Americana or Canadiana. We are selling hand-made. We are selling nostalgia... We are selling romance... Many of the people who grew up with maple syrup are getting older and consuming less and less. We are selling a product that many people think of only as pancake topping. Not many people eat pancakes for breakfast every day, or even every week, anymore. There is absolutely no way that we expect pancakes to maintain or increase the market for maple syrup' (cited in Lawrence and Martin, 1993).

Maple syrup may have some marketing hurdles ahead in its future if it is to maintain respectable, strong sales as a 'gourmet' product. Already, product substitution by cheaper corn syrup-based syrups has reduced its market share as a pancake topping. Sugar-makers may need assistance in the future to market their product and to develop new products that maintain market share and justify the relatively high costs of syrup production.

Certification potential

Maple sugarbushes pose interesting questions for certification assessment teams. For example, should a sugarbush be evaluated as a plantation or as a natural forest? Some sugarbush management practices run contrary to best management practices for timber. Because certification guidelines are geared primarily toward timber production, a method of fairly evaluating a forest's usage for non-timber goals needs to be weighed against the wisdom of the prevailing timber-oriented criteria and indicators. This does not mean that assessment teams should overlook deficiencies or problems with sugarbush management. For example, sugarbushes are acknowledged to be incompatible with wildlife habitat goals (Beattie, Thompson and Levine, 1993). The removal of non-maple species reduces available mast for wildlife and may make sugarbushes more susceptible to pest infestations. Excessive cleaning of saplings and understorey brush may retard development of a secondary canopy and have other negative impacts.

Certifiers must determine if some of the negative scores given to a sugaring operation for reductions in biodiversity and forest structure are mitigated or offset by the positive hydrological and aesthetic benefits provided by sugarbushes. Should sugarbushes be given positive points for encouraging older-aged stands in a region of the country where almost all old-growth forests have been cleared? Do sugarbushes, by their age and relative stability over time, serve as important

habitat for songbirds, fungi, insects, lichens and understorey plants?

Another important consideration involves scale. How does the size of a sugarbush influence its ability to meet certification standards? Most New England sugarbushes, even good-sized commercial operations, are less than 40 hectares in size. Globally, such a forest is small in size, although regionally it may be significant. The sugarbush's position in the surrounding landscape may also be critical. Does the sugarbush straddle important animal corridors or feeding areas? How is the sugarbush incorporated into the larger landholding if it is only part of a large estate? If the sugarbush is one of many in a region, is there a negative impact on floral and faunal diversity from the agglomeration of so many maple-dominated stands?

Certifiers must ensure that overtapping is not occurring and that managers are reducing the intensity of tapping when faced with signs of decline, disease or pest outbreaks. Rapid tap-hole closure (within two to three years of drilling) may serve as one easy-to-observe field indicator of tree vigour during assessments.

In general, assessing a sugarbush is much simpler than assessing management of small, portable NTFPs such as herbs or mushrooms. Tenure issues relating to ownership of and access to trees are easy to determine and inspect. The threats of theft or unmonitored access that make mushroom harvesting so complex are absent from an operation involving telltale buckets, taps and sugaring sheds. Maple trees, unlike understorey NTFPs, are included in traditional forest management plans, inventories and monitoring systems that are familiar to foresters. Chain-of-custody issues are also relatively simple for syrup because containers can be easily labelled, inventoried and tracked to sale at the farm gate or at local stores.

It is worth noting that many sugar-makers have not taken advantage of organic certification programmes long available to them. It appears that sugar-makers see little marketing advantage in organic certification, and are opposed to incurring any additional costs in what is already acknowledged as a marginally profitable venture. Many operations could achieve organic certification criteria with relative ease as few aspects of syrup production run contrary to existing regulations. Sugar-makers apparently resent the expense and intrusion of regulations that go beyond already strict state and federation codes governing quality and colour-grading of maple syrup.

If the organic movement has failed to muster support for certification of syrup among sugar-makers or the public, is it likely that the issue of forest management certification will have any greater resonance within the sugar-making industry or among the public? The certification movement may need to show independent-minded sugar-makers proof of new markets or market access to gain acceptance. Perhaps if markets for syrup as a pancake topping are drying up, certification could be used to develop a new marketing image for syrup, an image that vaunts forest stewardship as a means of perpetuating the working rural landscape and its attendant culture.

Chapter 16

American ginseng (*Panax quinquefolius*)

Alan R Pierce

Introduction

It is a Saturday morning at Bethel High School in central Vermont and the gymnasium is in use. But the usual cries of youths engaged in athletics and the odours of teen perspiration are absent. Instead, the air of the room is thick with the feral scent of animals. The heavy, musky overtone of castor permeates the gym, blending with the rank odours of blood, dried skin and gamey fur.

The pelts of many north-eastern furbearing mammals lie in long rows upon brown paper spread across the basketball court, paper that becomes grease-spotted from the furs by morning's end. Muskrat, otter, the round shapes of beaver stretched tight like drum

Illustration by Antônio Valente da Silva

American ginseng
*(*Panax quinquefolius*)*

covers, rabbit, coyote skins that stare with hollow eyes, fisher, fox and even a few skunks lay tagged and bunched by lot. The staccato voice of an auctioneer barks through a cheap public address system, announcing each trapper's harvest and eliciting bids from seven seated buyers.

In the school's cafeteria, trappers, farmers, rural blue-collar families, curious onlookers and state officials sip coffee and eat snacks. On several of the dining hall tables, more bounty from Vermont's wildlands is on display. Large, clear plastic bags of dried, gnarled, yellowish roots are arranged for discriminating inspection and eventual auction to two hardened buyers. The bags contain American ginseng (*Panax quinquefolius*) roots, and the event this early December weekend is the annual Vermont fur and ginseng auction. The auction draws an increasingly uncommon breed of rural Vermonters – old-timers, rough-and-tumble young men and rural families who live off the land and harvest the landscape's unique riches for sale to distant markets. Most of the furs bought this day will make their way to Canada, while the ginseng will travel a long route to East Asia.

A Jesuit priest, Father Lafitau, is credited with establishing the ginseng trade between eastern North America and East Asia over a quarter of a millennium ago. Lafitau was exposed to the writings of one Father Jartoux, a Jesuit missionary working in China, who chronicled the Chinese reverence for, and medicinal use of, Asiatic ginseng (*Panax ginseng*). Noting the reported similarity of floral genera between East Asia and eastern North America, Lafitau searched for a New World ginseng and ultimately found *Panax quinquefolius* growing in eastern Canada near the city of Montreal. Samples of the roots were subsequently sent to China where they were received with enthusiasm, and a lively, lucrative, foreign-currency-generating trade for settlers in Canada and the United States commenced.

At first, colonists paid Native Americans to collect ginseng. Over time, ginseng collection came to be the province of individuals who spent a great deal of time in the wilds – namely, trappers and frontiersmen. Early notable figures in the ginseng trade include frontiersman Daniel Boone and furrier tycoon John Jacob Astor. Ginseng provided trappers with an additional income source to scout while traversing the land and setting traps, and the confluence of the ginseng and fur trades, cemented in the early 1700s, con-

tinues in small part to the present day, although the furriers' dominance in the trade has waned considerably.

Ginseng has occupied an exalted position in traditional Chinese medicine for millennia. According to Chinese legend, ginseng was cultivated in heaven by the gods and brought to earth to ease human suffering (Steffey, 1984). It is claimed that ginseng increases performance during periods of fatigue, reduces stress, moistens the skin, lowers blood pressure, stimulates the central nervous and immune systems, acts as an aphrodisiac and ameliorates ailments such as anaemia, cancer, nausea, tuberculosis and rheumatism (Harriman, 1975; Duke, 1989; Persons, 1994a).

The presumed pharmacological constituents in ginseng are referred to as ginsenosides, which are thought to act as adaptogens. Adaptogens have been identified as substances that rectify human physiological imbalances (Proctor and Bailey, 1987) and increase 'the capacity of the body to adapt to a wide range of biological, chemical and physical stresses' (Halstead and Hood, 1984, in Duke, 1989). A round-table discussion on the pharmacological and medicinal uses of ginseng appears in Bailey et al (1995). Western medicine has yet to substantiate any of the miraculous properties attributed to ginseng by Eastern scientists and herbalists, although standardized testing of the root is ongoing. Foster (1991) points out that Eastern researchers culturally accept ginseng as a medicinal and focus on *how* the plant's compounds work in the human body, while Western researchers focus on determining *if* the plant provides medicinal benefits.

Ginseng is perhaps the most celebrated medicinal herb on the planet, and a wide body of literature and lore about the root, both popular and scientific in nature, exists. However, the quality of the ginseng literature is variable and many half-truths, contradictory statements and outright errors are continually perpetuated. Descriptions below will reveal some of the variations and gaps present in the ginseng literature. Controversy even lingers over the Latin binomial of the plant. Many authors insist on using the original neuter adjective *quinquefolium*, given by Linnaeus, rather than the now officially recognized masculine adjective *quinquefolius* (for a brief overview of the nomenclature debate, see Foster (1991), Tucker et al (1989) and Lewis and Zenger (1982)).

Because it is increasingly uncommon in the wild, American ginseng is now listed as a species of special concern under Appendix II of the Convention on International Trade in Endangered Species of Wild Fauna and Flora (CITES). Export of both wild and cultivated ginseng requires US government approval. The federal government delegates control and regulation of ginseng harvesters and dealers to individual states. States typically require ginseng diggers to:

- obtain harvesting permits;
- seek written or verbal permission from landowners when harvesting on land other than their own;
- limit harvesting to a specified season (usually late August to October);
- harvest only mature, seed-bearing plants; and
- plant all seeds from harvested individuals on site in an attempt to ensure continuation of the population.

State officials must weigh, inspect and certify the origin (usually recorded by county) of all wild ginseng roots before they can be legally sold for export out of state. Additional licences and regulations apply to ginseng dealers. Some wild ginseng trade goes unrecorded each year, though the magnitude of such illegal trade is unknown.

Biology and ecology

Ginseng (*Panax* spp.), family Araliaceae, is a disjunct genus made up of six species (Mabberley, 1987), found in eastern North America and East Asia. *Panax quinquefolius* is a leafy perennial herbaceous plant with a fleshy, tuber-like root, native to the eastern hardwood deciduous forests of North America. The genus name, *Panax*, is derived from the Greek *panakeia*, or panacea, meaning universal cure. *Quinquefolius* refers to the palmately compound structure of the plant's leaflets. The natural range of *Panax quinquefolius* extends from southern Quebec and southern Manitoba to Georgia, Alabama, Arkansas and eastern Oklahoma (Anderson et al, 1993). Like many temperate forest herbs, American ginseng is a k-selected species of stable habitats characterized by low but steady recruitment, a vulnerable juvenile period and a stable, long-lived adult stage (Charron and Gagnon, 1991; Bierzychudek 1982).

Ginseng grows to a height of less than 0.5 metres (m) and appears in April or early May when the forest canopy is partially to fully developed. The plant produces a single aerial stem from a gnarled rhizome attached to a taproot. Annual abscission of the aerial stem produces a scar on the rhizome. Many count the number of scars on the rhizome to estimate a plant's age. However, Anderson et al (1993) warn that 'although methods used to age plants range from counting rings of wrinkles on the root to stem scars on the rhizome, no morphological study has confirmed the accuracy of these techniques.' Some plants have been thought to live more than 60 years.

First-year ginseng seedlings have a single, trifoliate compound leaf that resembles a strawberry leaf. The plant later produces two, three and occasionally four or more whorls, or 'prongs', of leaves, palmately compound in structure. Ginseng produces a solitary umbel of small white flowers in early summer. Reports concerning the commencement of wild ginseng reproduction vary in the literature from three years (Charron and Gagnon, 1991), to four years (Anderson et al, 1993), to a high of eight years (Carpenter and Cottam, 1982).

Ginseng reproduction is mainly effected by sexual means; reports of asexual reproduction from root or rhizome fragmentation are rare (Lewis and Zenger, 1982). Ginseng flowers are self-compatible, so solitary plants are capable of reproducing. When cross-pollination occurs, it is thought to be performed by generalists such as halictids of the genera *Dialictus* (Lewis and Zenger, 1983; Schlessman, 1985; Duke, 1989) and *Erylaeus* (Lewis and Zenger, 1983), and syrphids of the genera *Toxomerus* (Lewis and Zenger, 1983; Duke, 1989), *Mesograpta* (Schlessman, 1985) and *Melanostomen* (Schlessman, 1985).

Ginseng flowers appear in late May or June. Fruit set occurs during June and July and ripened fruits fall from the plant in late August or early September. Fruits are bright-red pyrenes appearing in ball-like clumps on mature plants. Seeds fall in close proximity to the parent, although spring thaws may move seeds downslope from progenitors. The bright-red colour of the seed, the seed size and the moist fleshy nature of the exocarp suggests animal dispersal (Lewis and Zenger, 1982). Reported herbivores of ginseng seeds, and thus potential ginseng dispersers, include white-tailed deer (*Odocoileus virginianus*), ruffed grouse (*Bonasa umbellus*), turkey (*Meleagris gallopavo*), chipmunks (*Tamias striatus*), squirrels (*Sciurus* spp.), songbirds and small forest rodents (Steffey, 1984; Duke, 1989).

Seed dormancy is long, taking approximately 20 months from seed fall to germination (Lewis and Zenger, 1982; Charron and Gagnon, 1991). Natural fecundity of *P. quinquefolius* has been characterized as low (Hu et al, 1980; Lewis and Zenger, 1982; Schlessman, 1985). Lewis and Zenger (1982) reported a recruitment success of only 0.55 per cent in a wild Missouri population, albeit after a period of drought; however, once established, ginseng survivorship climbed to as high as 97 per cent. Similarly, Charron and Gagnon (1991) found a mortality rate of 69–92 per cent among small plants, while mortality rates among adult ginseng plants were less than 10 per cent. Interestingly, Anderson et al (1993) report that 66 per cent of all seeds planted from a natural population of ginseng in Illinois produced seedlings. While wild ginseng fecundity is low, Anderson et al's (1993) findings suggest that survivorship of ginseng seeds can be significantly improved on good sites through human manipulation (ie direct sowing of seeds). Indeed, many old-time ginseng diggers have 'wild-tended' ginseng patches for years, maintaining and even increasing recruitment by replanting seeds on site.

Ginseng requires dense shade (70–80 per cent or greater). The plant may be found in a variety of forest types, including northern hardwoods, oak–hickory woods, Appalachian cove forests, and occasionally even under conifers such as eastern white pine (*Pinus strobus*) and northern white cedar (*Thuja occidentalis*). Ginseng thrives in enriched hardwood coves and on benches where weathered material and organic matter collect. Ideal site conditions for ginseng are moist, well-drained, calcium-rich, moderately high pH (between 5.0 and 6.0), loamy soils beneath mature hardwoods on gentle north- or east-facing slopes. Typical overstorey species associates are sugar maple (*Acer saccharum*), white ash (*Fraxinus americana*), basswood (*Tilia americana*), hophornbeam (*Ostrya virginiana*), American beech (*Fagus grandifolia*), butternut (*Juglans cinerea*), tulip tree (*Liriodendron tulipifera*), oaks

(*Quercus* spp.) and hickories (*Carya* spp.). Commonly recorded understorey companion plants include maidenhair fern (*Adiantum pedatum*), wild ginger (*Asarum canadense*), Jack-in-the-pulpit (*Arisaema triphyllum*), bloodroot (*Sanguinaria canadensis*), trillium (*Trillium* spp.), blue cohosh (*Caulophyllum thalictroides*), baneberry (*Actaea* spp.), rattlesnake fern (*Botrychium virginianum*), bellworts (*Uvularia* spp.) and sweet Cicely (*Osmorhiza claytoni*) (Hu et al, 1980; Roberts and Richardson, 1980; Lewis and Zenger, 1982; Fountain, 1986; Anderson et al, 1993; Pierce, 1997).

Production and management

There are four distinct classes of ginseng roots: wild, simulated wild, woods grown and artificial-shade cultivated. Wild ginseng is collected from natural forests by rural inhabitants and commands the highest prices. Wild populations of *P. ginseng* have been hunted to near extinction in China and Korea, while American ginseng is becoming increasingly rare or threatened throughout much of its range. Simulated-wild ginseng is raised beneath natural forest canopy from seed or seedlings. Simulated-wild ginseng is planted at low densities to avoid risks of fungal disease and root rot, and is given little to no tending or chemical inputs in order to approximate the condition and appearance of wild ginseng. Simulated-wild roots are harvested after seven, or preferably more, years of growth and fetch prices close to those offered for wild roots. Woods-grown ginseng is more densely planted than simulated-wild roots, and requires usage of herbicides, fungicides and fertilizers. In the woods-grown method, labour-intensive beds are

dug beneath natural canopy, sometimes with the use of tractors or rototillers. Harvest takes place between five and eight years. Artificial shade-grown ginseng is the most labour- and capital-intensive method of ginseng cultivation and yields the lowest prices in the market. Because such ginseng is grown as an agricultural crop in fields, it will not be treated further in this section on forest management.

Prices paid for high-quality wild and simulated-wild ginseng roots can exceed US$500 per pound (per 0.45 kilograms) dry weight (Persons, 1996; Raver, 1996; Robbins, 1997). By contrast, artificial shade-grown roots currently sell for as little as US$20 per pound (Persons, 1996). The physical differences between a cultivated ginseng root and a wild ginseng root are readily apparent to ginseng cognoscenti. Asian consumers believe wild ginseng roots contain greater curative properties and accordingly pay much higher prices for such roots. Ginseng thus provides a very interesting case of a non-timber forest product (NTFP) that is more highly valued from the wild than from cultivated stocks, thereby challenging the paradigm that most NTFPs face ultimate replacement by agricultural systems. However, wild ginseng is increasingly uncommon, and woods cultivation techniques may need to be promoted as an alternative to the plant's ultimate extinction in the wild.

Most of the research on American ginseng cultivation has concentrated on the artificial-shade management technique, although the body of literature on woods-grown ginseng and simulated-wild ginseng is increasing. Much of the data about the latter two techniques is empirical, and the need for scientific trials of these cultivation methods is sorely needed, as is technology transfer of existing information to interested forest owners.

Wild-ginseng gatherers typically work individually or in family units. The actual number that obtains permission from landowners to harvest plants is likely small. Harvesters range from scrupulous to unscrupulous; while one will conscientiously wild-tend patches of ginseng for years, others will harvest all available plants with no regard for a population's survival. Because of its high value and easy portability, theft of ginseng is a serious issue for any individual who grows or wild-tends ginseng.

Despite Lewis's (1988) observation of a ginseng population recovery after decimation by collectors (a phenomenon he attributed to the presence of a ginseng seed bank), evidence appears to indicate that ginseng is extremely sensitive to harvesting pressure. Charron and Gagnon (1991) estimated that the maximum allowable annual harvest of ginseng ranged from 0 (during a poor growing season) to 16 per cent (during a good growing season, assuming a favourable and unchanging environment) of individuals from all age groups in a population. Nantel et al (1996) found that the maximum rate of annual harvest under stochastic environmental conditions would be only a little more than 5 per cent. Nantel et al (1996) report: 'extinction thresholds, the minimum number of plants required to rebuild a population, varied from 30 to 90 plants, and the minimum viable population size was estimated at 170 plants.' This research poses troubling prospects for the continuation of the species in the wild, as many surveyed wild-ginseng populations in Canada and the US do not exceed 170 individuals, much less 90 individuals. Long-term wild collection of the plant by rural gatherers may be threatened. Recently, ginseng collection has been suspended in several state and federal forests in the US midwest and south due to concerns over declining populations and rapacious harvesting practices.

Forest managers who cultivate woods-grown or simulated-wild ginseng need not worry as much about population dynamics because they are sowing large quantities of seeds purchased from commercial ginseng seed suppliers for one-time harvest. Management issues for woods-grown and simulated-wild ginseng cultivation involve monitoring the crop for signs of root and fungal diseases, as well as evidence of nutrient deficiencies. Ginseng cultivators may need to apply herbicides, fungicides or fertilizers to save their crops. Small woodland rodents have been known to feed upon ginseng roots, necessitating trapping, poisoning or the erection of physical barriers around ginseng populations.

Ginseng provides forest managers with the potential to diversify management goals and economic outputs. Pros of forest ginseng cultivation include:

- compatibility with multiple-use forestry;

- suitability as a management option on small forest parcels (<40 hectares) traditionally overlooked by many foresters;
- diversification of income sources;
- maintenance of future forest options (particularly with wild and simulated-wild crops);
- potential synergy with maple sugaring and recreational uses of forests; and
- compatibility with maintaining soil, hydrological, aesthetic and carbon-sink functions of forests.

Potential negative aspects of forest ginseng cultivation include:

- too long a time frame for profitability;
- a high degree of risk and uncertainty due to threats of theft, fungal diseases or limited site capabilities;
- negative impacts on populations of other understorey species removed as a result of ginseng cultivation;
- ginseng market volatility; and
- introduction of non-native seed stock and potential contamination of the local genotype.

Land-use changes

Although once common throughout eastern North America (Harding, 1908, reissued in 1972; Lewis and Zenger, 1982), *P. quinquefolius* is now considered vulnerable, threatened, rare or endangered across much of its natural range (Lewis, 1984; Schlessman, 1985; Charron and Gagnon, 1991; Nantel et al, 1996). Causes of the growing rarity of the herb include overcollection by gatherers, destruction of habitat through logging and forest conversion for agricultural or development purposes. In Canada, ginseng occurs in the most densely populated and developed areas of southern Quebec and Ontario. Nantel et al (1996) report that recent calculations estimate a 14 per cent disappearance of known ginseng populations in Quebec. Nantel et al (1996) add that 'fragmentation of mature forests has probably increased the vulnerability and accessibility of these plants.'

Increasing land prices across American ginseng's range promotes further subdivision of forest holdings, logging and construction. Rapid land turnover rates characteristic of today's highly mobile society also threaten ginseng habitat.

People residing in locations for short periods of time tend not to build attachments to land that ultimately breeds a stewardship ethic. The unfortunate, short-sighted, economically oriented trend to harvest timber before selling land to new owners has become a standard practice. As it requires deep shade, ginseng does not compete well in landscapes where frequent logging and subdivision are the norm. Ginseng is increasingly found on sites inhospitable to development or logging such as rocky cobbles and steep hollows.

Individual populations of ginseng are vulnerable to natural disturbances such as fire and windthrow. Maintaining canopy cover is a critical issue for ginseng cultivators. Atmospheric pollution poses a more problematic macro-scale threat to ginseng survivorship. Federer et al (1989) estimated that anthropogenically caused leaching (via acid precipitation) of soil calcium reserves, combined with intensive timber harvesting, may reduce total soil and biomass calcium by 20–60 per cent over only 120 years in eastern US forests. Such predictions bode ill for calcium-requiring, rich woods (biodiverse woods) species such as ginseng.

Markets and economic competition

Wild American ginseng has been exported to Asia for over 275 years. During this time, the price of wild ginseng has risen from US$0.07 per pound (per 0.45 kilograms), paid in 1717 (Persons, 1994b), to more than US$500 per pound (Persons, 1996; Raver, 1996). Early-1990s prices for woods-grown roots ranged from US$65–US$135 per pound, while simulated-wild root prices varied from US$65–US$300 per pound (Persons, 1994b). In 1994, the US exported 973,160 kilograms (kg) of cultivated ginseng worth an estimated US$49,969,100 and 104,329kg of wild ginseng worth approximately US$25,706,700 (US Department of Commerce, 1995).

The majority (>90 per cent) of ginseng produced in the US is shipped abroad, mostly to Hong Kong, where it enters the island duty free (Carlson, 1986; Persons, 1994b). Ginseng ranked third in value among all US exports to Hong Kong in 1975 (Carlson, 1986). It is interesting to note that American and Asian ginsengs are viewed by Chinese consumers as distinct medicinal products, and as such do not directly compete against each other in the Asian marketplace (Hsu, 1982; Guo et al, 1995). Ginseng is sold at auction markets in Hong Kong where roots are separated into 40 or more different classes based on a complex grading system that differentiates roots according to their size, shape, colour and wrinkles (Persons, 1994b). Further discussion of ginseng grading and desired root qualities in the Asian market is presented in Guo et al (1995) and But et al (1995). Much of the ginseng is re-exported from Hong Kong after the auctions, mainly to China, Taiwan, Singapore, Macao, Indonesia and Malaysia (Carlson, 1986).

American ginseng exports have fluctuated; but the past three decades show a marked increase in the quantity of roots shipped abroad. Ginseng exports increased by 200 per cent in quantity and 400 per cent in revenue between the years 1968 and 1978 (Patty, 1979), and recent export data (US Department of Commerce, 1995) reveal an increase of nearly 500 per cent in quantity and 200 per cent in revenue above 1970s figures. Wild ginseng exports fluctuated moderately between 1983 and 1994 (likely due to the vagaries of collection), but appear to demonstrate an average of roughly 65,000kg per year. Average prices for wild ginseng show an upward trend, and increased by more than 15 per cent between 1983 and 1994. However, recent economic downturns in Asia have depressed prices.

Foreign demand for wild and simulated-wild ginseng in Asia can still be characterized as steady. As China experiences greater prosperity and levels of disposable income rise, demand for wild ginseng may grow. However, it is unknown if younger, more Westernized, generations will continue to honour and use ginseng.

Historically the major market for ginseng has been the Far East, but new markets for ginseng in Europe and America may be emerging. Recent interest among Americans in alternative medicine (see Eisenberg et al, 1993), including herbal remedies, has sparked a boom in domestic sales of herbs. In 1990, Americans spent a total of US$13.7 billion on 'unconventional therapy' treatments, including herbal remedies (Eisenberg et al, 1993). According to a recent account, sales of ginseng products now top US$350 million per year, making it the second most popular herbal remedy in the US behind garlic (Foreman, 1997). It is unknown what percentage of the above-mentioned figure is represented by American ginseng (versus Asian ginseng or *Eleutherococcus* – see below).

Ginseng is also a commonly purchased herb in Europe. Laird (1999) reports that the second top-selling herbal remedy in Europe in 1996 was a ginseng product, with sales in excess of US$50 million. Ginseng now appears in Western markets in tinctures, in capsules, as whole roots, and as an ingredient in chewing gums, shampoos, teas and a plethora of other products. It remains to be seen whether US and European consumers will be able to appreciate the subtle distinctions between wild and cultivated ginseng to such a degree that they would be willing to pay US$300–US$500 per pound (per 0.45 kilograms) for wild or simulated-wild American ginseng roots.

In the US and European markets, American ginseng's greatest competition comes from Asian ginseng supplied by South Korea. Mainland China has begun to cultivate its own supply of *P. quinquefolius* under artificial shade from imported seed (Patty, 1982; Proctor et al, 1988; Xin, 1995). The Chinese are also experimenting with cultivation of *P. ginseng* under natural forest canopy (Wang et al, 1995). It may be only a matter of time before China attempts to raise woods-grown and simulated-wild *P. quinque-folius* in Chinese forests, thereby directly competing with American woods-grown and simulated-wild ginsengs. Xin (1995) makes this threat clear: 'Scientific cultivation techniques and production practices in the past 20 years have allowed the production of American ginseng in China to develop into a thriving new industry. Gone are the days when China relied on imports for its supply of American ginseng.'

American ginseng's greatest domestic competition may come from a Far Eastern herb known as 'Siberian ginseng' (*Eleutherococcus senticosus*). *Eleutherococcus senticosus* is not a true ginseng, but is a member of the same family (Araliaceae) as American ginseng and Asian ginseng. The 'Siberian ginseng' reputedly contains some of the same adaptogenic properties found in true ginsengs. The plant is an extremely common, thorny shrub native to Siberia, and is easily grown and propagated (Duke, 1989). Many consumers are unaware of the differences between the plants, and 'Siberian ginseng' is currently inexpensive to source in comparison with wild or woods-grown ginseng (Persons, 1994b). Some marketers distinguish 'Siberian ginseng' from *Panax* spp. on product claims, while others do not. The American Botanical Council is currently testing most of the ginseng products sold in the US to determine if these products contain *bona fide* ginseng (Blumenthal et al, 1995).

Certification potential

Certification of wild ginseng will be challenging. Ginseng diggers tend to be independent-minded, self-reliant rural people with a healthy scepticism for rules and regulations. Many ginseng gatherers collect the plant for the sheer enjoyment of being outdoors and the thrill of discovery, not unlike the thrill afforded by hunting or fishing. The adjectives used to describe ginseng collection convey an air of animation usually not attributed to plants: 'stalking ginseng', 'hunting ginseng' and 'ginseng poaching' are just a few examples. In many areas, 'sanging' or 'senging' (digging ginseng) is considered a God-given rite of autumn to be enjoyed.

Ginseng is often viewed as a common property resource. Ginseng gatherers dig the herb to earn supplemental, tax-free income to be used for Christmas gifts, car payments or general expenses. Hufford's (1997) interview with one Appalachian ginseng digger reveals the value of the plant to rural residents: 'We would dig ginseng to buy our school clothes and buy our books so we could go back to school in the fall.' Ginseng collection provides a connection to the landscape, a social identity, and a continuation of rural livelihood patterns in much of Appalachia. One ginseng collector, in a petition to document the cultural value of the mixed mesophytic forest of Appalachia, wrote: 'I work in construction, but really I consider myself a ginsenger' (Hufford, 1997). In Appalachia and across its range, ginseng is viewed as a natural bounty to inhabitants, a symbol of the wilds and a physical connection to place and identity. 'Wild ginseng, in fact, would seem to merit federal protection not because it is endangered but because within its limited range it is integral to the venerable social institution of the commons', writes Hufford (1997).

Chain-of-custody verification will present novel challenges. Many gatherers will begrudge any oversight of their activities. Ginseng gathering, in many ways, is an arcane activity that harvesters enjoy because of its very secretive nature. Management plans for wild ginseng are rare, tenure is problematic, and monitoring and security is extremely challenging. Ginseng diggers may not perceive the rigours of certification to be worth their while, particularly if the cost of certifica-

tion eats into much, if not all, of a year's profits. Pressure from middlemen and end-consumers might provide some leverage to change attitudes, but it is doubtful that a sea change will come soon to the ginseng industry. Chain of custody would currently work best for operations producing woods-grown and simulated-wild ginseng, where established tenure and documented baseline data already exist.

Certification may help to re-enforce ginseng CITES regulations by formalizing access rights between forest management operations and responsible gatherers with usufruct rights. Scrupulous harvesters may find such an arrangement preferable to competing with unscrupulous diggers in the commons. If forest managers cannot reach agreements with gatherers, safeguarding wild ginseng or simulated-wild/woods-grown ginseng populations will be difficult. Near-Draconian access measures would need to be enforced, and any certified management plan for ginseng production could be damaged by the silent incursion of one pilfering collector.

Ecological concerns with ginseng cultivation in woodland settings relate primarily to the impact of increased ginseng numbers on the populations of other understorey plants. Ginseng, as mentioned, grows in mature, stable, enriched habitats that tend to support other rare, threatened or endangered herbs. Managers who dedicate enriched sites to ginseng cultivation will reduce or exclude other herbs, thereby reducing or eliminating important habitat for other uncommon herbs on the forest property. Enriched habitats also tend to support the best development of important timber species such as sugar maple and white ash (Leak, 1980), making the temporal integration of ginseng and timber harvesting paramount. The environmental impact of any herbicides and fungicides used to protect ginseng crops would also need to be evaluated. The scale and intensity of ginseng cultivation will likewise warrant critical examination, as will the provenance of seed sources and their potential impact on local genetic diversity.

As most woods-cultivated and wild ginseng is primarily consumed in Asia, the receptivity of ginseng certification among Asian consumers should be thoroughly researched. Currently, knowledge of certification is low to non-existent among the general public in major ginseng-consuming countries, and the willingness of such countries to embrace certification remains unclear. At present, physical appearance, rather than environmental attributes, determines price. Widescale education will be needed, or support from major ginseng import–export houses obtained, before a serious push for wild- and woods-cultivated ginseng certification can be made. Since ginseng is ingested as a medicinal, linking forest certification with organic certification may be prudent.

Chapter 17

Mastic gum (*Pistacia lentiscus*), cork oak (*Quercus suber*), argan (*Argania spinosa*), pine nut (*Pinus pinea*), pine resin (various spp.) and chestnut (*Castanea sativa*)

Yorgos Moussouris and Pedro Regato

The Mediterranean eco-region

The Mediterranean eco-region is one of 233 such regions with outstanding biodiversity at a global scale. Located in the Northern hemisphere sub-tropical zone, between 28 and 45 degrees, the Mediterranean eco-region extends from the Atlantic coast to the Caspian Sea and from the mountain ranges of the Alps to the Saharan desert. This eco-region covers the lands surrounding the Mediterranean Sea, on the three continents of Africa, Europe and Asia, and constitutes a unique mosaic of terrestrial, freshwater and marine ecosystems. The rich natural landscape of the Mediterranean is a result of a distinct regional climate imprinted on a dynamic topography.

Illustration by Antônio Valente da Silva

*Mastic gum (*Pistacia lentiscus*)*

The climate is the main factor that shapes the physical environment in the Mediterranean. Yearly rainfall varies from 100 millimetres (mm) to more than 2500 mm, while the average temperature ranges from 5° Celsius (C) to 20° C. The existence of an intense summer drought period is the prevalent feature of Mediterranean climates at a global scale. The rich biodiversity of the Mediterranean flora results from a suite of adaptations to regional climatic conditions and, particularly, to the characteristic water shortage conditions during the dry summer period. The Mediterranean flora is extremely rich, with nearly 25,000 vascular plant species, half of which are endemic to the region (Regato, 1996).

In general, Mediterranean forest ecosystems constitute mosaic-like landscapes that reflect the complex climatic and geomorphological conditions of regional landforms. Human influence over the last 10,000 years has also intensively modified the natural structure and distribution of Mediterranean forest ecosystems. The advent of agriculture, the introduction of domesticated animals and pasture management, episodic plunder-ing of timber resources by ancient and modern civilizations, mining and smelting, and periodic settlement and abandonment of rural areas all precipitated periods of higher and lower human impacts on Mediterranean forests. The high levels of diversity that are found in today's Mediterranean forests, woodlands and *maquis* (evergreen short-tree and shrub communities) habitat types are a direct result of the interaction between humans and the natural environment.

Mediterranean traditional woodland management systems

Many of the traditional management systems of Mediterranean forests did not have a severe impact on ecosystem stability and have partly contributed to the maintenance of biodiversity. The traditional and familiar Mediterranean landscape of woodlands alternating with pastures and cultivated lands is a result of this type of sustainable rural management. Non-timber forest products (NTFPs) are one of the outputs of these management systems. Such traditional management systems portray the delicate balance between human presence and forest well-being and are worth preserving (Padulosi, 1999).

NTFPs have played an important role in the economies of Mediterranean cultures since prehistoric times. Preserved myth and lore reveal a reverence for forests, a tradition that still continues among many Mediterranean rural communities. In antiquity, sacred groves dotted the landscape, yielding products that were worshipped as divine. The 'Song of Solomon' compares the beauty of love to the bounty of the forest's gifts. The Greek philosopher Theophrastus, born around 370 BC, describes multiple-forest management practices that produced NTFPs; many of the practices described have survived to post-industrial times. His detailed accounts of cork extraction, pine-nut harvesting, aromatic plant gathering and resin extraction could easily apply to contemporary Mediterranean rural societies (Theophrastus, 1998a; 1998b).

The following species profiles provide a brief introduction to several of the diverse traditional Mediterranean forest-management systems that are associated with NTFPs: mastic gum from *maquis* woodlands, cork and argan oil from silvo-pastoral systems, pine nuts and pine resin from lowland coniferous forests and chestnuts from mountain woodlands.

Mastic gum production from *maquis* woodlands

Mastic gum is a natural resin extracted from a variety of *Pistacia lentiscus* growing on the Greek island of Chios. *Pistacia lentiscus* is one of the most characteristic evergreen species of the Mediterranean *maquis*. Although *Pistacia lentiscus* is a common species of the region, mastic resins are only secreted from trees on the island of Chios, where large-scale mastic production takes place.

Many ancient writers, such as Theophrastus, Pliny the Elder, Galenos and Dioscorides, referred to mastic gum, which was considered a panacea for many maladies. Information dating back to the middle of the 14th century reveals the importance of the gum production to Chios, which had peaks and lows as a result of political and socio-economic vicissitudes, including periods when production was completely abandoned. Production has fluctuated from 7000 kilograms (kg) to 390,000kg per year with an average of 250,000kg during the first half of the 20th century (Perikos, 1990).

Pistacia lentiscus var. *chia* is a slow-growing, cold-sensitive tree that grows in limestone soil. It reaches full size at 40 to 50 years and is able to produce gum after only the fifth or sixth year, but full production potential is reached between 12 and 15 years. Production averages 100 grams per year but sometimes can reach 650 grams.

Mastic gum production takes place between June and mid-October. Tapping preparations begin with cleaning of the tree, followed by sweeping and levelling the ground beneath the tree. Subsequently, the first vertical and horizontal cuts are made on the bark twice a week, for a period of five to six weeks. Collection follows crystallization of the first secreted gum. After that, the second cut is inflicted, and the 'tears' are collected once again. Mastic gum production regulation requires all collection activities to terminate after 15 October. After collection, the gum is sieved and then given to a cooperative for quality control. The cooperative sends the product to the Union of Mastic Producers, where final processing takes place.

There are many products of mastic gum. Drops of the gum have a unique, pleasant flavour and are sold as chewing gum, and confectionary from mastic has been processed, packed and marketed since 1995. Other products include mastic oil and rosin, which are derived from mastic gum distillation. Another mastic product, moscholivano, is a solid essence that, when burned, releases a pleasant odour. Mastic gum is a culinary ingredient in Mediterranean cuisine and patisserie and is also used to flavour ouzo (a sweet, aniseed-flavoured Greek spirit). Mastic by-products are used in varnishes and coatings and in a type of cement called asphalt mastic. Mastic is considered an astringent. Currently, there is extensive research to test all the medicinal properties attributed to mastic gum since ancient times.

Mastic from Chios is exported to 50 countries. Saudi Arabia is the largest importer. The trade delivers US$14.4 million per year to 21 villages located in the southern part of Chios. Since 1938, the village producers have held a monopoly on mastic gum collection and distribution. The future for the producers looks bright, especially now that current testing to identify additional medical properties in the gum has yielded positive results.

During a press conference held in Athens in December 1999, a team of experts from the University Hospital of Nottingham announced that there is strong evidence linking the consumption of mastic gum with a reduction in the incidence and recurrence of stomach ulcers. Their study indicates that daily digestion of 1 gram of raw mastic gum per day for two weeks can help cure peptic and duodenal ulcers. Tens of millions of people around the world suffer from duodenal ulcers, and mastic gum presents an opportunity for the development of a single, cheap and effective drug. To date, the treatment of ulcers has been based on the use of relatively expensive pharmaceuticals that kill (with a 90 per cent success rate) ulcer-causing *Heliobacter pylori* bacteria, formally recognized in 1994 by the World Health Organization (WHO) as one of the chief causes of stomach cancer. Recent tests have shown that mastic gum killed all *Heliobacter pylori* strains examined, thus expanding the commercial and medicinal potential of this ancient NTFP (Koromilas, 1999).

Cork production from silvo-pastoral woodlands

Cork is the name given to the thick outer bark of the evergreen Mediterranean oak *Quercus suber*. The largest cork oak forests are found in Portugal, where the species occupies an area of 660,000 hectares. In Spain, there are 500,000 hectares of pure cork oak stands and 121,000 hectares of mixed stands. In Algeria, there are around 480,000 hectares; in Morocco, 348,000 hectares; in Italy, 100,000 hectares;

Illustration by Bee Gunn

*Cork oak (*Quercus suber*)*

and resistant to heat and fire. Cork extraction begins when the tree is 15–20 years old. Cork is harvested by making horizontal and vertical cuts through the outer bark. Removal is made with great care so as not to cause any harm to the living inner bark. Cork is extracted from the stem and sometimes from the main branches of *Quercus suber*.

In Spain, regulation dictates that bark extraction should never exceed

in Tunisia, 45,000 hec-tares; and in France, around 43,000 hectares. Cork oak reaches 20 metres (m) in height, with an average height of 9m. Cork oak is a typical Mediterranean species, whose establishment outside its natural range has not been successful in terms of cork production.

Cork is an elastic, light, durable, homogeneous mass of flattened dead cells, including a fatty substance that makes it almost impermeable to water and gases a height greater than three times the length of the tree's circumference at breast height (measured at 1.3m above ground). The first extraction takes place when the girth at breast height (gbh) reaches 60 centimetres (cm) (Portuguese law stipulates 70cm as the minimum gbh for first stripping). The length of the first stripping cannot exceed 1.20m. Generally, in each producing region, quantifiable relations exist for the determination of stripping height. Optimum barking rotation depends upon the physiological effects that harvesting has on the tree, the quality of cork demanded by industry and climatic conditions. Extraction takes place every 10 years in south-western Spain and every 14 years in Catalonia. In Catalonia, the exposed stem is sprayed with anti-fungal medicine after barking to prevent infection of the tree.

The bark is seasoned and boiled following harvest, a process that removes tannic acid and makes the cork pliable. The outer bark regenerates after each stripping. The first stripping gives a coarse-textured cork, called 'virgin cork', that is combined with cork production residues in the manufacture of agglomerate cork. Subsequent stripping at intervals of ten years renders a better-quality product. Cork produced from the second stripping and afterwards is termed 'reproduction cork', and is mainly used in the manufacture of cork stoppers. An individual tree can produce cork for a period of 150 years or longer.

Thinning promotes vigorous growth in cork oak stands. Determination of the ideal density for cork production relates to many parameters depending upon management objectives, and can include hunting, grazing and agroforestry. Pruning is also applied, depending upon which oak product is in demand from a particular system (acorns, cork, shade, pasture, cereal crop, etc). However, excessive pruning is occasionally applied. Quantified relations between outputs do exist, and the type and intensity of management depends upon which of the many activities in a cork-producing woodland system need to be optimized.

Additional management activities accommodate barking. Understorey cleaning improves the efficiency of extraction operations and reduces fire hazard during the extraction year when trees with exposed stems are very vulnerable. Understorey cleaning results in partial or total elimination of underbrush in cork oak forests. Some experts believe that understorey cleaning protects cork trees from exposure to fungal infection, while others suggest that there is no evidence that the activity improves cork quality. Partial cleaning around individual trees is also applied in south-western Spain. Understorey corridors are occasionally cleaned to facilitate worker movement between trees. Cleaning takes place one to two years before barking to allow tree adjustment to new micro-environmental conditions, such as micro-climate, wind, steeper temperature gradients, etc.

One worrisome development in cork extraction concerns the availability of skilled labour. The traditional cork strippers are disappearing. Although there is more internal and external immigration of cork workers, many people who seek employment in cork woodlands and the cork industry have no experience in traditional management and production practices. Because cork extraction offers occupation for only four months out of the year, many people have shown a preference for more permanent employment positions in less labour-intensive, secure and profitable jobs, such as tourism offers. Lack of skilled labour may hold long-term ecological consequences for the cork resource.

The properties of cork have been known since antiquity, but it was not generally used until some centuries ago, when cork stoppers were manufactured for the newly introduced glass bottles. Extensive use of cork was initiated following the discovery of champagne during the 17th century by the Benedictine monk Dom Perignon. Since then, cork production has maintained strong ties with the wine industry. About 25 billion cork stoppers are used worldwide every year. Cork is also used in construction (insulation and floors), the naval industry (extensive use for lifebelts), transport, the textile industry, the chemo-pharmaceutical industries, the shoe industry (sole manufacturing), and for packing and linoleum.

More than 80 per cent of the global supply of cork is produced in Algeria, Portugal and Spain. Portuguese production reaches 175,000 tonnes per year (about 55 per cent of the global output), with a value of US$200 million. The greatest importer of cork products is the European Union (EU), which in 1989 imported 56 per cent of the total quantity and 57 per cent of the total value. Virgin cork production has decreased sharply over the past few decades and is presently about 35,000 tonnes per year. The reason behind the drop is not a reduction in cork oak woodland but rather a reflection of the rising cost of labour for cork extraction. In addition, synthetics are now used as a cork substitute for insulation and in other products that were originally manufactured from cork. Spirit manufacturers, such as gin- and whisky-makers, stopped using cork in the 1960s. A Norwegian factory recently patented a synthetic cork for stoppers made from ethyl vinyl acetate.

In 1990, more than 900 cork manufacturing factories were in operation in Portugal, occupying about 14,000 employees. The Corticeira Armorim, a family firm, currently controls around one-third of Portugal's cork manufacturing. Its case presents an example of the economies of scale for NTFP production and distribution, with production consolidation from small cooperatives to a single producer. The firm grew to its current sales of US$340 million because it established factories that use the remains from stopper manufacturing for other products, contrary to the traditional way, with most cork going to cottage industries that produced only stoppers. As a result, Corticeira Armorim became dominant in cork markets, making 70 per cent of the world's cork flooring and almost 95 per cent of the cork-based gaskets that Portugal produces for engine joints (FAO, 1997; Varela, 1995; Anonymous, 1996; Baldini, 1993; Direccao Geral das Florestas, 1990; Regato, pers comm, 1998).

The argan silvo-pastoral woodlands of Morocco

Argan (*Argania spinosa*) is a spiny evergreen tree, endemic to Morocco. It is a Tertiary relic species and is the only member of the tropical Sapotaceae to occur north of the Sahara on the African mainland. Argan's ecological and social values make it one of the most important tree species in North Africa. Argan woodlands cover an area of about 820,000 hectares in south-western Morocco (about 7 per cent of the total forest cover of Morocco). The woodlands exist in a region where rainfall rarely exceeds 200–300 millimetres per year; at times, rainfall is even lower than 120mm per year.

The species was probably known to the Phoenicians. A 13th-century medical book describes methods for oil extraction from its fruit. Argan oil was imported into Europe during the 18th century, but failed to maintain a market presence due to its strong flavour and competition from olive oil.

Argania spinosa plays a crucial role in the stabilization of environmental conditions. It prevents soil erosion, especially in overgrazed lands where the water absorption capacity of the soil is diminished. Its shade protects pasture grasses from the extreme evapo-transpiration that would result from direct exposure to sunlight. It facilitates water infiltration and aquifer replenishment. Finally, in areas of the extreme south of their range, argan woodlands form a green belt against desert advancement.

The argan tree is managed for oil production, pasture and fuelwood, commodities that ensure the subsistence of two million

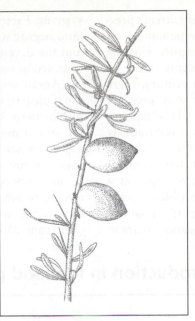

Illustration by Jamison Ervin

Argan (Argania spinosa)

people in rural Morocco. It has great potential to contribute to the economic development of rural populations and prevent rural emigration toward the large urban centres of the country. An indicator of argan's importance is the number of working days per year that argan management demands from Moroccan rural people. Specifically, there are estimations of 800,000 working days per year for fuelwood collection and 20,000,000 working days per year for oil extraction (the production of 1 litre of oil requires one and a half days of work) respectively.

The plum-sized argan fruit contains one to three kernels with a high oil content (over 50 per cent). The oil has a distinct flavour, resembling that of walnut oil. The ratio of total unsaturated to total saturated fatty acids is around 4 to 5, similar to that of olive oil. Argan oil contains about 80 per cent polyunsaturated fatty acids, of which 30 per cent is linoleic acid. This gives the oil a high nutritional value, since

it is one of the most important essential fatty acids in the human diet. Argan is a traditional staple for many Moroccans. A recent study reports that argan oil is bought by Moroccan immigrants in Israel, who number more than 600,000, at prices of up to US$43 per litre – a sum ten times greater than the cost of olive oil (Mizrahi and Nerd, 1996).

Argan oil production takes place at the family level and women undertake the entire task. The dried flesh of the fruit is separated from the nut, and the oil in the seeds is extracted. Next, the seeds are lightly roasted, ground and mixed with warm water. The floating oil is separated by rinsing and may be further purified by either emulsion with water or the addition of bread. Approximately 100kg of seed yields 1–2kg of oil and 2kg of pressed 'cake' (a pasty oil production by-product), as well as 25kg of dried husk.

In addition to cooking, the oil is used for lighting and soap manufacturing. The sun-dried cake residue is fed to livestock (although this reduces the quality of dairy cattle milk). The fruit and foliage are a valuable fodder source for livestock. The hard, heavy and durable argan timber gives good charcoal and argan brushwood is used for fencing. The tree also provides valuable shade for humans and livestock during hot days.

Despite the granting of protection status – which, since 1925, regulates the rights of use by local people – argan woodlands suffer continuing degradation.

Fuelwood collection applies extreme pressure to the tree and unsustainable fruit gathering and grazing magnify existing natural regeneration problems. Prior to the beginning of the 20th century, there was a balance between grazing pressure and natural regeneration. This balance has been disturbed by continuously increasing use of argan woodlands. At present, argan woodland regression is estimated at 600 hectares per year at a minimum. The principal problem comes from increasing demographic pressures, expressed as usage intensification of argan systems. Factors that lead to argan woodland degradation include intense plowing and the development of irrigated agriculture, wood removal and overgrazing.

Argan woodland conservation issues are typical of the plight of forest resources in Northern Africa. Among the priorities, the sound management (and survival) of argan forests is most important, as their loss will not only lead to the extinction of an important relic species but will also have adverse effects on the millions of people who rely on its resources (Benzyane Mohamed, undated).

Pine-nut production in lowland pine forests

Stone pine, *Pinus pinea*, is endemic to the Mediterranean. The total area covered by stone pine woodlands is 380,000 hectares (75 per cent in Spain; 9 per cent in Portugal; 9 per cent in Turkey; 5 per cent in Italy; and lower percentages in Greece, Lebanon and France). Stone pine woodlands are important in terms of their biodiversity (eg Doñana National Park in Spain), and their management yields a variety of products such as nuts, timber, firewood, resins, bark and honey, as well as pastures for livestock and hunting.

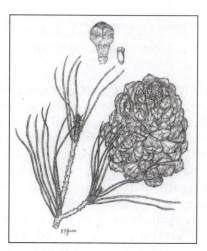

Illustration by Bee Gunn

*Stone pine (*Pinus pinea*)*

Stone pine can reach 15–25m in height and thrives on coastal sandy areas with a moist but well-drained ground, characterized by small temperature variations and a shallow water table. The special requirements of stone pine in terms of soil, hydrological and climatic conditions make the tree sensitive to environmental disturbance and difficult to regenerate. The distinct spherical shape of the crown allows the tree to achieve maximum benefits from solar radiation. The tree starts producing seeds after 12 to 18 years, depending upon its occurrence in isolation or in stands. Cones take three years to reach maturity, at which stage they are 10–15cm in length and 6–10cm in width.

Stone pine kernels are used in the Mediterranean as a culinary delicacy and have a protein value two-thirds that of lean steak. In addition to their nutritional value, stone pine nuts have been considered as an aphrodisiac all around the Mediterranean since ancient times. The

BOX 17.1 THE STROFILIA (*PINUS PINEA*) FOREST IN SOUTH-WESTERN GREECE

The Strofilia forest in south-western Greece provides a rather typical example of a rural community that is failing to reap the full benefits of products from an adjacent forest area. The Strofilia (*strofilia* is the Greek word for 'stone pine') forest constitutes the only remaining woodland of *Pinus pinea* in Greece that can still be characterized as a 'forest' and represents 80 per cent of the total stone pine forest in the country. Located in the western Peloponnese, the forest covers a north–south coastal strip with a length of 15km and an average width of 1.5km. *Pinus halepensis* and *Quercus aegilops* are also important tree species in the Strofilia forest. The forest belongs to a wider system of coastal dunes and wetlands that are included in the Ramsar Convention (an international convention on wetlands, signed in Ramsar, Iran, in 1971). In 1993, a Common Ministerial Decision gave special protection status to the whole ecosystem.

Pine-nut gathering is a popular activity in the Strofilia forest; but it does not take place in any organized way that could provide valuable income to adjacent communities. In addition, it is believed that this form of unsustainable gathering imposes a threat to the integrity of the forest because it may hinder stone pine regeneration. The lack of organized gathering is only one of the many threats to the Strofilia forest. Another existing problem is overgrazing, which disturbs the understorey and has a negative impact on maintenance of soil fertility. A recent study has shown that the grazing capacity of the whole area is only 7200 grazing units, much lower than the current 53,670 units that burden the forest. Moreover, habitat deterioration is compounded by unplanned tourist growth and the disturbance of soil and hydrologic conditions caused by intensification of agricultural activities, illegal road construction and sand mining. The overall result is a diminishment of the *Pinus pinea* population and, in many cases, the expansion of other less sensitive species, such as *Pinus halepensis*. Illegal hunting presents a threat to the wildlife of the forest. Recently, the killing of hundreds of tortoises (*Testudo hermanni* and *Testudo marginata*) and the consumption of tortoise eggs have been reported.

The lack of serious management in the forest may be detrimental to the forest's future welfare. In March 1998, a severe windstorm destroyed many stone pine trees (estimated at 10 to 20 per cent of the total population). Subsequently, the forest service allowed heavy vehicles to enter the forest area and remove the dead wood as part of an effort to reduce a potential fire hazard. However, only the trunks were removed (apparently to be used as firewood), while dead crowns were left in the forest and thousand of saplings were destroyed by the impact of the activities.

There is an urgent need for the implementation of a serious management plan that will protect the Strofilia forest and regulate human activities within it. A permanent Presidential Decree will implement the provisions of the management plan, including guidelines for the sustainable gathering of pine nuts. The guidelines should be based upon a stone pine-regeneration study and be accompanied by yield studies. Such research will provide a reliable measure of forest productivity in terms of pine nuts and define a sustainable harvest level. In parallel, socio-economic studies should indicate the most appropriate and efficient method to organize pine-nut production for the benefit of adjacent communities (cooperatives, enterprises, etc). A marketing plan will also be needed to promote the product to consumers (along with other existing forest products, such as honey), and could be accompanied by the potential benefits of eco-labelling.

The Strofilia forest is an example of a unique ecosystem that could benefit from serious protection efforts to ensure that its full potential to contribute to the economic well-being of rural communities who neighbour the forest is realized in a systematic and sustainable way.

Source: Kannelis, 1998

Roman poet Ovid (born in the 1st century BC), in his 'Ars amatoria – the Art of Love', a poem that challenged the serious moral reform efforts of Augustus, provides a list of aphrodisiacs, including 'the nuts that the sharp-leafed pine brings forth'. The Greek physician Galenos, of the 2nd century AD, suggests that a mixture of pine seeds, honey and almonds taken before bedtime for three consecutive evenings can increase sexual potency. Apicius, a Roman celebrity who loved good food and whose recipes (such as walnut-stuffed dormouse) were used until the Middle Ages, recommends a mixture of pine nuts, cooked onions, white mustard and pepper to achieve increased sexual appetite. Finally, the Arab text *Perfumed Garden*, referring to Galenos's writings, advises that in order to achieve sexual vigour a man should eat 20 almonds and 100 pine nuts, accompanied by a glassful of thick honey, for three nights before bedtime.

Spain has the most organized pine-nut production among Mediterranean coun-

tries. The production varies in cycles of two to six years. The number of pine cones per tree is a function of tree diameter, and the average yield is about 15–22kg of pine nuts per 100kg of cones. Collection takes place by men who climb the trees and gather the cones by hand or with a special tool. Each worker can collect about 400–600 cones per day. The collection period is from November to February. Extraction of the nut takes place by drying the cones in the sun. Empty cones can also be used as fuel for fires. Before reaching the market, the external hard cover of the pine seeds is removed by the use of special machines, a process that adds extra cost to the product.

The average annual production of pine nuts in Spain is about 6250 tonnes per year, representing 40 to 60 per cent of the world's production (including nuts coming from other pine species). Most of the production is exported, mainly to the US through Italy (Eutichidis, 1998; Regato, pers comm, 1998).

Pine-resin production

Resins are plant chemicals produced by several plant taxa in the order Coniferales. The term embraces a group of sticky, liquid, organic substances that usually harden into brittle, amorphous, solid substances when exposed to air. Natural resins are classified according to their physical and chemical properties into hard resins, oleoresins and gum resins.

Turpentine is a semi-fluid, yellow or brownish resin (oleoresin) secreted by pine trees. When a wound is inflicted, pine resin flows on the external surface of a tree to form a protective coat that seals

the opening, preventing sap loss and exposure to pathogenic micro-organisms. To obtain resin commercially, a tapping cut is made in the pine bark and the resin drops are collected into buckets or bags. The principal products of pine resin are rosin and turpentine oil. The most significant hard resin, from a commercial point of view, is rosin, which is obtained by distillation of pine resin. Rosin is used in paper glue and soap manufacturing, as a constituent of varnishes and paints, and for coating strings of musical instruments. Oil of turpentine is also produced by pine-resin distillation and is used for thinning and dissolving paint and varnish, as well as for shoe polish and the manufacture of sealing wax. Pine resin also has medical properties and can be used as a stimulant, anti-spasmodic, astringent, diuretic and anti-pathogenic. In the past, crude pine resin was used in sailing vessels as packing material and for waterproofing.

Resin collection activities in Mediterranean countries have always played a significant role in the welfare of forest communities, some of whom lived marginally at the edge of subsistence. In some low-income areas, resin collection was (and continues to be) the only reliable source of labour. In addition, many of the resin-producing forests are community forests, and production benefits go to resin community cooperatives. Another important aspect of these forests is that multiple-purpose forestry is applied and activities other than resin collection coexist. These include apiculture (usually honey production is undertaken individually and not by cooperatives), herbaceous plant-gathering (from the understorey), animal husbandry and employment in recreation. The preservation of resin production and the associated forest structure, along with several accompanying activities, are beneficial to both forest conservation and the economic viability of dependent rural communities in the Mediterranean. Income from the wood of a *Pinus halepensis* tree, for example, is only 2 per cent of the income generated from resin throughout the lifetime of the tree (an average-sized tree can produce 3–4kg of

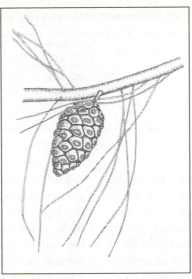

Illustration by Jamison Ervin

*Aleppo pine (*Pinus halepensis*)*

resin per year). Moreover, it has been observed that forests that have active resin production have a lower incidence of forest fires. This results from the fact that adjacent communities have an active interest in preserving the integrity of such forest ecosystems.

The low income and low market value of resin have reduced resin production in the Mediterranean, although world production of resin has remained almost constant since 1961 (despite the many changes that have occurred in the resin industry). What has occurred is a geographical displacement of resin production to developing countries, mainly due to the cost of labour. The data from the Mediterranean–Western European countries who produce pine resin is very informative and gives a clear picture of a declining trend. This trend is depicted in Table 17.1.

The case of France is characteristic; although the country has extensive potential stands for resin production, French resin-tapping and production ceased in 1991. Italian production ceased in 1980. Consider the following:

- The European deficit in resin is 128,000 tonnes per year.
- The deficit will increase.
- The total installed resin production capacity (in Portugal, Greece, Spain, France and Italy) is 290,000 tonnes per year.
- Mediterranean resin products are considered to be of top quality.

Table 17.1 *Annual resin production in Southern Europe, 1982 and 1997*

	1982 (tonnes)	1997 (tonnes)
Portugal	120,000	25,000
Greece	42,000	6000
Spain	60,000	3000
France	40,000	–
Italy	–	–

Source: Chozas Bermudez, 1997

It is thus obvious that resin production needs to be enhanced in all Mediterranean countries. Currently, resin deficits are supplemented by importing lower-quality products from abroad, particularly from China. However, the situation is complicated and innovative solutions need to be developed. The problems that must be considered are the abandonment of rural areas in Southern European countries and the high cost of production, which could make resin collection a non-viable activity. Furthermore, competition from petroleum-based synthetic resins presents an additional problem (Chozas Bermudez, 1997).

Chestnut production in mountain woodlands

The Parnon mountain range at the eastern part of Peloponnese in southern Greece spans a length of 70km, with its highest peak reaching 1936 metres (m). Forests mainly of Greek fir (*Abies cephalonica*) and black pine (*Pinus nigra*) cover the range. A relic juniper species, *Juniperus drupacea*, has its only European occurrence in Parnon. Chestnut (*Castanea sativa*) woodlands occur naturally in Parnon, but are also planted by local populations. Parnon forests have rich associated bird and reptile fauna. In addition, more than 80 threatened, rare and protected floral species occur in the Parnon, 12 of which are endemic.

Illustration by Antônio Valente da Silva

*Chestnut (*Castanea sativa*)*

Three sites in Parnon have been characterised as Natura 2000 network sites, in accordance with the European Union (EU) Habitats Directive. At the national level, the *Juniperus drupacea* stands and the chestnut woodland of Castanitsa have been declared natural monuments, while three Parnon villages have been characterized as cultural heritage sites. Future plans for Parnon concentrate on the establishment of a region-wide Parnon National Park, which will include the coastal wetland of Moustos, one of the most important wetlands along the eastern shores of the Greek peninsula. Representatives of local communities supported the initiative for the establishment of the protected area. A management plan for the park has already been produced.

Parnon has three main chestnut woodland areas: Castanitsa, Aghios Petros and Cosmas. The woodlands of Castanitsa cover an area of 450 hectares with about 35,000 trees. The woodlands are considered secondary or semi-natural forest and come from trees that were planted more than 150 years ago. For the chestnut tree woodlands of Castanitsa and Cosmas, the Greek Forest Service defines the forest management operations, while the Greek Bureau of Agriculture is responsible for fruit production. The two woodlands are subject to management plans produced by the Forest Service on a 10-year basis. The woodlands of Aghios Petros have a plantation structure, with trees interspersed among cultivated fields and terraces. In terms of land tenure, the woodland of Castanitsa has a community property status; it belongs to the dwellers of adjacent rural communities as a whole. The woodlands of Cosmas cover an area of 260 hectares, while the plantations of Aghios Petros cover about 300 hectares. Overall, Parnon chestnut woodlands and plantations cover an area of about 1000 hectares.

Fruit production starts when the tree reaches five years of age. Local varieties are edible, but fruit morphology limitations do not allow high competitiveness in the market (compared to Italian or French varieties), as Parnon chestnuts are more difficult to process. Local farmers in Parnon often graft chestnut trees with the maron variety, which has better confectionary properties. About one-third of the woodland has been certified under organic standards. Chestnut producers have organized themselves into a cooperative. Average chestnut production is about 250 tonnes per year.

Trees are not timbered. The chestnut tree woodland has a thin structure,

about eight chestnut trees per *stremma* ($1000m^2$). This density encourages crown development and does not allow the production of good-quality timber.

There are two main problems in the Castanitsa (and generally the Parnon) chestnut tree woodlands: chestnut blight and age structure. Chestnut blight is a fungal infection caused by *Cryptonectria* (*Endothia*) *parasitica* that inflicts severe damage to chestnut trees. In order to deal with the chestnut blight problem, two studies were undertaken. A four-year programme of biological 'treatment' based upon these studies is ready to be implemented. The treatment centres upon the introduction of weakened fungus, infected by a particular virus, in the hope of replacing the tree-damaging healthy fungus. To deal with the second problem, age structure, suggestions have been made to assist regeneration by planting the more productive maron variety (which is already grafted on Parnon chestnut trees). There is a need for a strategic study on chestnut woodland management. This study should take an integrated approach to chestnut woodland issues, including age structure. In order to preserve the woodland structure, young fir trees that grow among chestnut trees, threatening to eventually replace the chestnut canopy, are cut and sold for Christmas trees. Recently, a fir tree nursery was also established.

There is no management plan for chestnut harvesting. The fruit is harvested directly from the tree, or from the ground after the tree is shaken, causing the fruit to fall. The strategic study needs to incorporate issues such as yield, sustainable harvest levels, regeneration/replacement strategies and other issues. However, organized production will take place at the processing stage and no major intensification of harvesting is expected. No fires have occurred within the chestnut woodlands for more than 30 years (since 1966).

This is attributed to the fact that a continued human presence within the woodlands, with activities such as chestnut harvesting, results in good fire management of the forest.

There is a need to develop activities that target the sustainable management and production of chestnuts in the area, as well as activities that raise awareness at all levels about the importance of chestnut production for the conservation and development of the region. A positive step is the recent establishment of a cooperative to coordinate chestnut producers. The cooperative needs to lead the way in formulating appropriate management practices through all stages of production and needs to develop a dynamic strategy that will promote chestnuts within the market. Finally, an issue that requires more attention is the importation and use of foreign grafts, since they may threaten the local variety (Marinos, pers comm, 1998; Stefanos, pers comm, 1998; Papageorgiou, pers comm, 1998).

Overview of Mediterranean forest conservation issues

The conservation issues related to Mediterranean forests reflect the different socio-economic conditions prevailing in the northern, southern and eastern shores of the basin. In the north, rural abandonment has resulted in the collapse of many traditional sustainable forest-management activities. In the south, high birth rates result in overexploitation of forest resources and in forest depletion.

The total area (cover) and biomass of Mediterranean forests have increased in Southern Europe as a direct result of rural depopulation. In many cases, dense shrub communities have invaded land previously occupied by marginal agricultural activities. In certain locations, an increase in wildlife population densities has taken place, which means that rural abandonment was beneficial to forest integrity. However, in many cases, regenerated forests are of poor quality and of low biodiversity; this is because sustainable management methods that had been applied for centuries to woodlands were abandoned.

An example of these negative effects is the impact of forest fires. Although Mediterranean forests are fire adapted, they face severe fire problems as a result of a disruption in traditional fire management methods and the higher frequency of fire occurrence resulting from social pressure (such as the increasing demand among urban dwellers for holiday homes). Another example is the negative consequences of rural abandonment, in combination with other factors (such as the introduction of intensive agriculture methods), on the quality of silvo-pastoral systems.

Additional problems include overgrazing (which hinders forest regeneration), unplanned tourism development, especially in coastal forest areas, and massive afforestation initiatives that use exotic species, such as the extensive eucalyptus plantations in Spain and Portugal. In recent years, increases in non-local and foreign market demand have resulted in the unsustainable gathering of many NTFPs, mainly medicinal plants, herbs, bulbs, wild greens and other produce such as pine nuts.

Forests in southern Mediterranean countries face conservation problems of a different character: traditional forest management methods have become intensive as a result of rapid population growth. The situation in Turkey and the Middle East is somewhat between the situations in the north and the south.

Socio-economic benefits from NTFP commercialization in the Mediterranean

There are great economic incentives for countries in the Mediterranean to develop the NTFP production potential of their forests and to generate positive socio-economic benefits for rural populations that are compatible with conservation values. However, in order to deliver this potential there is a need to modify current economic notions that govern Mediterranean forest management. This modification will take place vis-à-vis conservation efforts and, in many cases, restoration of woodland resources. The entire process should be based on the verified belief that stable Mediterranean woodland ecosystems allow the production of a large number of NTFPs. Currently, with the possible exception of resins and cork, the production of NTFPs in the Mediterranean is highly neglected.

There are many factors that hinder the reintroduction of traditional NTFP production systems in the Mediterranean. Because NTFPs are often used locally for subsistence or trade in rural markets, they have been excluded from official forestry and agriculture statistics. The division of official governmental agencies between forestry and agriculture creates some practical inconvenience for the consideration of NTFP commodities that fall within a grey area of production for many experts. Finally, the mainstream forestry view that the value of a forest is clearly reflected by its timber production capacity has resulted in only incidental and fragmented consideration of NTFPs.

However, emerging trends may help to revert past biases. These trends can be summarized as follows:

- Deteriorating socio-economic conditions in the southern and eastern Mediterranean are instilling a new, sometimes subsistence, reliance on local natural resources.
- There is increasing awareness of the positive role that NTFPs can play in socio-economic development and in the conservation of natural resources.
- Green consumerism is growing, creating a demand for natural products.
- There is an increasing demand for traditional products.
- There is increasing awareness and demand for new biochemicals and pharmaceuticals.

Among the three groups involved in NTFP production and consumption (rural populations, traders and urban consumers), the numbers of traders and urban consumers are increasing, providing marketing opportunities. However, beyond any measurable economic benefits that may derive from revitalizing NTFP production systems, it is important to consider the cultural and religious significance of NTFPs to rural societies. Preservation of traditional forest management methods will not only maintain environmental and socio-economic integrity, but will also enhance cultural continuity.

NTFP certification issues in the Mediterranean

Certification may hold promise for some Mediterranean NTFPs. However, several issues will need to be tackled so that NTFP certification can proceed in the Mediterranean:

- Local or regional forest standards that incorporate the uniqueness and complexity of Mediterranean forest systems will need to be agreed upon.
- Mediterranean forest certification standards will need to encompass agroforestry and silvo-pastoral systems.
- Involvement of local experts who have knowledge of anthropogenically manipulated systems will be central to creating standards for Mediterranean ecosystems.
- The issue of grazing (timing and intensity) needs to be addressed, particularly for silvo-pastoral woodland systems where regeneration may be a critical issue.
- The treatment of fire – either its suppression or controlled use – will be an important issue.
- The issue of certification costs will need to be examined. Large units that are cooperatively managed may be able to afford certification, but the cost of certification for small properties that produce NTFPs could be burdensome.
- Regeneration studies, yield data and other basic biological and ecological information are still required to inform management of argan, pine and other Mediterranean NTFP-producing woodlands and agroforestry systems.
- Tenure and forest security issues pose potential problems for the certification of many Mediterranean NTFPs.

- Subsistence issues, resource rights and access issues will be complex in some areas of the Mediterranean.

Certification could sensitize the 'green consumer' to issues of sound forest management and, especially in the case of Parnon, sound management of protected areas. Thus, eco-labelling, apart from ensuring that NTFPs are produced in the most 'environmentally acceptable' way, could contribute to awareness about the importance of the human interface with forest areas and protected areas in the Mediterranean, where widespread human influence has been present for thousands of years.

Because demand for locally traded NTFPs is inelastic, the cost of certification may interfere with rural consumers' ability to pay. Thus, the best candidates for testing NTFP certification would be internationally traded NTFPs, such as nuts or cork. Any certification initiative, especially for medicinal plants, should be done in collaboration with other initiatives, such as TRAFFIC, the wildlife trade monitoring programme of WWF and the World Conservation Union (IUCN).

Overall, there are many cases where the prospect of NTFP certification could be positive, such as the development of 'gourmet' markets, which might enhance the livelihoods of rural Mediterranean people and bolster conservation efforts in their regions. However, certification efforts should proceed with caution because many of these populations rely on NTFPs (eg argan oil) and any increase in demand for the product outside local markets could negatively interfere with sensitive subsistence patterns. An important positive aspect of any certification initiative is that it could increase the awareness of landscape ecology in the region. Finally, putting an emphasis on NTFP certification will be a way of realistically evaluating the worth of non-timber-producing Mediterranean woodlands that, in the past, have been neglected or given only cursory attention.

Managing woodlands for NTFPs can contribute to maintaining the health, beauty and permanence of Mediterranean landscapes. To do so, investments need to locate and capitalize on existing knowledge about forest management for multiple outputs. Any aid given to introducing new economic activities should follow a piecemeal approach and be based on the existing potential of Mediterranean woodland resources. This applies equally to all Mediterranean countries. In the north, where abandonment has resulted in a decline of original management methods and left only migration as an option for rural populations, reconsidering the value of NTFPs could create small poles of economic attraction in the countryside. The situation is even more urgent in the south, where intensification of human use has disrupted the natural balance and has led experts to push for the adoption of imported land-management methods based upon monocultural models. It is time to act and to establish small- to medium-scale operations that would organize forest management for NTFPs, address the ecological and social needs of rural populations and preserve the rich, centuries-old natural and cultural landscape of the region.

Chapter 18

Griffonia (*Griffonia simplicifolia*)

Kodzo Gbewonyo

Introduction

Illustration by Bee Gunn

Griffonia (Griffonia simplicifolia)

Extracts from the seeds of a little-known African shrub recently became embroiled in an intense controversy between friends and critics of the dietary supplement industry. The story of griffonia plant extract 5-HTP appears to encapsulate the growing pains of the newly deregulated US dietary supplement industry and its impact on suppliers in source countries.

The species

Griffonia simplicifolia is a tropical shrub belonging to the botanical family Caesalpiniaceae found in abundance in the coastal and secondary forests of West Africa. The plant grows as a woody climber and flowers from August to November, producing 5-centimetre (cm) pods. The pods explode with a loud noise when ripe, releasing flat, disc-shaped seeds that are 1–2 millimetres (mm) in size, which are harvested and dried for export.

The characteristic explosive noise of the pods at harvest gave the plant its local names (ie *totolimo*, *gbogboto* (Ga); *wotowoto* (Ewe); *kagya* (Twi)). The potent medicinal properties of griffonia have been long identified by local people. Traditionally, various parts of the plant are used to treat a variety of ailments, including vomiting, diarrhoea and pelvic congestion. The plant is also used as a purgative, antiseptic for wounds and aphrodisiac. The twigs are used as chewing sticks while the leaves are fed to sheep and goats to stimulate reproduction, in addition to insecticide applications to ward off lice from poultry (Ayensu, 1978).

Active constituents

Modern research has revealed that the seeds of *Griffonia simplicifolia* are deficient in a key enzyme (5-HTP decarboxylase), required for tryptophan metabolism (Fellows and Bell, 1970). This deficiency leads to an accumulation of unusually high levels of the intermediate 5-hydroxy-L-tryptophan (5-HTP) in the mature seeds. Levels of 5-HTP in the range of 10–18 per cent on a dry weight basis have been reported by high performance liquid chromatography (HPLC) analysis (Adosraku, pers comm, 1998).

5-HTP is the direct precursor of the ubiquitous hormone serotonin (5-hydroxy-tryptamine: 5-HT), which serves an important function as the brain's chemical messenger (neurotransmitter) in the human body. Thus administration of 5-HTP can lead to increased serotonin synthesis, resulting in beneficial effects, especially in cases of serotonin deficiency. Furthermore, orally administered 5-HTP is believed to cross the blood–brain barrier, boosting serotonin release from the brain. Documented studies have demonstrated clinical effectiveness of 5-HTP for depression (Nardini et al, 1983), attention deficit disorder (Kahn and Westenberg, 1985), migraine headache (Titus et al, 1986), insomnia (Caruso et al, 1990; Puttini and Caruso, 1992) and appetite suppression (Cangiano et al, 1992).

Besides the accumulation of high levels of 5-HTP, griffonia seeds also provide the source of a well-known plant lectin (glycoprotein GSL II) with strong antigenic properties for N-acetyl-glucosamine residues, which is useful as an immunoreagent in blood-group typing as well as an affinity-labelling reagent in biochemical research (Hayes and Goldstein, 1974). Reagent grade preparations from griffonia seed extracts can be found listed in scientific research catalogues from well-known distributors such as Sigma-Aldrich (Sigma-Aldrich, 1999).

Exploding international markets

Demand for griffonia as a source of 5-HTP has brought this multifunctional medicinal plant species recent fame and notoriety. For years, griffonia has been sourced annually in relatively modest quantities as an item of medicinal plant trade from West Africa to Europe, along with *Voacanga africana*, *Pygeum africanum* and *Pausinystalia yohimbe*, to name a few. European extractors, notably Kadem (Germany) and Nuova Linnea (Switzerland), have supplied 5-HTP extracts from griffonia seeds to worldwide markets.

It was not until 1997 that the medicinal properties of 5-HTP came to the attention of the rapidly growing US dietary supplement industry. Rumours started circulating in industry circles about the potential of 5-HTP as the next 'hot herb' to capture market attention after the overwhelming popularity of St John's wort (*Hypericum perforatum*) and kava kava (*Piper methysticum*).

The interest in griffonia also coincided with the period immediately following the debacle of the popular weight-loss drugs Redux and 'Fen/phen', which were pulled off the market following reports of serious adverse effects on heart valves in some patients. Dietary supplement manufacturers did not miss out on the strategic opportunities presented by the sudden vacuum in the lucrative weight-loss product market. As such, 5-HTP, by virtue of its documented evidence as an appetite suppressant, was high on the list of substitute products of interest to supplement suppliers.

It is worthwhile viewing this period within the wider context of the resurgence of the US dietary supplement industry as a whole. The industry has been enjoying unprecedented growth, fuelled by greater public awareness of the linkages between health, wellness and nutrition. Consumer preferences for natural foods and remedies grew as synthetic drugs acquired negative associations. Record growth rates reaching 20 per cent annually have been reported for the industry in recent years, with estimated total annual sales exceeding US$12 billion. The herbal products category alone accounts for US$4.2 billion of this total (Brevoort, 1998).

Liberalization of the sector from stringent US Food and Drug Administration (FDA) regulation by enactment of the Dietary Supplement and Health Education Act (DSHEA) in 1994 (US FDA, 1995) gave rise to the boom in the natural product industry. Several new companies sprang up to play various roles as suppliers, manufacturers and distributors. The research and development capacity of these companies is still limited; as a result, they tend to borrow product ideas from the older and more established European herbal industry – particularly the German industry.

Besides sporadic adventures into native cultures for new product ideas (as typified by kava kava), the product portfolios of the US dietary supplement industry consist largely of imitation products from Europe. Nevertheless, interesting trends are emerging, such as niche product lines based on traditional Chinese medicine (TCM) and Indian Ayurvedic medicine. There is, however, very little systematic effort to tap into the rich culture of herbal medicines from Africa. The few products of African origin that are now gaining a foothold – such as Yohimbe and Pygeum – were initially promoted by the European natural product industry. Similarly 5-HTP was well known in European industry circles for over two decades before awareness was aroused in the US.

Supply

By the spring of 1997, 5-HTP was at the top of the 'most wanted list' of the US natural product industry. Manufacturers were busy trying to identify sources and availability of griffonia seeds. Attention was focused on the West African country of Ghana as the key source. Unfortunately, the 1996–1997 harvest season had just ended and there were no more seeds available for export. Pent-up demand for griffonia skyrocketed throughout the off-season as desperate inquiries were repeatedly received by medicinal plant exporters in Ghana.

Meanwhile, advance orders and export contracts were put in place between buyers and sellers in anticipation of the opening of the next griffonia harvest season. The 1997–1998 griffonia harvest season turned out to be a bumper crop, partly due to the El Niño effect, which brought considerable rain that year. Griffonia grows in the wild, throughout the southern regions of Ghana, as a climbing plant in the shade of large trees. Collection and post-harvest processing of the seeds are carried out in farm villages as a seasonal occupation to provide supplementary income.

During the harvest season the collection effort is organized through a network of purchasing agents who scout regions to assess availability and maturity of the seeds. As the mature seeds are released from the pods, village communities, including women and children, comb through the fields to hand pick the seeds in a very labour-intensive operation. Seeds are then laid out on sacks to dry in the sun for several days.

The dried seeds are then carted to designated purchase centres where an agent inspects the quality and weighs the material in order to negotiate an acceptable purchase price with the supplier. Cocoa-purchasing centres equipped with weighing scales and produce storage spaces are typically used for griffonia in some localities since its harvest does not unduly overlap with the cocoa harvest season. When enough seeds are accumulated, transport is arranged to move the seeds to warehouses closer to the point of export.

Major local buyers and exporters in Ghana for the 1997–1998 griffonia season included Bioresources, Getrade, Cashpro, Vicdoris and Madame Catherine, each of which had significant orders from their respective foreign customers. Non-governmental organizations (NGOs) such as Technoserve (Ghana) Ltd also played facilitating roles in organizing village communities to undertake griffonia collection as part of their rural development policies (Hicks, pers comm, 1998).

Business was brisk as several brokers from Europe, the US and Asia made their way to Accra, the capital city of Ghana, in search of griffonia seeds. The lobby of the plush Golden Tulip Hotel in Accra became the scene of intense negotiations and bargaining over truckloads of griffonia from the hinterland.

Prices on the first crop of the season started at US$6 per kilogram (kg) (twice the export price of the previous season). By mid-season the spot price rose to US$9 per kg, eventually reaching as high as US$14 per kg by the end of the harvest season as demand continued to grow while supply dwindled. It is estimated that between 300 and 500 tonnes of griffonia seeds were exported from Ghana during the 1997–1998 harvest season (Acquaye, pers comm, 1998).

Due to the urgency of 5-HTP demand, large quantities of griffonia were air freighted to extractors at additional cost (US$2–US$3 per kg for bulk air-freight rate). Besides Europe and the US, most of the griffonia was shipped to China and India for extraction to 5-HTP by contract manufacturers before trans-shipment to the US. This circuitous intercontinental business network was designed to take advantage of lower extraction costs in Asia.

Processing and products

Proprietary protocols are used by various manufacturers to extract 5-HTP from griffonia seeds. In general, processes involve grinding the seeds into powder and repeatedly extracting with hot or cold mixtures of alcohol and water. The alcoholic extracts are eventually concentrated to crystallize out the 5-HTP in solid form, with recovery yields of 8–12 per cent from the seeds. The purity of 5-HTP in the product is generally specified above 95 per cent by most manufacturers. The residual impurity profile will eventually prove to be the undoing of the 5-HTP market.

The price of purified 5-HTP rose steadily from US$1200 per kg at the beginning of 1998 to US$1600 per kg by mid-year at the peak of interest in the product. Suppliers and distributors of 5-HTP had the leverage on the market, entering into cut-throat contracts with end-users.

Meanwhile, dosage formulations of 5-HTP as 50 milligram (mg) and 100mg tablets began to appear in natural food stores. Products were packaged under major supplement labels, including Nature's Way, Natural Balance, Solgar and TwinLabs, and prominently displayed at natural food outlets such as general nutrition centres (GNCs) and the Vitamin Shoppe, as well as in pharmacies and food store aisles. Internet websites displayed 5-HTP products under provocative titles such as 'Forget Prozac'. Typically, a pack of 60–100 tablets of 5-HTP sold for about US$30.

Media interest feeds demand

News about the product spread among health food adherents by word of mouth. Bulge-conscious ladies shedding off winter coats in the spring began to hear of 5-HTP from vendors in health-food stores. Since DSHEA severely constrains the use of clinically unproven claims in labelling and advertising of dietary supplements, it is often difficult to disseminate information and create public awareness of new products in the industry.

A new book was released in May 1998 entitled *5-HTP: The Natural Way to Overcome Depression, Obesity and Insomnia*, written by Michael Murray, a well-known naturopath and strong advocate for the diet supplement industry (Murray, 1998). Public awareness came to a head in June when the ABC television news programme *PrimeTime Live* broadcast a lead story on 5-HTP as a promising supplement for weight control and insomnia. The programme featured an attractive New York model who attested to using 5-HTP to keep in shape and stay competitive as a fashion model, as well as a middle-aged woman who used 5-HTP to get relief from insomnia (ABC News, 1998).

This nationwide TV broadcast sparked a stampede for 5-HTP and within days shelves were completely empty of 5-HTP products. Stores were having difficulty replenishing stock and the limited supplies available were kept behind checkout counters and sold on demand to preferred customers. The media proclaimed 5-HTP a miracle drug with multiple effects to alleviate obesity, depres-

sion, headache and insomnia. Sales rode high on the media frenzy.

Manufacturers rushed into production only to find limited supplies of purified 5-HTP at exorbitant prices. The ripple effect spilled over to raw material suppliers in Ghana, and residual griffonia inventories remaining from the harvest season were quickly raided from warehouses at outrageous prices. Those few weeks of the summer of 1998 were the high point for 5-HTP and griffonia. There was anxiety over whether available supplies of 5-HTP could sustain market demand until the next griffonia harvest season (*Health Supplement Industry Insider*, 1998).

Concerns raised and media backlash

However, the 5-HTP honeymoon was destined to be short lived. The bombshell came in a short note published in the 'Letters to the Editor' column in the September 1998 issue of the medical journal *Nature Medicine*. A group of researchers from the Mayo Clinic in Rochester, Minnesota (Williamson et al, 1998), reported the presence of a contaminant code-named 'peak X' in samples of 5-HTP products from six different manufacturers bought from health-food stores. The researchers noted that the contaminant 'peak X' was implicated in an earlier adverse incident in 1991 involving a 28-year-old woman who became ill with the blood disease eosinophilia myalgia syndrome (EMS) (Michelson et al, 1994). The authors also cited another reported incident in 1980 associating EMS with 5-HTP (Sternberg et al, 1980).

Furthermore, the Mayo researchers alluded to similarities between the contaminant and the probable cause of an

outbreak of EMS in 1989 involving 1500 cases, including 38 fatalities. This later EMS outbreak was traced to a contaminated batch of L-tryptophan produced by fermentation from the Japanese company Showa Denko. As a result of this outbreak, the FDA banned the sale of L-tryptophan from the US market. The Mayo report concluded that the presence of 'peak X' in 5-HTP products represented 'another accident [epidemic] waiting to happen'.

The mass media, including the *San Francisco Chronicle* and *Los Angeles Times*, quickly picked up the Mayo Clinic report. To counteract the impact of bad press on 5-HTP and natural products as a whole, the leading industry association, National Nutritional Foods Association (NNFA), went on the offensive to control the damage. NNFA issued a press release challenging the motivation of the Mayo Clinic researchers, calling parts of the report 'speculative science' due to unsubstantiated claims associating the alleged contaminant of 5-HTP 'peak X' with the L-tryptophan incident (*Health Food Business*, 1998).

However, the FDA subsequently released its own independent evaluation confirming the presence of 'peak X' in samples of 5-HTP on the market. The agency further indicated that since there are uncertainties in establishing the cause of the 1989 EMS outbreak with regard to L-tryptophan and its contaminants, the 5-HTP situation 'warrants careful surveillance' (Centre for Food Safety and Applied Nutrition, 1998). Nevertheless the FDA did not find it necessary to issue a product recall on 5-HTP. Instead it recommended that 5-HTP manufacturers upgrade their processes to eliminate impurities in 5-HTP, provide mechanisms for the public to report any adverse events and notify the FDA, and undertake further research to address concerns about 5-HTP.

Although no cases of adverse events related to 5-HTP use actually materialized during this period, the media scare was sufficient to erode public confidence in 5-HTP. Product sales plummeted despite the efforts of a number of suppliers who claimed to provide 'peak X-free' 5-HTP. As interest waned, most suppliers moved on in pursuit of the next 'hot new herb'. Uninformed collectors and suppliers in Ghana and other source countries were disappointed as inventories of the 1998–1999 griffonia harvest accumulated in warehouses while buyers and orders failed to materialize.

A long-awaited NBC *Dateline* programme on 5-HTP and the 'peak X' controversy was finally aired in March, 1999, declaring that the jury is still out on whether or not 5-HTP and/or its associated contaminants pose any real public health threat (NBC News, 1999). Experts on both sides of the issue presented opposing views as the programme concluded that additional unbiased scientific evidence is needed to resolve the issues. Until then, the world has yet to hear the last word on the griffonia extract 5-HTP.

Lessons learned with relevance to marketing of NTFPs and certification

There are very important lessons to be learned by the natural products industry from the griffonia experience, with relevance to marketing and certification schemes, especially for players along the supply chain and in source countries:

- As constituted today, natural products represent a highly volatile market. Fortunes can be made quickly based on media hype, and likewise the media rumour mill can readily unmake products. Producers in source countries are often unaware of the volatility and trend-driven nature of these markets.

Botanical medicine markets in the US are particularly fickle, but all will respond strongly to scientific data emerging on products new to the market; products may ride a rollercoaster during their initial years.

- This volatile situation can be changed by building a solid foundation of good science to validate claims relating to the effectiveness and safety of products. It is highly important to maintain quality and purity of herbs and their extracts to maximize efficacy and minimize adverse side effects. Universally accepted standards and specifications for herbs and extracts established by a reputable body, such as the US Pharmacopoeia, will generate greater public confidence in herbal products. These standards might be incorporated within a certification programme, with ecological and social certifiers collaborating with industry quality-control and standards-setting bodies.

- Source countries such as Ghana can derive greater benefits from the fortunes of the industry by moving up the supply chain from their current role as bulk raw-material suppliers. Local extraction will streamline logistics and eliminate high freight costs for bulk material. As demonstrated in the pricing structure of 5-HTP extracts, source countries can increase their returns as much as tenfold by supplying extracts. By moving up the supply chain, source countries can also produce products for local and regional markets. The major gains to be made from botanical medicine markets are higher up the supply chain, and certification should seek to promote greater source-country processing and manufacturing of products.

Chapter 19

Baobab bark (*Adansonia digitata*)

Claudia Romero, Isla Grundy, Bruce Campbell and
Anthony B Cunningham

Introduction

The genus *Adansonia* (Bombacaceae) occurs in most countries of Africa south of the Sahara (one species), western Madagascar (seven species) and Australia (one species), at low altitudes in hot, dry woodlands (Wickens, 1981). Baobab trees (*Adansonia digitata*) in Zimbabwe are found in the valleys of the Zambezi River and its major tributaries, and in the Save-Limpopo lowveld. The species apparently prefers deep, well-drained soils at elevations of between 450 and 600 metres (m) and grows in areas that receive 180 to 1000 millimetres (mm) of precipitation per year, with extreme annual variation.

The baobab is a deciduous species that grows to 6m and more in diameter but rarely reaches heights greater than 20m. Baobab bark is smooth, reddish-brown or greyish-brown, with a thin

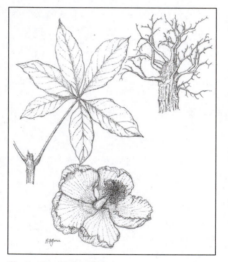

Illustration by Bee Gunn

Baobab (Adansonia digitata)

photosynthetic layer immediately under the surface of the outer bark. The wood is characterized by an abundance of water-storing tissue and high moisture contents (about 300 per cent of dry weight; de Villiers, 1951). Baobab trees reportedly start to flower at 25 years. The flowers are large, open only for a period of 24 hours and are pollinated by bats, though they are also visited by a range of other animals (eg moths, wasps and bush-babies; Wickens, 1981). Flowering occurs at the start of the rainy season. The fruits are a preferred food for monkeys, baboons, elephants and impala (Peters and O'Brien, 1980). In areas where there is little wildlife, fruits hang on the trees for several months.

The baobab has been known as the 'mammoth of the lowveld' (Pardy, 1953) and 'the upside down tree' (Wickens,

1981). Handicrafts made of baobab bark fibres represent one of the sources of income for rural inhabitants of the Save-Odzi Valley, in south-eastern Zimbabwe (Luckert et al, 2001).

Ecology

Baobab densities range from 3 to 21 trees per hectare in the lowveld of eastern Zimbabwe. Regeneration (individuals < 2m tall) is completely lacking in most communal areas. Deficiency of regeneration is apparently not due to lack of seeds or low seed viability; viability of baobab seeds is generally high (97 per cent; Mudavhanu, 1998). Monkeys, baboons (Peters and O'Brien, 1980) and particularly cattle and goats eat young seedlings. In areas where baobab is not commercially used (eg Sengwa Wildlife Research Area), as is the case in protected areas, baobab seedlings were very rarely found (Putz and Romero, pers comm).

Baobab trees reportedly die during severe droughts and less frequently are killed by lightning (de Villiers, 1951). Elephants are also known to kill baobabs and to be killed when the baobab trees whose stems they are gouging topple over. Annual mortalities ranged from 1.1 per cent (Mana Pools National Park; Swanepoel, 1993) to 7.3 per cent (Luangwa Valley in Zambia; Caughley, 1976). In the Save-Odzi Valley (eastern Zimbabwe), mortality rates of 0.33 trees per hectare per annum, with a mean tree density of 8.44 trees per hectare – no trees with circumferences < 20 centimetres (cm)

diameter at breast height (dbh) – were recorded (Romero et al, 2001).

Game and livestock cause extensive damage to baobab stems, especially in times of drought (de Villiers, 1951). Among the more subtle impacts of elephants on baobabs is the failure of damaged trees to produce mature pods (Swanepoel, 1993). Where elephants are abundant, baobab trees are often gouged out, far into the xylem, which suggests that more than just inner bark is eaten.

Baobab stem growth rates are positively correlated with rainfall (Piearce et al, 1994) and are extremely variable. Mean annual increment in dbh of 9 trees of known age (12–72 years) in three locations in Harare (Zimbabwe) was 2.01cm per year. Growth rate data from Messina and Hwange ranged from 0.30 to 1.50cm per year, respectively (Barnes, 1980). A source of error in using dbh as a metric to assess growth is seasonal shrinking and swelling of the trees.

Coates-Palgrave (1983) stated that baobabs of 8m dbh would be more than 3000 years old. A carbon-14 dating performed by Swart (1963) indicated that a baobab with a dbh of 4.5m found in Kariba, in the Zambezi Valley, was 1010 (+/– 100) years old.

Use

Baobab trees provide a variety of products that traditionally have been used throughout Africa. Fibres from its bark are used to make rugs, doormats, blankets, hats, handbags, baskets, tablemats, sandals, dolls, sewing thread, rope and whips. The inner bark is reportedly chewed as a cure for colds and made into a concoction for stomach-ache (Nkana and Iddi, 1991). The outer bark is boiled and used to ease toothaches. The woody exocarp of the fruit can be used as a cooking pot, ground and used for snuff, or used as a household receptacle. The seeds are embedded in a powdery sarcotesta that is widely consumed by humans and has a high concentration of vitamin C (Sidibe et al, 1996). Seeds can be ground into a butter, or roasted and ground to make a hot beverage sometimes consumed by people who cannot afford coffee (Kwaramba, 1995). Young roots, with their sweet taste and high water content, are sought after by children and herders. Bathing babies in water in which young baobab roots have been soaked is believed to ensure their plumpness and health. Slices of roots boiled in water are also eaten. Baobab leaves can be eaten as a vegetable (locally known as *gusha*) and provide a substitute to other vegetables during dry periods. Dead baobabs decompose relatively quickly and are used as compost (Mudavanhu, 1998). Finally, hollow baobabs can be used as water storage reservoirs, tombs or temporary shelters (Mullin, 1997).

Impact of bark harvesting and other stresses

Denudation of the baobab does not lead to land-use change; rather, it would mean that an element of the woodlands, and a very charismatic element at that, would eventually disappear. An important consideration in assessing the impact of bark harvesting on the future sustainability of baobab populations is whether and how the tree regenerates bark, and at what rate. Unlike most trees that regenerate bark slowly from the vascular cambium on the margins of a wound, baobab bark is produced from parenchyma cells underneath the surface of the exposed xylem. This peculiar mechanism of baobab bark regeneration was apparently first described by Fisher (1981).

Baobabs of a wide range of sizes (25–330cm dbh) in villages in the Save-Odzi Valley were harvested for bark (Romero et al, 2001). This study reported that harvesting was more prevalent during the dry season when people had available time due to reduced agricultural activities. Bark from 97.4 per cent of the baobab trees in the study area had been harvested at least once. More than 50 per cent of the trees had been harvested to heights of about 2m and above through the use of harvesting platforms set next to the trees.

Although local people reported that bark from the same portion of the stem could be reharvested after a recovery period of two years, or three years when a drought occurred, the study by Romero et al suggests a much longer recovery period. Experimentally harvested patches on baobab trunks recover their pre-harvesting bark thickness after six years. The mean rate of bark regeneration was 0.67cm per year ($n = 10$ trees per year) and did not vary over the four-year period of the study. The proportion of baobab bark fibre useful for handicrafts also increased with increasing recovery period. Based on the results of their experimental study, Romero et al (2001) established that the proportion (31.4 per cent) of usable bark from previously unharvested trees would be attained approximately ten years after the initial harvest.

Baobabs are susceptible to infection by a sooty mould of the *Antennulariella* type (Matose and Clarke, 1991; Maulka et al, 1995). Bark of infected trees becomes blackened or burned in appearance (hence the term 'sooty'). Other symptoms of infection include gum-sweating and crown die-back (Sharp, 1993). Sooty mould disease seems to be particularly prevalent during and soon after drought years. It has been suggested that the disease generally affects trees under environmental stress. Piearce et al (1994) hypothesized that drought causes physical contraction of the bark, leading to sap extrusion through weak points (ie cracks and wrinkles) where sooty moulds can colonize.

There appears to be a relationship between the intensity of bark harvesting in an area and the degree of infestation of the baobab (Mudavhanu, 1998). If such a relationship exists, it is unclear whether the high infection rate of harvested trees is due to harvesters spreading the disease from tree to tree, or whether trees are rendered more susceptible to the disease because of bark loss. The mean proportion of trees infected by the sooty disease in eastern Zimbabwe was 47.3 per cent (Romero et al, 2001). Because bark from all of the infected trees had been harvested in their plots, it was not possible for the researchers to establish a cause-and-effect relationship. The only tree they encountered in the sampling area from which bark had apparently never been harvested was completely infected by the mould disease.

Management

In the past, rules governing natural-resource management used to be dictated and enforced by local traditional leaders (Mukamuri and Kozanayi, 2000). Among the traditional rules governing natural-resource use in eastern Zimbabwe that still seems to be respected is the prohibition of felling fruit trees, including baobab (Romero et al, 2001). There are also traditional bans against completely stripping the boles of baobab trees and, specifically, against harvesting bark from trees infested by sooty mould disease (Matose and Clarke, 1991; Mukamuri and Kozanayi, 2000).

Villagers reported that in the study area there is no formal or informal control over baobab harvesting, except for the protection of some sacred trees. Although outsiders were technically not allowed to harvest bark in a village area, they could gain access to the resource through relatives. Village heads (*kraalheads*) tried to encourage harvesters not to strip bark from entire trees; but this advice was seldom adhered to and *kraalheads* reported that they did not have the time to enforce their rules. Individuals who were thought to be overexploiting the resource could be fined a goat or asked to brew beer for the village; but elders generally found it increasingly difficult to enforce the rules as harvesting pressure increased. Reportedly in the past, people stripped bark from one side of the tree at a time. Now they often remove bark from the whole circumference of trees, in two to three tiers, and sometimes de-bark the entire trunk. In this case study, harvesters were aware of the problem of overharvesting, but felt impelled to do so in order to prevent other people from de-barking the same trees – particularly if the trees produced bark of desirable quality (Romero et al, 2001). More recently, traditional leaders tried to discourage the use of baobab roots because it was thought to result in the death of trees (Mukamuri and Kozanayi, 2000).

Despite traditional taboos on selling baobab fruit, this widespread practice continues in many rural areas of Zimbabwe. This activity is likely to reduce the number of seeds available for regeneration and thus decreases the recruitment potential of the species. Given that extensive marketing of baobab fruits only began in the early 1990s and that Romero et al (2001) found no trees in their study area < 25cm dbh, seed availability was apparently not the major factor limiting baobab recruitment. Using the mean annual dbh increment rates estimated by the research team, a 25cm dbh tree would, on average, be at least 18 years old, which is twice as long as the period during which the baobab fruits have been extensively marketed.

The baobab craft industry is an important source of rural employment in the Save-Odzi Valley in eastern Zimbabwe, especially among women and young people (Kwaramba, 1995; Luckert et al, 2001). Up to 43 per cent of existing households in this area, mostly the poorest, were involved in bark harvesting and processing. Nevertheless, baobab bark harvesting was not uniformly practised throughout the study area; there were villages where just one or two members were involved (Luckert et al, 2001). Some villages were more endowed with the resource than others; and because of over-

harvesting, some harvesters had to walk to neighbouring villages to find trees from which they could collect bark.

Although the marketing of baobab products reportedly increased during the early 1990s (Braedt and Standa-Gunda, 1997), commercialization of baobab bark products seems to have been stable for the last four years (Veeman et al, 2001). The full concerns of commercialization of baobab bark products for the resource base have not yet been completely investigated. The implications of commercialization could be biophysical or institutional. One direct consequence is an increase in conflicts among traditional and governmental institutions over baobab management. Problems with managing baobab bark are currently being exacerbated by weak institutions and by poverty. Taking aside consideration of the baobab trees' longevity, which is very atypical for a tree, it is evident that the bark industry could eventually go into an economic boom-and-bust cycle, such as has been well described for other non-timber forest products (NTFPs) (eg Dove, 1993; Coomes, 1995). When a renewable natural resource is over-exploited, the deleterious impacts tend to be suffered mostly by the rural poor, who depend upon the resource the most (Arnold and Perez, 1998). This appears to be the case for baobabs in Zimbabwe. Therefore, in addition to environmental concerns about the destruction of the baobab resource, there are reasons relating to social welfare that impel an understanding of the impacts of current harvesting practices on this locally important NTFP.

Certification potential

Baobab trees in the Save-Odzi Valley in Zimbabwe are utilized as a common property resource (CPR). Despite long-standing

traditions concerning baobab trees and their use, there are many apparent failures in the capacities of local institutions to control the use of this resource in the face of poverty and high harvesting pressures. Most clearly, there is a frequent lack of enforcement of established rules by local communities (Mukamuri and Kozanayi, 2000).

Considering baobab bark in the context of the Save-Odzi Valley as a CPR, the responsibility of its management should go to the local communities and their institutions, with the additional collaboration of appropriate governmental agencies (eg the Zimbabwe Forestry Commission). Given the paucity of reliable information about baobab ecology, it seems appropriate that management should be carried out within the framework of an adaptive management system (Walters and Holling, 1990) that can be readily changed when new information becomes available or conditions change.

The reallocation of the right to manage the baobab bark resource to local communities needs to be accompanied by communities' acknowledgement of their responsibilities, as well. Several authors have identified this empowerment as a condition of obtaining effective commitment from local stakeholders to conservation and sustainable management, particularly in those situations where there is insecurity of tenure (Neumann, 1996). Collective management efforts are only likely to be successful when specific conditions are met. Among these conditions are the right to self-organize; the clear recognition of resource boundaries (ie harvesting areas for each village); the existence of rules that are clear and dynamic; the effective enforcement of rules; and the establishment of mechanisms for conflict resolution (McKean and Orstom, 1995).

These conditions are necessary preconditions for certification. Obviously, their compliance does not necessarily mean that certification is possible. An evaluation of the benefits of certification for community timber operations in Melanesia showed that although certification might imply access to international markets, restraints for small landholders were mostly related to the high cost of the certification process. In addition, the certification process increased work related to extra activities such as administration, book-keeping, monitoring and internal organization of local communities (Tofts, 1998).

Lack of natural-resource management, especially in response to expanding markets, often leads to biological and, ultimately, economic impoverishment (Nepstad et al, 1992). Active management programmes may help to counter this trend and rescue natural resources from being undervalued and thus overexploited (Panayotou and Ashton, 1993). Clar-ification of the connection between harvesters and the market for baobab bark products is critical given the increasing demand for baobab products. Perhaps this demand will cause an increase in prices, which may augment harvesting pressure and lead to overexploitation and the potential collapse of the resource base.

The maximum sustainable rate of baobab bark harvesting needs to be established for the Save-Odzi Valley. From the existing information, it seems that bark extraction rates are exceeding bark regeneration rates; this needs to be confirmed with evaluations at the population level. Given that baobab trees are not regenerating in the study area, the sustainability of bark resource use over the long term could be in severe doubt, particularly considering the unclear relationship between harvesting and sooty disease.

In addition to the informal nature of markets for baobab products (Veeman et al, 2001), demand for certification of baobab products in local markets is nonexistent. Certification may not be the most effective short-term tool to educate consumers or conserve the resource. This chapter concludes that under present conditions, the potential for certification of baobab bark products is low. It is hoped that further ecological and socio-economic research will clarify the future of baobab management and its certification potential in eastern Zimbabwe. With more ecological information and the emergence of local institutions that are committed to sustainability, certification of baobab products could contribute to the future survival of this species, as well as the people and organisms who depend upon it.

Acknowledgements

The authors would like to thank the people of the Save-Odzi Valley (eastern Zimbabwe) who facilitated the work. They also thank the institutions that funded the workshop at which most of the information presented was collected: the People and Plants initiative of the WWF; the Canadian International Development Agency (CIDA) through the Agroforestry: Southern African Project of the Institute of Environmental Studies (IES), University of Zimbabwe; and the Department of Rural Economy, University of Alberta.

Chapter 20

Yohimbe (*Pausinystalia johimbe*)

*Terry C H Sunderland, Marie-Laure Ngo-Mpeck,
Zacharie Tchoundjeu and Sarah A Laird*

Introduction

Pausinystalia johimbe is a tree native to the coastal forests of Central Africa and is distributed from southeast Nigeria to the Congolese mayombe (Vivien and Faure, 1985). Its bark contains up to 6 per cent of a mixture of alkaloids, the principal one being yohimbine (Tyler, 1993), which is also known as aphrodine, quebrachine or corynine (*Lawrence Review of Natural Products*, 1990). *P. johimbe* is used extensively as part of traditional health-care systems. Its many recorded uses vary from being employed directly as an aphrodisiac (Small and Adams, 1922; Greenish, 1929; Ainslie, 1937; Dalziel, 1937; Raponda-Walker and Sillans, 1961; Motte, 1980; Farnsworth, 1990; Oliver-Beyer, 1986; Tyler, 1993) to that of a local anaesthetic (Greenish, 1929; Oliver Beyer, 1986), a mild stimulant to prevent drowsiness

Illustration by Bee Gunn

*Yohimbe (*Pausinystalia johimbe*)*

(Raponda-Walker and Sillans, 1961; Obama, pers comm; authors' personal observation), a hallucinogen (Tyler, 1993), a treatment for angina (*Lawrence Review of Natural Products*, 1990), a hypertensive (Oliver-Beyer, 1986; *Lawrence Review of Natural Products*, 1990), a general tonic (Ainslie, 1937), a performance enhancer for athletes, a remedy to increase the clarity of the voices of singers during long festivals (Motte, 1980), an ichthytoxicant, and as a tonic to increase the resilience of hunting dogs (Raponda-Walker and Sillans, 1961).

In addition to the widespread local use, the species has been long exported to Europe for Western medicine in both prescription and herbal markets. The most common use of yohimbine-based prescription drugs today is in the treatment of diabetes-related male organic impotence

(*Lawrence Review of Natural Products*, 1990; Vaughan, pers comm). Sexual-stimulant products available over the counter often contain yohimbine. In the UK, yohimbine-containing drugs have become fashionable as one of the 'herbal highs' reported in the British press (Castle, 1997), and yohimbe-based products have long been a common sight in sex shops in Europe (Tyler, 1993).

Autoecology

Natural distribution and population structure

P. johimbe is found within the forest type classified by Letouzey (1985) as Atlantic Biafran evergreen forest in association with Caesalpiniaceae, an extensive forest formation extending from south-east Nigeria through Cameroon, Equatorial Guinea, Gabon and Congo Brazzaville. *P. johimbe* is a fast-growing tree, but does not reach a great diameter at breast height (dbh); it has a recorded maximum of circa 50 centimetres (cm) dbh (Letouzey, 1985). This seems to be a natural feature of the genus and is not regarded as a direct result of overexploitation of the larger size-class individuals.

P. johimbe has been referred to as being 'common' (Raponda-Walker and Sillans, 1960). However, it would seem that the species, while not rare, is far from regarded as common. Recent inventory data from Cameroon and Equatorial Guinea suggests that there are, on average, 15 trees > 1cm dbh per hectare, with only 4 trees > 10cm dbh per hectare that are potentially harvestable (Sunderland et al, 1997). With this number of trees per hectare, the authors could not support the premise that the species is common.

Reproductive ecology

The light winged seeds of *P. johimbe* are wind dispersed and their lightness and winged structure mean that they can travel long distances. Consequently, regeneration is not commonly found close to the mother tree and, in fact, in recent field surveys, the closest recruit found was 25 metres (m) from the parent (Sunderland et al, 1997). More commonly – in fact, almost exclusively – seedlings were found without the presence of parent trees, confirming this long-distance dispersal (Sunderland et al, 1997).

Although the species occurs mainly in closed-canopy forest, light is needed for seed germination and seedling development. Few seedlings survive in closed-canopy forest except in areas of light to moderate disturbance, and the survival rate of seedlings under a closed canopy is extremely low, suggesting that *P. johimbe* is a light-demanding species in the early stages of regeneration. Similar observations have recently been made with *Lovoa trichilioides*, an important commercial timber species (Tchoundjeu et al, 1999a; 1999b).

Sustainability

Current commercial *P. johimbe* bark exploitation practices in Cameroon

All *P. johimbe* bark is currently exploited from wild populations. This exploitation takes place exclusively in Cameroon, although interest also extends to Equatorial Guinea and Gabon. Interestingly, much of the exploitation of *P. johimbe* is related to timber prospecting, with individual stems of the species being identified during the inventories preceding exploitation. After the timber-harvesting activities are completed, the yohimbe trees are then also felled and stripped, often by the logging company employees.

Currently, Plantecam is the sole supplier of *P. johimbe* bark to Europe, and supplies around 100 tonnes annually (120 tonnes in 1996; Simons, 1997). Unlike the situation where Plantecam has its own collection teams providing *Prunus africana* bark (up to 33 per cent of the total) to its factory, all of the *P. johimbe* bark is exploited by outside contractors. These contractors are registered local businesses who have licences to exploit medicinal plants. These licences are provided by the Cameroon Forestry Department, and Plantecam states that it will not accept plant material from companies or individuals without these licences (Nkuinkeu, pers comm).

In actual fact, however, the majority of bark is collected by local people who are paid at the roadside for the delivery of bark. These local people do not have any permits or authorization to exploit *P. johimbe* and, unknown to Plantecam (who claim to be following the letter of the law), are supplying bark illegally to the contractors. Thus Plantecam, in turn, may be supplied by illegally exploited bark.

Prices paid per kilogram (kg) of bark by Plantecam range from 125–280 African Financial Community francs (CFA) per kilogram, depending upon the moisture content, with higher prices being paid for dried bark. However, the price paid at roadside to local collectors varies from 75 CFA (paid to pygmies, who supply fresh bark along the Kribi–Campo road) to 150 CFA (to Bulu suppliers at Bivoumba, who dry the bark over meat-drying racks). Recently, the president of the North-West Traditional Healers Association, Chief Fomentum, was asked to supply large quantities of bark to a contractor, to sell on to Plantecam, for 50 CFA per kilogram for *P. johimbe* and 75 CFA per kilogram for *Prunus africana*. Clearly, the profit margin for the contractors is high and local people do not receive a fair price for their work. However, none of the local collectors interviewed was aware of the true price of the bark and thought it worthwhile to collect bark to supply the contractors.

P. johimbe bark exploitation is a seasonal activity, as the yohimbine levels are highest during the rainy season (Paris and Letouzey, 1960). During the months of May to September, contractors travel into areas where *P. johimbe* is known to occur, contacting villagers in order to exploit the bark directly and promising to return subsequently with transport and payment in two to three weeks. Most contractors have been operating in the same regions for a number of years and use the same local exploiters.

The principles guiding the so-called sustainable exploitation of bark that have been applied to *Prunus africana* (ie removal of opposite two quarters of bark and then subsequent removal, years later,

217

of the other two quarters) have not been applied to *P. johimbe*. The exploited bark is often collected from the main stem only (except when the bark is harvested by pygmy exploiters) and not from the branches. This is surprising, given that yohimbine occurs not only in both the branches and young stems, but also in the leaves. Often, in order to increase outputs, the trees are felled, and Plantecam themselves admit that during exploitation '98 per cent of the trees exploited are probably felled' (Nkuinkeu, pers comm). According to the majority of informants interviewed, the trees can be harvested when they are around 10cm dbh. Although individuals all stated that it was easier and more ergonomic to harvest from larger diameter trees, these species were less common.

In the field, it was explained that whil the *P. johimbe* trees callus well after a small amount of bark removal,[1] removal of large quantities of bark leads to an attack by an (as yet unidentified) stemborer that penetrates the unprotected stem, killing the tree. That is why many harvesters prefer to fell the tree because 'the tree would die anyway' (Bivina, pers comm). Bakola (pygmy) harvesters, who are commonly employed to harvest yohimbe all along the Edea–Campo road, not only fell the trees but also cross-cut them into portable pieces. The bark is removed from the cut logs, carried to the roadside and sold. All the bark from the tree is removed, including that of the branches. The remaining logs are then used for fuelwood (Mana, pers comm).

Confusion between *P. johimbe* and *P. macroceras*

Henry (1939), in a study of *P. johimbe* and related species, concluded that *P. macroceras* contains a number of alkaloids, especially large quantities of the inactive alkaloid yohimbinine, which led to *P. macroceras* being named 'false yohimbe' (Small and Adams, 1922). Yohimbine is present in *P. macroceras*, although in very small quantities.

For most bark harvesters, these two species of *Pausinystalia* are reputedly distinguished through slash characters. Yohimbine becomes yellow-orange-brown on exposure to light. *P. johimbe* is said to oxidize red-brown very slowly, with *P. macroceras* oxidizing rapidly. However, from the authors' observations, it is clear that this character is unreliable. With the bark and bole characteristics of both species also being similar, the two species are almost impossible to tell apart using slash characters. This confusion between the species is not helped by the fact that the two species appear to be highly allopatric, meaning that direct comparison in the field is often impossible. However, the leaves of both species are highly distinctive, with *P. johimbe* having sessile, obovate leaves 15–25cm long, often in whorls of three with distinctive cordate leaf bases, while *P. macroceras* has petiolate, ovoid leaves 6–15cm long.

More subtle differences between the two species include the fact that the bark of *P. johimbe* is extremely bitter to the taste and is easy to peel, while *P. macroceras* bark is less bitter and is extremely difficult to peel, often needing beating first to loosen the cambial layer from the sapwood.

Plantecam states that *all P. johimbe* bark needs to be beaten before being removed; and, given that some bark supplied to Plantecam is known to have an extremely low yohimbine content, there can be no doubt that a good proportion (circa 60–70 per cent) of the bark received by Plantecam is that of *P. macroceras*, which is known to have very low levels of, and very poor-quality, yohimbine. The early markets for yohimbe-based products were also aware of this confusion and adulteration, which led to a series of guidelines being produced to distinguish between the bark of the two species (see Table 20.1).

With a simple field guide prepared for collectors, it would be a simple task to ensure that all bark received for processing is *P. johimbe*. This would both conserve the resource and avoid the unnecessary felling of individual trees of *P. macroceras*, while ensuring profitability.

Impacts of exploitation

Despite current levels of exploitation, *P. johimbe* presently has a healthy recruitment and there does not seem to be a problem with regeneration. However, data can be deceiving. Although the current regenerative capacity of the species is not yet compromised, removal through felling of reproductive individuals – especially at current rates of exploitation in certain areas – will ultimately affect future regenerative potential (ie fewer seed trees = fewer seedlings = reduced recruitment = fewer future harvestable trees).

Sustainable management

Potential for domestication

Due to the destructive harvesting methods employed and the rapidly growing market for aphrodisiac remedies, the International Centre for Research in Agroforestry (ICRAF) has begun a research programme to investigate the potential of *P. johimbe* for domestication and inclusion within its agroforestry systems programme.

One of the greatest dilemmas with initiating a domestication programme for any forest product is whether to begin work that could provide material for a hypothetical future market that will no longer exist when the products reach maturity. In contrast, one could decide that the volatile nature of such markets makes the investment prone to risk and that no action should be taken, inevitably leading to the extirpation of the species. In the case of *P. johimbe*, as for *Prunus africana*, along with the obvious biological urgency, the market seems secure enough in the short to medium term to warrant the development of cultivated systems. If the market no longer exists in the long term, the species can be used for other purposes, such as fuelwood, aside from serving a valuable ecological function.

In-situ management

While it is, of course, important to initiate a domestication programme for a potentially threatened species such as *P. johimbe*, it is also essential that this is implemented alongside a rational forest management regime. The ecology of *P. johimbe* (fast growing, reproductively gregarious, light-demanding) suggests that, with further work on the potential sustainability of bark harvesting from standing trees, a reasonable assessment could be made regarding the quantities that could be harvested from standing forest.

Table 20.1 *Diagnostic bark characters of* P. johimbe *and* P. macroceras

	P. johimbe	*P. macroceras*
Macroscopic characteristics:		
Thickness	4–20mm	2–5mm
Outer surface		
Colour	Grey to reddish-brown	Light or dark brown
Surface	Longitudinal furrows; many transverse cracks, 1–2cm apart	Often scraped; longitudinal furrows and ridges; few or curved transverse cracks
Lichens	Grey or white; few or many	Grey, usually numerous
Cork	Thin or thick, often easily detached	Thin, adhering closely
Inner surface		
Colour	Reddish-brown	Dark brown or reddish-brown
Surface	Finely striated and ridged	Ridged and wrinkled
Fracture	Short, fibrous, sometimes splintery on inside; surfaces soft, velvety	Same as *P. johimbe*
Microscopic characteristics:		
Cork		
Width of cork	one-twentieth to one-third	one-quarter to two-thirds
Width of cortex (number of cells)	3–30	2–40
Colour	Grey to dark brown	Dark brown
Phelloderm		
Number of cells wide	2–12	4–20
Colour	Yellowish-grey to reddish-brown	Same as *P. johimbe*
Cortex		
Width of cortex	one-sixteenth to 1	one-sixth to 1
Colour	Yellowish-brown to reddish-brown	Same as *P. johimbe*
Medullary rays		
TS inner bast width	1–4 cells	1–3 cells
Regularity	Straight	Straight
TS outer bast width	1–3 cells	1–3 cells
Regularity	Diverging, cells elongate tangentially	Curving irregularly, cells elongate tangentially
Ends	Straight or curved	Often distorted, curved
LS tangential width	1–3 cells	1–3 cells
Depth	6–35 cells	5–20 cells
Shape	Narrow spindle or rectangular	Somewhat rectangular with slightly tapering ends
LS radial depth	8–30 cells	5–20 cells
Bast fibres		
Grouping	Usually in one-cell-wide rows; 1–3 occur 'beaded'; no 'twinning' in outer bast	Radial rows 2–3 cells wide, common but not 'beaded'; 'twinning' in outer bast
Diameter	22–29µ	22–23µ
Length	0.7–1.6mm	0.6–1.9mm
Shape TS	Rectangular	Rectangular
Shape LS	Long spindle, pointed ends	Spindle with sharply pointed ends
Lumen	Punctiform or sometimes linear	Linear or sometimes punctiform
Wall	Thick, not striated	Thick, not striated

Note: TS = transverse section; LS = longitudinal section; µ = micron
Source: adapted from Small and Adams, 1922

In addition, it is also essential that local communities benefit from the exploitation of a resource such as yohimbe. In Cameroon, and soon in Gabon and Equatorial Guinea, the moves towards community management of forest resources, with a view to sustainability, should ensure that the communities managing such resources not only benefit from their exploitation but also are paid a fair price for the resource. This is not the case today. *P. johimbe* could undoubtedly provide a good case study for the equitable and sustainable management of such high-value forest products.

International markets

Interest in yohimbe outside of Africa was first recorded in Germany, where it was used as an aphrodisiac, as well as for treating painful menstruation and prostate inflammation with bladder complaints; it also served as a local anaesthesia for eye, ear and nose operations. Increasing use of yohimbe in the US herbal medicine market came about during the 1970s (Foster, 1999). Prior to the launch of Viagra, yohimbe was the medicine of choice for impotency for millions of men around the world. Markets for products that treat erectile dysfunction are substantial – it is estimated that 50 per cent of men between the ages of 40 and 70 suffer from some degree of erectile dysfunction (unpublished Massachusetts Male Aging Study 1987–89, conducted by New England Research Institutes, Watertown, MA).

Under US law, yohimbe is regulated as a dietary supplement, and yohimbine hydrochloride is a US Food and Drug Administration (FDA) approved pharmaceutical drug for impotence. The American Urological Association's clinical guidelines panel on erectile dysfunction classifies yohimbine as a second-line treatment for organic erectile dysfunction (Pure World Botanicals, 1999). Germany's Commission E monograph (Blomenthal et al, 1998) does not recommend yohimbe for impotence, citing mixed clinical evidence and the potential for adverse side effects, such as tremors, sleeplessness, high blood pressure and rapid heartbeat (Tyler, 1999).

Yohimbe bark contains up to 6 per cent of a mixture of alkaloids, the principal one being yohimbine (Tyler, 1993). Yohimbine was first isolated from yohimbe in 1896. The US FDA approved the use of yohimbine as a treatment for impotence, and the compound is now available in 11 prescription drugs, including Aphrodyne, Erex, Yocon, Yohimex and Yovital. A synthesized yohimbe pharmaceutical drug containing yohimbine hydrochloride has been available for decades. Yohimbine affects the autonomic nervous system and helps with male erection by increasing blood flow to the penis (Foster, 1999). Yohimbe tree bark has also been reported to increase energy and endurance, while building both strength and muscle mass by raising testosterone production. It is also used for weight loss. However, there is not sufficient medical evidence to prove these claims.

In 1995, the US FDA sponsored a study of 26 over-the-counter (OTC) yohimbe products and found only trace amounts of yohimbine in the products tested, ranging from 0.1 to 489 parts per million (ppm), probably not enough to have much effect, and much less than the average yohimbine content of yohimbe bark (7089 ppm). As Varro Tyler reports: 'There is almost a 100 per cent chance that the yohimbe product you purchase over the counter will be worthless' (Milman, 1999).

More importantly, yohimbe has been linked to serious health problems, and steps are being taken in the US to regulate yohimbe products more effectively. Included in the FDA 'Unsafe List', yohimbe can cause anxiety, sleeplessness and may react dangerously with a substance found in wine and cheeses, causing high blood pressure, nausea and vomiting (Milman, 1999). The 1997 FDA safety rules for ephedra-containing products included advising against the use of ephedra products mixed with caffeine or yohimbe (*Nutrition Science News*, 1997). Health Canada and the Health Protection Branch of the federal government banned the sale of yohimbe, along with dozens of other botanical products, due to safety concerns (Lake, 1998).

As a result, although the media attention on Viagra helped to create interest in botanical impotence drugs, concerns asso-ciated with yohimbe's safety have had a dampening effect on its widespread acceptance. Although yohimbe is the only botanical sex aid to be listed in the *Physicians Desk Reference*, and has been scientifically proven to improve sexual function, its side effects are considered as serious as those associated with Viagra – if not more so. Those individuals with hypertension, prostate problems or heart disease – in effect, those most likely to consume it – are warned against using yohimbe (EN, 1999). Ginkgo, garlic, ginseng, oatstraw (*Avena sativa*), muira puama, damiana and other botanicals tend to be promoted in the botanical medicine literature for widespread use over yohimbe, although for specialists, yohimbe appears to be holding its own (eg Haynes, 1998; Brody, 1998; *Natural Way*, 1998). In sum, yohimbe is considered a useful medicine, but one to be taken seriously and under the advice of a specialist. It should not be purchased from the widespread, self-medicating botanicals market.

Yohimbe products

Yohimbe is sold as both a pharmaceutical drug, containing synthesized yohimbine hydrochloride, and as botanical medicine (as bark extracts or ground-up bark). Yohimbe dietary supplement products are usually sold as capsules or tablets, but liquid extracts are also available. Yohimbe products are sold both for impotency and as a fat-burner/muscle-builder for men. Prescription drugs (today usually 5.4 milligrams (mg) per tablet) include Aphrodyne, Erex, Yocon (Palisades Pharmaceuticals), Yohimex and Yovital, as well as over-the-counter botanical preparations such as Yohimbe Power, Vigor Fit for Men, Inca Warrior Potent Male Formula, Yohimbe Backdraft, Men's X-Action Male-Performance Supplement, Super Man, Hot Stuff and Yohimbe Concentrate. In addition to the botanical and pharmaceutical industries, yohimbe is also featured increasingly in nutraceutical products designed to boost energy. For example, SoBe Beverages recently launched the Energy drink, with guarana, yohimbe and arginine. In one advertising spot launched in 1999 by SoBe (South Beach Beverage, Norwalk, Connecticut), the benefits of herbal ingredients, or 'functional beverages', is made explicit, including the sustained energy contribution of yohimbe to the SoBe Energy drink (guarana provides instant energy; arginine enhances physical performance) (Khermouch, 1999).

Botanicals are playing an increasing role in nutraceuticals, particularly sports nutrition. Key botanicals used to increase endurance and energy include yohimbe, ephedra, ma huang, guarana, kola nut and ginseng. Nutraceutical, or functional foods, include added ingredients that impart health benefits, and are growing rapidly in the mass market (Laird, 1999; Shugarman, 1999). Companies marketing yohimbe products include Univeral Labs, Twinlab, Ultimate Nutrition, HerbPharm, ActionLab, Only Natural, Vitol, Solaray and HerbPharm. The quality of capsulated powder and the concentration of liquid extracts vary greatly. Suppliers of yohimbe raw materials to manufacturers include AIDP, ATZ, Pure World Botanicals and Stryka Botanics Co (US); Nuova Linnea (Switzerland); Extractos Natra (Spain); and Schweizer Hall (Nigeria). Noga-Wills (Nigeria) Ltd specializes in the 'supply of tropical rainforest products used in pharmaceutical and cosmetic industries internationally.'

Certification potential

1 Demand for yohimbe is significant and – despite concerns associated with product safety – is projected to grow in the coming years. However, yohimbe is fed into two significantly different markets: the pharmaceutical and the botanical medicine market. The former is not a likely candidate for certified raw material, with the exception of raw material of certified quality and active constituents. The botanical medicine industry is a more likely candidate for certified raw material, and already some products carry claims of sustainability. In the US, HerbPharm markets an extract from the bark of trees 'custom wild-crafted', 'especially for use in their native habitat in Cameroon, Africa'. Given health concerns associated with yohimbe in the botanical medicine industry, however, a certifier should collaborate with groups who also certify quality and active constituents. Availability of substitute products should also be kept in mind as an additional factor influencing future yohimbe demand.

2 Yohimbe bark is currently collected from 100 per cent wild sources, is dispersed across a number of national borders and often takes place in remote areas. Chain of custody – the tracking of bark from source to the end-user – could prove extremely challenging in this case.

3 The ecology of yohimbe species is poorly understood, and a great deal of work is required to adequately develop sustainable management plans that will act as the basis for certification. While yohimbe species are fast growing and occur in relatively higher densities than many tropical forest trees, sustainable systems of wild harvest have not been developed to date, and there is little understanding of the impact of current harvesting practices on populations. However, research underway to domesticate the species (and thereby supplement wild supplies of raw material) and ecological stud-

ies on wild populations will yield data critical to the development of sustainable sources.

4 Existing collection, trade networks, processing and commercialization activities do not appear to significantly benefit local communities and those living in proximity to wild yohimbe. Wild harvesters earn less than half of the price paid at the gates of the processing company (Plantecam) within Cameroon, and prices paid for raw materials supplied by Plantecam are, in turn, a fraction of the final product sales. Certification would need to avoid encouraging existing inequity that is associated with the collection and trade system, and should seek to promote greater benefits for local communities.

5 It is unclear whether the legal and policy context supports the sustainable management of yohimbe, or supports increased benefit-sharing from market

tools such as certification, on a local or national level; this would need more investigation.

6 Yohimbe is often harvested by employees of logging companies, following the felling of timber in a given area. In some cases, therefore, certification of yohimbe might be conducted in conjunction with timber certification. In any case, the role of timber and road-building in creating access to yohimbe populations must be incorporated within assessments of yohimbe sources.

7 Chain-of-custody, social and sustainable-management issues would prove challenging to the process of certifying yohimbe. However, yohimbe's relatively high value, consistent international demand and relatively good potential for sustainable management argue for a consideration of this approach.

Acknowledgements

The authors would like to thank Anacletus Koufani, Augustin Njiamnshi, Crisantos Obama and Dinga Njingum Franklin for their diligent contributions to the study of *P. johimbe* in the field.

Note

1   A sample of this bark was collected to determine the amount and quality of yohimbine, the results of which have implications for potential sustainable management of wild populations.

Chapter 21

Rattan (various spp.)

Terry C H Sunderland and John Dransfield

Introduction

Rattans are climbing palms exploited for their flexible stems that form the basis of a significant market for cane and cane products. The thriving international and domestic trade in rattan and rattan products has led to substantial overexploitation of the wild rattan resource. This exploitation, coupled with the loss of forest cover through logging and subsequent agricultural activities, is threatening the long-term survival of the rattan industry, particularly in South-East Asia (Dransfield, 1988). The detrimental impact of the decline of wild rattan resources on local rattan collectors, who harvest the majority of the traded

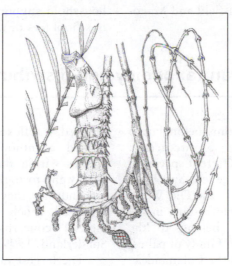

Illustration by Bee Gunn

*Rattan (*Calamus ornatus *var.* philippinensis)

cane, is often overshadowed by the more publicized concerns of the rattan industry itself. In many areas, the sustainable exploitation of the rattan resource is hindered by the lack of a sound taxonomic base in order that meaningful inventories and studies of population dynamics can be carried out. In addition, lack of resource tenure also precludes any attempts at long-term and sustainable harvesting; the fact that rattan is considered an 'open-access' resource throughout much of its range hinders any effective attempts at long-term management of rattan in the wild.

What are rattans?

The word rattan is derived from the Malay 'rotan', the generic name for climbing palms. Rattans are spiny palms found in the lowland tropical forests of the Old World and are the source of cane for the well-developed rattan industry, currently worth some US$6.5 billion per annum (ITTO, 1997). Most of the cane entering the world trade originates from South-East Asia and is collected, in the main, from wild populations, although considerable efforts have recently been focussed on the future provision of raw cane from cultivated sources (Dransfield and Mano-karan, 1992).

As well as forming the basis of a thriving export market, rattans contribute significantly to the subsistence economies of forest-based communities throughout their range. Many of these people utilize the cane resource as a means of direct cash income, especially during periods when other products are seasonally unavailable. Rattan harvesting is often a secondary activity for many farmers, who rely on the cash sale of rattan canes to invest in developing their agricultural base or during times when immediate cash is needed for household support, such as the payment of school fees or medical expenses.

Rattan taxonomy and distribution

Rattans are climbing palms belonging to the palm family (Palmae or Arecaceae). There are around 650 different species of rattan belonging to 13 genera and these are concentrated solely in the Old World tropics; there are no true rattans in the New World.[1] Rattans belong to the Calamoideae, a large sub-family of palms. All of the species within the Calamoideae are characterized by overlapping reflexed scales on the fruit, and all of these climbing palms are spiny, a necessary pre-adaptation to the climbing habit (Dransfield, 1992b).

Of the 13 genera of rattan, three are endemic to Africa: *Laccosperma*, (syn. *Ancistrophyllum*), *Eremospatha* and *Oncocalamus*. These taxa climb with the aid of a whip-like organ, a cirrus, that in the African genera represents a marked extension of the rachis between the distal leaflets. These leaflets are present as reduced, reflexed thorn-like organs termed acanthophylls. Although some species within these genera are utilized locally and form the base of a thriving cottage industry, they have not, until recently, attracted much attention from commercial concerns (Dransfield, 1992b; Sunderland, 1999).

The largest rattan genus is *Calamus*, with circa 370 species. It is represented in Africa by one very variable species, *C. deërratus*; however, *Calamus* is predominantly an Asian genus and ranges from the Indian sub-continent and south China southwards and east through the Malesian region (Malay Peninsula, Borneo and surrounding islands) to Fiji, Vanuatu and tropical and sub-tropical parts of eastern Australia. Most of the best commercial species of rattan are members of this genus. The remaining rattan genera, *Daemonorops*, *Ceratolobus*,

Table 21.1 *The rattan genera: number of species and their distribution*

Genus	Number of species	Distribution
Calamus L.	circa 370–400	Tropical Africa, India and Sri Lanka, China, south and east to Fiji, Vanuatu and eastern Australia
Calospatha Becc.	1	Endemic to Peninsular Malaysia
Ceratolobus Bl.	6	Peninsular Malaysia, Sumatra, Borneo, Java
Daemonorops Bl.	circa 115	India and China to westernmost New Guinea
Eremospatha (Mann and Wendl.) Wendl.	10	Humid tropical Africa
Korthalsia Bl.	circa 26	Indo-China and Burma to New Guinea
Laccosperma (Mann and Wendl.) Drude	5	Humid tropical Africa
Myrialepis Becc.	1	Indo-China, Thailand, Burma, Peninsular Malaysia and Sumatra
Oncocalamus (Wendl.) Wendl.	4	Humid tropical Africa
Plectocomia Mart.	circa 16	Himalayas and south China to western Malesia
Plectocomiopsis Becc.	circa 5	Thailand, Peninsular Malaysia, Borneo, Sumatra
Pogonotium J. Dransf.	3	Two species endemic to Borneo, one species in both Peninsular Malaysia and Borneo
Retispatha J. Dransf.	1	Endemic to Borneo

Source: adapted from Uhl and Dransfield, 1987

Korthalsia, Plectocomia, Plectocomiopsis, Myrialepis, Calospatha, Pogonotium and *Retispatha*, are centred in South-East Asia and have outliers further eastwards and northwards (Uhl and Dransfield, 1987; Dransfield, 1992a).

Despite the commercial importance of rattan, basic knowledge of the resource is somewhat limited and the rattan flora of Africa and much of South-East Asia and Malesia remains poorly known. Taxonomic work of this sort is not purely an academic exercise; it is an essential basis for the development of the rattan resource and underpins the conservation and sustainable development objectives much advocated for rattans. It is essential that species delimitation is clearly understood; we need to know which species are of commercial importance and how they may be distinguished from other species. This knowledge is essential in order to undertake meaningful inventories of commercially important taxa and to be able to assess the silvicultural potential of each species, based on sound ecological knowledge. Reference to a structured systematic framework also ensures that any experimental work undertaken is replicable.

Table 21.2 *Available rattan floras by region to date*

Region	Reference
Peninsular Malaysia	Dransfield, 1979
Sabah	Dransfield, 1984
Sarawak	Dransfield, 1992a
Brunei	Dransfield, 1998
Sri Lanka	de Zoysa and Vivekanandan, 1994
India (general)	Basu, 1992
India (Western Ghats)	Renuka, 1992
India (south)	Lakshmana, 1993
Andaman and Nicobar Islands	Renuka, 1995
Bangladesh	Alam, 1990
Papua New Guinea	Johns and Taurereko, 1989a; 1989b (preliminary notes only); Baker and Dransfield, in preparation
Papua (Indonesia)	Currently under study at Kew (Baker and Dransfield), in preparation
Indonesia	Dransfield and Mogea, in preparation; more field work needed
Laos	Evans, 2001
Thailand	Hodel, 1998
Africa	Sunderland and Profizi, 2001

The uses of rattan

The most important product of rattan palms is cane; this is the rattan stem stripped of its leaf sheaths and stem epidermis (although this is also often utilized for weaving). This inner stem is solid, strong and uniform, yet highly flexible. The canes are used either in whole or round form, especially for furniture frames, or are split, peeled or cored for matting and basketry.

Other plant parts of some species of rattan are also utilized and contribute to the indigenous survival strategies of many forest-based communities. A summary of these uses is listed in Table 21.3.

However, it is for their cane that rattans are most utilized. Rattan canes are used extensively across their range by local communities and play an important role in the subsistence strategies of many rural populations (Burkill, 1935; Corner, 1966; Dransfield, 1992d; Sunderland, 1998). The range of indigenous uses of rattan canes is vast; from bridges to baskets; from fish traps to furniture; from crossbow strings to yam ties.

Despite these many uses, there is a common misconception that all rattans are useful, and therefore all have potential commercial applications. However, while there may indeed be substantial spontaneous use for many species (Dransfield and Manokaran, 1994; Johnson, 1997; Sunderland, 1998), it is estimated that only 20 per cent of the known rattan species are of any commercial value (Dransfield and Manokaran, 1994). The remaining species are not utilized because of their inflexibility and because they are prone to breakage, because they possess other poor mechanical properties, or due to biological rarity.

Table 21.3 *Some traditional uses of rattans, excluding cane*

Product/Use	Species
Fruit eaten	*Calamus conirostris; C. dongnaiensis; C. longisetus; C. manillensis; C. merrillii; C. ornatus; C. paspalanthus; C. rhabdocladus; C. subinermis; C. viminalis; Calospatha scortechinii; Daemonorops hystrix; D. ingens; D. periacantha; D. ruptilis*
Palm heart eaten	*Calamus deerratus; C. egregius; C. javensis; C. muricatus; C. paspalanthus; C. rhabdocladus; C. simplicifolius; C. subinermis; Daemonorops fissa; D. jenkinsiana; D. longispatha; D. melanochaetes; D. periacantha; D. scapigera; D. sparsiflora; Laccosperma secundiflorum; Plectocomiopsis geminiflora*
Seeds chewed	*Calamus walkeri*
Fruit used in traditional medicine	*Calamus castaneus; C. longispathus; Daemonorops didymophylla*
Palm heart used in traditional medicine	*Calamus exilis; C. javensis; C. ornatus; Daemonorops grandis; Korthalsia rigida*
Fruit used as source of red dye	*Daemonorops didymophylla; D. draco; D. maculata; D. micracantha; D. propinqua; D. rubra*
Leaves used for thatching	*Calamus andamanicus; C. castaneus; C. dilaceratus; C. longisetus; Daemonorops calicarpa; D. elongata; D. grandis; D. ingens; D. manii*
Leaflet used as cigarette paper	*Calamus longispathus; Daemonorops leptopus*
Leaves chewed as vermifuge	*Laccosperma secundiflorum*
Roots used as treatment for syphilis	*Eremospatha macrocarpa*
Leaf sheath used as toothbrush	*Eremospatha wendlandiana; Oncocalamus spp.*
Leaf sheath/petiole used as grater	*Calamus burckianus; C. insignis*
Rachis used as fishing pole	*Daemonorops grandis; Laccosperma secundiflorum*

A word about local classification

The development of extensive indigenous classification systems for rattans often reflects the social significance of rattan, and these taxonomies have developed to reflect rattan as it grows in the forest, as well as to reflect how it is used. For example, a widespread species may be referred to by many names, since its range encompasses a number of dialectic groups. Often, one species can be given many names, reflecting the different uses of the plant or the various stages of development (from juvenile to adult with very distinct morphological differences between the two). Commonly, blanket names for 'cane' are given to a wide range of species.

Some species that have no use are often classified according to their 'relationship' to those that are utilized. These are often along kinship lines and species may be referred to as 'uncle of' or 'small brother of', reflecting their perceived relationship and similarity to species that are widely utilized. In the past, serious confusion has arisen from the uncritical use of vernacular names and has contributed to the misconception that all species are of commercial potential. Local names should be used in conjunction with classical Linnean taxonomic methods and not on a mutually exclusive basis.

Table 21.4 *The major commercial species of rattan as identified for Asia by Dransfield and Manokaran (1994), and for Africa by Tuley (1995) and Sunderland (1999)*

Species	Distribution	Conservation status
Calamus caesius Bl.	Peninsular Malaysia, Sumatra, Borneo, the Philippines and Thailand; also introduced to China and south Pacific for planting	Unknown
Calamus egregius Burr.	Endemic to Hainan Island, China, but introduced to southern China for cultivation	Unknown
Calamus exilis Griffith	Peninsular Malaysia and Sumatra	Not threatened
Calamus javensis Bl.	Widespread in South-East Asia	Not threatened
Calamus manan Miq.	Peninsular Malaysia, Sumatra, Thailand and Borneo and Sumatra	Threatened
Calamus merrillii Becc.	The Philippines	Threatened
Calamus mindorensis Becc.	The Philippines	Unknown
Calamus optimus Becc.	Borneo, and Sumatra; cultivated in Kalimantan	Unknown
Calamus ornatus Bl.	Thailand, Sumatra, Java, Borneo, Sulawesi, to the Philippines	Unknown
Calamus ovoideus Thwaites ex Trimen	Western Sri Lanka	Threatened
Calamus palustris Griffith	Burma, southern China, to Malaysia and the Andaman Islands	Unknown
Calamus pogonacanthus Becc. ex Winkler	Borneo	Unknown
Calamus poilanei	Thailand, Laos and Vietnam	Threatened
Calamus scipionum Loureiro	Burma, Thailand, Peninsular Malaysia, Sumatra, Borneo to Palawan	Unknown
Calamus simplicifolius Wei	Endemic to Hainan Island, China, but introduced to southern China for cultivation	Unknown
Calamus subinermis H. Wendl. ex Becc.	Sabah, Sarawak, East Kalimamtan and Palawan	Unknown
Calamus tetradactylus Hance	Southern China; introduced to Malaysia	Unknown
Calamus trachycoleus Becc.	South and Central Kalimantan; introduced to Malaysia for cultivation	Not threatened
Calamus tumidus Furtado	Peninsular Malaysia and Sumatra	Unknown
Calamus wailong Pei and Chen	Southern China	Unknown
Calamus zollingeri Becc.	Sulawesi and the Moluccas	Unknown
Daemonorops jenkinsiana (Hance) Becc.	India to south China	Unknown
Daemonorops robusta Warb.	Indonesia, Sulawesi and the Moluccas	Unknown
Daemonorops sabut Becc.	Peninsula Malaysia and Borneo	Unknown
Eremospatha macrocarpa (Mann and Wendl.) Mann and Wendl.	Tropical Africa, from Sierra Leone to Angola	Not threatened
Eremospatha haullevilleana De Wild.	Congo Basin to East Africa	
Laccosperma robustum (Burr.) J. Dransf.	Cameroon to Congo Basin	
Laccosperma secundiflorum (P. Beauv.) Mann and Wendl.	Tropical Africa, from Sierra Leone to Angola	Not threatened

The commercial rattan trade

The international trade in rattan dates from the mid 19th century (Corner, 1996), and this trade is now currently worth some $US6.5 billion a year (ITTO, 1997). A conservative estimate of the domestic markets of South-East Asia by Manokaran (1984) suggested a net worth of US$2.5 billion. This latter market includes the value of goods in urban markets and rural trade, as well as the value of the rural usage of the material and products. Dransfield and Manokaran (1994) estimate that 0.7 billion of the world's population use, or are involved in, the trade of rattan and rattan products.

South-East Asia

The majority of the international rattan trade is dominated by countries of South-East Asia. By the early 20th century, Singapore, despite having a very small rattan resource itself, became the clearing house for nearly the whole of South-East Asia and the western Pacific. Between 1922 and 1927, up to 27,500 tonnes of cane and cane products were exported, mainly to Hong Kong, the United States and France. During this same period, exports from Kalimantan and Sulawesi increased dramatically; from 9400 to 19,300 tonnes and from 10,300 to 21,800 tonnes respectively, with much of this also being re-exported through Singapore (Dransfield and Manokaran, 1994).

By the 1970s, Indonesia had become the supplier of about 90 per cent of the world's cane, with the majority of this going to Singapore for processing and conversion (from which Singapore earned more than US$21 million per annum). Thus, in 1977, Hong Kong imported some $US26 million of rattan and rattans products that, after conversion, was worth over US$68 million in export value. By comparison, Indonesia's share of the trade, mainly of unprocessed canes, was a mere US$15 million (Dransfield and Manokaran, 1994).

During the last 20 years, the international trade in rattan and rattan products has undergone rapid expansion. The increases in the value of exports from the major producing countries are indeed staggering; 250-fold for Indonesia over 17 years; 75-fold in the Philippines over 15 years; 23-fold over 9 years in Thailand; and 12-fold over 8 years in Malaysia. By the late 1980s, the combined value of exports of these four countries alone had risen to an annual figure of almost US$400 million, with Indonesia accounting for 50 per cent of this trade. The net revenues derived from the sale of rattan goods by Taiwan and Hong Kong, where raw and partially finished products were imported and then processed, together totalled around US$200 million per annum by the late 1980s.

During this same period, Thailand, the Philippines, Indonesia and Malaysia banned the export of rattan, except as finished products. These bans were imposed in order to stimulate the development of rattan-based industries in each country and to ensure that the value of the raw product was increased, (theoretically) protecting the wild resource. Recently, however, given the recession that has hit many countries in South-East Asia, Indonesia has lifted the ban on the export of raw cane and is currently flooding the market with relatively cheap supplies of cane, negatively impacting the cultivation industry of Malaysia, in particular (Sunderland and Nkefor, 1999a).

Africa

The restrictions in the trade of raw cane by some of the larger supply countries outlined above have encouraged some rattan dealers and gross users to investigate non-traditional sources of rattans, predominantly Indo-China, Papua New Guinea and, more recently, Africa. Some raw cane has recently been exported from Ghana and Nigeria to South-East Asia and there is a flourishing export trade of finished rattan products from Nigeria to Korea (Morakinyo pers comm). In addition, trade within and between countries is reported to be growing significantly across West and Central Africa (Falconer, 1994; Morakinyo, 1995; Sunderland 1999).

Historically, there has been a significant trade in African rattans. Cameroon and Gabon supplied France and its colonies (Hedin, 1929), and Ghana (formerly the Gold Coast) supplied a significant proportion of the large UK market during the inter-war period (Anon, 1934). The export industry was not restricted to raw cane, and in 1928 alone over 25,000 French francs (FF) worth of finished cane furniture was exported from Cameroon to Senegal for the expatriate community there (Hedin, 1929). More recently, an initiative promoted by the United Nations Industrial Development Organization (UNIDO) in Senegal exploited wild cane for large-scale production and export (Douglas, 1974), although this enterprise folded not long after its establishment due to problems securing a regular supply of raw material.

Rattan ecology and natural history

The large number of rattan species, and their wide geographic range, is matched by great ecological diversity. The majority of, admittedly crude, ecological preferences for rattan species have been generally made during taxonomic inventory work; yet these broad ecological summaries are invaluable as a basis for establishing cultivation procedures. A major gap in the knowledge of rattans, even of the commercial species, is an understanding of population dynamics and demography. The knowledge of the population structure, distribution, rate of regeneration, the number of harvestable stems per hectare, etc of each species is essential and forms the basis of an understanding of potential sustainability.

Forest type and light requirements

Throughout their natural range, rattan species are found in a variety of forest and soil types. Some species are common components of the forest understorey, while others rely on good light penetration for their development; hence, many species are found in gap vegetation and respond very well to canopy manipulation, particularly that caused by selective logging. Some species grow in swamps and seasonally inundated forest, while others are more common on dry ridge tops.

Despite this wide range of ecological conditions, the majority of rattans need adequate light for their development. Cultivation trials on many of the South-East Asia species, as well as recent germination trials of the African taxa, have indicated that seeds will germinate under a wide range of light conditions. The resultant seedlings will remain for long periods on the forest floor, waiting for light conditions to improve, such as through a tree fall. This seedling bank is a common feature of the regeneration of most species and is a well-recognized component of forests where rattans occur.

Life form

Rattans can be clustering (clump forming) or are solitary; some species, such as *Calamus subinermis,* can be both. Other species are acaulescent, having no discernable stem at all. Clustering species sometimes posses up to 50 stems of varying ages in each clump and produce suckers that continually replace those stems lost through natural senescence, or through harvesting. Some clumps can be harvested many times on a defined cycle if the light conditions are conducive to the remaining suckers being able to develop and elongate. Ensuring that stem removal through harvesting does not exceed that of stem replacement is the crux of rattan sustainability.

An even more crucial component of sustainability is the monitoring of the exploitation of solitary species. *Calamus manan,* one of the most commonly exploited rattan species, is single-stemmed; thus, the impacts of harvesting this species are much greater than harvesting from clustering rattans. Sustainability of such species relies on recruitment through sexual means, rather than through vegetative means.

Flowering

Another ecological feature of palms that is extremely important in terms of management is that rattans display two main modes of flowering: hapaxanthy and pleonanthy. In hapaxanthy, a period of vegetative growth is followed by the simultaneous production of inflorescence units from the axils of the uppermost leaves. Although often described as a 'terminal inflorescence', which it undoubtedly resembles, morphologically this is not the case. Flowering and fruiting is followed by the death of the stem itself. In single-stemmed palm species, the whole organism dies after the reproductive event. However, in clustering species of rattan, the organism continues to regenerate from the base and it is only the individual stem that dies. In pleonanthic species, axillary inflorescences are produced continually and flowering and fruiting does not result in the death of the stem. All of the species of *Korthalsia, Laccosperma, Plectocomia, Plectocomiopsis* and *Myrialepis,* and a few species of *Daemonorops,* are hapaxanthic. All other rattan species are pleonanthic. In terms of silviculture, the mode of flowering will affect the cutting regime and stem selection for harvest, particularly if the cultivated resource is to supply seed for further trials. Furthermore, in many hapaxanthic species, stems tend to be of low quality due to the presence of a soft pith that results in poor bending properties. These stems are also more prone to subsequent insect attack due to increased starch deposition.

Fruit and seed

Rattan fruits are usually brightly coloured (yellow, orange or red) and the sarcotesta is also attractive to birds and mammals. Hornbills and primates are the main dispersers of rattan seeds in both South-East

Asia and Africa, with primates and elephants also sharing a preference for the ripe fruit. Fruits are often ingested whole, where they pass through the intestinal tract of the agent concerned, or are sucked and spat out, with the seed intact.

In the Asian taxa, the seed is often covered with a sarcotesta. Incomplete removal of this sarcotesta often results in delayed germination, suggesting that it contains some chemical germination inhibitors. However, once this outer layer is fully removed, the germination of commercial species, such as *Calamus manan* and *C. caesius*, is both rapid and uniform. In contrast, propagation trials on the commercially important species in Africa have noted a physically induced dormancy resulting from the presence of a relatively robust seed coat surrounding the endosperm. Experiments have shown that, because of the barrier to imbibition, the germination times of some African rattan species can be prolonged, and it may take 9–12 months before germination commences. This physical dormancy has caused difficulty in cultivating some species, and numerous trials have been undertaken to reduce these germination times (Sunderland and Nkefor, 1999b).

Physical seed treatments, such as scarification or chitting, are somewhat effective means of reducing the germination times for some of the species; but soaking the seeds in water for at least 24 hours prior to sowing is probably the most effective means of inducing early germination (Sunderland and Nkefor, 1999b).

Rattan–ant relationships

Several species of rattan (*Laccosperma*, *Eremospatha*, *Korthalsia*, *Calamus* and *Daemonorops*) have developed morphological adaptations that provide nesting sites for ants. These adaptations include the hollowing out of acanthophylls, interlocking spines that form galleries or recurved proximal leaflets that tightly clasp the stem, or inflated leaf sheath extensions (ocreas). This relationship is extremely complex and has yet to be fully investigated. The 'farming' of scale insects by ants is also a common relationship. The scale insects feed on the rattan phloem cells, secreting a sweet honeydew that the ants then feed on; the ants, in turn, protect the rattan from other predators (unfortunately, this also includes rattan harvesters and unwitting botanists).

Harvest and management

Growth rates

Rattans are vigorous climbers with relatively high growth rates, and are thus able to be harvested on a short cycle. For the majority of rattans, stem production from the rosette stage (and the seedling bank) is initiated by exposure to adequate light. Stem elongation is also affected by light and, while continuous, varies – usually on a seasonal basis. While no data on the growth rates of rattans in the wild exists,

long-term studies have been undertaken in cultivation.

Management and harvesting

Examples of long-term in-situ management of rattans in the wild are rare (Belcher, 1999). However, based on experimental work in South-East Asia, four production systems of rattan exploitation can be identified:

Table 21.5 *The growth rates of some commercial rattans in cultivation*

Species	Growth rates (metres per year)
Calamus caesius	2.9–5.6
Calamus egregius	0.8
Calamus hainanensis	3.5
Calamus manan	1.2
Calamus scipionum	1.0
Calamus tetradactylus	2.3
Calamus trachycoleus	(5.0)*
Daemonorops jenkinsiana	(2.0–2.5)*

* Bracketed figures are estimates
Source: adapted from Dransfield and Manokaran, 1994

- *Natural regeneration in high forest.* This level of management requires the development and implementation of management plans based upon sound inventory data and an understanding of the population dynamics of the species concerned. This is particularly appropriate for forest reserves, community forests and other low-level protected areas. These 'extractive-reserve' models are highly appropriate for rattan: a high-value, high-yielding product that relies on the forest milieu for its survival.
- *Enhanced natural regeneration, through enrichment planting and canopy manipulation, in natural forest.* This is especially appropriate where forest has been selectively logged. Management inputs are fairly high, with the clearance of competing undergrowth vegetation and subsequent selective felling to create 'artificial' gaps. This has been practised in India, with some success for the rattan resource. Rattan planting in forest in East Kalimantan has also proved successful. The Forest Research Institute of Malaysia suggests that enrichment planting is perhaps the most beneficial form of cultivation, both in terms of productivity and the maintenance of ecological integrity (Supardi, pers comm).

- *Rattan cultivation as part of shifting cultivation or in formal agroforestry systems.* The incorporation of rattan within traditional swidden fallow systems in some areas of South-East Asia is well known (Connelly, 1985; Siebert and Belsky, 1985; Peluso, 1992; Weinstock, 1983; Kiew, 1991). The general principle is that, on harvesting ephemeral or annual crops, rattan is planted and the land is then left fallow. When the rotation is repeated, usually on a 7- to 15-year cycle, the farmer first harvests the rattan and then clears the plot again to plant food crops. The income generated from the harvesting of rattan in this way is significant.
- *Silvicultural trials* have concentrated on the incorporation of rattan within tree-based plantation-type systems. The need for a framework for the rattan to grow on is imperative and the planting of rattan in association with tree cash crops was begun in the 1980s. In particular, planting under rubber (*Hevea brasiliensis*) and other fast-growing tree crops has proven relatively successful, and both silvicultural trials and commercial operations are commonly encountered throughout South-East Asia.

The harvesting techniques employed in the extraction of rattan have an impact on potential sustainability, particularly for clustering species. The mature stems selected for harvesting are those without lower leaves (ie where the leaf sheaths have sloughed off) and usually only the basal 10–20 metres (m) is harvested. The upper 'green' part of the cane is too soft and inflexible for transformation and is often left in the canopy. In many instances, all of the stems in a clustering species may be cut in order to obtain access to the mature stems, even those that are not yet mature enough for exploitation and sale. This is particularly relevant when resource tenure is weak.

In general, two simple interventions can be implemented in order to improve rattan-harvesting practices.

For *clustering species*, younger stems, often indiscriminately cut during harvesting, should be left to regenerate and provide future sources of cane. Rotational harvesting systems could be increased if this was the case. However, better 'stool management' relies on adequate resource tenure.

For *all species*, harvest intensity and rotation should be based on long-terms assessments of growth rates and recruitment.

Inventory

Rattan inventory has proved to be a somewhat imperfect science. Initial attempts to determine stocking and yield have often been thwarted by a poor taxonomic base from which to begin; it is essential to know which species are being enumerated. Furthermore, inadequately sampling the correct parameters has led to much inventory information being discarded. When planning a rattan inventory, it is essential to:

- know the species concerned (collect herbarium specimens when in doubt);
- measure the correct parameters; these include number of stems per clump (for clustering species); number of clumps per hectare or, for solitary canes, stems per hectare; total stem length; and harvestable stem length (the lower stem portion with the leaves sloughed off);
- establish a protocol for measuring over time in order to determine growth rates and recruitment; this will determine the potential harvest and hence sustainable extraction rates.

Land tenure and socio-economic issues

Rattan management of whatever kind will only be successful if those involved have clear access to the forest, and/or long and easily renewable resource rights on it (de Fretas, 1992). Currently, rattan collectors rationally maximize their income by harvesting the best and most accessible canes because they are paid on a per item basis. Larger canes bring the best prices and it is also important to minimize the opportunity costs of collection (ie the rattans closer to the community will be harvested first, and probably more intensively).

Traditionally, many communities in South-East Asia and Africa have benefited from the harvesting of their rattan resource. Many of these groups are dependent upon high-value forest products, such as rattan, for access to the cash economy. However, local scarcity caused by uncontrolled harvesting is denying many local people access to this traditional means of income, let alone access to the resource for their own subsistence needs.

Cultivation

Many examples exist of rattans being cultivated in agroforestry systems in forest lands controlled by local communities (Weinstock, 1983; Connelly, 1985; Siebert and Belsky, 1985; Peluso, 1992), and a small proportion of cane from such systems supplies the formal markets. When it first became clear, during the period post World War II, in particular, that rattans were becoming scarce (with the associated market implications: scarcity = price increases), considerable attempts were made to include rattans within commercial-scale cultivation and silvicultural systems. Across South-East Asia, many plantations and trials were established. However, many of these plantations and cultivated sources of cane are owned and managed by sovereign forestry departments or private companies. Hence, the revenue accrued does not often find its way to local communities as it would if individuals were harvesting directly from their own agroforestry systems. In many ways, commercial cultivation leads to the removal of a resource from the informal forest economy and into the formal forestry sector; a system renowned for its inequity in terms of ensuring that benefits accrue to local people (Belcher, 1999). However, as discussed above, the attractiveness of these intensive cultivation systems has now been questioned, and many are systems being converted to oil palm plantations.

Table 21.6 *Commercial-scale rattan trials and plantations*

Country	Cultivation
Bangladesh	Trials of *Daemonorops jenkinsiana* established in early 1980s
Cameroon	1ha trial plot of *Laccosperma secundiflorum* under obsolete rubber near Limbe
China	1970s: 30,000ha of enrichment planting of forest on Hainan Island with *Calamus tetradactylus* and *Daemonorops jenkinsiana*; Plantations of *C. egregius* and *C. simplicifolius* in Guangdong Province; Cultivation trials of many species have been initiated since 1985
Indonesia	Trials of *C. manan* begun during the 1980s in Java; 1988–1993: several thousand hectares of *C. caesius* and, to a lesser extent, *C. trachycoleus* planted by Forestry Department in Java and East Kalimantan
Kenya	Trial plot *C. latifolius* under *Gmelina arborea* near Lake Victoria
Malaysia	1960: *C. manan* planted in Ulu Langat Forest Reserve; 1972: Cultivation trial of *C. manan* initiated in Pehang; 1975: Forest Research Institute of Malaysia (FRIM) cultivation trials of *C. scipionum* and *C. caesius* planted under rubber: 1100ha in total; 1980–1981: Sandakan area – 4000ha plantation in logged forest planted with *C. caesius* and *C. trachycoleus*, as well as 2000ha of abandoned rubber, *Acacia mangium*, and logged forest planted with *C. manan*, *C. caesius* and *C. merrillii*; 1982–1983: Two trial plots of *C. optimus* established in Sarawak; 1990: large-scale planting in Sarawak with *C. manan*, *C. caesius*, *C. optimus* and *C. trachycoleus*
The Philippines	1977: Cultivation trials of *C. merrillii* and *C. ornatus* var. *philippinensis* established in Quezon; 5000ha plantation of *C. merrillii* established in Mindanao; Early 1990: 500ha of *C. merrillii* and *C. ornatus* var. *philippinensis* planted under *Endospermum peltatum* (matchwood tree plantation) in Mindanao
Sri Lanka	*C. ovoideus* and *C. thwaitesii* trials established in recent years
Thailand	213ha of *C. caesius* in Narathiwat Province, established by 1978; *C. caesius* trials established in 1979 in Ranong, Surathani and Chuporn Provinces; 1980–1987: *C. caesius* and *C. manan* trials established – 930ha in Narathiwat Province

Source: adapted from Dransfield and Manokaran, 1994

Certification potential

The ecology and nature of rattans make them one of the few products that can be sustainably harvested, given the availability of crucial baseline information, the implementation of an appropriate management regime and adequate land and resource tenure. Rattan exploitation, whether in natural forest or in agroforestry systems, relies on an intricate and multilayered ecological balance between the rattan resource and the trees that rattan needs to support it. Rattan cannot be grown outside of this system and therefore its management lends itself to the ecological and management criteria for sustainability set by certifiers (Viana et al, 1996).

Rattan is relatively fast growing and high yielding and can be harvested on relatively short rotations. This allows for relatively short- to medium-scale returns for those involved in its management, whether local communities or companies. However, limited ecological data on growth rates and estimates of recruitment that are necessary to set harvesting levels and quotas will continue to hinder field assessments of sustainability. More basic ecological and applied research is urgently needed before management regimes for species of commercial interest can be drawn up and implemented. In this respect, it should be noted that managed high forest and/or agroforestry systems are more easily monitored for ecological sustainability than are intensively managed natural-forest systems.

Chain-of-custody (or 'production-to consumption') issues are complex for rattans harvested from the wild (Belcher, 1999). In many areas, collectors are small scale and widely dispersed, meaning that the trade is dominated by a series of middle men. In areas where rattan is more intensively managed by communities, such as in East Kalimantan, however, the chain of custody of material should be more straightforward because there are very clear, long-established links between these communities and the markets they supply.

Managed high forest and/or agroforestry systems also offer potentially great social rewards. By re-enforcing traditional tenure and management systems, certification can promote rights over resources and lands not commonly held by communities who manage rattan. However, technical issues remain important, and there are currently few documented traditional cultivation models for rattan. Little research has also been undertaken on the small-scale cultivation of rattans.

Commercial rattan plantations, albeit under a parent crop, do not usually reflect the diversity and complexity of traditional managed crops. In addition, the fact that the majority of commercial plantations are government or privately owned means that such systems offer only limited benefits to communities (de Fretas, 1992). However, when designed and maintained efficiently, commercial plantations can be both productive and highly profitable and should not necessarily be excluded from potential certification.

On a final note, and most importantly, the vigorous international and domestic markets for cane and cane products suggest that the additional costs incurred from certification, including better management practices and the equitable distribution of benefits, could readily be absorbed by consumers who pay a 'green premium' for certified products.

Note

1 Two other groups of palms confined to the New World have climbing representatives and are often mistaken as being closely related to true rattans. *Chamaedorea* (sub-family Ceroxyloxideae; tribe Hyophorbeae) and *Desmoncus* (sub-family Arecoideae; tribe Cocoeae) climb through the means of reflexed terminal leaflets. Indeed, *Desmoncus* is often exploited for its cane-like qualities and is used in the same way as the true rattans (Henderson and Chávez, 1993). In addition, a climbing palm (*Dypsis scandens*) has been discovered in Madagascar; it also is not related to the true rattans.

Chapter 22

Amla (*Phyllanthus emblica*)

Ganesan Balachander

Introduction

Phyllanthus emblica is a small- to moderate-sized tree, common in mixed deciduous forests throughout the greater part of tropical and sub-tropical India, and ascending the Himalayas to circa 1350 metres (m). It is not found in arid regions. Its trade name emblica is based on its old scientific name *Emblica officinalis* Gaertner. Its vernacular names include amla, in Hindi, and nelli, in Tamil. The main part used is the fruit, which is a very rich source of vitamin C (ascorbic acid). An alkaloid phyllembin and several tannins are also reported. 'An emblica fruit a day keeps the doctor at bay' is a rural

Illustration by Antônio Valente da Silva

*Amla (*Phyllanthus emblica*)*

Indian take on the Western refrain 'an apple a day keeps the doctor away'.

The fruits are one of the three constituents of the well-known Indian ayurvedic preparation Triphala, the other two being *Terminalia bellerica* and *Terminalia chebula*. Triphala is used as a laxative and is considered to be especially useful in the treatment of jaundice and stomach disorders, among other ailments.

Phyllanthus is derived from two Greek words: *phullon*, meaning a 'leaf', and *anthos*, a 'flower'. The whole meaning is a 'leaf flower' and apparently refers to the bearing of flowers on the leaves.

Ecology

P. emblica is commonly found in savanna and moist deciduous forests, while a related species, *P. indofischerii*, is relatively rare and restricted in distribution to dry deciduous forests. However, the latter's fruits are bigger in size and less acidic. Its leaflets, too, are bigger but in fewer numbers. *P. emblica* has a clumped distribution in the forest. It has feathery, light green foliage and small, narrow linear leaves. The leaves are 10–13 millimetres (mm) long and 2–3mm broad, very closely set in a pinnate fashion. The male and female flowers are borne on the same tree. Flowers are pale green/yellow, usually in small dense clusters. Female flowers are found in the lower axils, but mixed with the males, and with shorter pedicels. Fruits are 1.5–2.5 centimetres (cm) in diameter, fleshy, round and indistinctly marked into six lobes, which are pale green in colour. The fruits from cultivated farms are larger than those collected from the wild. Most of the trade from fruits grown in the south is from extraction, whereas in the north the trade is largely from cultivation.

The density of amla trees in the forest varies by forest type and is highest in deciduous forests – mean observed diameter at breast height (dbh) is 16cm. The dbh of trees is positively correlated with fruit productivity, with larger trees yielding greater amounts of fruits. In the scrub forest, by contrast, with its reduced canopy cover and stunted growth and low stature, amla trees with a dbh of between 5–10cm fruit quite frequently, but their productivity is limited. Table 22.1 presents an 'indicative' production from a south Indian forest.

Leaf-shedding, flowering and fruiting

Leaves begin to fall in November and the trees are leafless from about February to March or April, when new shoots appear. The tree has a peculiarity of shedding its twigs along with its attached leaves. The small yellow/pale green flowers, approximately 3mm across, appear from March until May, and are visited by swarms of bees. In addition to pollination by *Trigona* bees, the flowers are perhaps also wind pollinated.

The fruits, which ripen from November to February, have a six-ridged bony endocarp, containing about four to six dark brown, smooth seeds of which about 1800–1900 weigh approximately 30 grams. The seeds may be extracted by placing the ripe fruits in the sun until the hard putamen dehisces and the seeds escape. Various tests have shown that the percentage of fertility is comparatively low and that the seed does not retain its vitality long. Seeds kept for a year fail to germinate.

Table 22.1 *Estimated fruit production of amla from a south Indian forest.*

Vegetation type	Area (ha)	Density per ha	Fruit/tree (kg)	Fruit per ha (kg)
Evergreen	3510	1.8	19.6	35.3
Deciduous	33,264	20.5	20.2	414.1
Scrub	15,228	2.5	14.4	36.0

Source: Shankar et al, 1996

Impact of land-use change

The structure and composition of the Indian forests have been shaped by centuries of human use. Although shifting cultivation has been discontinued in recent decades, the collection of non-timber forest products (NTFPs) on a commercial scale, such as the fruits of *Phyllanthus emblica*, continues. There is evidence from a number of sites that extraction levels have increased over time.

Although there has been no commercial logging for several years, the forests, in general, have not yet recovered from past fellings. Weed infestation by species such as *Lantana camara* is rampant, presumably affecting regeneration of many indigenous species. Poor recruitment of *P. emblica* in forests may also result from fire and grazing (both linked to livestock management). Fires occur with relatively high frequency in most of the Indian forests, most set to promote a flush of grass with the onset of monsoon for cattle grazing.

Comparison of population stocks of amla trees within deciduous forests in the Biligiri Rangan Hills (1931 Forestry Department survey and 1992 census) indicates that the density of trees with a dbh greater than or equal to 45cm in 1992 was less than one half that in 1931. This indicates a radical shift of population structure to smaller size classes due to human impacts.

Management

Germination

Under natural conditions, the fruits fall during the latter part of the cold season and during a portion of the hot season. They lie on the ground until the fleshy covering dries up and the hard fruit stones split open, which they do with some force, the seeds thus escaping. Germination takes place early in the rainy season. Deer, which eat the fruits, disgorge the hard stones during rumination, which then dehisce on the ground especially during summer showers. Light and temperature conditions are then favourable for germination. Predators include porcupines. Regeneration also occurs through suckers, which take approximately ten years to mature. Natural reproduction is seldom found in any great abundance. This is partly due to the fact that the fertility of the seed is not high and also because of the sensitivity of the seedling in its early stages; the seedling is also vulnerable to insect attacks.

Silvicultural characters

Amla is a decided light-demanding species and is sensitive to both frost and drought. In severe frosts, the fruit becomes whitish, with the appearance of having been boiled. The trees coppice well and pollard moderately well, with the coppice shoots, in particular, growing vigorously. In cultivated areas, amla is commonly propagated from seed.

The seedling

Under favourable conditions, the growth of the seedling is rapid. In the north at an altitude of 1200m, seedlings on wooded but unwatered ground attained a maximum height in the first four years of 0.8m, 2.1m, 2.88m and 4.95m. The basal girth at the end of the fourth year was 0.18m. Weeding greatly stimulates development, while the presence of weeds retards it; however, after the seedlings have outgrown the weeds, their growth is rapid. In unweeded plots the growth is 0.13m, 1.1m and 2.95m during the first three years. Under natural conditions, growth is probably slower. The young plant is intolerant of shade or suppression of any kind, and when several young plants grow together, one or two vigorous specimens quickly tend to take the lead and to suppress the rest. During the first few months, the seedlings are somewhat delicate; they are sensitive to drought, are apt to be washed away or beaten down by heavy rains and are subject to the attack of insects, rats or squirrels.

Use and markets

The economic value of amla fruits (including formulations and extracts) is estimated at between 200 and 250 million rupees (Rs) (US$5–US$6.25 million) during 1996. The market potential is, however, several times higher. Another indicator of its importance is its frequency of occurrence in herbal formulations. Out of 1650 herbal formulations, Triphala (equal parts of the fruits of *P. emblica*, *T. chebula* and *T. bellerica*) occurs in 219.

Table 22.2 *The many uses of* Phyllanthus emblica

Use	Use group	Specific uses
Food	Leaves; infructescences	Green vegetables; fruits; condiments; pickles
Food additives	Wood	Water clarifier
Juice	Fruits	Tannins/shampoo
Fuelwood	Wood	Fuel
Medicine	Fruits	Treatment of jaundice and stomach ailment

Extraction

The extraction of amla fruits in the south begins around mid November and continues for about three months. The harvest is a highly organized activity, given the need for large quantities to reach the processing industries within a short time in order to avoid deterioration of quality. Harvesters arrive at specified sites for collection as determined by field surveys. The groups then split into families. Usually, the male member climbs the tree and lops off branches bearing fruits. Other family members beat the branches on the ground to separate the fruits. During a day's harvest, as many as five to ten amla trees may be exploited, resulting in a collection on average of 70 kilograms (kg) at a forest site in the Western Ghats of south India.

The collected fruits are pooled at the local cooperative society, where traders purchase fruit for transport to processing centres. The main use locally is as a fresh or dry fruit. It is also processed in the home, as well as in large-scale factories, into popular pickles. As mentioned, another major use of amla fruits is in Ayurvedic medicine for the preparation of Triphala.

Certification potential

Most of the amla fruits in today's trade come from forested areas, which are state properties. Local indigenous communities have the right to harvest these NTFPs. These are largely marketed by quasi-government cooperatives, such as large-scale Adivasi multipurpose societies (LAMPS), which were set up during the 1970s to stop the exploitation of forest collectors by forest contractors (see Figure 22.1). Local communities, however, do not have management responsibility. In some states, the tide seems to be turning as governments see the wisdom of granting local communities joint management responsibility alongside the Forestry Department. In the absence of resource governance and security of land tenure, the result is nonsustainable resource use. Lack of secure land tenure and resource rights would prove a major obstacle to effective field assessments and certification programmes.

Given that the forest fruits are 'naturally grown' or 'organically grown', there is no concern with soil contamination or pesticide use, making this product *de facto* organic and thereby overcoming one potential obstacle to certification. As a result of greater awareness by forest communities of the state of the resource, a greater willingness on the part of governments to involve local communities in natural resource management, and a sizeable environmentally conscious consumer class in India who is willing to vote with its pocket book, there is cautious optimism that the past misuses can be reversed. In this regard, certification could act as an incentive for sustainable management, if twinned with projects that promote local resource management, tenure and micro-enterprise. By the same token, there is a huge population who is very price conscious; if certification entails a significant premium, then certified products are likely to capture only a narrow niche in the market.

Involving local communities in resource monitoring and natural resource management, and setting up locally managed micro-enterprises for greater local value, would be the first key steps in the process of certification. In the longer term, and on a larger scale, the demands of the market, especially for those products that are in international demand, will force the Ayurvedic herbal manufacturers to adopt 'best practices' – practices that are ecologically sustainable and socially equitable – if they are to survive. Ayurvedic medicine has attracted increasing interest overseas, and consumers are likely to seek out confirmation that sources are high quality and sustainable. Certification could play a valuable role in assisting community-based projects that market sustainable amla to sell their products at a premium to aware consumers.

A forest site in the Western Ghats, India

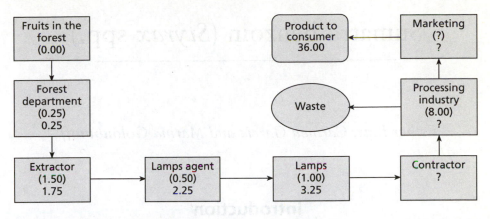

All values are in rupees (Rs per kg US$1 = Rs40)

Figure 22.1 *A value chain* of amla fruits: *from forest fruits to pickles*

Chapter 23

Sumatra benzoin (*Styrax* spp.)

Esther Katz, Carmen García and Marina Goloubinoff[1]

Introduction

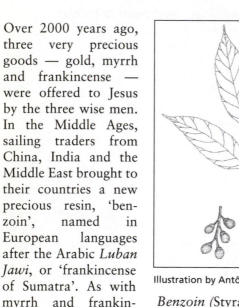

Illustration by Antônio Valente da Silva

*Benzoin (*Styrax paralleloneurum*)*

Over 2000 years ago, three very precious goods — gold, myrrh and frankincense — were offered to Jesus by the three wise men. In the Middle Ages, sailing traders from China, India and the Middle East brought to their countries a new precious resin, 'benzoin', named in European languages after the Arabic *Luban Jawi*, or 'frankincense of Sumatra'. As with myrrh and frankincense, it was used as incense, perfume and medicine. Between its place of origin and its destination, the resin was mixed, transformed and adulterated. After thousands of years of long-distance secretive trade, end-users rarely have any idea of what the original product looked like. Certification of internationally traded benzoin could be one way of revitalizing this ancient product.

The species

Benzoin is the resin of various species of *Styrax* trees (the Styracaceae family). The genus *Styrax* is distributed over Asia, Europe and America. Several species are exploited for their resin. In the Mediterranean, storax (*Styrax officinalis*) was used as incense since antiquity. In northern Laos and Vietnam, *S. tonkinensis* (Pierre) Craib ex Hartwiss and *S. benzoides* Craib, erroneously called 'Siam benzoin', are tapped for resin (Burkill, 1966; Svengsukas and Vidal, 1992;

Pinyopusarerk, 1994). Several species of benzoin are found in Malaysia and Indonesia, and at least two species are exploited commercially on the Indonesian island of Sumatra: *S. benzoin* Dryand and *S. paralleloneurum* Perk. *S. benzoin* also grows in Cambodia, Laos and Vietnam but is not tapped there (Svengsukas and Vidal, 1992).[2]

The information contained in this chapter is based on research conducted in North Sumatra since 1996. This profile focuses on Sumatra benzoin, produced from *S. benzoin* and *S. pararelloneurum*, called *kemenyan* in Malay and *haminjon*

in Batak Toba. Sumatra benzoin has been traded for centuries – perhaps even longer than 'Siam benzoin' (Wheatley, 1959),[3] but is less valued on the international market.

The main producing areas were historically located near the city of Palembang, in South Sumatra, and in the province of North Sumatra, particularly in the districts of North Tapanuli and Dairi. Although commercial production of benzoin from Palembang disappeared, according to recent estimations, about 3000 tonnes annually are still produced in the highlands of North Sumatra.[4]

Botanical description

Styrax trees are evergreen and medium in size. The leaves are simple, alternate, exstipulate, and entire or finely toothed. Flowers are bisexual, regular and in paniculate to racemose inflorescences. The fruit is a berry sitting on a persistent calyx. Each fruit usually contains a single seed, with a basal or sub-basal scar. Peculiar bark galls are found on *Styrax* trees, caused by specially adapted aphids (Van Steenis, 1949; Putz and Ng, 1978).

S. paralleloneurum Perk. (synonymous with *S. paralleloneurus*, *S. sumatranum* J.J. Smith and *S. sumatrana*) is a medium tree up to 27 metres (m) tall and 60 centimetres (cm) in diameter. The leaves of *S. paralleloneurum* differ from *S. benzoin* and have stellate hairs on the leaf undersurface, flattened into scales with arms radiating in one plane. The mature fruits are oblong-globose to ellipsoid, 2.5–3cm in diameter. Flowering occurs mostly from March to July, while fruiting lasts from July to November. It is found, in Sumatra and the Malay Peninsula, on mountains up to 1700m in

primary forest, rarely in secondary forest (old clearings), mostly on slopes, sometimes on ridges (Van Steenis, 1949; Putz and Ng, 1978).

Today, *S. paralleloneurum* is the species more commonly grown in the highlands of North Sumatra. Its resin is more valuable than other local *Styrax* species. It is usually planted in the forest, on slopes; yet according to some farmers, it also used to be planted in fallows. Its most common name in Batak Toba is *haminjon toba*, also mentionned by most botanists (Heyne, 1927; Burkill, 1966; Watanabe et al, 1996).

S. benzoin Dryand grows up to 34m tall and 100cm in diameter, occasionally with buttresses. The bark is smooth to vertically cracked or finely fissured. Leaves are ovate to elliptic. Flowers appear in racemes or panicles, and are terminal and axial. The maturing fruit is depressed-globose to globose, 2–3.8cm diameter and indehiscent. Swine and deer eat the fruit. Flowering and fruiting are not periodic and occur from January to

December. In Sumatra, the Malay Peninsula and West Java (rare), it is found in the lowlands up to 800m (rarely 1000m) in primary and disturbed forest, mostly on fertile soils (Van Steenis, 1949; Putz and Ng, 1978).

S. benzoin was historically cultivated in Palembang (de Vonck, 1891; Heyne, 1927) and is still cultivated in North Sumatra below 1000m. It is usually planted on dry rice fallows. Its most common local Toba name is *haminjon durame* ('rice straw benzoin'), also mentionned by most botanists (Heyne, 1927; Watanabe et al, 1996). *S. benzoin* has a continuous flow of fairly liquid resin. It takes longer to dry and is said to be less fragrant than *haminjon toba*. Today, it is also less val-

ued. Curiously, in older European pharmacopoeia (Hérail, 1927) and compilations on gums and resins (Jacob de Cordemoy, 1900; Howes, 1949), *S. benzoin* is mentioned while *S. paralleloneurum* is ignored. This suggests that its production was perhaps more important than *S. paralleloneurum* during the beginning of the 20th century.

Two varieties are recognized: *S. benzoin* var. *benzoin*, with depressed-globose fruits and seeds with small scars, and *S. benzoin* var. *hiliferum* Steenis, with globose fruits and seeds with large scars (Van Steenis, 1949; Putz and Ng, 1978), occasionally called *haminjon bulu* (Watanabe et al, 1992).

Ecology

There is little information available about the ecology of both *Styrax* species. *S. paralleloneurum* prefers primary forest on rich, clayey soils, or old secondary forest. It is a shade-tolerant species in the first stages, though it does not grow beneath dense primary or secondary forest cover. *S. benzoin* is a light-demanding species during its first stages. Its cultivation is related to swidden agriculture cycles in North Sumatra. It is established preferably in flat areas with good drainage. *S. paralleloneurum* is found at altitudes of 800–1700m, with a mean rainfall of 2050–2750 millimetres (mm), whereas *S. benzoin* is found between 100–700m and receives even higher amounts of rainfall.

This is in keeping with farmers' knowledge on establishment requirements for both species. Farmers explain that they plant *S. paralleloneurum* seeds or seedlings under forest cover to provide shade during the early stages of growth. Later they girdle other tree species in the garden as benzoin trees become shade intolerant. Farmers also report that this species grows well on very irregular terrain but later requires more time for tapping and harvesting the resin. By contrast, farmers report that *S. benzoin* is planted preferably in dry rice fields and on flatter lands because the species does not grow well on slopes.

Impact of land-use changes

Benzoin resin has been extracted for centuries from wild trees. In North Sumatra,

a small part of today's production still comes from this source. In Laos, benzoin trees are not cultivated; they are only managed in fallow lands where they grow spontaneously (Savathvong et al, 1997). Sumatra is thus the only place where benzoin has been cultivated for at least 200 years (Marsden, 1986), with a possible intensification of production during the 19th century.[5]

During the beginning of the 20th century, larger extensions of *Styrax benzoin* gardens existed; most were originally planted in dry rice fields (de Vonck, 1891; van Vuuren, 1908; de Braam, 1917; Schnepper, 1923; Heyne, 1927). Today, *S. benzoin* has disappeared from the lowlands (below 600m) and is common only at intermediate altitudes (600–900m) in a small part of the production area. A few *S. benzoin* trees occasionally grow in *S. paralleloneurum* gardens. *S. paralleloneurum* is now the dominant species; most gardens are located at higher altitudes (800–1500m) and were established on forest lands 50–60 years ago.

Many benzoin gardens were planted shortly after the Dutch achieved total control of the Batak region in 1907 (Braam, 1917), resulting in a surge of production in 1920, in spite of declining prices (Boomgard, 1994). In the meantime, lowland production of *Styrax benzoin* in North Sumatra and Palembang was abandoned in favour of rubber production, which boomed during the 1920s. At intermediate altitudes, mixed benzoin and rubber gardens are now still common. Populations of *Styrax benzoin* trees planted on flat lands that were previously under shifting cultivation cycles progressively decreased as these lands were converted to irrigated rice fields. This process reached a peak under Japanese occupation during World War II. Benzoin gardens not only provided income but were also a sign of land appropriation in fallows and in forests. Many of today's gardens were planted soon after Indonesian independence (1945), in order to secure forest lands from being seized and declared national lands (Michon and Saragih, 1999). In a few places, benzoin gardens were replaced by coffee or cinnamon plantations – these cash crops became profitable from the late 1970s onwards.

During the 1970s, benzoin farmers were much richer than other Batak farmers and would have been ashamed of cultivating annual plants. Today, however, younger farmers prefer to cultivate peanuts, corn or chili peppers, which are a quicker source of income. Nowadays, many farmers say that they are not motivated to plant new benzoin gardens or even to tend their old gardens because the price of benzoin has declined over the last few decades and theft of resin has risen. Some farmers have abandoned part or all of their benzoin gardens, allowing them to revert to forest. A few farmers have converted them into coffee gardens, although most farmers prefer not to cut the trees, as they still attach strong cultural values to them.

In some villages, large tracts of forest and even some benzoin gardens have been logged by Indorayon, a large regional pulp and paper company.[6] Today, local forests are affected by illegal logging. In some areas, benzoin gardens provide the only remaining forest cover. According to Indonesian law, forests are owned by the state. Farmers are no longer allowed to use forests for slash-and-burn agriculture or to plant benzoin trees. However, the authors recently observed that some young farmers with limited land are rejuvenating their gardens, tending wildlings or actually planting seedlings (Michon and Saragih, 1999). Future production of benzoin will depend not only upon farmers' motivation, but also upon widespread political and socio-economic changes at the regional and national levels.

Management

For *Styrax paralleloneurum*, farmers usually plant benzoin seeds, or preferably seedlings, inside forests in areas already colonized by benzoin trees.[7] The farmer selects a plot to establish the benzoin 'garden', normally no larger than 3 hectares (ha) and no smaller than 0.5 hectares. Before planting the seedlings, the farmer clears the garden of small- and medium-sized trees and shrubs, an activity that takes approximately ten days. Seedlings from the best resin-producing trees in other gardens are gathered and transplanted in the new garden. Two years after planting the seedlings, farmers progressively girdle the big trees left in the garden, which adds nutrients to the soil from the additional leaf litter and allows light to reach the young benzoin trees. Commencement of tapping begins after eight years. If done properly, resin may be extracted for nearly 60 years, although yields decrease after 30 years. When abandoned, the site is left to revert to secondary forest.

Management of the gardens involves annual selective clearing of woody species around the benzoin stands with a machete. Species with vegetative reproduction capabilities usually survive this treatment. Studies conducted in benzoin gardens show that management activities impact upon tree species composition, structure and diversity. A garden under intensive management exhibits low diversity and a very homogeneous structure, similar to a forest plantation. Besides the benzoin trees, farmers allow only those species with subsistence or economic value to grow within the garden sites (for instance, *petai* at higher altitudes, and occasionally coffee or cinnamon; rubber, durian, sugar palm, areca nut palm, *jengkol* and *langsat* at intermediate alti-

tudes).[8] Farmers also commonly plant food plants around the hut in the forest where they stay overnight for part of the week. When the garden is abandoned or managed less intensively, the population structure shifts to include species with very different life strategies, from early pioneers to primary tree species. Colonization of the site by new species takes place as a result of the long recruitment period of seeds in the soil, as well as the persistence of some species that reproduce vegetatively.

Tapping generally occurs from June to September for the trees that have already changed their foliage. Firstly, the farmers assess the colour of the leaves and the flowering stage of the tree to determine if it is ready for tapping. Trees considered ready for tapping have 'mature' leaves and young flowers. If trees have lost their leaves, they are tapped after changing foliage, between January and March.

Farmers clean competing vegetation from around the trunks of trees selected for tapping, up to a radius of 0.5–1m. Next, the tapping area is cleaned of any dead bark, lichens or mosses for a length of 5–6m up and down the trunk, scraping the bole down to a smooth red colour. The scraping preparation prevents resin from mixing with impurities as it flows out of the tree. According to farmers, the cleaned bark also allows the sun to shine directly on the tree trunk, warming it.

Farmers use a type of chisel to make a 2–3cm long wound in the bark. The chisel is inserted beneath the bark and pried upwards; the bark is then pounded with the chisel handle, which is shaped like a hammer. Usually five or six holes are made on one side of the tree, with an additional five to six holes tapped on the opposite side of the trunk, alternately spaced. Spacing between taps is 30–35cm, and tapping commences from the bottom of the tree upward, beginning at a height 5–10cm above ground. If the bark of a benzoin tree does not respond properly to tapping, the farmer leaves it for later.

Trees undergoing a first tapping receive only 10–12 taps. After two years of tapping, farmers will make tapping pockets throughout the length of the tree bole, to a height of 5–6m, but never exceeding 30 wounds per tree in order to avoid overexploitation of the resource. Special ropes of sugar palm fibre are used to climb the tree's bole to reach higher tapping pockets.

The first flow of resin (considered the best quality) can be harvested three or four months after tapping. Most of the resin (of a white colour) accumulates between the bark and the cambium; some resin (of a yellowish colour) flows outside of the tapping wound. The farmer uses a small, blunt, broad-bladed knife to pry away the bark to which the resin is attached and collects it in a basket. More resin continues to flow out of the wound for some time. Some farmers collect the resin a second time, two or three months later, by scraping it from the tree with the same type of knife. Part of this resin is white and part is dark brown, as it has oxydized and mixed with impurities from the trunk. Many farmers skip this harvest and collect all the leftover resin during the subsequent tapping season. The last resin is dark, sometimes slightly reddish, and if it is not collected, the tapping wound does not properly heal.

Styrax benzoin was commonly planted in rice swiddens. De Vonck (1891) described Styrax seeds being sown before the rice, so that the seedlings would grow in the shade of the paddy. After rice harvest, the land was temporarily abandoned or occasionally weeded. The trees were tapped after seven years, and tapping continued for another ten years. Batak farmers mention that, in the past, swiddens could bare two to three rice crops (sometimes associated with manioc) before being left fallow or being converted to benzoin and rubber gardens. In many cases, the gardens remained productive for 60–70 years.

The tapping and harvesting techniques are roughly the same for *S. benzoin* and *S. paralleloneurum*,[9] but it is more appropriate to collect *S. benzoin* resin after four or five months because it takes longer to dry. The first flow of resin is collected with the bark, but less S. benzoin resin accumulates under the bark. The outside resin flows all along the trunk, so it tends to be collected with more impurities, as the farmer gathers it up with a knife along the trunk. It is often collected into a cone made out of bark. The last flow of resin is harvested while tapping. *Haminjon bulu* resin does not accumulate under the bark at all; it is only collected from the trunk, hence its lower price.

Over the centuries, Batak farmers developed a very specific indigenous knowledge concerning benzoin. Benzoin has a strong cultural meaning to Batak farmers. Origin myths are told throughout the producing region about a poor, young and beautiful girl who turned into a benzoin tree. Benzoin is perceived as a nourishing tree and inspires respect. Its resin brought wealth to farmers and gave life to their villages. The farmers feel for their benzoin trees; they even sing a love song to the tree when cleaning its bark, preparing it (by caressing and warming it) for a sexual act (the tapping), which will 'give birth' to resin, often described as milk.

Use

Resin is the principal product of the *Styrax* tree.[10] Across the world, benzoin resin is used as incense, perfume, medicine and as a flavouring agent.

Batak and other people of Sumatra use benzoin as a medicine.[11] It is particularly important to traditional healers, who burn benzoin incense as they enter possession trances during curing rituals. In Sumatra and Java (above all, in Central Java, where benzoin consumption is the highest), benzoin is widely used in different types of traditional rituals: protection from bad spirits, rice-harvesting ceremonies, rain rituals, and offerings to the dead, house spirits and saints. It is burned in most Central Javanese sanctuaries. The incense is used in Christian, Muslim, Hindu and Buddhist ceremonies. After Java, the main consumers are Arabic countries, where benzoin is widely used in homes and mosques for religious and household rituals, and reputedly is also used to chase away bad spirits (Aubaile-Sallenave, 1997; El Alaoui, 1998). India is the third largest consumer of benzoin.[12]

Benzoin incense is rarely pure because the product would be too expensive for most incense customers to buy and because combustion of pure benzoin is too rapid for incense purposes. Factories in Java, Sumatra and Singapore mix benzoin with damar resin (from *Shorea* spp.) and other ingredients in order to make incense blocks. Damar is also fragrant and has the advantage of burning more slowly (it was traditionally used as a flammable agent in torches).

Benzoin is smoked with tobacco in a few places in Sumatra. In Central Java, it is still smoked by older men in a type of cigarette, either homemade or produced by small local industries, called *klembak menyan* (Goloubinoff, 1998). Benzoin is also a flavouring agent for some brands of *kretek* clove cigarettes, also produced in Java. *Kretek* represents an important national market, since production reached a level of 140 billion cigarettes in 1993 (Tarmidi, 1996). Benzoin is also used as a tobacco flavouring agent in other countries (Coppen, 1997).

Benzoin has been used for a long time in Chinese, Arabic, Indian and European pharmacopoeias and perfume industries (Pradal, 1895; Wheatley, 1959; Aubaile-Sallenave, 1997; Hew-Kian-Chong, 1998; Le Guérer, 1998). Some European countries such as France consider Siam benzoin superior to Sumatra benzoin, while others such as the UK prefer to use Sumatra benzoin. Such national predilections can be linked to traditional marketing channels (eg France and Indochina, UK and Singapore). Today, benzoin is employed only in a few Western medicines, since synthetic products have replaced many natural substances (Hew-Kian-Chong, 1998). The same substitution effect has occurred within the perfume industry. Benzoin used to be an important ingredient in Western perfumes, but is now employed only in small quantities (Vial-Debas, 1999).

Processing and marketing

Three-quarters of all Sumatra benzoin production is consumed by the Indonesian national market, while the remaining quarter is exported to the rest of the world via Singapore. Incense is the main outlet for both domestic and international markets (see Figure 23.1). No accurate trade statistics are available. Export figures from Indonesia to Singapore do not correspond to import statistics from Indonesia to Singapore (see statistics in Coppen, 1997). In customs statistics of other countries, benzoin is included under the general 'gums and resins' category.

Sumatra benzoin trade remains quite 'traditional' in its structure and behaviour, inside and outside Indonesia. It relies upon trading networks and relationships established over several generations, as well as upon a specific professional knowledge. In Indonesia, several stakeholder groups participate in the benzoin trade network: farmers, village collectors, regional traders, inter-island traders and exporters. At each level, benzoin resin is dried and sorted. When fresh, the resin is quite soft (toffee-like) and sticky. Firstly, the resin is dried for two weeks so that the bark and the dust can be removed. Secondly, the resin is sorted according to size, colour and consistency. Because benzoin melts during transport if not dried properly, traders allow three months to pass before shipping the resin from North Sumatra. At each step, intermediaries resort the resin. Sorting at each step is meant to adapt the product to the buyers' needs, but it is also a way of making additional profit. For each intermediary, the profit margin is quite small (less than 20 per cent); thus, to gain a little more, intermediaries often add some fairly good second-grade resin to the first-grade resin.

The structure of this trade allows for wider profit sharing and avoids creation of a monopoly.

The benzoin market is considered to be quite stable. However, it has experienced volatility over the last 150 years or so, often as a result of national and/or international political situations. At the end of the 19th century, prices declined (de Vonck, 1891); yet production increased after the Dutch managed to pacify the region in 1907. The 1929 financial crisis, World War II and the Japanese occupation of Sumatra had a negative impact upon benzoin production and/or trade. On the other hand, both farmers and traders remember the 1970s as a 'golden age'. During this time, trees planted in the 1950s, after independence, were reaching optimal production. Demand from the national market was high, especially within the cigarette sector (Tarmidi, 1996). Thanks to income from benzoin production and its trade, children attended schools and universities. Many Batak lawyers, teachers, army officers and civil servants, who today play an important role in national life, are 'benzoin children'.

Benzoin prices have progressively dropped in real terms since the peak production days of the 1970s, while nominal prices increased only slightly with the 1997–1998 South-East Asian monetary crisis. However, benzoin still provides a source of income for at least 100,000 people in North Sumatra, and benzoin money continues to contribute to school expenses. Yet, the incentives to continue cultivating benzoin are quite low. Plantations are growing older, farmers are ageing, the number of people willing to spend several days in the forest tending

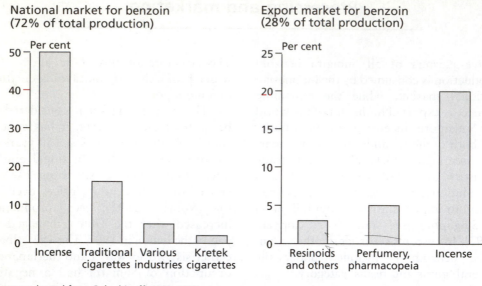

Figure 23.1 *National and export markets for benzoin*

benzoin gardens is diminishing, and those who do harvest benzoin tend not to cultivate all of their trees. Every year production drops. Farmer migration and the introduction of more lucrative cash crops contribute to the continuing decline of benzoin production. If too few people replace the old trees, regional production could drop significantly within the next decade, while demand is likely to remain stable. If end-users face a future benzoin shortage, they could turn to other products (in the case of incense) or to synthetic substitutes (in the case of perfumery and pharmacopoeia). The recent monetary crisis could still reverse the momentum, as some migrants are returning to the countryside from urban centres. Increasing farmers' confidence in their production methods could have an even greater effect.[13]

Certification potential

From a forestry perspective, *Styrax* management may need to be treated as either a plantation (when occurring in rice swiddens) or as a simplified natural forest in upland areas. While forest simplification goes against many forest certification criteria, the small size and scale of benzoin gardens may mitigate their overall impact on forest integrity. Once the gardens are abandoned, the biodiversity of the resultant secondary forest is similar to that of a primary forest, which seems to indicate a high resilience of forests formed under benzoin management practices. In some areas where forest concessions have been granted to logging companies, benzoin gardens provide the only remaining forest cover. Tenure issues may also pose some problems, particularly in cases where there are conflicting land claims.

Best tapping practices may need to be further investigated and elucidated before field criteria could be tested for the certification of this species. Yet, experiments on tapping techniques conducted by a Food and Agriculture Organization (FAO) team in Laos hold promise; the team found that local indigenous tapping techniques were the most efficient ones (M Fischer, pers comm, 1999). In Sumatra, farmers have managed to tap benzoin trees for well over 60 years, thus indicating that their techniques are likely sustainable.[14]

Any higher prices that certification may bring to benzoin producers may encourage production of this traditional product. However, a certain number of traders and end-users will likely not be keen to fulfill very strict criteria that would involve additional work or added costs, just as customs services have little motivation to separate benzoin from the general 'gums-and-resins' trade category. Although most end-users would not be willing to pay more to get a certified product, those interested in higher quality products might.

On the international market, Sumatra benzoin has the reputation of being a much lower-quality product than Laos benzoin. Most consumers and end-users only know Sumatra benzoin in a processed form, and only lower qualities of pure resin are most commonly traded on the world market. The best-quality resins are rarely known outside of Indonesia. At a local level, traders know that resin from certain villages is more fragrant than resins from other villages, but they habitually mix resins of different origins and different species. Little reliable published data is available on benzoin product quality. For instance, pharmacopoeia books are based on second-hand data, presenting Sumatra benzoin as blocks (ie it may not be pure benzoin). Furthermore, most published chemical analyses were conducted at the beginning of the century.[15] Certifying the chain of custody for benzoin may be difficult because:

- Record-keeping is inconsistent or non-existent.
- There are many intermediaries in the benzoin trade.
- Mixing resins of different origin is common practice.

While lower-quality resins are quite appropriate for incense, it may be worthwhile to promote certification for the best-quality resins used by specific end-users, such as perfume makers, both at national and international levels. The national market still has great potential because the population is large (Indonesia is the fourth most populated country in the world, with over 220 millions inhabitants). A higher-quality incense market is being developed in Europe. Marketing strategies for benzoin could capitalize on growing consumer interest in authentic natural products. After all, Sumatra benzoin is organically grown, as Batak farmers do not use fertilizers or pesticides in their benzoin plantations. Other niche markets may also be found. Certification could potentially help inform consumers about the origins of benzoin and its production methods, raising awareness of, and appreciation for, this ancient but little-known product.

Notes

1   The authors participated in two projects funded respectively by CIFOR and by the EU programme INCO III (Forresasia).
2   Fragrant trees of the genus *Liquidambar* (Hamamelidaceae) from Central America and the Middle-East are commonly called 'styrax', but they are very different from benzoin.
3   According to Wheatley (1959), Sumatra benzoin was exported to China since the 8th century (9th century according to a personal communication of F Obringer); a new source of benzoin was later discovered by the Chinese in continental South-East Asia.
4   According to official statistics, production equaled 5000 tonnes per year during 1993–1994 and 4000 tonnes per year in 1998. Marina Goloubinoff made an estimation from the sales of the largest traders of the region and Mardan Saragih (Forresasia project) from the production figures of individual villages. Both estimates totaled about 3000 tonnes. In comparison, Laos production of benzoin was only 50 tonnes per year and Vietnam 10 tonnes per year (Coppen, 1995).
5   In many villages, Batak farmers (who have a long genealogical memory) say that benzoin gardens were planted four to eight generations ago.
6   Indorayon operations were temporarily suspended after the 1998 political change, under pressure from local people; but the company's impact on the forests of North Sumatra Province during the previous ten years was devastating.
7   At the beginning of the 20th century, Heyne (1927) reported this cultivation method.
8   Respectively: *Parkia speciosa* Hassk., *Coffea canephora* Pierre var. *robusta* Cheval., *Cinnamomum burmanii* Blume, *Hevea brasiliensis* Muell. Arg., *Durio zibethinus* Murr., *Arenga pinnata* (Wurmb) Merr., *Areca catechu* L., *Pithecellobium jiringa* Prain, *Lansium domesticum* Corr.
9   But De Vonck (1891) and Van Vuuren (1908) describe other types of harvesting techniques.
10 Sumatra farmers also occasionally use dead benzoin trees as firewood and sell (at a low price) the slightly fragrant bark attached to the resin, which is subsequently ground and mixed into benzoin incense blocks. In Vietnam, in recent years, *Styrax tonkinensis* has been planted for use by the pulp and paper industry (Pinyopusarerk, 1994).
11 Curiously, in Laos, farmers extract benzoin resin for trade but do not use it themselves (A Hubert, pers comm, 1996; Chagnaud, 1996).
12 Data on exports to Arabic countries and India come from Singapore exporters.
13 In Lampung, damar farmers have gained much pride since scientists began studying the management of their gardens. In a North Sumatra village visited by our team between 1996 and 2000, some young farmers told us recently that they were more motivated to work in their benzoin gardens because scientists had begun taking an interest in benzoin.
14 Many farmers who do not work their garden prefer not to rent it out because careless or inexperienced workers might damage their trees. It takes several months or years to acquire the proper tapping techniques. Tapping is supposed to be a most delicate operation.
15 Private perfume or medicine companies lead their own research but rarely publish their results.

Chapter 24

Sustainable harvesting of epiphytic bromeliads in the highlands of Chiapas, Mexico: a pilot study

Jan H D Wolf and Cornelis J F Konings

One factor exacerbating worldwide forest decline and degradation is an economic system that rewards over-exploitation of resources and agricultural uses for short-term benefits, but economically under-values natural habitats (WRI et al, 1992).

Harvesting epiphytic bromeliads from natural popu-lations may augment the direct economic value of forests for local communities through the application of the concept of canopy farming© for bromeliads (the term canopy farming is copyrighted by Dr R A A Oldeman). Canopy farming has been advanced as a way to access the potential of the forest canopy for sustainable pro-duction. Because canopy farming leaves the natural canopy habitat largely intact, it shows potential as a forest conservation tool (Neugebauer et al, 1996).

In the highlands of Chiapas, Mexico, certain bromeliads have traditional uses.

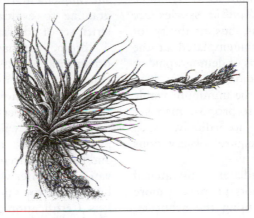

Illustration by Antonio Rodríguez

*Bromeliad (*Tillandsia vicentina*)*

For example, the highland indigenous people of Mayan des-cent use the flowers of *Tilland-sia eizii* L.B. Smith for ceremonies (Breedlove and Lauglin, 1993). Current har-vesting of these flowers appears to be unsustainable. Commonly used species have nearly disappeared from the most accessible mature forests. How-ever, the most severe threat to these species is probably the loss of mature forests. Between 1974 and 1994, the area of dense forest in the central Chiapas highlands decreased by 42 per cent (Ochoa-Gaona and González-Espinosa, 2000).

Bromeliads from Chiapas may provide a commercially viable canopy product because many similar plants are already exported to floral markets from neigh-bouring countries, such as Guatemala (Jenkins and Oldfield, 1992; Rauh, 1992). Between 1993 and 1995, Guatemala alone exported circa 14.5 million *Tillandsias* annually (Véliz-Pérez, 1997). According to Rauh (1992), information from WWF in Germany suggests that in the first three months of 1988 alone, 150 tonnes of these 'airplants' (circa six million plants) were exported from Guatemala. Rauh (1992) estimates that at least 75 per cent of the plants in *Tillandsia* farms are collected from the wild.

Since harvesting of bromeliads may be regarded as a means of forest conservation, the question of sustainability is of mayor importance. In a pilot study in disturbed pine-oak forest, the authors focused on the sustainability of offtake, omitting ecological and socio-economic aspects. Because *Tillandsia* species are ecologically different, sustainability of offtake should be contemplated at the species level. By means of demographic or genetic studies and modelling, one may attempt to establish the minimum viable population size and to propose management interventions accordingly. Such studies, however, require observations over a long period of time.

For the immediately threatened bromeliads, the authors propose a more empirical approach using the arbitrary, but generally accepted, definition of the strictest criteria for sustainable harvesting:

- high population density;
- individuals evenly distributed in space; and
- minimum impact on reproductive capacity.

In this pilot study (Wolf and Konings, 2001), one epiphytic bromeliad, *Tillandsia vicentina* Standley, was identified that met the criteria. This species does not have a current local use. The species is sold as a houseplant in the US and in Europe. The authors prefer targeting export markets before developing a national market for the plants, which may be difficult to control against competitors who operate unsustainably. The authors estimate that it is possible to harvest sustainably nearly 700 rosettes of *T. vicentina* per hectare per year from the understorey and forest floor of the study site. Implementation of a monitoring programme to evaluate this arbitrary, yet strict, set of criteria is recommended.

Bromeliads have a ready market as ornamental plants in many Northern countries. While many of the bromeliads entering international trade are cultivated, significant numbers of plants are still harvested from the wild. This project seeks to produce income for local communities and to create incentives for forest conservation by offering sustainably sourced bromeliads for sale to international markets. Certification could bolster initiatives such as the bromeliad pilot project by creating market differentiation for sustainably harvested wild bromeliads, and by raising awareness of forest conservation issues for Northern consumers of ornamental houseplants.

Chapter 25

Reducing the ecological footprint of the 'wooden rhino': the case for certification of Kenyan woodcarvings[1]

Susanne F Schmitt and Anthony B Cunningham

The success of the Kenyan woodcarving industry and the realization of the size of the footprint

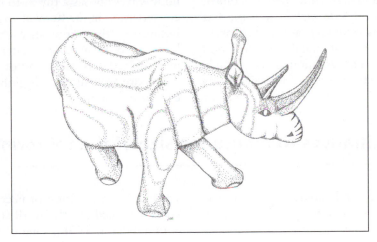

Illustration by Jamison Ervin

Wooden rhino

The Kenyan woodcarving industry is a rural development economic success, but it now faces the collapse of locally available hardwood stocks for commercial carving production. Focused mainly upon exports, this industry has grown significantly over the last 80 years. The annual value of exports has expanded from UK£75,000 (at 1950s rates) to US$20 million today, over half of which is exported to North America, with most of the remainder to Europe and Japan. This developmental success owes much to the high carving and business skills of the WaKamba people, who started and still dominate the trade. A total of about 60,000 carvers (with some 300,000 dependants) work in Kenya (Obunga, 1996).

The increasing demand of the market, coupled with the fact that many of the species used are slow-growing hardwoods, has led to the depletion of some of the favoured species. Surveys conducted under a People and Plants Initiative project (Obunga and Sigu, 1996) have documented this decline, particularly in the case of *mpingo*, or 'ebony' (*Dalbergia melanoxylon*), and *muhugu*, or 'mahogany' (*Brachylaena huillensis*). Many of the carvers are aware of the problem of hardwood supply and the threat this poses to their future livelihoods. Some carvers have sought alternatives through cultivation or by testing other tree species for the suitability of carving. All of the most suitable alternative species identified are exotics (eg neem, jacaranda, grevillea, mango), one of which, neem (*Azadirachta indica*), has become invasive in coastal forest areas.

Apart from sustainability of the wood base, further conservation issues include possible genetic erosion of the species (as some populations are decimated or destroyed) and degradation of the Kenyan coastal forests. The latter, with their many endemic species, are internationally recognized for their importance in biodiversity conservation. Today, only isolated coastal forest fragments remain. These face many pressures, one of which is exploitation of valuable hardwoods for woodcarving. Based on counts of logs bought by Kenyan woodcarver cooperatives, Simon Choge of the Kenya Forestry Research Institute (KEFRI) has shown that over 40,000 trees are felled each year for the carving industry, most of which are forest species. Research by the East African Wildlife Society, funded by People and Plants, has shown that almost half of *muhugu* logs that are used by carvers at Mombasa and Malindi are hollow. Destruction of these hollow trees poses a threat to biodiversity conservation in the Kenyan coastal forests because of the importance of these hollows as nest sites or shelter for small mammals, birds and reptiles, several of which are endemic to this globally threatened forest habitat.

Initiatives to reduce the size of the footprint

It is clear to all stakeholders involved that the Kenyan woodcarving industry needs to be placed on a sustainable footing. There are two main reasons for this:

1   to secure the livelihoods of thousands of carvers and their dependants; and
2   to conserve globally important biodiversity in forests in Kenya and in other East African countries.

There is no doubt that bringing such a large woodcarving industry onto a sustainable basis will be a challenging process, involving a multitude of interventions. At a workshop held in December 1997, a 20-year vision of necessary steps was developed jointly by all stakeholders (Cunningham, 1998). One of these steps concerned the use of a marketing initiative involving certification of 'Good Woods' as a tool to switch demand away from slow-growing hardwoods to fast-growing exotics. As a follow-up, a course on certification of Kenyan woodcarving was held in Kenya in March 1999, and agreement was reached to develop a certification system (Cunningham, 1999).

Certification is considered a potentially powerful tool in providing an economic incentive for a shift away from ecologically damaging and unsustainable exploitation of East African coastal forests for carving. Certification of woodcarving also has the potential to be the entry point for wider adoption of timber certification for plantation and natural forests in East Africa in the medium to long term. The People and Plants initiative has been working with the Forest Stewardship Council (FSC)-approved certifiers SmartWood and, subsequently, the Soil Association Woodmark Programme to develop a suitable certification system for Kenyan woodcarvings.

The certification approach: piloting FSC certification for woodcarvings

Certification, in the context of the Kenyan woodcarving industry, will firstly aim at distinguishing carvings made from slow-growing and increasingly depleted hardwoods from carvings made from fast-growing 'Good Wood' species. At the course held in March 1999, participants agreed that developing a form of certification is the right way forward. Arguments for using this approach included the following:

1   Many preconditions for certification are fulfilled:
    - Large stocks of alternative 'Good Woods' are available. All are introduced species to Kenya that are acceptable to, and already used by, Kenyan carvers. 'Good Woods' are locally available along the coast – in particular, neem (*Azadirachta indica*) and old mango trees (*Mangifera indica*); in central Kenya – mostly grevillea (*Grevillea robusta*) and jacaranda (*Jacaranda mimosifolia*). All are multipurpose trees, which should ensure their replacement because of the many benefits that can be derived from them.
    - Several large cooperatives have already taken steps in using 'Good Wood' alternatives by increasing the proportion of carvings made from 'Good Woods', such as

neem. This is largely due to temporary shortages of hardwoods and, in particular, to the absence of large diameter logs for large carvings.
    - The FSC has recently started to adapt its site-based certification requirements, which are based on proving sustainable forest management of a forest operation. Now, for example, group certification of small woodland owners, or even certification of wood from street tree cuttings, is possible. This gives hope that certification can be applied in this case, effectively centred around exotic carving species that come from diffuse sources (municipal land, small holdings, private land, plantations, etc) within, for example, a district or sub-district.
    - Examples of ethical sourcing already exist. For example, the Mennonite Central Committee (MCC), who buy approximately US$250,000 worth of carving exports each year from Kenya, have pledged to increase the amount of 'Good Wood' carvings by 10 per cent each year and to return 3 per cent of the value of carvings purchased to support nurseries for carving wood production.

- Five major woodcarving cooperatives already have a detailed system of record-keeping of logs bought and carving items sold. Thus, chain-of-custody monitoring of 'Good Wood' logs bought and carvings sold should only require simple modifications.

- Experience in raising 'Good Wood', as well as hardwood species, already exists in some of the cooperatives. The oldest nursery, owned by the Makindu Carvers Cooperative, has been running for ten years.

- Carvers are well aware of the resource scarcity situation, and a 20-year vision was developed jointly by the carvers and other interest groups in December 1997. This was followed up by a 'Good Wood' labelling and certification course, held in March 1999. Furthermore, awareness-raising amongst carvers, tourists and importers through drama, production of a poster, videos, a slide pack, exhibitions and the establishment of 'Green Corners' displaying only 'Good Wood' carvings in the cooperatives' showrooms has already taken place.

- Kenya Airways has agreed to screen a short (ten-minute) video as part of in-flight awareness-raising for people visiting Kenya.

- A new director of the Kenya Forestry Department was appointed who is favourably inclined towards certification and supports stricter enforcement of logging bans of hardwoods and the protection of forest reserves.

2 Availability of certified 'Good Wood' carvings provides consumers with an ethical choice by allowing them to distinguish between carvings made from sustainably produced wood and those that are not.

3 When combined with an effective campaign, certification – as a marketing tool – has the potential to result in a switch in consumer demand to certified carvings made from 'Good Wood' species. Such a campaign will be aimed at North America, Europe and Kenya respectively, with the main target audience being importers and tourists. The intention is to create consumer-led demand that will provide the right incentives for carvers to switch to alternative 'Good Wood' species or, in the long term, sustainably produced hardwoods.

The goal is to achieve FSC certification of woodcarving timber produced through agroforestry systems on-farm, in plantations or potentially with savanna species such as ebony (*Dalbergia melanoxylon*), produced through coppice rotation in managed savanna. In the short to medium term, certification in Kenya will have to be restricted to 'Good Wood' species; hardwood stocks are very depleted and recovery is gradual due to very slow growth rates. Furthermore, plantation and natural forest management will require major improvements in order to achieve certification. Great interest in certification, shown by the new director of the Kenya Forestry Department (who was one of the participants in the People and Plants certification course in March 1999), provides some hope that a more favourable, institutional environment for sustainable forest management in Kenya is developing.

The attempt to develop an FSC-approved certification system for Kenyan 'Good Wood' carvings represents a pilot case and will require flexibility in FSC policy, or amendments to existing FSC policies. However, the FSC is becoming more favourably inclined towards certifying non-timber forest products (NTFPs) and atypical timber operations. For example, the FSC is exploring pragmatic ways to improve access to certification for smallholder farmers (Scrase, 1999). In the woodcarving case, FSC certification will have to be extended to on-farm production of carving trees and the harvesting of 'Good Wood' species from existing stocks on public, private or communal land. This would mean that the supply of 'Good Wood' will often not be from a clearly defined source area, where management practices are clearly documented and prescribed. However, the argument is that management and securing replacement of harvested trees are of no major concern in the case of 'Good Woods' for several reasons:

- All favoured species are exotic, multipurpose trees that people already plant and are therefore likely to replace, especially given the added incentive of being able to sell the wood when the tree has reached sufficient size.
- In the humid coastal zone, neem (*Azadirachta indica*) has become an invasive species and now poses a problem in natural forests. Removing it from these areas and elsewhere will, in fact, be a benefit for conservation. On farms and in municipal areas, the replacement of neem trees can be encouraged by nurturing wildlings.
- The existing stock of trees is large and trees often have to be removed for building purposes, safety (eg in the case of *Jacaranda* street trees) and restocking to improve yields (eg old mango trees with a small yield).
- Maintenance of 'Good Wood' stock can also be ensured through simple agreements made with farmers and landowners to ensure the replacement of cut trees.

Increasingly, the FSC label is becoming the standard for certified wood products. Increased publicity and awareness among the general public will help to make certification of 'Good Woods' a powerful tool in the ongoing efforts to reduce the ecological footprint of the 'wooden rhino'.

Additional information

Two videos about the woodcarving project are available:

- *Saving the wooden rhino: ethnobotanical methods and the Kenya woodcarving industry* (1998); camera and direction: Anthony B Cunningham; editing: Nick Chevalier Productions. This is a methods and training video (25-minutes long).
- *Carvers, conservation and consumers* (1998); camera and direction: Anthony B Cunningham; editing: Nick Chevalier Productions. This is a shorter (ten-minute) awareness-raising video aimed at importers and exporters of carvings and at tourists.

Both videos are available from:

- NHBS (National History Book Service Ltd)
  2–3 Wills Road
  Totnes
  Devon
  TQ9 5XN
  UK
  Tel: +44 (0)1803 865 913
  Fax: +44 (0)1803 865 280
  Email: sales@nhbs.co.uk
  Web: www.nhbs.com

Note

1 The information contained in this chapter is based partly on the unpublished work of Raymond Obunga, Gordon Sigu and Simon Choge, with support from the Kenya Crafts Cooperative Union, Kenya Forest Research Institute, National Museums of Kenya and TRAFFIC. Much of the information regarding eco-labelling and certification was gathered, with the help of all participants, at a People and Plants Initiative course on certification, held in Kenya in March 1999. The course was attended by all relevant stakeholders and was organized jointly by WWF International and the United Nations Educational, Scientific and Cultural Organization (UNESCO). A representative from a Forest Stewardship Council (FSC)-accredited certifier, SmartWood, provided insights into certification and eco-labelling. Funding has been made available by the UK Department for International Development (DFID), the UK National Lottery Charities Board (NLCB) and WWF-UK.

Section III

THE CORE ELEMENTS OF NTFP CERTIFICATION

Chapter 26

Ecological issues

Alan R Pierce and Patricia Shanley

Introduction

Illustration by Antônio Valente da Silva

*Bacuri (*Platonia insignis*)*

To manage non-timber forest products (NTFPs) properly, it is imperative to have a basic understanding of the biology and ecology of the target species, the site capabilities of the forest under management and the response of the target species to harvesting and other human and natural disturbances. This chapter will explore ecological issues relating to NTFP harvest, including knowledge of species harvested, harvest impacts and the importance of trained harvesters. The chapter will also focus on specific ecological issues brought to light by the certification field trials and will outline additional environmental issues that managers and certifiers alike need to consider when evaluating NTFP operations. Ecological elements touching on certification are also covered in the NTFP guidelines (see Appendix I) and the technical elements discussion presented in Chapter 30.

In general, when non-timber forest products are properly managed, they protect many forest services (eg hydrological functions, aesthetics, soil retention and carbon sequestration) and cause less biotic impoverishment than other land uses (Peters, 1994; Nepstad et al, 1992). This observation, however, must be tempered by the sheer variety of non-timber forest products and NTFP production systems. Some intensively managed NTFP production systems result in localized loss of biodiversity. Thiollay (1995) found that avian species richness, diversity and equitability was significantly lower in Sumatran agroforestry systems producing rubber (*Hevea brasiliensis*), damar (*Shorea javanica*) and durian (*Durio zibethinus*) than in primary forests. As

reported in the maple syrup (*Acer saccharum*) and benzoin (*Styrax* spp.) species profiles in Chapters 15 and 23, intensive production of these exudates may also lead to forest simplification and loss of diversity. Yet, in comparison to other land uses, NTFP management can play a positive role in forest conservation. From the Dayak forest fruit gardens (*tembawangs* – see de Jong, 1995) of Kalimantan, Indonesia, to the silvopastoral (*dehesas*) systems of the Mediterranean (see the Mediterranean species profiles in Chapter 17), NTFP management supports the maintenance of forests and many of their attendant ecosystem services. While some might not consider silvopastoral systems as 'true forests', such systems do provide important ecological services, help maintain biodiversity and are perceived as stable ecological systems by local environmentalists (Moussouris, 1999).

Ecological knowledge

Lack of information concerning species ecology was anticipated as an obstacle to sustainable management and certification of the species reviewed in the field tests on palm heart (*Euterpe oleracea*), chicle (*Manilkara zapota*) and Brazil nut (*Bertholletia excelsa*); but this was actually found not to be one of the most problematic aspects of the trial assessments. In the cases of chicle, palm heart and Brazil nut, all species had been managed for lengthy periods of time and traditional management techniques had been empirically developed. Scientific understanding of these species was also advanced, and though admittedly incomplete, was believed to be sufficient to determine whether or not the species were managed according to best known practices.

In the cases of poorly studied species

that make up the majority of NTFPs, lack of ecological understanding of species growth requirements, regeneration niche, production/yield and appropriate harvesting techniques could be a tremendous barrier to the adequate assessment of species' ecological requirements for sustainable extraction (Peters, 1994). Even species that have been widely used for centuries, such as benzoin, copaíba (*Copaifera* spp.) and pine nuts (various spp.), are lacking in definitive studies elucidating particular aspects of their population ecology. For instance, the ecology, response to harvest and growth requirements of marapuama (see Box 26.1) are so little known that even the most basic information needs for certification or sustainable management are unavailable today.

BOX 26.1 IRRESPONSIBLE MARKETING OF AMAZONIAN VIAGRA

Maria Constanza von der Pahlen and Patricia Shanley

Marapuama (*Ptychopetalum olacoides*) is a primary forest species endemic to Brazil that grows as a bush or small tree. Its roots have been harvested for medicinal purposes for many years. Complete harvest of the root results in the death of the plant. In eastern Amazonia, severed sections of the root are sold in open-air markets, medicinal plant shops and in makeshift booths along sidewalks. Marapuama is costlier than other medicinals, but demand for the root is high, even by individuals of modest means. The strong demand for marapuama indicates that, in the public's mind, the root is unique and without substitutes.

In Amazonia, where pharmaceutical preparations are not available to a majority of the general public for financial reasons, the plant is an important remedy. Marapuama is principally used for diseases of the nervous system and impotence. Phytochemical and pharmacological research has indicated that an alcohol infusion prepared with the roots produced effects on the nervous system, potentially by interacting with the dopaminergic and/or noradrenergic systems (Elisabetsky et al, 1986).

Historically, the root has been exported to Europe. In England, marapuama is used to combat impotence and infertility. In Germany, it is primarily employed as a tonic. In France, the root has gained popularity as an aphrodisiac (von der Pahlen, 1999). More recently, interest has escalated in the US, due in part to Internet advertising promulgating marapuama as the Amazonian natural equivalent of Viagra.

Serious problems exist with such Internet marketing schemes. Firstly, the density, distribution, germination, growth rate, regeneration niche and production of *P. olacoides* are all unknown. Secondly, as recently as a decade ago, species identification of the plant was still being questioned. Thirdly, interviews with collectors in eastern Amazonia make it clear that marapuama is increasingly difficult to find in the wild, even to meet local demand. With little to nothing known about its ecology, and uncertainty regarding species identification, export of this destructively harvested primary forest root is a cause for concern.

Setting harvest levels, modelling and the importance of technological transfer

Determining sustainable harvest levels for NTFPs is difficult. Some technical tools are available, as described by Cunningham (2001), Peters (1996; 1994; 1990) and Hall and Bawa (1990). In most cases, NTFP harvest prescriptions have been arrived at through years and years of field observation and experimentation. Harvest levels, whether set by computer models or practical experience, must be supported by data gleaned from inventories, yield studies and monitoring, and readjusted over time in response to new information. Most operations applying for NTFP certification rely upon the principle of adaptive management and set harvest levels based upon observation and experience, supplemented by information gained from monitoring the impact of harvesting over time – what Peters (1996) terms 'successive approximation'. Few operations have the technical expertise, equipment, time and finances to perform more indepth scientific analyses (eg matrix models). Matrix models, as Peters (1996) relates, are useful because 'overexploitation occurs first in [the] computer simulation, not 50 or 60 years later in the field when it may already be too late to remedy the situation'. Transition matrices can also give important insight into the influence of stochastic events on long-term population viability, as shown by Nantel et al (1996) in the case of ginseng. More complex mechanistic modelling, according to Boot and Gullison (1995), may also be used to predict changes in population and ecosystem structure, thus adding rigour to the formulation of NTFP management plans. In sum, transference of technological support and knowledge to NTFP operations is critical. Non-governmental organization (NGOs) and donor agencies can facilitate the transfer of technology to NTFP producers, thereby supporting best management practices and, in cases, reinforcing certification eligibility of operations.

Harvest impact

The impact of harvest regimes on NTFP resources will vary according to harvest intensity, resource density, site productivity, harvester training and the plant part harvested. While a firm knowledge of NTFP biology and ecology is necessary for management, the plant part harvested often determines the focus of management actions, monitoring activities and certification assessments. A firm grasp of general functional ecology is also extremely important for resource managers, particularly in cases where baseline knowledge and data may be limited or lacking.

- With reproductive propagules, attention to the target species' ability to regenerate and the impacts of management actions on wildlife (animals that depend upon the resource or that act as pollinators or seed dispersal agents) will be the primary ecological concerns (unless sprouting is a major means of reproduction).
- Harvest of vegetative structures that can result in the death of a plant – eg ginseng roots (*Panax* spp.), marapuama, pau d'arco (*Tabebuia* spp.)

bark or single-stemmed palms (*Euterpe precatoria*) – necessitates a firm understanding of the species' reproduction strategies, population structure, density and distribution.

- Harvest of other vegetative structures that do not necessarily cause mortality, such as xate leaves (*Chamaedorea* spp.) for the floral industry, baobab (*Adansonia digitata*) bark for crafts and oak bark for cork (*Quercus suber*), requires a grasp of species' recovery rates, physiological impacts of harvesting (eg on photosynthesis and reproduction) and harvesting techniques.
- Collection of exudates, such as chicle, amapá (*Parahancornia* spp. and *Brosimum* spp.), pine resin (various spp.), mastic gum (*Pistacia lentiscus*), benzoin and maple sap, requires evaluation of tapping procedures, extent of tapping injury, recovery rates, understanding of the physiological impacts of tapping and assessment of harvester skills and techniques. In addition, evaluation of the secondary impacts of tapping on species growth, reproduction, resistance to disease

and insect attack and potential loss of nutrients is important.

- In cases of species with complex inter-relations (specific pollinators, symbiotic relationships such as mycor-rhizal fungi), management will need to review the population biology of the interlinked species and any environmental factors that may upset such ecological balances.

Ecological importance of trained harvesters

The knowledge and skill of the harvester is central to minimizing environmental damage associated with NTFP collection. Cork oak harvesters must be skilled in stripping trees in order to avoid causing damage to the living inner bark (the bast and cambium) of *Quercus suber*. Overharvesting of fiddlehead ferns can precipitate a decline in the number, size, flavour and tenderness of ferns from frequently collected sites (von Aderkas, 1984). The placement, depth, periodicity and number of taps made by rubber (*Ficus elastica*), maple, benzoin, croton (*Croton lechleri*) and chicle harvesters carry critical consequences for tree vigour and long-term survival. Even ginseng and other destructively collected herbs depend upon knowledgeable gatherers to carefully select mature individuals for harvest and to replant all viable seeds in order to ensure continuance of the population. Mushroom harvesters who allow a portion of the fruiting bodies they encounter to mature and release their spores likewise assist resource recovery.

Reliable indicators of sustainable NTFP management for many species are often unrecorded in the scientific literature. With many species, such as chicle, maple, ginseng, rattan and palm heart, indicators of sustainable management were not first documented through scientific study; rather, they were documented by collectors who had observed the response of the resource over time under many different harvest regimes. It is thus critical to respect and record the ecological knowledge and harvesting techniques found within traditional harvest regimes.

Harvesters often have a wealth of empirically gained knowledge that can provide practical lessons for NTFP managers. For example, in the case of açai (*Euterpe oleracea*), some harvesters had managed the resource for a greater number of years than others, thus offering a test of their techniques. Their experience served to demonstrate that sustainable management of açai for palm heart also served to extend the harvest season of its highly valued fruit (Johnson, 1999). Families managing açai for successive years were enjoying its fruits throughout the entire year, instead of only during the six- to eight-month season when the species generally produces fruit. Highly beneficial for subsistence consumption by the family, the extra harvest also serves to meet the heavy demand for açai during the off-season, when the fruit commands exceptionally high sale prices.

Fitting traditional ecological knowledge and practices with certification

Ecological requirements of certification guidelines proved problematic in cases where harvesters were not accustomed to documenting their management techniques and observations on paper. Many extractivists conduct frequent visual inventories of their resources, monitoring harvest, regeneration and growth, as well as conducting post-harvest assessments. The majority of wild plant harvesters, however, do not necessarily record these in a systematic fashion. In addition, unless a community has received outside support regarding forest management, it may not have a formally documented management plan or forest inventory. Such factors do not signify that a community does not understand and manage its resource base – only that its knowledge and manipulation of the resource is not recorded in the way stipulated by certification programmes.

Although cumbersome and foreign to most small landholders, formalization of inventories and management plans can hold a number of benefits for community forest management, some of which became evident during field assessments. Because both of the community forest operations assessed (in Mexico and Brazil) had received significant support for resource management, each had the opportunity to develop formal management plans, to conduct inventories and to decide upon sustainable harvest regimes. The process of formalizing what had previously been informal served a number of useful functions. Most importantly, the process encouraged gatherers to openly share their different management techniques, to compare and evaluate them, and to determine which aspects were most beneficial to resource management. Although informal exchanges occur between gatherers, the process of registering their management techniques served as an impetus to discuss them among a wider range of harvesters, in a more profound manner than might have occurred informally.

External support to meet ecological requirements of certification agencies

While uncomfortable with certain aspects of the documentation necessary for certification, harvesters found that discussions during the assessments helped them to realize the added benefits of conducting regular inventories and documenting their findings. Realistically, however, communities without external support are unlikely to meet requirements delineated by certification guidelines. Although harvesters may be highly knowledgeable about forest composition and structure, without training, most are unfamiliar with how to compose a forest management plan – a core requisite of sustainable forest management for certifiers and outside agencies.

Furthermore, documentation may be detrimental to many gatherers. Clearly, ginseng and fiddlehead fern (*Matteucia struthiopteris*) gatherers in Vermont would not benefit from mapping out a resource or designing a forest management plan for goods that they gather surreptitiously from other people's prop-

BOX 26.2 BOWS AND ARROWS: TOOLS FOR PALM HEART MANAGEMENT?

Georges Schnyder (Agroindustrial Ita, Belém, Brazil)

A forward-thinking palm heart industry leader in Brazil envisioned that the wild stands of açai he was harvesting might not prove sufficient to meet the growing demand for palm heart projected for the future. Researching the use of *Bactris gasipaes* as a cultivated alternative, the owner invested funds in planting an experimental area with *B. gasipaes* in the Atlantic Forest in the state of São Paulo.

He and the workers responsible for maintaining the area patiently waited the few years necessary for the palms to establish themselves and reach harvesting age. However, as soon as the plants became established, capivaras (*capybaras*: large Amazonian rodents) entered the area, consuming the young palm trees. Frustrated, the company sought help from specialists and was told that lights would repel the marauding wildlife. The company followed this advice, installing lights and fencing around the periphery of the site. These measures did not deter the wildlife from consuming the palms. Next, the owner decided to hunt the *capivaras*, thus lowering the population. He was informed by the Brazilian environmental protection agency IBAMA that hunting capivaras in this area would be legal only for Indians using bows and arrows. As a result, the owner employed Indians to cull the herd. The Indians arrived with bows and arrows. However, it had been quite some time since they had wielded bows and arrows and they were unsuccessful in the hunt. Returning to IBAMA, the owner was informed that if the area was fenced and designated as a wildlife farm for *capivaras*, as opposed to a palm heart plantation, it would be permissible to shoot the animals.

erty. Likewise, non-literate, indigenous tribes in Brazil are highly unlikely to see the benefits of designing forest management plans for breu (*Protium* spp.), titica (*Heteropsis* spp.) and amapá, when they collect and sell relatively small quantities of each for scant prices (see Chapters 9–12).

Cat's claw (*Uncaria* spp.) gatherers in Peru, rattan collectors in Indonesia, gatherers of yohimbe (*Pausinystalia johimbe*) in Cameroon and harvesters of açai fruit in Brazil and Bolivia – although they hail from different corners of the globe – share two things in common: they generally receive scant cash for hard labour. Documenting the ecological impacts of harvest is not a priority with such harvesters.

Onerous documentary requirements inherent in certification, and the added costs of certification, combine to make the process a challenge for many, especially small producers. Firstly, many producers and industries must already comply with strict governmental requirements for land use and management (see the *Croton* profile in Chapter 10). The fetters of sometimes-arbitrary government requirements may even inhibit certain environmental activities, as illustrated in Box 26.2. Since narrow niche markets compose much of the interest in sustainably managed non-timber forest products, additional requirements to procure certification may gain little to no marketing advantage, and therefore may prove counterproductive.

Setting ecological indicators for assessment

One of the benefits of investigating management regimes and developing indicators and verifiers of sustainable management is that the process can help elucidate simple, elegant and effective keys to determine sustainable harvesting and management techniques. In the case of maple trees tapped for syrup, minimum diameter at breast height (dbh) for tapping, depth of tap hole and number of tap holes per tree are widely cited as management indicators. Promptness of tap-hole closure may be viewed as an additional manifestation of responsible tapping. According to experienced tappers, rapid tap-hole closure indicates good tree vigour and a well-drilled tap (see Appendix II). Rate of tap-hole closure thus provides an example of an easy-to-implement field indicator for certification evaluators.

The field trials in Latin America permitted the testing and refining of the generic NTFP guidelines presented in Appendix I. The field trials demonstrated that for some collectors of internationally marketed species, the process of certification might prove useful regardless of whether or not certification is attained. In the following section, some of the ecological concerns and benefits regarding each of the field assessment species are described. More indepth descriptions of the ecology of each species are provided in the species profiles in Chapters 4, 5 and 6.

Ecological aspects of the three field assessments

Palm heart

In eastern Amazonia, two sites of palm heart extraction were assessed: a comparatively small community forest operation (approximately 300 hectares) and one of the largest industrial producers of palm heart in the region (approximately 3000 hectares). In both cases, the multistemmed palm, *E. oleracea* (which produces basal shoots and reproduces by seed) was harvested. Because forest management of açaí palms represents an atypical forest certification challenge, it is useful to place açaí in an environmental context (Johnson, 1999).

Originally, palm heart extraction (of single-stemmed *E. precatoria* – which generally takes longer to reach reproductive age than *E. oleracea* and reproduces from seed) took place in the Atlantic Forest of southern Brazil. Only during the late 1960s and 1970s did the industry become established in eastern Amazonia, where *E. oleracea* was also extracted. At the time, collection was predatory. By 1980, rampant clear-cutting of the açaí stands left the resource base in a degraded state, seriously threatening açaí fruit supply (the principal use of the palm throughout the region). Regionally, there is no custom of consuming the palm heart (the whitish, tender immature leaves of the palm, found just above the growing point on each stem). However, the fruit of the açaí palm is widely appreciated, representing one of the most important subsistence and market items throughout the eastern Amazon. Açaí can make up to 50 per cent of the caloric intake of families living in *várzea* forests. In Belém, the fruit is so highly appreciated that during the fruit season, sales of US$30 million each month are projected (Clay, 1997a).

Management

Forest management of açai palm (*Euterpe oleracea*) has evolved through trial and error by local inhabitants and can entail various techniques. Some of the most common management practices include: thinning competing understorey vegetation, girdling economically unimportant species to open the canopy, direct seeding, enrichment planting and extracting only select shoots in each cluster while leaving the remainder for a subsequent harvest or fruit production (Anderson and Jardim, 1989; Anderson, 1991; Jardim, 1992). The canopy is opened to allow growth of *Euterpe oleracea*. The effect is to maintain the *várzea* forest association at a slightly earlier stage of succession, when the açai palm occurs in greater numbers. Açai occurs naturally in densities of 230 to 600 clumps per hectare, considering only stems higher than 2 metres (m) (Anderson and Jardim, 1989; Clay, 1997a). In one of the field assessment sites, the management plan envisioned maintaining a density of 800–1000 açai palm clusters per hectare.

In the community site, harvesting regimes were widely practiced and set at reducing the total number of stems to six. This comprised two stems of medium height (2–10 centimetres (cm) in diameter), two small stems (up to 2m) and two basal suckers. Harvestable stems were defined as having a dbh of 10cm or greater. One of the community's plans called for harvesting one third of all commercial stems in each of three consecutive years. Each participating family pledged to manage an area of at least 1 hectare for the primary purpose of providing palm hearts for processing in the community factory. Where economic tree species such

as ucuúba (*Virola surinamensis*), andiroba (*Carapa guianensis*), sumaúma (*Ceiba pentandra*) and esponja (*Parkia pendula*) occurred in the family management units, they were protected and managed. The community discovered that managing for palm heart inadvertently increased the length of time throughout the year during which açai produces fruit, thus offering substantial subsistence and market benefits directly to the families.

In the areas managed by industry, management regimes are less clear and contracted labour is employed to extract palm hearts. Because they are paid by the piece (ie by volume) of palm heart they extract, there is a strong tendency for harvesters to cut every palm they come upon. Such destructive harvesting impacts upon the population by not leaving any stems for future growth, and by extracting stems of small diameter.

The community forest establishment had significantly better management regimes than those practiced by the large industry due to the relatively small land areas involved, direct involvement of property owners in land management, the presence of a strong, local organization, and intimate know-how of management techniques. Inventories, assessment of regeneration dynamics, enrichment plantings, careful thinnings and silvicultural treatments to promote, enhance and increase populations of açai palms are part of the regular routine for the small landholders. By comparison, the large palm heart operation encountered serious difficulties in açai management because harvesters did not own much of the land and traditional management regimes were lacking.

The following is a summary of some ecological lessons from the palm heart assessment:

- NTFP management may be appropriate in *várzea* forests because such areas have been disturbed, have naturally high densities of palm hearts and are in a naturally arrested state of succession.
- Traditional management practices may inform ecologically sensitive management planning.
- Management can increase yields of palm hearts and palm heart fruit over time.
- Setting harvest prescriptions by volume can cause destructive harvesting and ecological damage.
- Harvester ownership and involvement have positive ecological ramifications.
- Operations that produce important subsistence NTFPs such as açaí fruits need to account for local consumption in their planning.
- Functional ecology can and should guide development of NTFP guidelines and selection of species for management (in the case of palms, *E. oleracea* has many advantages over *E. precatoria*).

Chicle

Chicle trees have been widely used since the Mayan civilization. The sticky white latex exuded from fissures in the bark is used in the manufacture of gum, and historically served for construction purposes. Like palm heart, however, chicle is not currently utilized locally, but extracted solely for commercial ends. Trees are fire resistant and occur in high densities. Favoured by locals for centuries, it is the most abundant tree species, along with *Brosimum alicastrum* (ramon), in the Noh Bec *ejido* (indigenous forest community). The tree is also currently in demand as a timber species.

Management

The techniques utilized to extract the latex have been employed for centuries by Indians and *mestizos*. The current techniques have changed little since the earliest days and are evidenced by the diagonal slash marks found along the trunks of mature *M. zapota* trees. Based on centuries of management and local understanding on the part of chicleros (chicle harvesters), Mexican law (Norma oficial NUM-009-RENAT, 1996) established norms to regulate various aspects of chicle harvest (minimum diameter, rest periods between harvest, depth of incisions, etc).

At the assessment site, it is general practice to harvest from trees with a minimum height of 20cm from the base of the tree, at an inclination of approximately 45–60 degrees with respect to the trunk. The cut is a zig-zag that should occupy less than half the circumference of the tree. Key factors determining sustainability of harvest of chicle include minimum diameter, harvesting intensity and rest period. The harvest levels of a tree with a dbh of 25–34cm are noted to be approximately 0.59 kilograms (kg) per tree, and for larger trees of 75cm dbh and above, 2.4kg per tree. At the site visited, the annual projected production was 25 tonnes.

Factors affecting tree recovery include the time elapsed since last tapping and the healing condition of the tree. If properly tapped, trees suffer no damage to the vascular cambium. Tree injury occurs when the cambium is mistakenly cut or trees are excessively tapped. Damage can be evaluated through visual appraisal of tapping scars. Bark peeling and/or the formation of knots indicate poor healing. When overtapped, trees often die.

The following is a summary of some of the ecological findings from the Mexican field trial:

- Traditional ecological knowledge and management practices are the basis for national chicle extraction laws and local management plans.
- Knowledgeable tappers are essential to the proper harvesting of the resource.
- Cultural preference for particular resources, combined with natural disturbance such as fire, has created a change in the species composition of the Quintana Roo forests over the centuries.
- Although manipulated by human disturbance, the forests are complex and support great diversity.
- New markets for *M. zapota* timber have potential positive and negative ecological and social consequences. Removal of chicle trees may promote the growth of shade-intolerant trees that are currently decreasing in abundance throughout the forest. However, the chicle resource base may be threatened if markets for *M. zapota* wood prove more lucrative than chicle gum markets (which are now low).

Brazil nut

Brazil nut trees are a keystone species in Amazonian forests occurring in upland, dry *terra firme* forests. Characteristically, canopy emergent trees attain heights of 30–50m and are 1–2.5m in diameter (Mori and Prance, 1990). Historically, Brazil nut and rubber have been the largest extractive income generators in Amazonia.

Brazil nut trees grow slowly and take several decades to produce fruit. In tree-fall gaps or forest openings, trees begin bearing fruit at 12 years, reaching commercial production at 16 years. Seedlings are gap dependent, needing canopy openings to reach reproductive size (Meyers et al, 2000; Kainer et al, 1998; Clay, 1997b). Production varies widely. One tree may

produce about 36 litres or 20kg of raw nuts. A year of high production is generally followed by a year of low production; this alternative-year bearing is common in non-domesticated species (Rosengarten, 1984; Clay, 1997b; Clement, 1993).

Management

The present density and distribution of Brazil nuts is thought to be anthropogenically influenced, resulting from the management techniques of indigenous Amazonians. Thus, present harvests are, in part, a result of past management. In addition to planting by indigenous populations, the seeds are dispersed by agoutis (*Dasyprocta* spp.) and squirrels (Mori and Prance, 1990). However, in the field assessment site, besides the trail network created to collect the nuts, little active management of the species (ie planting seeds, transplanting seedlings, enrichment plantings) currently takes place. Though not pristine, the large forest holding is of significant conservation value because of its size, biodiversity and the lack of roads and heavy human disturbance. However, hunting by harvesters is taking a toll on animal populations in the region.

Although Brazil nuts have been harvested and utilized for centuries, it is unclear if current levels of nut harvest will be sustainable without additional active management to maintain populations. For example, studies in some regions indicate that the density of Brazil nut seedlings is very low, with scant regeneration (Lisboa et al, 1990; Nepstand et al, 1992; Boot and Gullison, 1995). The lack of saplings and seedlings indicates that the species is not replenishing itself and that current levels of harvest may not be sustainable for the future.

The relationship identified between gap size and regeneration of Brazil nuts may indicate that Brazil nut trees could benefit from silvicultural interventions, such as liberation thinning, specifically the single-tree selection system (Meyers et al, 2000). Such silvicultural interventions depend upon the presence of advance regeneration as well as sufficient light availability to facilitate growth (Uhl et al, 1988). In areas with scant regeneration, enrichment plantings may be considered.

However, in some regions of Brazil, the most serious threat to Brazil nut trees is not a lack of regeneration but deforestation. The research of Viana et al (1994) discovered high mortality in areas of pasture where all trees but the Brazil nut (which is protected by Brazilian law) were removed. Their study reported high Brazil nut mortality, no regeneration in pastures, and little to no fruit production. The Brazilian case provides a warning for other regions.

A summary of some of the ecological lessons learned from the Bolivian field trial follows:

- Indigenous management of Brazil nuts probably influenced the present density and distribution of the species in many forests.
- NTFPs such as rubber and Brazil nut, not timber, have traditionally provided income in most parts of the region.
- Management for NTFPs has helped to maintain many of the ecological and conservation values of the forest, which would clearly not be the case with other land uses.
- Hunting by NTFP harvesters has negative ecological impacts on wildlife, particularly endangered species and important seed-disperser populations.
- Brazil nut does not thrive in pastures and heavily disturbed areas; rather, it requires a complex forest setting for its survival.
- Where Brazil nut regeneration is sparse, silvicultural treatments such as liberation thinning and enrichment planting may be required to manage the resource sustainably.

Other ecological observations

A number of other ecological lessons are worth pointing out for the benefit of NTFP managers, NTFP certifiers and policy-makers.

Managing forest ecosystems is complex and information is incomplete

Tropical trees receive critical pollination services from a number of creatures that range in size from midges to large bats. Mammals and birds play significant roles in dispersing seeds from tropical trees. Tropical forest managers must ensure that

their forest management activities do not destroy critical habitats (nesting, breeding, feeding areas) of pollinators and dispersers such as birds, bats, mammals and insects. For example, durian (*Durio zibethinus*), an economically valuable fruit in South-East Asia, is exclusively pollinated by *Eonycteris* bats who depend upon the flowers of *Sonneratia alba*, a coastal mangrove tree (Peters, 1994). *Eonycteris* bats, on their journeys to coastal mangrove stands, only incidentally pollinate durian trees. Durian survival is thus contingent upon the maintainence of healthy populations of *Eonycteris* bats

---

BOX 26.3 MARKETING SUCCESS: ECOLOGICAL AND SOCIAL FAILURE

Jean Allan

Over a decade ago, a project mounted with an indigenous community in Bolivia sought markets for string (sisal: *Agave sisalana*) bags. Women of the tribe collected the sisal wild from the forest, processed it laboriously by hand and then wove it into bags. Located far from the city, the tribe had relatively few opportunities for income generation.

The project was successful in finding markets in Europe and assistance from an airline to move the bags at low cost from Bolivia. The women began making bags and their enterprise proceeded smoothly. However, as time went by and money came in, the women experienced more purchasing power than they had ever had, and sisal collection and bag production began to increase exponentially. Soon, the women found it more rewarding to make bags than to work in the fields. Furthermore, the women began harvesting increasing quantities of raw material until sisal populations became depleted in areas surrounding their village. Thus, by virtue of its economic success, the project contributed not only to depletion of the sisal resource but to social disruption. Fortunately, the focus of the project was realigned, thereby enabling the resource to regenerate and the community to regain its social equilibrium. However, the community and project leaders learned to beware of the successful marketing of non-timber forest products (NTFPs). If a resource has not been adequately inventoried or sustainably managed, overenthusiasm for marketing can prove both socially and environmentally destructive.

---

and mangrove stands that lie outside the borders of durian management areas.

Commercialization of NTFPs, access to markets or proximity to markets have ecological consequences

Echinacea (*E. purpurea*, *E. angustifolia* and *E. pallida*), golden seal (*Hydrastis canadensis*) and ginseng are examples of widely used medicinal species whose native populations have declined due to habitat destruction/degradation and over-harvesting to fulfill market demand. Widespread commercialization can exacerbate factors affecting vulnerable plant species, and may potentially imperil wild populations of plants, particularly primary forest species that occur in low densities (see Cunningham, 1993).

Assessment of sustainability may be less difficult for species that occur in abundance and about which management practices are widely known. However, as is demonstrated in the example from Bolivia (see Box 26.3), overenthusiastic harvesting can deplete local stands of even commonly occurring plants and can jeopardize the long-term viability of the population.

Bovi and de Castro (in Clay and Clement, 1993) report that the markets of the Brazilian city of Belém consume more than 50,000 litres of açaí fruits per day during the palm's fruiting season. Such fruits are highly perishable and spoil after 24 hours. Areas within 24 hours' reach of Belém are managed for this highly valued and marketable fruit. Outside the 24-hour transportation radius, report Bovi and de Castro (in Clay and Clement, 1993), açaí stands are largely decimated and sold as palm hearts. Thus, proximity to markets, especially for perishable products, has great ecological and management implications.

Some ecological factors are beyond a manager's control

Occasionally, ecological vectors beyond the control of a forest manager precipitate a loss of biodiversity or forest decline. For example, atmospheric pollution in Europe is thought to be causing forest decline and attendant declines in mushroom yields (Molina et al, 1993). More recent studies by DeHayes et al (1999) have provided evidence linking red spruce (*Picea rubens*) freezing injury and decline in eastern North America to the effects of acid rain.

Landscape ecology issues can also be difficult for individual landowners to address under certification, particularly for small-sized parcels. Because certification focuses on individual land management units, it has inherent limitations with respect to maintaining many ecosystem functions and structures that are considered cornerstones of landscape ecology principles (Pierce and Ervin, 1999).

Detrimental effects of timber harvest on NTFPs

Rising world demand for timber has exponentially increased the number of species extracted by the timber industry. While advantages exist to using lesser-known timber species, some of these species serve important ecological and subsistence functions in forest ecosystems. In addition, especially in some geographical regions in which diminutive fees are offered for timber, fruit and medicinal species can offer a market value far in excess of their wood value (Shanley, 2000;

Peters, 1989). Therefore, it is increasingly important for certifiers of timber operations to take into account species that offer important fruit, game-attracting and/or medicinal properties to regional populations. NTFPs with waning markets and desirable timber can be heavily exploited, leading to a cessation of any future NTFP potential, as is shown by the case of Borneo camphor (see Box 26.4).

Pau d'arco is another example of a primary forest species that occurs in low densities and is in danger of overexploitation (see Chapter 7). Its bark is extensively used by local populations for basic health care, including internal inflammations, tumours and skin diseases (von der Pahlen, 1999). Among populations with scant access to costly pharmaceuticals, the bark of the tree provides critical health needs for both rural and urban citizens. A valuable timber species, pau d'arco is highly sought after by the timber industry, thus posing a potential threat to its future sustainability and to the health care of millions of Brazilians who rely upon its healing properties. Similarly, amapá (*Parahancornia* spp.), piquiá (*Caryocar villosum*), maçaranduba (*Manilkara* spp.), chicle (*Manilkara* spp.), *Shorea* spp. and hundreds of other non-timber species are extracted by timber companies, thereby lessening the potential economic benefits from non-timber forest products as well as the actual subsistence benefits to local populations.

Some NTFPs require complex forest environments

The fate of many NTFPs, argue some, is domestication under plantation systems or substitution (see Homma, 1992). However, some NTFPs, such as chicle and Brazil nut, defy domestication efforts. Such products require complex forest environments to thrive. The same is true

BOX 26.4 BORNEO CAMPHOR: DECLINE OF A HISTORICALLY IMPORTANT NTFP

Esther Katz

Borneo camphor (*Dryobalanops aromatica* Gaertn. f.), or Barus camphor (in Malay, *kapur Barus*), was one of the oldest and most valuable non-timber forest products (NTFPs) traded from Sumatra (Barus harbour), Borneo and the Malay Peninsula. Due to its rarity, it was extremely expenisve. It was considered a miracle medicine and used as a stimulant, diaphoretic and poultice, as well as ingested for the treatment of stomach and bowel complaints. It was used not only for medicinal applications but also for embalming purposes (China and Sumatra) and as incense (China and India). *Dryobalanops* wood is insect resistant, making it a favourite material for the construction of chests in China and natural history cases in Europe. In Borneo, local people still make canoes out of its wood and walls and floors out of its bark.

Although the exploitation of *Dryobalanops* trees has been sustainable for more than ten centuries, the future of this narrowly distributed gregarious Dipterocarpaceae may be threatened. Since the beginning of the 20th century, its extraction for timber has eclipsed its collection for camphor. As the suite of timber species extracted for plywood has expanded, *Dryobalanops* is commonly logged, both legally and illegally. As smaller size-class diameters of *D. aromatica* are harvested, potential future stands of camphor are extirpated. Moreover, in many of the areas where Borneo camphor is endemic, forests have been converted into oil-palm and fast-growing tree plantations.

Camphor is a white aromatic substance found inside the trunk of particular, large-diameter aged trees. It crystallizes out of an oil (*umbil* in Malay), and is still used locally for its medicinal properties. It is traditionally collected by felling the tree. Some external signs give indications about the possible occurrence of camphor, but they are not sufficient to ensure its presence. In Malaysia, shamans took charge of finding camphor-containing trees through divination. Only a secret language could be used when cutting the tree. According to an old Punan informant in Borneo, whose father looked for camphor in the days when the country was still a Dutch colony, the finding of camphor was announced through premonitory dreams.

Historical records indicate that trade in Borneo camphor occurred as early as the eighth century, and likely earlier. The product was exported to China, India and as far as the Middle East. In the 16th century, Chinese camphor, produced at low cost and in large quantities from chips of *Cinnamomum camphora* and leaves of *Blumea balsamifera*, started competing with the expensive Borneo camphor. However, the chemical properties and medicinal uses of the two camphors differed, and Chinese camphor was less valued. The peak of the international demand for camphor occurred in the 19th century, when it was utilized for medicine and, in the case of Chinese camphor, in the manufacture of celluloid. Export was principally to China and Europe. Prices were high and volumes were generally small, totaling about 500kg per year from Borneo at the close of the 19th century. With the invention of synthetic camphor and plastic (replacing celluloid) after World War II and the growing interest for camphor timber, the Borneo camphor trade declined. Today, it is generally collected by loggers and may be traded illegally to Singapore. True Borneo camphor can no longer be found on the open market (Baillon, 1884; van Breda de Haan et al, 1906; van Vuuren, 1908; Oever, 1911; Heyne, 1927; Wheatley, 1959; Burkill, 1966; Grieve, 1973; Marsden, 1986; Goloubinoff, 1997; Guillot, 1998).

of rubber (*Ficus elastica*) within its native range in South America (the rubber plantations of South-East Asia have been able to flourish only due to the absence of a South American leaf blight that makes creation of rubber plantations in the New World impossible). Other NTFPs are more valued from wild systems than plantations. For example, wild ginseng receives substantially higher prices in the marketplace than cultivated ginseng (see Chapter 16). Many timber and non-timber species require the maintenance of complex, diverse forested ecosystems, and NTFP management can occasionally play a supportive role in bolstering the rationale for forest conservation in many regions.

Intensive management of NTFPs is not necessarily negative

The silvopastoral and agroforestry systems of the Mediterranean region provide examples of anthropogenic systems that (although they originally created reductions in biodiversity) are today considered sound, productive multiple-use forest systems. *Várzea* forests are also highly disturbed and in a state of arrested succession, making them well suited for intensive NTFP management in some areas. The setting of an NTFP operation and the history of land use within the region where the NTFP is managed thus tempers perceptions about the ecological trade-offs involved in NTFP management.

Conclusions

Timber and non-timber forest product management is occurring in forests throughout the world, based upon an imperfect understanding of forest ecology and the consequences of human disturbance. There is an urgent need to improve forest management in many parts of the globe. Certification may provide a tool for recognizing good forest practices and may improve those operations over time. Management planning, inventory methods, yield studies and monitoring systems are all required to obtain certification.

In some cases, documentation of practices and rationale may be weak or unrecorded, particularly for those operations based upon traditional practices. Most NTFP operations will require assistance to obtain certification. Certification, however, should not be viewed as an end in itself. Rather, it is a tool that can help explore, through practical, field-based analysis, issues of ecological sustainability and provide a process for instilling best management practices over time.

Chapter 27

Social issues

Alan R Pierce

Introduction

'All forestry', wrote Westoby (1989), 'should be social'. Yet practising forestry that is truly inclusive of social issues is exceedingly difficult. Of forest certification's three underlying tenets – ecological integrity, social equity and economic viability – evaluating the social aspects of forest operations, and particularly non-timber forest product (NTFP) operations, is the most challenging.

It would be fool hardy to suggest that one mere initiative, such as certification, could rectify the complex and myriad social issues present in many NTFP operations. Certification is a relatively narrow policy tool that has little influence over macroscopic political, social and economic trends and prevailing

Illustration by Antônio Valente da Silva

*Buriti (*Mauritia flexuosa*)*

cultural norms. This chapter will examine how certification can address particular socio-cultural aspects of NTFP management, harvest, use and marketing on a case-by-case basis. The chapter covers tenure and resource access as well as worker rights and community benefits, drawing upon information from the three field trials, the species profiles and the NTFP literature. The theme of subsistence usage of NTFPs, an area not well covered under certification, was deemed so important that it is treated separately in Chapter 28 through the presentation of one study from the North (US) and one from the South (Brazil).

Background

Timber-oriented forestry programmes typical of most academic, government and research institutions have given scant attention to non-timber forest products. The very terms used to describe the field of study encompassing forest fruits, nuts, resins, exudates, medicinal plants and fungi are illustrative: minor, secondary, special, alternative and non-timber/non-wood forest products all convey a dismissive tone.

Non-timber forest product research touches upon the fields of forestry, geography, anthropology, economics, sociology, natural resource management and a host of other disciplines, yet claims none. The fragmented nature of NTFP research, combined with the political powerlessness of most NTFP gatherers, has effectively marginalized the issue from academic and political circles. Furthermore, the weighty cultural and social complexities and idiosyncrasies inherent in NTFP gathering and use make the subject difficult for policymakers to address. Government policies around the globe, still dominated and driven by commodity-production paradigms, often overlook NTFP-dependent people and local communities.

NTFP markets are widely scattered and difficult to quantify. Researchers often refer to trade in NTFPs as 'invisible economies'. NTFP harvesters themselves are often 'invisible' to society and policymakers, eking out livelihoods at the margins of mainstream economic and social systems. Yet, NTFPs are far from trivial resources. Hundreds of millions of people worldwide depend upon them for food, shelter and subsistence income. Nearly 80 per cent of rural populations in developing countries rely upon traditional medicines, many derived from forests, for primary health care (Farnsworth, 1988; WWF, 1988). NTFPs have been overlooked by traditional resource-management scientists and economists in the past, but are beginning to garner attention from policy-makers and environmental organizations. It is clear that any new policy aimed at NTFPs, certification included, needs to be applied with extreme prudence because the outcome will affect some of society's poorest and most politically powerless people.

Applying the market metaphor to NTFPs

The spread of capitalism and global commerce has been linked with a concomitant rise in social fragmentation, the dissolution of social and emotional links between people, place and community and ecological destruction (Landy and Plotkin, 1982). Gray (1990) and Dove (1994) have been particularly critical of applying green marketing initiatives to tropical forest products, noting that such initiatives often produce negative social impacts and provide benefits for few local people. However, in some cases, certification may have the potential to validate, re-enforce and reward good NTFP management, provide a small buffer between communities and the international market, and strengthen social and cultural norms involving NTFP harvest and sale.

One of the aims of certification is to incorporate the true social and environmental costs of producing goods, thereby internalizing formerly externalized costs. The trend to incorporate formerly externalized environmental and societal costs of production is laudable and necessary if the bonds between people and place that make conservation possible are to be preserved. However, the current economic market is indifferent to the loss of a language or a culture, and is ill equipped to measure the intrinsic value of NTFPs. Neo-classical economics cannot adequately value the identity NTFPs confer to individuals and communities, the spiritual value of plants and forests, the social value of bonds forged over NTFP gift-giving, or the personal satisfaction gained from wearing new clothes or carrying new school books bought with money gleaned from NTFP-gathering.

Certification is a market-based tool based upon traditional economic assumptions, and as such it may reveal certain limitations when applied to the full array of social and cultural aspects of NTFP harvest and sale. The introduction of international market mechanisms may create negative social impacts in certain situations, particularly in subsistence and traditional economies (see Box 26.3 in Chapter 26). The central question at hand, then, is whether certification – a market-driven tool of an economic system that is acknowledged to cause ecological and social degradation – can help to maintain NTFP-dependent communities and provide a measure of improvement in NTFP management and, if appropriate, NTFP marketing.

Social issues

Hussain (1999) identifies several social issues that affect sustainable resource use, including literacy, population growth, urbanization, economic structures and institutions, links with international trade, political ideology and tenure. Certification is limited in its scope to affect most of the macroscopic-level issues listed above. Certification must instead concentrate on issues that directly influence resource use within forest management units such as land tenure, resource and access rights, rights to control use of traditional knowledge, workers' safety, workers' living conditions, workers' compensation and community participation and responsibility.

Land tenure, forest resource rights and access

'Land is our physical life and our social life; it is marriage; it is status; it is security; it is politics; in fact, it is our only world. We have little or no experience of social survival detached from the land. For us to be completely land-less is a nightmare that no dollar in the pocket or dollar in the bank will allay; we are threatened people' (Dove, Miriung and Togolo, 1974, quoted in Kula, 1999).

In general, long-term resource utilization is only possible in areas characterized by social stability, where clear rights and responsibilities governing land, resources and traditional knowledge are outlined and respected. Of the many social issues intrinsic to forest management, several authors have identified tenure and forest access rights as central to long-term resource sustainability (Poffenberger, 1990; Perl et al, 1991; Johnston, 1994; Oglethorpe, 1999). Understanding of 'tenure' varies considerably from region to region and continent to continent, and the number of traditional tenure systems is myriad.

For the purposes of this discussion, tenure refers to ownership or use rights to land, and the attendant 'bundle of rights' and duties that follow from recognition of land title or usufruct rights (see Oglethorpe, 1999; Fortmann and Bruce, 1988). A 'bundle of rights' refers to the 'rights to use land, trees and their products in certain ways and sometimes to exclude others from use' (Fortmann and Bruce, 1988). 'Such rights', continue Fortmann and Bruce (1988), 'can be held by individuals, communities or the state, and it is not at all unusual for a village to have a certain tenure over a piece of land while an individual or family has another tenure over part of the same land, and the state asserts a residual title to the same land.' Box 27.1 provides a brief introduction to issues relating to access and knowledge.

Pre-colonial societies across the globe maintained relatively sustainable relationships with their environment through local tenure systems based upon the familial, communal and tribal unit and enforced by geography, customs, rituals, pacts, taboos and belief systems. Relatively low population levels enhanced resource conservation. The link between traditional societies and natural resources was, and remains in some areas of the world today, a powerful force that shaped identity, culture and functional resource management norms (see Poffenberger, 1990; Chandrasekharan, 1998; DeBeer

and McDermott, 1996; Oglethorpe, 1999).

Colonization, the replacement of communal tenure with private property and state property, the rise of industrialism, the imposition of the 'nature-as-commodity' paradigm and the introduction of global commerce weakended or effectively dismantled many local customs and institutions that once facilitated sustainable resource management across the globe (Poffenberger, 1990; Clay, 1994; Oglethorpe, 1999). Newly formed governments alienated people from the land through privatization, issuance of logging or mining concessions to industries or imposition of state ownership, while lacking the means to enforce and monitor edicts due to corruption and/or lack of human and financial resources.

The erosion of traditional rights and the exclusion of local communities from involvement in resource management decisions often led to environmental degradation and, occasionally, civil unrest. Government attempts to undermine the authority of local communities and wrest control of forest resources are cited as contributing factors to insurrections in the Philippines, northern Thailand, Indonesia and Burma (Poffenberger, 1990), as well as in Mexico, Bolivia, Colombia, Ecuador, Brazil and Guatemala (Vargas, 1999).

A World Conservation Union (IUCN)-sponsored conference on tenure and sustainable natural resource use concluded that 'replacement of customary tenure systems with government management regimes has operated largely to the detriment of conservation of biological diversity' (Oglethorpe, 1999). The report further suggests: 'where well-defined tenure and access rights have been devolved to the local level (ie landholders and communities who live with, know or use the resources), sustainability of

Box 27.1 Ethical and legal obligations of commercializing traditional knowledge and resources

Sarah A Laird

The marketing of non-timber forest products (NTFPs) takes place within the context of international and national law and policy, and the customary laws of local communities. The equity of marketing relationships is dependent upon established rights for indigenous peoples and local communities, including the right to self-determination, autonomy and territory, as well as basic human and cultural rights. If these rights are not established, the intended objectives of certification – sustainable use, conservation and benefit-sharing – will not be realized.

As the International Alliance of Indigenous-Tribal Peoples of the Tropical Forests and the International Working Group for Indigenous Affairs (IWGIA, 1996) state:

'...partnership and participation can only take place between equals and in conditions where our fundamental rights remain intact. We are rights holders, not stakeholders. No activity should take place on our territories without our free and informed consent...our consent is a prerequisite for any access agreement or commercial contract. Whereas we support benefit-sharing, this must be based on principles of fair trade, with a priority focused on empowering our diverse local economies and markets.'

In some cases, NTFPs marketed to consumers through labels certifying environmental, organic or social standards are based upon long histories of traditional use and knowledge. For example, most of the botanical medicines in trade – including cat's claw, pau d'arco, yohimbe and croton – grow from traditional medical systems. The management, formulation and processing of products are also often based upon traditional knowledge and expertise developed over many years. It is critical, therefore, that certification systems for NTFPs address community rights to control access to not only resources and land, but also knowledge. In fact, benefit-sharing and prior informed consent (PIC) of communities is required under a range of international policy instruments today. These include binding conventions such as the Convention on Biological Diversity (CBD) and the International Labour Organization (ILO) Convention 169 Concerning Indigenous Peoples, and non-binding instruments such as the Rio Declaration, Agenda 21, the Forest Principles, and the Universal Declaration of Human Rights.

Demands for control over access to lands and resources, knowledge and requirements for benefit-sharing also come from indigenous peoples' groups through a number of statements, such as the 1993 Mataatua Declaration on Cultural and Intellectual Property Rights of Indigenous Peoples, the 1994 Statement from the Coordinating Body of Indigenous Organizations of the Amazon Basin (COICA)–United Nations Development Programme (UNDP) Regional Meeting on Intellectual Property Rights and Biodiversity ('The Santa Cruz Declaration'), and the Leticia Statement of 1996. It behoves certifiers and projects to become aware of these documents, and the concerns of communities as articulated by groups established to represent their interests (see links at www.rbgkew.org.uk/peopleplants/manuals).

A central aspect of social standards for the certification of NTFPs, therefore, will involve respect for a 'bundle' of traditional resource rights with emerging and strengthening legal status (Posey and Dutfield, 1996). Without these rights built into the marketing and certification process, local communities are unlikely to benefit significantly from commercial activities over time.

resource use has been significantly enhanced'. The report concludes that 'tenure, per se, does not necessarily have a positive influence on sustainability. Rather, tenure can provide an incentive, which, in turn, can be used to promote sustainability and accountability of the users' (Oglethorpe, 1999).

The fight for recognition of tenure and resource access rights has gained international attention during the past decade, particularly in Brazil and Borneo. A number of treaties covering indigenous peoples' rights to tenure, resource access, benefit-sharing and intellectual property rights have been recently drafted (see Box 27.1), and have strong implications for certifiers working in territories populated by indigenous peoples. While certification itself does not actively promote tenure transfer or recognition of resource access rights, it may bolster institutions and policies that promote recognition of traditional tenure rights or usufruct resource rights. NTFP certification will thus require flexibility in application if it is to respect and reinforce different tenure arrangements and resource-access expectations from region to region.

With respect to tenure and access, certification requires:

- clear evidence of rights to land or resources (legal title, customary rights or lease agreements);
- free and informed consent in cases where communities devolve their legal or customary tenure or rights to other agencies,
- clear and fair mechanisms for disputes over tenure and use rights;
- fair compensation for the application of any traditional knowledge.

Working conditions

A number of international and national laws and conventions govern workers' rights, workers' safety issues, fair compensation and the right to organize, particularly the edicts of the International Labour Organization (ILO). However, enforcement of national and international labour laws is haphazard, particularly in the NTFP sector. Entire families often work in NTFP collection or processing, and while families might consider their children's work to be an asset to household income, the practice is often in violation of international laws governing child labour.

NTFP harvesters are often seasonal employees. Wages and working conditions vary tremendously across the globe. For many NTFP harvesters working in remote areas, access to adequate health care and legal advice is limited or non-existent. Safety conditions differ according to the product harvested and the associated jobs. For example, work such as palm heart harvesting involves potential injury from the use of sharp tools such as machetes, while jobs in NTFP canning factories have associated machine-related accidents. Wages, living conditions, sanitary conditions and medical care likewise vary, with regular employees often receiving more benefits and better working and living conditions than seasonal employees.

With respect to working conditions and worker welfare, certification requires that:

- Local communities are given opportunities for employment, training and other services.
- There is adequate (at or above the industry norm) reimbursement for labour.
- Safe working (and, if applicable, living) conditions are provided.
- Social services exist, such as adequate health care and access to medical attention.

- Employee training programmes are provided.
- Workers have the right to organize and collectively negotiate.
- There is adherence to national and international labour laws.

For some NTFP operations, these requirements pose idealized situations that may not fit the current realities of NTFP harvest. Such requirements may deny certification to small family operations, as well as large NTFP operations that rely on brigades of seasonal employees. Indeed, individual and family operations, which make up the majority of the NTFP sector worldwide, operate under entirely different situations that are largely ill suited to certification. Many such operations would not be able to afford the direct or indirect costs of certification, and could not comply with the minimum safety and health standards, labour laws and other formal-sector norms governing working conditions.

Community relations and participation

Community relations and employee participation are important components in ensuring long-term resource viability. In one sense, community involvement touches upon the themes of benefit-sharing and respect for intellectual property rights discussed previously. Community participation in management also implies a working relationship between forest management and local stakeholders. This requires forest managers to pursue 'good neighbour' policies with local communities and affected stakeholders, offering employment opportunities to local people and sharing benefits with the local populace.

Building positive relations with local communities can yield long-term gains for forest management, particularly in the form of a loyal workforce. Forest man-

agers also can benefit from community participation in management planning and decision-making. Involved employees have a greater sense of ownership and pride in operations and are likely to perform their jobs with greater care than disenfranchised workers. Involved employees who have input in management planning and understand and support the goals of management are likely to be better trained and more effective workers. Systems-based certification programmes, such as the International Organization for Standardization (ISO) 9000 series programme, have proven that goals such as total product quality management can be achieved through direct employee participation.

Certifiers seek to gauge a company's 'good neighbour' policy when conducting an assessment. They interview company employees and members of local communities. They review worker training programmes, accident rates, company hiring practices and company commitments to its workers and local community. For forestry operations, it is critical that field employees are well trained and understand the goals of management planning. Without such expertise, understanding and involvement in management and implementation of best forest practices are unlikely. Security of the NTFP management areas from illegal logging or NTFP collection is also heavily dependent upon the goodwill of employees and local communities.

With respect to community benefits and community participation, certification evaluates:

- the 'good neighbour' policies of forest operations, including community consultation;
- the operation's sensitivity to local needs for benefits, employment, training and participation;

- the operation's sensitivity to local usage of NTFPs and other forest resources;
- degree of employee participation in management planning and execution;
- avenues for democratic decision-making;
- efficacy of mechanisms for resolution of employee or community grievances.

These conditions apply mostly to NTFP operations that operate within the formal economy. In such instances, participation is an issue. In the largely informal sector where much of the world's NTFP gathering and marketing takes place, participation is not an issue. Rather, for individuals and families engaged in NTFP collection, adherence to tacit or formal rules spelling out rights and responsibilities to resources is more of a critical issue, particularly in societies with traditional tenure systems. It is probably unavoidable that the bulk of certifications will apply to more formal, organized NTFP operations – hence, the emphasis in this section on working conditions and participation vis à vis larger NTFP companies.

Observations of social issues from the field trials

Three field trials were conducted in Mexico, Bolivia and Brazil to test NTFP certification criteria and the general feasibility of NTFP certification. Tenure is a key social issue in Latin America, where the majority of land is held by governments or under legal ownership by a small, elite upper class. The NTFP certification field trials in Latin America provided a good opportunity to examine the interaction between certification and land tenure issues in three different settings. In addition, the field trials afforded a chance to examine certification issues relating to working conditions, workers' rights and community relations and community consultation at different NTFP operations. The following summarizes the observations of social issues from the field trials.

Mexico

The first NTFP certification field trial, evaluating chicle gum extracted from the sapodilla (*Manilkara zapota*) tree, was conducted in Quintana Roo State, on the Yucatan Peninsula of Mexico. The forest operation under consideration, Noh Bec, is a community forestry operation organized as an *ejido*. The *ejido* system of communal land tenure was born in the Mexican Revolution, codified into the Mexican Constitution of 1917 and has been formally recognized and enacted by the Mexican government since 1942. The *ejido* system grants land and usufruct rights over natural resources to communities, who in turn collectively manage resources for use by and among their members, known as *ejidatarios*.

In 1954, timber concessions in the *ejidos* of Quintana Roo were granted to the state-owned enterprise Maderas Industriales de Quintana Roo (MIQRO). Rapacious harvesting practices by MIQRO and other socio-economic and political factors led *ejidatarios* to refuse renewal of logging contracts with MIQRO in 1983. Political and technical support led to the formation of a new organization, the Plan Piloto Forestal, which gave greater empowerment, and even more direct control over forest extraction activities, to *ejidatarios*. The Plan Piloto Forestal was built from the 'bottom up', relatively free from government intervention, giving high importance to building local decision-making and negotiation capacities (Kiernan and Freese, 1997). In the Noh Bec community today, the *ejido* holds regular general assemblies to discuss forest management planning, forest product marketing, distribution of forest-generated revenues and other issues relating to forest usage. Each *ejidatario* has a voice, a vote and the power to propose amendments or additions to existing community resource-management policies at such assemblies.

Working conditions within the *ejido* were found to be safe and salaries are consistent with, and at times higher than, the regional average. *ejido* members carry out the majority of jobs related to timber and chicle extraction. In addition, profits for timber sales are equally shared among the community, as well as a portion of the chicle revenues (although those members registered as chicleros retain a greater percentage of the chicle income earned). Training programmes assist *ejido* members in implementing forest management plans and forest product harvesting. Local processing of chicle and timber products adds value to the community's forest products and earns additional income for the *ejido* and its members.

Unlike many other areas of Latin America, tenure is secure within the Noh Bec *ejido*. Vargas (1999) cites secure tenure as the cornerstone of the Plan Piloto Forestal's success, a point echoed by Kiernan and Freese (1997). Community vigilance committees periodically monitor the communal forestlands for signs of settler encroachment, illegal timber and non-timber harvesting, illicit hunting and forest fires. The Noh Bec chicle harvesting cooperative received exemplary scores for social issues and was

eventually certified under the Forest Stewardship Council. Fair Trade eV and a US organic certifier also endorsed Noh Bec's chicle operation. This triple certification is a testament to the strength of the democratic processes within the *ejido*.

The success of the Plan Piloto Forestal has brought the participating *ejidos* domestic and international recognition and the project is now seen as a model for other states in southern Mexico. Certification has also 'helped to reinforce progress to date toward achieving sustainability (Kiernan and Freese, 1997).' However, authors (Vargas, 1999; Kiernan and Freese, 1997) warn that looming technical, social and economic forces may challenge the *ejido*'s structure and processes. For now, the Noh Bec *ejido* experience provides a hopeful lesson, proving that secure tenure and open, democratic participation of community members in management planning and benefit-sharing can lay the groundwork necessary for long-term resource conservation.

Bolivia

The second NTFP certification field trial, evaluating Brazil nut (*Bertholletia excelsa*) and palm heart (*Euterpe precatoria*) harvest in a sub-tropical humid forest located in north-eastern Bolivia, represents a more typical Latin American tenure arrangement, as described in Vargas (1999). The large forest holding (more than 250,000 hectares) has been owned by a single entity for many years. In the early half of the 20th century, rubber from the siringa tree (*Hevea brasiliensis*) was the principal product of the forest, attracting a stream of workers to the remote forest area. After the decline of the rubber boom, brought about by the introduction of synthetic rubber, some rubber extractors settled in the forest. Three generations later, a number of families – descendants of the original rubber tappers – live on in the forest, working as Brazil nut harvesters in the rainy season and palm heart gatherers in the dry season. Several hundred additional migrant workers descend upon the forest during Brazil nut and palm heart harvest seasons.

The resident families of the forest have no recognized rights or tenure to the land where they live, despite a residency of three generations. The families are completely dependent upon the company for housing, jobs and wages, education, medical attention, supplies (there is a company store where the families are given running tabs for goods that are subsequently deducted from wages) and other basic necessities. All leases and contracts between the forest residents and the company are tenuous, since they are only verbal in nature. Seasonal workers have no tenure rights, lack verbal contracts with the company and are dependent upon intermediary labour foremans for their wages and other needs.

The loose arrangements between the company and the forest residents and seasonal workers did not strengthen and clarify tenure rights, roles and responsibilities for all interested parties. Rather, forest residents and seasonal workers are tacitly allowed to gather forest resources for their own consumption or sale, in addition to the Brazil nut and palm heart harvesting activities. For example, forest residents and seasonal workers regularly hunt game, including certain endangered species, with bullets supplied by the company store. The company does not formally recognize the resident community and its use of the forest resource, fails to include the NTFP harvesters in management planning and provides no guarantee that housing leases or job opportunities will be renewed from year to year. Such a situation does not guaran-

tee proper implementation of best harvesting practices or good worker morale.

Working conditions in the forest are extremely hard. Harvesters work in remote areas for days at a time, in bad weather, sleeping in crude shelters. Because of the remoteness of the area, safety and medical conditions were far from exemplary. While local medical care was available, workers often had to be transported long distances from the forest to receive care, and serious injuries required evacuation to larger cities. Safety conditions in the NTFP processing factories, while far from deplorable, did not meet all national and international laws. Children also worked in the forest, helping their families to earn income, although this situation also runs against national and international laws. Wages were considered consistent with, or above, many other similar NTFP operations in the region, although payment of wages had become tardy in recent years.

The company's land owning is large and its conservation significance is great. While not pristine, the area is intact and home to numerous endangered species, in part because it has been used for NTFP extraction and has not been sub-divided, logged or cleared. The field trial found significant problems with the management of the forest, mostly in relation to social issues. Yet, the social conditions found during the field visit are not unique when compared to many large-scale NTFP operations in South America. In fact, the company is considered to be one of the more progressive NTFP operations in the region. Browder (1992) has been critical of the social conditions prevalent in many extractive communities. If incentives can be found to raise the social standards of NTFP operations while conserving the forest, the import could be significant. The task may be too great for certification alone to address. However, certification may be a useful mechanism to increase profit-sharing from Brazil nut sales to forest workers and forest companies, thereby supporting the additional investments in social infrastructure and the management needed to encourage viable long-term use of this forested area.

Brazil

The third NTFP certification field trial, conducted in the riverine (*várzea*) forests of the Lower Amazon in Brazil, involved two different operations harvesting palm heart (*Euterpe oleracea*). The first operation was community managed, while the second operation was larger and was company run.

The community forest area has been managed for palm heart for decades and, until recently, was controlled by several individual landowners, or *patrons*, who claimed rights over most of the river valley and historically hired brigades of palm heart harvesters to cut the resource. Within the past ten years, the community, with financial and political support from oversees donors and a local non-governmental organization (NGO), organized itself into an association of palm harvesters. The association is composed of individual family units, each with their own family plots for growing palm hearts. Families work on their individual properties and in common as harvesting brigades on properties held by project participants. Each family tends its own plot but people band together to harvest palm heart.

The insecurity of tenure has been noted as a major social and ecological problem in Amazonia (Ianni, 1978; Nugent, 1993; Pace, 1998). Brazilian laws that cover tenure acquisition are also exceedingly complex. At present, most members of the palm heart harvesting association have secured provisional title to their individual family plots. However,

steps remain to be completed in the finalization of tenure recognition for association members. The issue of usufruct rights over *terra firme* forest areas, located inland from the river, remains an outstanding issue in the valley, as access to this forest area is not fully legalized and recognized for other forest users, many of whom may be potential future association members. The creation of the palm harvester association has given its members greater political voice and power than previously held at the individual family level, and has improved access to legal counsel and political standing in disputes with local patrons.

While the association has made positive steps towards empowering its membership and securing legal and political recognition, several outstanding tenure-related issues must still be addressed. The importance of legitimizing land tenure and recognizing usufruct rights to forest resources in this forest community is paramount. In the past, overharvesting of palm hearts had a negative impact on families who relied upon nutritious açaí fruits for subsistence use. Furthermore, the collection of game is not covered in the association's management plan, nor is harvest of economically valuable trees. Such loopholes do not secure the long-term forest resource against incremental degradation because they perpetuate open-access attitudes towards game and timber by association members and non-members.

The association of palm harvesters has provided a good vehicle for families to have direct involvement in forest management, palm harvesting and distribution of income derived from palm heart and palm fruit sales. Processes are democratic and involve open meetings and the election of association representatives to conduct negotiations with outside entities. Despite women's involvement in the production of palm fruit wine and forest jams, the assessment did note that female participation in decision-making processes was weak. Training videos for proper harvest and processing of açaí are available to workers in the community. Nevertheless, formal community agreements on forest uses and benefits are needed in order to reach collective understanding of rights, duties, enforcement measures and monitoring needs. Such community agreements and resolution of tenure and use-rights issues will be necessary before certification can be granted.

Social scientists conducting the evaluation of the community also noted a danger of 'cultural capital depletion' (erosion of traditional food bases, activities, intercommunity ties, etc), brought about by reliance upon a single product and the market economy. Decline in varieties of cultivated crops, amount of game captured and reliance upon currency and river traders who charge exorbitant prices for goods were just some of the negative results brought about by the community's decision to concentrate time, labour and capital on palm heart extraction. The question of whether certification can bolster retention of cultural capital remains to be seen.

The company-owned palm heart harvesting operation had more problematic social conditions than the community-based operation. Primary among the social issues requiring resolution was the issue of tenure and forest use rights. The company claimed land that was previously inhabited or claimed by local residents, embittering many locals. The certification team determined that a transparent resolution process was necessary in order to resolve land ownership issues. The assessment team also asked the company to devise a formal mechanism to resolve future grievances and disputes. Lastly, neighbouring properties were to be formally identified, in order to avoid future property disputes.

Control of, and access to, forest resources within the company ownership were unclear and required formalization with clear delineation of roles and responsibilities. For example, hunting, fuelwood gathering, illegal logging and NTFP harvesting were all found to occur on company land, yet no guidance documents or agreements spelled out if and how such activities were to be undertaken. The level of community dependence upon the company land's resources was great, but not quantified. The lack of agreement on alternate forest uses seriously compromised forest security and long-term resource viability. There was no system for monitoring forest security or community vigilance groups to enforce forest security.

Worker participation in forest management and NTFP processing was minimal, and communication between the company and workers was poor. Gender inequity was also noted and highlighted as an issue to be resolved. The company also lacked training courses to improve employees' knowledge of environmental, safety and technical issues.

Emergency medical equipment for workers in the field was found to be in need of improvement. In general, health security was minimal for field and factory workers, particularly for workers in small factories outside company lands who supply the company with processed palm heart. As in Bolivia, agreements with seasonal workers were lacking and seasonal workers generally had fewer rights and benefits than did regular employees.

Additional social issues

Common property resources

Communities treat many NTFPs as common property resources (CPRs). They often protect CPRs from overexploitation through taboos, rules or regulations, many times arrived at through participatory processes. Government land title claims and socio-economic pressures sometimes diminish the strength and application of norms to protect CPRs. Community stewardship of CPRs also can go unnoticed and unrecognized by government and other institutions. Yet, to view such resources as 'open-access' goods (resources that harvesters view as 'free for the taking') that require strict regulation or privatization would threaten local communities and the long-term viability of the resource itself. Certification needs to be sensitive to the complexities of CPRs and the bundle of rights that communities and community members may hold over particular resources. Certification's formal recognition of CPRs and their attendant NTFPs may permit the concentration of harvested products, a result that could facilitate sales negotiations, political representation and profit-sharing.

Open access

True situations of open access, on the other hand, pose some dilemmas for certification of NTFPs. If forest security cannot be guaranteed, then NTFP populations, particularly portable NTFPs, may be jeopardized over the long term.

Social, cultural and religious significance of NTFPs

NTFPs are palpable manifestations of the intimate links people develop with plants, ecosystems and a sense of place. NTFPs are unique, particular to certain regions or forest types, with distinctive tastes, odours, textures, curative properties, and building, manufacturing or weaving characteristics. In many regions, NTFPs are imbued with cultural and spiritual significance and are linked to a sense of personal, communal or cultural identity. Seasons become associated with the gathering and partaking of particular greens and fruits. Seasonal celebrations and rituals have evolved around individual plants or products, such as maple syrup festivals in New England, durian (*Durio zibethinus*) festivals in South-East Asia and piqui (*Caryocar brasilensis*) and açaí (*Euterpe oleracea*) festivals in Amazonia. The forest itself comes to be viewed as medicine cabinet, larder, provider and protector.

NTFP use can be an integral part of many cultural and spiritual traditions. NTFP use also builds ecological literacy between people and the plants and animals of particular ecosystems – a literacy that is declining steadily the world over. Certification requires that forest operations respect sites of cultural or religious significance, such as sacred groves. This provision may need to be extended to cover the protection of individual NTFPs used for cultural and religious purposes. However, the cultural context of NTFP-dependent peoples is so complex that certification itself will not be adequate to ensure preservation of local traditions, customs and cultures.

During the last decade, the right of countries and indigenous peoples to maintain their resources against attempted biopiracy has arisen as a new economic, social, cultural and political issue. The case of ayahuasca (see Box 27.2) provides a troubling example of cultural contamination and appropriation of resources. Westerners seeking new experiences have spurred the creation of a tourist trade centred on psychoactive plants and the shamanistic practices of indigenous peoples. Influxes of tourists can have negative repercussions for the social and cultural integrity of local cultures. More troubling still is the attempt to patent ayahuasca by a US citizen. As the economic value of certain plant resources comes to light, particularly in the medicinal sector, the possibility of their attempted appropriation by outsiders, through legal and political means such as patents, grows.

Application of social criteria in the field

NTFP certification is extremely contextual by nature and depends upon very site-specific circumstances. Operations located in the same region of a country producing the same NTFP may manifest widely varying social issues. Certification criteria for social issues are arguably more difficult to measure in the field than ecological and economic criteria. Often, social issues require long periods of observation and interaction before a thorough analysis can be completed, a luxury not afforded by the relatively rapid time frames typical of most certification assessments. Forest certification may benefit by exchanging information and experiences with organizations (eg the Center for International Forestry Research (CIFOR) Fair Trade and Tropenbos) that have developed and tested social criteria in the field. Assessments can also benefit by exchanging information with local NGOs that have ongoing relationships with forest communities, forest-based industries and governmental representatives.

Access to certification

Certification is often dependent upon an operation's access to finances, technology and information. Many NTFP operations are small scale. It is incumbent that certification is available to small-scale and large-scale NTFP producers. This implies that NTFP certification will need to be cost sensitive to smaller operations. If certification cannot be tailored to fit a variety of operations, new inequities may be put into play. For example, organic certification of coffee has allowed cooperatives access to green markets and higher prices – market advantages denied to small, poor farmers who are default organic producers but lack the funds necessary to become certified (Rice and Ward, 1996).

It will be difficult or impossible for individual gatherers, family groups and some communities to meet the technical requirements of certification, particularly remote and semi-literate communities. Certification requires operations to have a management plan. One certification organization is experimenting with the use of video to record community members explaining management planning and implementation, rather than requiring a formal written document (Rezende, pers comm, 1998). It remains to be seen if such innovations as use of video will be practical or acceptable. What this exercise does point out is the need for maintaining the rigour of certification audits while experimenting with the flexibility of its application in the field, particularly for small operations.

Potential limitations of NTFP certification

Certification focuses on forest activities within the boundaries of discrete management units. Many NTFP harvesters are landless or do not own the land upon

Box 27.2 Ayahuasca (*Banisteriopsis* spp. and admixtures): appropriation and globalization of a sacred NTFP

Miguel N Alexiades

Ayahuasca is a tropical forest liana, most commonly *Banisteriopsis caapi* (Malpighiaceae), used for its psychoactive and medicinal properties in much of Amazonia, as well as in parts of the Orinoco Basin and along the Pacific Coast forests of Colombia and Panama (Dolmatoff, 1972; Schultes and Raffauf, 1990). Ayahuasca (in Quechua *aya* means 'soul' and 'dead', and *huasca* means 'vine') is typically combined with one or more, often psychoactive, admixtures to make a beverage known by the same name.

Use of ayahuasca in shamanistic and other ritual contexts was once largely restricted to the health and religious practices of indigenous peoples, farmers and the urban lower and middle class. Recently, ayahuasca's use as a religious, symbolic and psychoactive resource has undergone a socially upward movement, leading to its appropriation by middle- and upper-class consumers in cities and industrialized nations. One of the expressions of this 'globalization' of ayahuasca is the emergence of a relatively small, localized but thriving ayahuasca tourism industry, particularly in Peru, Ecuador and Brazil (Grunwell, 1998). More than a dozen lodges in the area around the Amazonian city of Iquitos, Peru, alone now offer travellers ayahuasca sessions guided by local healers (Elton, 1999).

A number of anthropologists have voiced concerns over the ethical and socio-cultural implications of 'the selling of the shaman' (Joralemon, 1990, p105) and of the emerging 'drug tourism' industry in Amazonia (Dobkin de Rios, 1994). These concerns are part of a broader set of questions regarding the effects of cultural and economic globalization on indigenous societies and cultures.

Ayahuasca became the focal point of a bitter, well-publicized international dispute after an American citizen applied for, and received, a US patent for a putative variety of ayahuasca originally cultivated by an indigenous community of Ecuador. When indigenous leaders – principally the Coordinating Body of Indigenous Organizations of the Amazon Basin (COICA) – activists and environmental lawyers at the Centre for International Environmental Law (CIEL) learned of the patent, they mobilized an international campaign to repeal the patent. The coalition filed a request for re-examination with the US Patent Trade Office (PTO). The PTO eventually suspended the patent in November 1999. The suspension was made on the narrowest grounds possible, whereby issuance of a patent is prohibited when the invention has been patented or described in a printed publication more than one year prior to the date of patent application (Ho, 1999; Wiser, 1999).

The image of an individual claiming as private property a plant considered by thousands of indigenous peoples as their sacred heritage has been interpreted by many as a powerful reminder that private property has expanded too far into the public domain. As such, the ayahuasca patent case resonated with growing concerns among environmental and indigenous activists that bioprospecting and international patent law favour the misappropriation of genetic resources and cultural knowledge, a concern most vocally articulated by the concept of biopiracy (Shiva, 1999). Indeed, at the same time that the ayahuasca patent was being challenged, the government of India was challenging several US patents on a number of traditionally utilized Indian plants (Srinivas, 1999).

As ayahuasca becomes increasingly well known and its use continues to spread away from geographically, politically and economically marginal areas into centres of economic and political power, it is likely that its use will become more contested. Widening use of ayahuasca adds a particularly complex cultural, social and political dimension to this extraordinary plant and its future as a medical and religious non-timber forest resource.

which they conduct their gathering activities. Their rights to gather NTFPs may be unresolved or unrecognized by legal landowners. Certification's focus on the land base rather than the harvester may be problematic for many NTFPs. In such instances, more appropriate mechanisms to foster better NTFP stewardship, in addition to (or as an alternative to) land-based certification, may include NTFP harvester training or certification of NTFP harvesters or associations of harvesters.

Lastly, certification requires conformance to standards, oversight by an outside body and formal record-keeping. Many NTFP harvesters live on the periphery of formal economic and social systems. Many harvesters may resent any type of oversight or perceived 'red-tape' regulations implied by certification and may interpret such intervention as an infringement or barrier to basic needs and freedoms.

Conclusions

Certification is not a tool that can be used to hand tenure over to worthy recipients. Nor is certification a labour and safety regulatory instrument. Such roles remain the province of government institutions. However, certification can, in some cases, bolster progressive management and provide leverage for projects that seek to enhance local acquisition of tenure, community participation and implementation of safe working conditions.

Chandrasekharan (1998) and Ruiz-Pérez and Byron (1999) stress the need for strategic changes in local political, social and economic policies and institutions if policies are to properly encourage NTFP conservation and local community participation, a viewpoint certification proponents would do well to keep in mind. Clearly, many of the social issues discussed in this chapter are beyond the ability of certification to tackle alone. They will need to be addressed by a number of policy instruments and government, human rights and conservation groups if they are to be successfully resolved.

Chapter 28

Subsistence issues

Alan R Pierce

Introduction

Non-timber forest products (NTFPs) provide food, medicine, shelter and income for hundreds of millions of people worldwide. In subsistence economies, NTFPs serve as barter or gifts, and their exchange maintains friendship and kinship ties, enhances local traditions, enforces the concepts of mutual aid and respect and supports other norms that stabilize and enrich community life. The issue of subsistence use of NTFPs is so complex and critical that it deserves special attention as a subject area within social issues that deal with forest operations. Any forest policy or initiative, certification included, seeking to fully address social and equity issues requires a deep and respectful understanding of subsistence.

The following two sections describe cases of subsistence use of NTFPs by individuals and communities in the North (US) and in the South (Brazil). While there are dramatic differences in the cultural, environmental and socio-economic settings of these two studies, there are also striking similarities in the reliance upon, and use of, NTFPs for basic needs. The profile from the Upper Peninsula of Michigan, US, demonstrates the importance of NTFPs in a region traditionally beset by high unemployment rates and few job opportunities. Largely failed by the formal market, rural residents of the Upper Peninsula utilize NTFPs for food, medicine, barter and income, cobbling together a living from year to year in a close relationship with the surrounding forest and the rhythms of the seasons.

The second profile details the wide array of trees used by rural communities

Illustration by Antônio Valente da Silva

*Inajá (*Maximiliana maripa*)*

in the Amazon Basin of Brazil. Recent logging events in the area have resulted in dramatically negative impacts on NTFPs used for subsistence. Shanley's (2000) research shows that NTFP contributions to annual family food needs fell drastically in less than a decade as a result of localized forest degradation. Shanley's Brazilian study presented in this chapter is particularly instructive because it touches upon the importance of game (a critical NTFP not treated elsewhere in this book) to protein-poor local diets. Shanley also demonstrates that harvesting lesser-known timber species (LKS), a conservation strategy often promoted for improving utilization of standing tropical forests, can produce negative consequences for local communities who use such species for medicinal, nutritional and game-attracting qualities.

To underscore the value of NTFPs to skeptical academics and policy-makers, researchers have stressed the economic potential of such resources, particularly as competitive alternatives to timber-generated revenue on a hectare-per-hectare basis (eg Peters et al, 1989, Grimes et al, 1994). While such studies have gained some much-needed attention for NTFPs, there have been unintended negative consequences. Some policy-makers have simplified the lessons of the NTFP literature to the point where they believe additional revenue is eluding capture from forest systems. Such simplification results in the introduction of new legislation aimed at increasing taxes on NTFPs, raising fees for NTFP collection permits and limiting or curtailing access to NTFPs.

In the US, two new legislative proposals illustrate the problem of overinflating the potential profits to be made from NTFPs while ignoring the social ramifications of such proposals, particularly upon subsistence users. In the first case, the federal government is proposing to increase revenues from NTFP permits on US Forest Service lands from the US$3 million currently collected to more than US$12 million dollars in the coming years (see Rogers, 1999). Protecting resources on federal lands is a laudable goal, but the proposed legislation appears to be more about increasing profits than ensuring resource security. The US$9 million in increased revenue that the law would create is a paltry sum when compared to government accounts, as the government loses such sums daily through corruption, misguided appropriations and wasteful, redundant or obsolete programmes. The end result of such legislation has the potential to be socially regressive, hurting the poorest and least politically powerful who depend upon NTFPs from federal lands and who can ill afford to purchase costly permits or drive for hours to obtain such permits.

The second case involves proposed legislation before the state of Florida that would restrict collection of saw palmetto (*Serenoa repens*) berries. Under the proposed legislation, possession of more than 45 kilograms (kg) of saw palmetto berries (used as a medicinal for prostate treatment) without proper documentation and permission from the landowner where the berries were harvested would be treated as a criminal offence. The legislation is supported by large private landowners in Florida who seek to legally control access to palmetto berries on their lands and to capture profits from their trade. Saw palmetto berry harvesters are traditionally poor migrant farm workers, many of Hispanic, Native American or African-American descent, who heavily depend upon income from palmetto berry sales during the agricultural off-season in mid summer (see Coalition of Immokalee Workers, 1999).

Forest managers and certification assessment teams must seriously consider the impacts of their actions and recommendations on NTFPs used for subsistence if they are to avoid socially regressive consequences. In some cases, turning a blind eye towards subsistence use of forest resources may be warranted if such usage does not compromise resource integrity, does not interfere with forest operations and does not compromise local livelihood considerations. In other instances, conscientious retention of certain fruit trees or game-attracting trees by management may go a long way towards improving relationships between management and local communities. Such good-faith efforts could build trust and ultimately benefit resource security by involving and respecting local communities' use of the forest. Lastly, in cases of community forest management, management plans may need to balance the desire for income from timber with the subsistence needs of the community for nutrition, medicine and shelter provided by NTFPs.

Certain steps may lessen impacts on NTFPs that are used for subsistence. Managers and certification teams should actively seek to:

- consult with local communities to determine NTFPs important for subsistence use;
- identify traditional gatherers of subsistence NTFPs;
- monitor populations of commonly used NTFPs.

Actions may need to be taken to secure NTFP resources or perhaps limit access if and when one or more of the following events take place:

- An influx of new harvesters puts additional pressure on traditional resources.

- A rise in the price and/or a rise in the demand for a particular NTFP increase harvest intensity.
- A decline in NTFP populations is noted due to overharvesting or other reasons.

If forest operations decide to commercialize NTFPs, managers and certifiers should guard against:

- promoting commercialization of vulnerable or culturally/religiously significant NTFPs;
- excluding local communities from work opportunities;
- depleting NTFP stocks so that communities no longer have access to traditional resources;
- dismissing local knowledge or gathering norms;
- rapid immersion in market economies (particularly in the case of indigenous groups or poor households).

It is important that certifiers conduct thorough social work to ascertain which gatherers have traditional or usufruct rights to NTFPs for subsistence use and to encourage forest managers to grant long-term access to traditional users over newer settlers or profit-seekers. However, as Emery's study demonstrates, social consultations, can be exceedingly difficult and may be coopted by the interests of elite groups within communities. Of the three subject areas certification covers – environmental, social and economic – consensus on social aspects is the most difficult to achieve, and measuring and enforcing social criteria are extremely challenging activities. Certification may not be equipped to solve subsistence issues fully, but it should always seek ways to mitigate, and not contribute to, social inequities in forest management and use.

Space outside the market: implications of NTFP certification for subsistence use (US)

by Marla R Emery[1]

'*Contrary to much contemporary policy wisdom, leaving social and environmental problems to the market may be better for the market than for the problems*' (Nepstad and Schwartzman, 1992).

Introduction

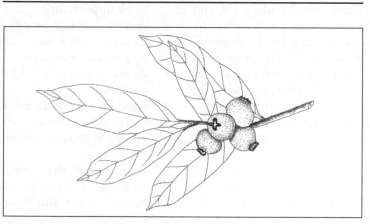

Illustration by Antônio Valente da Silva

*Blueberry (*Vaccinium *spp.)*

Non-timber forest product (NTFP) certification is a market mechanism that is advanced to attain the dual goals of protecting global forests and promoting economic development (Nepstad and Schwartzman, 1992; Pierce, 1999; Viana et al, 1996). Certification criteria and indicators emphasize the rationalization and control of each step of the NTFP process from forest to consumer. The creation of markets for items produced through such systems is a central focus of the strategy. There is a danger, however, that these very processes may undermine the achievement of certification goals, particularly those aimed at social equity and the protection of subsistence uses.

Critiques of market-based environment and development initiatives identify inherent contradictions. Schroeder (1995) describes how tree crop programmes introduced to promote environmental restoration and stabilization in the Gambia relied upon women's work while creating economic benefits for men. He notes that 'commodification of nature can lead to the imposition of new forms of property claims and the introduction of inequitable labour relations' (p337). Crook and Clapp (1998) analyse three market strategies for conserving global forests, including NTFPs. While they focus primarily on the potentially perverse environmental consequences of marketing NTFPs, they also note the social hazards of such an approach: 'The introduction of novel market mechanisms will not alter existing unequal power relations, but provide yet another field in which those inequalities are played out' (p142).

This contention is reinforced by the historical example of the 19th-century gum arabic trade, which consolidated the power of local elites in Western Africa and led to the increased use of slave labour in the region (Hanson, 1992).

Based upon a Northern profile, this case study examines the potential contradictions lurking in certification efforts to promote NTFPs as 'green' commodities while ensuring equitable access to their benefits, including protection of subsistence uses. The case study draws upon an ethnographic study conducted in the US Upper Great Lakes region and the work of economic anthropologists and historians to explore the implications of certification projects for NTFP subsistence uses.

Subsistence and the market

Subsistence is defined by Webster's dictionary as 'a source or means of obtaining the necessities of life' (Merriam-Webster, 1999). Thus, subsistence refers to the acquisition or production of goods for direct consumption or for use as gifts.[2] Subsistence also includes limited use of NTFPs for their exchange values. This encompasses their barter or trade for other items and their sale in raw or value-added forms for small amounts of cash that are used to pay for basic necessities.

Subsistence activities principally take place outside of the formal market economy. However, exchange-value uses may be articulated along a continuum from the strictly informal economy to transactions with agents who transfer products to the formal market (see Figure 28.1). Studies of the informal economy have identified distinctions between its primary motivating and regulating factors and those of the formal economy (see Table 28.1). Transactions in the informal economy are motivated primarily by the desire to satisfy specific needs and are governed by social structures and networks. The logic of the formal market economy emphasizes

Informal economy — Formal market economy

barter/trade — sale to user/consumer* — sale to middle person**

* Often as a value-added craft or food stuff, usually within the local area.
** Most frequently in a raw form, often for consumption in a regional, national or international market.

Figure 28.1 *NTFP exchange-value continuum. NTFPs contribute to gatherer livelihoods through both use values and exchange values. Exchange values can be thought of as taking place along a continuum from transactions that occur strictly in the informal economy to those that are closely linked to the formal economy*

Table 28.1 *Motivational factors in informal and formal economies. The informal and formal economies are motivated and regulated by distinct factors*

	Motivators	*Regulators*
Informal economy	Satisfaction of needs	Social structures and networks
Formal market economy	Maximization of the utility of scarce needs	Market forces; the state

maximizing the utility of scarce resources in a system where production, distribution and consumption are driven by market forces and regulated by the state (Castells and Portes, 1989; Gaughan and Ferman, 1987; Mingione, 1994; Roberts, 1994; Smith, 1989).

Extending these principles to exchange uses of NTFPs, the closer a use takes place to the informal economy end of the continuum, the more likely it is to be motivated by the desire to satisfy a finite, identified need and to be subject to social norms regarding appropriate prac-tices. By contrast, the closer a transaction tends towards the formal economy end, the more likely it is that the NTFP will be regarded as a commodity to be maximized in the near term. Once viewed as a commodity, the likelihood of increased capitalization to secure and control the terms of NTFP production, distribution and consumption, using the state or state-like entities if possible, strongly increases. As the following study suggests, these characteristics of the formal market are in potential conflict with subsistence uses of NTFPs.

Gatherers and subsistence in the US Upper Great Lakes

The Upper Peninsula (UP) is located in the north-central United States. Bordered on three sides by Great Lakes – Lakes Superior, Huron and Michigan – it is part of the US state of Michigan, although its only land link is with the state of Wisconsin. Archaeological evidence sug-gests human occupation of the region since the 'Woodland' era (3000 BP to 300 years BP) (Cleland, 1992). However, per-manent year-round settlement appears to be relatively recent, dating to the disloca-tion of the Ojibwa from their eastern territories during the Iroquois War and the efforts of European missionaries dur-ing the 1600s to convert and settle the region's indigenous population (Cleland, 1983).

In addition to providing subsistence resources for resident Native and European Americans, the UP has been a source of furs, timber, copper and iron that fuelled political expansion and eco-nomic development elsewhere on the North American continent (Cronon, 1991; Karamanski, 1989; Williams, 1989). Its present-day population includes people of both European and indigenous ancestry. Average human population den-sity in 1990 was less than 18 individuals per square mile (259 hectares) (US Census Bureau, 1990b). Forest cover in 1993 was 3,566,419 hectares (83.9 per cent total land base) of mixed hardwood and conif-erous species in largely second- and third-growth stands. Located between 47 degrees and 45 degrees North latitude, average annual growth is comparatively slow at 4.25 million cubic metres during the period of 1980–1992 (Schmidt, Spencer and Bertsch, 1997).

From August 1995 to July 1996, the author conducted ethnographic fieldwork in the UP to learn what NTFPs residents might be gathering in the forests, the social and biophysical processes associated with that gathering, and how this fits into gatherers' household livelihoods. At the conclusion of the year, 139 products were identified from over 100 botanical species. These products can be categorized in two ways in order to help understand the subsistence role of NTFPS in the UP:

1 product types; and
2 livelihood uses.

Product-type categories emphasize the direct material uses of NTFPs and include ceremonial/cultural, edible, floral/nursery/craft and medicinal. Livelihood uses distinguish between means by which NTFPs contribute to gatherers' household economies, with economics understood as any strategy that provides the material means for meeting human needs (Gudeman, 1986; Halperin, 1988; Polanyi, 1977). In the case of UP NTFPs, these comprise personal consumption, gift-giving, sale in a raw form and sale in a processed form.

Table 28.2 extracts a sub-set of ten products from the UP NTFP database (Emery, 1998) and illustrates the multiple ways in which Upper Peninsula non-timber forest products are used. Blueberries and birch bark provide especially good examples of the multiple products that may be derived from a single species and the diverse livelihood resources that these may provide. Blueberries fall into just one product-type category – edibles – but all four livelihood uses. People pick and con-

sume them directly and they are often given as gifts, freshly picked or preserved as jams and baked goods. Blueberries also provide a modest source of cash income for some gatherers. At the height of the season, makeshift roadside stands displaying small containers of the deep purple berries are a common sight where wild blueberries are plentiful. At least a dozen individuals in the region make and sell blueberry preserves, largely to the local market.

Birch bark also furnishes both multiple-product types and livelihood uses. Its traditional medicinal applications include use as a treatment for blood diseases (Meeker, Elias, and Heim, 1993; Moerman, 1998), with personal consumption and gift-giving being the only reported livelihood uses for birch bark in this product-type category.[3] As a ceremonial product, the bark is the primary construction material for long houses, where rituals and other important social functions are performed by individuals trying to observe traditional Native American practices. Finally, birch bark is used to make baskets and other crafts (floral/nursery/craft-product type) that are generally given as gifts or sold.

Figure 28.2 shows patterns in the relationship between the product types and livelihood strategies of UP NTFPs. Both edibles and floral/nursery/craft products contribute to gatherers' domestic economies through all four livelihood strategies. However, the relative proportion of use values (personal consumption and gift-giving) and exchange values (sale in raw and processed forms) are virtual mirror images of each other: use values account for 60 per cent of all mentions of edibles while exchange values constitute 62 per cent of floral/nursery/craft mentions. By contrast, UP gatherers employ medicinals and ceremonials almost exclusively for their use values. From this

Table 28.2 *Multiple uses of Michigan NTFPs. A single UP NTFP may provide multiple types of products and contribute to gatherers' household livelihoods in one or more ways*

Common name	Botanical name	Product types				Livelihood uses			
		M	C	E	F	PC	GG	SR	SP
Blueberries	*Vaccinium* spp.			x		x	x	x	x
Birch bark	*Betula papyrifera*	x	x		x	x	x		x
Cattail, corn	*Typha* spp.			x		x		x	
Cattail, down*	*Typha* spp.				x		x		
Cattail, shoots	*Typha* spp.			x		x			
Cedar, boughs	*Thuja occidentalis*	x	x		x	x		x	x
Gold thread	*Coptis trifolia*	x				x	x		
Sheep sorrel	*Rumex acetosella*			x		x			
Sketaugen	*Inonutus obliquus*		x			x			
Wild leek	*Allium tricoccum*			x		x		x	

* 'Down' is the fluffy filament of mature seed heads.

Key: Product types   Livelihood uses
       M: medicinal   PC: personal consumption
       C: ceremonial   GG: gift-giving
       E: edible   SR: sale in a raw form
       F: floral/nursery/craft SP: sale in a processed form

breakdown of livelihood strategies it is clear that edible, medicinal and ceremonial products are especially important for their use values while floral/nursery/crafts products are important sources of exchange values, especially cash income. There are also some differences in the patterns of various demographic groups. The women interviewed mentioned use values for the NTFPs they gather 40 per cent more frequently than did the men. 80 per cent of NTFP livelihood strategies of gatherers 60 years of age or over were use values, compared to 58 per cent for people between the ages of 20 and 60.

The UP economy and gatherers' individual and household livelihood strategies shed light on NTFPs' persistent subsistence role in this post-industrial setting. Like resource-based economies throughout the world, the UP has experienced cycles of economic boom and bust. Between 1832 and 1834, John Jacob Astor's American Fur Company virtually eliminated populations of every commer-

cially profitable fur-bearing animal in the region (Catton, 1976). During the ten-year period preceding the fieldwork, annual unemployment rates (see Figure 28.3) and intra-annual unemployment fluctuations were consistently higher (see Figure 28.4) than those for the state of Michigan or the US as a whole. Furthermore, 31 per cent of UP households had no formal earnings whatsoever in 1989 (US Census Bureau, 1990a).

Clearly, the market is not performing well for many in the UP. Given this regional economic profile, it is not surprising that much of UP gatherers' livelihoods are derived outside the formal market. Of the 42 individuals included in the survey on income sources, fewer than half (20) had formal employment and only 9 of these had full-time, year-round jobs. 30 people mentioned informal or self-employment, 10 were on social security (government-administered retirement pensions) and 4 received disability payments from public or private sources.

Livelihood uses

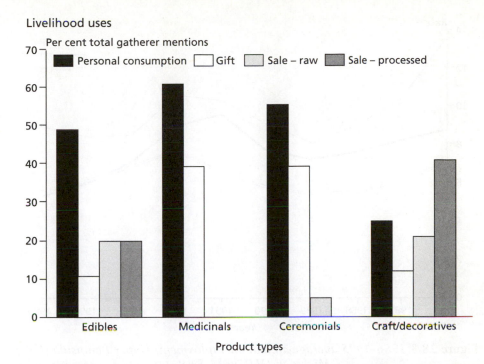

Figure 28.2 *Product types and livelihood uses of Michigan NTFPs. The relative importance of livelihood uses varies for each product type, with edibles, medicinals and ceremonials contributing most heavily to gatherers' domestic economies through their use values (eg personal consumption and gift-giving). Floral/nursery/craft products are turned to most frequently for their exchange values (eg sale in raw and processed forms)*

Additional household strategies shed further light on the flexibility and diversity of livelihoods in the region. 31 gatherers lived in households with one or more additional residents. These individuals contributed income from another 42 sources: 7 full-time, year-round and 2 full-time, seasonal jobs; 3 part-time jobs; 23 informal or self-employment sources; 3 social-security payments; and 4 other types of government-transfer payments. In total, the 42 gatherer households drew upon 108 income sources to meet at least some of their needs. The prevalence of episodic, part-time and low fixed-income sources meant that people simultaneously or sequentially pursued a number of strategies in order to meet their needs throughout the year. Livelihood strategies were diversified throughout the course of gatherers' lifetimes as well.

NTFPs were one element among many in these diverse livelihood systems. Their proportional contribution to a particular gatherer's material sustenance varied in good part according to need and other available income sources. The stories of four gatherers and the role of NTFPs in their livelihoods illustrate this diversity and temporal flexibility.

Lorraine[4] lives with her two grown sons. Their household income consists of her social security pension (she worked for 22 years in a factory making hood latches and locks for cars) and one son's disability

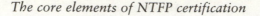

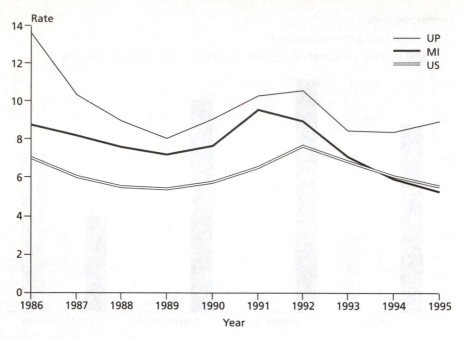

Figure 28.3 *1986–1995 average annual unemployment: Upper Peninsula (UP), Michigan (MI) and US rates*

payments. These funds are not enough to support three adults, however, and they rely heavily on gathering. Blueberries are a source of both food and income. Lorraine and her sons pick enough to sell more than 300 quarts (600 pints), eat plenty of fresh berries and can a few dozen quarts for personal consumption every year. Lorraine also makes birch-bark baskets according to traditional designs. Income from the sale of these baskets is the single most important supplement to her livelihood. Lorraine indicates that the NTFPs are critical to her survival from month to month.

James grew up on a farm in the UP. As a child he gathered mushrooms, berries and other NTFPs. In the family diet, these complemented the vegetables and animals they raised and staples purchased with income from his father's jobs as a trucker and iron dock worker. As a young man,

James went to work in a large manufacturing plant in the area. There were few alternative employment sources when he and 2000 other labourers lost their jobs. So James turned to the forests, cutting evergreen boughs for the seasonal floral market for two years to help support himself, his wife and daughter. At the time of interview, both he and his wife were employed and had adequate incomes to support themselves. James no longer gathered. although he said that he missed the time in the woods.

Caroline has worked as a journalist, librarian and educator. When her husband, a skilled labourer, suffered an on-the-job accident he was left permanently disabled and they abruptly lost over 50 per cent of their household income. Working with her parents, they began harvesting birch bark, making baskets, and selling the baskets at regional

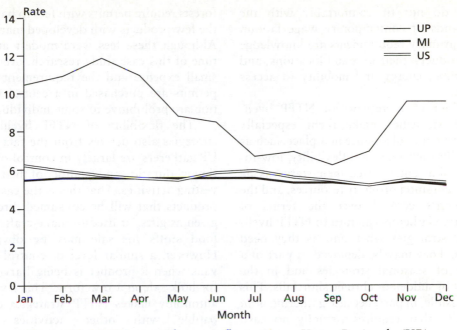

Figure 28.4 *1995 unemployment fluctuations: Upper Peninsula (UP), Michigan (MI) and US rates*

gatherings of Native Americans. The activity helped to keep Caroline's husband's mind off the chronic pain he was suffering, and the income allowed them to pay their bills for several months until Caroline was able to find a higher-income job. When interviewed, Caroline and her family were still making baskets, but on a much smaller scale than they had before. She indicated that it was important to maintain the skill in case their economic circumstances should take a dramatic downturn again.

Robert remembers camping in blueberry fields with his whole family, especially during the great economic depression of the 1930s. They lived out of a tent and picked from the time the berries ripened until the first hard frost of winter. He has also picked princess pine (*Lycopodium obscurum* complex) almost every year since he was six or seven years' old. As an

adult, he worked primarily as a logger but also did a bit of construction work and spent a couple of years working in a steel mill. At 76 years of age, he was living off social security with his wife in a comfortable new mobile home on family land. With dozens of grandchildren and great-grandchildren, Robert indicated that the money he makes gathering and selling princess pine during the years when his health permits makes it possible to buy Christmas presents.

For these individuals, in particular, and for UP gatherers in general, NTFPs serve as a buffer and refuge from the vagaries of the formal market. This is a strategy that can be pursued by workers who find themselves between jobs and by individuals whose employment opportunities are chronically limited by age, gender and/or disability. The independent nature of the activity also makes it suitable for people who do not fit comfortably with the demands of contemporary wage labour. The primary requirements are knowledge of products, their uses and locations, and the time, energy and mobility to access them.

Four characteristics of NTFP livelihood strategies make them especially valuable for subsistence in a place such as the UP: their temporal flexibility, low-to-no-capital entry costs, their status as *de facto* common property resources, and the gatherer's control over the terms of labour. Gatherers can turn to NTFP livelihood strategies when and as they need them. They may be deployed as part of a suite of seasonal strategies and in the event of sudden or chronic shortfalls. This is possible, in part, because gathering is an activity that requires virtually no cash investment. Harvesting equipment, where this is needed, is generally confined to inexpensive hand tools such as knives or clippers, which are often available as household implements. For gathering that cannot be done within walking distance of home, petrol is frequently the greatest expense. Indeed, NTFP buyers report that they occasionally loan a gatherer petrol money so that the individual can get to the product and bring it back to the buying location.

As a rule, gatherers in the region do not have the means to own land, and loosely formalized usufruct rights facilitate access to NTFPs for subsistence uses. Where products are located on small private holdings, UP gatherer norms dictate that they obtain permission to enter onto the land and harvest.[5] Often this involves no more than an informal conversation with a neighbour. Large industrial landowners in the region seem largely indifferent to NTFP harvesting provided gatherers stay out of active timber-cutting areas. Michigan state and US national forests require permits with fees to harvest the few products with developed markets. Although these fees were modest at the time of this case study research, even the small expense and the requirement that permits are purchased in a central location are prohibitive to some individuals.

The flexibility of NTFP livelihood strategies also derives from the fact that UP gatherers are largely in control of the timing, duration and quantity of their harvesting activities. That this is the case for products that will be consumed directly, given as gifts, or used to make crafts and food stuffs for sale may be obvious. However, a similar level of control prevails when a product is being harvested for bulk sale in a raw form. This level of autonomy makes NTFP strategies compatible with other activities and responsibilities, a characteristic that may be especially important for women with children.

Several sources report that, as a rule, gatherers who sell raw NTFPs are seeking to meet a specific need or desire. Frequently mentioned goals were money for holiday celebrations, annual real-estate taxes and vehicle expenses. Once gatherers arrive at their monetary goals they generally stop harvesting. A number of buyers reported that raising the price paid for products resulted in their obtaining less rather than more because gatherers arrived at their goal sooner. In cases where more than one buyer in the region purchases a product, gatherers' status as independent contractors also leaves them free to choose their buyers. Interestingly, more than one individual indicated that price was not the sole determinant of their preferred buyer. Rather, they indicated that they sold to the buyer who treated them with respect and/or with whom they had a long-standing reciprocal relationship.

Market logic, certification programmes and NTFP subsistence uses

As a market-based initiative, NTFP certification relies upon formal economic logic and structures to achieve its environmental and social goals. Not surprisingly, then, proposals for certification programmes dedicate intensive efforts to rationalizing and regulating NTFP production by identifying each step from forest to consumer and specifying measurable ecological and market indicators of compliance. Emphasis is also placed on developing sustained markets for products, as well as guarantees of exclusive access to them that will maximize returns to producers over the long term and, presumably, create disincentives for unsustainable harvests in the short term.

Numerous contradictions lurk in the characteristics of the formal market, NTFP certification programmes and subsistence uses. The drive to specify who has access to products in a given location is likely to privilege those who are identified as gatherers at the time such terms are set and exclude those who are not, thus reducing the temporal flexibility of NTFP subsistence uses. The designation of areas reserved for subsistence gathering may place the resources beyond the reach of individuals with limited mobility and/or concentrate previously extensive activities such that they become unsustainably intensive (McLain and Jones, 1997). The introduction of market strategies to create demand and produce sustained revenues for both capital investors and the state can be expected to engender efforts to control the terms of labour in order to maximize profits. This process might well convert independent contractors into wage labourers, reducing gatherers' ability and incentive to stop harvesting when they achieve their personal goals or feel that the resource necessitates it. It also raises the specter of previously traditional practices being converted into criminal offenses. Finally, NTFP certification documents generally propose negotiations with local communities to set the terms of programmes in specific areas. Yet, criteria and indicators for assessing local communities and the internal dynamics of NTFP use do not appear to be spelled out with anything approaching the detail devoted to ecological and economic issues, such as chain of custody. As Neumann and others have pointed out, communities are not harmonious, egalitarian units and negotiations with outside entities are often captured by local elites (Neumann, 1996; Peluso, 1992). Given that subsistence gatherers are typically among the least powerful members of their communities, a naive faith in undifferentiated community participation is unlikely to protect their interests.

Certification and subsistence use: conclusion

Even when it involves exchange uses, the most striking feature of NTFP subsistence practices is their location outside of the formal market. It is precisely this position that makes NTFPs a continuously viable resource for individuals who are let down by the market. The return to their labour has immediate survival benefits. Where products have not entered the intensive commodity market, there is minimal competition for the resource and little or no investment is required beyond time and effort. Certification programmes introduced to such areas run a high risk of introducing the contradictions between market processes and subsistence uses of NTFPs, to the detriment of the latter. The introduction and/or strengthening of market processes can be reasonably expected to introduce or strengthen market forces, such as the competition for scarce resources. The likely result is the displacement of people from spaces (both geographic and economic) that they had previously occupied.

However, where NTFPs have been heavily commoditized, market processes may already jeopardize subsistence uses, and appropriately designed certification programmes might be used to provide some protection for them. There may be opportunities for certification programmes to do so when focused upon products that have long-standing exchange value and do not have a traditionally important use value where they are harvested (eg many floral/nursery/craft items in the UP). In such instances, programmes may provide some protection for subsistence use by including provisions to secure continued access for gatherers without formalized tenure, to reinforce gathering norms and to preserve gatherers' control over the terms of their labour.

Realization of such benefits will require certifiers to value and make space for NTFP uses outside of the formal market. At least one certification initiative (Fairtrade) stresses equity for forest workers in the distribution of NTFP benefits. While this represents an encouraging recognition of social values in relation to ecological and economic considerations, to the extent that it assumes standard labour–capital relationships, this emphasis is unlikely to protect subsistence gatherers' interests. Instead, certification programmes should begin with social inventories that parallel ecological inventories in the depth and vigour with which they seek to document all existing NTFP uses and users. Furthermore, they must specify criteria for monitoring and evaluating the social results of certification programmes with the same level of detail currently dedicated to biophysical and market dynamics. With such additions, certification programmes might counteract some of the inherent contradictions between market forces and subsistence use of NTFPs.

Notes

1 The author wishes to thank the US Department of Agriculture (USDA) Forest Service, Northern Global Change Programme for support of the research on which this case study is based.
2 Gifts have important survival benefits because they help to create and maintain social networks that may be called upon in times of need.
3 Native American gatherers trying to observe traditional practices were the only individuals who reported using birch bark for medicinal purposes. Their norms expressly prohibit the sale of medicines. Thus, their livelihood uses were intentionally confined to personal consumption and gift-giving.
4 Fictitious names are used to protect the identity of gatherers.
5 However, it is unlikely that this norm, or any norm, is observed at all times by all people.

The interface of timber and non-timber resources: declining resources for subsistence livelihoods (Brazil)

Patricia Shanley, Leda Luz and Margaret Cymerys[1]

Introduction

For rural and urban populations world-wide, non-timber forest resources meet crucial subsistence needs and play vital roles in local and regional trade. Non-timber forest products (NTFPs) are often gathered out of necessity; they offer sustenance in times of food deficit, protection from agricultural shortfalls, and oppor-

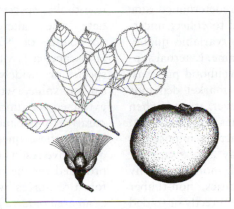

Illustration by Antônio Valente da Silva

*Piquiá (*Caryocar villosum*)*

tunities for less advantaged groups such as women and children (Arnold and Ruiz-Pérez, 1996). In spite of the essential role that NTFPs occupy in fulfilling the nutritional and health needs of the rural and urban poor, governmental agencies and policy-makers have customarily demonstrated scant interest in subsistence and local uses of non-timber forest products. During the last decade, however, aid agencies and environmental sectors have shown circumspect interest in non-timber forest products through their promotion in national and international trade.

The increased attention given to NTFPs is, in part, due to favourable projections of financial gain from the trade of specific species documented during the

1980s and 1990s (Peters et al, 1989; Balick and Mendel-sohn, 1992; Plotkin and Famolare, 1992; Clay and Clement, 1993; Wollenberg and Ingles, 1998). Studies of the potential economic value of non-timber forest products offered hope that the harvest of non-wood resources from the forest could present an economically promising alternative to logging. While possibly beneficial in select scenarios, market-based conservation incentives that promote NTFPs generally overlook the inestimable worth of subsistence and local trade of NTFPs worldwide.

For gatherers of non-timber forest resources who occupy marginal niches in society, the assumption that increased trade in NTFPs to global markets is likely to be favourable may be erroneous. Many gatherers face substantial difficulties accessing local, much less national or international, markets. In *terra firme* (upland dry) forests of Amazonia, for example, low resource density, unpredictable fruiting, inconsistent production, lack of transportation, perishable products and insufficient knowledge about market prices generally place gatherers at a conspicuous disadvantage in the marketplace (Phillips, 1993; Pendelton, 1992).

Furthermore, cultural and socio-economic characteristics of subsistence livelihoods render them inherently contradictory to the formal market economy (Crook and Clapp, 1998; Emery, 1998; Pierce, 1999). Whereas industries generally require large quantities of products of a certain quality in a predetermined time frame, forest users tend to collect uncertain volumes of highly variable quality during a flexible time frame. External support may alter these livelihood patterns, molding them to meet market demands more effectively. However, if and when external support vanishes, organizational and socio-economic structures imposed by the external system may also disappear. For these reasons and more, in many isolated rural communities, non-timber forest resources are used directly or traded locally, but rarely sold to external markets.

By contrast, timber is easily sold. Loggers show up with cash in hand, extract trees and haul them away. Although the money offered might be meager, for a majority of rural Amazonians, sale of timber rights to logging companies offers a singular means to acquire a lump sum of cash. In a cash-poor economy, the detrimental consequences of forest disturbance, such as decreased abundance of game, fruit, fibres and medicinals, accrue over time and are rarely considered prior to sales.

Given the importance of non-timber forest resources to subsistence livelihoods, the increased rate of logging in Amazonia, and the pronounced overlap of timber and non-timber species, it is important to evaluate the altered composition and abundance of NTFPs. In this changing landscape, it is vital to understand which species are widely utilized for their non-timber value, which NTFP species are extracted for timber and what their comparative timber and non-timber value is. To answer these questions, quantitative and qualitative results of a seven-year study are provided on the use of plant and animal forest resources by 30 households residing in an area of *terra firme* (upland dry) forest undergoing selective logging. This case study offers a better understanding of the potential role of certification for locally valued NTFPs, particularly the growing number of species that, at one time sourced primarily for medicines and fruits, are currently felled for their timber.

Research site and methods

Trade in oils, pelts, latex and game thrived along Amazon River tributaries in the Brazilian state of Pará in eastern Amazonia from the last half of the 19th century until the 1960s. During the 1970s and 1980s, the expansion of the region's timber trade, increasing sale of agricultural produce and growing use of substitute products brought about a sharp decline in the region's national and international trade of non-timber forest products. Within 150 kilometres (km) of sawmills, logs became the principal market commodity extracted from the region's forests.

Since the 1970s, many villages in remote settings of Pará have been presented with a new forest-based income opportunity. Road networks constructed during the 1960s and 1970s have allowed the timber and cattle industries to penetrate formerly inaccessible areas. Although timber companies offer a fraction of what processed wood is eventually sold for, this meager sum (US$2–US$15 per tree) represents an enticing offer in a cash-poor economy. Currently, in times of agricultural shortfall, resource deterioration, illness or need, villagers in forested areas within the proximity of sawmills tend to market not NTFPs but trees.

Today, in rural regions throughout Pará, villagers persist in extracting game, fruits, fibres and medicinals from forests for subsistence use and derive income from the sale of agricultural produce, such as *farinha* (a non-perishable, cassava-based flour), bananas, corn, rice and squash. Field research presented in this case study was conducted in three rural communities, collectively occupying 3000 hectares of selectively logged forest and agricultural land along the Capim River. The communities are composed of *caboclos* (rural peasant farmers of mixed descent) who have occupied the land for close to a century.

Results are derived from an ethnobotanical forest inventory, marketing surveys, five year study of the production/yield of three fruit species and NTFP consumption studies. From 1993 to 1994, the volumes of fruit, fibre and game used by 30 households were counted and weighed daily. From 1994 to 1999, during three consecutive logging episodes, participant observation, studies of fruit production/yield and interviews were used to estimate levels of consumption of fruit, fibre and game.

Regionally important NTFPs

To understand the impact of the timber industry on the subsistence use of non-timber forest products, it is necessary, first, to examine which are the NTFPs of greatest local value and to determine whether they occur in mature forest or fallow. The composition of NTFPs, of course, varies greatly by region; this section describes those with a fairly wide distribution throughout eastern Amazonia, specifically in the *terra firme* forest, which makes up over 50 per cent of Amazonia. Notably, the species most valued locally had received scant scientific study.

Within *terra firme* forests of the region studied, the most highly valued fruits are sourced from mature forest and include piquiá, (*Caryocar villosum*), uxi (*Endopleura uchi*), bacuri (*Platonia insig-nis*), jatobá (*Hymenaea courbaril*) and sapucáia (Lecythis pisonis). The bright yellow, oily flesh of piquiá contains a substantial amount of vitamin A, often lacking in Amazonia diets. The sweet white pulp of bacuri is eaten straight from the tree or used in the preparation of juices and desserts. The oily, grainy texture and high caloric value of the pulp of the egg-shaped fruit of uxi is also highly esteemed. In the city of Belém, uxi is one of the favourite popsicle flavours. The nut of sapucáia (similar to Brazil nut) offers protein to both humans and animals.

While forest fruit is directly eaten and adds critical nutrition to diets, these forest fruit trees offer another enormous advantage to subsistence livelihoods – they attract game. For example, the pale yellow, protein-rich flowers of piquiá 'call'

Table 28.3 *Medicinal tree species extracted as timber, Pará, Brazil*

Species	Common name	Use
Copaifera spp.	Copaíba	Deep wounds, 'nature's antibiotic'
Carapa guianensis	Andiroba	Sprains, rheumatism, insect repellent
Dipteryx odorata	Cumaru	Rheumatism, muscular pains
Himatanthus sucuuba	Sucuúba	Worms, herpes, uterine infection
Hymenaea coubaril	Jatobá	Tonic, flu, expectorant
Paraharcornia spp.	Amapá	Respiratory diseases, tonic
Tabebuia spp.	Pau d'arco	Inflammations, tumors, ulcers
Virola michelii	Ucuuba	Fever, hepatis, cicatrizant

over three times more game than any other species in the region. During the three- to four-month fruiting season of uxi, hunters place traps beneath the branches of the tree in order to catch game that arrive to feast on the oily fruit. Some hunters are so successful they daily dine on armadillo, a tremendous contribution to the family diet. Game capture by one Amazonian community of 30 families over the course of one year demonstrated the importance of primary forest as a source of game: approximately 80 per cent of game came from mature or logged forest, with the remaining 20 per cent captured in fallow, fields, marshes and river habitats.

Hunters weave fibres into sling-like carriers to carry game home from long hunts. Fibres are a fundamental material used not only in hunting but also in nearly all aspects of everyday life, used to make brooms, baskets, sieves, backpacks, fences, lashing material, fasteners and fishing traps. Principal fibres used in the region include titica (*Heteropsis jenmanii*) and timboaçu (*Thoracocarpus bissecta*), epiphytes harvested from mature forest.

Due to long distances to reach health care, lack of funds to expend on pharmaceutical products, and a long history of plant-based knowledge, Amazonians make use of a wide variety of medicinal plants, many of which are now extracted by the timber industry (see Table 28.3). Although many medicinals are sourced from fallows and gardens, the popular Amazonian medicinals listed above are sourced from forests.

Direct impact of logging on NTFPs

Thirty years ago, the relationship between villagers and loggers was a relatively symbiotic one – a timber sale did not appear to significantly damage a villager's forest. A handful of up to 20 high-value timber species was selectively extracted from area forests, pulled out by men and floated downstream. Villagers obtained cash and a cleared soccer field, without loss of the fruits, fibres, medicinals and game-attract-ing species that they relied upon for subsistence use. In the late 1980s, as stocks of the most highly valued timber declined in the immediate vicinity of sawmills, loggers began to extract an ever-growing number of species at ever-greater distances.

Currently, of the 15 most highly valued non-timber resources in the Capim region (ranked according to the methods of Prance et al, 1987), all are targeted by

Table 28.4 *Fifteen of the most useful tree species (> 10cm dbh) to caboclos of the Capim River, Brazil, in a 1ha forest plot (200m x 50m)*

Species	Common name	Use
Caryocar villosum	Piquiá	A, B, E, G
Platonia insignis	Bacuri	A, B, d, E, g
Endopleura uchi	Uxi	A, b, E, G
Copaifera spp.	Copaíba	b, D, E, G
Lecythis pisonis	Sapucaia	a, b, d, E, G
Hymenaea parvifolia	Jutai	a, d, E, G
Brosimum acutifolium	Mururé	b, D, f, G
Manilkara huberi	Maçaranduba	a, B, d, e, g
Couratari guianensis	Tauari	c, E, f, G
Manilkara amazonica	Maparajuba	a, B, e, g
Eschweilera coriaceae	Maturi	b, c, d, e, g
Manilkara paraensis	Maçaranduba	a, B, e, g
Virola michelii	Ucuúba	b, D, E
Dipteryx odorata	Cumaru	b, D, E
Eschweilera grandiflora	Mata mata ci	b, d, e, G
Licania heteromorpha	Caraipé	B, c, e, g

Note: Upper case indicates major use value; lower case indicates minor use value.
A or a = food. B or b = construction.
C or c = technology. D or d = remedy.
E or e = commerce. F or f = other use.
G or g = animal food.

the timber industry (see Table 28.4). These include each of the fruit and medicinal species described above, as well as species used for technological purposes (signifying items such as resins, gums, fibres, dyes and inner barks). Examination of the list reveals not only species directly used as food, but also game-attracting species that indirectly contribute substantially to rural diets (Shanley, 2000).

To place these results in a wider regional perspective, during the last three decades in eastern Amazonia, the number of species extracted by loggers has escalated from a select few to over 300 (see Figure 28.5). Of the 300 species currently logged in eastern Amazonia, one third are also valued for food, medicines and/or gums and resins (Martini et al, 1994). Moreover, while secondary forest species offer substantial fruit, fibre and medicinals in other regions of Latin America, many of the principal fruit, fibre, game-attracting and medicinal species used in the study region are sourced from mature forest.

In a longitudinal study of the volume of extractive products consumed pre- and post-logging events in three eastern Amazonian forest communities, results demonstrated that in 1993, even after several logging events, households continued to consume substantial volumes of game, fruit and fibre (Shanley, 2000). Six years later, in 1999, after three additional logging episodes and fire, average volumes of game, fruit and fibre dropped drastically (see Figure 28.6). Villagers accustomed to consuming hundreds of forest fruits during the four-month fruiting season in the early 1990s complained that they had not consumed wild fruit the entire year and that fibres for constructing fundamental household implements such as brooms and baskets were no longer accessible. The findings underscore that there is a

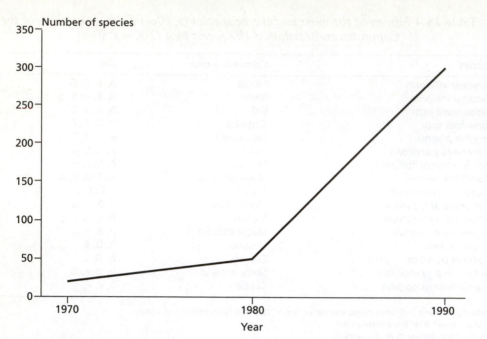

Source: Veríssimo et al, 1992; Martini et al, 1994

Figure 28.5 *Number of species extracted by the timber industry in eastern Amazonia, Pará, Brazil*

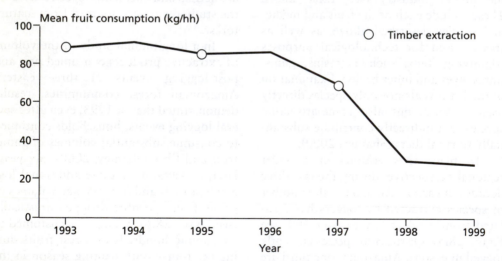

Source: Shanley, 2000

Figure 28.6 *Fruit consumption in three Capin River communities, Pará, Brazil*

critical limit to the volume of timber that can be extracted from forests, after which present and future harvests of non-timber resources plummet.

Indirect impact of logging on NTFPs

Depending upon the equipment used and the number of hectares of forest logged, logging episodes in the Capim Basin lasted between two months and two years. Today, logging roads penetrate forests, trucks or bulldozers extract trees and 16-wheelers or large barges carry logs to nearby cities. Communities suffer not only because of the loss of the species upon which they rely for their livelihoods, but also because of the substantial collateral damage associated with predatory timber extraction.

In Amazonia, logging operations that aimed to extract one tree damaged 16 more trees that were > 10 centimetres (cm) diameter at breast height (dbh). During selective logging, tree felling per hectare damaged 124 trees (Johns et al, 1996). Canopy cover can be reduced by close to one half in such logging events (Uhl and Vieira, 1989). Collateral damage associated with tree harvesting, such as seedling destruction, soil compaction, top-soil removal and soil erosion, directly affect present and future harvests of both timber and non-timber forest products (Laird, 1995).

After logging events, animal and plant resources are not only less abundant, but more distant and inconvenient to extract. Once collected within only 1 kilometre (km) of their homes, residents of many regions must now search for fibres and fruits at distances of 3–10km. Deep-flooded tractor tracks, felled trees and thick secondary growth filling tree-fall gaps and logging roads obstruct passage through the forest and obscure vision, making harvest of perishable products particularly difficult.

In addition to collateral damage, selectively logged forests burn easily because timber extraction creates conditions that favour fire by opening the canopy to solar radiation, by drying slash and by increasing the fuel load on the forest floor (Uhl and Kaufman, 1990; Cochrane et al, 1999). For example, following closely on the heels of a logging event in the Capim Basin, two accidental fires raged for close to one month, burning an estimated one third of one community's forest. Fruit trees that had been deliberately spared from logging caught fire, causing fruit to fall prematurely. The open nature of the logged, burned forest permitted winds to move swiftly through the landscape, blowing down 100-year-old fruit trees. In addition to such immediate effects of fire and logging, some valuable species do not regenerate readily after fire; these include the medicinal oil trees andiroba and copaíba, the game-attracting fruit tree uxi, and the most commonly utilized forest fibre, titica.

In spite of the crucial significance of floral non-timber resources, for many forest peoples, fauna is the non-wood resource of greatest value. However, due to habitat loss, fire and overhunting, game populations in many regions are severely depleted. Whereas a decade ago in the Capim River Basin game was consumed weekly, for some households consumption is now as infrequent as a few times a year.

Timber certification: its potential impact on regionally and locally important NTFPs

To understand the potential impact of timber certification on non-timber forest products, let us look at the products described above in eastern Amazonia. Of the scores of products utilized within the region, very few reach an international market. Consumers of açaí wine, bacuri ice cream, marapuama root and andiroba oil have no need of, or interest in, a 'green' label. In fact, these products are often purchased in their crude form, bearing no label at all. The culture, health and dietary customs of eastern Amazonians habituate them to consume forest products independent of their source. For example, marketers state that the intestines of Paraenses (Pará residents) require açaí; babies imbibe the palm fruit drink at six months of age, and by adulthood, consumption of 3 litres a day of the thick, purple drink is not uncommon.

While certification of these products is unlikely to be useful within the region, certification of the forests from where they come (in the event of timber extraction) most certainly could be. For example, andiroba oil (*Carapa guianensis*) is one of the most popularly consumed medicinals in urban and rural areas of Amazonia. Heavily logged, its numbers are in decline, prohibiting its use by many rural villagers who previously depended upon it as an insect repellant and remedy for bruises, sprains and rheumatism. Uxi (*Endopeura uchi*) is a tree bearing a distinctly flavoured fruit utilized in the ice cream and juice industries. Eluding domestication, it is still largely gathered

from wild sources. Occurring in densities of only 0.3–3.0 trees per ha in mature forests, its value as a timber species has precipitated its decline in particular regions. These and many other fruit and medicinal oil species are not only important for the nutrition and health care of the rural and urban poor, but may offer a greater economic value standing than cut (Shanley et al, 1998).

But would a certification assessment team entering a forest where andiroba and bacuri are being extracted know that these and additional species (eg copaíba, sucuúba, piquiá, uxi, amapa) hold important economic value locally and are regionally in decline? Most likely, not. While NTFPs are mentioned in the Forest Stewardship Council (FSC) principles, the concept is not elaborated upon. As with any certification assessment, attention, or lack thereof, to non-timber products would depend upon the make-up of the assessment team. Since few individuals sufficiently understand the ecology or socio-economics of non-timber forest products, chances are that these resources would be inadequately represented during an assessment. Although lack of attention to non-timber forest products need not concern a Northern consumer who purchases 'certified' tropical timber to construct a garden bench, it can most certainly have lasting and detrimental effects on local populations who rely upon forest products for rudimentary health care and nutrition.

Recognizing regionally and locally valued NTFPs

If regionally valuable NTFPs are identified and singled out for conservation, would this not negatively impact overall timber production? Perhaps, not. In fact, in upland forests of Amazonia, due to the low densities at which many non-timber forest products occur (less than one per ha), conservation of important NTFP species need not significantly reduce timber output. Within 1 hectare in the Capim region, for example, less than two to three trees per hectare might be singled out as particularly important game-attracting, fruit or medicinal oil trees in need of active conservation. However, to date, negotiations between loggers and smallholders have been largely uninformed, resulting in timber extraction methods that neglect to consider the basic nutrition and health-care needs of forest-based communities. A full assessment of the relative value and contribution of the forests' timber and non-timber resources to the region's economic, nutritional and health status is needed.

To conduct certification assessments more adequately, assessors need to be familiar not only with species listed in the Convention on International Trade in Endangered Species of Wild Fauna and Flora (CITES), but with species used by local populations to meet their subsistence and regional marketing needs. Integration of NTFPs into timber certification programmes could have a geographically broad impact. In order to accomplish this, harvesters and regional experts might work together to develop broad-based, region-specific lists of species that are widely utilized and may be vulnerable to logging, overharvest or other land-use or market changes. If the certification movement pursues these goals, it has an opportunity to not only improve timber certification processes, but to promote ecologically and socially sustainable management of forests. With such improvements, certification will strengthen its social mission, conserving woodlands not only for the interests of Northern environmentalists, but for the interests of rural people who, out of bare necessity, daily depend upon the forests.

Notes

1   This study would not have been possible without the patient collaboration and hard work of over 30 Capim River families and research assistants Jurandir Galvão, Gloria Gaia and Gabriel Medina. The authors would like to thank the US Agency for International Development (USAID/GCC), the Educational Foundation of America, the Earth Love Fund and the International Center for Research on Women for support to conduct the research on which this case study was based. The research was begun with the Woods Hole Research Center and completed in collaboration with the Amazon Institute of People and Environment (IMAZON) and the Center for International Forestry Research (CIFOR).

Chapter 29

Marketing issues

Sarah A Laird and Abraham Guillén

Introduction

The focus of this chapter is on the minority of non-timber forest products (NTFPs) found in international trade. These include Brazil nut (*Bertholletia excelsa*), palm heart (various spp.), chicle (*Manilkara zapota*), rattan (various spp.) and a wide range of medicinals. Earlier chapters have made clear that NTFPs are most important in local and regional markets and for subsistence use, with communities who live in and around forests often relying upon a range of products with economic, medical, nutritional and cultural value. However, certification is a valuable tool only in cases where products are traded in volume and to consumers receptive to the objectives certifiers promote through their labels, primarily those in developed countries.

The types of industries into which NTFPs feed, the size of these industries

Illustration by Bee Gunn

*Yohimbe (*Pausinystalia johimbe*)*

and the scale of trade in individual products varies significantly (see Table 29.1). For example, the International Tropical Timber Organization (ITTO, 1997) estimated the international rattan market at US$6.5 billion. The 1996 global trade in more than 440,000 tonnes of medicinal and aromatic plant material to pharmaceutical, botanical medicine, food and flavouring, cosmetic, cleaning product, insecticide and other industries was valued at US$1.3 billion (Lange, 1998). Worldwide sales of commercial botanical medicine products, dominated by European and Asian markets, average around US$20 billion a year (Gruenwald, 1998; 1999). However, any single medicinal plant product is unlikely to generate sales of more than a few hundred million dollars, and most sell for less than US$10 million per year. Most individual NTFPs have relatively small annual turnovers. Annual cork (*Quercus suber*) sales come to around US$240 million (see Chapter 17); palm heart (various spp.) exports from Boliva in 1997 came to just over US$12 million (see Chapter 6); wild American ginseng (*Panax quinquefolius*) sales in 1993 totalled US$25 million (see Chapter 16); and maple syrup (*Acer sacharum*) sales in the US in 1998 were US$32 million (see Chapter 15).

Incorporating NTFPs into market-based conservation strategies

NTFPs are important for local livelihoods and the harvest of many species has relatively less impact on forest habitats than other land uses such as logging and clearing for agriculture. As a result, NTFP marketing and management strategies are often incorporated within conservation and development programmes. These programmes seek to develop sustainable livelihoods and alternative incomes for local communities, thereby reducing pressure on forests – with mixed results over the years (Crook and Clapp, 1998). Some projects work on a local level to develop sustainable management and local marketing strategies for highly threatened and/or valuable species. Others have focused on international markets for NTFPs, seeking to improve corporate relationships with raw material sources and to increase benefits for local communities.

The ways in which international markets are incorporated within conservation and development programmes vary, and local groups' ability to benefit from commodification of NTFPs varies widely by product and type of market (Arnold and Ruiz-Pérez, 1996). For example, during the late 1980s and 1990s, conservation groups such as Cultural Survival (CS) and Conservation International (CI) began to act as brokers between communities and international companies such as Ben and Jerry's (ice cream) and Croda Inc (personal care products and cosmetics) (Clay, 1992;

Morris and Laird, 1999). In other cases, companies have established direct partnerships with community groups in order to ensure that a larger portion of raw material sourcing and processing benefits those living in areas from which products derive. In many cases, the aim was also to build higher-quality and more affordable sources of raw material. Nature's Way struggled for a number of years to strike an agreement with groups in Vietnam to source a 'new' ginseng species, *Panax vietnamensis* (Laird and Burningham, 1999). Aveda Corporation collaborates with the Yawanawa community of Acre, Brazil, to source *Bixa orellana* (annatto) – a natural colourant used in lipsticks, shampoos and other products (Waddington and Laird, 1999). The Body Shop has established partnerships to source raw materials such as Brazil nut oil, shea butter and blue corn with community groups around the world as part of its Community Trade Programme.

In another approach, conservation and social rights organizations have launched certification and labelling schemes to promote sustainably and ethically sourced forest products (Pierce, 1999). Certification and labelling of NTFPs comprise a viable strategy for only a few of the 'charismatic' forest products with high profiles and significant international markets. These include, for example, Brazil nut, chicle, palm heart, rattan and medicinal species such as pygeum (*Prunus africana*), yohimbe (*Pausinystalia johimbe*) and cat's claw (*Uncaria tomentosa* and *U. guianensis*). Furthermore, certification and labelling will be effective only in cases where social and political conditions allow local communities to capture the increased economic benefits generated by certification. For those few species managed in appropriate social, ecological and political contexts, and with adequate international markets, however, certification can help harness market forces to serve sustainable and equitable management and trade.

Certification can be used not only as a tool to develop economic alternatives for local communities – and thereby potentially help forest conservation indirectly – but also to ameliorate negative impacts of international trade on species' survival. In many cases, the wild harvest of NTFPs for international markets is unsustainable. This has proven most dramatically the case for botanical medicine species such as pygeum, devil's claw (*Harpagophytum procumbens*), echinacea (*Echinacea* spp.), golden seal (*Hydrastis canadensis*) and pau d'arco (*Tabebuia* spp.). Some of these species – such as golden seal and pygeum – have made their way onto Appendix II of the Convention on International Trade in Endangered Species of Wild Fauna and Flora (CITES). Other species are victims of the boom-bust cycle created by media-driven sales, in which they are replaced in the market by the next 'hot' herb just as local producers come online with large quantities of raw material (eg *Griffonia simplicifolia* – see Chapter 18). If not replaced, however, demand over time can significantly erode wild populations. Demand for pygeum, echinacea and golden seal, for example, has diminished wild populations over many years. Although cultivation is underway, threats to wild populations continue.

The World Conservation Union's (IUCN's) Species Survival Commission (SSC) Medicinal Plant Specialist Group, and organizations such as the Rocky Mountain Herbalist Coalition and United Plant Savers in the US, are studying and developing guidelines for threatened medicinal plant species in trade. A multipronged strategy is required for those species most threatened, incorporating efforts to domesticate species and develop standards for sustainable wild harvest. Certification is a valuable tool in these strategies, combining the creation and implementation of standards for sound management practices, as well as consumer education about the manner in which raw material is sourced, and rewarding the conscientious producer and company.

While certified products provide an important recourse for consumers who seek to purchase environmentally and socially sound products, certification programmes can also promote increased awareness and accountability within industry. In general, botanical medicine, personal care and cosmetic, food and beverage, and other industries marketing NTFPs are unaware of the conditions in which raw materials are sourced. A tradition of cheap raw materials, traded as bulk commodities, persists, leaving limited room for exploring sustainable and equitable practices. However, sustainability and equity in sourcing are within the scientific, financial and logistical reach of most companies. Incentives can be created and pressure brought to bear on internationally marketed products through a combination of approaches that include consumer awareness campaigns, innovative brokering, technical assistance to domesticate or sustainably wildcraft species, and the certification and labelling of sustainable and fairtrade products.

Marketing issues to consider before undertaking certification of NTFPs

There are a number of reasons why managers choose to obtain certification. The decision to undergo a certification evaluation requires strategic choices based upon best available information. Managers should consider the following marketing issues before engaging the services of a certifying agency.

Information needed to evaluate existing markets

Is the product already marketed?

'All things being equal, start with products already being produced and that have markets' (Clay, 1996). Launching new products onto the market is a difficult and risky undertaking. Certification is most valuable as a tool to promote improved management of existing products, thereby reducing risks incurred by local groups.

Marketing information

Certification is a market-based tool. It is therefore critical that market information flows to all involved stakeholders. For example, chicle producers in Quintana Roo, Mexico, certified by the SmartWood Project in 1999 work in partnership with one company – Wild Things – but need market outlets for their remaining chicle. The more market information that can be supplied to local groups through the certification process (eg price, distribution channels, product quality demands and companies with potential interest), the better they can market their product.

Recent history of market's stability

It is important to understand the fluctuations in a product's history before embarking upon a costly international marketing and certification scheme. Have price and demand remained steady, decreased or increased over the past 5 years, 10 years, 20 years? How elastic is demand?

Know your market: the type of international markets into which products feed

International trade in NTFPs supplies a wide range of industries, each with its own research, manufacturing, and marketing requirements. Pharmaceuticals, botanical medicines, cosmetics, and food and beverage industries are just a few of the sectors that widely use NTFPs. It is critical that certification programmes incorporate the unique features of the industries into which they feed, and where possible assist in diversifying markets for raw materials. The botanical medicine industry today, for example, is often fickle and trend driven (eg griffonia, pau d'arco and cat's claw); and labels in the food industry would most likely need to incorporate organic and quality-control concerns (eg chicle, palm heart and Brazil nut).

Relationship between markets and local use

What local, regional or international markets do products feed into, and what is the relationship between markets; how finely is this balanced? Could certification of products for international markets increase demand in such a way that supplies for local markets and subsistence use are significantly reduced?

For example, in Brazil, marapuama (*Ptychopetalum olacoides*) is an increasingly popular botanical medicine, used to treat nervous disorders and impotence. But marapuama is a low-density species with an unknown ecology, and harvesting of the root is highly destructive. A surge in international demand for this species, in part as a 'natural Viagra', may decrease availability of marapuama in local markets and threaten wild populations (see Box 26.1 in Chapter 26).

Information needed to evaluate threats, challenges, barriers and competition

Availability of substitutes and alternatives

In the early stages, certification schemes incorporate a premium to cover the increased costs of sustainable management incurred by local groups. Groups must be aware of pricing and other issues that inform the private sector and consumer selection of products for purchase. If possible, certified products should not be priced out of the mainstream market. In any case, a product's marketing niche and relationship to synthetic and alternative products should be well understood.

Natural chicle, for example, propelled the modern chewing gum industry in the late 19th century, and by the mid 20th century chicle extraction was the most important industry in the Yucatan Peninsula of Mexico and the Petén region of Guatemala.

By 1960, however, petroleum-based gum had replaced natural chicle, and today only a limited demand for natural chicle exists (see Chapter 4). In addition, because prices for synthetic gum are a fraction of those for natural chicle, chicle must be marketed in alternative niche markets.

Alternative sources of raw material

It is important to understand the nature of raw material sources against which certified products and material will compete. NTFPs in trade take the form of both complete products (eg palm hearts, Brazil nuts, pine nuts (various spp.) and maple syrup) and raw material that will act as ingredients or components of commercial products (eg *Bixa orellana* as a colourant for cosmetics). Many of these products are traded as bulk commodities today (eg Brazil nuts and medicinal plants). While a significant portion continue to be harvested from the forest, international demand for consistency in quality and supply often leads to large-scale cultivation of high-value NTFP species. Large investments have been made in the search for low-cost material, for example, in efforts to cultivate the pharmaceutical compound-yielding forest species *Pilocarpus jaborandi* and *Taxus brevifolia*; the colourant *Bixa orellana*; botanical medicine species such as croton (*Croton lechleri*), ginseng (*Panax* spp.), cat's claw, devil's claw, golden seal and echinacea; and other species covered in this manual such as rattan and palm heart.

It is likely that increased commercial demand will create incentives for large-scale commercial agriculture to enter the market. If certification is successful, and larger quantities of materials are sought, what are the chances that small producers will be squeezed out by bigger competitors? How can the role of smaller producers in such a case be bolstered?

Logistical and infrastructure issues

Sustainable management of NTFPs in natural forests is only part of the certification equation. NTFPs also raise a number of issues associated with transport, processing, storage and associated infrastructure that should be incorporated within a certification programme. How perishable is the product, and do means exist to transport it efficiently to intended markets? What potential exists to add value locally to products? Can post-harvest losses be reduced and, therefore, yields and income increased? What are the estimated costs, time, equipment and infrastructure necessary to scale-up management and processing of products to serve expanded markets? Because NTFPs represent a diverse range of products, these questions cannot be answered in a generalized fashion – as they might be, say, for timber. The many ways in which NTFPs can contribute to local livelihoods, and the diverse roles local groups can play in adding value and preparing products for market, should be assessed and incorporated within a certification programme.

Producers must have the capacity and infrastructure in place to provide products with consistent quality and reliable quantities over time (eg Brazil nuts with acceptable levels of aflatoxin). It is not only the product itself that must live up to market standards, but also the services attached to its development and delivery. This often creates a 'Catch 22' situation, where the demands of large buyers for volume and high quality over time cannot be filled by smaller producers of sustainable material.

The legal and policy environment

Laws and policies often influence the success or failure of NTFP initiatives; therefore, an understanding of local, regional and international laws and policies is paramount. Some questions that should be answered include:

- Are local and national laws and policies conducive to creating comp-

etitively priced and processed certified materials?
- Is land tenure and access to resources by local groups secure?
- Do price controls or distortions exist that could dampen returns to local producers?
- Do mechanisms exist that allow local groups to benefit, ensuring that certification improves both management and local livelihoods?
- Will increased income attract taxation, which might prove prohibitive?
- Are incentives for other land uses too great to make NTFP management profitable over time?
- Will international trade policies (eg those set by the World Trade Organization – WTO) create obstacles to marketing products – or can they aid in marketing?
- Does the legal environment recognize local rights to control the use of, and benefit from, traditional knowledge?

Additional opportunities, challenges and strategies for utilizing certification

Niche versus mainstream markets

The intended market, potential buyers and consumers of products should be clearly identified from the start. Selling products to mainstream markets is probably beyond most NTFP producers, and in most cases 'green' or 'fairtrade' niche markets will be the most useful starting point. By carefully identifying and targeting appropriate niche markets, and partner companies, producers of certified NTFPs may enjoy increased market access, market share and possible market premiums. In timber certification, an ongoing problem has been the mismatch between supply and demand. Because no single NTFP producer can probably supply the needs of even a small company in the US, cooperatives and other ways to increase available volume should be investigated, in order to increase opportunities in both niche and mainstream markets (Clay 1996).

Processing

The potential to build local capacity through increased processing, in ways that meet international standards, should be assessed. Whether through innovative partnerships between communities, cooperatives or domestic companies, adding value locally should be emphasized and the provision of bulk raw material for overseas markets de-emphasized as projects develop.

For example, the Noh Bec *ejido* in Mexico is seeking to add value to their chicle by processing and producing ready-to-chew gum (see Chapter 3). Palm hearts are processed locally at the field site in Brazil (see Chapter 3). Clay (1997c) demonstrates the ways in which local producers might gain from investments made in processing. While harvesters receive US$0.03 per pound of Brazil nuts, by the time processors' profits (and costs, waste and spoilage) are factored in, the price per pound reaches US$0.70; taxes, customs and handling in Brazil bring the free-on-board (FOB) price to US$0.85 cents per pound.

Potential to market by-products

NTFPs often yield useful by-products that can be sold to local, regional or international markets. It is important to ask at the onset of certification whether by-products from processing have value, and if they could be certified and marketed. It is also important to note if by-products create environmental problems of their own.

Marketing channels and chain of custody

Chain of custody is a major challenge in the certification of NTFPs. NTFPs are often widely distributed, have decentralized harvest and trade patterns, and involve a large number of intermediaries. Chain-of-custody issues are central to marketing, as certified materials must be followed through the entire marketing process – a potentially expensive undertaking for NTFPs (see Chapter 30).

In order to identify how certification might operate most effectively, it is critical to understand the ways in which products make their way from the forest to markets. This would include the number and nature of intermediaries or wholesale traders, relationships between different parties, and the likely impact of certification on the existing web of involved groups. Although intermediaries are often portrayed negatively, they serve an important function and create opportunities for marketing that would otherwise not be available. Certification should not re-enforce exploitative relationships, but should also not seek to artificially replace those existing structures that fairly facilitate trade.

Relationship to other land uses and markets

Production of NTFPs for international markets should take place within the context of other land uses, and other uses for species, and should seek to diversify – rather than dominate – local economies and livelihoods. Certification and marketing of an NTFP should complement other economic activities, rather than squeezing them out; a package of products and sources of income should be the objective.

In cases where certification of timber is the objective, certification of NTFPs can help to provide additional income and incentives for sustainable forest management. For example, in the Noh Bec *ejido*, certification of chicle was seen as a valuable way to enhance income from the forest, which otherwise might derive only from timber, resulting in overexploitation of species that local groups now feel can be sustainably managed. It can also help to offset pressure to fell chicle trees for use as structural wood and flooring (see Chapter 3). Properly managed and marketed NTFPs can also out-compete more destructive uses of forests. For example, maple syrup may have the potential to yield greater returns on a per-hectare basis than timber in some areas (see Chapter 15).

In Pará state, Brazil, palm heart estates supply the international palm heart market – for which certification is a useful tool – as well as the more significant domestic market, which absorbs 85 per cent of production. Moreover, these estates also supply local markets with critically important açaí fruits worth an estimated US$30 million per month in the city of Belém during fruiting season (see Chapter 3). Well-managed palm hearts appear to be an ideal product for certification because there is a significant domestic market for the product, which minimizes producers' risks, as well as a 'secondary' product, açaí, that has tremendous local economic and nutritional value.

Can certification help promote products overseas?

If certifiers or other groups based in the home countries of potential consumers do not shoulder some responsibility for marketing certified products, then local producers will often be unable to sell the products they produce. In cases where commercial companies spur certification of products, and use labels to help promote and sell their products (eg Wild Things' Jungle Gum), certified NTFPs will be brought to the attention of consumers, who might then demand that other companies in an industry provide confirmation of the sustainability of their sources – thus creating a domino effect. But if producer groups request certification – for example, Brazil nut producers in Boliva (see Chapter 3) – a commitment from certifiers or other collaborators may be needed to help ensure that markets and interested companies are in place to purchase certified material, as well as to catalyse the process.

In the case of timber certification, buyers' groups largely undertook the marketing of the concept to consumers, led by large suppliers such as B&Q in the UK, who had committed to sell sustainably sourced timber. For certification to work, a long chain of events must come together, and marketing is a significant element. If all the pieces are not assembled, certification is unlikely to help local groups promote sustainably managed NTFPs. Given the diversity and range of products grouped under NTFPs, and the relatively small volume of NTFP trade, marketing will prove more challenging for this group than for timber.

There is also a great deal of national and regional variation in markets for certified products that must be incorporated within certified NTFP marketing strategies. European consumers generally appear more willing to pay more for fairtrade and environmentally sound products, such as chewing gum, Brazil nuts and palm heart, while US consumers are more sensitive to price variation and are less willing to pay premiums for certified products. US consumers respond well to products that are considered 'healthier' or 'health enhancing', however. NTFP marketing should therefore be tailored to the concerns and priorities of end-consumers.

What is driving certification?

Companies, producer groups and others seek certification for a range of reasons, which should be clarified at the start. Companies, for example, usually seek to differentiate themselves in the marketplace with eco-brands or certified products. If this is the case, will they ask, in return, for exclusivity? Will they help to link producers to other companies? The relationship between company and producer group should be clear from the start.

Some producer groups seek a premium in return for sustainable management, while other producers see certification as a way to access markets that they might otherwise lack the skills or contacts to reach. Although in some cases certification alone will lead to a premium for local producers and companies, it has been most effectively used to date as a tool to better market value-added products – thereby increasing value, not volume.

In some countries, local governments and consumers require that only certified sustainable and fairtrade material is locally used (eg city ordinances requiring use of, or preference for, certified wood in municipal construction contracts). The palm heart estate in Pará, Brazil (see Chapter 3), sought out certification in order to secure a bank loan for which the managers had to prove the production system was environmentally sound. The myriad of motivations underlying certification should be clarified by all involved parties – producer groups, certifiers, companies, governments, lending agencies, etc – before initiating the programme.

Combining information needs: the critical role of collaboration

Certification of some NTFPs may be achieved most effetively through a combination of social (fairtrade), organic and ecological/forest conservation standards. In addition, for medicinal products, information on quality and active constituents – increasingly addressed on product labels – should be integrated within the labelling, and sometimes field assessment, process. For food products, quality control is paramount. For example, European import regulations strictly control the aflatoxin (a mycotoxin) content of Brazil nuts, which is threatening the industry's viability in South America.

Representing these various issues will require collaboration among certifiers with expertise on different aspects of NTFP management and product development (as seen in the field assessments for chicle, palm heart and Brazil nuts), or the creation of a new breed of certifier that reflects and combines a wide range of concerns. Given the relatively low cost per volume of NTFPs, a series of relatively costly field assessments is unlikely to make sense (Scrase, 1999). Multi-disciplinary collaboration and sharing of perspectives will be critical in developing a workable field methodology, and transmitting a coherent message to consumers.

Conclusions and recommendations

- Efforts to link international marketing of NTFPs and conservation, including NTFP certification, are most useful for a small suite of internationally marketed products, and less valuable for locally and regionally consumed products, which make up the majority of NTFP use. This argues for complementary approaches to incorporate NTFPs within conservation and development programmes in which certification can act as one of a number of 'tools' to achieve programme objectives.

- In some domestic markets – for example, in most developed countries and in the case of woodcarvings sold to tourists in East Africa (see Chapter 25) – labels can prove useful. In most developing countries, however, the market for certified products is likely to remain small, and markets will need to be sought overseas in developed countries, particularly in Europe and North America. In some cases, locally or regionally developed labels may be effective, such as those used by the NeoSynthesis Research Institute in Sri Lanka and by cooperatives in the state of Acre, Brazil.

- Some species gain rapid popularity in international markets – eg marapuama, cat's claw and kava (*Piper methysticum*) – and certification efforts must take care not to exacerbate existing problems associated with sourcing shortages. Certification can educate consumers about the social and environmental problems associated with unsustainable sourcing, and encourage the purchase of sustainably managed products.

- Certification of NTFPs destined for medicinal plant, food and other industries should incorporate not only social (fairtrade), health (organic) and biodiversity conservation criteria, but also quality control (eg International Organization for Standardization – ISO) and Good Manufacturing Practices (GMP). Assessments can incorporate these issues for harvest, cultivation, processing, storage, handling and manufacture.

- Marketing of certified products will only prove effective if consumers are sufficiently educated about the problems associated with existing sources. If consumer demand is not sufficient, the expense of certification will not be warranted, and local producers could suffer from overly optimistic expectations of future markets. Certifiers and other groups should therefore ensure that their programmes include strong consumer awareness campaigns.

- Trade in NTFPs takes place within existing economic, marketing and political frameworks; if these are exploitative, it is possible that certification could re-enforce existing practices that draw benefits away from local groups, and fail to create economic incentives for biodiversity conservation. Certifiers serving wider conservation and development objectives must ensure that projects do not perpetuate existing exploitative practices.

Box 29.1 An industry perspective: Shaman Botanicals' view on the certification of NTFPs

Beto Borges and Steven R King

In principle, Shaman Botanicals views certification of non-timber forest products (NTFPs) very favourably. When the certification process as a whole is better defined and its requirements clearer, it is likely that Shaman will apply for certification of its supply of *Croton lechleri* latex – the raw material for our SB-Normal Stool Formula product – through a Forest Stewardship Council (FSC) accredited organization or its equivalent. The challenge for the FSC is to make NTFP certification an attractive incentive for both producers and consumers.

Obtaining certification may present important benefits to NTFP producers and industry alike. Perhaps the most important benefit of all, from a company's perspective, is the assurance of a minimal environmental impact on the target product and its associated species. Generally, responsible producers and industries are well aware of the need to manage their raw materials wisely. Wise management ensures that resources are not depleted and that harvesting does not cause environmental degradation, which would compromise future supply. However, few existing market mechanisms assist and support investments in sustainable sources.

Shaman Botanicals conducted extensive scientific studies to obtain sound baseline data on the primary ecological and biological characteristics of Croton lechleri over ten years. Some of these studies were recently published in *Desarrollando Nuestra Diversidad Biocultural: Sangre de Grado y el Reto de su Producción Sustentable en el Peru (Developing Our Biocultural Diversity: Sangre de Grado and the Challenge of its Sustainable Production in Peru)* by Peruvian forester and scientist Elsa Meza (1999c). This book discusses indepth biological, ecological, anthropological and legal aspects of *Croton lechleri*. The need to acquire scientific knowledge on this NTFP and to learn how to manage it in an ecologically sound way has been a significant component of our research and development process for *Croton lechleri*.

In addition to scientific research and publication, Shaman has been complying with all environmental regulations set forth by local governments, such as producing extensive and independent management plans and obtaining all necessary government permits. To further minimize environmental impacts, Shaman requires that producers replant three *Croton lechleri* trees for each one harvested. Shaman provides a financial incentive for the replanting of *Croton lechleri* by paying a value-added price for latex collected by conscientious harvesters. Shaman has also produced and distributed 5000 copies of a field manual on the sustainable management and reforestation of *Croton lechleri* and sponsored several community workshops about the species.

Evaluation of social impacts, operational accountability and benefit-sharing should be integral components of a good certification process. Shaman's local staff conduct regular field visits to monitor the impact of harvesting, reforestation and sale of *Croton lechleri* latex on the communities we work with. Field assessors produce detailed written reports that are useful for measuring positive impacts and identifying remaining challenges that need to be overcome. In addition, Shaman commissions independent impact assessments and evaluations from respected professionals. Evaluation of reforestation efforts is also conducted by local government agencies on a routine basis.

Shaman has made significant investments in compiling baseline data and implementing environmentally and socially sound sourcing of *Croton lechleri* latex. Shaman considers such long-term investments worthwhile and wise; but this perspective is not always shared by others in the private sector. However, as environmental protection becomes an increasingly important factor in consumers' decision-making processes, certified products may offer a differential advantage that, at times, may supersede cheaper alternatives. Marketing certified products imparts a positive image for a company as a whole, potentially resulting in a series of spin-off benefits, such as attracting environment-friendly investors.

Certification can also serve as a tool to ensure quality control. Considering the cost of obtaining certification, it would be necessary, from an industry perspective, that the process maximizes quality control and quality assurance of the final product. Comprehensive certification processes may also provide additional opportunities for technological improvements in harvesting and manufacturing equipment, general know-how, forest management systems, and other aspects; this, in turn, may result in overall cost reduction and/or higher production efficiency.

From Shaman's perspective, the main challenge to obtaining certification is that the certification process for NTFPs is not yet finalized. We are therefore not sure what to expect in terms of meeting the necessary requirements. It is only natural to avoid entering a process that is still clear. Shaman believes that there are some specific concerns that need to be properly addressed before NTFP certification can be viewed as an attractive financial and philosophical venture.

One obvious concern involves the organization that evaluates the NTFP production system. Does the certification agency have the necessary technical expertise and knowledge of the particular resource in question to perform a sound assessment? Knowledge of the ecological and biological characteristics of a plant species is key in determining its utilization. Fast appraisal studies without sound scientific reasoning may generate a great deal of conflict between the parties involved in the certification process.

Chain of custody also presents difficult challenges. For example, who should be certified in the chain of custody for a particular NTFP that has different kinds of producers, middlemen and companies that add further value to the product? Is it fair to expect indigenous collectors to comply with the same certifying requirements expected of community-based small enterprises? Are middlemen, who in many cases are necessary players in the chain of custody, to be certified as well? How can we ensure that the middlemen are buying from certified collectors? Should a company that adds value to a certified NTFP be certified as well? These are not hypothetical questions; rather, they realistically reflect the realm of players whom a company such as Shaman deals with when sourcing *Croton lechleri*.

Lastly, the cost of certification to both NTFP producers and the industries that transform raw materials into consumable goods is of prime importance. In general, commodity markets characterized by high demand easily absorb the value-added cost of certification. Such is the case with certified coffee, which may cost US$0.05–US$0.10 more per pound – a premium many consumers are willing to pay. To what extent will the cost of certification be prohibitive for products that do not have the same demand and consumer appeal? How will the cost of certified products and other certification requirements affect supply and demand?

In spite of the challenges associated with the certification of NTFPs, it is clear that there are several potential benefits. As NTFP producers and industries come to understand what certification is and consider the benefits of becoming certified, they will have to evaluate what is potentially wrong ('not certifiable') with their production systems and enact policies to change poor practices. At the very least, those who entail the risks of obtaining the certification prize will probably be better equipped to minimize the environmental impacts of their businesses, and that is a real positive change.

Table 29.1 *Markets for selected NTFPs and examples of marketing limitations and opportunities afforded by certification*

Species	Existing markets	International market sector	Examples of marketing-based limitations to certification	Examples of marketing-based opportunities for certification
Brazil nut	L,R, I*\nBolivia, Brazil and Peru: combined annual exports of US$40–70 million	Food	Quality control (aflatoxins). Local capacity and infrastructure. Ability for any one producer to produce volume needed. Social fairness of the commercial production is still a serious challenge.	Large market and international demand for certified products. Consumer awareness of links with rainforest and local communities.
Benzoin	L,R,I	Fragrance; flavouring; incense; cigarettes	Three-quarters sold to domestic markets, certified products. International consumers are in the Middle East, also not likely to be interested in certified products.	European and US consumers of incense appear likely candidates for 'green' certified products.
Cat's claw	L,R,I\nUS$3.3 million in exports from Peru in 1995	Botanical medicine	Botanical medicine raw material is traded as a bulk, cheap commodity – certification would need to overcome this tradition and industry's historical lack of investment in sustainable supplies. Markets for this product in the future are uncertain. It rose quickly to prominence in the 1990s, but might fall out of favour.	International markets are significant. Consumers are increasingly aware of the need to certify sources of raw material as sustainable.
Chicle	L,R,I\nChewing gum industry: US$1.5 billion in 1986	Food	Chain of custody could prove challenging. International markets are dominated by cheaper synthetics, leaving only niche markets open to natural chicle.	Producer groups are experienced and in search of markets for sustainable chicle. Consumers in niche green and fairtrade markets, particularly in Europe, appear receptive to certified sustainable chicle.
Cork oak	L,R,I\nUS$240 million	Beverage material	Existence of cheaper synthetic materials. Consumers of beverages only indirectly purchase cork, so it might be difficult to impact consumer purchasing choices. It is difficult to influence the market for industrial materials through certification, unless required by law.	Consumer interest in certified cork material, particularly organic, could be developed.

Croton	L,R,I	Botanical medicine	There is a need to ensure that any increased demand from international markets does not impact local use and markets, which are significant. Chain-of-custody issues might prove challenging.	International market is emerging, if still small, and is represented by a handful of companies. A major marketer of croton products (Shaman Botanicals) in the US has a public commitment to sustainably and equitably sourced materials (see Box 29.1). Increasing consumer awareness of the need to pay attention to sustainable sourcing practices for botanical medicines.
Wild ginseng (American)	L,R,I US$25 million in 1993 (US Department of Commerce, 1995)	Botanical medicine	Chain-of-custody issues could prove challenging. Alternative sources of *Panax* spp., substitute species or cultivated ginseng might make more expensive certified wild/woods-grown American ginseng unattractive to some consumers.	Well-established international markets. Increasing consumer awareness of the need to pay attention to sustainable sourcing practices for botanical medicines.
Griffonia	L,R,I	Botanical medicine	Concerns associated with safety make already volatile botanical medicine markets unpredictable in this case. Quality-control demands are significant.	Demand persists, and supplies exist that were developed to serve a much larger market than exists today. Scientific research is underway to validate use; could help create standards for quality control and safety.
Maple syrup	L,R,I US sales: US$31.5 million in 1998 Canadian sales: Cdn$115 million in 1998	Food	It is not clear that producers need an additional entry into the market, or that they would benefit from a premium from certification.	International markets are significant. Existing consumer interest in organic maple syrup and organic labels could be paired with certification of sound forest management.
Palm heart	L,R,I 1997 exports from Bolivia: US$12, 355,420 US 1997 consumption: US$8 million	Food	The industry is not well integrated, and chain of custody and adherence to management plans might prove problematic. Cultivated sources will likely replace wild-harvested sources in the near future.	International markets are significant. Consumer demand for sustainable palm heart is established and has potential to grow. Palm heart also provides an important local fruit, açaí, thereby increasing the economic viability of management.

Table 29.1 *continued*

Species	Existing markets	International market sector	Examples of marketing-based imitations to certification	Examples of marketing-based opportunities for certification
Phyllanthus	L,R, I US$5–US$6.25 million in 1996	Botanical medicine	Primarily a domestic and regional market, not generally receptive to certified products.	Increasing use of Ayurvedic and Indian medicinal species overseas.
Rattan	L,R,I US$6.5 billion in 1997	Furniture	Chain of custody could prove challenging for rattan harvested from smallholder forest. Rattan management under certification principles is challenging for small producers.	Efforts to sustainably manage rattan in the wild, and large-scale cultivation, could supply volumes needed by international markets. Significant international markets exist. A diversity of end-products and markets would help to reduce risk involved in marketing certified material.
Yohimbe	L,R,I	Pharmaceutical and botanical medicine	Little local infrastructure. Concerns associated with product safety make the botanical medicine market uncertain. Chain of custody could prove extremely difficult. Existing trade networks, and legal and policy structure, do not create significant benefits for local communities or incentives for sustainable management. Botanical medicine raw material is traded as a bulk, cheap commodity – certification would need to overcome this tradition and industry's historical lack of investment in sustainable supplies.	Demand and markets are significant, and have been so for many years. Consumers are already informed that raw material is 'sustainable', although no such certified sources exist to date. Management could be integrated with timber management.

* L = significant local markets or subsistence use; R= regional markets; I = international commercial markets (primary target of certification schemes

Chapter 30

Technical issues

Abraham Guillén, Alan R Pierce and Richard Z Donovan

Introduction

Non-timber forest products (NTFPs) are some of the latest forest resources to be proposed for inclusion under the Forest Stewardship Council (FSC) accreditation system. Traditionally, many NTFPs have been harvested from the wild without a formal understanding of sustainable harvest levels, without long-term forestry planning and without being adequately incorporated within forest management plans. From the

Illustration by Jamison Ervin

Sangre de drago
(Croton lechleri)

preceding chapters, it is clear that there are many outstanding issues in need of further research if knowledge and professionalism of NTFP management is to advance. The greatest technical challenges to NTFP certification involve management planning, setting sustainable harvest levels, monitoring, chain of custody, policies and regulations affecting NTFP practices, and the size and scale of operations.

Differences between timber assessments and NTFP assessments

An NTFP certification assessment follows the same general process, and addresses the same general subject areas, as a timber assessment. However, the focus of an NTFP assessment may differ from a timber assessment, particularly with respect to social issues and management planning. An NTFP assessment will also involve different expertise from a timber assessment – expertise in the specific species harvested, integrated forest management and social sciences relating to tenure, use rights and harvester welfare. The timing of certification audits may also be more critical for NTFPs than for timber. Areas harvested for timber can be easily monitored post-harvest by looking at basal area, evaluating regeneration, assessing residual stand damage, inspecting road and skid-trail construction and viewing the size and number of stumps left behind. By contrast, assessors visiting areas managed for mushrooms or forest herbs may not get an accurate picture of the resource, its abundance, worker conditions (and related social issues) and the harvesting practices employed unless the assessment visit occurs during or shortly after harvest.

Management planning

Management planning is the most basic and formidable requirement for achieving certification of an NTFP. Most existing guidance for forest management revolves around timber objectives. There are few examples of good management plans for commercially harvested NTFPs, despite their long history of harvesting, although increased efforts to develop effective and affordable management regimes are underway (Peters, 1996). NTFPs are not normally incorporated within long-term timber management plans.

For example, Brazil nuts have been harvested in Bolivia for over 30 years, but the first Brazil nut management plan was not designed until 1998, under the auspices of the US Agency for International Development (USAID) Bolivia Sustainable Forestry Management Project (BOLFOR). The Bolivian government issues permits for the harvest and export of Brazil nuts despite a lack of sound technical information about the species. Many widely collected medicinal herbs have never been included in forest management plans, nor have sustainable harvesting regimes been created for their collection. Despite 300 years of trade, and its current Convention on International Trade in Endangered Species of Wild Fauna and Flora (CITES) listing, wild American ginseng is rarely included in forest management plans.

FSC guidelines provide a framework for designing and implementing forest management plans that, with modification, can be tailored to address non-timber resources as one of many management goals to be addressed within the bounds of a forest ownership. The maple syrup guidelines provide a good example of how to use the FSC framework to accommodate an NTFP (see Appendix II).

In contrast to maple syrup, NTFPs that fruit irregularly in space, time and abundance pose more serious challenges to forest management planning and marketing. In the paleo-tropics, some trees such as *Shorea* spp., which produce commercially important illipe nuts, fruit irregularly during 'masting years' (Peters, 1994; Salafsky et al, 1993). Estimating the harvest intensity and yield of irregularly fruiting trees is a difficult management planning task. Furthermore, maintaining markets for fruits that appear with irregularity is difficult, especially when such fruits are highly perishable (Salafsky et al, 1993).

In general, however, management plans for NTFPs may evolve to include

Box 30.1 Management planning requirements for certification of NTFPs

Abraham Guillén, Alan R Pierce and Richard Z Donovan

The Forest Stewardship Council (FSC) requires certification applicants to have formal management plans with the following elements:

- description of management objectives;
- description of forest resources under management, environmental limitations, land use and ownership status; description of adjoining properties;
- maps of the forest resource base and delineation of management areas;
- layout of access roads or trails;
- description of the silvicultural and/or other management systems based upon site capabilities and information gathered through resource inventories;
- a resource inventory system;
- yield studies;
- rationale for species selection and rate of harvest, with a description and justification of harvesting techniques and equipment used;
- a monitoring system;
- protection measures for rare, threatened and endangered species and special management areas;
- multiyear planning.

For non-timber forest management (NTFP) management, certifiers will specifically focus on the species ecology and biology, justification for harvest levels and monitoring systems. Because setting harvest levels for many NTFPs is complex, adequate monitoring (inventory systems, population surveys) with strong decision-making processes for adjusting harvest levels or modifying forest operations to enhance regrowth or regeneration will be a certification necessity.

some of the basic characteristics of management plans for timber, with the exception that many NTFPs require greater monitoring, shorter spans for harvest readjustment and more adaptive management than timber. Boxes 30.1 and 30.2 list the basic elements required of NTFP management plans, and provide a brief description of the decision-making process involved in selecting NTFPs to manage.

Integration of timber and non-timber resources

Timber and NTFPs are not normally integrated in long-term forest management planning. This situation presents an area of opportunity for researchers and forest managers to develop sound integrated systems. However, little technical guidance on how to integrate both product types currently exists. Everson and Gremaud

Box 30.2 Steps to establish production systems for NTFPs

Róger Villalobos and Daniel Marmillod

Initial species knowledge

The first step includes researching the ethnobotany, biology, ecology and economics relating to the targeted species and its by-products. Managers will need to determine:

- variables to differentiate growth stages;
- biological factors affecting these variables that will guide and inform development of the forest management system.

Developing tools to characterize population structure

To estimate a product's sustainable harvest over time, and the productive potential of the population as a function of its demographic structure, it is necessary to define:

- reasonable and sufficient description of age classes to characterize the population based upon available information;
- observable or measurable biological characteristics to categorize individuals by age class and to determine if individuals are productive.

Developing tools to estimate allowable harvest

The product's allowable harvest within a particular management unit is determined through census or inventories. These tools are only technically and economically reasonable if reliable and precise information is available about the product requirements for harvest. This implies that managers determine:

- minimum sufficient variables, measurable in the field, that permit a precise estimation of the quantity of product to harvest from each individual;
- the mathematical relation and degree of variability between data from field measurements and estimations of product quantity (eg from modelling exercises).

Developing the forest management system

Definition of tools for an adequate characterization of the target population permits the establishment of optimal conditions for species growth and production, and the characterization of the population's distribution relative to the main environmental gradients within the management unit. The main factors that determine the behaviour of a species selected for production in tropical forests include:

- species requirements for environmental resources, particularly light and water;
- species phenology;
- species response to forest management activities;
- annual production of the species within the proposed forest management system; and
- the optimal harvest system to obtain a sound product without diminishing the population's productive capacity.

(1995) have created an ecosystem/NTFPs assessment handbook to quantify and qualify plant communities in Oregon, US. Such a technical assessment tool is useful as an example for temperate Oregon, but will require extensive modification to suit complex tropical forest systems. Inventing more tools to assess the ecological (and economic) potential of a forest for timber and non-timber values and benefits is a research priority. Assessment tools will need to be technologically appropriate to the scale and intensity of the management unit, as well as to the social context of the production area.

Integrated management for timber and non-timber resources cannot be easily generalized due to the wide variety of forest types and diverse classes of NTFPs with varying biological and ecological requirements. In some cases, NTFP management may complement timber management. For example, golden seal (*Hydrastis canadensis*), American ginseng (*Panax quinquefolius*) and other shade-requiring valuable medicinals can be grown beneath temperate hardwood stands awaiting maturation to veneer-size quality, thus providing managers with income from several crops over time. In Brazil, sale of epiphytes from harvested caixeta trees (*Tabebuia cassinoides*) may offset current low prices paid for caixeta wood, thus improving the overall eco-nomic viability of caixeta management (Rezende, pers comm, 1996).

In integrated operations, planning, timing and implementation of harvest operations and avoidance of collateral damage (from timber harvest to NTFPs and vice versa) become issues of paramount importance. Some NTFP populations will require liberation thinnings, followed by weeding, to regenerate and take hold. Other species will require disturbances, such as soil scarification or fire. Other species react poorly to disturbance and require an intact canopy or viable populations of a specific pollinator or seed disperser. In tropical systems, knowledge of traditional management systems for NTFPs may provide valuable lessons for creating and managing integrated forest management regimes. Even those operations primarily oriented towards timber production have an obligation to local communities and stakeholders to learn about widely used NTFPs, and to incorporate those NTFPs within management plans in order to avoid damaging locally important NTFPs during harvesting operations.

Integrating NTFPs within forest planning adds additional expenses to management and monitoring budgets. Many timber certification plans are based upon well-documented ecological information and tested management systems for well-known species, facilitating evaluation for certification purposes. With NTFPs, the challenge will be to develop and implement plans that are conducive to good management and that are cost effective. When financially stable private companies manage NTFPs, planning and monitoring requirements are not always financially insurmountable, as demonstrated by the field trials. However, the costs of designing and implementing an NTFP management plan may serve as a major impediment to certification for communities and small forest owners. The field trials found that unless community-run or small-scale operations are subsidized by supporting organizations, they may have difficulties in obtaining certification. At present, internationally or regionally traded NTFPs are the main products justifying the investment necessary to develop sound forest management planning. Management of such products is more likely because they have the potential to provide positive financial returns and because they are sufficiently well studied enough to enable formulation of sound management plans.

Harvesting

Determining sustainable harvest levels for NTFPs is challenging. Some of the issues involved in setting harvest levels are presented in Chapter 26, while more thorough treatments of the subject can be found in Cunningham (2001), Peters (1996; 1994; 1990) and Hall and Bawa (1993). Simply put, the intricacies of setting harvest levels for NTFPs are based upon the basic biological and ecological data available for the species, and are informed by monitoring the yield of product and the target species' population demographics. Data collected from monitoring is then used to adjust harvest levels to reflect the actual response of the species to harvesting within its particular environment.

Harvest of many NTFPs is labour intensive and often takes place in remote forest areas. The competency of harvesters to enact environmentally sensitive practices presents a technical challenge for managers and certifiers. Implementation of established harvest levels is dependent upon a trained workforce. Seasonal migrant workers who perform short-term labour in forests, and quickly leave the management area once the NTFP season is over, may not strictly follow best harvesting practices unless companies provide training and incentives for conscientious work. It is important that certifiers carefully evaluate training programmes for harvesters, interview seasonal workers and visit management areas during or soon after harvest.

Harvesting cycles for NTFPs, in general, are shorter than harvesting cycles for timber. This characteristic makes NTFPs an interesting source of revenue for forest managers because they can expect income in more immediate time frames than typically offered by timber. If properly integrated within forest management, NTFPs may make forest operations more economically viable by yielding differing products with different markets at staggered time horizons. However, integrating forest management for both NTFPs and timber requires intensive oversight and monitoring because potentially negative ecological impacts can become pronounced over a short time.

Security

A further characteristic of NTFPs worth noting is that they are sometimes perceived as 'free-access' products in certain countries, a situation that raises serious security issues. Because the harvest of many NTFPs can be done without the use of heavy equipment, illicit harvest threatens the continuity of proper management planning and carries unavoidable forest security issues for certification assessors and managers alike. Roots, leaves and exudates may be overharvested when they exist in open-access conditions and on tenured properties alike, particularly if market conditions encourage their harvest. Establishing a control system to ensure respect for proper harvesting and silvicultural practices is a basic certification requirement and presents a particular challenge when applied to NTFPs, especially for products gathered from public lands. The most promising models found during the field trials were communities that were integrally involved in the planning and implementation of NTFP management systems.

Monitoring

Monitoring is one of the most critical components for a sustainable NTFP management system. NTFPs from tree species are simpler, in a way, to include within management plans because some of the data about the target population (eg size and age-class distribution; density) are likely to be already reflected in continuous forest inventory (CFI) plots and other data bases. Integrating understorey herbs within CFI systems may pose more challenges to traditional forest managers and assessors. Certification does not require that managers follow one particular system of sampling (eg random or systematic). Rather, management must demonstrate that the monitoring system is comprehensive for the species harvested and is representative of the species' population distribution across the management unit (and, potentially, different habitats) and tailored to the plant part harvested. The last point is critical – harvesting reproductive propagules is quite different from harvesting vegetative structures such as roots and carries vastly different implications for management.

Monitoring must not only reflect population demographics but a species' response to a particular harvest regime. Yield studies complement inventory data and provide a picture of a species' productivity within a management unit. Monitoring inventory data and yield studies over time informs the rationale for harvest levels. Ideally, productivity should be randomly measured across the management unit (to account for differences in site and habitat) and across age or size classes within the target population. Post-harvest recovery period is another monitoring variable to consider with respect to certain NTFPs, particularly in cases such as bark harvest (see the cork oak and baobab profiles in Chapters 17 and 19) or moss collection.

Many NTFP operations do not have the expertise or funding to carry out state-of-the-art monitoring. Some operations may base their harvest levels upon traditional practices or empirical observation. Certification may initially approve some operations that do not have state-of-the-art monitoring practices – as long as such monitoring practices are shown to be effective. In such cases, certifiers may impose recommendations or conditions for improving the sophistication of the monitoring system over time.

Most monitoring systems focus upon gathering inventory data, studying yields and detailing community structure and composition. Attention to other ecological functions, particularly in tropical forest systems, is critical. Monitoring changes in wildlife diversity, pollinators, seed dispersers, specific inter-relations between plants and animals, genetic diversity and other issues is important, but rarely done for either timber or non-timber operations due to a lack of clear indicators and a paucity of resources to conduct such exhaustive studies. Such monitoring is expensive and requires technological transfer. Further elucidation of streamlined, elegant and cost-effective monitoring procedures is clearly needed.

Chain of custody

Certification requires that forestry operations have tracking systems in order to ensure that products offered for sale come from well-managed forests, and that certified products are not mixed with non-certified products on their way to market. Large products (eg timber) coming from discrete certified forest areas are more easily traceable than small goods (many NTFPs) that come from multiple sites. Products such as palm hearts and Brazil nuts, for example, are often harvested from several different management areas by a number of individuals, making them difficult to track and identify. Solutions to the problems posed by multiple management areas or multiple numbers of harvesters include:

- designing the forestry plan to cover all areas harvested;
- labelling of product at various checkpoints (eg blocks of chicle are embossed with marks denoting the harvester's identity);
- creating centralized collection points for certified material;

- designing a clear production flow chart and establishing control mechanisms at every link where necessary;
- identifying the main risk points in the production flow chart (where the mixing of certified material with non-certified material is more likely) and setting specific controls, at a minimum, at the highest risks points;
- developing clear and simple paper trails and physical control systems that enable the personnel from the different processing links to provide accurate data input;
- physically differentiating the certified products through use of paint, tags, special containers, etc;
- designating specific areas for storage of certified products;
- implementing training programmes for personnel (from harvesters to suppliers, manufacturers, warehouse workers, sales staff, management and accounting) in the proper handling and tracking of certified material.

When timber and NTFPs are to be harvested within the same management unit, a 'master' or 'integrated' plan should be designed that details specific prescriptions and tracking mechanisms for each product.

Once NTFPs have left the forest, chain-of-custody challenges remain. For example, products such as Brazil nuts are traded in bulk as commodities, making it virtually impossible to separate certified from non-certified nuts. Possible chain-of-custody solutions to this problem, in addition to some of the relevant points made above, include:

- creating physical and documentary controls at every stage in the process (input, manufacturing, assembling, packing, sales, etc);
- packaging nuts in small, clearly marked units (bags or boxes);
- certification of middlemen who specifically deal in certified product;
- creating direct contracts between the certified operation and the end retailer;
- umbrella certification for operations or traders through an organization such as a trade association;
- clearing any processing units of non-certified material prior to processing certified material;
- pure 'batch runs' of 100 per cent certified product at processing plants;
- using separate certification identification codes that enable differentiation of products (for computerized systems);
- using seals or different coloured paper to indicate the certified status of the product (for non-computerized sys-

tems using paper forms and record-keeping);
- using separate filing space for storage of records relating to certified products.

In general, certifiers work with operations to utilize as many of the existing control features within an operation as possible, making additional adjustments when necessary to ensure the reliability of the tracking system, always with an eye towards reducing unnecessary expenses.

Organic, Fairtrade, FSC and conventional agriculture systems have all demonstrated that product tracing and product labelling are feasible for a number of goods. Supermarkets currently stock conventionally grown nuts and fruits that are individually labelled with the producing company's name. Organic and Fairtrade coffee is packed in specially marked bags for export, and its volume and shipping routes are carefully recorded. Greens are often bundled with distinctive wrappers or shipped in clearly marked bags for sale at markets and florists. Such examples prove that tracking mechanisms and labelling opportunities exist for a number of NTFPs.

Chain of custody requires documentary controls in addition to physical tracking systems. Typically, small operations do not document product flow from forest through processing to sales outlets with great detail, nor do they maintain rigorous inventory control systems. Such documentary requirements may be onerous; but the certifiable systems need not necessarily be complex as long as they are effective in capturing the requisite data.

Research, knowledge and access to technical assistance

Historically, timber has received the bulk of attention from forest researchers, an orientation facilitated through partial subsidization by governments and private organizations. Throughout the field trials in Latin America, the recurrent technical questions for NTFP certification revolved around defining sustainable harvesting levels for NTFPs and understanding the ecology of targeted species. Where communities or small forest owners manage NTFPs, there is a need to conduct research in conjunction with government, private organizations and international assistance projects in order to offset onerous costs and technical burdens.

However, species with long histories of management by local communities tend to be well understood, and some local groups have developed sustainable management regimes over the years (eg chicle). This does not necessarily mean that traditional management systems can sustain increased commercial demand for products, but it does offer a base of ecological and management expertise upon which to draw.

Funding for forestry issues has traditionally supported timber-oriented research, and NTFP research has remained seriously underfunded. Dissemination of information about new NTFP research and technologies is minimal because most research is done by university students or is undertaken as a minor component of regional research projects that receive limited coverage and distribution. A major impediment to improving NTFP management practices is lack of technical assistance to NTFP producers. Lack of technical exchange is also a major impediment to improving NTFP management and marketing. Access to research funds is more justifiable for commercially traded NTFPs, such as rattan, Brazil nut and palm heart. Normally these types of products are produced by an entire region, which provides even greater economy of scale.

Government permitting, forest policies and regulations

Government permitting systems often set harvesting quotas, or otherwise regulate the gathering of commercial NTFPs. Certifiers and forest managers must incorporate government regulations about management planning, land tenure, access rights and harvest levels into their field operations because certification requires compliance to all existing national and international laws. However, laws are occasionally contradictory and require resolution. Laws may indicate harvesting levels that are not appropriate for particular situations or operations. Laws may also discourage the sale of NTFPs by prohibiting the trade of products or mandating stringent conditions for the transport or sale of NTFPs.

In South America, most forestry concessions are granted for timber, while NTFPs are harvested without management plans through short-term (one- to five-year) permits and government mandated quotas. In other cases, given the poor understanding of law-makers, NTFP management falls under agricultural legislation.

In order for NTFP producers to gain land rights, many must designate NTFPs as agricultural production systems because forestry regulations only allow granting of concessions or long-term forestry permits to operations that produce timber. Vast forest regions where natural NTFPs are the dominant species (eg palm hearts in Amazonian *várzea* forests) are simply not considered for long-term management due to conflicting government policies. Many forestry laws are also mere copies of neighbouring countries' forestry laws, a significant factor that impedes NTFP management and reinforces a poorly conceived common approach towards NTFPs management across regions.

Because NTFPs regularly fall under the oversight of different government ministries, certifiers and managers may have to work with a variety of actors and agencies in order to produce certified NTFPs. Some laws actually discourage production of NTFPs or subsume them under legislation for timber or agriculture. The legal and policy arena is an area where international organizations have been, and could be, of greater assistance to the improvement of NTFP legislation and guidance, given that forest managers and governments do not have sufficient funds or incentives to invest in long-term research. Historically, there has been little financial motivation for policy-makers to include NTFP management in legislative activities because such products generate small amounts of taxable income for state and national coffers. International pressures to protect forests, initiated by environmental and social organizations, are bringing the importance of NTFPs to the attention of governments and international multilateral organizations. Governments and multilateral organizations have begun to respond by developing the legal framework for expanding forest management beyond timber. Certification may serve to catalyse nascent efforts of governments and multilateral organizations that positively reinforce NTFP projects and legislation.

Scale and demand for certified products

Currently, NTFP certification under the FSC umbrella is aimed at products derived principally from natural forests. Many commonly produced agricultural products (eg cocoa and coffee) were originally NTFPs that have been 'domesticated' under plantation systems in response to market demand. NTFP certification is designed mainly for products that come from natural forests in order to distinguish such goods as contributing to forest conservation and as being separate from agricultural systems. Many NTFPs are not well suited for competition in international markets. For example, Clay (1992) reports that a large candy company in the US uses 70 metric tonnes of nuts per eight-hour production shift, equivalent to a year's production of Brazil nuts from the Xapuri, Brazil, processing plant.

The size and scale of an operation may determine its access to certification. Small-scale operations may not be able to afford assessment fees; documentation requirements of certifying agencies; added costs of validating and monitoring NTFP harvest levels; research and development for creating management and marketing plans; and monitoring costs associated with ensuring quality control for international markets.

Possible solutions to the problem of making certification more accessible to small-scale producers may be found in existing FSC models for timber certification of small parcels, particularly certified resource manager and group certification models. The resource manager model allows certified foresters to pool multiple properties under a single management certificate, thus lowering certification costs to landowner clients using these services. Group certification similarly permits an aggregation of landowners to pool properties and resources, thereby lowering the cost of certification. Similar innovative models need to be developed for NTFPs. Producer associations may be one potential avenue for lowering certification costs (the chicle producers' association in Mexico provided technical expertise and marketing assistance to the Noh Bec *ejido*) or aggregating producers.

Combining different systems for NTFP certification

It may take a long time to clarify the role and scope of agricultural, forestry and agroforestry certification programmes. In the interim, it may be useful for edible forest products falling under forest certification programmes to also meet organic and, possibly, fairtrade standards. NTFPs that meet forest certification, organic and fairtrade standards will appeal to a broader consumer market and dissipate confusion that might otherwise arise from a single programme's label and claims. For example, consumers may incorrectly assume that the FSC label, because it is an 'ecological' label, guarantees that a product meets organic standards – when, in fact, it may not.

Processing and quality-control issues areas that are typically addressed by organic certification systems are not well covered by the FSC system. For example, the Bolivian field trial found levels of aflatoxin (a mycotoxin) contamination in harvested Brazil nuts that effectively rendered them unsaleable to the European Union (EU). This sanitation and processing issue was new to FSC certifiers but quite familiar to organic certifiers. Botanical products also present challenges, since species identification, percentage of active chemical constituents and quality control are of increasing importance to manufacturers and consumers. The integration of forest certification, fairtrade and organic standards will be critical if processing, sanitation, benefit-sharing, social and worker welfare and chain-of-custody criteria are to be addressed in a harmonized and cost-effective way.

Conclusions

Evaluating a forest for NTFP production is inherently different than for timber production. NTFP operations will require specialized personnel to conduct certification assessments. Ideally, such personnel should be competent in NTFP management, the target species managed, social sciences, and various certification systems (organic, Fairtrade, International Organization for Standardization – ISO) for issues relating to sanitation, product processing and product purity. Many

NTFP managers will also require specialized assistance and financial support or incentives in order to achieve the technical requirements of certification assessments.

The first field trials concentrated on well-known NTFPs from tree species. In a sense, these field trials began with 'low-hanging fruits' – that is, products that had rich documentation, a history of management and international markets. The field trials demonstrated that certification may be applicable to a select group of NTFPs. However, certification has room to improve its technical assessment procedures for NTFPs. It remains to be seen how certification will handle more challenging products, such as epiphytes, mushrooms and primary forest herbs, particularly when such products are harvested from public lands.

Section IV

CONCLUSIONS AND RECOMMENDATIONS

Chapter 31

Conclusions and recommendations

Patricia Shanley, Sarah A Laird, Alan R Pierce and Abraham Guillén

NTFP certification: opportunities and challenges

Non-timber forest products (NTFPs) are not inherently ideal candidates for certification. They are most commonly consumed at a subsistence level, are traded locally and regionally, and most are not featured in markets open to 'green' or 'fairtrade' messages. Only in a few exceptional cases do NTFPs find their way into international markets that may be receptive to eco-labelling – for instance,

Illustration by Antônio Valente da Silva

*Uxi (*Endopleura uchi*)*

NTFPs themselves are also poorly understood. Little is known about the ecology of most species, their social and cultural role in communities is often complex, and many are harvested from areas with uncertain tenure. At the same time, those systems that do exist for NTFP management are usually oriented towards serving local needs or small markets, and are not often able to accommodate increased commercial demand.

the luxury food, medicinal herb and floral trades. Many NTFPs are harvested from forest areas by individuals who live at the margins of economic and political systems. Such harvesters are loath to comply with added regulations, not only because the regulations are anathema in and of themselves, but also because such added oversight involves extra costs and monitoring that may lower or negate their profits.

However, for some of the NTFP species in trade, certification offers a way to improve market access, to capture a greater share of benefits at a local and community level, and to promote wider conservation objectives. Many of the most valuable NTFPs are also those most poorly managed, and certification offers consumers a chance to buy wisely and responsibly, rewarding companies and producers who seek to purchase and produce sustainable and fairly traded raw and processed materials. In cases where populations of valued NTFPs have been depleted, certification may not have much to offer as far as accessing markets; rather, certification could be used in concert with other initiatives to promote guidelines for species recovery projects or sensitive enrichment planting/cultivation efforts.

The NTFP Marketing and Management Project (known as the NTFP certification project), through the evaluation of guidelines in the field and the examination of issues presented in species profiles, tested assumptions and teased out some of the themes central to NTFP certification. In addition to yielding important lessons, the book has highlighted some of the opportunities and challenges intrinsic to NTFP certification. The following sections discuss some overarching lessons learned by the NTFP certification project and review potential opportunities and challenges. The chapter concludes with some recommendations for 'next steps' in developing and implementing effective NTFP certification.

Some lessons learned

- NTFP certification may be most useful for a limited number of products with international markets. Markets for environmental and fairtrade-certified products are primarily found in Europe and, to a lesser extent, in North America. Developing country consumers do not typically prioritize the concerns of Northern certifying agencies.
- Limitations in ecological knowledge are not always severe. The field trials demonstrated that for a few widely marketed species with long histories of management, such as chicle and palm heart, sufficient information may be available to develop adequate guidelines. Maple syrup is a notable example of a product with a long documented history of harvesting techniques, management regimes and marketing channels.
- NTFP certification should integrate elements of forest/ecosystem certification (eg Forest Stewardship Council – FSC), 'responsible sourcing/ethical wild-crafting' guidelines, organic, fairtrade and – in the case of edibles and medicinals – quality control standards (eg International Organization for Standardization (ISO), Good Manufacturing Practices (GMPs) and basic health and sanitation standards). The cost of conducting assessments under each programme would probably prove prohibitive for most forest products; certifiers, therefore, should collaborate and integrate approaches to field assessments, chain-of-custody inspections and labelling.
- Generic guidelines help to provide a framework for issues that should be addressed; but plant-class indicators and verifiers, and species specific and area/region-specific guidelines, provide the level of detail necessary to most effectively certify NTFPs. Development of guidelines is best accomplished in close collaboration with both harvesters and scientific authorities.
- NTFP certification is a market-based tool that requires a primed market

and educated consumers. If consumers are unaware of the issues raised by NTFP sourcing, and demand is insufficient, certified products might not achieve market differentiation, market access or market premiums.

- The practices required to meet certification guidelines can assist producers in moving their operations towards more sustainable management. Whether or not certification results, the process of developing and implementing standards for wise management can contribute to broader efforts at sustainable forest management and accountability.

- NTFPs should be more effectively integrated within timber certification efforts which, to date, have not adequately addressed the inter-relationship between these types of forest products. Species-specific appendices (see Appendix II) for certification of NTFPs from forest areas where timber is the primary product is one approach. A more integrated approach to addressing NTFPs – many with important local uses are not always recognized by loggers and forest managers – is also required; this would include accounting for NTFPs in management plans and harvesting activities.

- Externally supported communities, particularly in Southern countries, are more likely to fulfill the requirements of NTFP certification than community forest operations that lack outside fiscal, technical or infrastructural support. Such subsidies are, however, double-edged swords; once they disappear, many projects are likely to regress or fail if adequate provisions (eg training, good market links, strong political and technical infrastructure) are not in place to ensure their continued success.

- Certification can bolster the positive progress made to date by NTFP operations, raise morale and ensure the incremental improvement of operations through annual audits.

- Of the three underlying tenets of certification – ecological integrity, social equity and economic viability – evaluating and ensuring maintenance of the socially beneficial aspects of NTFP operations will be most challenging for many assessments.

- Most NTFP harvesters will find certification difficult or impossible to obtain due to financial, technical and organizational reasons. The majority of the world's NTFPs are collected by individuals and families, many desperately poor, who have little chance of benefiting from certification unless it is subsidized and applied with the greatest sensitivity. Indeed, many NTFP researchers argue that certain NTFPs should continue to remain as unregulated goods of the informal sector, where they often serve as a safety net.

- Forest product certifiers who emphasize timber production will need to build capacity to address NTFPs. New capacity must be built in order to address the planning, harvest and inventory of different vegetative structures and plant forms not normally covered by traditional certification assessments. NTFPs will also require new expertise on assessment teams to cover the unique social and cultural aspects of NTFPs. Monitoring and chain-of-custody issues may raise additional technical and financial challenges as well.

- Forest certification programmes will need to extend the patents of their labelling trademarks to include non-wood products. Labelling claims covering products that use only a percentage of certified NTFPs in their manufacture will also need to be reviewed. Lastly, the FSC and certifiers will need to strengthen

frameworks for NTFP certification to provide clarity and consistency of application.

Opportunities in NTFP certification

NTFP certification can provide a range of opportunities for a number of species. The following sub-sections provide a brief review of points that have emerged throughout the course of this project.

Promoting sustainability

Many NTFPs sold in international markets are harvested unsustainably, with little benefit accruing to local communities. Consumers in developed nations are often unaware that the expensive herbal medicine, chewing gum or wild edible that they consume is sourced for pennies, and that such products are subsidized by low payments to harvesters while the forest resource base for many species is being rapidly degraded. Consumer awareness campaigns are important for drawing attention to exploitative sourcing strategies. However, it is also important to provide positive alternatives – 'conscientious' producers, processors and retailers whom consumers can turn to and support. Responsible business practices also help to ensure that, as a result of good intentions, local harvesters are not denied even their minimal income from harvesting forest products through boycotts. Certification could thus provide companies and consumers with a real alternative to the exploitative use of resources and local labour by highlighting the source and practices associated with the manufacture of consumer goods.

Industry accountability

The growth in 'green' and fairtrade markets has been accompanied by increasing claims of environmental responsibility from a number of companies. These claims engender wide publicity and imply an environmentally and socially responsible image that is often misleading or untrue. As a result, companies that genuinely seek to 'do the right thing' receive no reward in the marketplace, and consumers remain ignorant of problems associated with sourcing. Third-party certification can separate responsible companies from companies who engage in marketing hype, ensure accountability, alleviate consumer confusion and reward sound management. Certification might also assist in identifying dependable, sustainably managed and equitably produced sources of raw material for companies, an area of increasing concern in some corporate circles.

Integrating NTFPs into timber certification assessments

Increasing the attention given to non-timber forest products heightens their visibility to forest product certifiers who might otherwise focus solely upon timber. Heightened awareness of the role of NTFPs in forest use and management could encourage timber certifiers to press for the retention of species more valuable for their non-wood products than for their timber. Optimally, certifiers will recommend that NTFPs are factored into harvest planning and felling operations, silvicultural treatments and management plans.

Training certifiers and forest managers in the ecology, use and management of NTFPs

Forest management is still largely defined by timber, and forest product certification largely grows from traditional timber-based approaches to forest management. To effectively manage forests for use by local, regional and international stakeholders, however, greater attention must be paid to non-timber forest products. Training of forest managers and certifiers in the basics of NTFP ecology and use can be an important first step in moving forest management practices towards a more holistic approach.

Decreasing logging of valuable non-timber forest species

Increased harvest of lesser-known species for timber may diminish populations of species with important local and regional use as medicines, fruits, fibres or game attractants. Because some of these species exist in low densities, widespread extraction can rapidly alter species composition and the value of forests as used for subsistence, local and regional marketing purposes. NTFP certification can increase awareness of these important local and regional values, generate commercial revenues, and slow logging of what are otherwise considered 'minor' species.

Promoting consumer education on sustainable forestry and fairtrade

Because the issue of forest value and sustainable harvest is a complicated one, any attempt to promote certification of non-timber forest products will require a widespread consumer education campaign. A result of this campaign will be greater consumer awareness of the environmental and social conditions in which products are harvested, and the need for sustainable and fairtrade models of forest product extraction.

Increasing the knowledge base about the ecology, traditional harvesting practices and management of NTFPs

Developing effective certification guidelines depends upon detailed, species-specific knowledge regarding the density, distribution, regeneration, harvesting and management practices for particular species in particular areas, as well as the plant part being harvested. Because so little information of this type has been recorded to date, the process of collecting this information, as part of a wider effort to develop management plans for certification, is extremely valuable. Collaborative partnerships with NTFP harvesters can also yield valuable keys to management strategies.

Providing market access and increased revenues

NTFP certification can provide market access and increased revenues for local producers. This was evident in the cases of chicle and palm heart, where consumer interest in sustainable products led to greater sales and earnings by local producers.

Supporting community forestry

Forests are not always exploited on an industrial scale for timber; rather, they are managed by communities for numerous outputs, including timber, fuelwood and

NTFPs. To the extent that certification can elucidate best management practices for NTFPs and develop easy-to-use field guidelines for assessing management efficacy, it may provide positive models for managers, donors, companies and non-governmental organizations (NGOs) working with community forestry operations.

Managing long-term prospects

Managing for sustainability has the obvious benefit of ensuring a resource exists for the long term, avoiding the boom-bust phenomenon in resource extraction, and providing for local livelihoods in a consistent manner over time.

Certification should work with existing products

Certification can serve as a useful tool in times of rapid transition within industries (eg upheavals caused by new 'hot' products – see Chapter 18 on griffonia), allowing companies to identify well-managed sources of raw material. Whenever possible, however, certifiers should seek to work with existing products, and existing commercial demand, rather than try to build markets from 'scratch'.

Challenges of NTFP certification

Challenges in certifying NTFPs will vary by product; however, there are some recurring themes and these are reviewed in the following sub-sections.

Inaccessibility of certification for small producers

Certification requires an administrative and institutional infrastructure, and has built-in fixed costs that few small community groups can muster. Management plans, monitoring, unfamiliarity with national laws, uncertain knowledge of market opportunities, and other factors combine to make certification a difficult enterprise for the small producer. Few operations have the funds to cover the direct (eg assessment fees) and indirect (eg additional investments in management and marketing) costs of certification. As a result, certifiers need to consider ways of covering the initial start-up and auditing costs, assist with legal and marketing expertise, and undertake training in man-

agement plan and monitoring design. Communities organized into cooperatives – as in the case of the Noh Bec *ejido* in Mexico – can effectively undertake certification, but will likely need a sponsor to do so. Certifiers are addressing this issue for small-scale timber producers, and there is much to be learned from their experiences. However, the general absence of economies of scale in the NTFP sector might make organization into cooperatives unavoidable – an option that will be unattractive to some harvesters, thus reducing the applicability of certification to a wide range of situations.

Uncertain tenure and access

NTFPs are often harvested across large geographic areas and from marginal lands over which legal tenure and access are uncertain. In most cases, certification requires a level of legal certainty that is not possible to verify. Certification also focuses on land units, not harvesters.

Many NTFP gatherers do not own the land where they gather, are landless or do not have legal rights over resources. Currently, certification does not cover those without formal land rights; therefore, the rigorous regulations required by certification can be viewed as exclusionary and will not provide a good fit for many NTFP situations.

Lack of market knowledge and expertise

Timber certifiers work within a well-defined and bounded market, but NTFPs are sold to a wide range of commercial sectors. The scale of NTFP markets is slight when compared with timber markets, and investment in the sector is minimal. Local producers and certifiers need to be well versed about the markets into which certified NTFPs will feed. Timber certification has benefited significantly from the active involvement of companies seeking sustainable sources, and NTFP certification might also be best driven by company demand for particular products. Otherwise, certifiers must undertake or partner with brokers to ensure that certified materials find their way to the marketplace – and, in some cases, receive the premium that the market will bear. In sum, NTFP certification may not thrive as a purely market-driven tool; rather, it might require assistance in the short as well as long term.

Lack of ecological knowledge for many species

Baseline ecological data on many NTFP species is limited (ie density, distribution, growth rate, regeneration niche, production/yield). Similarly, other areas critical to sustainable management remain poorly understood. These include harvesting techniques, sustainable harvest levels, forest inventory and monitoring techniques, and potential declines in biodiversity due to increased densities of commercial species.

Capacity-building in the forestry sector

Assessment of NTFP operations poses new challenges to forest certification organizations traditionally oriented towards timber production. New expertise, and new species-specific knowledge, will be required to undertake a thorough evaluation of candidate NTFP operations. Operations managing multiple NTFPs present even greater challenges to both forest managers and certification assessors with regard to technical expertise. The skills of trained individuals familiar with NTFP management and ecology will be needed by forest operations and certifying agencies alike. In addition, certifiers and the FSC itself will need to strengthen frameworks for NTFP certifications if the field grows in order to provide clarity and consistency of application.

Chain of custody

NTFPs are harvested from wide geographic areas and often occur in low densities. Physical labelling of NTFPs is more difficult than for timber, although NTFPs might be tracked by volume (ie using labelled bags or crates). The processing of NTFPs also creates the added risk of 'contamination' – the mixing of certified products with uncertified products. Some NTFPs are sold mixed with raw material from a wide range of sources. For example, cocoa manufacturers blend beans from a wide range of countries and regions into a single candy bar. In such cases, certification would need to ensure pure 'batch runs' of 100 per cent certified NTFPs, or else target niche markets with clear, certified supply chains.

Narrow and unpredictable markets

NTFPs are often sold in international markets as luxury goods, which are part of very elastic markets characterized by relatively inelastic supply and unpredictable demand over time. This is not the case with raw materials for the pharmaceutical industry or some herbal medicine products. However, demand for wild foods, natural ingredients in cosmetics and chewing gum, and some botanical medicines will come and go with a rapidity that will shock unprepared producers.

In the case of NTFPs that are principally traded in local markets, the majority of consumers will likely be unable or unwilling to pay a premium for certified products. Many vendors and consumers of forest products have built-in, informal systems of recognizing and indicating which goods are of premium quality, are well processed and/or unadulterated. Considerations of where and under what conditions the product was managed and gathered are simply not of the utmost concern to most consumers.

In cases where NTFPs are staple products, they are commonly replaced by synthetics, although this fear is occasionally overstated. For example, *Bixa orellana* was used for years as a colourant in cosmetics and foods, only to be replaced by red dye #3, which was subsequently found to be carcinogenic. Demand for 'natural' *Bixa orellana* colourant (primarily from Brazil) has risen dramatically in recent years. It is found in niche markets that make use of the natural origins of the colourant in marketing (eg Aveda's cosmetics and shampoos), as well as in mainstream food products that make no mention of the 'naturalness' of the colouring agent.

NTFP producers do have difficulties meeting the volume and quality specifications of the marketplace, however, and small producers, in particular, have significant difficulties accessing international markets as a result. Moreover, some well-established companies with well-defined brand names and images may not consider it necessary or desirable to carry a certification label on their products. Unpredictable and complex market dynamics must be understood and monitored by certifiers, small producers and others who seek to make the link between sustainability, fairtrade and the marketplace.

Lastly, how a country implements the Convention on International Trade in Endangered Species of Wild Fauna and Flora (CITES) and other international treaties (eg the Convention on Biological Diversity – CBD) determines how plant collectors and industries are regulated at the local level (see Chapters 8 and 13). Certification will need to conform to different national laws and policies that directly affect people, plants, management systems and trade.

Recommendations

NTFP certification has the potential to broaden the rubric of forest management options and raise awareness about these critical resources among forest managers, certification agencies and the public. NTFP certification requires prudent application because the ecological knowledge base necessary for the management of many species is limited. More importantly, the management, harvest and sale of NTFPs is loaded with weighty social implications that require great sensitivity from certifiers and policy-makers. The fol- lowing recommendations are intended to help spur the effective exploration and implementation of NTFP certification when and where it is warranted.

Recommendations for NGOs

Educate consumers

While consumer awareness of destructive logging has been heightened in recent years, few are concerned or even aware that harmful NTFP harvest occurs. In fact, many consumers erroneously assume that NTFPs are inherently 'green' products that promote forest conservation. NGOs, concerned governments, multilateral agencies and certifiers need to raise public awareness about the ecological and social importance of NTFPs, and highlight the vulnerability of many currently traded species. NTFPs play a part in numerous markets, and consumers are only partly informed of the many links between their consumption patterns and the viability of forest resources. Only with strong consumer demand – of the kind generated in Europe through widespread campaigns – are companies likely to become proactive in seeking out sustainable sources.

Identify the key species under threat

The NTFP certification project began by focusing upon species in danger of poor management, but not largely under threat. Other researchers might wish to target key species in high demand by the international market. Botanical medicine species such as pygeum (*Prunus africana*), yohimbe (*Pausinystalia yohimbe*), devil's claw (*Harpagophytum procumbens*), kava (*Piper methysticum*), pau d'arco (*Tabebuia* spp.) and golden seal (*Hydrastis canadensis*), for example, could, in some cases, be potentially good candidates for certification. Research is underway on sustainable harvesting regimes and consumer awareness for a few species has been raised; but no direct market link has been made between environmentally and socially sound producers and the consumer. Species under significant threat should receive priority attention. The species mentioned above are also likely to be a great deal more difficult to certify than Brazil nut, palm heart, and chicle since less is known about their ecology. Local knowledge of traditional management practices will prove invaluable in these cases.

Partner with other efforts to promote sustainable NTFP management

Certification is only one tool among many in a kit that seeks to address resource management issues associated with NTFPs. Sustainable harvesting regimes, domestication, producer education and training, policy revision, direct brokerage and marketing, and other efforts will necessarily complement certification. Producer groups and NGOs might seek out certifiers at key points in their work to better make use of the marketplace to effect change. Certifiers cannot provide 'all in one' services (ie technical expertise, certification services and marketing assistance) to communities due to obvious conflict-of-interest issues. Thus, many NTFP producers or producer associations will require external technical support to achieve sustainable management of NTFPs – a role well suited to NGOs. It is therefore important that NTFP certification is viewed as a step in the process towards good management and is closely integrated with a range of approaches and actors.

Recommendations for research institutions and forest managers

Support integrated studies of timber and NTFPs

Universities and forest research institutions need to stress integrated forest management and should produce new methods and practical expertise necessary for managing timber and non-timber resources together. Attention should be given to the broad array of species utilized and traded at the local and regional level, in addition to internationally traded products. Because so little is known about the ecology and management of many NTFPs, and since smallholders are repositories of this knowledge, more research should focus on partnerships with local harvesters.

Thoroughly research NTFP certification before committing to a programme

Managers interested in obtaining NTFP certification should consider the following questions:

- What expectations do you hold for NTFP certification: access to expert advice, leverage for funding and access to resources, new markets, etc?

- How realistic are these expectations?
- Will the benefits of certification outweigh the costs?
- Are the NTFPs that you produce well documented in management plans, and are those plans integrated with the overall plan for the entire property?
- What is the basis for setting NTFP harvest rates?
- Is it validated by either scientific data or traditional management norms?
- Are your harvesters well trained so that their activities cause the least amount of ecological damage?
- Have you read certifier criteria for forest management certification and, in particular, NTFP certification?
- Do you have a ready market for certified NTFPs or an already established market that may be sympathetic to certified products?
- What are the current social issues in your operation, and have you fairly addressed workers' rights, worker safety, housing and wages, and any subsistence issues?
- Are community relations positive, and do workers and the community feel a vested interest in maintaining the resource?

Recommendations for certifiers

Monitor early pilot projects and expand the focus

It is difficult to predict the impact of NTFP certification in the short term. It is likely that only well-supported community operations and producers of internationally traded products will initially seek NTFP certification. It will therefore be imperative to monitor the successes or failures of the first NTFP certifications and learn from the experiences of these 'early adopter' producers.

The first field trials focused upon edible NTFPs from trees and palms. More field trials will be necessary to better understand the implications of certification for understorey herbs, medicinal plants, fungi and resins used for industrial applications. Markets for medicinal plants, industrial resins and edibles vary greatly from each other and have very different quality-control needs. Likewise, the management, ecology and monitoring of fungi and understorey herbs present greater management challenges than managing NTFPs from trees.

Make certification accessible to small producers

Certifiers need to find ways of making NTFP certification more affordable and accessible to small-scale producers and rural inhabitants. Group certification, certification through NTFP producer organizations, a sliding fee-scale based upon size of operation, and other innovations will be necessary to ensure equitable access to certification. Some experimental models for small producers have been created, but widespread application is still slow and the procedures require further fine tuning. In the end, the cost of certification will remain a burden and a potential barrier to many NTFP producers, particularly poor, decentralized families and individuals.

Training in NTFPs

Certification programmes will need to train a new cadre of NTFP professionals in certification procedures. Since few people know specific NTFPs indepth, it is imperative that certifiers seek out collaborations with knowledgeable international, regional and local experts. Such professionals will strengthen forest certification programmes and should be included in the planning and implementation of assessments and training exercises.

Collaboration is critical

Discussions between forest certification, organic and fairtrade programmes should continue, and should aim to make NTFP certification comprehensive and cost effective. NTFP certification will only work if it incorporates a range of existing certifier priorities. Producers likewise need access to the widest array of marketing programmes and tools available in order to increase their competitive edge. Collaboration between certifiers and research institutions could also strengthen NTFP criteria used in the field.

Continue to evolve NTFP guidelines

Species-specific guidelines will be necessary for the effective certification of many NTFPs. Social indicators and verifiers will also require further elaboration and testing in order to assure that certification causes the least amount of disruption to, and significantly benefits, traditional societies and rural communities. Market access and fair and safe working conditions should also be established.

Encourage further involvement by the FSC

The FSC should consider finding additional funding sources to support NTFP research and should work closely with accredited certifiers in order to enrich NTFP certification protocols and models. A strong commitment to NTFPs would enable the organization to cover a wider variety of forest operations and certification applicants, particularly small forest owners and community forestry operations. Such a commitment would require flexibility on the part of the organization; but a proactive approach could go a long way towards ensuring that a proliferation of confusing, competing labels for NTFPs does not occur.

Recommendations for funders

Support locally and nationally relevant research

NTFP certification is relevant for only a select handful of widely traded products, and is thus limited as a conservation tool. If forest conservation initiatives and forest policies are to have a meaningful impact upon forests and forest-based livelihoods, they must pay attention to the many species traded at the local and regional level. Due to rapid changes in forest cover worldwide, research is urgently needed on forest products that are vital to local and regional health care and nutrition, but which are vulnerable to continuing land-use change or overexploitation. In addition, research that actively attempts to fill in gaps regarding the ecology, use and management of widely traded, but little known, species (eg many tree exudates, fibres and forest-based medicinals) will be valuable domestically and internationally.

Support small producers

Although there is a drive to certify volume in timber certification circles, NTFP certification should emphasize the catalysing role that certification can play in improving forest management and social practices. Small NTFP producers will require donor support to implement sound management practices and create the political and social infrastructure necessary to maintain viable production systems. Certifiers and NGOs likewise need donor support to better train and assist small producer groups.

Support efforts to raise consumer awareness

NTFP certification is likely to have a limited impact unless widespread marketing campaigns and education programmes raise consumer awareness. Funders should support groups who specialize in consumer education (not usually certifiers) in order to ensure that the message about non-timber forest products – their importance to local livelihoods, and the social and ecological damage wrought by exploitative harvesting practices – makes its way to a broad range of consumers.

Fund an NTFP management working group

Scientists, certifiers, conservationists, and others working on NTFPs do not often share the same literature and do not attend the same conferences. In order to advance a more holistic approach to NTFP management and marketing (an approach that, in part, also incorporates certification), a working group comprised of representatives from a range of disciplines and backgrounds could be formed. Ideally, this group would be an independent network, based at an existing institution, but without institutional constraints.

Recommendations for companies

Educate consumers through your marketing; don't mislead them

Corporate marketing can be useful for sending messages to consumers about environmental and social responsibility. Companies need to ensure that their message is clear and honest. They should also create a process for ensuring the sustainability of their sources of raw materials. To do so, input will be required from ecologists and resource managers knowledgeable about the forest resource. Many companies will not achieve 100 per cent sustainable and fairtrade sourcing immediately, but can make a commitment to do so within a realistically expedient time frame.

Research your supply chain and the existing options

One of the first steps towards certification should involve a comprehensive examination of a company's supply chain. Where are your products coming from? What countries and, more specifically, which forests supply your suppliers? What is the social and environmental reputation of your supplier(s)? Are there particularly egregious sources of supply from endangered habitats and regions with poor human rights records; if so, what alternatives exist? Does your company have staff members with a social or environmental background who understand the issues surrounding the responsible sourcing of materials or, at least, have access to NGOs, research institutions and individuals who can assist your company with these issues?

Organize your industry through associations and conferences

Companies should raise issues of sustainable sourcing at industry meetings. They should request that their industry associations explore issues associated with sourcing. Lastly, industries should coordinate trade association working groups to identify ways in which members can address these issues.

Work with and assist small producers

Companies can help build capacity within small producer groups to supply the volume and quality required over time, and can help build the necessary infrastructure to undertake the certification of products. In the case of timber certification, some industries have shouldered all or a portion of the certification costs incurred by their suppliers. Companies might consider working cooperatively with suppliers to phase-in certified lines of NTFPs as they become available.

365

Generic guidelines for assessing the management of NTFPs

NTFP certification project team

Introduction

Non-timber forest products (NTFPs) are biological resources/products, other than timber, that can be harvested from forests for subsistence and/or for trade. NTFPs may come from primary and natural forests, secondary forests and forest plantations or agroforestry systems. NTFPs include a wide range of products, including medicinal plants, fibres, resins, latex, oils, gums, fruits,

Illustration by Antônio Valente da Silva

*Tucumã (*Astrocaryum vulgare*)*

nuts, foods, spices, flowers, crafts, dyes, construction materials, rattan, bamboo, fish and game. This chapter will deal solely with plant products taken from a variety of life forms and plant parts, including reproductive propagules, plant exudates and vegetative structure, such as roots and bark (drawn from Peters, 1994; FSC, 1997).

The hierarchical framework: principles, criteria and indicators

The main conceptual tools for guiding assessments are principles, criteria and indicators. This hierarchical framework breaks down the goal of sustainable forest management and, in this case, sustainable NTFP species management into levels and parameters that can be assessed. Principles break the overall goal into more specific

components; criteria add meaning and operationalize the principles; indicators add a performance value; and verifiers add greater specificity to measure an indicator. Terms are defined as follows (definitions drawn from CIFOR, 1997; FSC, 1997; Lammerts van Bueren and Blom, 1997; and from field experience):

- *Principle:* a fundamental truth or law as the basis of reasoning or action; an essential rule or element.

- *Criterion:* a means of judging whether or not a principle has been fulfilled. A criterion adds meaning and operationality to a principle without itself being a direct yardstick of performance.

- *Indicator:* qualitative or quantitative parameter that can be assessed in relation to a criterion. It describes in an objectively verifiable way the features of the ecosystem or a related social system. Minimum or maximum allowable value of an indicator is known as threshold value (ie a way of quantifying or qualifying or measuring performance).

Thus, in the context of this appendix, an indicator is assumed to include a performance value and is therefore called a performance indicator.

- *Verifier:* describes the way an indicator is measured in the field (ie data points or information that enhance the specificity or the ease of assessment of an indicator). The intention in this process is not to prescribe a minimum set of verifiers, but to allow room for verifiers that are specific to region, product, class, operation size, etc. Verifiers add meaning, precision and usually also site-specificity to an indicator. Numerical parameters might be assigned to a verifier on a case- and site-specific basis.

The generic NTFP guidelines

The following generic guidelines are designed for areas where NTFPs are the primary product being assessed for certification. For operations where timber is the main product being managed and there is NTFP utilization, an NTFP addendum has been designed for the existing SmartWood *Generic Guidelines for Assessing Natural Forest Management* (2000) (see Appendix II). These guidelines focus solely upon the plant kingdom and do not address game, fish or invertebrates. Although these products are critically important NTFPs, the development of guidelines for fauna will require additional research and experimentation.

These generic NTFP guidelines are based upon the framework of Forest Stewardship Council (FSC) principles and criteria, numbers 1–10, and draft principle number 11: non-timber forest products, developed by the FSC–NTFP working group. These guidelines incorporate all aspects of the FSC-approved SmartWood

Generic Guidelines for Assessing Natural Forest Management so that, in theory and practice, if applied, an FSC-approved SmartWood certification of NTFPs could occur. Based upon an already approved FSC policy (memo to FSC members by Dr Timothy Synnott, 20 April 1998), some 'commercial' tests of the guidelines are occurring during this pilot project, whereby actual FSC-approved NTFP certification could result.

In these guidelines, FSC principles form 'subject areas' and are followed by criteria drawn from the FSC *Principles and Criteria for Forest Management* (2000) and numerous other standards and source materials. Class (plant part) ecological indicators and verifiers follow. Social and cultural issues are covered in these generic NTFP guidelines; however, given the complexity of this aspect of NTFP use, management and marketing, experience may dictate that additional social indicators and verifiers should be developed.

NTFP guidelines criteria

1.0 Commitment to FSC principles and legal requirements

Non-timber forest products (NTFPs) shall be managed in accordance with principles and criteria numbers 1–10 of the Forest Stewardship Council (FSC) and (draft) principle number 11 (non-timber forest products) and its criteria. NTFP certification will also take place within the ethical and legal framework of international environmental and human rights law and policy, and national, state/provincial and local laws in the country where forest management takes place.

1.1 The forest management operation (FMO) clearly demonstrates a long-term commitment to adhere to the FSC principles and criteria.
1.2 The FMO meets national, state/provincial, and local environmental, labour and forestry laws.
1.3 The FMO is up to date in payment of local taxes, resource rights or leases, fees, royalties, etc.
1.4 The FMO is in accordance with local customary law governing exploitation of the resource. If local communities (landowners or administrators) are not actively involved in the forestry operation, prior informed consent for all forest management operations on their lands, or for exploitation of traditionally managed resources, must be granted. In most cases, prior informed consent (consent based upon understanding and agreement with the proposed plan) takes written form (agreements, memoranda of understanding, etc).
1.5 The FMO is in accordance with international environmental, human rights and labour conventions; field operations must meet the intent of such conventions.
1.6 Forest managers are willing to make available a public certification summary of forest management operations according to the certifier's requirements.

2.0 Land tenure and use rights and responsibilities

NTFPs are often spread across great distances, and are managed according to traditional systems that incorporate complex customary legal and management norms. The forest operation must respect and incorporate customary law with regard to tenure and forest and species stewardship. Clear land tenure – guaranteeing rights and access to resources – enables forest managers and communities to invest in long-term forest management strategies of the kind NTFP certification is intended to promote.

2.1 The rights to use the property and access to resources are secured for the long term.
2.2 Land is dedicated by owners to long-term forest management.
2.3 Local communities with legal or customary tenure or use rights maintain control, to the (legally acceptable) extent that they are able to protect their rights

or resources over forest operations unless they delegate control with free and informed consent to other agencies.

2.4 Resource conflicts with adjoining landowners or other resource users are resolved or are addressed in a systematic and effective manner.

2.5 A monitoring system exists to maintain security over forest areas (eg protection from illegal logging, occupation, hunting, resource extraction, commercial agricultural development, ranching or land conversion to other uses).

3.0 Forest management planning and monitoring

A management plan – appropriate to the scale and intensity of the operations, modified as necessary to reflect conditions on the ground, and resulting from consultations with relevant stakeholders – shall be written, implemented and kept up to date. The long-term objectives of management, and the means of achieving them, shall be clearly stated.

Forest management and planning should be seen as a process and not just a document, although the value of a written plan is that it improves understanding of the management approach by staff and others involved, and facilitates consistency in the face of personnel and landholder changes, etc. Scale, location and intensity of harvests are important factors in determining expectations in terms of management planning. In diverse ecosystems, monitoring a suite of species is difficult; therefore, limited monitoring is the realistic expectation. However, vulnerable species can be anticipated based upon life form, plant part harvested, habitat, sprouting ability and harvest intensity; effective monitoring systems can be developed in response.

Large operations will require a more systematic management plan with greater detail than plans for smallholders. Plans need to respond to the economic and social interests of local communities. Certified operations are expected to balance production with environmental and social objectives, weigh the advantages and disadvantages of each forest management approach, and select techniques that maintain or restore ecosystems, while responding to social and economic realities.

Internal monitoring systems are crucial in order to provide quality control for forest management operations, to identify sustainability and operational challenges, and to report on the success or failure of management interventions to resolve problems.

3.1 A multiyear forest management plan is written and available for the whole area under management that integrates all commercialized NTFPs and timber products.

3.2 The forest management plan is comprehensive, site specific and detailed, appropriate to the scale and intensity of the forest operations, and should include the following elements:
- clear statement of management objectives;
- description of forest resources being managed (including NTFP and, if applicable, timber forest resources) environmental limitations and land use;
- description of measures for protecting or enhancing regeneration;
- description of actions taken to protect rare, threatened and endangered species and ecosystems;
- description of, and rationale for, selected harvesting systems;

- maps that describe total forest management area, including the harvest areas, strict conservation and/or other protection areas, road system, buildings;
- plan for forest protection against encroachment, uncontrolled fires, etc;
- sales plan;
- description of local communities, including total population, number of participants in the activity, history of harvesting, form of organization, organizations involved;
- plan for periodic monitoring, and a description of how results will be used to adjust the forest management plan.

3.3 Rationale behind harvesting prescriptions is documented (ie based upon regional or site-specific field data, local knowledge or published regional forest research, as well as government requirements).

3.4 Allowable harvest has been set based upon conservative and documented estimates of growth, ensuring that the rate of harvest does not exceed sustainable levels (use attached indicators and verifiers).

3.5 Maps and work plans are available to indicate locations of extraction trails or roads, conservation areas and main infrastructure at a scale that is useful for supervision of management activities and to facilitate onsite monitoring.

3.6 Summary of the main elements of the management plan, or related annual operating or harvesting plans, are available to stakeholders.

3.7 The management plan is periodically revised (at least every five years) to incorporate the results of field monitoring and new scientific or technical information, as well as to respond to changing environmental, social, cultural and economic conditions.

3.8 If timber products are harvested, they have been inventoried and their management is incorporated within the management plan.

3.9 Monitoring is conducted appropriate to the scale and intensity of forest management in order to assess the condition of the forest. Forest management includes systematic research and data collection needed to monitor the following:
- estimated production of forest products harvested;
- regeneration and condition of the forest;
- observed changes in flora and fauna;
- environmental impacts of harvesting and related operations;
- social impacts of harvesting and related operations.

3.10 Indicators and verifiers, as applicable, are addressed in the management plan (include indicators and verifiers (I&Vs) according to class as discussed in subsection 10.0: 'Performance indicators and verifiers).

4.0 Forest management practices

In many cases, the harvesting of NTFPs has proven destructive, either through poor technique, equipment or disregard for an individual's long-term survival (such as girdling a tree, or felling it to collect fruits). In order to minimize the impact of NTFP harvesting on species populations, as well as overall forest structure and species diversity, proper harvesting techniques must be employed. For specific harvesting and management practices of NTFP classes, evaluate according to sub-section 10.0: 'Performance indicators and verifiers'.

4.1 Allowable harvesting is complied with in the forest.

4.2 Harvesting prescriptions are adhered to.

4.3 Monitoring is implemented according to plan (see criterion 3.9)

4.4 Trail or road construction, maintenance and closure standards are implemented in the field, according to local standards or best practice, in order to minimize drainage problems, soil erosion, and/or sedimentation of watercourses.

4.5 Trees are not felled or uprooted in order to harvest NTFPs unless specified as necessary and acceptable in the management plan or other management documents.

5.0 Environmental impacts and biological conservation

Certifiable NTFP management shall ensure long-term ecological viability of NTFP populations. NTFP harvesting and management generally have lower impacts on forest ecosystems than timber harvesting; but care must be taken that species are not overharvested, and appropriate protection must be provided for vulnerable species in residual stands.

5.1 Field assessments of the forest condition are completed prior to the commencement of activities (appropriate to the scale, intensity of forest management and the uniqueness of the affected resources) and are adequately integrated within management systems. Assessments include landscape-level considerations, as well rare, threatened and endangered species.

5.2 Non-timber and timber species on either local/or international endangered or threatened species lists (eg Appendix 1, national list, of the Convention on International Trade in Endangered Species of Wild Fauna and Flora – CITES) are not harvested.

5.3 Conservation zones and protected areas are established, appropriate to the scale and intensity of forest management and the uniqueness of the affected resources.

5.4 Conservation zones are preferably contiguous blocks, though they may be a series of smaller blocks linked by corridors.

5.5 Conservation zones are clearly demarcated on maps and in the field, and forest operations are carefully controlled in these areas.

5.6 Threatened (ie rare, endangered) species are protected. Harvesting of products in protected areas will account for ecological requirements of other species (eg food for frugivorous birds and mammals).

5.7 Desirable habitat features for wildlife are maintained (eg wildlife food, mast-producing species, downed logs, standing trees suitable for nesting, diverse cover of vegetation).

5.8 Ecological functions and values are maintained intact, enhanced or restored, including forest regeneration; genetic, species and ecosystem diversity; and natural cycles that affect the productivity of the forest ecosystem.

5.9 Change in species diversity and composition as a result of human intervention are maintained within critical limits, and emphasize the maintenance of natural diversity patterns wherever possible.

5.10 The building of rails and/or roads avoids damage to residual forest, under-storey, non-target species, wildlife habitat and waterways. Canopy cover reduction through road-building is minimized. Use of trails or roads is restricted in inappropriate seasons.

5.11 Steps are taken to minimize damage to soils, including erosion and compaction.

5.12 Synthetic chemical inputs and biological control agents are not used unless part of a well-designed, environmentally sensitive production system, and as articulated in the management plan.

5.13 Genetically modified organisms are not used.

5.14 Waste from processing is properly handled and disposed of. NTFP processing by-products may have a range of uses that should be investigated and potentially integrated within commercial activities.

5.15 Hunting is regulated and controlled.

5.16 Harvesting or collection of non-certified timber (eg firewood) or NTFPs that have not been certified are regulated and controlled.

5.17 Enrichment planting, if carried out, should use native species.

5.18 Introduction of exotic species is discouraged. However, naturalized NTFP species (exotic species that are reproducing on their own over a long time frame) may be certifiable, as long as known negative ecological impacts are controlled, since they may now form an integral part of local forests and the management of resources.

6.0 Social and cultural impacts

NTFPs are integral to local societies, economies and cultures, and as such contribute in a range of ways to how people perceive of, and manage, their forests. Certification must not create imbalance in existing traditional management systems, many of which are based upon complex histories of use and belief. NTFP certification should bolster local economies in culturally and socially appropriate ways. Certification should strive to avoid creating new dependency relationships that can disrupt cultural balance and integrity. NTFP certification efforts should attempt to minimize any potentially negative impacts of market forces on traditional local use and the management of forests and forest products.

Forest management shall not threaten or diminish, either directly or indirectly, the resources or tenure rights of indigenous peoples or local communities. Forest management operations should not impinge upon local communities' existing access to NTFPs or forest areas.

6.1 Forest management identifies and recognizes the value and use of forest functions and resources for the local community.

6.2 NTFP management or harvest for commercial purposes does not negatively impact upon subsistence utilization and traditional harvesting practices of the commercial species/products. Unless negotiated otherwise with local people, marketing should only be of surplus products, above subsistence needs.

6.3 Forest management respects the cultural and religious significance of NTFP species and forest areas. Harvest of NTFP species is not conducted in sacred forests, or sites of special cultural, ecological, economic or religious significance, unless with the explicit permission of local community stakeholder groups.

6.4   Forest management and the processing of NTFPs are conducted in accordance with cultural traditions and norms, where possible and when sustainable.

6.5   Detrimental social and cultural changes resulting from the influx of workers to harvest products are minimized.

7.0 Community and worker relations

NTFP certification is intended to increase and/or stabilize long-term local income from the forest resource. It is not only the owner(s) of the business who should receive a premium from the production of certified NTFPs – the wider community and workers should benefit as well, wherever possible. As much value as possible should be captured at the local level. The active involvement and ongoing participation of individuals and groups from the local community will help to promote long-term sustainable forest management, a primary objective of NTFP certification.

Community relations

7.1   Communities within, or adjacent to, the forest management area are actively involved in forest management activities, including first rights to employment, training and other opportunities.

7.2   Local organizations or individuals directly affected by forest management activities are given an opportunity to participate in forest management planning.

7.3   Ongoing communication with affected local communities and governing bodies is maintained during the implementation of forest management operations.

7.4   Appropriate and effective mechanisms are used to resolve grievances and to provide fair compensation in the case of loss or damage affecting the legal or customary rights, property, resources or livelihoods of local peoples. Measures are taken to avoid such loss or damage.

7.5.   When feasible and locally desired, processing of products is conducted as close to harvesting locations as possible in order to maximize the benefits that accrue to communities living in the forest area.

Worker relations

7.6   Workers must be paid at least equivalent to the sector average, the union negotiated rate or the legal minimum wage. Men and women must receive equal pay for equal work. Other benefits (eg health, retirement, workers' compensation, housing, food) for full-time staff and contractors must be consistent with (not lower than) prevailing standards.

7.7   Forest management must meet or exceed applicable laws and/or regulations covering the health and safety of employees and their families, and the rights of workers to organize and voluntarily negotiate with their employers.

7.8   Forest workers must receive adequate training and supervision to ensure proper implementation of the management plan. (ie orientation programmes, courses, written manuals and policies).

8.0 Benefits from the forest and economic viability

NTFPs can provide a range of social and economic benefits at local, regional and international levels. The intent of NTFP certification is to optimize the socio-economic potential of certain marketable species, in order to provide a larger economic return from a given forest area for local communities and forest managers, without negatively impacting local use of these or other NTFP species.

8.1   Mechanisms for sharing benefits are perceived as fair by local community groups, and will adapt to the changing economic conditions of these communities.

8.2   If traditional knowledge is used to develop a marketable product, informed consent must be given by the traditional or local community prior to the marketing of any product. Mutually agreed upon terms must be reached regarding access to this knowledge and the equitable distribution of benefits arising from its use.

8.3   Indigenous and local communities receive fair and adequate benefits for any use of their name or image in marketing.

8.4   Based upon local experience and markets, payment for products or other rents that are paid to local landholders for uses or products derived from their forest property are at or above the norm (ie average), and are perceived by landholders to be a positive incentive for encouraging long-term forest management.

8.5   The revenue received from forest operations should be sufficient to cover the costs of forest management activities in the long term, including conservation investments.

8.6   In the case of externally supported operations, a plan exists to reduce the level of dependency upon external support (technical, financial) to maximize the level of self-sufficiency and control.

8.7   Forest management strives to strengthen and diversify the local economy, avoiding – wherever possible – dependence upon a single forest product.

8.8   Forest management operations recognize, maintain and, where appropriate, enhance the value of forest services and resources, such as watersheds and fisheries.

8.9   Forest management operations and processing centres minimize waste associated with harvesting and processing activities and avoid damage to other natural resources.

8.10 Smallholders are able to participate in negotiating contracts for the sale of their products.

9.0 Chain of custody in the forest

Chain of custody (CoC) is a tracking system that enables certifiers to trace each forest product from its origin through harvesting, processing, storage and sale. CoC ensures that certified products are not mixed with non-certified products (otherwise known as 'contamination'). NTFP chain-of-custody issues can be highly problematic. NTFPs are often gathered from a wide geographic area, they can be channelled into bulk as well as specialty markets, processing facilities might be used for both certified and non-certified products, and there might be extremely complicated internal chains of custody. In some cases, the costs of resolving the chain-of-custody issues might outstrip the return that can be made from attempting to produce certified NTFPs. However, product inventory and handling up to the point of sale, or transport of the product to other parties outside of the forest (ie resolving its internal chain of custody), are critical to NTFP certification.

9.1   Volume and source data on raw materials are available (ie scaled, inventoried, measured) at intermediate storage facilities, processing and distribution centres.
9.2   Invoices, bills of lading, certificates of origin and other applicable documentation related to shipping or transport specify the certified status of the products.
9.3   Certified forest products are clearly distinguished from non-certified products through marks or labels, separate documented storage, or accompanying invoices or bills of lading. Unique marking or identification of certified products exists at all stages of processing and distribution up to the point of sale or transport either outside of the forest (ie up to the 'forest gate') or to a third party.
9.4   All marketing materials and public representation of certified forest products are consistent with certifier policy.

10.0 Performance indicators and verifiers

Depending upon many factors, including density, regeneration and pollination, an NTFP species may be more or less susceptible to exploitation than others. Parameters that will determine the impact of harvest include the intensity of collection, the initial density or size of the population, the regeneration and growth requirements of the species, and the degree to which the plant depends upon animals for pollination and dispersal. Geographic and climatic variations, such as elevation and moisture, will influence production and desirable levels of harvest.

The previous principles and criteria are a relatively unchanging foundation, while the following indicators and verifiers will be adapted based upon regional and site-specific considerations. A range of verifiers is supplied for the following indicators, not all of which will be used in each case. Certifiers will need to select those that are most effective in a given situation.

The performance indicators and verifiers apply to following classes of NTFPs:

*   exudates;
*   vegetative structures: apical bud, bark, root, leaves;
*   reproductive propagules: fruit, seed.

The broad category of NTFPs has been divided into classes that are based upon the product, or plant part, harvested. This will allow for more effective field assessments by providing the information necessary to determine sustainability. Species-specific performance indicators, verifiers and other guidance documents will also be developed and employed in some field assessments – in particular, for internationally marketed species such as palm heart, Brazil nut, rattan and chicle.

These indicators and verifiers are based upon the draft FSC principle and criterion number 11.2:

management plans, operational activities and monitoring shall ensure long-term ecological viability of NTFP populations. Management systems should address the ecological processes of, and implement activities to minimize the ecological impacts of harvesting upon, various types of NTFPs, including but not limited to, products that:

- require the removal of the individual;
- affect the species' growth or productivity;
- when harvested, cause damage to trees or other forest products;
- are critical to nutrient cycling;
- have high wildlife value;
- have very specific ecological interdependencies;
- are harvested for subsistence use.

10.1 Exudates

Plants produce many useful exudates, including, latex, resin, oleoresin and gums. Harvest of exudates may entail tapping the tree or the creation of incisions within a tree's bark. The impact of this type of harvest is determined by the maturity of the plant and the frequency and intensity of harvest. If properly conducted, tapping will not kill the exploited tree. However, in addition to felling a tree to collect exudates, excessive tapping can result in the death of the individual. Moderate tapping of a tree may weaken its vigour by diverting the energy needed to produce seeds to be used in the production of latex. When extracting exudates, the physiological demands on the tree to produce additional latex or oleoresin compete with the tree's ecological necessity to produce seeds (Peters, 1994).

Management indicators and verifiers for exudates

1   *Indicator (knowledge)*: rates of harvesting intensity, frequency and seasonality are defined based upon a combination of scientific study and/or long-term local experience and knowledge.
    Verifiers:
    - Scientific information is available.
    - Local management/use of selected species exists.
    - Harvest rates are documented in writing.
    - Analysis of implications of different harvest rates is available.

2   *Indicator (diameter and/or age)*: minimum diameter or age of trees for commencement of tapping has been determined, which explicitly aims to reduce negative impacts upon long-term vigour and production.
    Verifiers:
    - Maximum number of taps/incisions per tree is specified.
    - Minimum diameter/age is established on a species- and site-specific basis.

3   *Indicator (quantity)*: the quantity of exudate extracted that reduces negative impacts upon long-term vigour and production is determined.
    Verifiers:
    - Records of volumes extracted are documented.
    - Data (or recorded visual observations) on the relationships between volume extracted and tree health are available.

4   *Indicator (frequency)*: the frequency of harvest from an individual in a given time period has been determined in a way that reduces negative impacts upon long-term vigour and production.

Verifiers:
- Frequency of harvest does not exceed stipulated frequency.
- Frequencies are adjusted according to the diameter at breast height (dbh)/age of the harvestable tree.
- Records of harvest frequency are documented.
- Information on frequency is based upon the observations of a number of different sources.

5   *Indicator (**timing/seasonality/precipitation**):* harvesting is explicitly timed and designed to reduce stress during reproductive periods and to minimize impacts upon reproductive capacity.
Verifiers:
- Harvesting takes place according to a specified timing.
- Information is available on the reproductive cycles.
- Written instructions exist on periods to avoid and when to concentrate on harvesting.
- There is clear evidence that collectors are avoiding harvests during reproductive periods.

6   *Indicator (**density/abundance**):* the percentage of individuals harvested from the entire population will allow for the retention of mature reproducing individuals, and will reflect natural diversity in composition and structure.
Verifiers:
- The portion of mature reproducing individuals to retain is specified.
- A portion of mature reproducing individuals is retained.
- The number of individuals harvested is according to a pre-agreed density (trees per hectare).
- Structural and genetic diversity is maintained.

7   *Indicator (**techniques**):* exudates will be collected according to best harvesting practices.
Verifiers:
- Trees will not be felled unless part of approved silvicultural operations.
- Appropriate heights for taps/incisions are determined.
- Taps/incisions are located at a specified height.
- Appropriate depth of tap is determined.
- Tap does not exceed specified depth.
- Negative, indirect impacts of harvesting are minimized.

Monitoring indicators and verifiers for exudates

8   *Indicator (**growth rates and regeneration**):* growth rates and regeneration are regularly monitored using a well-designed inventory system.
Verifiers:
- Frequency of monitoring is specified.
- Periodic regeneration surveys are conducted as specified.
- Size-class distribution includes seedlings to large adults.
- Seedling or sapling densities as recorded in a vegetation or regeneration survey remain equal to or above baseline values.
- If, over time, seedling or sapling densities significantly decline, harvest adjustments are made by limiting the total area from which the resource can be harvested; regulating the number or size of the plants being harvested; and/or enrichment-planting of harvested species.

9   *Indicator (**visual appraisal of health and vigour**)*: regular visual appraisals of the behaviour and condition of harvestable plants/trees are conducted pre- and post-harvest.
    Verifiers:
    *   Over a specified period of time, harvestable plants/trees do not display loss of vigour, disease, aborted fruit/ leaves or stunted growth.
    *   If harvested individuals display a weakened condition, harvest volumes are reduced to allow for individual and population recovery.
    *   If visual assessments and inventories indicate a decline in the density of non-targeted species in the area of harvest, adjustments are made in the management regime to recover density.

10.2 Vegetative structures

Vegetative structures signify a variety of different plant parts such as stem, leaf, root, bark and apical bud (the primary growing point at the tip of the stem). This vast array of NTFP products is regularly harvested for use as food, medicine, crafts and building materials. The impact of harvesting plant tissues will depend upon the plant growth form and the technique and intensity of harvest. Intense and uncontrolled harvest of vegetative structures may result in the death of the plant. However, with proper harvesting techniques, plants may recover from damage due to the harvesting of leaves, sprouts and branches as they realize compensatory growth. This can result in a net higher biomass production compared to an undisturbed plant. The ability to produce a higher net biomass or to remain stable depends upon:

*   harvesting techniques;
*   harvesting intensity; and
*   growth form of the plant (Ros-Tonen et al, 1995; Peters, 1994).

Monitoring indicators and verifiers for all types of vegetative structures

1   *Indicator (**growth rates and regeneration**)*: growth rates and regeneration are regularly monitored by a well-designed and documented inventory system.
    Verifiers:
    *   Periodic regeneration surveys are conducted.
    *   Size-class distribution includes seedlings to large adults.
    *   Seedling or sapling densities as recorded in a vegetation or regeneration survey remain equal to or above baseline values.
    *   If seedling or sapling densities decline, harvest adjustments are made by limiting the total area from which the resource can be harvested; regulating the number or size of the plants being harvested; and/or enrichment-planting of harvested species.
    *   Relationships between resource stock and resource yield are assessed.

2   *Indicator (**visual appraisal**)*: regular visual appraisals of the behaviour and condition of harvestable plants/trees are conducted pre- and post- harvest.
    Verifiers:
    *   Harvestable plants/trees do not display loss of vigour, disease, aborted fruit/ leaves or stunted growth.

- If harvested individuals display a weakened condition, acceptable harvest volumes will be reduced to allow for individual and population recovery.
- If visual assessments and inventories indicate a decline in the density of non-targeted species in the area of harvest, adjustments will be made in the management regime to recover diversity.

Management indicators and verifiers for specific vegetative structures

Apical bud

1   *Indicator (**species selection**)*: multistemmed species that have the ability to resprout are harvested preferentially.
Verifiers:
- In areas where numerous species produce a similar product, multistemmed species and those with the ability to resprout are preferentially harvested (eg palm heart *Euterpe oleracea* in lieu of *Euterpe precatoria*), or provisions are made to enhance the preferred species.
- Commercial harvesting of hapaxanthic palm is prohibited except in cases where it occurs across large areas, with strictly controlled rotation of a fast-growing species (ten years to maturity).

2   *Indicator (**knowledge**)*: rates of harvesting intensity, frequency, and seasonality are defined based upon a combination of scientific study and/or long-term local experience and knowledge.
Verifiers:
- Scientific information is available.
- Local management/use of selected species exists.
- Harvest rates are documented in writing.
- Analysis of implications of different harvest rates is available.

3   *Indicator (**diameter and/or age**)*: minimum age or height at which apical buds may be harvested has been determined in a manner that explicitly aims to reduce negative impacts upon long-term vigour and production.
Verifiers:
- Minimum age (mature and fruiting and flowering) and height for first and subsequent harvests are specified.
- Individuals are harvested at or above the minimum dbh/age.

4   *Indicator (**quantity**)*: the quantity of plant tissue removed minimizes negative impacts upon long-term vigour.
Verifiers:
- Volumes extracted are documented.
- Data (or visual observations) on the relationships between volume extracted and plant health are available.

5   *Indicator (**frequency**)*: the frequency of harvest from an individual in a given time period has been determined in a way that reduces negative impacts upon long-term vigour and production.
Verifiers:
- Frequency of harvest does not exceed stipulated frequency based upon the rate of replacement of an adult tree.
- Frequencies are adjusted according to the age or height of the harvestable tree.
- Records of harvest frequency are documented.

- Information on frequency is based upon the observations of a number of different sources.

6   *Indicator (timing/seasonality):* harvesting is explicitly timed and designed to reduce stress during reproductive periods and to minimize impacts upon reproductive capacity.
    Verifiers:
    - Harvesting takes place according to a specified timing.
    - Information is available on the reproductive cycles.
    - Written instructions exist on periods to avoid and when to concentrate harvesting.

7   *Indicator (density/abundance):* the percentage of individuals harvested from the entire population will allow for the retention of mature reproducing individuals.
    Verifiers:
    - The portion of mature reproducing individuals to retain is specified.
    - A portion of mature reproducing individuals is retained.
    - The number of individuals harvested is according to a pre-agreed density (trees per hectare).
    - Structural and genetic diversity is maintained.

Bark

1   *Indicator (knowledge):* rates of harvesting intensity, frequency and seasonality are defined based upon a combination of scientific study and/or long-term local experience and knowledge.
    Verifiers:
    - Scientific information is available.
    - Local management and use of selected species exist.
    - Harvest rates are documented in writing.
    - Analysis of implications of different harvest rates is available.

2   *Indicator (diameter and/or age):* minimum dbh or age at which bark may be harvested has been determined in a manner that explicitly aims to reduce negative impacts upon long-term vigour and production.
    Verifiers:
    - Minimum age and dbh for first harvest are specified.
    - Individuals are harvested at or above the minimum dbh/age.

3   *Indicator (quantity):* the quantity of bark removed will minimize negative impacts upon long-term vigour.
    Verifiers:
    - Volumes extracted are documented.
    - Data (or visual observations) on the relationships between volume extracted and plant health are available.

4   *Indicator (frequency):* the frequency of harvest from an individual in a given time period has been determined in a way that reduces negative impacts upon long-term vigour and production.
    Verifiers:
    - Frequency of harvest does not exceed stipulated frequency.
    - Frequencies are adjusted according to the dbh of the harvestable tree.
    - Records of harvest frequency are documented.
    - Information on frequency is based upon the observations of a number of different sources.

5   *Indicator (timing/seasonality)*: harvesting is explicitly timed and designed to reduce stress during reproductive periods and to minimize impacts upon reproductive capacity.
Verifiers:
- Harvesting takes place according to specified timing/seasonality.
- Information is available on the reproductive cycles.
- Instructions exist on periods to avoid and when to concentrate harvesting.
- There is clear evidence that collectors avoid harvests during reproductive periods.

6   *Indicator (density/abundance)*: the percentage of individuals harvested from the entire population will allow for the retention of mature reproducing individuals, and will reflect natural diversity in composition and structure.
Verifiers:
- The portion of mature reproducing individuals to retain is specified.
- A portion of mature reproducing individuals is retained.
- The number of individuals harvested is determined according to a pre-agreed density (trees per hectare).
- Structural and genetic diversity is maintained.

7   *Indicator (techniques)*: bark will be harvested according to specified techniques that minimize negative impacts upon vigour.
Verifiers:
- Trees will not be girdled.
- Trees will not be felled in order to harvest bark unless part of a coppicing system.
- Bark can be collected from trees felled as part of approved silvicultural operations.
- Appropriate heights for bark harvest are determined.
- Bark is harvested only at agreed-upon heights.
- Bark is harvested only from an agreed-upon percentage of the diameter.
- The stemwood will not be damaged.
- Negative, indirect impacts of harvesting are minimized.

Root

1   *Indicator (knowledge)*: rates of harvesting intensity, frequency and seasonality are defined based upon a combination of scientific study and/or long-term local experience and knowledge.
Verifiers:
- Scientific information is available.
- Local management/use of selected species exists.
- Harvest rates are documented in writing.
- Analysis of implications of different harvest rates is available.

2   *Indicator (diameter and/or age)*: root harvest is conducted at specified maturity that will not excessively affect the species population.
Verifiers:
- Minimum age for first harvest is specified.
- Individuals are harvested at or above the minimum age.
- Individuals are harvested following reproductive maturity.

3   *Indicator (quantity)*: the quantity of root collected in a defined area will be in accordance with what is specified.

Verifiers:
- Volumes extracted are documented.
- Data (or visual observations) on the relationships between volume extracted and plant health are available.
- Mortality does not exceed recruitment.

4   *Indicator (**frequency**):* the frequency of harvest from a population in a given time period has been determined and is conducted in a way that reduces negative impacts upon population structure and production.
Verifiers:
- Frequency of harvest does not exceed stipulated frequency.
- Frequencies are adjusted according to the age/size of the harvestable plant.
- Frequencies are adjusted according to recruitment in the population.
- Records of harvest frequency are documented.
- Information on frequency is based upon the observations of a number of different sources.

5   *Indicator (**timing/seasonality**):* harvesting is explicitly timed and designed to reduce stress during reproductive periods and to minimize impacts upon reproductive capacity.
Verifiers:
- Harvesting takes place according to specified timing/seasonality.
- Information is available on the reproductive cycles.
- Root harvest is conducted after the fruit/seed of an individual plant has matured.
- Instructions exist on periods to avoid and when to concentrate harvesting.
- There is clear evidence that collectors are avoiding harvests during reproductive periods.

6   *Indicator (**density/abundance**):* the percentage of individuals harvested from the entire population will allow for the retention of mature reproducing individuals.
Verifiers:
- The portion of mature reproducing individuals to retain is specified.
- A portion of mature reproducing individuals is retained.
- The number of individuals harvested is determined according to a pre-agreed density (trees per hectare).
- Structural and genetic diversity is maintained.

7   *Indicator (**techniques**):* roots are harvested according to specified techniques.
Verifiers:
- The correct portion of the root, bulb or rootbark to be harvested is determined.
- Only the specified portion of the root, bulb or rootbark is harvested.
- Harvest techniques will be in accordance with the species' ability to sprout or to spread by root and/or seed.
- If a plant is capable of recovery, only a portion of the root is harvested and a viable portion left to resprout.
- Seed collected from a mature plant prior to harvest will be planted in the vicinity of the harvested individual in a habitat that is preferential to germination (eg ginseng).
- Negative, indirect impacts of harvesting are minimized.

Leaves

1   *Indicator (**knowledge**)*: rates of harvesting intensity, frequency and seasonality are defined based upon a combination of scientific study and/or long-term local experience and knowledge.
    Verifiers:
    - Scientific information is available.
    - Local management and use of selected species exist.
    - Harvest rates are documented in writing.
    - Analysis of implications of different harvest rates is available.

2   *Indicator (**diameter and/or age**)*: leaf harvest is conducted at specified dbh/age that will not excessively affect the species population.
    Verifiers:
    - Minimum age for first harvest is specified.
    - Individuals are harvested at or above the minimum age.

3   *Indicator (**quantity**)*: the quantity of leaves harvested will be in accordance with what is specified.
    Verifiers:
    - Volumes extracted are documented.
    - Data (or visual observations) on the relationships between volume extracted and plant health are available.
    - The appropriate proportion of healthy leaves needed for photosynthesis is determined.
    - A sufficient proportion of healthy leaves remains on each individual to allow for photosynthesis.

4   *Indicator (**frequency**)*: the frequency of harvest from an individual in a given time period has been determined and is conducted in a way that reduces negative impacts upon vigour and production.
    Verifiers:
    - Frequency of harvest does not exceed stipulated frequency.
    - Frequencies are adjusted according to the age of the harvestable plant.
    - Sufficient time is allowed between successive harvests for plants to produce new leaves (new leaves must be present on previously harvested individuals).
    - Records of harvest frequency are documented.
    - Information on frequency is based upon the observations of a number of different sources.

5   *Indicator (**timing/seasonality**)*: harvesting is explicitly timed and designed to reduce stress during reproductive periods and to minimize impacts on reproductive capacity.
    Verifiers:
    - Harvesting takes place according to specified timing/seasonality.
    - Information is available on the reproductive cycles.
    - Instructions exist on periods to avoid and when to concentrate harvesting.

6   *Indicator (**density/abundance**)*: the percentage of individuals from which leaves are harvested will be limited to specified levels in order to retain a vigorous population.
    Verifiers:
    - The portion of mature reproducing individuals to be retained is specified.
    - Mature reproducing individuals are retained.

- The number of individuals from which leaves are harvested is determined according to a pre-agreed density (trees/plants per hectare).
- Structural and genetic diversity is maintained.

7   *Indicator (techniques)*: leaves will be harvested according to specified techniques that minimize negative impacts upon vigour.
   Verifiers:
- Individual plants are not destroyed during harvest.
- Trees/shrubs are not felled.
- Reproductive structures and apical buds remain intact and do not show signs of post-harvest damage.
- Branches are not removed for the picking of leaves.
- Leaves are not collected from felled trees unless part of approved silvicultural operations.

10.3 Reproductive propagules: fruit/seed

The reproductive propagules of a plant, its fruits, nuts and oil seeds, are frequently harvested for use as food, oil, crafts and medicines. Harvest of fruits and seeds from beneath the crown of a tree may, in the short term, represent the least amount of direct damage to any NTFP because a population produces more offspring (seeds) and immature individuals (seedlings, saplings, juveniles) than is necessary to maintain its number of reproducing adults. The surplus of seeds is necessary to compensate for the extremely high risk of mortality in the juvenile phase.

The continual removal of significant quantities of offspring, however, can directly affect the ability of a plant to reproduce. Over the long term, mortality may exceed recruitment. A shortfall in recruitment can cause a notable change in population structure, resulting in decreased plant densities and modified size-class structure. Continued harvest can also affect the genetic composition of the tree population being exploited. In addition, in areas where commercial collectors diminish the quantities of fruits and seeds, frugivores that play a critical role in germination and seed dispersal may migrate to more isolated forest (Peters, 1994).

Management indicators and verifiers for reproductive propagules (fruit/seed)

1   *Indicator (knowledge)*: rates of harvesting intensity, frequency and seasonality are defined based upon a combination of scientific study and/or long-term local experience and knowledge.
   Verifiers:
- Scientific information is available.
- Local management and use of selected species exist.
- Harvest rates are documented in writing.
- Analysis of implications of different harvest rates is available.

2   *Indicator (quantity)*: research, documentation or systematic observations of population dynamics have been used to develop growth and to yield predictions that determine the quantity of fruit or seed harvested.
   Verifiers:
- Volumes extracted are documented.

- The productive capacity of the species has been determined through weighing, counting or measuring the quantity of the resource produced by different sample trees during the harvest season.
- No more than a determined percentage of the harvestable yield is extracted.

3   *Indicator (**techniques**)*: fruit will be harvested according to specified methods that minimize negative impacts upon populations.
Verifiers:
- Trees are not felled.
- Fruit, seeds and nuts are harvested from the tree itself or directly from the ground after falling from the tree.
- Trees are not damaged to induce premature fruiting.
- A determined portion of fruits remains in the forest for wildlife (disperser) populations.

Monitoring indicators and verifiers for vegetation propagules

1   *Indicator (**growth rates and regeneration**)*: growth rates and regeneration are monitored by a suitable inventory system.
Verifiers:
- Periodic regeneration surveys are conducted.
- Size-class distribution demonstrates a population structure from seedlings to large adults.
- Seedling or sapling densities as recorded in a vegetation or regeneration survey remain equal to or above baseline values.
- If seedling or sapling densities decline, harvest adjustments are made by limiting the total area from which the resource can be harvested; regulating the number of fruits harvested; and/or enrichment-planting of harvested species.

2   *Indicator (**visual appraisal**)*: regular visual appraisals of the behaviour and condition of harvestable plants/trees are conducted pre- and post-harvest.
Verifiers:
- Harvestable plants/trees do not display loss of vigour, disease, aborted fruit/ leaves or stunted growth.
- If harvested individuals display a weakened condition, acceptable harvest volumes will be reduced to allow for individual and population recovery.
- If visual assessments and inventories indicate a decline in the density of non-targeted species in the area of harvest, adjustments will be made in the management regime to recover diversity.

3   *Indicator (**wildlife/dispersors**)*: periodic assessments are conducted in order to evaluate populations of animals that disperse seeds and fruits.
Verifiers:
- Within the area of harvest, populations of animals that disperse fruits remain stable.
- If populations of animals that disperse the seed decline, harvest adjustments are made (see above).

Species-specific NTFP certification guidelines for the production of maple syrup

(to be used with SmartWood's *Generic Guidelines for Assessing Natural Forest Management*)

Alan R Pierce

Introduction

This appendix provides specific guidelines that must be used in every assessment of a commercialized non-timber forest product (NTFP). These guidelines are NTFP-specific sub-criteria that are to be nested under the existing Rainforest Alliance SmartWood programme generic sub-criteria for assessing forest management. Thus, for a complete picture of certification requirements for NTFPs, this appendix must be reviewed alongside SmartWood's *Generic Guidelines for Assessing Natural Forest Management* (2000).

This appendix also provides specific guidance for the certification of maple sugaring operations. Maple-specific guidelines are listed below the generic NTFP guidelines, in italics.

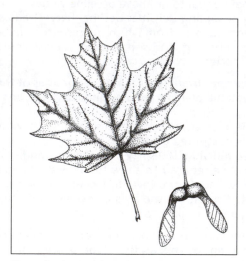

Illustration by Jamison Ervin

*Sugar maple (*Acer saccharum*)*

Principle 1: compliance with laws and Forest Stewardship Council (FSC) principles

Non-timber forest product harvest shall take place within the ethical and legal framework of international environmental and human rights law and policy, as well as national, state/provincial, and local laws in the country where forest management takes place. NTFP harvest and processing may involve laws and regulations not normally covered under a typical SmartWood assessment. Laws concerning NTFP harvest and use may fall under the Convention on International Trade in Endangered Species of Wild Fauna and Flora (CITES), national tenure and usufruct rights laws and national forest management legislation. Collection of some NTFPs requires legal permits or licences. Furthermore, for edible products, a variety of laws may govern quality control, transport, packaging and labelling requirements. Assessors must check with relevant government agencies and other stakeholders to verify that an operation is dealing with legal requirements for NTFP management, harvest, processing and sale in a responsible fashion.

Because maple syrup is an edible product, it is subject to a number of state and federal laws regarding quality control, sanitation measures and labelling. SmartWood will not assess the actual legal compliance of the sugaring operation to the relevant laws because that is the mandated task of government institutions. However, SmartWood must be assured that operators have the proper tools and facilities to comply with all relevant laws governing maple syrup, and may check with government agencies and other stakeholders to verify that an operation adheres to legal requirements in a responsible fashion.

1.1 NTFP processing equipment, processing methods and transport meet all applicable international, national and local laws governing licence fees, sanitation standards, quality control, and packaging and labelling requirements.
The sugar-maker adheres to national and state laws governing acceptable syrup density, colour grading, packing and labelling regulations and other relevant laws.
Verifiers:
- The sugar-maker maintains an up-to-date colour kit and an accurate, periodically tested hydrometer.
- Enrollment in an organic or state certification programme (eg Vermont's Seal of Quality programme).
- No formal complaints have been filed with the sugar-maker about product quality.

1.1 The forest management operation (FMO) or NTFP harvester(s) maintains up-to-date harvesting permits, collecting licences and collecting contracts or cultivation permits, and pays any fees, leases, royalties, etc in a timely manner.
Any invoices for purchasing sap/syrup from other sugar-makers or lease fees to tap trees on land not directly owned by the sugar-maker are up-to-date in payment.

1.5 Collection of NTFPs, firewood, timber, game and other forest resources by forest workers and local communities is monitored and, if necessary, controlled.

Principle 2: tenure and use rights and responsibilities

Non-timber forest products are important resources for rural and even urban populations worldwide. Clear land tenure – the guaranteeing of rights and access to resources – enables forest managers and communities to invest in long-term forest management strategies of the kind NTFP certification is intended to promote. Forest managers shall demonstrate sensitivity to the dependence of local individuals and communities on NTFPs, as long as such NTFP usage does not threaten forest integrity. Forest managers may take proactive steps to improve community relations by improving understanding of NTFP usage, permitting continued access to such resources and by being mindful of maintaining NTFP resources in management planning. However, increased market demand, higher prices for particular NTFPs or new settlement may increase pressures on NTFPs. In such instances, management may need to restrict NTFP access to those with traditional rights or, in drastic cases, temporarily curtail access to protect resources.

Maple sugaring takes place in regions of North America that have strong private property traditions. Tenure to maple stands is usually very well defined, though in some regions outstanding resource claims may be encountered. Unlike NTFPs such as herbs or mushrooms, policing illegal harvest of maple sap is facilitated by the visibility of tapping equipment and the length of the harvest season. For sugar-makers who collect sap from properties not directly under their ownership or control, tapping leases or written permission is necessary.

2.1   When applicable, the rights of forest workers to use, occupy (and own) the property is secure.
When land is not directly owned or controlled by the NTFP harvester, NTFP harvest is undertaken with the permission of the landowner and is preferably outlined in writing (eg a lease contract or other agreement outlining harvest area, species collected, estimated volume extracted, etc).
The sugar-maker secures written permission or a lease contract for tapping any trees on land not under his/her direct ownership or traditional control.

2.3   Commercialization and large-scale harvesting of NTFPs is described to affected communities in public meetings, mailings or other types of communications in advance, when harvest of such products has the potential to impact local subsistence use.
Any conflicting claims over traditional access to sugaring stands are addressed in a systematic and effective manner.

Principle 3: indigenous peoples' rights

The rights of indigenous peoples to use NTFPs for subsistence needs are to be protected. NTFPs play central roles in cultural and religious ceremonies for local communities, and their protection may ensure cultural survival and positive relations with stakeholders. Certification should seek to minimize any potentially negative impacts of market forces upon the traditional local use and management of forests and forest products. Certification should also avoid creating dependency relationships that may disrupt cultural balance, integrity and belief systems.

North American settlers learned the art of making maple syrup from Native Americans. Settlers have manufactured maple syrup for over 200 years, embracing the product as their own and giving the product a special cultural status in rural areas. As far as is known, maple syrup commercialization does not disrupt any religious or cultural significance to indigenous communities, and there are no outstanding indigenous claims for compensation due to the use of traditional knowledge.

3.2   The FMO or NTFP harvester(s) does not commercialize vulnerable NTFPs, particularly NTFPs that are used for subsistence or have cultural or religious significance to local communities.

3.2   Plants and animal resources of cultural and religious significance are identified and protected.

Collateral damage from harvesting timber and non-timber products to culturally and religiously significant sites, groves, plants and animals is controlled.

3.2   Local communities receive fair and adequate benefits for any use of their name or image in the marketing of NTFPs.

When local or indigenous knowledge forms the basis of an NTFP-related patent, informed consent is obtained and the affected community receives fair and adequate benefits.

Principle 4: community relations and workers' rights

NTFP operations should follow a 'good neighbour' policy with their workers and with local communities. Certification of NTFPs should benefit not only forest managers, but also forest workers and the wider community. Active community involvement in forest management operations can strengthen long-term worker relations and sustainable forest management, which is the primary goal of certification.

Working conditions in some remote NTFP operations may be below health and safety norms. However, to achieve certification, SmartWood expects candidate operations to make every effort to ensure that working conditions are safe and well paid, with adequate amenities and benefits (compared to local norms). Workers from local communities are expected to have preferance when hiring. Where appropriate, worker access to living quarters and forest resources such as timber, fibres, game and subsistence NTFPs should be agreed upon in some formal manner. In addition, NTFP operations should make every effort to ensure that harvesting methods and processing methods and facilities are safe and sanitary for both workers and end-consumers.

Sugaring operations are often family run. However, additional help is sometimes needed for thinning, tapping or boiling the sap. When help is hired for sugarbush operations, wages are expected to be fair, and the operation should maintain insurance to cover any injuries that occur on the property.

Lead contamination from old buckets, rusty storage tanks or lead-soldering on evaporator pans can be a problem for some sugaring operations. SmartWood expects candidate operations to have samples of their syrup tested for lead contamination by third-party facilities. Lead levels exceeding 250 parts per billion will require corrective steps to lower the lead content, either by replacing the most egregious equipment or blending with other certified syrup to achieve lower lead levels.

4.1 *If sugar-makers require extra help with the sugaring operation, local communities and residents are given first preference for jobs involving sugarbush thinning, tapping, processing, packing or sale of maple products.*

4.2 Health, retirement, workers' compensation, housing, food and other benefits for full-time staff and contractors involved with NTFP harvest are consistent with (not lower than) prevailing standards.

Hired help for sugarbush management, tapping or work in the evaporating shed or sales area is fairly compensated in accordance with local laws and norms.

Sugarbush and evaporator workers are insured for any injuries arising from accidents sustained on the job.

For edible items, management undertakes proactive product quality-control actions to ensure that its products pose no health risks to the final consumer.

If a defoamer is used in the sugaring shed, it meets organic certification standards.

Sugar-makers have their syrup independently tested for lead contamination over a period of at least three years.

Verifiers:

- Independently verified results of lead sampling are sent to SmartWood headquarters or are available for inspection during the site visit.
- Enrollment in organic or state certification programmes (eg Vermont's Seal of Quality programme).

4.4 Social impacts of NTFP harvest and commercialization on local communities are addressed and incorporated within management planning, particularly with respect to subsistence NTFP users.

Consultations with local NTFP gatherers and users identify important NTFP species or habitats. Management shares information on harvesting objectives with affected stakeholders.

Detrimental social and cultural change resulting from the influx of NTFP harvesters or commercialization of NTFPs is minimized.

4.4 The FMO or NTFP harvester(s) maintains viable populations of NTFPs and other locally important forest resources, when and where possible.

Principle 5: benefits from the forest

NTFPs can provide a range of social and economic benefits at local, regional and international levels and have the potential to diversify income sources for forest operations. The intent of NTFP certification is to optimize the socio-economic potential of certain marketable species, in order to provide a larger economic return from a given forest area for local communities and forest managers, without negatively impacting local use of these or other NTFP species. Some NTFPs may favourably compete with timber revenues on a hectare-per-hectare basis. Many other NTFPs do not compete well with timber revenues, but serve important local needs. Other NTFPs go through economic boom-and-bust cycles. Like timber extraction, NTFP commercialization should follow rational marketing plans and have sound financial investments to ensure long-term viability, forest conservation and the stability of local communities.

Traditionally, maple syrup has provided income to labour-rich but cash-poor rural farmers and woodlot owners. Small operations may not be economically viable according to classical economic formulae; yet, people continue to produce the product out of tradition and a need for income. Sound investments are necessary to keep sugarbushes and sugaring operations viable, and include sugarbush thinning, building maintenance and purchases of new equipment, such as tubing, evaporators and/or evaporator parts, packing materials and storage tanks. Maple syrup has a strong domestic market and a small but growing international market. While its use as a pancake topping has diminished, due to substitution by corn syrup-based 'maple syrups' and a diminishment in overall pancake consumption, its use in 'luxury' food items is very promising.

Tapping results in direct injury to individual trees. Proper tapping can ensure the longevity and productivity of the sugarbush. Traditional tapping guidelines specified tapping to commence at 10 inches (25.5cm) diameter at breast height (dbh), with a second tap being added at 15 inches (38cm) dbh, a third at 20 inches (51cm) dbh and a fourth on trees greater than 25 inches (64cm) dbh. Newer, more conservative tapping guidelines now recommend commencement of tapping at 12 inches (30cm) dbh, and recommend that no more than two taps be used on any tree with a dbh greater than 18 inches (46cm). Introduction of the 'narrow spout' or 'health spout' may cause tapping guidelines to be modified yet again.

SmartWood's philosophy of forest management is in alignment with the newer, more conservative tapping guidelines. Rather than require prescriptive adherence to a particular set of tapping guidelines, SmartWood may allow variance from conservative guidelines (eg the addition of a third tap at 30+ inches – 76cm – dbh) if such tapping is well justified by the sugar-maker, the site is very productive and trees show rapid tap-hole closure (closure within two to three years). Tree vigour is enhanced by proper thinning, integrated pest management (IPM) and maintenance of soil fertility, and is manifested, in part, by rapid tap-hole closure. Tapping should be reduced in trees showing reduced vigour, die-back or damage.

Tap-hole depth should optimally be less than 2.5 inches (6cm) in depth and should not exceed 3 inches (8cm) in depth. Tap holes should be distributed over as large an area as possible of the maple's available tapping shell. Guidelines recommend placing new taps at least half a foot (0.15 metres) to the side and two feet (0.6m) above or below any old tap holes. 'Cluster tapping', the placement of many taps within a small area of the overall tapping band of the tree, is to be avoided because injuries from closely placed tap wounds can coalesce and hasten rot and decay.

5.1 Based upon local experience and markets, payments or fees paid to local landowners for the use of products derived from their forest property are at or above the norm (ie average), and are perceived by landowners to be a positive incentive for encouraging long-term forest management.

The FMO or NTFP harvester(s) keeps abreast of current NTFP harvest methods, harvesting equipment and processing equipment, and (within fiscal constraints) makes every effort to invest in new tools and equipment that minimize ecological damage to NTFPs or improve the overall economic viability of the operation.

Sugar-makers keep up to date on sugarbush management and syrup processing developments and technology.

Verifier is:

- *Attendance at annual sugar-maker meetings, interaction with extension agents, subscriptions to, or purchase of, maple-oriented literature and maple research or technical papers, participation in the North American*

Sugar Maple Decline Project, participation in maple-pest research projects or programmes experimenting with new tapping techniques.

When it occurs, advance payment to NTFP supervisors and harvesters is timely, and cash-flow issues do not jeopardize the forest operation or worker relations. In the case of externally supported operations, a plan exists to reduce the level of dependency upon external support and to maximize levels of self-sufficiency and control.

5.1 Utilization of lesser-known species does not compromise local NTFP needs (eg for fruits, medicines, game-attracting species, etc) and does not negatively affect forest diversity.

5.3 The FMO or NTFP harvester(s) explores options to utilize or commercialize NTFP processing waste, when feasible and appropriate.

5.5 Interviews with communities and individuals indicate a positive or neutral impact upon NTFPs used for subsistence.

5.5 The intensity, frequency and seasonality of NTFP harvest, by area and volume, are based upon a combination of scientific study and/or long-term local experience and knowledge and do not exceed sustainable levels.

The area of the sugarbush is delineated on maps and the number of taps used within the area is prescribed.

Minimum tapping diameter and the number of taps used per size class are documented.

Tapping is judicious and does not deliberately hasten a decline in tree health or vigour.

Verifier is:
* *Two-year-old tap holes, of traditional 7/16-inch diameter, are completely closed or closing to such an extent that a standard number 2 pencil cannot be inserted into the tap wound.*

NTFP harvest rates, cultural techniques and harvest methods are appropriate for the particular plant part used (exudate, reproductive propagule, vegetative structure), and management activities maintain viable populations of target NTFPs.

Silvicultural treatments ensure proper spacing of trees and adequate regeneration of sugar maple.

Verifier is:
* *Thinning is based upon spacing and tree vigour. Retention of sugar trees may be supported by measuring sugar content of the trees (through use of a refractometer).*

Use of paraformaldehyde pellets in tap holes is prohibited.

Allowable NTFP harvest rates are being followed in the forest.

Verifiers:
* *Trees smaller than the minimum allowable tapping diameter are not tapped.*
* *Number of taps used per size class follows management prescription.*

Appropriate NTFP harvest prescriptions are being implemented in the field.

Verifiers:
* *Taps are immediately pulled from trees at the end of the sugaring season.*
* *Tap holes are drilled with a slight upward angle and are not excessively deep (ie exceed 2.5 inches – 6cm – in depth).*
* *'Cluster tapping' is not practised.*

- *Drop lines on tubing systems are of sufficient length to preclude cluster tapping (ie the drop line is long enough so that the tap can reach all sides of the tree and can be placed sufficiently above or below old tap holes).*

Population levels of targeted NTFPs are monitored and recorded.

Sugarbush monitoring systems monitor and record size class, distribution, growth and regeneration of sugar maple.

Principle 6: environmental impact

NTFP management, if properly handled, may enhance overall forest integrity. However, NTFP management may result in forest simplification in some cases. Such simplification may be offset by the temporal or operational scale of the NTFP management activity, or the relatively reduced destruction to forest integrity by NTFP harvest when compared to timber harvest. Nevertheless, harvest of many NTFPs can be destructive to forest resources due to poor technique, shoddy equipment or disregard for an individual plant's long-term survival (eg felling a tree to collect its fruits). Proper harvest techniques, tailored to the individual target species and incorporating the impact of NTFPs' removal on population structure, can ensure long-term NTFP population viability. Producers of edible NTFPs should make every effort to meet organic standards because ecological labels on NTFPs may confuse consumers if they do not ensure that the product is pesticide free. Exudates, reproductive propagules and vegetative structures all entail differing harvest regimes and impacts, and management activities should reflect such differences.

Sugarbush management results in the simplification of natural forests. However, the size of many sugarbushes, even large operations, almost never exceeds 81 hectares, and is often quite smaller. The overall impact and placement of the sugarbush should be considered in management planning. Sugarbushes are generally thought to have negative wildlife impacts (due to the removal of mast species and the simplification of the forest); but conclusive studies on the wildlife impacts of sugarbushes have not been documented (including the wildlife impact of tubing systems on animal movement). Wildlife, particularly squirrels, can cause great damage to tubing systems. Quite a few sugar-makers trap, poison or otherwise exclude squirrels and other damaging wildlife.

6.1 The environmental assessment includes impacts of NTFP commercialization.
Management considers the impact of the sugarbush upon diversity at the stand level, and upon wildlife at the watershed and landscape level.

6.1 NTFPs on either local and/or international endangered or threatened species lists (eg CITES Appendix 1, national lists, etc) are not harvested.

6.1 NTFP management minimizes impacts to forest composition and structure, as well as soil structure and fertility.
Management encourages the retention of non-maple species in the sugarbush to promote diversity and, potentially, to promote the pest resistance of the stand.
Management practices avoid heavy cleaning of the sugarbush understorey. Grazing is prohibited in the sugarbush.
Access roads are kept to a minimum to avoid soil damage during spring snow melt.

Harvesting of NTFPs accounts for the ecological requirements of the target NTFP and other species (eg food for frugivorous birds and mammals, animal dispersal of seeds, maintenance of specific ecological interdependencies, etc). *Sugaring takes place on sites well suited to sugar maple growth.*
NTFP management and harvest ensure the retention of mature, reproducing individuals of NTFP target populations, and maintain a natural diversity in the composition and structure of such populations. *Adequate sugar maple regeneration is present.*
Enrichment planting of NTFPs minimizes impacts upon overstorey or understorey diversity across the forest.

6.5 Construction, maintenance and closure standards for NTFP access trails and roads are implemented according to local standards or best practices in order to minimize forest resource damage, drainage problems soil erosion and/or sedimentation of watercourses.
Sugarbush operations comply with or exceed current federal, state and municipal laws and regulations, including best management practices (BMPs), and avoid rutting and off-site transport of soils (ie into streambeds).

6.5 Use of chemical pesticides in harvest areas for comestible NTFPs is prohibited, unless these chemicals are allowed under local, national or international organic standards.
Any wildlife control measures (eg squirrel trapping or poisoning) are judicious.
Verifiers:
- *Evidence of consultation with wildlife experts to determine best methods for wildlife control.*

6.8 Use of biological control agents in NTFP harvesting areas meets local, national and international organic standards and is documented, minimized, monitored and strictly controlled.

6.9 Naturalized NTFP species (exotic species that reproduce on their own over a long time frame) do not demonstrate any known negative ecological impacts and are strictly controlled.

6.10 Severe forest simplification arising from NTFP management is allowed only when it is temporally or spatially bound; provides a limited impact upon the overall forest management unit; maintains high-conservation value forest attributes; or provides secure, outstanding conservation benefits to local communities or forest protection efforts.

Principle 7: management plan

Management plans should specifically incorporate NTFPs destined for commercial sale and should enumerate management objectives, harvest rates and harvest techniques for target NTFPs. Harvest levels and methods should be firmly rationalized through published literature, site-specific data and/or local knowledge. Poorly trained NTFP harvesters can cause great damage to forest resources. Forest worker training is central to realizing good management planning and implementation of proper harvesting techniques in the field.

Sugarbushes should be incorporated within the management plan, and specific objectives for management must be documented. Maps should depict, at least, the sugarbush area, sugaring access road and the sugaring shed. Tapping prescriptions, equipment used and other parameters relating to sap harvest should also be reflected in the management plan. Any hired help should be well trained in order to ensure proper implementation of ecologically sensitive tapping in the field.

7.1   The management plan or appendices to the plan specifically address and incorporate commercially managed NTFPs.

The sugarbush is incorporated within the management plan and is depicted on management maps; clear management objectives exist.

Maps delineate the sugarbush area and indicate sugaring access roads and the sugaring shed.

Silvicultural prescriptions for the sugarbush, whether under even-aged or uneven-aged management, are documented and followed.

The management plan includes the rate and quantity of NTFPs to be harvested based upon plant part used (exudate, reproductive propagule, vegetative structure) and the established best management practices for each NTFP.

The management plan states the number of taps used in the operation and future tapping targets.

Numbers of taps used, volumes of sap extracted and volumes of syrup produced per annum are recorded.

The management plan includes a description of, and justification for, the amount of each NTFP harvested, the implemented harvesting technique and the equipment used.

The number of allowable taps per size class, the depth of taps and the placement of taps on the tapping band are specified in the management plan.

Rationale for the equipment used is justified.

If prescribed tapping rates vary from well-established norms, compelling evidence justifies the deviation.

The rationale behind NTFP management activities is well documented (ie based upon site-specific field data, local knowledge or published regional forest research and government requirements).

Tapping rates are justified by prompt tap-hole closure, published tapping guidelines and relevant site-specific data and observation.

The NTFP management plan(s) is technically sound and sufficiently detailed, given the size, complexity and intensity of the forest operation.

7.1   NTFP management and harvesting practices are adjusted to incorporate new scientific or technical information.

Use of 'health spouts' or 'narrow spouts' on small diameter trees (< 25.4cm dbh) is conservative until research shows such usage is ecologically and economically viable.

7.1   NTFP harvesters receive adequate training and supervision in order to ensure that ecologically sensitive harvesting techniques are being properly implemented in the field.

Workers receive adequate instruction on proper tapping techniques and processing issues.

Verifiers:

- Cluster tapping is not observed in the field.
- Tap holes are properly drilled (at a proper depth, with a new sharp drill bit, showing infrequent splitting of the bark from driving taps too deeply or into frozen tissue).

Principle 8: monitoring and assessment

Internal monitoring systems are crucial in order to provide quality control for forest management operations, to identify social, ecological, economic and operational challenges, and to report on the success or failure of management interventions to resolve problems. In some NTFP management operations, monitoring may be adequate but extremely informal. Assessors may need to move some operations towards more formal and documented monitoring systems, which in the end can serve to improve management quality and effectiveness.

Sugarbush monitoring should ideally follow guidelines for continuous forest inventories. Sugarbush monitoring should include the basal area, dbh and species mix present in the sugarbush. Recording growth rates of sugar maples is also important. Sugaring trees should exhibit enough growth of new sapwood (in excess of 1/8 inch – 0.3cm – per year) so that spacing of tap holes around the tree avoids the creation of large decaying areas through an agglomeration of tap wounds or tapping into dead brown wood of old compartmentalized tap wounds. The general condition of the trees in the sugarbush should be noted and recorded, and declines in health and vigour of trees should precipitate reduced levels of tapping. In addition, IPM should be incorporated as part of the sugarbush monitoring, with observations of pest populations recorded. Ideally, aspects such as tap-hole closure rates should be recorded. The sweetness of sap from trees, measured with a refractometer, is also useful information to obtain, particularly when making decisions to retain or remove trees during thinnings – however, this information needs to be properly interpreted (for example, stressed trees can contain very sweet sap). Lastly, the number of taps used per year, volume of sap collected and volumes and grades of syrup produced and sold should be documented.

8.1 Monitoring reports indicate how management prescriptions should be changed for NTFP management based upon results of new social information.

Sugarbush monitoring is incorporated within the overall monitoring plan for the forest management operation.

Sugarbush monitoring includes monitoring of pest populations and overall health of trees within the sugarbush.

8.2 The monitoring plan identifies and describes observed changes in conditions relating to:

- NTFP populations (impact of harvest, growth rates, loss of vigour or decline, recruitment);
- any outstanding environmental changes from NTFP management affecting flora, fauna, soil and water resources;
- socio-economic aspects of NTFP use and harvest (changes in community and worker relations or conditions, changes in NTFP use or demand, etc).

The sugarbush monitoring plan is technically sound and identifies/describes changes in the condition of:

- *sugar maple growth rates and regeneration;*
- *sugar maple health (decline, die-back or even poor tap hole closure rates);*
- *presence of pests.*

The monitoring plan documents the number of taps used, volume of sap collected and volume and grades of syrup produced.

8.2 Volume and source data on loads of NTFPs are available (ie scaled, inventoried, measured) in the forest, in transport, and at processing and distribution centres controlled by the FMO or NTFP harvester(s).

The volume and source of sap collected and the volume and grades of syrup produced are recorded for future tracing.

Invoices of syrup or sap sales are documented and available for inspection.

For operations with multiple (certified and non-certified) sources of sap, 100 per cent batch runs are devised for production of certified sap.

Each batch of syrup is coded as packed for future tracking.

Storage barrels are appropriately labelled, particularly in operations with multiple (certified and non-certified) sources of sap.

Invoices for certified syrup or sap sales are kept separate from non-certified syrup or sap sales, and certified syrup or sap is clearly distinguished from non-certified products through marks, bar codes, labels or other means.

8.2 NTFP harvest is adjusted when populations exhibit decline or weakened condition.

Tapping is reduced or halted when trees exhibit decline, poor tap-hole closure or symptoms of severe stress, or after a heavy thinning of the stand.

Thinnings do not take place after several defoliation events or stress events in the sugarbush (eg ice damage).

Principle 9: maintenance of high conservation-value forests

NTFP management may contribute to the maintenance of high conservation-value forests (HCVF). FSC definitions require consultation in order to determine the status of HCVFs, including social consultations. Current definitions allow forests to be considered HCVFs if they provide basic needs for local communities, either for subsistence use or for the maintenance of cultural identity. In such cases, NTFPs may play a large role in determining if forests are to be considered HCVFs from a social perspective.

Sugarbushes may or may not contribute to the maintenance of high conservation-value forests, depending upon regional definitions and stakeholder interests. For example, simplifying a remnant old-growth Eastern forest into a sugarbush may not retain many HCVF values. However, existing old stands of sugar maples used for sugaring may represent old seral stages in areas otherwise lacking in older growth stands. Old sugarbushes may provide stable habitats for unique understorey plant communities, or may provide habitat and refugia for species of mosses, lichens, fungi or animals requiring old den trees (eg pileated woodpeckers).

9.1 Consultations to determine the status of a HCVF specifically include NTFPs as an element of the social analysis section covering forest importance to local communities (as per definition 'd' of HCVF, provided by the FSC; for further information, see FSC, 1999).

9.3 NTFP management does not diminish attributes that cause a forest to be listed as a HCVF.

Principle 10: plantations

NTFPs may come from plantations or agroforestry systems as primary products or as by-products. For the production of some NTFPs, a long continuum from purely agricultural settings to forestry settings exists. The challenge for SmartWood assessors is to determine where in the continuum the NTFP fails. Regional forest standards and consultations with experts will help in determining when to treat certain NTFPs as forest or agricultural products.

NTFP plantations may be created through sowing, planting, intensive silvicultural treatments or intensive understorey clearing in natural forests. NTFP plantations that exhibit few or none of the characteristics and key elements of native ecosystems, and are not established on lands committed to long-term forest cover, will normally be disqualified from certification. In addition, extensive cultivation of exotic understorey plants not found in local ecosystems will normally be excluded from certification. Such crops may be better addressed by agroforestry, organic or fairtrade initiatives that primarily focus upon pesticide use, fair wages and working conditions, and actions that seek to mitigate biodiversity losses due to intensive agricultural production. In the case of forest gardens that retain some of the characteristics and key elements of native forests, SmartWood may work in tandem with other initiatives to provide certification on a case-by-case basis.

NTFP production can balance management objectives and outputs for some plantation systems, and as such should be encouraged, particularly if production of the NTFP in question from natural forests is endangered or otherwise controversial. NTFPs potentially provide additional challenges to the plantation principle because many products are understorey plants that are not well covered by existing FSC criteria.

Sugar maple stands are occasionally established on abandoned pasture or otherwise open land. As long as the trees are well suited to the site, and the site is not an ecologically important non-forest habitat (eg a remnant prairie fragment, a wetland, etc), the sugarbush can be certified as long as it meets the FSC and SmartWood criteria for plantation management.

10.1 The plantation management plan articulates objectives for NTFP production, whether as the primary product of the management plan or as a by-product of the timber plantation.

10.1 Intensive management or cultivation of understorey NTFPs in natural forests does not adversely impact the diversity of shrubs and herbs across the forest landscape.

10.6 Intensive management or cultivation of understorey NTFPs in natural forests does not cause erosion, reduce water quality or adversely impact soil structure or fertility.

10.6 Use of chemical pesticides in plantations of comestible NTFPs is prohibited unless such chemicals meet local, national or international organic standards.

10.6 Establishment of NTFP plantations does not adversely impact resources or the rights of local communities or local people.

Resource directory

The NTFP certification project team found the following resources valuable to their work.

Documents

- African Timber Organization (ATO), *Draft Principles for African Tropical Forests*, 1996
- Amazon Cooperation Treaty A C, *Tarapoto Proposal on Criteria and Indicators of Sustainability for the Amazon Forests*, 1995
- 'Bolivian Council for Voluntary Forest Certification Brazil Nut Standards', second draft, (Estándares para la Certificación Forestal Voluntaria de Castaña (*Bertholletia excelsa*), 'El Comitéde Estándares de Castaña, Consejo Boliviano para la Certificación Forestal Voluntaria'), 1998
- Canadian General Standards Board, *Draft Standard for Organic Agriculture*, 1997
- Center for International Forestry Research (CIFOR), *Testing C&I for Sustainable Management of Forests: Phase 1 Final Report*, 1996
- CIFOR, *A Basic C&I Knowledge Base for 'CIMAT'(C&I Modification and Adaptation Tool)*, Project 4, 1998
- Crafter, S, J Awimbo and A Broekhoven, *Non-timber Forest Products Value, Use and Management Issues in Africa, Including Examples from Latin America*, IUCN, 1997
- Cunningham, A B, *African Medicinal Plants: Setting Priorities at the Interface Between Conservation and Primary Healthcare*, People and Plants Working Paper 1, UNESCO, 1993
- Cunningham, A B, *Applied Ethnobotany: People, Wild Plant Use and Conservation*, Earthscan/WWF, 2001
- Cunningham, A B and F T Mbenkum, *Sustainability of Harvesting* Prunus africana *Bark in Cameroon: A Medicinal Plant in International Trade*, People and Plants Working Paper 2, UNESCO, 1993
- De Beer, J and M McDermott, *The Economic Value of Non-Timber Forest Products in Southeast Asia*, IUCN, 1996 (1989)
- Deskundigenwerkgroep Duurzaam Bosbeheer, *Evaluating Sustainable Forest Management*, 1994
- Fairtrade Labelling Organizations (FLO), *General Criteria for Awarding the Fairtrade Mark*, 1998
- FLO, *Banana Criteria*, 1998
- Fairtrade Federation (FTF), *Principles and Practices*, undated
- Fairtrade Foundation, *Fairtrade Mark General Criteria*, 1996
- Food and Agriculture Organization (FAO), *More Than Wood: Special Options on Multiple Use of Forests*, FAO Forestry Topics Report No 4

- Forest Garden Products, *A Standards Manual*, first draft, 1998
- Forest Stewardship Council (FSC), *Principles and Criteria for Forest Management*, 1996
- Freese, C, *Wild Species as Commodities*, Island Press, 1998
- FSC, *NTFP Working Group Draft Principle 11*, 1997
- *Goods & News*, 'Guidelines for Fairtrade Products', 1998
- Institute for Sustainable Forestry (ISF), *Pacific Certified Ecological Forest Products*, 1995
- International Federation for Alternative Trade (IFAT), *Code of Practice*, 1995
- International Federation of Organic Agriculture Movements (IFOAM), *Basic Standards*, third version, July 1998
- IFOAM, *Guidelines on Social Rights and Fair Trade*, 1994
- International Tropical Timber Organization (ITTO), *Criteria for the Measurement of Sustainable Tropical Forest Management*, 1992
- Instituto de Manejo e Certificação Florestal e Agrícola (IMAFLORA), *Draft Standards for Rubber and Brazil Nuts*, 1995
- Laird, S A *The Natural Management of Tropical Forests for Timber and NTFPs*, Oxford Forestry Institute Occasional Paper, 1995
- Max Havelaar Foundation, 'Max Havelaar Basic Principles' (fairtrade), undated
- Ministerial Conference on the Protection of Forests in Europe, *European Criteria and Most Suitable Quantitative Indicators for Sustainable Forest Management*, 1994
- Montreal Process, *Criteria and Indicators for the Conservation and Sustainable Management of Temperate and Boreal Forests*, 1995
- Naturland-Verband fur Naturgemassen, *Naturland Standards on Organic Forest Use*, 1997
- Network of European World Shops (NEWS), *Fair Trade Criteria*, undated
- Neumann, R and E Hirsch, *Commercialization of Non-Timber Forest Products: Review and Analysis of Research*, CIFOR, 2000
- North-East Organic Farmers Association (NOFA), *Organic Maple Syrup Standards*, undated
- Organic Crop Improvement Association (OCIA), *International Certification Standards*, 1998
- Pierce, A, S A Laird and R Malleson, *Annotated Collection of Guidelines, Standards, and Regulations for Trade in Non-Timber Forest Products (NTFPs) and Botanicals*, Sustainable Botanicals Project, Rainforest Alliance, 2002
- Posey, D and G Dutfield, *Beyond Intellectual Property: Toward Traditional Resource Rights for Indigenous Peoples and Local Communities*, IDRC, 1996
- Rainforest Alliance (Laird et al), *Introductory Handbook to Cocoa Certification*, 1996
- Rainforest Alliance–ECO-OK, *Principles of the Conservation Agriculture Network*, 1998
- Shanley, P et al, *Fruitiferas da Mata na Vida Amazonica*, 1998
- Silva Forest Foundation, *Silva Forest Foundation Summary of Standards for Ecologically Responsible Forest Use*, 1998
- Scientific Certification Systems (SCS), *Forest Conservation Programme*, 1995
- SmartWood, *Generic Guidelines for Assessing Natural Forest Management*, SmartWood programme, Rainforest Alliance, 2000
- Societé General du Surveillance (SGS), *Qualifor Forestry Programme Standards*, 1996
- Soil Association, *Standards for the Certified Products Scheme*, 1993
- Soil Association, *Responsible Forestry Programme*, 1994
- State of Vermont, *Regulations for Ginseng Harvest and Regulations Relating to the Certification of Ginseng*, 1987
- Tropenbos (Ros-Tonen et al), *Commercial and Sustainable Extraction of Non-Timber Forest Products*, 1995

- Tropenbos (Lammerts van Bueren and Blom) *Hierarchical Framework for the Formulation of Sustainable Forest Management Standards*, 1997
- US Bureau of Land Management, *Oregon/Washington BLM Handbook for Special Forest Products*, 1997
- 'Windhorse Farm Standard for Restoration and Maintenance of the Natural Forest', 1997
- Wollenberg, E and A Ingles, *Incomes From the Forest*, CIFOR, 1998
- WWF-US (Clay), *Generating Income and Conserving Resources: Twenty Lessons from the Field*, 1996
- WWF-US (Freese), *The Commercial, Consumptive Use of Wild Species: Managing It for the Benefit of Biodiversity*, 1996

Internet resources

- Amazon Conservation Association (Brazil nut project in Peru): www.amazonconservation.org
- Bromeliad research (from Wolf and Konings's work): www.ecosur.mx/bromelias/brom.htm
- Center for International Forestry Research (CIFOR): www.cifor.org
- Conservation International (CI) (Andean Network of Sustainable Alternative Products and other NTFP information): www.conservation.org
- Fairtrade information: www.fairtrade.net
- Forest Garden Programme information: www.forestgarden.org
- Forest Stewardship Council (FSC) information: www.fscoax.org
- Forest, Tree and People Programme and Network: www-trees.slu.se
- International Centre for Research in Agroforestry (ICRAF): www.cgiar.org/icraf
- International Federation of Organic Agriculture Movements (IFOAM) information: www.ifoam.org
- International Network for Bamboo and Rattan (INBAR): www.inbar.org.cn
- Institute for Culture and Ecology (IFCAE): www.ifcae.org
- International Union of Forest Research Organizations (IUFRO) Non-Wood Forest Products Group: www.ersac.umn.edu/iufro/iufronet/d5/hp51100.htm
- Jungle Gum (certified chicle): www.junglegum.com
- Kenyan woodcarving project: www.rbgkew.org.uk/peopleplants
- Mediterranean NTFP information (from Moussouris and Regato's work): www.fao.org/docrep/x5593e/x5593e00.htm
- NTFP livelihoods research, Michigan, US (from Emery's work): www.fs.fed.us/ne/burlington/nontimb/index.htm
- People and Plants Initiative online: www.rbgkew.org.uk/peopleplants
- Plant Resources o South-East Asia (PROSEA): www.prosea.nl
- ProFound: www.ntfp.org
- Rainforest Alliance information: www.rainforest-alliance.org
- Scientific Certification Systems (SCS) information: www.scs1.com
- SmartWood certification programme information: www.smartwood.org
- Societé General du Surveillance (SGS), Qualifor programme information: www.sgs.co.uk
- The Soil Association certification information: www.soilassociation.org
- TRAFFIC: www.traffic.org
- Tropenbos Foundation: www.tropenbos.nl

- United Nations Food and Agriculture Organization (FAO): www.fao.org
- United States Department of Agriculture, Forest Service, Northwest Research Station: www.fs.fed.us/pnw/proglk.htm
- Virginia Tech special forest products site: www.sfp.forprod.vt.edu

Acronyms and abbreviations

ABS	access and benefit-sharing
ACPC	Asociación para la Conservación del Patrimonio Cutiriveni
AIDESEP	Asociación Interétnica de Desarollo de la Selva Peruvana
AIDS	acquired immune deficiency syndrome
ANAP	Apatayawaca Nampitzi Ashaninka Pichis
APHA	American Pharmaceutical Association
ATO	African Timber Organization
BMP	best management practice
BOLFOR	Bolivia Sustainable Forestry Management Project (USAID)
BOSCOSA	Osa Peninsula Forest Conservation and Management Project (Costa Rica)
BP	before present
C	Celsius
C&I	criteria and indicators
CATIE	Centro Agronómico Tropical de Investigación y Enseñanza
CBD	Convention on Biological Diversity
CCMSS	Consejo Civil Mexicano para la Silvicultura Sostenible
CDC	Centro de Datos para la Conservación
Cdn$	Canadian dollars
CEIBA	Certificación Integral de Bosques Americanos
CFA	African Financial Community franc (*Communauté Financière Africaine*)
CFI	continuous forest inventory
CI	Conservation International
CIDA	Canadian International Development Agency
CIEL	Centre for International Environmental Law
CIFOR	Center for International Forestry Research
CIMAR	Centro de Investigacion y Manejo de Recursos Naturales Renovables
CITES	Convention on International Trade in Endangered Species of Wild Fauna and Flora
cm	centimetres
CoC	chain of custody
COICA	Coordinating Body of Indigenous Organizations of the Amazon Basin
CPR	common property resource
CS	Cultural Survival
CVRD	Companhia Vale do Rio Doce
DBH	diameter at breast height
DFID	Department for International Development (UK)
DNA	deoxyribonucleic acid

DSHEA	Dietary Supplement and Health Education Act (US)
EMS	eosinophilia myalgia syndrome
EPA	US Environmental Protection Agency
EU	European Union
FAO	Food and Agriculture Organization
FDA	Food and Drug Administration (US)
FECONAYA	Federación de Comunidades Nativas Yaneshas
FF	French franc
FLO	Fairtrade Labelling Organizations International
FMO	forest management operation
FOB	free on board
FRIM	Forest Research Institute of Malaysia
FSC	Forest Stewardship Council
FSC P&C	Forest Stewardship Council *Principles and Criteria for Forest Management*
FTF	Fairtrade Federation
gbh	girth at breast height
GMP	Good Manufacturing Practice
GNC	general nutrition centre
ha	hectare
HCVF	high conservation-value forests
HPLC	high performance liquid chromatography
5-HT	5-hydroxy-tryptamine
5-HTP	5-hydroxy-L-tryptophan
IATP	Institute for Agriculture and Trade Policy
IBAMA	Instituto Brasileiro do Meio Ambiente e dos Recursos Naturais Renováveis (Brazilian environmental protection agency)
ICRAF	International Centre for Research in Agroforestry
IDRC	International Development Research Centre
IES	Institute of Environmental Studies
IFAT	International Federation for Alternative Trade
IFCAE	Institute for Culture and Ecology
IFOAM	International Federation of Organic Agriculture Movements
ILO	International Labour Organization
IMAFLORA	Instituto de Manejo e Certificação Florestal e Agrícola
IMAZON	Amazon Institute of People and Environment
INBAR	International Network for Bamboo and Rattan
INRENA	Instituto Nacional de Recursos Naturales
IOAS	International Organic Accreditation Service
IPEF	Instituto de Pesquisas e Estudos Florestais
IPM	integrated pest management
IPR	intellectual property right
IRB	Institute of Research for Development (France)
ISF	Institute for Sustainable Forestry
ISO	International Organization for Standardization
ITTA	International Tropical Timber Agreement
ITTO	International Tropical Timber Organization

IUCN	World Conservation Union
I&V	indicator and verifier
IWGIA	International Working Group for Indigenous Affairs
KEFRI	Kenya Forestry Research Institute
kg	kilogram
km	kilometre
LAMPS	large-scale Adivasi multipurpose societies
lb	pound
LKS	lesser-known timber species
LS	longitudinal section
m³	cubic metre
MCC	Mennonite Central Committee
mg	milligram
MIQRO	Maderas Industriales de Quintana Roo
ml	millilitre
mm	millimetre
MTE	Menominee Tribal Enterprises
n	sample population size
NCI	National Cancer Institute (US)
NEWS	Network of European World Shops
NGO	non-governmental organization
NLCB	National Lottery Charities Board (UK)
NOFA	North-East Organic Farmers Association
NNFA	National Nutritional Foods Association
NTFP	non-timber forest product
NYBG	New York Botanical Garden
ODI	Overseas Development Institute (UK)
OCIA	Organic Crop Improvement Association
OFI	Oxford Forestry Institute
OTC	over the counter
PIC	prior informed consent
ppm	parts per million
PTO	US Patent Trade Office
R&D	research and development
RBG	Royal Botanic Gardens, Kew
RNA	ribonucleic acid
Rs	rupees
SCS	Scientific Certification Systems
SGS	Societé General du Surveillance
SPEFQR	Sociedad de Productores y Ejidos Forestales de Quintana Roo
SSC	Species Survival Commission
TCM	traditional Chinese medicine
TRIPS	Trade-Related Aspects of Intellectual Property Rights
TS	transverse section
TVE	Television Trust for the Environment
UK	United Kingdom
UNCED	United Nations Conference on Environment and Development

UNEP	United Nations Environment Programme
UNESCO	United Nations Educational, Scientific and Cultural Organization
UNDP	United Nations Development Programme
UNIDO	United Nations Industrial Development Organization
UP	Upper Peninsula (US)
US	United States
USAID	United States Agency for International Development
USDA	US Department of Agriculture
WHO	World Health Organization
WRI	World Resources Institute
WTO	World Trade Organization
WWF	*formerly* World Wide Fund For Nature (World Wildlife Fund in Canada and the US)

References

Abate, T. 1999. 'Shaman quits the drug business'. *The San Francisco Chronicle*. 3 February, Final Edition, Business Section, pD1

ABC News. 1998. *Prime Time Live* (segment 2), broadcast 17 June

Acquaye, D. 1998. Pers comm. Project Coordinator, BioResources (Gh) Ltd

Adosraku, R. 1998. Pers comm. Senior Lecturer, Faculty of Pharmacy, University of Science and Technology, Kumasi, Ghana

Agreda, V. 1999. *Análisis socio-económico de la actividad castañera de Madre de Dios*. Informe final. Proyecto Castañales y CANDELA-PERU. Junion de 1999

Agriculture Canada. 2000. Online information: www.agr.ca

Aguirre R A, J R Botina and D A Arias. 1999. 'Plan de manejo ambiental para el aprovechamiento del Sangre de Grado, *Croton lechleri* Mull. Arg. (Euphorbiaceae), en el Departamento del Putumayo'. Hylea Ltda: Mocoa, Putumayo, Colombia

Ainslie, J R. 1937. 'A list of plants used in native medicine in Nigeria'. *Imperial Forestry Institute Paper*, no 7, p57

Alam, M K. 1990. *The Rattans of Bangladesh*. Bangladesh Forest Research Institute, Dhaka

Alarcón, R, P Mena and A Soldi. 1994. 'Etnobotánica, valoración económica y comercialización de recursos florísticos silvestres en El Alto Napo, Ecuador'. Unpublished report

Albán C J. 1996. *Investigaciones entorno a la uña de gato del Perú*. Museo de Historia Natural *'Javier Prado'*, Universidad Nacional Mayor de San Marcos, Lima

Alcorn, J. 1993. 'Indigenous peoples and conservation'. *Conservation Biology*, vol 7, no 2, pp424–426

Alcorn, P W. 1994. 'The chicle tree (*Manilkara zapota*) in Northwest Belize: Natural history, forest floristics, and management'. Unpublished MSc thesis. University of Florida. Department of Botany, Gainesville, FL

Alencar, J C. 1981. 'Estudos silviculturais de uma população natural de *Copaifera multijuga* Hayne (Leguminosae) na Amazônia Central. I. Germinação'. *Acta Amazonica*, vol 11, no 1, pp3–11

Alencar, J C. 1982. 'Estudos silviculturais de uma população natural de *Copaifera multijuga* Hayne (Leguminosae) na Amazônia Central. II. Produção de óleo-resina'. *Acta Amazonica*, vol 12, no 1, pp75–89

Alencar, J C. 1984. 'Silvicultural studies of a natural population of *Copaifera multijuga* Hayne: Leguminosae, in Central Amazonia'. *Acta Amazonica*, vol 14, no 1–2, pp255

Allen, O N and E K Allen. 1981. *The Leguminosae: A Source Book of Characteristics, Uses and Nodulation*. University of Wisconsin Press, Madison, WI, p812

Alonso, J. 1998. 'El lapacho (*Tabebuia impetiginosa*)'. *Fitociencia*, vol 3, pp22–27

Anderson, A and M Jardim. 1989. 'Costs and benefits of floodplain forest management by rural inhabitants of the Amazon estuary: A case study of açai palm production' in J O Browder (ed) *Fragile Lands of Latin America: Strategies for Sustainable Development*. Westview, Boulder, CO

Anderson, A B. 1991. 'Forest management strategies by rural inhabitants in the Amazon estuary' in A Gomez-Pompa, T C Whitmore and M Hadley (eds) *Rainforest Regeneration and Management*. UNESCO, Paris

Anderson, R, J Fralish, J Armstrong and P Benjamin. 1993. 'The ecology and biology of *Panax quinquefolium* L. (Araliaceae) in Illinois'. *American Midland Naturalist*, vol 129, no 2, pp357–372

Andersson, L and C M Taylor. 1994. 'Rubiaceae-Cinchoneae-Coptosapelteae' in G Harling and L Andersson (eds) *Flora of Ecuador 50*. Botanical Museum, Copenhagen, Denmark

Anesini, C and C Perez. 1993. 'Screening of plants used in Argentine folk medicine for antimicrobial activity'. *Journal of Ethnopharmacology*, vol 39, pp119–128

Anonymous. 1922. 'Replies to correspondents: How to dose a boar with Yohimbe'. *Pharmaceutical Journal*, vol 55, p578

Anonymous. 1934. *Shipments of Rattans to the UK and USA from the Gold Coast*. Gold Coast Forestry Department Annual Report

Anonymous. 1982. 'Scorned African aphrodisiac scores against organic impotence'. *Medical World News*, vol 23, p115

Anonymous. 1996. 'It grows on trees'. *The Economist*, vol 339, no 7964, p64

Anonymous. 1999. 'Super immunity'. *Business and Industry*, vol 45, no 7, p16

Aquino, R, C Conti and M L Stein. 1989. 'Plant metabolites: Structure and in-vitro antiviral activity of quinovic acid glycosides from *Uncaria tomentosa* and *Guettarda platypoda*'. *Journal of Natural Products*, vol 52, no 4, pp679–685

Aquino, R, V De Feo, F De Simone, C Pizza and G Cirino. 1991. 'Plant metabolites: New compounds and anti-inflammatory activity of *Uncaria tomentosa*'. *Journal of Natural Products*, vol 54, no 2, pp453–459

Arnason, J T, R Mata and J T Romeo. 1994. *Phytochemistry of Medical Plants*. Vol 29. Plenum Press, New York, NY

Arnold, J E M and M Ruiz-Pérez. 1996. 'Framing the issues relating to non-timber forest products research' in M Ruiz-Pérez and J E M Arnold (eds) *Current Issues in Non-Timber Forest Products Research*. CIFOR, Bogor, Indonesia

Arnold, J E M and M Ruiz-Pérez. 1998. 'The role of non-timber forest products in conservation and development' in E Wollenberg and A Ingles (eds) *Incomes from the Forest: Methods for the Development and Conservation of Forest Products for Local Communities*. CIFOR, Bogor, Indonesia

Ashcraft, N. 1973. *Colonialism and Underdevelopment: Processes of Political and Economic Change in British Honduras*. Teachers College Press, New York, NY, pp48–54

Assiess, W. 1997. *Going Nuts for the Rainforest: Non Timber Forest Products, Forest Conservation and Sustainability in Amazonia*. Thela Publishers, Amsterdam

Aubaile-Sallenave, F. 1997. 'Le monde traditionnel des odeurs et des saveurs chez le petit enfant maghrébin' in B Schall (ed) *Enfance. L'odorat chez l'enfant: perspectives croisées*. Presses Universitaires de France, Paris, pp186–208

Ayala, F. 1992. 'Estudio ecológico: Distribución, densidad y capacidad de latex de *Croton lechleri* M. Arg'. Manuscript. Iquitos, Peru

Ayala, F. 1993. 'Control de la altura y diametro de *Croton lechleri* M. Arg'. Shaman Pharmaceuticals Inc, Iquitos, Peru

Ayala, F. 1997. 'De Amazonian Natural Products a Shaman Pharmaceutical Inc'. Informe confidencial. Iquitos, Peru

Ayensu, E S. 1978. *Medicinal Plants of West Africa*. Reference Publications, Michigan, MI

Bailey, W, C Whitehead, J Proctor and J Kyle. 1995. *The Challenges of the 21st Century: Proceedings of the International Ginseng Conference – Vancouver 1994*. Simon Fraser University, Vancouver

Baillon, H. 1884. *Traité de Botanique Médicale*. Hachette, Paris

Baldini, S. 1993. Produits 'Forestiers non lignieux dans la region Mediterraneenne'. FAO Report. FAO, Rome

Balée, W L. 1994. *Footprints of the Forest: Ka'apor Ethnobotany – The Historical Ecology of Plant Utilization by an Amazonian People*. Columbia University Press, New York, NY

Balick, M J and R Mendelsohn. 1992. 'Assessing the economic value of traditional medicines from tropical rain forests'. *Conservation Biology*, vol 6, no 1, pp128–130

Balsam, M S and E Sagarin (eds). 1974. *Cosmetics: Science and Technology*. Vol 3. John Wiley and Sons, New York, NY, p787

Barbour, T. 1945. *A Naturalist in Cuba*. Little, Brown and Company, Boston, MA

Barnes, R F W. 1980. 'The decline of the baobab tree in Ruaha National Park, Tanzania'. *African Journal of Ecology*, vol 18, pp243–252

Barreto, P. 1999. Pers. comm. Director of the Instituto do Homem e do Meio Ambiente na Amazonia (IMAZON)

Bartlett, H H. 1935. 'A method of procedure for field work in tropical American phytogeography based upon a botanical reconnaissance in parts of British Honduras and the Peten forest of Guatemala'. *Publications of the Carnegie Institution*, no 461

Basile, A C, J A A Sertie, P C D Freitas and A C Zanini. 1988. 'Anti-inflammatory activity of oleoresin from Brazilian *Copaifera*'. *Journal of Ethnopharmacology*, vol 22, pp101–109

Basu, S K. 1992. *Rattan (Canes) in India: A Monographic Revision*. Rattan Information Centre, Kuala Lumpur

Baumann, H. 1993. *The Greek Flora in Myth, Art and Literature*. Hellenic Society for the Protection of Nature, Athens

Beattie, M, C Thompson and L Levine. 1993. *Working with Your Woodland: A Landowner's Guide* (revised edition). University Press of New England, Hanover, New Hampshire

Belcher, B. 1999. 'A production to consumption systems approach: Lessons from the bamboo and rattan sectors in Asia' in E Wollenberg and A Ingles (eds) *Incomes from the Forest: Methods for the Development and Conservation of Forest Products for Local Communities*. CIFOR/IUCN, Bogor, Indonesia

Belize Customs Reports, 1942–1952. Government Printing Office, Belize, British Honduras

Benzyane Mohamed. Undated. 'Administration of National Forestry Commission and the Conservation of the Grounds'. Moroccan Ministry for Agriculture, Morocco

Beretsos Marinos. 1998. Pers comm (chestnut certification)

Berg, M E van den. 1982. *Plantas Medicinais na Amazônia – Contribuição ao seu Conhecimento Sistemático*. CNPq/PTU, Belem, p233

Bianco, A, P Passacantilli and G Polidori. 1983. 'Two new natural esters of 6-epimonomelittoside'. *Iridoids in Equatorial and Tropical Flora* (VII), vol 113, pp465–467

Bierzychudek, P. 1982. 'Life histories and demography of shade-tolerant temperate forest herbs: A review'. *New Phytologist*, vol 90, pp757–776

Blake, S. 1942. 'The ostrich fern as an edible plant'. *American Fern Journal*, vol 32, pp61–68

Blumenthal, M. 1995. 'Uña de gato (cat's claw): Rainforest herb gets scientific and industry attention'. *Whole Foods*, October, pp62–64

Blumenthal, M, D Awang, H Fong, J Fitzloff, J Arnason, I Ibraham and T Hall. 1995. 'Analysis of North American commercial ginseng: American Botanical Council's ginseng evaluation program' in W Bailey, C Whitehead, J Proctor and J Kyle (eds) *The Challenges of the 21st Century: Proceedings of the International Ginseng Conference – Vancouver 1994*. Simon Fraser University, Vancouver

Blumenthal, M, W R Busse, A Goldberg, J Gruenwald, T Hall, C W Riggins and R S Rister (eds). 1998. *The Complete German Commission E Monographs: Therapeutic Guide to Herbal Medicines*. S Klein and R S Rister (translators). American Botanical Council/Integrative Medicine Communications, Austin, TX/Boston, MA

Boom, B M. 1996. *Ethnobotany of the Chácabo Indians, Beni, Bolivia*. Second Edition. New York Botanical Garden, New York, NY

Boomgaard, P (ed). 1994. *Forests and Forestry, 1823–1941. Changing Economy in Indonesia. Volume 16: A Selection of Statistical Source Material from the Early 19th Century up to 1940.* Royal Tropical Institute, Amsterdam

Boot, R G A and R E Gullison. 1995. 'Approaches to developing sustainable extraction systems for tropical forest products'. *Ecological Applications*, vol 5, no 4, pp896–903

Borges, J R, S R King, K Hughes, E Meza, S Nelson and C Romero. In press. 'Conservation of biocultural diversity in the Amazon: *Croton lechleri*, a traditional indigenous resource'. *Advances in Economic Botany*

Bown, D. 1988. *Aroids: Plants of the Arum Family.* Timber Press, Portland, Oregon

Braam, J S (Van). 1917. 'Het Boschwezen in Tapanoeli'. *Tectona*, vol 10, pp209–214

Braedt, O and W Standa-Gunda. 1997. 'The woodcraft industry in Zimbabwe: an overview'. Paper presented at the II CIFOR Workshop on The Contributions of Non-Timber Forest Products to Socio-economic Development, Riberalta, Bolivia. 7–11 September

Braun, A. 1994. 'The sowing of palm seeds in the tropic and germination results'. Privately published. Caracas, Venezuela

Breedlove, D E and R M Laughlin. 1993. 'The Flora' in D E Breedlove and R M Laughlin (eds) *The Flowering of Man: A Tzotzil Botany of Zinacantán.* Volume 1. Smithsonian Contributions to Anthropology 35, Washington, DC

Brevoort, P. 1998. 'The booming US botanical market: A new overview'. *Herbalgram*, vol 44, p33

British Pharmaceutical Codex. 1949. London, pp949–950

Brokaw, N V L and E P Mallory. 1993. 'Natural history of the Rio Bravo Resource Management and Conservation Area'. Manomet Bird Observatory. Unpublished manuscript

Browder, J. 1992. 'The limits of extractivism: Tropical strategies beyond extractive reserves'. *BioScience*, vol 42, no 3, pp174–182

Burkhill, I H. 1966. *A Dictionary of the Economic Products of the Malay Peninsula.* Government of Malaysia and Singapore/Ministry of Agriculture of Malaysia and Singapore, Kuala Lumpur (originally published in 1935)

Burkill, I H. 1935. *A Dictionary of the Economic Products of the Malay Peninsula.* Crown Agents, London. 2 volumes

But, P, S Hu and H Cao. 1995. 'The ginseng plant: Products and quality' in W Bailey, C Whitehead, J Proctor and J Kyle (eds) *The Challenges of the 21st Century: Proceedings of the International Ginseng Conference – Vancouver 1994.* Simon Fraser University, Vancouver

Cabieses, F. Undated. *La Uña de Gato y su entorno.* Segunda Edición. Universidad de San Martin de Porres, Lima

Cáceres, N C. 1995. 'Contribución a la química de Uncaria II'. *Revista de Química*, vol 9, p66

Calzavara, B B G. 1972. 'As possibilidades do açaizeiro no estuário Amazônico'. *Boletim No 5*, Faculdade de Ciências Agrárias do Pará, Belém

Camargo, P B, R de P Camargo, S Trumbore and L A Martinelli. 1994. 'How old are Brazil-nut trees (*Bertholletia excelsa*) in the Amazon?' *Scientia Agricola*, Universidade de São Paulo, Piracicaba, vol 51, no 2, pp389–391

Cangiano, C, F Ceci, A Cascino, M Del Ben, A Laviano, M Muscaritoli, F Antonucci and F Rossi-Fanelli. 1992. 'Eating behavior and adherence to dietary prescriptions in obese adult subjects treated with 5-hydroxytryptophan'. *American Journal of Clinical Nutrition*, vol 56, pp863–867

Carlson, A. 1986. 'Ginseng: America's botanical drug connection to the Orient'. *Economic Botany*, vol 40, no 2, pp233–249

Carpenter, S and G Cottam. 1982. 'Growth and reproduction of American ginseng (*Panax quinquefolius*) in Wisconsin, USA'. *Canadian Journal of Botany*, vol 60, pp2692–2696

Caruso, I, P S Puttini, M Cazzola and V Azzolini. 1990. 'Double-blind study of 5-hydroxytryptophan versus placebo in the treatment of primary fibromyalgia syndrome'. *The Journal of International Medical Research*, vol 18, pp201–209

Castanel, M, V Yumbo and M Yumbo. 1995. *Informe de actividades de siembra de sangre de drago, Croton lechleri, en la Amazonia Ecuatoriana*. D T M Cia, Quito

Castells, M and A Portes. 1989. 'World underneath: The origins, dynamics and effects of the informal economy' in A Portes, M Castells and L Benton (eds) *The Informal Economy: Studies in Advanced and Less Developed Countries*. The Johns Hopkins University Press, Baltimore

Castle, S. 1997. 'Jail for retailers of "herbal highs"'. *The Independent*, 24 August, p7

Catpo V R. 1998. 'Inventario de Sangre de Grado (*Croton lechleri*) en Madre de Dios para el desarrollo de un plan de manejo y aprovechamiento sostenible por comunidades locales'. Conservación Internacional, Lima, Perú

Catton, B. 1976. *Michigan: A Bicentennial History*. W W Norton & Company, New York, NY

Caughley, G. 1976. 'The elephant problem – an alternative hypothesis'. *East African Wildlife Journal*, vol 14, pp265–283

Centre for Food Safety and Applied Nutrition. 1998. FDA memorandum, released 24 September. US Food and Drug Administration, Washington, DC

Chagnaud, F. 1996. 'La valorisation des sous-produits agroforestiers au Laos: Une alternative pour le développement durable' in C M Hladik, A Hladik, H Pagezy, O F Linares, G J A Koppert and A Froment (eds) *L'Alimentation en Forêt Tropicale: Interactions Bioculturelles et Perspectives de Développement*. UNESCO, Paris, pp1065–1074

Chambers, R. 1983. *Rural Development: Putting the Last First*. John Wiley and Sons, New York, NY

Chandrasekharan, D. 1998. *NTFPs, Institutions and Income Generation in Nepal: Lessons for Community Forestry*. International Centre for Integrated Mountain Development, Kathmandu, Nepal

Charron, D and D Gagnon. 1991. 'The demography of northern populations of *Panax quinquefolium* (American ginseng)'. *Journal of Ecology*, vol 79, no 2, pp431–445

Chase, S. 1996. 'Season's sweet rewards'. *The Burlington Free Press*, Business Monday section, 15 April, pp1, 4

Chen, Z-P, Y Cat and J D Phillipson. 1994. 'Studies on the anti-tumour, anti-bacterial, and wound-healing properties of dragon's blood'. *Planta Medica*, vol 60, pp541–545

Chichignoud, M, G Déon, P Détienne, B Parant and P Vantomme. 1990. *Tropical Timber Atlas of Latin America*. International Tropical Timber Organization (ITTO), Yokohama, and Centre Technique Forestier Tropical (div. CIRAD), Nogent-Sur-Marne Cedex, France, p218

Chozas Bermudez, A. 1997. 'Forest exploitation operations for non-timber purposes: Resin' in A K Mukerji (ed) *XI World Forestry Congress, Antalya, Turkey*, Volume 3, Topic 15. FAO, Rome

Clay, J. 1992. 'Some general principles and strategies for developing markets in North America and Europe for non-timber forest products' in M Plotkin and L Famolare (eds) *Sustainable Harvest and Marketing of Rain Forest Products*. Island Press, Washington, DC

Clay, J and C R Clement. 1993. 'Selected Species and Strategies to Enhance Income Generation from Amazonian Forests'. FAO Working Paper. FAO, Rome

Clay, J. 1994. 'Resource wars: Nation and state conflicts of the twentieth century' in B Johnston (ed) *Who Pays the Price? The Sociocultural Context of Environmental Crisis*. Island Press, Washington, DC, pp19–30

Clay, J. 1996. *Generating Income and Conserving Resources: Twenty Lessons from the Field*. World Wildlife Fund, Washington, DC

Clays, J W. 1997a. 'The impact of palm heart harvesting in the Amazon Estuary' in C H Freese (ed) *Harvesting Wild Species: Implications for Biodiversity Conservation*. The Johns Hopkins University Press, Baltimore and London, pp283–314

Clay, J W. 1997b. 'Brazil nuts. The use of a keystone species for conservation and development' in C H Freese (ed) *Harvesting Wild Species: Implications for Biodiversity Conservation*. The Johns Hopkins University Press, Baltimore and London, pp246–282

Clay, J. 1997c. 'Business and biodiversity: Rainforest marketing and beyond' in N Vance and J Thomas (eds) *Special Forest Products: Biodiversity Meets the Marketplace*. USDA, Washington, DC

Cleland, C E. 1983. 'Indians in a changing environment' in S L Flader (ed) *The Great Lakes Forest: An Environmental and Social History*. University of Minnesota Press, Minneapolis

Cleland, C E. 1992. *Rites of Conquest: The History of Michigan's Native Americans*. University of Michigan Press, Ann Arbor, MI

Coalition of Immokalee Workers. 1999. 'Coalition Members Traveling to Tallahassee to Testify at Hearing on Palmetto Berry Bill'. Press Release, 17 April, Immokalee, FL

Coates-Palgrave, K. 1983. *Trees of Southern Africa*. Struik, Cape Town

Cochrane, M, A Alencar, M Schulze, C Souza Jr, D Nepstad, P Lefebvre and E Davidson. 1999. 'Positive feedback in the fire dynamic of closed canopy tropical forests'. *Science*, vol 284, pp1832–1835

Conelly, W T. 1985. 'Copal and rattan collecting in the Philippines'. *Economic Botany*, vol 39, no 1, pp 39–46

Coomes, O T. 1995. 'A century of rain forest use in Western Amazonia: Lessons for extraction-based conservation of tropical forest resources'. *Forest and Conservation History*, vol 39, pp108–120

Coppen, J J W. 1995. *Gums, Resins and Latexes of Plant Origin*. Non-Wood Forest Products, FAO, Rome

Coppen, J J W. 1997. *Gum Benzoin: Its Markets and Marketing and the Opportunities and Constraints to Their Improvement in Lao PDR*. FAO, Rome

Corner, E J H. 1966. *The Natural History of Palms*. Weidenfeld and Nicolson, London

Correia Lopez, L, S dos Santos Marques and F C M Piña-Rodrigues. 1994. 'Sistema de Plantio Adensado pata a Revegetação de Áreas Degradadas'. Paper presented at Simposio Brasilero de Recuperacao de Areas degradadas, Curitiba, PR, Brasil

Costa, M F da, M R C Loureiro, C R A Albuquerque de and Z P Amaral Filho do. 1974. 'Perspectivas para o aproveitamento integral da palmeira do açaí'. *Série Monografias 14*. IDESP, Belém

Courville, S. 1999. *Evaluation of Certification Systems that Promote Socially and Environmentally Responsible Production and Consumption: Fair Trade (FLO International), Forest Protection (FSC, SmartWood) and Organic (IFOAM, CERTIMEX) Standards on Coffee*. Institute for Agriculture and Trade Policy (IATP), Minneapolis, Minnesota

Cronon, W. 1991. *Nature's Metropolis: Chicago and the Great West*. W W Norton & Company, New York, NY

Crook, C and R A Clapp. 1998. 'Is market-based forest conservation a contradiction in terms?' *Environmental Conservation*, vol 25, no 2, pp131–145

Cuéllar, E. 1996. 'Estudio comparativo de propagación por estacas de *Uncaria tomentosa* (Widl) DC en diferentes condiciones micro ambientales'. Unpublished MSc thesis. Universidad Nacional Agraria 'La Molina', Lima, Peru

Cunningham, A B. 1993. 'African medicinal plants: Setting priorities at the interface between conservation and primary health care' in *People and Plants Working Paper 1*. UNESCO, Paris

Cunningham, A B and F T Mbenkum. 1993. 'Sustainability of harvesting *Prunus africana* bark in Cameroon: A medicinal plant in international trade'. *People and Plants Working Paper 2*. UNESCO, Paris

Cunningham, A B. 1998. *Kenya Woodcarving: Steps Towards Sustainable Sourcing*. Final workshop report for the WWF/UNESCO/Kew People and Plants initiative, National Museums of Kenya

Cunningham, A B. 1999. *Woodcarving, Certification and 'Good Wood' labelling – Searching for Practical Systems*. Final report on a course held by the People and Plants initiative in Nairobi and Malindi, Kenya, 15–20 March

Cunningham, A B. 2001. *Applied Ethnobotany: People, Wild Plant Use and Conservation*. Earthscan, London

Dalziel, J. 1937. 'The Useful Plants of Tropical West Africa'. Supplement to *The Flora of West Tropical Africa*. Royal Botanic Gardens, Kew

Danusa, M. 1999. Pers comm (mara.danusa@telnet.com.br). Journalist and historian

Davis, W. 1999. 'Vanishing cultures'. *National Geographic*, vol 196, no 2, pp62–89

Drug and Cosmetic Industry (DCI). 1992. 'Raw Material Directory'. *Drug and Cosmetic Industry*, July, p137

de Beer, J H and M J. McDermott. 1996. *The Economic Value of Non-Timber Forest Products in Southeast Asia* (second revised edition). The Netherlands Committee for IUCN, Amsterdam

de Cordemoy, H J. 1900. *Gommes, résines d'origine exotique et végétaux qui les produisent, particulièrement dans les colonies françaises*. Augustin Challamel, Paris

de Fretas, Y. 1992. 'Community versus company-based rattan industry in Indonesia' in S Counsell and T Rice (eds) *The Rainforest Harvest: Sustainable Strategies for Saving the Tropical Forest*. Friends of the Earth, London

de Jong, W. 1995. 'Recreating the forest: Successful examples of ethnoconservation among Dayak groups in Central West Kalimantan' in Ø Sandbukt (ed) *Management of Tropical Forests: Toward an Integrated Perspective*. Centre for Development and the Environment, Oslo, Norway

de Jong, W and R Utama. 1998. 'Turning ideas into action: Planning for non-timber forest product development and conservation' in E Wollenberg and A Ingles (eds) *Incomes from the Forest: Methods for the Development and Conservation of Forest Products for Local Communities*. CIFOR and IUCN, Bogor, Indonesia

de Jong, W, M Melnyk, L Alfaro, L M Rosales and M García. 1999. *Uña de Gato: Fate and Future of a Peruvian Forest Resource*. Unpublished manuscript

de Jong, W, M Melnyk, L Alfaro, L M Rosales and M García. 2000. 'A concerted approach to uña de gato development in Peru'. *International Tree Crop Journal*, vol 10, no 4, pp321–336

de Zoysa, N and K Vivekenandan. 1994. *Rattans of Sri Lanka*. Sri Lanka Forest Department, Batteramulla

Defo L. 1999. 'Rattan or porcupine? Benefits and limitations of a high-value non-wood forest products for conservation in the Yaounde region of Cameroon' in T C H Sunderland, L E Clark and P Vantomme (eds) *The Non-Wood Forest Products of Central Africa: Current Research Issues and Prospects for Conservation and Development*. FAO, Rome

DeHayes, D, P Schaberg, G Hawley and G Strimbeck. 1999. 'Acid rain impacts on calcium nutrition and forest health'. *BioScience*, vol 49, no 10, pp789–800

Desmarchelier, C, F Witting, S J Coussio and G Cicca. 1997. 'Effects of sangre de drago from *Croton lechleri* Muell.-Arg. on the production of active oxygen radicals'. *Journal of Ethnopharmacology*, vol 58, pp103–108

Diamatis, S. 1998. Pers comm (chestnut certification)

Diener, B. 1998. 'Portico, SA: Strategic decisions 1982–1997' in Sustainable Forestry Working Group *The Business of Sustainable Forestry: Case Studies*. Island Press, Washington, DC

Direccão General das Florestas. 1990. *Report on Cork*. Lisbon, Portugal

Dirzo, R and A Miranda. 1991. 'Altered patterns of herbivory and diversity in the forest understory: A case study of the possible consequences of contemporary defaunation' in P W Price, M Lewinsohn, G W Fernandes and W W Benson (eds) *Plant Animal Interactions: Evolutionary Ecology in Tropical and Temperate Regions*. John Wiley and Sons, New York, NY

Dobkin de Rios, M. 1994. 'Drug tourism in the Amazon'. *Jahrbuch für Ethnomedezin*, vol 3, pp307–314

Dolmatoff, G E. 1990. 'The cultural context of an aboriginal hallucinogen: *Banisteriopsis caapi*' in P T Furst (ed) *Flesh of the Gods. The Ritual Use of Hallucinogens*. Waveland Press, Prospect Heights, IL, (originally published in 1972) pp84–113

Domínguez T G. 1997. *Uña de gato y produccións sostenible.* Universidad Nacional Agraria La Molina, Lima, Peru

Douglas, J S. 1974. *Utilisation and Industrial Treatment of Rattan Cane in Casamance, Senegal (Return Mission).* Unpublished report to United Nations Industrial Development Organization

Dove, M R. 1993. 'A revisionist view of tropical deforestation and development'. *Environmental Conservation,* vol 20, pp17–24, 56

Dove, M R. 1994. 'Marketing the rainforest: "Green" panacea or red herring?' *Asia-Pacific Issues,* no 13. East–West Centre, Honolulu, Hawaii

Dove, M R. 1996. 'Center, periphery and biodiversity: a paradox of governance and a developmental challenge' in S B Brush and D Stabinsky (eds) *Valuing Local Knowledge: Indigenous People and Intellectual Property Rights.* Island Press, Washington, DC, pp41–67

Dransfield, J. 1979. *A Manual of the Rattans of the Malay Peninsula.* Malayan Forest Record No 29. Forestry Department, Malaysia

Dransfield, J. 1984. *The Rattans of Sabah.* Sabah Forest Record No 13. Forestry Department, Malaysia

Dransfield, J. 1988. 'Prospects for rattan cultivation' in M J Balick (ed) *The Palm – Tree of Life: Biology, Utilization and Conservation. Advances in Economic Botany,* vol 6, pp190–200

Dransfield, J. 1992a. *The Rattans of Sarawak.* Royal Botanic Gardens, Kew/Sarawak Forest Department, Kew

Dransfield, J. 1992b. 'The taxonomy of rattans' in R W M Wan, J Dransfield and N Manokaran (eds) *A Guide to the Cultivation of Rattan.* Forest Record No 35. Forest Research Institute, Kuala Lumpur

Dransfield, J. 1992c. 'The ecology and natural history of rattans' in R W M Wan, J Dransfield and N Manokaran (eds) *A Guide to the Cultivation of Rattan.* Forest Record No 35. Forest Research Institute, Kuala Lumpur

Dransfield, J. 1992d. 'Traditional uses of rattan' in R W M Wan, J Dransfield and N Manokaran (eds) *A Guide to the Cultivation of Rattan.* Forest Record No 35. Forest Research Institute, Kuala Lumpur

Dransfield, J. 1998. *The Rattans of Brunei Darussalam.* Forestry Department, Ministry of Industry and Primary Resources, Brunei Darussalam/Royal Botanic Gardens, Kew

Dransfield, J and N Manokaran (eds). 1994. *Plant Resources of SE Asia – Rattans.* PROSEA, Indonesia

Duke, J A. 1985. *The CRC Handbook of Medicinal Herbs.* CRC Press, Boca Raton, FL

Duke, J. 1989. *Ginseng: A Concise Handbook.* Reference Publications, Inc, Algonac, MI

Duke, J A. 1991. 'Tropical botanical extractives'. Text for a lecture presented at the Symposium on Rainforest Conservation, Panama, 18–21 June

Duke, J A and J L Cellier. 1993. *CRC Handbook of Alternative Cash Crops.* CRC Press, Boca Raton, FL, p536

Duke, J and R Vásquez. 1994. *Amazonian Ethnobotanical Dictionary.* CRC Press, Boca Raton, FL

Dwyer, J D. 1951. 'The Central American, West Indian and South American species of *Copaifera* (Caesalpiniaceae)'. *Brittonia,* vol 7, no 3, pp143–172

Dykeman, B. 1985. 'Effects of crozier removal on growth of the ostrich fern'. *Canadian Journal of Plant Science,* vol 65, pp1019–1023

Dykeman, B and B Cumming. 1985. 'In vitro propagation of the ostrich fern (*Matteuccia struthiopteris*)'. *Canadian Journal of Plant Science,* vol 65, pp1025–1032

Edwards, C R. 1986. 'The human impact on the forest in Qunitana Roo, Mexico'. *Journal of Forest History,* vol 30, no 3, pp120–127

Efe News Services Inc. 1999. 'Campesinos sustituirán cultivos de coca por plantas medicinales'. 21 May

Efe News Services Inc. 1999. 'España autoriza venta "uña de gato" en mercado medicamentos'. 16 January

Egler, F E. 1947. 'The role of botanical research in the chicle industry'. *Economic Botany*, vol 1, pp188–209

Eisenberg, D, R Kessler, C Foster, F Norlock, D Calkins and T Delbanco. 1993. 'Unconventional medicine in the United States'. *The New England Journal of Medicine*, 28 January, pp246–252

El Alaoui, N. 1998. *Les routes des benjoins. Usage et commerce des benjoins par les Maghrébins (France et Maroc)*. Draft report, CIFOR, Bogor, Indonesia

Elisabetsky, E, S F Taniguchi, S Thorup and B A S Moura. 1986. 'Plantas medicinais como fonte potencial de agents antiparkinsonianos: *Ptychotetalum olacoides, Chaunochiton kappleri* e *Maytenus guianensis*'. Paper presented at the annual meeting of the Sociedade Brasileira Para o Progresso da Ciência, Brasil

Elliott, C. 1999. 'Forest certification: Analysis from a policy network perspective'. Unpublished PhD thesis. École Polytechnique Federale de Lausanne, Switzerland

Elton, C. 1999. 'Day trippers'. *Outside Magazine*, vol 24, no 10, p34

EMBRAPA-CNPF. 1988. *Anais 1° Encontro Nacional de Pesquisadores em palmito*. EMBRAPA/CNPF, Curitiba

Emery, M R. 1998. 'Invisible livelihoods: Non-timber forest products in Michigan's Upper Peninsula'. Unpublished PhD thesis. Department of Geography, Rutgers University, New Brunswick, New Jersey

Emmons, L H. 1984. 'Geographic variation in densities and diversities of non-flying mammals in Amazonia'. *Biotropica*, vol 16, no 3, pp210–222

Empresa Hecker Hermanos SA. 1998. 'Plan de Manejo Forestal para Castaña: Área de Fortaleza', Empresa Hecker Hermanos SA, Riberalta, Bolivia

Environmental Nutrition. 1999. 'Yohimbe bark: Herbal Viagra better gotten by Rx'. New York, NY, February

Ervin, J, C Elliott, B Cabarle and T Synnott. 1996. 'Accreditation process' in V Viana, J Ervin, R Donovan, C Elliott and H Gholz (eds) *Certification of Forest Products: Issues and Perspectives*. Island Press, Washington, DC

Espinoza, S and T Paspuel. 1993. 'Plan de manejo para el aprovechamiento de corteza y/o savia de la especie forestal "Sangre de drago" *Croton* spp. en el sector "El Km 36"'. Parroquia Cotundo, Provincia del Napo. D T M Cia Ltda, Tena, Ecuador

Eutichidis, Y. 1988. 'The last stone pine stand'. *Nea Oikologia*, April (in Greek), pp30–31

Everson, B and P Gremaud. 1995. *Special Forest Products Inventory: Ecosystem Assessment*. Rogue Institute for Ecology and Economy, Ashland, Oregon

Falconer, J. 1994. *Non-Timber Forest Products in Southern Ghana – Main Report*. Natural Resources Institute, University of Greenwich, Oxon, UK

Food and Agriculture Organization (FAO). 1986. 'Food and Fruit-Bearing Forest Species, 3. Examples from Latin America'. FAO Forestry Paper. FAO, Rome

FAO. 1991. 'Non-Wood Forest Products: The Way Ahead'. FAO Forestry Paper 97. FAO, Rome

FAO. 1995. 'Non-Wood Forest Products 1: Flavours and Fragrances of Plant Origin'. FAO Forestry Paper. FAO, Rome

FAO. 1995. 'Non-Wood Forest Products 3: International Expert Consultation on Non-Wood Forest Products'. FAO Forestry Paper. FAO, Rome

FAO. 1995. 'Non-Wood Forest Products 7: Non-Wood Forest Products for Rural Income & Sustainable Forestry'. FAO Forestry Paper. FAO, Rome

FAO. 1995. 'Non-Wood Forest Products 8: Trade Restrictions Affecting International Trade in Non-Wood Forest Products'. FAO Forestry Paper. FAO, Rome

FAO. 1995. 'Non-Wood Forest Products 9: Domestication and Commercialization of Non-Timber Forest Products in Agro-Forestry Systems'. FAO Forestry Paper. FAO, Rome

FAO. 1997. 'Non-Wood Forest Products 11: Medicinal Plants for Forest Conservation and Health Care'. FAO Forestry Paper. FAO, Rome

Farnsworth, N. 1988. 'Screening plants for new medicines' in E O Wilson (ed) *Biodiversity*. National Academy Press, Washington, DC, pp83–97

Farnsworth, N R. 1990. 'The role of ethnopharmacology in drug development' in J Chadwick and J Marsh (eds) *Bioactive Compounds From Plants*. Wiley, Chichester, pp2–21

Federer, C, J Hornbeck, L Tritton, C Martin and R Pierce. 1989. 'Long-term depletion of calcium and other nutrients in Eastern US forests'. *Environmental Management*, vol 13, no 5, pp593–601

Fellows, L E and E A Bell. 1970. '5-Hydroxy-L-Tryptophan, 5-Hydroxytryptamine and L-Tryptophan-5-Hydroxylase' in *Griffonia simplicifolia*. *Phytochemistry*, vol 9, pp2389–2396

Figliuolo, R, S Naylor, J Wang and J H Langenheim. 1987. 'Unusual nonprotein imino acid and its relationship to phenolic and nitrogenous compounds in *Copaifera*'. *Phytochemistry*, vol 26, no 12, pp3255–3259

Finol Urdaneta, H. 1981. *Planificación silvicultural de los bosques ricos en palma manaca (Euterpe oleracea), en el delta del río Orinoco*. Universidad de Los Andes, Mérida

Fisher, J B. 1981. 'Wound healing by exposed secondary xylem in *Adansonia* (Bombacaceae)'. *International Association of Wood Anatomists Bulletin*, vol 2, pp193–199

Flores, S and N Revelo. 1993. *Ensayo de procedencias de sangre de drago*. Croton *aff*. lechleri. *en Jatun Sacha*. Tesis de grado. Facultad de Ingeniería en Ciencias Agropecuarias y Ambientales, Universidad Técnica del Norte, Ibarra, Ecuador

Foreman, J. 1997. 'Ginseng: $350 million for not much?' *The Boston Globe*, 3 February, ppC1, C4

Forero, L E. 1992. *Ethnobotanical Observations on* Croton lechleri Muell.-Arg. *in the Amazon Valley (Colombia)*. Final report. Shaman Pharmaceuticals Inc, South San Francisco, CA

Forero, L E, J F Chávez and H Y Bernal. 2000. 'Agrotecnología para el cultivo de sangre de drago o sangregrado' in J V Martínez, H J Y Bernal and A Cáceres (eds) *Fundamentos de Agrotecnología de Cultivo de Plantas Medicinales Iberoamericanas*. CYTED/SECAB, Santafé de Bogotá, Colombia, pp157–190

Forest Stewardship Council (FSC). 1997. 'Draft principle 11: Non-timber forest products'. FSC, Oaxaca, Mexico

FSC. 1998. 'FSC strategic plan (draft 1998)'. FSC, Oaxaca, Mexico

FSC. 1999. *Principles and Criteria for Forest Stewardship*. Revised February 1999. Document 1.2. FSC, Oaxaca, Mexico

FSC. 2000. *Principles and Criteria for Forest Management*. FSC, Oaxaca, Mexico

Forsyth, K, D Haley and R Kozk. 1999. 'Will consumers pay more for certified wood products?' *Journal of Forestry*, vol 97, no 2, pp18–22

Fortmann, L and J Bruce (eds). 1988. *Whose Trees? Proprietary Dimensions of Forestry*. Westview Press, Boulder, CO

Foster, S. 1991. *American Ginseng (*Panax quinquefolius*)*. Botanical Series No 308, American Botanical Council, Austin, Texas

Foster, S. 1999. 'Yohimbe: An African aphrodisiac to treat with caution'. *Herb for Health*, March/April, pp15–17

Fountain, M. 1986. 'Vegetation associated with natural populations of ginseng (*Panax quinquefolium*) in Arkansas'. *Castanea*, vol 47, no 3, pp261–265

Fralish, J, F Crooks, J Chambers and F Harty. 1991. 'Comparison of presettlement, second-growth and old-growth forest on six site types in the Illinois Shawnee Hills'. *American Midland Naturalist*, vol 125, pp294–309

Frieswick, T and A Malley. 1985. *Forest Statistics for Vermont 1973 and 1983*. Forest Service, Northeastern Station Resource Bulletin NE-87. USDA, Broomall, PA

Furnemore, H. 1926. *The Essential Oils*. Ernest Benn Ltd, London, p880

Gabriel, S E, S E Davenport, R J Steagall, V Vimal, T Carlson and E J Rozhon. 1999. 'Novel plant-derived inhibitor of cAMP-mediated and chloride secretion'. *American Journal of Physiology*, vol 39, ppG58–G63

Gabriel, W. 2000. Pers comm. Retired USDA Forest Service Researcher

Ganesan, B. 1993. 'Extraction of non-timber forest products, including fodder and fuelwood, in Mudumalai, India'. *Economic Botany*, vol 47, no 3, pp268–274

Ganzhorn, J U, A W Ganzhorn, J P Abraham, L Andriamanarivo and A Ramananjatovo. 1990. 'The impact of selective logging on forest structure and tenrec populations in western Madagascar'. *Oecologia*, vol 84, pp126–133

Gaughan, J P and L A Ferman. 1987. 'Toward an understanding of the informal economy'. *The Annals of the American Academy of Political and Social Science*, vol 493, September, pp15–25

Gentry, A H. 1980. 'Bignoniaceae – Part I (Crecientieae and Tourrettieae)'. *Flora Neotropica Monographs*, vol 25, pp1–150

Gentry, A H. 1992. 'Bignoniaceae – Part II'. *Flora Neotropica Monographs (Tribe Tecomeae)*, vol 25, no II, New York Botanical Garden, New York, NY

Gentry, A H. 1992a. 'A synopsis of Bignoniaceae ethnobotany and economic botany'. *Annals of Missouri Botanical Garden*, vol 79, pp53–64

Gentry, A H. 1993. *A Field Guide to the Families and Genera of Woody Plants of Northwest South America (Colombia, Ecuador, Peru) with Supplementary Notes on Herbaceous Taxa.* The University of Chicago Press, Chicago, and Conservation International, Washington, DC

Gilly, C L. 1943. 'Studies in the Sapotaceae, II. The Sapoodilla-Nispero complex'. *Tropical Woods*, vol 73, p1

Godman, R, H Yawney and C Tubbs. 1990. '*Acer saccharum* Marsh. – Sugar maple' in R Burns and B Honkela (eds) *Silvics of North America, Volume 2: Hardwoods.* Agricultural Handbook 654. USDA Forest Service, Washington, DC, pp78–91

Goloubinoff, M. 1997. 'Commerce et usages du benjoin et du camphre en France'. Draft report. CIFOR, Bogor, Indonesia

Goloubinoff, M. 1998. 'Senteurs de miel et d'encens. Le benjoin à Java Centre' in C Guillot (ed) *Histoire de Barus. Le site de Lobu Tua.* Cahier d'Archipel no 30. Association Archipel-EHESS, Paris, pp265–280

Goloubinoff, M. 1999. 'Non-Timber Forest Products Trade in Indonesia. Case Studies'. Draft report. CIFOR, Bogor, Indonesia

Goutarel, R. 1964. 'Alcaloides in Apocynaceae. Les Alcaloides steriodiuques des Apocynaceas. Actualities Scientifiques et Industrielles 1302'. *Chimie des Substances Naturelles, Volume 5*

Graham, A. 1977. 'The tropical rain forest near its northern limits in Veracruz, Mexico: Recent and ephemeral?' *Boletin de la Sociedad Botánica de México*, vol 36, pp13–18

Gray, A. 1990. 'Indigenous peoples and the marketing of the rainforest'. *The Ecologist*, vol 20, no 6, pp 223–227

Grazziotin, J D, E E S Schapoval, C G Chaves, J Gleye and A T Henriques. 1992. 'Phytochemical and analgesic investigation of *Tabebuia chrysotricha*'. *Journal of Ethnopharmacology*, vol 36, no 3, pp249–251

Greenish, H G. 1929. *Materia Medica.* J & A Churchill, London

Grieve, M. 1973 (revised). *A Modern Herbal: The Medicinal, Culinary, Cosmetic and Economic Properties, Cultivation and Folklore of Herbs, Grasses, Fungi, Shrubs and Trees with all Their Modern Scientific Uses.* Tiger Books International, London

Grimes, A, S Loomis, P Jahnige, M Burnham, K Onthank, R Alarc, W Palacios Cuenca, C Ceron Martinez, D Neill, M Balick, B Bennett and R Mendelsohn. 1994. 'Valuing the rain forest: The economic value of non-timber forest products in Ecuador'. *Ambio*, vol 23, no 7, pp405–410

Gruenwald, J. 1998. 'Herbal sales close to $17 billion worldwide'. *Nutrition Business Journal*, October/November, p24

Gruenwald, J. 1999. 'The international herbal medicine market'. *Nutraceuticals World*, January/February, p5

Grunwell, J N. 1998. 'Ayahuasca Tourism in South America'. *Newsletter of the Multidisciplinary Association for Psychedelic Studies* (MAPS), vol 8, no 3: www.maps.org/news-letters/v08n3/08359gru.html

Gudeman, S. 1986. *Economies as Culture: Models and Metaphors of Livelihood*. Routledge and Kegen Paul, London

Gudiño, E, F Gutierrez and S Espinoza. 1991. *Lineamientos preliminares para el manejo de Croton spp. en la Amazonía Ecuatoriana*. D T M, Cía Quito, Ecuador

Guillot, C (ed). 1998. *Histoire de Barus. Le site de Lobu Tua*. Cahier d'Archipel no 30. Association Archipel-EHESS, Paris

Guo, Y, W Bailey and K van Dalfsen. 1995. 'North American ginseng (*Panax quinquefolium* L.) root grading' in W Bailey, C Whitehead, J Proctor and J Kyle (eds) *The Challenges of the 21st Century: Proceedings of the International Ginseng Conference – Vancouver 1994*. Simon Fraser University, Vancouver

Hadden, S. 1986. *Read the Label: Controlling Risk by Providing Information*. Westview Press, Boulder, CO

Hall, E R and K R Kelson. 1959. *The Mammals of North America*. Vol 1 Ronald Press Co, New York, NY

Hall, P and K Bawa. 1993. 'Methods to assess the impact of extraction of non-timber tropical forest products on plant populations'. *Economic Botany*, vol 47, no 3, pp234–247

Halperin, R. 1988. *Economies Across Cultures: Towards a Comparative Science of the Economy*. St Martin's Press, New York, NY

Hammond, N. 1982. *Ancient Maya Civilization*. Rutgers University Press, New Brunswick, New Jersey

Hansen, E and J Punches. 1998. 'Collins pine: Lessons from a pioneer' in Sustainable Forestry Working Group *The Business of Sustainable Forestry: Case Studies*. Island Press, Washington, DC

Hanson, J H. 1992. 'Extractive economies in a historical perspective: Gum arabic in West Africa' in C Nepstad and S Schwartzman (eds) *Non-Timber Products from Tropical Forests: Evaluation of a Conservation and Development Strategy*. The New York Botanical Garden, Bronx, New York, NY

Harding, A. 1972. *Ginseng and Other Medicinal Plants: A Book of Valuable Information for Growers as well as Collectors of Medicinal Roots, Barks, Leaves, etc* (revised from 1908). Emporium Publications, Boston, MA

Harlow, W, E Harrar and F White. 1979. *Textbook of Dendrology: Covering the Important Forest Trees of the United States and Canada* (sixth edition). McGraw-Hill, New York, NY

Harriman, S. 1975. *The Book of Ginseng*. Pyramid Books, New York, NY

Hartshorn G S. 1980. 'Neotropical forest dynamics. Tropical succession' (supplement). *Biotropica*, vol 12, pp23–30

Hawken, P. 1993. *The Ecology of Commerce: A Declaration of Sustainability*. HarperCollins Publishers, Inc, New York, NY

Hayes, C E and I J Goldstein. 1974. 'An alpha-D-galactosly-binding lectin from Bandeiraea simplicifolia seeds. Isolation by affinity chromatography and characterization'. *Journal of Biological Chemistry*, vol 249, no 6, pp1904–1914

Haynes, K. 1998. 'The Viagra alternatives'. *Vegetarian Times*, October, pp12–13

Health Canada. 1997. 'Raw or uncooked fiddleheads can cause illness'. *Health Canada Information Bulletin*, vol 1997–37, 4 June, Health Canada, Ottawa

Health Foods Business. 1998. '5-HTP alarm called politically motivated', October, p8

Health Supplement Industry Insider. 1998. '*Prime Time Live* report spurs 5-HTP sales', 29 June, p3

Hedin, L. 1929. 'Les Rotins au Cameroun'. *Revue de Botanique Appliquée et d'Agriculture Tropicale*, vol 9, pp502–507

Heithaus, E R, T H Fleming and P A Opler. 1975. 'Foraging patterns and resource utilization in seven species of bats in a seasonal tropical forest'. *Ecology*, vol 56, no 4, pp841–854

Henderson, A. 1986. 'A review of pollination studies in the Palmae'. *The Botanical Review*, vol 52, no 3, pp221–259

Henderson A and F Chávez. 1993. '*Desmoncus* as a useful palm in the western Amazon basin'. *Principes*, vol 37, pp184–186

Henderson, A and G Galeano. 1996. '*Euterpe, Prestoea* and *Neonicholsonia* (Palmae)'. *Flora Neotropica 72*, New York Botanical Garden, New York, NY

Hendrickson, R. 1976. *The Great American Chewing Gum Book*. Chilton Book Co, Radnor, PA

Hendrikx, H J A. 1935. 'De geschiedenis der pogingen tot reboisatie van alang-alang-terreinen in de Residentie Tapanoeli' (History of reforestation attempts in Alang-Alang areas in Tapanuli residence). *Tectona*, vol 28, pp844–849

Henry, T A. 1939. *The Plant Alkaloids*. J & A Churchill, London

Hérail, J. 1927. *Traité de Matière Médicale. Pharmacographie*. J Baillère & Fils, Paris

Hew-Kian-Chong, H. 1998. *Benjoins, Styrax et Storax*. Diplôme d'etat de docteur en pharmacie. Université Montpellier-I, Faculté de Pharmacie de Montpellier

Heyder, H M. 1930. 'Sapodilla tapping in British Honduras'. *Empire Forestry Journal*, vol 9, no 1, pp107–113

Heyne, K. 1927. *De Nuttige Planten van Nederlandsch-Indië*. Dept van Landbaouw, Nijverheid & Handel in Nederlandsch-Indië, Buitenzorg (originally published in 1917)

Hicks, F. 1998. Pers comm. Programme Director, Technoserve (Gh) Ltd

Hill, A F. 1937. *Economic Botany: A Textbook of Useful Plants and Plant Products*. McGraw-Hill Book Company, Inc, New York, NY

Hladik, C M et al (eds). 1996. *L'alimentation en foret tropicale: Interactions bioculturelles et perspectives de developpement*. UNESCO, Paris

Ho, D. 1999. 'Patent Office suspends patent for hallucinogenic plant'. The Associated Press. 5 November, Friday, PM cycle. *Business News*; Washington dateline

Hodel, D. 1998. *The Palms and Cycads of Thailand*. Allen Press, Kansas

Hoffman, B. 1997. 'The biology and use of nibbi *Heteropsis flexuosa* (Araceae): The source of an aerial root fiber product in Guyana'. Unpublished MSc thesis. Florida International University, Miami, FL

Homma, A K O. 1983. 'Esgotamento de recursos finitos – o caso do extrativismo vegetal na Amazonia'. *Bol. FBCN*, vol 18, pp44–48

Homma, A K O. 1992. 'The dynamics of extraction in Amazonia: A historical perspective' in D C Nepstad and S Schwartzman (eds) *Non-Timber Forest Products from Tropical Forests: Evaluation of a Conservation and Development Strategy*. Advances in Economic Botany 9. New York Botanical Garden, Bronx, New York, NY, pp23–31

Howes, F N. 1949. *Vegetable Gums and Resins*. Chronica Botanica Company, Waltham, Massachusetts

Hsu, P. 1982. 'Domestic and foreign use for ginseng' in C Roberts and J English (eds) *Proceedings of the Fourth National Ginseng Conference*. University of Kentucky, Kentucky

Hu, S, L Rudenberg and P del Tredici. 1980. 'Studies of American ginsengs'. *Rhodora*, vol 82, pp627–636

Hufford, M. 1997. 'American ginseng and the culture of the commons'. *Orion*, vol 16, no 4, pp11–14

Hughes, K and T Worth. 1999. *Cat's Claw*. New Crop Fact Sheet: www.hort.purdue.edu/newcrop/CropFactSheets/catsclaw.html

Hulssen, C J (Van). 1940. 'Sumatra-Benzoë'. *Pharmaceutisch Tijdschr*, vol 1, p13

Hurtado, F. 1998. *Posibilidades de manejo de Sangre de drago en la amazonia ecuatoriana*. Fundación Jatún Sacha, Ecuador

Hussain, S. 1999. 'Tenure in the context of sustainable use of natural resources in Asia' in J Oglethorpe (ed) *Tenure and Sustainable Use*. IUCN, Gland, Switzerland, and Cambridge, UK, pp21–29

Ianni, O. 1978. *A luta pela terra: Historia social da terra e da luta pela terranuma area da Amazonia*. Brasil Vozes, Petropolis

International Federation of Organic Agriculture Movements (IFOAM). 1998a. 'Fact sheet' in G Rundgren (ed) *Building Trust in Organics: A Guide to Setting Up Organic Certification Programmes*. Tholey-Theley, Germany

IFOAM. 1998b. *Basic Standards*. Tholey-Theley, Germany

Indian Medicinal Plants. 1997. 'A Sector Study', Occasional Papers 54. Export Import Bank of India, India

Instituto de Pesquisas e Estudos Florestais (IPEF). 1999. Online information centre for forestry sciences in Latin America with 60,000 bibliographic references: www.florestal.ipef.br/bibliotecas

International Organic Accreditation Service (IOAS). 1998. *Operating Manual for the IFOAM Accreditation Programme*. Jamestown, ND

International Tropical Timber Organization (ITTO). 1997. 'Bamboo & rattan: Resources for the 21st century?' *Tropical Forest Update*, vol 7, no 4, p13

International Work Group for Indigenous Affairs (IWGIA). 1996. *Indigenous Peoples, Forests and Biodiversity*. Document no 82. International Alliance of Indigenous-Tribal Peoples of the Tropical Forests/IWGIA, Copenhagen

Ip, C and D J Lisk. 1994. 'Bioactivity of selenium from Brazil nut for cancer prevention and selenoenzyme maintenance'. *Nutrition and Cancer*, vol 21, no 3, pp203–212

Jardim, M. 1992. *Orientacoes técnicas no manejo da palmeira Açai (*Euterpe oleracea *Mart.) paca producaõ de frutos e palmito*. Museu Paraense Emílio Goeldi, Belém, Brazil

Jenkins, M and S Oldfield. 1992. *Wild Plants in Trade: A TRAFFIC Network Report*. TRAFFIC International, Cambridge

Johns, A D. 1988. 'Effects of "selective" timber extraction on rainforest structure and composition and some consequences for frugivores and folivores'. *Biotropica*, vol 20, pp31–37

Johns, J S, P Barreto and C Uhl. 1996. 'Logging damage during planned and unplanned logging operations in the eastern Amazon'. *Forest Ecology and Management*, vol 89, pp59–77

Johns, R and R Taurereko. 1989a. *A Preliminary Checklist of the Collections of* Calamus *and* Daemonorops *from the Papuan Region*. Rattan Research Report 1989–1992

Johns, R and R Taurereko. 1989b. *A Guide to the Collection and Description of* Calamus *(Palmae) from Papuasia*. Rattan Research Report 1989–1993

Johnson, D V. 1997. *Non-Wood Forest Products: Tropical Palms*. Food and Agriculture Organization (FAO), Rome

Johnson, D. 1999. *Forest Certification Assessment Report for Palm Heart*. SmartWood, Rainforest Alliance, New York, NY

Johnston, B (ed). 1994. *Who Pays the Price? The Sociocultural Context of Environmental Crisis*. Island Press, Washington, DC

Joralemon, D. 1990. 'The selling of the shaman and the problem of informant legitimacy'. *Journal of Anthropological Research*, vol 46, no 2, pp105–117

Jordan, E. 1996. *Estudio de Mercado de Sangre de drago (*Croton lechleri*)*. INEFAN, GTZ, Ecuador

Jorgenson, A B. 1993. 'Chicle Extraction and Forest Conservation in Quintana Roo, Mexico'. Unpublished MSc thesis in Latin American studies, University of Florida, Gainesville, FL

Joseph, G M. 1987. 'The logwood trade and its settlements' in L H Krohn, M Murray, C Gill, M Mahler, L Ysaguirre and J Robinson (eds) *Readings in Belizean History*, second edition. Belizean Studies, St John's College, Belize City, Belize, pp32–47

Kahn, F and J-J de Granville. 1992. *Palms in Forest Ecosystems of Amazonia*. Springer-Verlag, Berlin

Kahn, R S and H G M Westenberg. 1985. 'L-5-Hydroxytryptophan in the treatment of anxiety disorders'. *Journal of Affective Disorders*, vol 8, pp197–200

Kainer, D A, M L Duryea, N Costa de Macedo and D Williams. 1998. 'Brazil nut seedling establishment and autecology in extractive reserves of Acre, Brazil'. *Ecological Applications*, vol 8, no 2, pp397–410

Kalem, Sedat. 1998. Pers comm (styrax oil)

Kam, T S, K H Lee and S H Goh. 1992. 'Alkaloid distribution in Malaysian *Uncaria*'. *Phytochemistry*, vol 31, no 2, pp2031–2034

Kannelis, Y. 1998. 'Strofilia'. *Nea Oikologia*, July (in Greek), pp 7–8

Karamanski, T J. 1989. *Deeps Woods Frontier: A History of Logging in Northern Michigan*. Wayne State University Press, Detroit, MI

Karling, J S. 1934. 'Dendrograph studies on *Achras zapota* in relation to the optimum conditions for tapping'. *American Journal of Botany*, vol 21, no 4, pp113–159

Karling, J S. 1942a. 'Collecting chicle in the American tropics: Part 1'. *Torreya*, vol 42, pp38–49

Karling, J S. 1942b. 'Collecting chicle in the American tropics: Part 2'. *Torreya*, vol 42, pp69–81

Karling, J S. 1942c. 'The response of *Achras zapota* in latex yield to wounding by the ibidem method of tapping'. *Bulletin of the Torrey Botanical Club*, vol 69, no 8, pp552–560

Keplinger, K, G Laus, M Wurm, M P Dierich and H Teppner. 1999. '*Uncaria tomentosa* (Willd.) DC – Ethnomedical use and new pharmacological, toxicological and botanical results'. *Journal of Ethnopharmacology*, vol 64, pp23–24

Khermouch, G. 1999. 'SoBe Radio ads flog herbal bennies'. *Brandweek*, New York, NY, 3 May

Kiernan, M and C Freese. 1997. 'Mexico's Plan Pilot Forestal: The search for balance between socio-economic and ecological sustainability' in C Freese (ed) *Harvesting Wild Species: Implications for Biodiversity Conservation*. The Johns Hopkins University Press, Baltimore, Maryland and London, pp93–131

King, S R and M S Tempesta. 1994. 'From shaman to human clinical trials: The role of industry in ethnobotany, conservation and community reciprocity' in G T Prance, D J Chadwick, J Marsh (eds) *Ethnobotany and the Search for New Drugs*. Ciba Foundation Symposium 185. John Wiley and Sons, Chichester, pp197–213

King, S R et al. 1997. '*Croton lechleri* and the sustainable harvest and management of plants in pharmaceuticals, phytomedicines and cosmetics industries' in D S Wozniak, S Yuen, M Garrett and T K Shuman (eds) *International Symposium on Herbal Medicine*. San Diego State University, San Diego, CA

King, S R, E N Meza, T J S Carlson, J A Chinnock, K Moran and J R Borges. 1999. 'Issues in the commercialization of medicinal plants'. *HerbalGram*, vol 47, pp46–51

Kircher, M and J Meier. 1997. 'Investigación sobre la cantidad y las edades de árboles "Sangre de drago" (*Croton* spp.) en Sucumbíos, Ecuador'. Unpublished manuscript

Koelling, M and R Heiligmann (eds). 1996. *North American Maple Syrup Producers Manual*. Ohio State University Extension, Bulletin 856, Ohio

Koromilas, K. 1999. 'Chios mastic therapeutic for peptic ulcer, say scientists'. *Athens News*, 10 December, p1

Kula, G. 1999. 'Influence of tenure and access rights on the sustainability of natural resource use' in J Oglethorpe (ed) *Tenure and Sustainable Use*. IUCN, Gland, Switzerland, and Cambridge, UK, pp43–48

Kwaramba, P K. 1995. 'Potential commercialization of common property resources: The case of baobab (*Adansonia digitata*) bark around the Hot Springs area'. Unpublished report. Institute of Environmental Studies, University of Zimbabwe, Harare

LaFleur, J R. 1992. *Marketing of Brazil Nuts: A Case Study from Brazil*. FAO, Rome

Laird, S A. 1995. *The Natural Management of Tropical Forests for Timber and Non-Timber Products*. Oxford Forestry Institute, Occasional Papers No 49, University of Oxford, Oxford

Laird, S A. 1999. 'The botanical medicine industry' in K ten Kate and S A Laird *The Commercial Use of Biodiversity: Access to Genetic Resources and Benefit-Sharing*. Earthscan, London, pp78–116

Laird, S A and M Burningham. 1999. 'The development of a benefit-sharing partnership in Vietnam: *Panax vietnamensis* – a "new" ginseng' in K ten Kate and S A Laird *The Commercial Use of Biodiversity: Access to Genetic Resources and Benefit-Sharing*. Earthscan, London, pp112–115

Laird, S A and K ten Kate. 1999. 'Natural products and the pharmaceutical industry' in K ten Kate and S A Laird *The Commercial Use of Biodiversity: Access to Genetic Resources and Benefit-Sharing*. Earthscan, London, pp34–77

Lake, R. 1998. 'Health Canada's X-rated natural health products'. *Alive*, no 194, 31 December, p7

Lakshmana, A C. 1993. *The Rattans of South India*. Evergreen Publishers, Bangalore, India

Lama, A. 2000. 'Ills of unregulated medicinal plant exports'. *IPS News Wires*, 3 February: www.ips.org

Lambrecht, B. 1999. 'Botanist sows seeds of enterprise in Ecuador to save forests, people; David Neill searches for options to opportunism'. *St Louis Post Dispatch*, 11 October 1998, pA9

Lammerts van Bueren, E M and E M Blom. 1997. *Hierarchical Framework for the Formulation of Sustainable Forest Management Standards: Principles, Criteria and Indicators*. The Tropenbos Foundation/Backhuys Publishers, Wageningen/Leiden, The Netherlands

Landis, S. 1997. 'Home depot shelves certified line'. *Understory* (the *Journal of the Good Wood Alliance*) vol 7, no 1, pp1, 12

Landy, M and H Plotkin. 1982. 'Limits of the market metaphor'. *Society*, vol 19, no 4, pp8–17

Lange, D. 1998. *Europe's Medicinal and Aromatic Plants: Their Use, Trade and Conservation*. TRAFFIC International, Cambridge, UK

Langenheim, J H. 1973. 'Leguminous resin-producing trees in Africa and South America' in B J Meggers, E S Ayensu and W D Duckworth (eds) *Tropical Forest Ecosystems in Africa and South America: A Comparative Review*. Smithsonian Institution Press, Washington, DC, p350

Laus, G, D Brössner and K Keplinger. 1997. 'Alkaloids of Peruvian *Uncaria tomentosa*'. *Phytochemistry*, vol 45, no 4, pp855–860

Law, K H and N P Das. 1990. 'Studies on the formation and growth of *Uncaria elliptica* tissue culture'. *Journal of Natural Products*, vol 53, no 1, pp125–130

Lawrence Review of Natural Products. 1990. 'Yohimbe. Facts and Comparisons'. St Louis, MO

Lawrence, J and R Martin. 1993. *Sweet Maple: Life, Lore and Recipes from the Sugarbush*. Montpelier and Shelburne, Vermont Life and Chapters Books, Vermont

Lazarte, F J. 1998. *Estudio de mercado de especies seleccionadas*. Volume 1. Resumen Ejecutivo. Proyecto INRENA-ITTO PD 9/95 'Repoblación Forestal con Especies Tropicales Valiosas en Sistemas Agroforestales en la Provincia de Tambopata'. INRENA, Ministerio de Agricultural Región Agraria Madre de Dios, Lima, Peru

Le Cointe, P. 1947. *Amazonia Brasiliera III Arvores e Plantas Uteis*. Biblioteca Pedagógica Brasiliera, Serie 5, vol 251. Companhia Editora Nacional, São Paulo, p506

Le Guérer, A. 1998 (1988). *Les Pouvoirs de l'Odeur*. Opus, Odile Jacob, Paris

Leak, W. 1980. 'Influence of habitat on silvicultural prescriptions in New England'. *Journal of Forestry*, vol 78, pp329–333

Leite, A, A Alexandre, C Rigamonte-Azevedo, C A Campos and A Oliveira. 2002. *Recommendacoes paro o manejo sustentavel do óleo de copáiba*. Série: Manejo Sustentavel de Florestas Tropicais. UFAC/SEFE, Acre, Brazil

Lenko, K and N Papavero. 1996. *Insetos no folclore* (revised second edition). Pleide, São Paulo

Letouzey, R. 1985. 'Notice de la carte phytogeographique du Cameroon'. Institute de la Carte Internationale de la Vegetation, Toulouse, France

Leung, A L. 1980. *Encyclopedia of Common Natural Ingredients used in Food, Drugs and Cosmetics*. John Wiley and Sons, New York, NY, p409

Lewis, W. 1984. 'Population structure and environmental corollaries of *Panax quinquefolium* (Araliaceae) in Delaware County, New York'. *Rhodora*, vol 86, pp431–438

Lewis, W. 1988. 'Regrowth of a decimated population of *Panax quinquefolium* in a Missouri, Wisconsin, climax forest'. *Rhodora*, vol 90, pp1–6

Lewis, W and V Zenger. 1982. 'Population dynamics of the American ginseng *Panax quinquefolium* (Araliaceae)'. *American Journal of Botany*, vol 69, no 9, pp1483–1490

Lewis, W and V Zenger. 1983. 'Breeding systems and fecundity in the American ginseng, *Panax quinquefolium* (Araliaceae)'. *American Journal of Botany*, vol 70, no 3, pp466–468

Lewis, W H and M P F Elvin-Lewis. 1977. *Medical Botany: Plants Affecting Man's Health*. John Wiley and Sons, New York, NY

Likens, G, C Driscoll and D Buso. 1996. 'Long-term effects of acid rain: Response and recovery of a forest ecosystem'. *Science*, vol 272, pp244–246

Lisboa, P L B, U N Maciel and G T Prance. 1990. 'Some effects of colonisation on the tropical flora of Amazonia: A case study from Rondonia'. *Kew Bulletin*, vol 46, pp187–204

Long, S. 1995. 'Healthy rivers are made in the shade'. *Vermont Woodlands*, vol 2, no 2, pp10–13

Loos, H. 1922. 'Lets over benzoe in Tapanuli' (in Dutch). *Teysmannia*, vol 32, pp397–408

Lopes, A V F, J M S de Souza and B B G Calzavara. 1982. *Aspectos econômicos do açaizeiro*. SUDAM, Belém

Luckert, M K, N Nemarundwe, L Gibbs, I Grundy, G Hauer, D Maruzane, S Shackleton and J Sithole. 2001. 'Contribution of baobab production activities to household livelihoods' in Hotsprings Working Group *Household Livelihoods, Marketing and Resource Impacts: A Case Study of Bark Products in Eastern Zimbabwe*. IES Working Paper, no 18. Institute of Environmental Studies, University of Zimbabwe, Harare, pp1–18

Lundell, C L. 1933a. 'The agriculture of the Maya'. *Southwest Review*, vol 19, pp65–77

Lundell, C L. 1933b. 'Chicle exploitation in the sapodilla forest of the Yucatan Peninsula'. *Field & Laboratory*, vol 2, pp15–21

Lundell, C L. 1934. 'Preliminary sketches of the phytogeography of the Yucatan Peninsula'. *Contributions to American Archaeology*. Publication 436. Carnegie Institute, Washington, DC

Lundell, C L. 1937. *The Vegetation of Peten*. Publication 478, Carnegie Institution of Washington, Washington, DC

Mabberley, D. 1987. *The Plant-Book: A Portable Dictionary of the Higher Plants*. Cambridge University Press, Cambridge, UK

Macbride, J F. *Flora of Peru*. Vol 13, part 6. Field Museum of Natural History, Chicago

Mann, J. 1992. *Murder, Magic and Medicine*. Oxford University Press, Oxford, p105

Marcelo, A J and E N Meza. 1999. 'Propiedades biológicas de metabolitos secundarios de "Sangre de Grado" (*Croton* spp.)' in E N Meza (ed) *Desarrollando Nuestra Diversidad Biocultural: 'Sangre de Grado' y el Reto de su Producción Sustentable en el Perú*. Universidad Nacional Mayor de San Marcos, Lima, Peru, pp165–196

Marks, P and S Gardescu. 1998. 'A case study of sugar maple (*Acer saccharum*) as a forest seedling bank species'. *Journal of the Torrey Botanical Society*, vol 125, no 4, pp287–296

Marsden, W. 1986. *The History of Sumatra* (reprint of 1811, Longman et al, London). Oxford University Press, Oxford

Martinez, M. 1959. *Plantas utiles de la flora Mexicana*. Ediciones Botas, Mexico, DF

Martini, A M, N Rosa and C Uhl. 1994. 'An attempt to predict which Amazonian tree species may be threatened by logging activities'. *Environmental Conservation*, vol 21, no 2, pp152–162

Mason, C. 1987. 'Maple sugaring again: The dog that did nothing in the night'. *Canadian Journal of Archaeology*, vol 11, pp99–109

Mason, H. 1972. *Gilgamesh: A Verse Narrative*. Mentor Books, New York, NY

Mater, C. 1998a. 'Emerging technologies for sustainable forestry' in *The Business of Sustainable Forestry: Case Studies*. Island Press, Washington, DC

Mater, C. 1998b. 'Menominee tribal enterprises: Sustainable forestry to improve forest health and create jobs' in *The Business of Sustainable Forestry: Case Studies*. Island Press, Washington, DC

Mater, C and S Mater. 1998. 'Vernon forestry: Log sorting for profit' in *The Business of Sustainable Forestry: Case Studies*. Island Press, Washington, DC

Matose, F and J Clarke. 1991. *Sooty Baobabs – Survey of Local Knowledge*. Zimbabwe Forestry Commission, Division of Research and Development, Harare

Maugh, T H II. 1979. 'Unlike money, diesel fuel grows on trees'. *Science*, vol 206, p436

Maulka, A J, L Ryvanden and R Mazodze. 1995. *A Guide to Forest and Timber Protection in Zimbabwe*. FORAGI Environmental Group, Harare

Maxwell, N. 1990. *Witch Doctor's Apprentice*, third edition. Citadel Press, New York, NY

May, P. 1999. Pers comm. Executive Director, Pro-Natura (tabebuia)

McKean, M A and E Ostrom. 1995. 'Common property regimes in the forest: Just a relic from the past?' *Unasylva*, vol 46, pp3–15

McLain, R J and E T Jones. 1997. *Challenging 'community' definitions in sustainable natural resource management*. International Institute for Environment and Development (IIED), London

McNeil, J R. 1992. *The Mountains of the Mediterranean World*. Cambridge University Press, Cambridge

Medical Letter. 1968. 'Afrodex and impotence'. *Medical Letter Drugs Therapy*, vol 10, p97

Medina C D and E N Meza. 1999. 'Estudio morfoanatómico de *Croton lechleri* Muell. Arg. (*Crotoneae, Euphorbiaceae*)' in E N Meza (ed) *Desarrollando Nuestra Diversidad Biocultural: 'Sangre de Grado' y el Reto de su Producción Sustentable en el Perú*. Universidad Nacional Mayor de San Marcos, Lima, Peru, pp77–94

Meeker, J E, J E Elias and J A Heim. 1993. *Plants Used by the Great Lakes Ojibwa*. Great Lakes Indian Fish and Wildlife Commission, Odanah, Wisconsin

Merriam-Webster. 1999. *Webster Dictionary*. Merriam-Webster, Inc, New York, NY

Meza, E N. 1991. *Estudio preliminar del potencial de producción de sangre de grado (*Croton *spp.), selva alta, Peru*. Fundación Peruana para la Conservación de la Naturaleza, Lima, Perú

Meza, E N. 1992a. *Informe de trabajo de Puerto Bermudez, Peru. Agosto-Setiembre 1992*. Report, Shaman Pharmaceuticals, Lima, Perú

Meza, E N. 1992b. *Informe de trabajo de Alto Marañón, Grupo Etnico Huambisa. Peru. Diciembre 1992*. Report, Shaman Pharmaceuticals, Lima, Perú

Meza, E N. 1992c. *Estudio preliminar de mercado de Sangre de Grado*. Report, Shaman Pharmaceuticals, Lima, Perú

Meza, E N. 1993a. *Segundo informe del trabajo de alto Marañón grupo étnico Aguaruna Huambisa, Peru*. Report, Shaman Pharmaceuticals, Lima, Perú

Meza, E N. 1993b. *Un tema para reflexionar: Indigenas en el comercio de planta medicinal*. Report, Shaman Pharmaceuticals, Lima, Perú

Meza, E N. 1994. *Reforestación de tierras indígenas de la selva Peruana con plantas medicinalles para la exportación*. Report, Shaman Pharmaceuticals, Lima, Peru

Meza, E N. 1995. *Informe No 001. Año 1995. Viaje a Puerto Bermúdez (CCNN El Milagro)*. Report, Shaman Pharmaceuticals, Lima, Perú

Meza, E N. 1996. *Organización y ejecución de taller de capacitación y difusión sobre organización comunal, manejo de pequeños proyectos y agroecología Indígena. Comunidad Nativa 'El Milagro', Puerto Bermudez, Pasco, Peru*. Confidential Report, Shaman Pharmaceuticals Inc, Lima, Perú

Meza, E N. 1997a. *Viaje a Pucallpa departamento de Ucayali, Peru.* Report, Shaman Pharmaceuticals, Lima, Perú

Meza, E N. 1997b. *Viaje a Puerto Bermudez Departamento de Pasco, Peru.* Report, Shaman Pharmaceuticals, Lima, Perú

Meza, E N. 1998a. *Viaje a selva nororiental. Asistencia Consejo Aguaruna Huambisa, Peru.* Report, Shaman Pharmaceuticals, Lima, Perú

Meza, E N. 1998b. *Planteamiento de la demanda de látex de 'Sangre de Grado' en el ámbito nacional en el Perú, invitación a diferentes instituciones para la reforestación con las especies de interés. Distribución de manuales educativos.* Report, Shaman Pharmaceuticals, Lima, Perú

Meza, E N. 1998c. *Viaje a selva central. Palcazú, Pichis (Departamento Pasco), Pucallpa (Departamento Ucayali), Peru.* Report, Shaman Pharmaceuticals, Lima, Perú

Meza, E N. 1998d. *Viaje a la zona sur de Peru. Puno-Cuzco-Madre de Dios.* 17–22 de Agosto de 1998. Report, Shaman Pharmaceuticals, Lima, Perú

Meza, E N. 1998e. *Viaje a la region San Martín, Perú.* 27–28 de Agosto de 1998. Report, Shaman Pharmaceuticals, Lima, Perú

Meza, E N. 1998f. *Viaje a la selva central. Provincia Padre Abad (Departamento de Ucayali), Provincia Coronel Portillo (Departamento Huanuco), Perú.* Report, Shaman Pharmaceuticals Inc, Lima, Peru

Meza, E N. 1999b. 'Cosecha de "Sangre de Grado" (*Croton* spp.) y factores que influyen en su abundancia' in E N Meza (ed) *Desarrollando Nuestra Diversidad Biocultural: 'Sangre de Grado' y el Reto de su Producción Sustentable en el Perú.* Universidad Nacional Mayor de San Marcos, Lima, Perú, pp45–76

Meza, E N. 1999c. 'Diagnostico del potencial de producción de "Sangre de Grado" (*Croton* spp.) Oxapampa, Perú' in E N Meza (ed) *Desarrollando Nuestra Diversidad Biocultural: 'Sangre de Grado' y el Reto de su Producción Sustentable en el Perú.* Universidad Nacional Mayor de San Marcos, Lima, Peru, pp95–121

Meza, E N and A J Marcelo R. 1999. 'Patentes registradas para "Sangre de Grado" (*Croton* spp.) con relación a la propiedad intelectual en la legislación Peruana' in E N Meza (ed) *Desarrollando Nuestra Diversidad Biocultural: 'Sangre de Grado' y el Reto de su Producción Sustentable en el Perú.* Universidad Nacional Mayor de San Marcos, Lima, Peru, pp197–259

Meza, E N and C Calderón M. 1999. 'Micorrización vesicular arbuscular en *Croton lechleri* Muell. Arg' in E N Meza (ed) *Desarrollando Nuestra Diversidad Biocultural: 'Sangre de Grado' y el Reto de su Producción Sustentable en el Perú.* Universidad Nacional Mayor de San Marcos, Lima, Peru, pp151–164

Meza, E N and C E Lara. 1997. *Estudio de mercado de sangre de grado.* Report, Shaman Pharmaceuticals, Lima, Peru

Meza, E N and M Pariona. 1999. 'Nombres aborigenes Peruanos de las especies de *Croton* que producen el látex denominado "Sangre de Grado"' in E N Meza (ed) *Desarrollando Nuestra Diversidad Biocultural: 'Sangre de Grado' y el Reto de su Producción Sustentable en el Perú.* Universidad Nacional Mayor de San Marcos, Lima, Peru, pp25–44

Meza, E N. Undated. *Mis experiencias con Shaman Pharmaceuticals Inc y 'Sangre de Grado' en el Perú.* Manuscript, Lima, Peru

Meza, E N and M Valencia R. 1999. 'Estudio comparativo de suelos con relación al crecimiento y calidad de "Sangre de Grado" en *Croton lechleri* Muell. Arg' in E N Meza (ed) *Desarrollando Nuestra Diversidad Biocultural: 'Sangre de Grado' y el Reto de su Producción Sustentable en el Perú.* Universidad Nacional Mayor de San Marcos, Lima, Peru, pp123–149

Meza, E N (ed). 1999a. *Desarrollando Nuestra Diversidad Biocultural: 'Sangre de Grado' y el Reto de su Producción Sustentable en el Perú.* Universidad Nacional Mayor de San Marcos, Lima, Peru

Meza, E N, F Ayala, M Castañel, L E Forero, M Peñsa, A Ortiz, S R King and J R Borges. 1998. *El Manejo Sostenible de drago o Sangre de Grado: Material Educativo.* Shaman Pharmaceuticals Inc, Lima, Peru

Michelson, D, S W Page, R Casey, M W Trucksess, L A Love, S Milsten, C Wilson, S G Massaquoi, L J Crofford, M Hallett, P W Gold and E M Sternberg. 1994. 'An Eosinophilia-Myalgia syndrome related disorder associated with exposure to L-5-hydroxytryptophan'. *The Journal of Rheumatology*, vol 21, no 12, pp2261–2265

Michon, G and M Saragih. 1999. 'Regional survey: Global evolution of benzoin management'. *Forressasia INCO III Report. Appendix 3*

Miller, C J. 1990. 'Natural History, Economic Botany and Germplasm Conservation of the Brazil Nut Tree (*Bertholletia excelsa*, Humb & Bonpl.)'. Unpublished MSc thesis. University of Florida, Gainesville, FL

Miller, W W. 1968. 'Afrodex in the treatment of male impotence: A double-blind crossover study'. *Current Therapeutic Research*, vol 10, p354

Millman, C. 1999. 'Natural disasters'. *Men's Health*, April, p52

Mingione, E. 1994. 'Life strategies and social economies in the postfordist age'. *International Journal of Urban and Regional Research*, vol 18, no 1, pp24–25

Mizrahi, Y and A Nerd. 1996. 'New crops as a possible solution for the troubled Israeli export market' in J Janick (ed) *Progress in New Crops*. ASHS Press, Alexandria, Vermont

Moerman, D E. 1998. *Native American Ethnobotany*. Timber Press, Portland, Oregon

Molina, R, T O'Dell, D Luoma, M Amaranthus, M Castellano and K Russell. 1993. *Biology, Ecology and Social Aspects of Wild Edible Mushrooms in the Forest of the Pacific Northwest: A Preface to Managing Commercial Harvest*. USDA Forest Service, General Technical Report, PNW-GTR-309. US Forest Service Pacific Northwest Research Station, Portland, Oregon

Montague, A. 1997. 'Love is here to stay'. *The Guardian*, 15 July, pp13–14

Mora Urpí, J, A Bonilla, C R Clement and D V Johnson. 1991. 'Mercado internacional de palmito e futuro de la explotación selvaje vs. cultivado'. *Pejibaye – Boletín Informativo*, vol 3, no 1/2, pp6–27

Morais, P B, M B Martins, L B Klaczko, L C Mendonça-Hagler and A N Hagler. 1995a. 'Yeast succession in the Amazon fruit *Parahancornia amapa* as resource partitioning among *Drosophila* spp.'. *Applied and Environmental Microbiology*, vol 61, no 12, pp4251–4257

Morais, P B, C A Rosa, S A Meyer, L C Mendonça-Hagler and A N Hagler. 1995b. '*Candida amapae*, a new amino acid-requiring yeast from the Amazonian fruit *Parahancornia amapa*'. *Journal of Industrial Microbiology*, vol 14, pp531–535

Morakinyo, A B. 1995. 'Profiles and Pan-African distributions of the rattan species (Calmoideae) recorded in Nigeria'. *Principes*, vol 39, no 4, pp197–209

Morales, A et al. 1981. 'Nonhormonal pharmacalogical treatment of organic impotence'. *Journal of Urology*, vol 128, pp45–47

Morales, A et al. 1982. 'Yohimbine for treatment of impotence in diabetes'. *New England Journal of Medicine*, vol 305, pp1221

Morgan, P et al. 1994. 'Ostrich fern poisoning – Western Canada and New York, 1994'. *Canada Communicable Disease Report 1994*, vol 20. Health Canada, Ottawa, pp160–163

Mori, S A and G T Prance. 1987. 'Species diversity, phenology, plant-animal interactions, and their correlation with climate, as illustrated by the Brazil nut family (Lecythidaceae)' in R E Dickenson (ed) *The Geophysiology of Amazonia*. John Wiley and Sons, New York, NY

Mori, S A and G T Prance. 1990. 'Taxonomy, ecology and economic botany of the Brazil nut (*Bertholettia excelsa* Humb. and Bonpl; Lecythidaceae)'. *Advances in Economic Botany*, vol 8, pp130–150

Morris, J and S A Laird. 1999. 'Cohune oil: Marketing a personal care product for community development and conservation in Guatemala – an overview of the Conservation International and Croda Inc partnerships' in K ten Kate and S A Laird *The Commercial Use of Biodiversity: Access to Genetic Resources and Benefit-Sharing*. Earthscan, London, pp287–290

Mors, W B and C T Rizzini. 1966. *Useful Plants of Brazil*. Holden-Day Inc, San Francisco

Morton, J M. 1987. *Fruits of Warm Climates*. Julia F Morton, Miami, pp393–410

Motte, E. 1980. *Les plantes chez le pygmies Aka et les Monzombo de la Lobaye (Centrafrique)*. Societé d'éudes Linguistiques et Anthropologiques de France, Paris

Moussouris, Y. 1999. *Cork Certification According to FSC Principles and Criteria*. Unpublished manuscript. WWF Mediterranean Programme

Mudavanhu, H T. 1998. 'Demography and Population Dynamics of Baobabs (*Adansonia digitata*) Harvested for Bark in South-Eastern Zimbabwe'. Unpublished MSc thesis. University of Zimbabwe, Harare

Mukamuri, B B and W Kozanayi. 2000. 'Institutional dynamics in the exploitation of the bark of three tree species: *Adansonia digitata Berchemia discolor* and *Warburgia salutaris*'. IES working paper 14. Institute of Environmental Studies (IES), University of Zimbabwe, Harare

Mullin, L J. 1997. 'The baobab giant of Zimbabwe's lowveld' in M J Kimberly (ed) *Succulent Plants of Zimbabwe and Their Conservation. Excelsa*, vol 18, pp41–45

Murray, M. 1998. *5-HTP: The Natural Way to Overcome Depression, Obesity and Insomnia*. Bantam Books, New York, NY

Myers, G P, A C Newton and O Melgarejo. 2000. 'The influence of canopy gap size on natural regeneration of Brazil nut (*Bertholletia excelsa*) in Bolivia'. *Forest Ecology and Management*, vol 127, pp119–128

Nantel, P, D Gagnon and A Nault. 1996. 'Population viability analysis of American ginseng and wild leek harvested in stochastic environments'. *Conservation Biology*, vol 10, no 2, pp608–621

Napier, I A. 1973. 'A brief history of the development of the hardwood industry in Belize'. *Coedwigwr*, vol 26, pp36–43

Nardini, M, R DeStefano, M Annuccelli, R Borhesi and N Battistini. 1983. 'Treatment of depression with L-5-Hydroxytryptophan combined with Chlorimipramine, a double-blind study'. *International Journal of Clinical Pharmacological Research*, vol 3, no 4, pp239–250

Natural Way. 1998. 'Herbal aphrodisiacs'. *Natural Way for Better Health*, vol 3, no 6, 28 February, p45

NBC News. 1999. *NBC Dateline* (segment 1), broadcast 6 April

Nearing, H and S Nearing. 1950. *The Maple Sugar Book: Together with Remarks on Pioneering as a Way of Living in the Twentieth Century*. Schocken Books, New York, NY

Nelson, A. 1951. *Medical Botany*. E & S Livingstone, Edinburgh, p426

Nepstad, D C and S Schwartzman (eds). 1992. *Non-Timber Products from Tropical Forests: Evaluation of a Conservation and Development Strategy. Advances in Economic Botany*, vol 9, New York Botanical Garden, Bronx, New York, NY

Nepstad, D, L Brown, L Luz, A Alechandre and V Viana. 1992. 'Biotic impoverishment of Amazonian forests by rubber tappers, loggers and cattle ranchers' in D Nepstad and S Schwartzman (eds) *Non-Timber Products from Tropical Forests, Evaluation of Conservation and Development Strategy. Advances in Economic Botany*, vol 9, New York Botanical Garden, Bronx, New York, NY, pp1–14

Neugebauer, B, R A A Oldeman and P Valaverde. 1996. 'Key principles in ecological silviculture' in T V Østergaard (ed) *Fundamentals of Organic Agriculture*. 11th IFOAM International Scientific Conference, Copenhagen, pp153–175

Neumann, R P. 1996. 'Questions and issues for non-timber forest product research in relation to conservation policies in Africa' in J E M Arnold and M Ruiz-Pérez (eds) *Current Issues in Non-Timber Forest Products Research*. CIFOR, Bogor, Indonesia

Niese, J and T Strong. 1992. 'Economic and tree diversity trade-offs in managed northern hardwoods'. *Canadian Journal of Forest Research*, vol 22, pp1807–1813

Nkana, Z G and S Iddi. 1991. *Utilisation of Baobab (*Adansonia digitata*) in Dondoa District, Central Tanzania*. Record No 50, Sokoine University of Agriculture, Morogoro, Tanzania

Nugent, S. 1993. *Amazonian Caboclo Society: An Essay on Invisibility and Peasant Economy.* Berg Publishers, Providence

Nutrition Science News. 1997. 'FDA Stops Short of Banning Epherdra'. *Nutrition Science News*, vol 2, no 7, 31 July, pp307

Obregón V L E. 1997. 'Uña de Gato', 'Cat's Claw'. *Género Uncaria. Estudios botánicos, químicos y farmacológicos de Uncaria tomentosa, Uncaria guianensis*, third edition. Instituto de Fitoterapia Americano, Lima

Obunga, R. (1996) *Sustainable Development of the Woodcarving Industry in Kenya.* Draft technical progress report (Phase 1). Unpublished report for the WWF/UNESCO/Kew People and Plants Initiative, National Museums of Kenya

Obunga, R. & Sigu, G. (1996) Sustainable development of the woodcarving industry in Kenya. Draft technical progress report (Phase 2). Unpublished report for the WWF/UNESCO/Kew People and Plants Initiative, National Museums of Kenya

Ocampo, P. 1994. Uncaria tomentosa, *aspectos etnomédicos, médicos, farmacológicos, botánicos, agronómicos, comerciales, legales, antropológicos, sociales y políticos.* Instituto de Desarrollo Rural Peruano, Lima, Peru

Ochoa-Gaona, S and M González-Espinosa. 2000. 'Land use patterns and deforestation in the highlands of Chiapas, Mexico'. *Applied Geography*, vol 20, pp17–42

Oever, H Ten. 1911. 'De vooruitzichten der kamferkultuur'. *Tectona*, vol IV, pp623–631

Oficina de Planificación Agraria. 1998. *Cultivo de Sangre de Drago.* Ministerio de Agricultura, Dirección Regional Agraria Loreto, Iquitos, Peru

Oglethorpe, J (ed). 1999. *Tenure and Sustainable Use.* IUCN, Gland, Switzerland, and Cambridge, UK

Oliver-Beyer, B. 1986. *Medicinal Plants in Tropical West Africa.* Cambridge University Press, Cambridge, p62

Olizar, M and A Olizar. 1968. *A Guide to the Mexican Markets*, third edition. Mexico, DF, p178

Orecklin, M. 1999. 'Savor the peach: The slow food movement wants you to honor your roots and vegetables'. *Time*, vol 153, no 19, p86

Orlande, T, J Laarman and J Mortimer. 1996. 'Palmito sustainability and economics in Brazil's Atlantic coastal forest'. *Forest Ecology and Management*, vol 80, pp257–265

Ortiz, E. 1991. *Early Recruitment of Brazil Nut Trees (Bertholletia excelsa Humb. & Bonpl.): Preliminary Results, Discussion and Experimental Approach.* A proposal report, August. Wildlife Conservation International, New York, NY

Ortiz, E. 1995. 'Survival in a nutshell'. *America*, September–October. Organization of American States, Washington, DC, pp12–15

Osol, A and Farrar, G E (eds). 1947. *The Dispensatory of the United States of America*, 24th edition. J B Lippincott Co, Philadelphia

Ozanne, L and R Vlosky. 1998. 'Environmental certification of wood products'. *Women in Natural Resources*, vol 19, no 3, pp4–8

Pace, R. 1998. *The Struggle for Amazon Town: Gurupa Revisited.* Lynne Ryenner, Boulder, CO

Padulosi, S. 1999. *Conservation and Use of Underutilized Mediterranean Species.* Final report. International Plant Genetic Resources Institute, Regional Office for Central and West Asia and North Africa (CWANA), Aleppo, Syria

Panayotou, T and P S Ashton. 1993. *Not by Timber Alone: Economics and Ecology for Sustaining Tropical Forests.* Island Press, Washington, DC

Papageorgiou, Aristotelis. 1998. Pers comm (Parnon chestnuts)

Pardy, A. 1953. 'Notes on indigenous trees and shrubs of S. Rhodesia. *Adansonia digitata* L. (Bombacaceae)'. *Rhodesian Agricultural Journal*, vol 50, pp5–6

Paris, R and R Letouzey. 1960. 'Repartition des alcaloides le Yohimbe (*Pausinystalia johimbe*) (K. Schum.) ex Pierre (Rubiaceae)'. *Journal d'Agriculture Tropicale et de Botanique Appliquée*, vol 7, no 4–5, pp256–258

Paspuel, A.1998. 'Analisis de sobrevivencia y crecimiento inicial de Sangre de drago'. *Bosques y Desarrollo*, vol 17, pp49–50

Passos, L and S O Ferreira. 1996. 'Ant dispersal of *Croton priscus* (Euphorbiaceae) seeds in a tropical semideciduous forest in Southeastern Brazil'. *Biotropica*, vol 28, no 4, part B, pp697–700

Patty, G. 1979. 'Trends in commerce with American ginseng' in D Hensley, S Alexander and C Roberts (eds) *Proceedings of the First National Ginseng Conference*. University of Kentucky, Kentucky

Patty, G. 1982. 'Use of and competition for US ginseng in foreign markets' in C Roberts and J English (eds) *Proceedings of the Fourth National Ginseng Conference*. University of Kentucky, Kentucky

Peattie, D. 1948. *A Natural History of Trees of Eastern and Central North America*. Houghton Mifflin Company, Boston, MA

Pedrosa Macedo, J H, F O Rittershofer and A Dessewffy. 1975. *A silvicultura e a indústria do palmito*. IPRNR, Porto Alegre

Peirce, A. 1999. *The American Pharmaceutical Association Practical Guide to Natural Medicines*. Stonesong Press Inc, New York, NY

Peluso, N L. 1992. 'The rattan trade in East Kalimantan, Indonesia' in D Nepstad and S Schwartzman (eds) *Non-Timber Products from Tropical Forests: Evaluation of a Conservation and Development Strategy, Advances in Economic Botany*, vol 9, New York Botanical Garden, Bronx, New York, NY, pp115–127

Peña Claros, M. 1996. 'Ecology and Socio-Economics of Palm Heart Extraction from Wild Populations of *Euterpe precatoria* Mart'. in Eastern Bolivia. Unpublished MSc thesis. University of Florida, Gainesville, FL

Pendelton, L H. 1992. 'Trouble in paradise: Practical obstacles to non-timber forestry in Latin America' in M Plotkin and L Famolare (eds) *Sustainable Harvest and Marketing of Rain Forest Products*. Island Press, Washington, DC

Pennington, T D. 1990. 'Sapotaceae'. *Flora Neotropica, Monograph 52*. New York Botanical Garden, New York, NY

Perikos, Y. 1990. *The Mastic Gum of Chios*. Perikos Publications, Chios, Greece

Perl, M, M Kiernan, D McCaffrey, R Buschbacher and G Batmanian. *Views from the Forest: Natural Forest Management Initiatives in Latin America*. WWF-US, Washington, DC

Persons, W. 1994a. *American Ginseng: Green Gold* (revised edition). Bright Mountain Books, Inc, Asheville, North Carolina

Persons, W. 1994b. 'Growing American ginseng in its native woodland habitat' in A Kestner, J Simon and A Tucker (eds) *Proceedings of Herbs '94: The Ninth National Herb Growing and Marketing Conference*. International Herb Growers and Marketers Association, Mundelein, IL

Persons, W. 1996. *Ginseng News from Tuckasegee Valley*. Tuckasegee Valley Ginseng, Tuckasegee, North Carolina

Peters, C M. 1983. 'Observations on Maya subsistence and the ecology of a tropical tree'. *American Antiquity*, vol 48, no 3, pp610–615

Peters, C M, A H Gentry and R O. Mendelsohn. 1989. 'Valuation of an Amazonian rainforest'. *Nature*, vol 339, pp655–656

Peters, C M. 1990. 'Population ecology and management of forest fruit trees in Peruvian Amazonia' in A Anderson (ed) *Alternatives to Deforestation: Steps Towards Sustainable Use of the Amazon Rain Forest*. Columbia University Press, New York, NY, pp86–98

Peters, C M. 1994. *Sustainable Harvest of Non-Timber Plant Resources in Tropical Moist Forest: An Ecological Primer*. Biodiversity Support Programme and World Wildlife Fund, Washington, DC

Peters, C M. 1996. 'The Ecology and Management of Non-Timber Forest Resources'. World Bank Technical Paper No 322. World Bank, Washington, DC

Peters, C R and E M O'Brien. 1980. *Wild-Plants Genera Exploited for Food by Humans, Chimpanzees and Baboons in Eastern and Southern Africa.* University of Georgia, Athens, Georgia, US

Phillips, O L B. 1993. 'The potential for harvesting fruits in tropical rainforests: New data from Amazonia Peru'. *Biodiversity and Conservation*, vol 2, pp18–38

Piearce, G D, G M Calvert, C Sharp and P Shaw. 1994. 'Sooty Baobab – Disease or Drought?' Zimbabwe Forestry Commission, Research Paper 6, Harare

Pierce A. 1996. 'Certification of non-timber forest products'. *FSC Notes*, vol 1, no 3, Forest Stewardship Council, Oaxaca, Mexico

Pierce, A. 1997. 'Simulated-wild ginseng: A feasible crop for non-industrial private forest owners in Vermont?' Unpublished MSc thesis. University of Vermont, Burlington, Vermont

Pierce, A R. 1999. 'The challenges of certifying non-timber forest products'. *Journal of Forestry*, vol 97, no 2, pp34–37

Pierce, A R and J B Ervin. 1999. 'Can Independent Forest Management Certification Incorporate Elements of Landscape Ecology?' *Unasylva*, vol 50, no 196, pp49–56

Pieters, L, T De Bruyne, B van Poel, R Vingerhoets, J Tott, D van den Berge and A Vlietink. 1995. 'In vivo wound healing activity of dragon's Blood (*Croton* spp.), a traditional South American drug, and its constituents'. *Phytomedicine*, vol 2, no 1, pp17–22

Piña-Rodrigues, F. 1999. Pers comm. Professor Adjunct, Deptartment of Silviculture, Forestry Institute, UFRRJ, Brazil

Pinedo R R. 1997. 'Informe No 013-97-DRA-CRI/RPR. Inspección a plantación de Sangre de Grado'. Comité de Reforestación de Loreto, Dirección Regional Agraria, Ministerio de Agricultura, Peru

Pinyopusarerk, K. 1994. *Styrax tonkinensis: Taxonomy, Ecology, Silviculture and Uses,* ACIAR Technical Reports, ACIAR, Canberra

Pires, N. 1993. Pers comm. Anthropologist working with the Tembé Indians in the Alto Rio Guamá Reserve, Para, Brazil

Pittier, H. 1926. *Manual de las Plantas Usuales de Venezuela,* (1939 compendium). Editorial Elite, Caracas, p458

Plantecam. 1993. *Pygeum Bark and Yohimbe Received by Plantecam (Mutengene) from 1/7/92 to the 30/6/93.* Internal report for Plantecam company, Mutengene, Cameroon

Plotkin, M and L Famolare (eds). 1992. *Sustainable Harvest and Marketing of Rain Forest Products.* Island Press, Washington, DC

Plowden, C. 2001. 'The Ecology, Management and Marketing of Non-Timber Forest Products in the Alto Rio Guamá Indigenous Reserve (Eastern Brazilian Amazon)'. Unpublished PhD thesis. Penn State University, University Park, PA

Plowman, T. 1984. 'The ethnobotany of coca (*Erythroxylum* spp., Erythroxylaceae*).' Advances in Economic Botany*, vol 1, pp62–111

Poffenberger, M (ed). 1990. *Keepers of the Forest: Land Management Alternatives in Southeast Asia.* Kumarian Press, Hartford, Connecticut

Polanyi, K. 1977. *The Livelihood of Man.* H W Pearson (ed) Studies in Discontinuity. Academic Press, New York, NY

Politis, Yorgos. 1998. Pers comm (chestnut certification)

Pollack, A. 1999. 'Shaman says it is exiting drug business'. *The New York Times*, 2 February, Late Edition, section C, p9, column 1

Pollack, H, M Mattos and C Uhl. 1995. 'A profile of palm heart extraction in the Amazon estuary'. *Human Ecology*, vol 23, no 3, pp357–385

Portes, A, M Castells and L Benton. 1989. *The Informal Economy: Studies in Advanced and Less Developed Countries.* The Johns Hopkins University Press, Baltimore

Posey, D A and W Balee (eds). 1989. *Resource management in Amazonia: Indigenous and folk strategies. Advances in Economic Botany,* 7. New York Botanical Garden, New York, NY

Posey, D and G Dutfield. 1996. *Beyond Intellectual Property: Toward Traditional Resource Rights for Indigenous Peoples and Local Communities*. IDRC, Ottawa

Posey, D A (ed). 1999. *The Cultural and Spiritual Value of Biodiversity*. UNEP, Nairobi

Poucher, W A. 1950. *Perfumes, Cosmetics and Soaps with Special Reference to Synthetics*. Chapman and Hall Ltd, New York, NY, vol 1, p459; vol 2, p430

Powell, A H. and G V N. Powell. 1987. 'Population dynamics of male Euglossine bees in Amazonian forest fragments'. *Biotropica*, vol 19, no 2, pp176–179

Prabhu, R, C J P Colfer and R G Dudley. 1999. *Guidelines for Developing, Testing and Selecting Criteria and Indicators for Sustainable Forest Management: A C&I Developer's Reference*. The Criteria & Indicators Toolbox Series, no 1. Center for International Forestry Research (CIFOR), Bogor, Indonesia

Pradal, Malepeyre and Villon. 1895. *Nouveau Manuel Complet du Parfumeur*. Roret, Paris

Prance, G T, W Balée, B Boom and R L Carneiro. 1987. 'Quantitative ethnobotany and the case for conservation in Amazonia'. *Conservation Biology*, vol 1, pp296–310

Proctor, J and W Bailey. 1987. 'Ginseng: Industry, botany and culture' in J Janick (ed) *Horticultural Reviews*, vol 9. Van Nostrand Reinhold Company, New York, NY

Proctor, J, T Wang and W Bailey. 1988. 'East meets west: Cultivation of American ginseng in China'. *HortScience*, vol 23, no 6, pp968–973

Propper, D, T Lent, M Skelly and R Crossley. 1998. 'Marketing products from sustainably managed forests: An emerging opportunity' in Sustainable Forestry Working Group *The Business of Sustainable Forestry: Case Studies*. Island Press, Washington, DC

Puttini, P S and I Caruso. 1992. 'Primary fibromyalgia syndrome and 5-Hydroxy-L-tryptophan: A 90-day open study'. *The Journal of International Medical Research*, vol 20, pp182–189

Putz, F and F S P Ng. 1978. 'Styracaceae' in F S P Ng (ed) *Tree Flora of Malaya*. Longman, London, Kuala Lumpur, Singapore

Quebec Maple Federation. 2000. Online information: www.maple-erable.qc.ca/sirop.html

Quevedo G A. 1995. *Silvicultura de la uña de gato*. CRI-IIAP Ucayali, Pucallpa, Peru

Raffauf. R F. 1970. *A Handbook of Alkaloids and Alkaloid-Containing Plants*. Wiley-Interscience, New York, NY

Rainforest Alliance. 1999. *Draft Generic Guidelines for Assessing the Management of NTFPs in Natural Forest*. The NTFP Certification Project. Rainforest Alliance, New York, NY

Raintree. 1999. Raintree Nutrition Inc, Austin, Texas, online information: www.raintree.com/paudarco.htm

Ramirez, N and M K Arroyo. 1987. 'Spatial and temporal variations in seed depredation of *Copaifera pubiflora* Benth. (Leguminosae: Caesalpinioideae) in Venezuela.' *Biotropica*, vol 19, no 1, pp32–39

Rao, M M and D G I Kingston. 1980. 'Plant anticancer agents (XII). Isolation and structure elucidation of new cytotoxic quinones from *Tabebuia Cassinoides*'. *Journal of Natural Products*, vol 45, no 5, pp600–604

Raponda-Walker, R A and S Sillans. 1961. *Les Plantes Utiles de Gabon*. IRA, Paris

Rauh, W. 1992. 'Are Tillandsias endangered plants?' *Selbyana*, vol 13, pp138–139

Raver, A. 1996. 'Ginseng is a tonic for its growers'. *The New York Times*, 14 July, p39

Record, S J and C D Mell. 1924. *Timbers of Tropical America*. Yale University Press, New Haven, p610

Regato, P. 1996. 'Mediterranean forests: An introduction' in P Regato *SILVA 96 Handbook – a WWF Course on Mediterranean Forests*. WWF Mediterranean Programme Office, Madrid

Regato, P. 1998. Pers comm (cork certification, pine nuts)

Regato, P, S Jiménez-Caballero, U Elena-Rossell and M Castejón. In press. In S Mazzoleni, P DiMartino, G DiPasquale and F Rego (eds) *Dynamics of Mediterranean Vegetation Landscape*. Gordon & Bread Publishing, Reading, UK

Reinhard, K H. 1999. '*Uncaria tomentosa* (Willd.)D.C: Cat's Claw, Uña de Gato or Savéntaro'. *The Journal of Alternative and Complementary Medicine*, vol 5, no 2, pp143–151

Reining, C, R Heinzman, M C Madrid, S Lopez and A Solorzano 1991. *A Socio-Economic and Ecological Analysis of Non-Timber Forest Products in the Peten, Guatemala*. Conservation International. Washington, DC

Reitz, R. 1981. *Flora Ilustrada Catarinense: Burseráceas*. Conselho Nacional de Desenvolvimento Científico e Tecnológico – CNPq, Itajaí

Renuka, C. 1992. *Rattans of the Western Ghats: A Taxonomic Manual*. Kerala Forest Research Institute, India

Renuka, C. 1995. *A Manual of the Rattans of the Andaman and Nicobar islands*. Kerala Forest Research Insititute, India

Rezende, T. 1996. Pers comm Executive Director of Instituto de Manejo e Certificacão Florestral e Agrícola (IMAFLORA), Piracicaba, Brazil

Rezende, T. 1998. Pers comm. Executive Director of Instituto de Manejo e Certificacão Florestral e Agrícola (IMAFLORA), Piracicaba, Brazil

Rezende, T. 1999. Pers comm. Executive Director of Instituto de Manejo e Certificacão Florestral e Agrícola (IMAFLORA), Piracicaba, Brazil

Rice, D S. 1991. 'The Maya rediscovered: Roots; resourceful Maya farmers enabled a mounting population to survive in a fragile tropical habitat'. *Natural History*, February, pp10–14

Rice, R and J Ward. 1996. *Coffee, Conservation and Commerce in the Western Hemisphere: How Individuals and Institutions Can Promote Ecologically Sound Farming and Forest Management in Northern Latin America*. Smithsonian Migratory Bird Centre and NRDC, Washington, DC

Robbins, C. 1997. 'US medicinal plant trade studies'. *TRAFFIC Bulletin*, vol 16, no 3, pp121–125

Roberts, B. 1994. 'Informal economy and family strategies'. *International Journal of Urban and Regional Planning*, vol 18, no 1, pp6–23

Roberts, C and J Richardson. 1980. *Wild Ginseng in Kentucky 1978–1979*. Progress Report 247, University of Kentucky Agricultural Experiment Station, Lexington, Kentucky

Roberts, N. 1994. *The Holocene: An Environmental History*. Blackwell Publishers, Oxford, UK

Rogers, D. 1999. 'Despite surplus boasts, lawmakers search for revenue'. *The Wall Street Journal*, 7 September, pA26

Rogers, E. 1995. *Diffusion of Innovations*, fourth edition. The Free Press, New York, NY

Romell, R. 1996. 'Cash crop herb rings up big sales, but some doubt firm's claims'. *Milwaukee Journal Sentinel*, 17 October, p1

Romero, C, D Dovie, J Gambiza, E Luoga, S Schmitt and I Grundy. 2001. 'Effects of Commercial Bark Harvesting on *Adansonia digitata* (Baobab) in the Savi-Odzi Valley, Zimbabwe, with Considerations for its Management' in Hotsprings Working Group *Household Livelihoods, Marketing and Resource Impacts: A Case Study of Bark Products in Eastern Zimbabwe*. IES Working Paper, no 18. Institute of Environmental Studies, University of Zimbabwe, Harare, pp28–51

Ros-Tonen, M, W Dijkman and E Lammerts van Bueren. 1995. *Commercial and Sustainable Extraction of Non-Timer Forest Products: Towards a Policy and Management Oriented Research Strategy*. The Tropenbos Foundation, Wageningen, The Netherlands

Rosengarten, Jr F. 1984. *The Book of Edible Nuts*. Walker & Company, New York, NY

Roys, R L. 1931. *The Ethno-Botany of the Maya*. Deptartment of Middle American Research, Tulane University, New Orleans, LA

Ruiz-Pérez, M and N Byron. 1999. 'A methodology to analyze divergent case studies of non-timber forest products and their development potential'. *Forest Science*, vol 45, no 1, pp1–14

Salafsky, N, B Dugelby and J Terborgh. 1993. 'Can extractive reserves save the rain forest? An ecological and socio-economic comparison of non-timber forest product extraction systems in

Petén, Guatemala, and West Kalimantan, Indonesia'. *Conservation Biology*, vol 7, no 1, pp39–52

Salomao, R.de P. 1991. 'Estrutura e densidade de *Bertholletia excelsa* H. & B. ('Castanheira') nas regioes de Carajas e Maraba, Estado do Para'. *Boletim do Museu Paraense Emílio Goeldi, série Botânica*, Belem, vol 7, no 1, pp47–68

Salwasser, H, D MacCleery and T Snellgrove. 1993. 'An ecosystem perspective on sustainable forestry and new directions for the US national forest system' in G Aplet, N Johnson, J Olson and V Sample (eds) *Defining Sustainable Forestry*. Island Press, Washington, DC

Sanabria, R. 1999. *Palm Hearts Market Review*. Rainforest Alliance, New York, NY

Savathvong, S, M Fischer and K Pinyopusarerk. 1997. 'Fallow Management with *Styrax tonkinensis* for Benzoin Production in Upland Cultivation Systems in Northern Lao PDR', Communication, *Indigenous Strategies for Intensification of Shifting Cultivation in Southeast Asia*, ICRAF/Cornell University, Bogor, Indonesia

Schlessman, M. 1985. 'Floral biology of American ginseng (*Panax quinquefolium*)'. *Bulletin of the Torrey Botanical Club*, vol 112, no 2, pp129–133

Schmidt, T L, J S Spencer, Jr and R Bertsch. 1997. *Michigan's Forests 1993: An Analysis*. Resource Bulletin NC-179. North Central Forest Experiment Station, St Paul

Schnepper, W C R. 1923. 'Benzoëcultuur en volkswelvaart in Tapanoeli (Sumatra)', *Tectona*, vol 16, pp264–275

Schroeder, R A. 1995. 'Contradictions along the commodity road to environmental stabilization: Foresting Gambian gardens'. *Antipode*, vol 27, no 4, pp325–342

Schultes, R E and R F Raffauf. 1990. *The Healing Forest: Medicinal and Toxic Plants of the Northwest Amazonia*. Dioscorides Press, Portland, Oregon

Schultz, A M et al. 1987. 'Agroforestry in Greece'. Working document. Aristotle University of Thessaloniki/School of Forestry & Natural Environment/Department of Range & Wildlife Science/Laboratory of Range Science, Thessaloniki

Schwartz, N B. 1990. *Forest Society: A Social History of Peten, Guatemala* . University of Pennsylvania Press, Philadelphia, PA

Scrase, H. 1999. *Certification of Forest Products for Small Businesses: Improving Access – Issues and Options. Final Report*. DFID, RNRKS, FRP, UK

Sfikas, Y. 1995. *Medicinal Plants of Greece* (in Greek). Efstathiadis Group, A E, Athens

Shaman Pharmaceuticals Inc. 1998. 'Environmental Impact Statement (EIS). *Croton lechleri* and SP-303' (draft). Shaman Pharmaceuticals, Inc, Department of Ethnobotany and Conservation, San Francisco, CA

Shankar, U, K S Murali, R U Shaanker, K Ganeshaiah and K S Bawa. 1996. 'Extraction of Non-Timber Forest Products in the Forests of Biligiri Rangan Hills, India. 3. Productivity, Extraction and Prospects of Sustainable harvest of Nelli (Amla) *(Emblica officinalis)*'. *Economic Botany*, vol 50, no 3, pp270–279

Shanley, P. 2000. 'As the forest falls: The changing use, ecology and value of non-timber forest resources for caboclo communities in Eastern Amazonia'. Unpublished PhD thesis. The Durrell Institute of Conservation and Ecology, University of Kent, Canterbury, UK

Shanley, P, M Cymerys and J Galvão. 1998. *Frutíferas da Mata na Vida Amazônica*. Editora Supercores, Belém, Brazil

Sharp, C. 1993. 'Sooty baobabs in Zimbabwe'. *Hartebeest*, vol 25, pp7–14

Sheldon, J W, M J Balick and S A. Laird. 1997. *Medicinal Plants: Can Utilization and Conservation Coexist? Advances in Economic Botany*, vol 12, New York Botanical Garden, New York, NY

Shiva, V. 1999. 'Biopiracy: Need to change Western IPR systems'. *The Hindu* (New Delhi), 28 July, online: www.hinduonline.com/today/stories/05281349.htm

Shugarman, A E. 1999. 'Suppliers Say'. *Nutraceuticals World*, vol 2, no 1, 28 February, p59

Shumacher, E F. 1993. *Small Is Beautiful*. Vintage, London

Sidibe, M, J F Scheuring, D Tembely, M M Sidibe, P Hofman and M Frigg. 1996. 'Baobab – homegrown vitamin C for Africa'. *Agroforestry Today*, vol 8, pp13–15

Siebert, S and J M. Belsky. 1985. 'Forest-product trade in a lowland Filipino village'. *Economic Botany*, vol 39, no 4, pp522–533

Sigma-Aldrich. 1999. *Biochemical and Reagents for Life Science Research*, Company catalogue for 2000–2001. Sigma-Aldrich, St Louis, MO, p2080

Simons, T. 1997. *Cameroon Trip Report*. 1–10 May, International Centre for Research in Agroforestry (ICRAF), Nairobi

Small, J and F M J Adams. 1992. 'Yohimbe bark: Its history and identification in commerce'. *Pharmaceutical Journal*, vol 108, no 3051, pp282–286

SmartWood. 2000. *Generic Guidelines for Assessing Natural Forest Management*. SmartWood, Rainforest Alliance, Richmond, VT. Available online at: www.smartwood.org/guidelines/forest-management-generic.html

Smith, M E. 1989. 'The informal economy' in S Plattner (ed) *Economic Anthropology*. Stanford University Press, Stanford

Sokolov, R. 1985. 'Tough nuts'. *Natural History*, vol 3/85, pp78–80

Sociedad de Productores Forestales Ejidales de Quintana Roo, S C (SPFEQR). 1993. *Primer encuentro regional de productores de chicle Guatemala*. Unpublished report, Belice, Mexico

Srinivas, N N. 1999. 'Opposing patents is not government's job'. *Economics Times* (New Delhi), 29 July, online: www.economictimes.com/290799/29opin03.htm

Standley, P C. 1925. 'An enumeration of the Sapotaceae of Central America'. *Tropical Woods*, vol 4, pp1–11

Standley, P C and S J Record. 1936. 'The forests and flora of British Honduras'. *Field Museum of Natural History*. Publication 350, Botanical Series, Volume 12

Steenis, C G G J (Van). 1949. 'Styracaceae' in C G G J van Steenis (ed) *Flora Malesiana*, series 1, vol 4. Noordhoff-Kolff, Djakarta, Indonesia, pp49–56

Steffey, J. 1984. 'Strange relatives: The ginseng family'. *American Horticulturalist*, vol 63, no12, pp4–9

Sternberg, E M, M H van Woert, S N Young, I Magnussen, H Baker, S Gauthier and K Osterland. 1980. 'Development of a scleroderme-like illness during therapy with L-5-Hydroxytryptophan and Carbidopa'. *The New England Journal of Medicine*, vol 303, pp782–787

Stoffelen, P. 1993. 'Systematische studie van de Afrikaanse genera *Corynanthe* en *Pausinystalia* (Rubiaceae – Coptosapelteae)'. Unpublished PhD thesis. Katholieke Universiteit Leuven, Leuven

Stoffelen, P, E Robbrecht and E Smets. 1996. 'A Revision of *Corynanthe* and *Pausinystalia* (African Rubiaceae – Coptosapelteae)'. *Botanical Journal of the Linnean Society*, vol 120, pp287–326

Sunderland, T C H. 1998. *The Rattans of Rio Muni, Equatorial Guinea: Utilisation, Biology and Distribution*. Report to the Proyecto Conservacion y Utilizacion Recional de los Ecosystemas Forestales (CUREF) – Fondo Europeo de Desarrollo, Proyecto No 6, ACP-EG 020

Sunderland, T C H. 1999. 'New research on African rattans: An important non-wood forest product from the forests of Central Africa' in T C H Sunderland, L E Clark and P Vantomme (eds) *The Non-Wood Forest Products of Central Africa: Current Research Issues and Prospects for Conservation and Development*. FAO, Rome

Sunderland, T C H. 2001. *Taxonomy, Ecology and Utilisation of African Rattans (Palmae: Calamoideae)*. University College London/Royal Botanic Gardens, Kew

Sunderland, T C H, L E Clark and P Vantomme. 1999. *Non-Wood Forest Products of Central Africa: Current Research Issues and Prospects for Conservation and Development*. FAO, Rome

Sunderland, T, M L Ngo-Mpeck, Z Tchoundjeu and A Akoa. 1999. 'The ecology and sustainability of *Pausinystalia johimbe*: An over-exploited medicinal plant of the forests of Central Africa' in T C H Sunderland, L E Clark and P Vantomme (eds) *The Non-Wood Forest Products Of Central Africa: Current Research Issues And Prospects for Conservation and Development*. FAO, Rome

Sunderland, T C H, A Njiamnshi, A Koufani, M L Ngo-Mpeck, C Obama and D F Njingum. 1997. *The Ethnobotany, Ecology and Natural Distribution of Yohimbe (*Pausinystalia johimbe*); An Evaluation of Current Bark Harvesting Practices and Recommendations for Domestication and Management*. A report prepared for the International Centre for Research in Agroforestry (ICRAF), Nairobi

Sunderland, T C H and J P Nkefor. 1999a. 'Technology transfer between Asia and Africa: Rattan cultivation and processing'. African Rattan Research Programme Technical Note No 5

Sunderland, T C H and J P Nkefor. 1999b. 'The propagation and cultivation of African rattans'. Paper presented at the international workshop African Rattans: A State of the Knowledge, held at the Limbe Botanic Garden, Cameroon, 1–3 February 2000

Sunderland, T C H and J P Profizi. 2002. *New Research on African Rattans. Proceedings of an International Expert Meeting on African Rattans. Limbe Botanic Garden, Cameroon, 1–3 February 2000*. International Network for Bamboo and Rattan, Beijing

Svengsuksa, B and J E Vidal. 1992. 'Styracacées' in P Morat (ed) *Flore du Cambodge, du Laos et du Viêtnam, Volume 26*. Muséum National d'Histoire Naturelle, Paris, pp145–195

Svoronou, E. undated. *Literature Anthology on Mediterranean Forests* (in Greek). Unpublished document. WWF-Greece, Athens

Swanepoel, C M. 1993. 'Baobab damage in Mana Pools National Park, Zimbabwe'. *African Journal of Ecology*, vol 31, pp220–225

Swart, E R. 1963. 'Age of the baobab tree'. *Nature*, vol 198, p708

Swygert, L A, E F Maes, L E Sewell, L Miller, H Falk and E M Kilborne. 1990. 'Eosinophilia-Myalgia syndrome: Results of national surveillance'. *Journal of the American Medical Association*, vol 264, pp1698–1703

Tabora, P C Jr, M J Balick, M L A Bovi and M P Guerra. 1993. 'Hearts of palm (*Bactris, Euterpe* and others)' in J T Williams (ed) *Underutilized Crops: Pulses and Vegetables*. Chapman and Hall, London, pp193–218

Tarmidi, L T. 1996. 'Changing structure and competition in the Kretek cigarette industry', *Bulletin of Indonesian Economic Studies*, vol 32, no3, pp85–107

Tchoundjeu, Z, B Duguma, M L Tienchu and M L Ngo Mpeck. 1999a. 'The domestication of indigenous agroforestry trees: ICRAF's strategy in the humid tropics of West and Central Africa' in T C H Sunderland, L E Clark and P Vantomme (eds) *The Non-Wood Forest Products Of Central Africa: Current Research Issues And Prospects for Conservation and Development*. FAO, Rome, pp161–169

Tchoundjeu, Z, M L Ngo Mpeck, T Simons and T Sunderland. 1999b. *Domestication of Pausinystalia johimbe through Vegetative Propagation Techniques*. ICRAF, Yaounde

ten Kate, K and S A Laird. 1999. *The Commercial Use of Biodiversity: Access to Genetic Resources and Benefit-Sharing*. Earthscan, London

Theophrastus. 1998a. *Aetiology of Plants* (2 volumes, in Greek). Kaktos, Athens

Theophrastus. 1998b. *History of Plants* (3 volumes in Greek). Kaktos, Athens

Thiollay, J M. 1995. 'The role of traditional agroforests in the conservation of rain forest bird diversity in Sumatra'. *Conservation Biology*, vol 9, no 2, pp335–353

Tibor, T. 1996. *ISO 14000: A Guide to the New Environmental Management Standards*. Irwin Professional Publications, Chicago

Titus, F, A Dalavos, J Alom and A Codina. 1986. '5-Hydroxytryptophan versus Methysergide in the prophylaxis of migraine'. *European Neurology*, vol 25, pp327–329

Tofts, A. 1998. 'How appropriate is certification for small-scale timber producers in Melanesia?' Network paper, 23rd Rural Development Forestry Network, Overseas Development Institute (ODI), London

Tomlin, E S, J H Borden and H D Pierce, Jr. 1996. 'Relationship between cortical resin acids and resistance of Sitka spruce to the white pine weevil.' *Canadian Journal of Botany*, vol 74, pp599–606

Troy, A and A Harte. 1998. *The Liana Project: Traditional Arts, Conservation, and Economic Development in the Amazon*. Rainforest Action Network, San Francisco

Troup, R S. 1921. *The Silviculture of Indian Trees*, vol III. Clarendon Press, Oxford, UK

Tucker, A, J Duke and S Foster. 1989. 'Botanical nomenclature of medicinal plants' in L Craker and J Simon (eds) *Herbs, Spices and Medicinal Plants: Recent Advances in Botany. Horticulture and Pharmacology*, vol 2. Oryx Press, Phoenix, Arizona, pp169–242

Tuley, P. 1995. *The Palms of Africa*. Trendrine Press, UK

Tyler, V. 1999. 'Six man-loving herbs that really work'. *Prevention*, April, vol 51, pp118–121

Tyler, V E. 1993. *The Honest Herbal – A Sensible Guide to the Use of Herbs and Related Remedies*, third edition. Haworth Press, London, pp327–330

US Census Bureau. 1990a. '1990 census of population' in D E System (ed) *1990 Census Lookup*, generated by Marla Emery, 18 September 1997

US Census Bureau. 1990b. 1990 Census of Population and Housing, online: www.venus.census.gov/cdrom/lookup

US Department of Commerce. 1995. *Merchandise Trade – Imports and Exports by Commodity: Ginseng Roots, Cultivated, and Ginseng Roots, Wild* (CD-ROM). Available from National Trade Data Bank – the Export Connection Programme, US Trade Information, Washington, DC

US Department of Agriculture (USDA). undated. *Copaiba*. Internal leaflet DRP-26(13) prepared by USDA, Agricultural Research Administration, Bureau of Plant Industry, Division of Drug and Related Plants

USDA. 2000. *New England Agricultural Statistics Service*, online: www.nass.usda.gov/nh/

US Food and Drug Administration (FDA). 1995. *CFSAN, Dietary Supplement Health and Education Act of 1994*. 1 December 1995. US FDA, Washington, DC

Ubillas, R, S D Jolad, R C Bruening, M R Kernan, S R King, D F Sesin, M Barrett, C A Stoddart, T Flaster, J Kuo, F Ayala, E Meza, M Castañel, D McMeekin, E Rozhon, M S Tempesta, D Barnard, J Huffman, D Smee, R Sidwell, K Soike, A Brazier, S Safrin, R Orlando, P T M Kenny, N Berova, and K Nakanishi. 1994. 'SP-303, an antiviral oligomeric proanthocyanidin from the latex of *Croton lechleri* (Sangre de Drago)'. *Phytomedicine*, vol 1, no 2, pp77–106

Ueda, S, T Umemura, K Dohguchi, T Matsuzaki, H Tokuda, H Nishino and A Iwashima. 1994. 'Production of anti-tumour-promoting furanonaphthoquinones in *Tabebuia avellanedae* cell cultures'. *Phytochemistry*, vol 36, no 2, pp323–325

Uhl, C and I C Vieira. 1989. 'Ecological impacts of selective logging in the Brazilian Amazon: A case study from the Paragominas Region of the State of Pará'. *Biotropica*, vol 21, no 2, pp98–106

Uhl, C and J B Kaufmann. 1990. 'Deforestation effects on fire susceptibility and the potential response of tree species to fire in the rainforest of the eastern Amazon'. *Ecology*, vol 71, pp437–449

Uhl, C, K Clark, K Dezzeo and P Maquirino. 1988. 'Vegetation dynamics in Amazonian treefall gaps'. *Ecology*, vol 69, no 3, pp751–763

Uhl, N and J Dransfield. 1987. *Genera Palmarum*. Allen Press, Kansas

Ulh, C, R Buschbacher and E A S Serrão. 1988. 'Abandoned pastures in Eastern Amazonia: Patterns of plant succession'. *Journal of Ecology*, vol 76, pp663–681

Uphof, J C Th. 1968. *Dictionary of Economic Plants*. Verlag Van J Cramer, New York, NY

US Environmental Protection Agency (EPA). 1993. *Status Report on the Use of Environmental Labels Worldwide.* EPA Report 742-R-9-93-001. EPA, Washington, DC

van Andel, T, P Huyskens and K Bröker. 1998. *Palm Heart Harvesting in Guyana's North-West District: Exploitation and Regeneration of Euterpe oleracea Swamps.* Tropenbos Interim Report 98-1, Tropenbos-Guyana Programme/Herbarium Utrecht University, Wageningen, The Netherlands

Van Breda de Haan, J, W R Tromp de Haas and H G Wigman. 1906. 'Kamfer'. *Teysmannia,* vol XVII, pp595–605

van den Berg, M E. 1984. 'Ver-o-Peso: The ethnobotany of an Amazonian market'. *Advances in Economic Botany,* vol 1, pp140–149

Van Vuuren, L. 1908. 'De handel van Barus als oudste haven op Sumatra's Westkust verklaard en voor de toekomst beschouwd', *Tijdschrift van het Koninklijk Nederlansche Aardrijkskundige Genootschap,* vol 25, pp1389–1402

Vance, N and J Thomas (eds). 1997. *Special Forest Products: Biodiversity Meets the Marketplace.* USDA, Washington, DC

Varela, M C. 1995. 'Previous activities of the Quercus suber Network' in E Frison, M C Varela and J Turok (eds) *Quercus suber Network Report of the First Two Meetings, 1–3 December and 26–27 February 1995.* International Plant Genetic Resources Institute (IPGRI), Rome

Vargas, A. 1999. 'Tenure in the context of sustainable use in Latin America' in J Oglethorpe (ed) *Tenure and Sustainable Use.* IUCN, Gland, Switzerland, and Cambridge, UK, pp49–56

Veeman, M, M Cocks, A Muwonge, S Choge and B Campbell. 2001. 'Markets for three bark products in Zimbabwe: A case study of markets for bark of *Adansonia digitata, Berchemia discolor* and *Wartburgia salutaris*' in Hotsprings Working Group *Household Livelihoods, Marketing and Resource Impacts: A Case Study of Bark Products in Eastern Zimbabwe.* IES Working Paper, no 18. Institute of Environmental Studies, University of Zimbabwe, Harare, pp51–70

Velásquez, R C. 1998. *Inventario de Sangre de Grado (Croton lechleri) en Madre de Dios para el desarrollo de un plan de manejo y aprovechamiento sostenible por comunidades locales.* Conservación Internacional, Programa Perú, Fundación Conservación Internacional, Perú

Véliz-Pérez, M E. 1997. 'Los biotopos universitarios y la renitroduccion de flore silvestre' in *Proceedings Taller: Rescate, Rehabilitación y Reintroducción de Vida silvestre.* Universidad de San Carlos de Guatemala, pp63–70

Veríssimo, A, P Barreto, M Mattos, R Turita and C Uhl. 1992. 'Logging impacts and prospects for sustainable forest management in an old Amazonian frontier: The case of Paragominas'. *Forest Ecology and Management,* vol 55, pp169–199

Vial-Debas, C. 1999. 'Sumatra benzoin trade and uses in French and European perfume industry'. *Forressasia INCO III Report. Appendix 12*

Viana, V, J Ervin, R Donovan, C Elliott and H Gholz (eds). 1996. *Certification of Forest Products: Issues and Perspectives.* Island Press, Washington, DC

Viana, V, R Mello, L Morais and N Mendes. 1994. *Ecology and Management of Brazil Nut Populations in Extractive Reserves in Xapuri, Acre.* University of São Paulo, Piracicaba, Brazil

Viana, V M, A R Pierce and R Z Donovan. 1996. 'Certification of non-timber forest products' in V M Viana, J Erwin, R Z Donovan, C Elliot and H Gholz (eds) *Certification of Forest Products: Issues and Perspectives.* Island Press, Washington, DC

Viana, V M, R A Mello, L M de Morais and N T Mendes. 1998. 'Ecologia e manejo da castanha do Pará em reservas extrativistas no Xapuri, Acre' in C Gascon and P Montinho (eds) *Floresta Amazônica: Dinâmica, regeneração e manejo.* IPAM, INPA, Manaus, Brazil

Viera, L S. 1992. *Fitoterapia da Amazônia: Manual das Plantas Medicinais.* Editora Agronômica Ceres Ltda, São Paulo, p347

Villiers, P C, de. 1951. 'The baobab tree (*Adansonia digitata,* L)'. *Journal of South African Forestry,* vol 29, pp9–18 (translated from Afrikaans by L Gibbs and C Smit)

Vivien, J and J J Faure. 1985. *Arbres des forets denses d'Afrique Centrale.* Ministre des Relations Exterieures Cooperation and Developpement et Agence de Cooperation Culturelle et Technique, Paris

Vokou, D. 1996. *Mediterranean Forests.* Unpublished report. WWF-Greece, Athens

von Aderkas, P. 1984. 'Economic history of ostrich fern, *Matteuccia struthiopteris*, the edible fiddlehead'. *Economic Botany,* vol 38, no 1, pp14–23

von Aderkas, P, A Rogerson and A de Freitas. 1986. 'Silicon accumulation in fronds of the ostrich fern, *Matteuccia struthiopteris*'. *Canadian Journal of Botany,* vol 64, pp696–699

von der Pahlen, M C. 1999. *Marapuama: An Amazonian medicinal.* Unpublished manuscript

Vonck, L M de. 1891. *Nota over de benzoecultuur in de residentie Palembang (Note over the cultivation of the benzoin tree in Palembang Residency).* Tijdschr. Orgaan Ned, Maatschappij Bevordering Nijverheid, Sekajoe

Vuuren, L (Van). 1908. 'De handel van Barus als oudste haven op Sumatra's Westkust verklaard en voor de toekomst beschouwd'. *Tijdschrift van het Koninklijk Nederlansche Aardrijkskundige Genootschap,* vol 25, pp1389–1402

Waddington, M and S A Laird. 1999. 'The production and marketing of species in the "public domain": The Yawanawa and Aveda Corporation *Bixa orellana* Project, Brazil' in K ten Kate and S A Laird *The Commercial Use of Biodiversity: Access to Genetic Resources and Benefit-Sharing.* Earthscan, London, pp281–286

Walter, Sven. 1998. Pers comm (NTFP definition). FAO

Walters, C and C S Holling. 1990. 'Large scale management experiments and learning by doing'. *Ecology,* vol 71, pp2060–2068

Wang, H, J Fan, X Yang, G Fan, Q Liou and H Dai. 1995. 'A study on ginseng cultivation under forest conditions and its physiological and ecological characteristics' in W Bailey, C Whitehead, J Proctor and J Kyle (eds) *The Challenges of the 21st Century: Proceedings of the International Ginseng Conference – Vancouver 1994.* Simon Fraser University, Vancouver

Waridel, L and S Teitelbaum. 1999. *Fair Trade: Contributing to Equitable Commerce in Holland, Belgium, Switzerland and France.* Equiterre, Montreal, Quebec

Warner-Lambert, Inc. 1986. Press release, Newswire, 3/25. Morris Plains, New Jersey

Watanabe, H, K I Abe, K Kawai and P Siburian. 1996. 'Sustained use highland forest stands for benzoin production from Styrax in North Sumatra, Indonesia'. *Wallaceana,* vol 78, pp15–19

Wateringen, S van de. 1997. 'USA Pushes Ecuador to Sign IPR Agreement'. *Biotechnology and Development Monitor,* vol 33, pp20–22

Webster, G. 1993. 'A provisional synopsis of the sections of the genus *Croton* (Euphorbiaceae)'. *Taxon,* vol 42, pp794–823

Weinstock, J A. 1983. 'Rattan: Ecological balance in Borneo rainforest swidden'. *Economic Botany,* vol 37, no 1, pp58–68

Westoby, J. 1987. *The Purpose of Forests: Follies of Development.* Basil Blackwell, Ltd, Oxford, UK

Westoby, J. 1989. *Introduction to World Forestry: People and Their Trees.* Basil Blackwell, Ltd, Oxford, UK

Wheatley, P. 1959. 'Geographical notes on some commodities involved in Sung maritime trade'. *Journal of the Malayan Branch of the Royal Asiatic Society,* Tien Wah Press Ltd, Singapore

Wickens, G E. 1981. 'The baobab: Africa's upside down tree'. *Kew Bulletin,* vol 37, pp173–209

Williamson, B L, K Klarskov, A J Tomlinson, G J Gleich and S Naylor. 1998. 'Problems with over-the-counter 5-hydroxy-L-tryptophan'. *Nature Medicine,* vol 4, no 9, p983

Williams, M. 1989. *Americans and Their Forests: A Historical Geography.* Cambridge University Press, Cambridge

Willits, C. 1965. *Maple Syrup Producers Manual.* Agriculture Handbook No 134. USDA Agricultural Research Service, Washington, DC

Wiser, G. 1999. *PTO Rejection of the 'Ayahuasca' Patent Claim: Background and Analysis.* Centre for International Environmental Law: www.ciel.org/ptorejection.html

Wolf, J H D and C J F Konings. 2001. 'Toward the sustainable harvesting of epiphytic bromeliads: A pilot study from the highlands of Chiapas, Mexico'. *Biological Conservation*, vol 101, pp23–31

Wollenberg, E and A Ingles. 1998. *Incomes from the Forest: Methods for the Development and Conservation of Forest Products for Local Communities.* CIFOR and IUCN, Bogor, Indonesia

World Resources Institute (WRI), World Conservation Union (IUCN) and United Nations Environment Programme (UNEP). 1992. *Global Biodiversity Strategy: Guidelines for Action to Save, Study, and Use Earth's Biotic Wealth Sustainably and Equitably.* WRI/IUCN/UNEP, Washington, DC

WWF-UK. 1995. *Truth or Trickery: Timber Labeling Past and Future.* WWF-UK, Godalming, Surrey, UK

WWF. 1988. *Mission Report on the WHO/IUCN/WWF International Consultation on the Conservation of Medicinal Plants.* WWF International, Gland, Switzerland

Xin, J. 1995. 'The present and future prospects for American ginseng in China' in W Bailey, C Whitehead, J Proctor and J Kyle (eds) *The Challenges of the 21st Century: Proceedings of the International Ginseng Conference – Vancouver 1994.* Simon Fraser University, Vancouver

You, C and W H Petty 1991. 'Effects of Hurricane Hugo on *Manilkara bidentata*, a primary tree species in the Luquillo Experimental Forest of Puerto Rico'. *Biotropica*, vol 23, no 4a, pp400–406

Youngken, H W. 1943. *Text-Book of Pharmacognosy.* The Blakiston Co, Philadelphia, p1038

Zak, V. 1991. *Study of the Sangre de Drago Tree.* Report prepared for Shaman Pharmaceuticals. D T M Cía Ltda, Quito, Ecuador

Zavala, C Z. 1996. *Taxonomía, distribución geográfica y status del genero Uncaria en el Perú.* Universidad Nacional Agraria La Molina, Lima, Peru

Zoghbi, M D G B, J B G Sigueira, E L A Wolter and O L P Junior. 1994. 'Chemical constituents of Protium paniculatum (Burseraceae).' *Acta Amazonica*, vol 24, no 1–2, pp59–62

Zona, S and A Henderson. 1989. 'A review of animal-mediated seed dispersal of palms'. *Selbyana*, vol 11, pp6–21

Zucas, S M, E C Silva and M Fernandes. 1975. 'Farinha de castanha-do-Pará: Valor de sua proteína'. *Revista Farmacêutica e Bioquimica da Universidade de São Paulo*, vol 13, pp133–143

Index

Page numbers in *italics* refer to figures, tables and boxes

açaí *see* palm heart
accreditation 9, 10, 11, 13, *332*
Acer saccharum see maple syrup
ActionLab 223
Adansonia digitata see baobab
Africa 226, 227, 228, *230, 232, 234*, 236
  see also East Africa; Sub–Saharan Africa;
    West Africa
Agave sisalana see sisal
Agenda 21 287
agriculture 9, 10–11, *12*, 145, 235, 326, 345,
  346–7
agroforestry
  Brazil nut production 71
  for NTFP production 23, 36, 48, 198, 282
  palm heart production 78
  rattan production 235, 237, 238
  sangre de drago production 143, 145, 149,
    154
  yohimbe production 219
AIDP 223
Aleppo pine *see* pine resin
Algeria 186, 188
Allium tricoccum see wild leek
alternative medicines *see* botanical medicines
  industry
amapá *123*
  animal interaction 124
  biology 123, 124
  certification 125
  ecology 124
  economic value 48, 125
  habitat 124
  harvesting/production 124–5, 270, 271
  and indigenous peoples 124
  management 124–5, 273
  medicinal properties 123, 124, 125, *316*
  profile 47, 123–5
  species compared 124–5
  threats to production 124
  as timber product 125, 280

  uses 123, 124, 125, *316*
Amazon region
  amapá 123, 124, 125
  ayahuasca 297
  Brazil nuts 61, 62, 64, 65, 66–7, 73, 277
  breu resin 111
  cat's claw 93, 94, 104, 106
  copaíba 127, 128, 129, 132
  land-use change impacts 90, 129
  logging 314, 317–21
  marapuama 269
  NTFP distribution 315
  palm hearts 37–8, 75, 76, 77, 78, 80, 81,
    82–4, 274–5
  pau d'arco 85, 87, 88
  sangre de drago 138, 142, 144, 145, 147,
    151
  subsistence issues 299–300, 313–14
  titica vine 116, 119
Amazonian nut *see* Brazil nut
Amazonian Treaty 8
Amazonian Viagra *see* marapuama
Amburana cearensis see roble
American Chicle 52
American ginseng *172*
  animal interaction 175
  biology 174–5
  certification 180–2, *335*
  competition 180
  cultivated 175, 176, 177–8, 180, 181–2,
    282
  ecology 174–6
  economic value 4, 48, 176–7, 179, 323
  habitat 174, 175–6
  harvesting/production 174, 176, 177,
    180–1, 270
  and indigenous peoples 173
  land-use change impacts 178
  legal restrictions 174
  management 176–8, 181, 271, 272–3, 338,
    341

medicinal properties 173–4, 176, 179–80
organic certification 182
profile 48, 172–82
sustainability 174, 176, 177, 181, 270, 271
threats to production 178
amla *240*
  biology 241, 242
  certification 244, *336*
  cultivated 241, 242, 243
  distribution 240
  ecology 241
  economic value 48, 243
  habitat 48, 240, 241
  harvesting/production 243–4
  and indigenous peoples 244
  land tenure issues 244
  land-use change impacts 242
  management 242–3, 244
  medicinal properties 240, 243, 244
  productivity *241*
  profile 48, 240–5
  regeneration 242
  species compared 241
  sustainability 244
  as timber product *243*
  uses 240, 243, 244, *336*
Ancistrophyllum spp. *see* rattans
Andaman Islands *228, 230*
andiroba *316*, 320
Angola *230*
annatto 323, 326, 360
Apatayawaca Nampitzi Asháninka Pichis
  (ANAP) 146
argan *47, 189*
  economic value 48, 189
  habitat 48, 188
  management 190, 198
  profile 48, 188–90
  sustainability 189–90
  as timber product 189
  uses 188, 189
Argania spinosa see argan
Argentina 80, *82*, 85, 86, 87, 90, 127
arginine 222, 223
asai *see* palm heart
Asháninka Indians, Peru 102, 104, 108, 145,
  146
Asia 94, 179, 182, 203, 204, 322
Asian ginseng 173, 176, 179, 180
Asociación Interétnica de Desarollo de la
  Selva Peruvana (AIDESEP) 146

Asociación para la Conservación del
  Patrimonio Cutiriveni (ACPC) 102
Astrocaryum vulgare see tucumã
ATZ 223
Australia 208, 226, *227*
Aveda Corporation 323, 360
ayahuasca *296, 297*
Azadirachta indica see neem

Bactris gasipaes see pejibaye palm
bacuri *267*, 315, *317*, 320
Bangladesh *228, 237*
Banisteriopsis spp. *see* ayahuasca
baobab *208*
  animal interaction 208, 209
  bark 208, 209–14
  biology 208, 209
  certification 212–14
  distribution 208
  ecology 209
  economic value 48, 212
  habitat 48, 208
  harvesting/production 210, 211–12, 213,
    343
  and indigenous peoples 209, 210, 211–13
  management 211–12, 213
  medicinal properties 210
  profile 48, 208–14
  regeneration 209, 210, 212, 213
  sustainability 210, 213–14
  threats to production 209, 211
  uses 209–10
bark 47, 48, 343
  baobab 208, 209–14
  birch 305, *306*, 308
  Brazil nut 72
  cat's claw 95, 98, 99, 100, 101, 105, 106
  pau d'arco 88, 90, 92, 280
  root bark 97, 98, 101, 105–6
  sangre de drago 143, 147, 150, 151
  yohimbe 215, 217–19, 220, 221–2, 223
  see also cork
Belize 50, 51, 52, 54, 57, *84, 93*
Belle of Maine 157–8, 161
Ben and Jerry's 8, 16, 323
benzoin 246
  biology 247–8
  certification 246, 254–5, *334*
  cultivated 248, 249, 250
  distribution 246–7, 248
  ecology 248

economic value 48, 247, 248, 249, 253, 255

habitat 48, 247, 248

harvesting/production 250–1, 253–4, 255, 268, 270, 271

and indigenous peoples 251, 255

land tenure issues 254–5

land-use change impacts 248–9

management 250–1, 254, 268

medicinal properties 252

profile 47, 246–55

species compared 246–7, 248, 249, 250–1

sustainability 255

uses 246, 252, 334

Bertholletia excelsa see Brazil nut

Betula papyrifera see birch

biodiversity loss 70, 170, *191*, 254, 260, 268, 280, 282, 319

Bioresources 203

birch 305, *306*, 308

Bixa orellana see annatto

blueberry *302*, 305, *306*, 308, 309

The Body Shop 8, 323

Bolivia

Brazil nuts

certification 6, 20, 28, 34–7, 278

harvesting/production 36, 63, 64, 70, 338

production 61, 62, 63, 64, 67, 73, *334*

logging 36, 69

palm hearts 40, 77, 78, 80, *82*, *83*, *84*, 335

pau d'arco 87

sangre de drago 146, 147–8

sisal bag industry *279*

social issues 37, 291–3

Bolivia Sustainable Forestry Management Project (BOLFOR) 338

Borneo 226, *227*, *228*, *230*, *281*

Borneo camphor 280, *281*

botanical medicines industry

dietary supplements 179–80, 200, 202–7, 222–3

herbal remedies

amla 240, 243

cat's claw 94, 95, 104, 106

copaíba 131

marapuama *269*

pau d'arco 86, 88, 89, 324

sangre de drago 138, 144, 154

yohimbe 215, 221–2

marketing issues 322, 324, 325, 326, *334*, *335*, *336*, 356, 360

species under threat 90, 91, 219, 324, 331, 361

see also pharmaceutical industry

B&Q 329

Brachylaena huillensis see muhugo

bracken fern 158

Brazil

Brazil nuts 61, 62, 63–4, 67, 69, 70, 72, *334*, 347

cat's claw 93, 95

copaíba 126, 127, 130, 131, 133–4, 135

logging 69, 70

marapuama *269*, 325–6

palm hearts

certification 6, 13, 20, 25, 28, 37–44

production 75, 78, 79, 80, *82*, *83*, *84*, *273*

pau d'arco 86, 87, 88, 89–90

sangre de drago 139, 140

social issues 40–1, 43–4, 293–4, 300

subsistence issues 299–300, 314–21

titica vine 116, 117, 118, 119–20

see also Amazon region

Brazil nut 7, *28*, *61*

aflatoxin contamination 36, 330, 348

animal interaction 36, 67, 68, 69, 70

biology of trees 61–2, 65–7, 68, 278

certification 5, 10

challenges 35–7

ecological issues 36, 65, 73, 323

economic issues 36–7, 73–4

field trials 6, 20, 28, 34–7, 277–8, 291–3

and indigenous peoples 34–5, 37, 74

land tenure issues 37, 74, 291–2

marketing issues 16, 36–7, 323, 328, 329, *334*

monitoring 36, 37

opportunities 35, 65, 70, 74, 293–4, *334*

social issues 37, 291–3

technical issues 35–6

distribution of trees 62–3, 65

ecology of trees 61–2, 65–9, 277

economic value 3, 4, 48, 64, 72, 73, 322

habitat of trees 35, 48, 62, 65, 66

harvesting/production 36, 63, 64, 67–8, 70–1, 72, 73–4, 277

and indigenous peoples 37, 63–4, 70–1, 72, 292

land-use change impacts 36, 69–70

management 69, 70–2, 74, 268, 277–8, 338

medicinal properties 62, 72
nutritional value 62
productivity of trees 36, 64, 66, 71, 277
profile 48, 61–74
regeneration of trees 71, 73, 277–8
sustainability 37, 69–70, 71, 73, 74, 277
threats to production 36, 278, 330, 348
and timber production 69, 72
uses 62, 69, 72–3
breu amescla 111, 113
breu resin *110*
   biology of plants 111
   certification 114
   distribution of plants 111
   ecology of plants 111
   economic value 48, 112–13, 114
   habitat of plants 111
   harvesting/production 111, 112–13,
      114–15
   insect interaction 110, 111–12, 114, 115
   management 112–13, 273
   medicinal properties 110, 113
   profile 47, 110–15
   species of plant compared 111, 112, 113,
      114
   sustainability 114, 115
   and timber production 114
   uses 110, 113–14
bromeliads *257*
   certification *258*
   economic value 48, 257, 258
   harvesting 257, 258
   profile 257–8
   sustainability 257, 258
   uses *257*, 258
Brosimum acutifolium see mururé
Brosimum alicastrum see ramon
Brosimum spp. *see* amapá
buriti *283*
Burma *227*, *230*

C-MED-100 105
caixeta 341
Calamus spp. *see* rattans
Calospatha spp. *see* rattans
Cambodia 247
Cameroon 216, 217–18, 221, 223, 224, *230*,
   232, *237*
camphor *see* Borneo camphor
Canada 168, 169
   fiddlehead fern 156, 157, 158, 159, 161

ginseng 177, 178
maple syrup 163, 164, 167, *335*
cane *see* rattans
caraipé *317*
caranday palm 80
Carapa guianensis see andiroba
Caryocar brasilensis see piqui
Caryocar villosum see piquiá
Cashpro 203
castaña *see* Brazil nut
Castanea sativa see chestnut
cat's claw *93*
   biology *95*, *96–7*, *98–9*
   certification
      challenges 106–9, *334*
      ecological issues 106–7, 108–9, 323–4
      ethical issues 108
      marketing issues 107–8, 323–4, 331, *334*
      opportunities 106, *334*
   commercialization 94–5, 99–100, 108
   cultivated 102–3, 106, 108–9
   distribution *93*, *95*
   ecology *97–9*
   economic value 4, 48, 93–5, 99–100, 104,
      106
   habitat *95–6*, *97–8*, 108–9
   harvesting/production 98, 99–100, 101–2,
      106, 273
   and indigenous peoples *93*, *95*, 99, 101,
      102, 106, 109
   land-use change impacts 99
   legal restrictions 100–1, 108
   management *95*, 101–3, 106, 108–9
   medicinal properties *93*, 94, *97*, 103–6
   patent rights 108
   profile 48, 93–109
   regeneration 98, 102
   species compared *95*, *96*, 99, 103, 104–5,
      107
   sustainability 100–1, 331
   as timber product 106
   uses *93*, 94, *95*, *97*, 103–6, *334*
cattail *306*
cedar 35, *306*
Cedrela spp. *see* cedar; Spanish cedar
Center for International Forestry Research
   (CIFOR) 21, 296
Central America 51, 75, *82–4*, 88, 90, *93*,
   140
Centre for International Environmental Law
   (CIEL) *297*

Centro de Datos para la Conservacíon (CDC) 100
Centro de Investigación y Manejo de Recursos Naturales Renovables (CIMAR) 5, 21
Ceratolobus spp. *see* rattans
Certificación Integral de Bosques Americanos (CEIBA) 5
certification (of NTFPs)
  challenges 5, 198, 273, 296, 298, 311, *333–6*, 353, 358–60
  collaboration 9–13, 18–19, 21, 348, 354, 361–2, 363, 365
  company involvement 15–18, 31, 38–41, 329–30, *332–3*, 356, 359, 365
  costs 5, 24, 198, 273, *333*, 353, 354, 358, 363
  cultural issues 5, 22, 25
  ecological issues 4, 24, 26, 198–9, 280, 323–4, 342, 359, 360–1
  economic issues 311, 355
  field tests 6, 20, 21, 24–7, 28, 349, 354–6, 363
  and governments 18, 19, 122, 153, 154, 244, 346, 347, 360
  guidelines 5–6, 20–7, 47, 354–6, 357, 363–4
  and indigenous peoples 4, 5, 23–4, 26, 283–90, 355
  land tenure issues 22, 24, 25, 198, 285–8, 298, 312, 327, 358–9
  marketing issues 4–5, 14–18, 22, 198, 311–12, 324–31, *332–6*, 353–60
  monitoring 342, 343–4, 363
  and NGOs 18, 21, 296, 358, 361–2
  and NTFP management 4, 16–17, 21, 122, 198, 199, 282, 338–49, 355
  opportunities 13–18, *332–3*, *334–6*, 353–4, 356–8
  performance indicators/verifiers 21, 22, 24, 47–8, 269–70, 274, 363–4
  social issues 4, 22, 23–4, 25, 26, 198, 285–98, 361, 363–4
  subsistence issues 24, 37, 198, 299, 300–1, 302, 311–12, 321, 364
  technical issues 23, 337–49, 359–60
  see also under individual NTFPs
certification (of timber products) 4, 8, 16–18, 30, 260–3, 337–8, 341–2
  NTFP involvement 14–18, 125, 134, 135, 224, 280, 320–1, 337–8, 355–6

Chaemaedorea spp. *see* xate
chain-of-custody issues 23, 311, 328, *333*, 344–5, 354, 359–60
  amla 244, *245*
  benzoin 255
  Brazil nuts 36–7, 344, 345
  chicle 31, 32, 59, *334*, 344
  copaíba 135
  fiddlehead ferns 161
  ginseng 181, *335*
  maple syrup 171
  palm hearts 39–40, *335*, 344
  pau d'arco 91
  rattans 238, *336*
  sangre de drago *335*
  timber 344, 345
  titica vine 122
  woodcarvings 262
  yohimbe 223, 224, *336*
chestnut *194*
  certification 6
  economic value 48, 196
  habitat 194–5
  harvesting/production 195–6
  and indigenous peoples 195, 196
  management 195
  profile 48, 194–6
  threats to production 195
chewing gum 29, 30–1, 49, 52–3, 57, 58, 326, *334*, 356
Chiapas, Mexico 257–8
chicle *28*, *49*
  animal interaction 50–1
  biology 49, 50–1
  certification 5, 10, 13, 29
    challenges 32–4, 58–9, *334*
    ecological issues 31, 32–3, 58, 59, 276–7, 323
    economic issues 31, 32, 33, 59
    field trials 6, 13, 20, 28, 29–34, 276–7, 290–1
    and indigenous peoples 29, 30, 33–4, 59–60, 277, 290–1
    land tenure issues 290
    marketing issues 31–2, 33, 58–9, 323, 325, 328, 329, *334*, 357
    monitoring 32, 59
    opportunities 31–2, 58, 291, *334*
    social issues 33–4, 290–1
    technical issues 32
  distribution 50, 51

ecology 49–51, 276
economic value 3, 4, 48, 49–50, 51, 52–3,
    276, 322
fairtrade certification 30, 31, 32
growth rates 51
habitat 29–30, 50
harvesting/production 29, 55, 56, 58, 59,
    270, 271, 276, 344
land-use change impacts 53–4
management 33, 57–8, 268, 271, 276–7,
    354
medicinal properties 33
organic certification 31
producers' association 30, 57, 348
productivity 29, 51, 58
profile 29–30, 47, 49–60
species compared 49
sustainability 54, 56, 57, 58, 271, 276
as timber product 33, 276, 277, 280
uses 29, 33, 52, 276, *334 see also* chewing
    gum
chicle, inferior 49
chicozapote *see* chicle
Chile 27, 137, 151
China
    camphor trade *281*
    cat's claw trade 94
    ginseng trade 173, 179, 180
    griffonia trade 204
    pine-resin trade *194*
    rattans 226, 227, *230*, 237
cigarette manufacture 252, *254*, *334*
Clarisia spp. *see* mururé
cocoa 359
coffee 11, *12*, 249, 296, *333*, 345
Collins Pine 15, 16, 17
Colombia
    ayahuasca *297*
    Brazil nuts 62
    breu resin 113
    palm hearts 80, *82*, *83*, *84*
    pau d'arco 87
    sangre de drago 138, 141, 142, 145
    see also Amazon region
companies
    and certification 15–18, 31, 38–41,
        329–30, *332–3*, 356, 359, 365
    environmental responsibility 4, 8, 16, 217,
        323, *332–3*, 356, 365
    marketing issues 4–5, 14–18, 325, 329–30,
        332, *333*, 353–4, 360, 365

social responsibility 4, 5, 37, *332*, 356, 365
Congo 215, 216, *230*
Consejo Aguaruna-Huambisa 146
Consejo Civil Mexicano para la Silvicultura
    Sostenible (CCMS) 5, 21, 29
Conservation International (CI) 323
consumers 4–5, 31, 331, *333–6*, 348, 356,
    357, 361, 364, 365
    see also green consumerism
Convention on Biological Diversity (CBD)
    152–3, *287*, 360
Convention on International Trade in
    Endangered Species of Wild Fauna and
    Flora (CITES) 100, 174, 181, 321, 324,
    338, 360
Coordinating Body of Indigenous
    Organizations of the Amazon Basin
    (COICA) *287*, 297
copaíba *126*
    biology 127, 128
    certification 134–5
    distribution 127
    ecology 127–8
    economic value 48, 129, 131, 132, 133,
        135
    habitat 127
    harvesting/production 126–7, 129–30, 133,
        134–5
    and indigenous peoples 126–7, 130
    land-use change impacts 128–9
    management 129–30, 134, 268
    medicinal properties 104, 126, 131, 132–3,
        316, *317*
    profile 47, 126–35
    species compared 127, 130
    sustainability 126, 129, 131–2, 134–5
    as timber product 125, 128–9, 134
    uses 104, 125, 126, 128–9, 131–4, *316*,
        317
Copaifera spp. *see* copaíba
Copernicia alba see caranday palm
Coptis trifolia see gold thread
cork 186, 187–8
cork oak *186*
    certification 6, *334*
    distribution 186
    economic value 48, 188, 323
    habitat 48
    harvesting/production 186–7, 270, 271,
        343
    management 186, 187

profile 48, 186–8
regeneration 187
Costa Rica 15–16, 81, *84*
Couma guianensis see amapá
Couratari guianensis see tauari
craft industry 48, 209, 210, 212, 305, 306,
   307
Croda Inc 323
Croton spp. *see* sangre de drago
Cuba 85
Cultural Survival (CS) 323
cumaru *316, 317*

Daemonorops spp. *see* rattans
Dalbergia melanoxylon see mpingo
damar 252, 268
deforestation 8, 30, 36, 76, 128, 278
devil's claw 324
Dietary Supplement and Health Education
   Act (US, 1994) 203, 204
dietary supplements industry *see* botanical
   medicines industry
Dipteryx odorata see cumaru
Dominica *83*
dragon's blood *see* sangre de drago
Dryobalanops aromatica see Borneo camphor
durian 268, 278–9, 295
Durio zibethinus see durian

East Africa 260, 261
East Asia 173
'ebony' *see mpingo*
echinacea 324
ECO-OK programme 21
Ecuador
   palm hearts 80, *82, 83, 84*
   pau d'arco 86
   sangre de drago 138, 141, 142, 146, 148,
      149, 151, 152, 153
   see also Amazon region
ejido system, Mexico 29, 30, 32, 51, 290,
   291, 328
Eleutherococcus senticosus see Siberian
   ginseng
emblica fruit *see* amla
Endopleura uchi see uxi
ephedra 222, 223
epiphytes 341, 349
epiphytic bromeliads *see* bromeliads
Equatorial Guinea 216, 217, 221
Eremospatha spp. *see* rattans

Eschweilera spp. *see* mata mata ci; maturi
Europe
   benzoin trade 252
   botanical medicines industry 88, 106, 180,
      202, 215, 322
   Brazil nut trade 72, 330, 348
   bromeliad trade 258
   camphor trade *281*
   cat's claw trade 94, 105, 106
   certified product market 4, 32, 33, 40, 329,
      331, 354, 361
   chewing gum market 32, 33
   copaíba trade 132
   ginseng trade 179, 180
   griffonia trade 202, 203
   palm heart trade 40, 75
   pau d'arco trade 86, 88
   pine-resin production 193, *194*
   sisal bag trade *279*
   woodcarving trade 259, 262
   yohimbe trade 215, 217
European Union (EU) 94, 188, 194, 348
European Union (EU) Habitats Directive 194
Euterpe spp. *see* palm heart
Extractos Natra 223
exudates 21, 47, 49, 72, 270–1, 343
   see also breu resin; latex; maple syrup; mas-
      tic gum; oleoresin; pine–resin

Fair Trade eV 30, 31, 32, 291
fairtrade certification 9, 11, 13, *14*, 21, 312,
   348, 354
Fairtrade Foundation 11, 21
Fairtrade Labelling Organizations
   International (FLO) 9, 11, 13, *14*
fairtrade products 4, 13, 329, 330, 345, 357
FDA 203, 205, 206, 221–2
Federación de Comunidades Nativas
   Yaneshas (FECONAYA) 146
Ficus elastica see rubber
fiddlehead fern *156*
   biology 157
   certification 160–1
   commercialization 157–8
   consumption 156–7, 158, 159, 161
   distribution 156
   ecology 157
   economic value 4, 48, 158, 159
   habitat 48, 157
   harvesting/production 158, 159–60, 161,
      271

and indigenous peoples 156–7, 159
land-use change impacts 160
management 159–60, 272–3
profile 48, 156–61
sustainability 159–60, 161
Fiji 226, *227*
5-HTP 200, 201–6, *207*
Florida, US 300
Florida Growers Association 31
Food and Agriculture Organization (FAO) 255
Food and Drug Administration (US) *see* FDA
food safety 36, 39, 58, 158, 205–6, *207*, 222, 330
forest management
    ecological issues 7–8, 21, 43, 181–2, 184, 196–7, 257, 357, 364
    by indigenous peoples 29, 30, 43, 122, 184, 196–7, 290–1, 301, 357–8
    NTFP involvement 21, 184, 197–9, 301, 329–30, 338–49, 356–7, 360–4
    socio-economic issues 4, 8, 24, 30, 43, 184, 257, 283
Forest Stewardship Council 9–10, 261, 262–3, 291, *332*, 338, 348, 356, 364
    Principles and Criteria 8, 10, 21
forests
    canopy farming 257, 258
    enrichment planting 23, 71, 79, 90, 181, 235
    fires 53, 128, 167, *191*, 193, 196, 198, 242, 319
    forest gardens *12*, 48, 249, 250, 254
    habitats 48, 183–4
    inventories 32, 217, 236, 272, 343
    maquis 184, 185–6
    silvicultural systems *see* plantations
    silvo-pastoral systems 48, 184, 186–90, 198, 268, 282
    sustainability 4, 5, 7–8, 9, *12*, 21, 196, 260, 272
    várzea forests 37, 38, 41, 120, 127, 275, 282
    see also forest management; logging
France 81, 151, 186, 190, 193, *194*, 231, 252, *269*
fuelwood 39, 48, *243*, 294, 357
functional foods 222–3

Gabon 216, 217, 221, 232
Gambia 302–3

game 23, 35, 48, 293, 294, 300, 315, 316, 319
    see also hunting
garabato *see* cat's claw
Germany 64, 73, 202, 221, *269*
Getrade 203
Ghana 203, 207, 232
Gibson Guitar 17
ginseng *see* American ginseng; Asian ginseng
gold thread *306*
golden seal 324, 341
Good Manufacturing Practices (GMP) 331, 354
'Good Woods' 260, 261, 262–3
Goods & News 21
governments
    NTFP certification 18, 19, 122, 153, 154, 244, 346, 347, 360
    NTFP management 39, 100–1, 102, 145, 146, 244, 273, 284, 346
    NTFP regulation 122, 138, 153, 154, 174, 300, 327, 346–7, 360
Greece 6, 185, 190, *191*, 193, 194–6
green consumerism 7, 33, 197, 198, 238, 244, 262, 329
green premiums 15, 16, 238, 244, *355*
grevillea 260, 261
griffonia *200*
    biology 201
    certification 206–7, *335*
    ecology 201
    economic value 48, 202–5, *207*, 324
    harvesting/production 203
    and indigenous peoples 201, 203
    medicinal properties 201–2, 204–5
    profile 48, 200–7
    uses 200, 201–2, 204–5
Griffonia simplicifolia see griffonia
guarana 222, 223
Guatemala 50, 51, 52, 53–4, 56, 57, 58, *84*, 258
gum, synthetic 29, 33, 53, 55, 56
gum arabic 303
gum latex *see* latex
Guyanas 62, 80, *82*, *83*, *84*, 87, 95, 118

Harpagophytum procumbens see devil's claw
herbal remedies *see* botanical medicines industry
HerbPharm 223
Heteropsis spp. *see* titica vine

Hevea brasiliensis see rubber
Himatanthus sucuuba see sucuúba
Hispaniola 85
Hong Kong 231
hunting 35, 36, 68, 74, 111, 278, 292, 294
  see also game
Hydrastis canadensis see golden seal
Hymenaea courbaril see jatobá
Hymenaea parvifolia see jutai
Hypericum perforatum see St. John's Wort

illipe 338
inajá *299*
incense 252, 253, *254, 255, 281*
India
  amla production 240, *241,* 242, 243–4, *245*
  benzoin trade 252
  camphor *281*
  griffonia trade 204
  rattans 226, *227, 228, 230,* 235
indigenous peoples
  access rights 225, 285–8, *294, 295, 297,*
    301, 310
  community relations 43, 44, 289–90, 291,
    293–4, 311, 358
  forest management 29, 30, 43, 122, 184,
    196–7, 290–1, 301, 357–8
  land tenure issues 29, 30, 285–8, 290, 292,
    293, 294, 298, 312
  and NTFP certification 4, 5, 23–4, 26,
    283–90, 355
  NTFP management 122, 184, 267, 268,
    270–1, 272–3, 289, 293, 346
  social issues 23–4, 29, 30, 37, 40–1, 43, 44,
    198, 285–98
  subsistence issues 3, 24, 37, 284, 299–301,
    304, 313–21
  traditional knowledge 106, 267, 268,
    271–2, 286, 287, 288, 294
  working conditions 37, 40–1, 288–9, 291,
    292, 294
  see also under individual NTFPs
Indonesia 22, *228, 230,* 231, *237,* 247, 249,
  253, 255
Indorayon 249
Inonutus obliquus see sketaugen
Instituo Brasileiro do Meio Ambiente e dos
    Recursos Naturais Renováveis (IBAMA)
    120
Instituto de Manejo e Certificação Florestral e
    Agrícola (IMAFLORA) 5, 21

Instituto Nacional de Recursos Naturales
    (INRENA) 100
intellectual property rights 108, 137, 138,
    153, *287, 288, 296, 297*
International Centre for Research in
    Agroforestry (ICRAF) 219
International Federation of Organic
    Agriculture Movements (IFOAM) 9,
    10–11, *12,* 21
International Labour Organization (ILO) 23,
    287, 288
International Organization for
    Standardization (ISO) 289, 331, 348, 354
International Tropical Timber Agreement
    (ITTA) 8, 23
International Tropical Timber Organization
    (ITTO) 129, 146, 322
Italy 52, 73, 137, 151, 186, 190, 193, *194*

jacaranda 260, 261, 263
Japan 31, *52, 56,* 133, 259
jatobá 113, 315, *316*
Java *227, 230,* 248, 252
juçara *see* palm heart
junco vine *see* titica vine
'Jungle Gum' 31–2, 329
juniper 194
jutai *317*

Kadem 202
Kalimantan *230,* 231, 235, 238, 268
kava kava 4, 202, 331
Kayapó Indians, Brazil 62
Kenya *237,* 259–63
Korea 232
Korthalsia spp. *see* rattans

labelling 7, 11, 13, 323–4, 331, 344, 345,
    354, 355–6
Laccosperma spp. *see* rattans
land tenure issues
  and indigenous peoples 29, 30, 285–8, 290,
    292, 293, 294, 298, 312
  in NTFP certification 22, 24, 25, 198,
    285–8, 298, 312, 327, 358–9
  in NTFP production 29, 30, 37, 236
land-use impacts
  of logging 54, 69–70, 78, 128–9, 178, 242,
    249, 314, 319
  see also under individual NTFPs
Laos *228, 230,* 246, 247, 248–9, *255*

large-scale Adivasi multipurpose societies
(LAMPS) 244, *245*
latex
amapá 123, 124–5
chicle 29, 31, 32, 33, 47, 49, 55–6
sangre de drago 136–9, 141–4, 145–8,
149–50, 151–2, 154
Latin America
cat's claw 94
land tenure issues 290, 291
NTFP certification project 5, 20, 48,
274–8, 290–4, 346
palm hearts 79, 80, 81, *82–4*
sangre de drago 136
see also Amazon region
Lebanon 190
Lecythis pisonis see sapucáia
Lesser Antilles *83*
Leticia Statement (1996) *287*
Licania heteromorpha see caraipé
Liofilizadora de Pacífico/Omniagro 94, 102
Lithuania 137, 151
local communities *see* indigenous peoples
logging
illegal 36, 249, *281*, 294
land-use issues 54, 69–70, 78, 128–9, 178,
242, 249, 314, 319
NTFPs affected 114, 125, 278, 280, *281*,
300, 314–15, 316–21, 357
Lycopodium obscurum see princess pine

maçaranduba 280, *317*
Madagascar 208
Madame Catherine 203
Maderas Industriales de Quintana Roo
(MIQRO) 290
mahogany 29, 54
'mahogany' *see muhugo*
Makindu Carvers Cooperative 262
Malaysia *226*, *227*, *228*, *230*, *231*, *237*, 247,
248, *281*
mango trees 260, 261
mangroves 278, 279
Manilkara chicle see chicle, inferior
Manilkara spp. *see* maçaranduba;
maparajuba
Manilkara zapota see chicle
maparajuba *317*
maple syrup *162*
biology of trees 164
certification 10, 22, 170–1, *335*

distribution of trees 164
ecology of trees 164
economic value 3, 4, 48, 168–70, 323
habitat of trees 48, 164
harvesting/production 165, 166, 167, 170,
268, 270, 271, 274
and indigenous peoples 165, 167
land tenure issues 170
land-use change impacts 167
management 166, 271, 274, 354
organic certification 171
profile 47, 162–71
regeneration of trees 164, 166
species of tree compared 163
sustainability 271
threats to production 167–8, 170
and timber production 163, 329
marapuama 268, 269, 270, 320, 325–6, 331
mastic gum
economic value 48, 185
harvesting/production 185, 270
medical properties 185, 186
profile 47, 185–6
uses 185, 186
mata mata ci *317*
Mataatua Declaration on Cultural and
Intellectual Property Rights of Indigenous
Peoples (1993) *287*
Matteucia struthiopteris see fiddlehead fern
maturi *317*
Mauritia flexuoso see buriti
Max Havelaar Coffee 11, 21
Maximiliana maripa see inajá
Mayan civilization 29, 30, 51, 53–4, *57*
McCain's 161
Mediterranean region 183–99, 246, 268, 282
Mennonite Central Committee (MCC) 261
Menominee Tribal Enterprises (MTE) 17
Mexico
bromeliads 257–8
chicle
certification 6, 13, 20, 28, 29–34, 276–7,
290–1
production 50, 51, 52, 56, 57, 58
logging 29, 54, 290–1
pau d'arco 85, 87
social issues 33–4, 290–1
Middle East 197
Montreal Process 8
Morocco 186, 188–90
mpingo ('ebony') 260, 262

muhugo ('mahogany') 260
mururé 34, *217*
mushrooms 3, 4, 48, 170, 271, 280, 308, 338, 349
Myrialepsis spp. *see* rattans

National Nutritional Foods Association (NNFA) 205–6
Natura 2000 network 194
Natural Balance 204
Nature's Way 204, 323
Naturland 21
neem 260, 261, 263
Neosynthesis Research Institute, Sri Lanka 27, 331
Netherlands 64
New Guinea *227*
NGOs
    NTFP certification 18, 21, 296, 358, 361–2
    NTFP management 102, 138, 145, 146, 203, 270, 358
Nicaragua *84*
Nigeria 215, 216, 223, 232
Noga-Wills (Nigeria) Ltd 223
non-governmental organizations *see* NGOs
non-timber forest products *see* NTFPs
North Africa 188, 190
North America
    certified product market 22, 27, 331, 354
    fiddlehead fern 156, 157, 158, 160
    ginseng 174, 178
    maple syrup 22, 162, 163, 164
    woodcarving trade 259, 262
    see also Canada; United States
Northeast Organic Farmers Association 21
NTFP Exchange Programme, PROFOUND 27
NTFPs
    access rights 225, 285–8, 294, 295, *297*, 301, 310, 343
    in barter systems 299, 303, 304, 311
    biology 270, 271, 278, *340*, 359
    certification
        challenges 5, 198, 273, 296, 298, 311, *333–6*, 353, 358–60
        collaboration 9–13, 18–19, 21, 348, 354, 361–2, 363, 365
        company involvement 15–18, 31, 38–41, 329–30, *332–3*, 356, 359, 365
        costs 5, 24, 198, 273, *333*, 353, 354, 358, 363

cultural issues 5, 22, 25
ecological issues 4, 24, 26, 198–9, 280, 323–4, 342, 359, 360–1
economic issues 311, 355
field tests 6, 20, 21, 24–7, 28, 349, 354–6, 363
and governments 18, 19, 122, 153, 154, 244, 346, 347, 360
guidelines 5–6, 20–7, 47, 354–6, 357, 363–4
and indigenous peoples 4, 5, 23–4, 26, 283–98, 355
land tenure issues 22, 24, 25, 198, 285–8, 298, 312, 327, 358–9
and management 4, 16–17, 21, 122, 198, 199, 282, 338–49, 355
marketing issues 4–5, 14–18, 22, 198, 311–12, 324–31, *332–6*, 353–60
monitoring 342, 343–4, 363
and NGOs 18, 21, 296, 358, 361–2
opportunities 13–18, *332–3*, *334–6*, 353–4, 356–8
performance indicators/verifiers 21, 22, 24, 47–8, 269–70, 274, 363–4
social issues 4, 22, 23–4, 25, 26, 198, 285–98, 361, 363–4
subsistence issues 24, 37, 198, 299, 300–1, 302, 311–12, 321, 364
technical issues 23, 337–49, 359–60
commercialization 3, 4, 24, 197, 279, *287*, 301
cultivation 23, 195, 196, 280, 282
cultural issues 295–6, *297*, 305, 306, *307*
ecological issues 3, 267, 268, 270–1, 278–80, 282, 323–4, 330–1
economic value 3, 284, 299, 300, 303–4, 313, 323
exotic species 24, 25, 196
in forest management 21, 184, 197–9, 301, 329–30, 338–49, 356–7, 360–4
government regulation 122, 138, 153, 154, 174, 300, 327, 346–7, 360
harvesting 267, 268, 269–71, 272, 289, 301, 310, 338, 342–3
logging affects 114, 125, 278, 280, *281*, 300, 314–15, 316–21, 357
management
    and certification 4, 16–17, 21, 122, 198, 199, 282, 338–49, 355
    by governments 39, 100–1, 102, 145, 146, 244, 273, 284, 346

by indigenous peoples 122, 184, 267,
268, 270–1, 272–3, 289, 293, 346
NGO involvement 102, 138, 145, 146,
203, 270, 358
marketing issues 279–80, 284–5, 287,
303–4, 311–12, 313–14, 322–4, 338,
347–8
medicinal uses 4, 48, 279, *281*, 287, 305,
316, *317*
nutritional value 315, 320
overharvesting 4, 24, 196, 279, *281*, 301,
324, 343
research 3, 21, 284, *332*, 346, 362, 364
social issues 21, 22, 283, 284, 295–6
species under threat 90, 91, 219, 324, 331,
361
subsistence issues 3, 299–301, 303–10,
313–20
substitutes 90, 118–19, 120, 280, 326
sustainability 196, 269–71, 279, 324, 331,
342, 356, 358, 361–2
in timber certification 14–18, 125, 134,
135, 224, 280, 320–1, 337–8, 355–6
uses 4, 48, *281*, 305–6, *307*, *317 see also*
medicinal uses above
wild-harvested 4, 11, *12*, 48, 161, 324
see also under individual NTFPs
Nuova Linnea 202, 223
nutraceutical products 222–3

oleoresin 126–7, 128, 129, 130, 131, 133,
135, 192
Oncocalamus spp. *see* rattans
Only Natural 223
organic certification 9, 10–11, *12*, 21, 296,
348, 354
Organic Crop Improvement Association
(OCIA) 21
organic products 4, 10, 11, *12*, 21, 325, 330,
334, 345
ostrich fern *see* fiddlehead fern

Palisades Pharmaceuticals 222
palm heart *28*, 75
biology of plants 76–7
certification 5, 10, 13
challenges 36, 39–41, 43–4, 81, *335*
ecological issues 39, 40, 43, 274–6, 323
economic issues 40, 43
field trials 6, 13, 20, 22, 28, 34, 37–44,
274–6, 293–4

and indigenous peoples 39, 40, 41–4,
275, 293–4
land tenure issues 40, 43, 44, 293, 294
marketing issues 39, 40, 43, 323, 328,
329, 330, *335*, 357
monitoring 39, 43
opportunities 38–9, 42, 81, 276, *335*
social issues 40–1, 43–4, 288, 291–4
technical issues 39–40, 43
commercialized 37–41, 75, 78, 80–1, *82–3*,
274, 275
cultivated 81
distribution of plants 75, *82–4*
ecology of plants 76–7
economic value 3, 4, 48, 75, 76, 80–1, 275,
322, 323
in forest management initiatives 41–2
habitat of plants 38, 48, 75, 76, 77, 78,
82–4
harvesting/production 36, 39, 78–9, 80, 81,
270, 271, *273*, 275–6
and indigenous peoples 40–1, 43, 44, 75,
78, 80, 271
land-use change impacts 40, 77–8
management 39, 42, 78–9, 81, 268, 271,
273, 275–6, 354
medicinal properties 76, 80, 82
non-commercialized 41–4, 75, *83–4*
nutritional value 38, 41, 79, 274
organic certification 38–9
profile 42, 48, 75–84
regeneration of plants 78, 79, 81
species of plants compared 75, 76, 77, 78,
79, 80, *82–4*
sustainability 37, 42, 80, 81, 271, 275
uses 38, 41, 75–6, 79–80, *82–4*, 274, 320,
335
palmito *see* palm heart
Pan-European Criteria 8
Panama *82*, *84*, *95*, 297
Panax ginseng see Asian ginseng
Panax quinquefolius see American ginseng
Papua New Guinea *228*, *232*
Pará, Brazil 314–21, 329, 330
Paraguay 80, *82*, *86*, *93*, *95*, 140
Parahancornia spp. *see* amapá
patent rights 108, 137, 138, 153, 287, 288,
296, *297*
Patent Trade Office (PTO) *297*
pau d'arco *85*
biology 85, *86–7*, 87

certification 91–2
distribution 85, 86, 87
ecology 86–7
economic value 4, 85, 86, 89–90
habitat 48, 86, 87
harvesting/production 89–90, 92, 270, 280
and indigenous peoples 86, 88
land-use change impacts 89–90
management 90–1
medicinal properties 85, 86, 88–9, 92, 280, *316*, 324
as ornamental tree 85–6, 88, 92
profile 48, 85–92
regeneration 90–1
species compared 85, 86–7, 89, 90–1
substitutes 90
sustainability 90, 91, 324
as timber product 85, 86, 88, 89–90, 280
uses 85–6, 88–90, 92, 280, *316*
Pausinystalia johimbe see yohimbe
Pausinystalia macroceras see yohimbe, false
pejibaye palm 81, *273*
People and Plants initiative 260, 261
perfume manufacture *see* personal care industry
personal care industry 114, 133, 135, 252, *254*, 322, 323, 325, 360
Peru
  Brazil nuts
    certification 37, 70
    harvesting/production 63, 64, 70, 72
    production 61, 62, 63, 64, 66, 67, 69, 72, *334*
  cat's claw 93–4, 98, 99–101, 102, 103–4, *334*
  NTFP certification 27
  palm hearts 40, 76, 77, 80, *83*, *84*
  pau d'arco 87, 90
  sangre de drago
    harvesting/production 143, 144, 147–8
    medicinal use 104, 136, 151
    production 138, 141, 142, 145, 146
    trade in 151–2, 153
  see also Amazon region
Petén Basin, Guatemala 50, 51, 53–4, 57, 58, 326
pharmaceutical industry 19, 105–6, 132–3, 137–8, 152, 322, 325, *336*, 360
  see also botanical medicines industry
Philippines *230*, 231, *237*
Phyllanthus emblica see amla

Phyllanthus indofischerii see amla
pine nuts *190*
  distribution of trees 190
  economic value 48, 192
  habitat of trees 190, *191*
  harvesting/production *191*, 192
  management *191*, 192, 268
  medicinal properties 190, 192
  nutritional value 190
  profile 48, 190–2
  regeneration of trees *191*
  sustainability *191*
pine resin *193*
  certification 5
  economic value 3, 5, 48, 193–4
  harvesting/production 192, 270
  and indigenous peoples 193
  management 198
  medicinal properties 193
  profile 47, 192–4
  and timber production 193
  uses 192–3
Pinus halepensis see pine resin
Pinus pinea see pine nuts
Piper methysticum see kava kava
piqui 295
piquiá 3, 280, *313*, 315–16, *317*
Pistacia lentiscus see mastic gum
Plan Piloto Chicero, Mexico 30, 31, 32, 57
Plan Piloto Forestal, Mexico 290–1
plantations 23, 51, 170, 195, 196, 235, 237, 262, 280
Plantecam 217, 218, 224
Platonia insignis see bacuri
Plectocomia spp. *see* rattans
Plectocomiopsis spp. *see* rattans
Pogonotium spp. *see* rattans
pollution 167–8, 178, 280
Portico SA 15–16
Portugal 186, 188, 190, 193, *194*, 196
Pouteria reticulata see chicle, inferior
princess pine 309
Pro-Naturaleza 102
Protium spp. *see* breu resin
Provir 137, 138, 144
Prunus africana see pygeum
Pteridium aquilinum see bracken fern
Ptychopetalum olacoides see marapuama
Puerto Maldonado, Peru 64, 72
Pure World Botanicals 223
pygeum 217–18, 219, 323–4

Quercus suber see cork oak

Rainforest Alliance 5, 20
ramon 27629
rattans *225*
  animal interaction 233–4
  biology 226, 233–4
  certification 22, 238, 323, *336*
  commercialization 231–2, *234*, 235, 237,
    238
  cultivated 227, 234, 235, 237, 238
  distribution 226–7, *230*
  ecology 232–4
  economic value 3, 4, 48, 226, 231, 236,
    238, 322
  growth rates 234, *235*, 238
  habitat 226, 232–3
  harvesting/production 226, 233, 236, 238,
    273
  and indigenous peoples 228, 229, 236, 238
  insect interaction 234
  land tenure issues 238
  land-use impacts 225
  management 234–7, 238, 271, *336*
  profile 225–38
  regeneration 235
  species compared 226–7, 229, *230*, 233,
    234, *235*, 237
  sustainability 225, 233, 237, 238, 271
  uses 120, *225*, 228, 229, *336*
reforestation 138, 145, 146, 149, 196
reproductive propagules 21, 47, 48, 271, 343
resin *see* benzoin; breu resin; mastic gum; ole-
    oresin; pine resin
Retispatha spp. *see* rattans
Rio Declaration *287*
roble 35
Rocky Mountain Herbalist Coalition 324
root bark 97, 98, 101, 105–6, 118
roots 47, 48, 343
  baobab 210, 212
  cat's claw 97, 98, 100, 101–2, 105
  palm hearts 76, 80
  titica vine 116, 117–18
rosin 192
rubber 34, 52, 142, 235, 249, 268, 280, 282,
    291–2
Rumex acetosella see sheep sorrel
Russia 137, 151

Salix viminalis see vime
sangre de drago *136, 337*
  animal interaction 141
  biology 139–40, 142
  certification 153–4, *335*
  commercialization 136–8, 144, 145, 147,
    148, 151–2
  distribution 139, 141
  ecology 140–3, 145
  economic value 4, 136–7, 143, 144, 148,
    151–2, 154
  growth rates 141–2, 149
  habitat 140, 142, 143
  harvesting/production 142–3, 144, 145,
    146–8, 151–2, 154, 271
  and indigenous peoples 136, 145, 146, 147,
    148, 151–2
  land-use change impacts 140, 144
  management 137, 143, 144–9, 154
  medicinal properties 104, 136, 137–8, 143,
    149–50, 151
  patent rights 108, 137, 138, 153
  productivity 142–3, 147
  profile 47, 136–54
  regeneration 142, 145–6, 148–9
  species compared 139, 140, 141
  sustainability 144, 153–4
  as timber product 150
  uses 104, 136, 137–8, 149–52, *335*
Santa Cruz Declaration (UNDP) *287*
sap *see* maple syrup
sapucáia 315, *317*
sarara see breu resin
Saudi Arabia 185
saw palmetto 300
SB-Normal Stool 138, 144, 152, *332*
Schweizer Hall 223
Scientific Certification Systems 21
Senegal 232
Serenoa repens see saw palmetto
Seven Islands 16
SGS Silviconsult 21
Shaman Group 137–8, 144, 145–6, 148, 152,
    154, *332–3, 335*
sheep sorrel *306*
Shorea javanica see damar
Shorea spp. *see* illipe
Siberian ginseng 180
Sierra Leone *230*
Singapore 231, 252, 253, *281*
sisal *279*

sketaugen *306*
Slow Foods movement 161
SmartWood 5, 10, 21, 29, 261, 325
SoBe Beverages 222–3
Sociedad de Productores y *ejidos* Forestales de
  Quintana Roo (SPEFQR) 30
Soil Association 21, 261
Solaray 223
Solgar 204
South America
  copaíba 127
  NTFP regulation 122, 346
  palm heart production 75, 77, *82–4*, 93
  pau d'arco production 88, 90
  sangre de drago 139, 140
South-East Asia 17, 27, 225, 226, *230*, 231,
  233–5, 236, 278
South Korea 52, 180
South Pacific *230*
SP-303 137, 143, 150
Spain
  cat's claw trade 94
  cork production 6, 186, 187, 188
  forest conservation 196
  pine-nut production 190, 192
  pine-resin production 193, *194*
  sangre de drago trade 137
  yohimbe trade 223
Spanish cedar 29, 54
Species Survival Commission (SSC) Medicinal
  Plant Specialist Group (IUCN) 324
Sri Lanka 27, *227, 228, 230, 237,* 331
St. John's Wort 200
stewardship 4, 10, 134, 178, 295
stone pine *see* pine nuts
strofilia see pine nuts
Stryka Botanics Co. 223
Styrax spp. *see* benzoin
Sub-Saharan Africa 200–24
sucuúba *316*
sugar 163, 164, 165, 166, 168
sugar maple *see* maple syrup
sugarbushes *see* maple syrup
Sulawesi *230,* 231
Sumatra *227, 230,* 247–9, 251–3, 255, 268,
  281
Sumatra benzoin *see* benzoin
Surinam *82, 83*
sustainability
  of forests 4, *5,* 7–8, *9, 12,* 21, 196, 260,
  272

of NTFPs 196, 269–71, 279, 324, 331,
  342, 356, 358, 361–2
of timber 7–8, 54, 260–3
see also under individual NTFPs
Swietenia macrophylla see mahogany
Switzerland 202, 223
synthetic gum 29, 33, *53, 55, 56,* 326

Tabebuia cassinoides see caixeta
Tabebuia spp. *see* pau d'arco
Taiwan 231
tauari *317*
Technoserve (Ghana) Ltd 203
Thailand *227, 228, 230,* 231, *237*
Thoracocarpus bissecta see timboaçu
Tillandsia spp. *see* bromeliads
timber
  certification 4, 8, 16–18, 30, 260–3, 337–8,
  341–2
    NTFP involvement 14–18, 125, 134, 135,
    224, 280, 320–1, 337–8, 355–6
  marketing issues 4, 15–16, 17–18, 314,
  327–8, 329
  sustainability 7–8, 54, 260–3, 329
  in woodcarving industry 260–3
  see also logging
timboaçu 120, 316
titica vine *116*
  biology 116, 117
  certification 121–2
  distribution 117
  ecology 117
  economic value 48, 116, 120
  in forest management initiatives 122
  habitat 48, 116, 117
  harvesting/production 117–18
  and indigenous peoples 116, 118, 119–20
  land-use change impacts 121
  management 118–19, 121–2
  profile 48, 116–22
  regeneration 118, 121
  species compared 117
  substitutes 118–19, 120
  sustainability 121–2
  uses 116, 119–20, 316
Tom's of Maine 8
tourism 196, 262, 263, *296, 297*
Trade-Related Aspects of Intellectual Property
  Rights (TRIPS) Agreement (WTO) 153
TRAFFIC (WWF) 198
training 32, 36, 41, 289, 294, 298, 342, 344,

357, 363
Transfair Network 11
Trattinnickia spp. *see* breu amescla
Trinidad and Tobago 82, *83*, 95
Triphala 240, 243, 244
Tropenbos Foundation 21
tucumã *366*
Tunisia 186
Tupi Indians, Brazil 127, 131
Turkey 190, 197
turpentine 192–3
TwinLabs 204, 223
Typha spp. *see* cattail

ucuuba *316*, *317*
Ukraine 137
Ultimate Nutrition 223
UN Industrial Development Organization
    (UNIDO) 232
uña de gato *see* cat's claw
Uncaria spp. *see* cat's claw
UNCED Forest Principles 8, *287*
UNDP Regional Meeting on Intellectual
    Property Rights *287*
United Kingdom 7, 64, 73, 216, 252, *269*
United Plant Savers 324
United States
    ayahuasca 296, *297*
    botanical medicines industry
        dietary supplements 179–80, 200, 202–6,
        222–3
        herbal remedies 88, 89, 95, 106, 131,
        202, 221–2, 269
    Brazil nut trade 63, 64, 73, 347
    bromeliad trade 258
    cat's claw trade 94, 95, 105, 106
    certified product market 7, 32, 33, 329
    chewing gum market 32, 33, 52–3
    copaíba trade 131, 132, 133
    fiddlehead fern 156–61
    ginseng 172–3, 175, 177, 178, 179, 181
    griffonia trade 200, 202–6
    maple syrup production 162–71
    marapuama trade *269*
    NTFP regulation 300
    palm heart trade 75, 81, *335*
    pau d'arco trade 86, 88, 89
    pine-nut trade 192
    rattan trade 231
    sangre de drago trade 136–7, 151
    subsistence issues 299, 304–10, 312

woodcarving trade 261
yohimbe trade 221–3
United States Agency for International
    Development (USAID) 5, 20, 338
Universal Declaration of Human Rights *287*
Universal Labs 223
Upper Peninsula, Michigan, US 299, 301–10,
    312
US Food and Drug Administration *see* FDA
uxi *20*, 315, *317*, 320, *353*

Vaccinium spp. *see* blueberry
Vanuatu 226, 227
vegetative structures 21, 47, 48, 270, 343
Venezuela 62, 80, 82, *83*, *84*, 86, 130, 131
Vicdoris 203
Vietnam *230*, 246, 247, 323
vime 118–19, *120*
Virend 137
Virola michelii see ucuuba
Vitamin Shoppe 204
Vitol 223

Warner Lambert 52
Wells (W.S.) and Son Company 157–8, 161
West Africa 201, 202, 232, 303
'white' breu *see* breu resin
'wild' foods 4, 11, *12*, 48, 161, 360
wild leek 4, *306*
Wild Things 30, 31–2, 325, 329
woodcarving industry 48, 259–63, 331
Woodmark Programme 261
World Conservation Union (IUCN) 198, 324
World Trade Organization (WTO) 153, 327
Wrigleys 52, 55

xate 270

Yanesha Indians, Peru 102, 104, 108, 146
yohimbe *215*, *322*
    biology 216
    certification 223–4, 323–4, *336*
    cultivated 219
    distribution 215, 216
    ecology 216, 223–4
    economic value 4, 48, 217
    habitat 216
    harvesting/production 217–18, 219, 223,
        224, 273
    and indigenous peoples 217, 218, 221, 224
    management 219, 221, 224, *336*

medicinal properties 215–16, 221–2
nutritional value 222–3
products 221, 222–3
profile 48, 215–24
regeneration 216, 219
species compared 218–19, *220*
sustainability 217–19, 221, 223, 224, *336*
uses 215–16, 221, 222–3, *336*

yohimbe, false 218–19, *220*
Yucatan, Mexico 29, 30, 32, 51, 53–4, 57, 58, 326

Zimbabwe 208, 209–14